D0643076

PANZER ACES II

More Battle Stories of German Tank Commanders in WWII

Franz Kurowski
Translated by David Johnston

STACKPOLE BOOKS
Essex, Connecticut
Blue Ridge Summit, Pennsylvania

STACKPOLE BOOKS
An imprint of Globe Pequot, the trade division of
The Rowman & Littlefield Publishing Group, Inc.
4501 Forbes Blvd., Ste. 200
Lanham, MD 20706
www.rowman.com

Distributed by NATIONAL BOOK NETWORK

Copyright © 2000 by J. J. Fedorowicz Publishing Inc.
First Stackpole Books edition 2022

All rights reserved. No part of this book may be reproduced in any form or by any electronic or mechanical means, including information storage and retrieval systems, without written permission from the publisher, except by a reviewer who may quote passages in a review.

British Library Cataloguing in Publication Information available

Library of Congress Cataloging-in-Publication Data

A previous edition of the book was cataloged with the Library of Congress.

LCCN 2004005895

ISBN 9780811739252 (paperback) | ISBN 9780811769198 (electronic)

∞™ The paper used in this publication meets the minimum requirements of American National Standard for Information Sciences—Permanence of Paper for

Table of Contents

Sepp Brandner outfitted for the winter fighting in Courland.

Major Sepp Brandner

"Leutnant Brandner reporting as ordered!"

"Thank you, Brandner, stand at ease." Hauptmann Handrick, battery commander of the 202nd Assault Gun Battalion, shook hands with his technical officer. "Brandner, you know that Leutnant Böhm was severely wounded in the assault on Yelnya and is out of action. Would you take over the 1st Platoon in his place?"

At first Sepp Brandner thought he had heard wrong. He was being offered what he had been striving for since beginning the Russian campaign as a gun commander.

"I would like to very much, sir."

"Good. I have already informed the battalion commander. He agrees, because Leutnant Narbutt can replace you as technical officer. Come, we'll go to your platoon."

The two assault guns of the 1st Platoon were parked close together. Feldwebel Preinlinger, commander of the second vehicle, reported. Speaking quickly, Hauptmann Preinlinger informed him that they had received a new platoon commander. No further explanation was required, for it had been Leutnant Brandner who had gone into the minefield with the 18-ton prime mover to rescue the two assault guns during the first breakthrough attempt near Yelnya. That had been on 18 July 1941. Now they were stuck in the Yelnya salient. Before them were nine Russian rifle divisions and two tank units arrayed in a broad arc. The battalion itself was under the command of the 10th Panzer Division. To the north was the SS Division *Das Reich.*

The 10th Panzer Division had destroyed fifty enemy tanks in one day. The 202nd Assault Gun Battalion, which General Schaal had deployed at the hot spots, played a part in this success. Yelnya was taken. But then the division became stalled in front of the well-fortified Russian positions. One-third of the division's vehicles were put out of action. Ammunition had to be brought in over a 450-kilometer land route. The SS Division *Das*

Reich was stalled north of Yelnya, between the city and Dorogobush. That was the situation in July 1941.

"Russian counterattack. Enemy has reached the main line of resistance and has driven our troops in the trenches back to the windmill and Hill 16.7. The assault gun battalion is to attack the enemy forces which have broken in and drive them back in a counterattack."

The battalion commander had assembled the leaders of the three batteries. The alert report had come from up front an hour earlier and the division commander, General Schaal, had immediately alerted the assault guns.

"Are we to split up, sir?"

"No. First a concentrated attack by all twenty-seven guns on Point 16.7. Then we turn toward the windmill and retake it. Departure in five minutes."

The battery commanders hurried back to their batteries. Hauptmann Handrik reached the seven assault guns and waved over the gun commanders. They gathered round and looked at him expectantly.

"Comrades, we are going to retake the main line of resistance from the enemy. Everyone fully armed? Enough fuel on board?"

"All set, sir!"

The engines of the assault guns roared to life. They rolled out of cover and moved into the specified attack formation. Sepp Brandner looked ahead through the "scissors" (binocular telescope). He saw the movements at the west end of the village. He was about to report this when the battery commander's voice came over the radio:

"Tiger to Marten and Polecat. Each take one enemy antitank gun at the village exit. Advance quickly and open fire from close range. Out."

After five-hundred meters Brandner ordered his driver to take the assault gun out of the ditch. When he could see the village again he saw one of the antitank guns not 300 meters in front of him. The barrel of the enemy weapon was turning toward him.

"High-explosive round Schranzl!"

"Jammed, sir!"

"Damn it, get going or we've had it!"

Through the "scissors" Brandner saw feverish activity around the antitank gun. It must fire at any moment.

"Turn right. Full power!"

The "Marten" leapt forward. The enemy fired at the same instant. The shell passed two meters behind the assault gun. The remaining guns of the battery opened fire. Amid the din Brandner heard the second antitank gun fire. Then to the left and right he saw German infantry emerging from the ditches and crevices where they had dug in.

Possibilities and orders whirled through Sepp Brandner's head. The jam had still not been cleared and the third shot from the Soviets might come at any time. He had only seconds to do the right thing. If he failed he placed the assault gun and the lives of its crew at risk. Then he heard a bang from behind and to the right.

"The Polecat, sir!"

"Antitank gun taking aim at Polecat!" shouted Brandner, and then it came to him. "We're going to run it over. Get going, step on the gas Rakowitz!"

The "Marten" raced forward at full throttle. The assault guns of the 3rd Battery fired in turns. Exploding shells ripped apart the houses at the west end of the village. Machine-guns opened fire.

A jet of flame left the barrel of the antitank gun aiming at "Polecat." Then the gun crew recognized the approaching threat. A Maxim machine-gun opened fire. The bullets bounced off Marten's frontal armor. It rumbled and shook inside the assault gun. Driver Rakowitz turned slightly, heading the assault gun straight towards the antitank gun position.

The Russians could not swing the gun around in time. The scattered in all directions just before the tracks reached the gun. A jolt shook the assault gun as it struck the antitank gun head on. The sound of breaking metal filled the inside of the vehicle, which leaned dangerously to the left. The crew hung on tight. Then the assault gun returned to the horizontal. Brandner heard a relieved shout from the gunner.

"Jam cleared, Leutnant!"

"Open fire on the attacking infantry!"

The first shot left the barrel. The shell burst in the midst of the mass of attacking Red Army troops. Loader Lubisch rammed the next round into the breech and closed it. The gun cracked again. The assault gun jerked back. The flanking group came into sight. A third shot. The men now heard the rumble of "Polecat" which had immediately followed them. The commander's vehicle turned toward them.

"Our infantry are sitting on it," shouted Brandner. He emerged briefly from his hatch and saw German infantry.

"Get on. Quickly, quickly!"

"Tiger to everyone!" called Hauptmann Handrik. "Drive through the village and take Hill 16.7 in a concentric attack. Let the infantry ride on the vehicles."

The assault guns began to move again. They came under fire and answered with their own guns. Shells smashed the lightly-constructed houses. Another Russian antitank gun opened fire. Under fire from two assault guns, it was destroyed in a huge explosion.

"Marten" rolled east, leaving the cover of some houses. Before it Hill 16.7 rose up from the flat plain. A quick look and Brandner saw that the others were in attack position.

"Keep going Brandner! Watch out for the hedge on the right flank," warned the Hauptmann.

A Russian cannon opened up a rapid fire, sending shells at the assault guns. The noise inside Brandner's vehicle was tremendous. It swung to the right and made an arc, disappearing into the shadows of a clump of willows. Rakowitz turned, reached the depression that led up the hill and raced the assault gun upwards. With a quick glance Brandner surveyed the trenches of the German main line of resistance, which had been lost to the Russians that morning.

"Range 200, direction 12 o'clock!"

Gunner Schranzl fired, and the enemy machine-gun post that had been firing at the advancing infantry went up in a cloud of smoke and dust. They rolled toward the Russian trenches. Enemy soldiers appeared right in front of them. Marten drove right over them. Schranzl fired again. Then the other assault guns appeared.

Faced with this mass assault, the Russians broke and ran. The German infantry fired after them, down the hill toward the east.

"Battalion commander to everyone!" called Major Buchner. "First battery north windmill, second middle, third south. Stay on their heels, don't let them settle down at the windmills."

"Sir, they're turning left. They probably want to get to the birch wood!"

Brandner had also seen this movement. He was about to instruct his driver to turn when Hauptmann Handrik's voice rang out over the radio:

"Third Platoon follow the enemy into the wood. Everyone else continue south in the general direction of the windmills."

"Oh, we want to have a go. But . . ."

The next words were taken from Leutnant Brandner's mouth. A huge explosion shattered the noontime quiet, then another. Two bursts of flame shot up where the Third had reached the edge of the wood.

"They have driven over mines, sir!"

"Damn, that doesn't look good. Polecat, follow me. Get going Rakowitz, turn left. We're going to go over there and get them out."

Through the "scissors" Brandner saw that the crews had bailed out. They had taken cover in a shell hole and now Russians were running toward them from three sides to capture them.

"Fire!"

Marten's first shot slammed into the leading group of enemy soldiers and caused them to go to ground. Polecat fired as well. Then they were there. The mounted infantry got down and chased off the enemy troops. The crews from the two assault guns climbed onto the vehicles, which turned around.

An infantryman under cover from a *Sturmgeschütz* awaits its advance.

"Thanks, Sepp!" shouted Leutnant Marischka, platoon leader in the Third Battery. "That was close!"

"Nonsense. You would have done the same for us."

"Sir, there ahead!"

The driver's voice was a little high with excitement and Brandner immediately turned to see what was happening. In front of them were four Russian armored cars. They turned toward the two assault guns. The gunners loaded armor-piercing shells. A second later the battalion commander's vehicle emerged from some bushes and set the first armored car on fire with a single shot.

"Look at the old man! He's going after them!" shouted Leutnant Marischka enthusiastically. Hauptmann Handrik turned and knocked out the last armored car, which were now in full retreat.

"Ahead at the windmills! Something's going on there!"

They raced at full throttle to the scene of the fighting, where the 2nd Battery was already engaged with the Russian 76.2-mm antitank guns. But they did not get to intervene, for the enemy guns were silenced before they got within firing range. There, too, the enemy had turned and fled toward the safety of his own main line of resistance.

When the enemy continued his attacks in front of Yelnya on 26 July, Generaloberst Guderian sent in the 268th Infantry Division to bolster that sector of the front. On the same day Generaloberst Hoth's Panzer Group 3, which was deployed to the north of Guderian's Panzer Group 2, succeeded in closing the pocket east of Smolensk from the north. As a result, Panzer Group 3, which had been pulled back somewhat, could now be moved forward again. However, in the opinion of Panzer Group 2 the most dangerous foe was near Roslavl and east of Yelnya. This assessment proved to be accurate. The enemy repeatedly attacked Yelnya and each time the 202nd Assault Gun Battalion was in the thick of the action. Thirteen Russian attacks were repulsed on 30 July alone. By now Leutnant Brandner was well accustomed to his new position. It was as if he had been a platoon commander from the very beginning.

Roslavl was taken on 3 August. But at Yelnya the enemy showed no sign of yielding and Generaloberst Guderian had to commit his last reserves there. It was the panzer group command post's security company. On 4 August 1941 there was a conference at Novy Borisov attended by Hitler and the commanders of Army Group Center. An evacuation of the

Yelnya salient was rejected, because it was still uncertain whether it might yet be needed as a jump-off position for an attack on Moscow. On 14 August Generaloberst Guderian again asked for permission to give up the Yelnya salient and once again the OKH refused. Finally the German forces broke through at Yelnya. The advance continued in the direction of Orel. Leutnant Brandner scored successes against enemy antitank guns and against machine-guns and enemy infantry. The 202nd Assault Gun Battalion neared Orel.

✠

"First Platoon from battery commander. Attack the village and advance along the road to Briansk and secure there."

The platoon's two assault guns rolled out of the assembly area. There was still nothing to be seen. The infantry advanced behind the assault guns to take possession of the terrain that was won. Peering through the "scissors," Brandner saw the enemy before the infantry could. Then everyone could see the dense waves of Russian infantry storming out of the village to cut off and destroy the two assault guns. The machine-gun installed on the rear of the assault gun began to rattle. The first shells left the main gun. The Russian assault began to lose steam. But suddenly they regrouped and Leutnant Brandner heard his own infantrymen shout: "Tanks, tanks!" Seconds later he saw the gray-green colossus as it rolled from right to left between two houses, directly in front of him about 120 meters away. It was followed closely by a second tank.

"T-34 in front of us. Load armor-piercing! T-34 from the right, fire!"

The shot rang out. His forehead pressed against the periscope, Leutnant Brandner watched the T-34. He saw an armor-piercing shell strike the turret and ricochet high into the air. The second shot brought the same result.

"We can't make a hole, sir!"

The first shot from the enemy flew over the assault gun. The first T-34 was hit twice more. When "Polecat" joined the battle the two Soviet tanks turned and disappeared behind the houses.

"Damn it to hell! We can't penetrate their armor. What a useless gun we have!" cursed Unteroffizier Schranzl.

"Aim at the tracks!" ordered the Leutnant when two more T-34s appeared. The first shot wrecked the track of the lead tank. With their vehicle immobilized, the crew bailed out. Small arms fire knocked them to the ground.

"Marten" turned. As soon as he had a clear shot at the rear of the T-34 the gunner fired again. A jet of flame shot from the engine compartment. They had destroyed their first enemy tank.

The village seemed to spit flame as they rolled into it. The other two platoons arrived. Thirty minutes later the village was in German hands. The assault guns stayed in their staring positions at the exit from the village.

✠

"Sir, we have to have better guns and ammunition."

"I know Brandner. We have already spoken to corps many times. We will be receiving the new hollow-charge shells in a few days. With them you will be able to handle the T-34."

"The gun is too short, sir!"

Hauptmann Handrik tried to smile but it disappeared immediately. He nodded.

"You're right Brandner. But all that is supposed to change. We're soon going to reequip with the long seventy-five-millimeter gun."

The two officers had just come back from the repair workshop. The attack on the village and the Russian position beyond had demonstrated clearly that they needed better weapons to deal with the Russian T-34.

"We'll be moving on before dark Brandner." The two officers stopped in front of the battery command post.

"Do you know anything more precise, sir?"

"Not yet."

Brandner walked into the hut which served as quarters for his gun crews.

"We have a few eggs left, sir."

"Fine, Lubisch. Actually I am rather hungry."

When he had finished eating and lit the obligatory cigarette, Feldwebel Preinlinger turned to him.

"How's it look? Will we be spending the night here?"

"We're moving out toward evening. We are going to drive through the villages north of Briansk and then turn south."

Five hours later the assault guns of the 202nd Assault Gun Battalion moved off. They came to a wide belt of forest and passed several abandoned villages. Standing in the open hatch, Brandner saw the broad back of Hauptmann Handrik emerge from the commander's vehicle in front of him. It would be dark in an hour. If they hadn't reached the communications road by now they would surely have lost their way in the forest. The assault guns rolled into another wood. A loud bang caused Leutnant

Brandner to duck involuntarily. He suddenly saw four muzzle flashes simultaneously.

Hauptmann Handrik's voice came over the radio: "Take cover!" Brandner ducked inside the assault gun.

"First Platoon, open fire!"

Shells flitted through the forest lane that stretched before them, landing in the bushes from where the enemy had ambushed them. Another burst of machine-gun fire flashed through the twilight. A single round from Polecat's gun silenced the Maxim machine-gun. The two assault guns began to move again.

"Partisans, men. I don't think we've seen the last of them."

Leutnant Brandner's prediction would soon be borne out. Before the night was over the advance detachment, of which they were a part, was fired on several times by partisans. The assault guns answered the fire from on the move, refusing to allow it to stop them. When morning came they had passed the forested zone and were in the assembly area for the assault on Briansk.

"Attention everyone, enemy tanks ahead."

The attack had been under way for ten minutes. The entire battalion was rolling in line abreast formation toward the enemy positions, from which the tanks now emerged.

Hauptmann Handrik's battery rolled toward a ravine. When Rakowitz saw flashes from the approaching tanks he wanted to turn in order to pass them. A warning from Leutnant Brandner held him back. He turned to the other side. However at that moment there was a loud crash on the right side and then the steering went slack.

"Disabled, sir!"

There was another crash, a hit on the superstructure. Luckily the shell failed to penetrate; it bounced off and struck the left wall of the ravine.

"Bail out! Don't forget the submachine-gun and the assault rifle."

Sepp Brandner was the first one out the hatch, the assault rifle in his fist. A burst of fire hissed over his head. He leapt to the ground and landed in a clump of bushes. Brandner turned around immediately, the assault rifle raised. He saw a muzzle flash and fired. The enemy fire fell silent; his three men were able to bail out. They took cover beside the Leutnant. The enemy fired again. Armor-piercing shells whizzed over the heads of the assault gun crew.

"Polecat, sir!"

Unteroffizier Schranzl's cry of dismay caused Brandner to turn around. He saw that his platoon's second assault gun was smoking. Just then a second armor-piercing shell whizzed across and blew off its right track.

Enemy tanks rolled toward them. Four tanks were driving up the ravine. At that moment Feldwebel Preinlinger bailed out of "Polecat," the first member of its crew to get out, and zigzagged to the side. A burst of machine-gun fire pursued him but he dodged out of the way. His men followed. The last out was driver Pischel. He ran behind the others. A solid armor-piercing shot flitted towards him. He tried to jump out of the way but it was too late. The shell struck him in the chest.

"Pischel," said loader Lubisch, "our Pischel."

"Look out! There's infantry coming behind the tanks!"

The four tanks had approached to 150 meters when they saw the Red Army troops appear behind them. Leading the way was a group hauling a Maxim machine-gun on a cart. Behind followed others armed with rifles and submachine-guns.

"Crawl to the rock wall. Don't show yourselves!"

Sepp Brandner saw the boulders lying against the rock wall thirty meters to the right. The tanks could not reach them there and they would also have a chance of holding off the enemy. Clutching the assault rifle, he crawled forward on elbows and foot tips. When he reached the cover of the first boulder a single shot was fired. He stood up, looked over the jagged edge of the boulder and saw one of the machine-gun crew fall. The second shot knocked the next man off his feet. Then the Russians began to run.

For a moment Leutnant Brandner had tried to crawl behind the rocks. He was relatively safe there. But before it was over he was raising the assault rifle again. He emptied the entire magazine on rapid fire. The enemy fell, but not all of them. Two submachine-guns turned toward him. Bullets knocked splinters of stone from the boulders, striking him in the face. He ducked quickly, inserted a fresh clip of ammunition and then reappeared on the other side of the rock. At that moment all four Russian tanks fired. He heard the shells exploding. High-explosive shells! Forty meters in front of him Soviets appeared, advancing at a crouch, trying to reach the flank of the small group of Germans while they were pinned down by tank fire. Brandner fired when they were all in sight. Once again the enemy went down, but four men turned toward him.

Sepp Brandner saw flames shoot from the muzzles of their submachine-guns with the round magazines. Then his assault rifle was empty. He threw it aside and pulled out his pistol. Bursts of fire caused him to take cover. He crawled back into the rocks, heard guttural shouts and then a sharp order. But his comrades had been warned, even if he should end up being stuck there.

The first face appeared from out of the shadows, followed by a second. The figures carried submachine-guns. Brandner fired. Both enemy soldiers fell. A Russian submachine-gun rattled from behind the rocks. Brandner heard bullets hitting the stone above his head. Then the Russian appeared around an outcropping of rock and was cut down by a bullet. The frightful sound of tank tracks sounded doubly loud. The air stank of oil. Brandner saw the first tanks fifty meters in front of him. They continued to fire and then they were upon him.

At that moment Lubisch came running up. He dashed toward the first tank, disappeared from the Leutnant's field of view ten reappeared on the rear of the tank. Then he jumped down and took cover. His two comrades fired their assault rifles at the Russian soldiers, who had taken cover.

A mighty blast caused the tank turret to tip forward slightly. The tank cannon's long barrel pointed toward the ground. A huge pillar of flame shot from the rear of the enemy tank. The first of four T-34s was burning, but the other three came nearer. They rolled straight toward where Brandner's men had taken cover. Sepp Brandner was about to run over to them when he heard the sound of assault gun cannon firing from the mouth of the ravine, from where they had come.

"They're coming, sir!" shouted Feldwebel Preinlinger through the din. Then the Feldwebel was at Brandner's side; the other two crew members followed close behind him.

"Did you . . . ?"

"I was able to call them before we had to bail out. The Hauptmann radioed that he was sending Leutnant Marischka."

"There, they've got the first one."

A mighty crash signaled that a T-34 had been hit. Black smoke spiraled from the tank. The two remaining enemy tanks turned. One of them was hit when it showed its flank to the assault guns. The shell smashed into its engine and set it on fire. One of the assault guns stopped by Brandner and his men while the second continued on. Leutnant Marischka appeared in the hatch for a second.

"Thanks for getting us out, Poldi."

Instead of an answer Leutnant Marischka shouted, "You should get out of here if your crate is to be repaired!" Then he ducked back into his assault gun. It moved off with a jerk and followed the other vehicle, which had just fired again.

"Anybody hit?"

"No, sir!"

"Then get to work, fix that track!" Brandner turned to Preinlinger. He nodded in the direction of where Pischel had fallen.

Loading ammunition during a break in operations was hard work for the ammunition resupply crews. These soldiers are from the 226th Assault Gun Battalion.

When they reached Polecat's driver they saw that he was beyond human help. Brandner kneeled down beside his young comrade, who came from Vienna. He removed his identity disk and his valuables.

"We'll bury him afterward if we have time, Preinlinger."

"Yes, sir. We owe Pischel that."

"See what you can do with Polecat, Preinlinger. If you can't fix it here I'll send a report to the repair echelon."

The other two members of Polecat's crew came over to their fallen comrade. Lutter had tears in his eyes as he looked down at the Feldwebel. Sepp Brandner went over to him.

"Hang on, Lutter! It's over for him now."

"Yes, sir!" The volunteer's baby-blue eyes looked at Sepp Brandner. Lutter swallowed and walked over to the others, who were already working on the assault gun.

Leutnant Brandner went over to the platoon commander's vehicle. Lubisch and Schranzl were just breaking out the spare track, while Rakowitz stood in the turret and waited.

"Move it a bit, Toni!"

Rakowitz disappeared. The assault gun turned slightly on its intact track.

"Stop! That's perfect."

As they worked to drag the track over the roadwheels, the crew heard the roar of the battle, which had erupted in all fury in front of them. The sharp crack of the short-barreled seventy-fives alternated with the deeper boom of the Russian tank cannon. Meanwhile the division artillery fired away for all it was worth.

"That's not too bad, eh Lubisch?"

"Done, sir!" reported Schranzl.

"Hey, Preinlinger, how's your crate coming?"

"We'll be all right, sir, but it's going to take a while."

"Good, finish up. Then move forward slowly. We're moving on toward the village."

Sepp Brandner swung himself into his seat. He adjusted the "scissors" and Marten moved off. The assault gun passed the last part of the ravine. When Brandner had a clear view he saw flashes of gunfire.

"Enemy tanks ahead on the hills in front of the village," Brandner informed his men. "They're probably dug in there."

"Marten and Polecat advance on the right flank. Direction of advance south flank of the village."

"Marten to battery commander: understood. Polecat is still being repaired. Marten advancing."

"Good, Brandner. If you encounter serious resistance fight a delaying action and divert the enemy's attention."

The assault gun turned and drove into a depression. Water sprayed as it forded a brook. Marten's nose ran into a boulder. The engine roared and died. Before Schranzl could start it again the crew heard the sound of tanks from the direction of the village.

"T-34! Schranzl, move up through that narrow gully."

The assault gun forced its way through the gully. The tracks ground into both sides. Bushes collapsed over them and when they suddenly parted Brandner saw the first T-34 not a hundred meters in front of him. The enemy tanks were advancing for a counterattack against the Handrik battery. The two leading tanks had just stopped. Their turrets rotated, but not towards Brandner's assault gun, but toward the others, which had already opened fire.

"We'll put a shell through the gratings into its body. It will penetrate there. Rakowitz, fifty meters to the right, full throttle! Stop over there where the saplings are. Schranzl, get ready. The first shell has to fly as soon as Rako points the crate in the right direction."

The motor roared and the assault gun moved in the specified direction. Sepp Brandner now also saw the three or four T-34s farther to the right, advancing along the stream in the cover of a line of willows. But he did not change his order; he intended to carry out the maneuver.

"Stop!" he shouted. The heavy assault gun immediately turned on the spot. The shell hissed toward the T-34, bored into the weak gratings just above the engine and set it on fire.

"Turn toward the second one!"

Rakowitz turned the assault gun further. At the same instant the T-34's turret also began to move. But it was still not in position to fire when Schranzl fired. Lubisch rammed another shell into the breech. The second T-34 was hit.

"Now, move, or else . . ." There was a loud bang which shook the vehicle, and the crew heard the howl of the ricocheting shell. Marten leapt forward and avoided the shells fired by the T-34s, which were now within firing range and advancing out of the bushes. The assault gun zigzagged toward the village at high speed. Through the crack of tank cannon Brandner suddenly heard the roar of assault guns firing. Then, to his left and slightly behind, he saw the guns roll out of cover. Then he heard the guns of his own battery firing as well.

"We're attacking!" he roared. The first houses were already dangerously near. Bursts of fire from machine-guns and automatic rifles sprayed the armored sides of the assault gun with bullets.

The wall of a house came dangerously close. "Look out, turn left!" shouted Brandner. The driver turned the vehicle but its right flank rammed the wall. The mud wall tumbled down onto Marten. The assault gun's engine roared and with a jolt the vehicle was free.

"Fire high-explosive!"

The shell detonated near the spot where the muzzle flashes from the enemy machine-guns had been seen. The weapons had been firing at the German infantry advancing behind the assault guns. Houses went up in flames, walls collapsed. Then the assault gun rolled on. The German assault guns pressed into the village from all sides. The infantry, some of them riding on the assault guns, cleared the village of enemy troops house by house. They had reached their objective.

While the Battle of Briansk was still raging, the 202nd Assault Gun Battalion continued to advance as part of the drive toward Orel. The new armor-piercing ammunition finally arrived. Now the assault guns could successfully engage the T-34 from in front. The German forces advanced through partisan country. During the night of 7 October (the Handrik battery had just driven into the assembly area for the attack on Orel) it began to snow. Sepp Brandner knew all too well that things were going to get much tougher for the armored units from now on. And that they did. The following rains transformed the roads into muddy channels. The advance continued at a snail's pace. The units had to be ready to be fired on at any moment.

Orel was taken. The men of the 202nd Assault Gun Battalion were able to rest for a dew days. Men and equipment were brought back to peak performance. Sepp Brandner pitched in to help overhaul the assault guns and check the vehicles. He was his own repair officer. The work went on well into the night.

After the assault on Moscow literally became stuck in the mud near Mtsensk at the end of October, at the beginning of November an "armored battle group" was formed which included the 202nd Assault Gun Battalion. Mtsensk had to be taken, because the only paved road from Orel to Tula passed through the town. Oberst Eberbach, brigade commander of the 4th Panzer Division, led the battle group.

Mtsensk was taken. The advance made rapid progress. Chern was also taken. The assault guns rolled forward with infantry riding on them. But by the time Plavskoye was reached the armored battle group, too, was exhausted. The spearhead of the 3rd Panzer Division was already at the gates of Tula, 150 kilometers east of Mtsensk. But the necessary forces and fuel needed for an immediate attack on the city were lacking. For all practical purposes the XXIV Panzer Corps's large-scale armored thrust toward Moscow came to an end there.

The assault guns were in action constantly and it became increasingly obvious to Sepp Brandner that the short-barreled seventy-five was inadequate to deal with the T-34, which had received thicker armor. The assault gun had to approach to within 600 meters of the T-34 to engage it with any hope of success, while the T-34 could fire with effect from almost twice that distance. The assault guns had no other choice but to approach to what was almost point-blank range to engage the Soviet tank.

In December the mercury fell to minus thirty degrees; it was the start of a bitter time for the German forces, including the assault guns. But whenever the infantry called for the assault guns they came, as at Venev, Stalinogorsk and Kashira. The assault guns repeatedly drove forward, clearing the way for the infantry. The supply units stayed on the heels of the fighting forces and the assault guns rearmed during the night.

But then everything ground to a halt. General Winter was stronger than the will to fight. The inadequately-clad German infantry cowered in their foxholes. How often Leutnant Brandner drove forward to bring back another pitiful cargo of men with frozen limbs. Assault guns had to be blown up because their fuel had frozen and the enemy attacked without warning. Supply dumps were blown up and the German forces retreated. Although ammunition was in short supply, the assault guns drove into the counterattacking Russians to rescue trapped comrades of the infantry. Men with frozen limbs were placed on the assault guns and evacuated to hospital.

The battle group commanded by Oberst Munzel held on to the area around Posnyahovo. The battle group, which had lost many of its tanks, fought in the trenches, spurred on by Oberst Munzel himself, who stayed in the foxholes with his men. In their black uniforms the tank soldiers were easily seen in the snow. Nevertheless they refused to give up. The assault guns supported the infantry in dozens of actions, and wherever there was an especially difficult mission Sepp Brandner was there. The actions of the Brandner platoon were lauded in a special division order of the day. And then came 12 February 1942, a day which still causes Sepp Brandner to shudder.

"Combat echelon is ready to move, sir."

"Thank you, Brandner. Today you are leading the entire battery. The village that the Soviets have taken must be recaptured, because it projects into our main line of resistance."

"Yes, sir. We will take the village."

"Watch out for mines Brandner. Don't drive through the balkas (ravines). The Ivans have mined them all."

"We will be careful. Combat echelon—forward!"

Sepp Brandner raised his arm three times. His command vehicle moved off. The soft snow was pushed aside by the grinding tracks.

"Sir, the crate is much too heavily loaded," reported driver Rakowitz.

"Let it shake a little, Rako. After all we have loaded 120 shells instead of the usual forty."

Sepp Brandner was still not used to being addressed as Leutnant, even though his promotion had come through on 16 January, at the same time as his Iron Cross, First Class. But he would have time to get used to it, for it no longer looked like this would be a blitz campaign.

Standing in the open hatch, Brandner looked around his assault guns. The battery's three platoons, which he was leading as the combat echelon, had been bolstered to ten vehicles. His command vehicle, the faithful "Phoenix," and the other nine assault guns, three to a platoon, drove sin-

A *Sturmgeschütz* III photographed at the assault artillery school at Burg.

gle file to avoid hitting mines. There was no sound from the front. Then suddenly, about 600 meters from the village, "Phoenix" was shaken by a mighty blast. The men inside the assault gun were thrown against equipment and weapons. Leutnant Brandner managed to hang on with both hands. He heard a moan.

"Anyone wounded?" he asked. His ears were ringing from the explosion of the Russian mine, and even though he was shouting he could scarcely hear his own voice.

"Everyone's all right, sir!"

"The vehicle's disabled!"

"Load armor-piercing!" Leutnant Brandner turned to the radio: "Guns fire at recognized targets."

The assault guns opened fire. As they did so enemy antitank guns opened up from the village. Not thirty meters in front of the assault guns the infantry waved from their trenches and foxholes. They were preparing to storm into the village behind the assault gun and eliminate the enemy infantry.

"Schranz, fire at whatever targets in the village you can reach by traversing the cannon."

"Phoenix" also began to fire. Ten guns fired shells into the middle of the enemy-held village.

"All guns carry out central attack," radioed Brandner.

The assault guns moved off. When they reached the infantry positions the soldiers left their trenches. They ran behind the slowly advancing assault guns carrying machine-guns and submachine-guns, assault rifles and explosives. One of the assault guns was hit and disabled by enemy fire. Before the soldiers advancing behind it could take cover, the assault gun's ammunition exploded, killing everyone in its immediate vicinity. Brandner looked into the melee.

"Target the antitank gun. Four-hundred straight ahead Schranzl!"

The high-explosive shell shot from the barrel and flew straight to the enemy gun position. The antitank gun fell silent. The crew heard the fierce shouts as the infantry stormed into the village and disappeared. Hand grenades exploded, explosive charges destroyed entire houses. Repeatedly shots from the assault guns rang out through the sounds of battle.

"Continue firing at targets of opportunity."

"What are you doing, sir? That's not a good idea. Let me . . . !"

But Leutnant Brandner was no longer listening. He handed the driver his headset and left the vehicle.

"Damn it!" shouted the Leutnant when he saw what had happened.

"What is it?" the driver shouted back over the noise.

"Both tracks are gone. One roadwheel has been blown off."

"Watch out for more mines, sir. They usually place them in groups.

Sepp Brandner grinned involuntarily. He wasn't going to find any more mines here. Nevertheless he began poking into the soft snow with a stick. He struck something hard and began carefully digging it out. A Russian box mine appeared and within a few minutes he had found two more.

By now the men ahead had fired a "red" signaling the all clear. Schranzl, who had also climbed out, said: "If we had driven there, sir . . ."

". . . then we would have a free pass to heaven in our pocket, Schranzl."

"Would have been a working accident, sir. Assault guns are not life insurance like our comrades in the infantry think."

"Get to work. We can manage the track. As well we have a spare roadwheel with us."

"Sir, Marischka is calling us. They need help urgently."

"You help, Rako! I'll take the radio again."

Rakowitz climbed out and went over to lend a hand to the other two, who were already at work. An antitank gun on the extreme right end of the village began to fire. The shells howled close over the Phoenix and landed somewhere behind in the saplings.

"They're trying to do us in, sir."

"Keep going, fast, fast! Phoenix to Cheetah, come in."

"Cheetah here, come in."

"Cheetah with Lion and Lynx destroy antitank gun at south end."

"Understood. Attack antitank gun."

"Marischka, come in."

The commander of the Third Platoon answered instantly: "Marischka here."

"What's happening, Marischka?"

"Dug-in tanks at the edge of the ravine east of the village, sir."

"Drive past them to the north, Marischka. Then roll them up from the flank. We'll come in a few minutes as soon as damage is repaired."

Sepp Brandner also called the commanders of the 1st and 2nd Platoons. They were also facing dug-in enemy tanks. He briefed them with a few words.

"Finished, sir."

"Then get into the crate! Full throttle Rako! Follow your nose!"

Rakowitz grinned and set the assault gun in motion. For minutes everyone listened to the sound of the vehicle. Then they were certain that the track was one-hundred percent in order.

Peering through the periscope, Brandner saw several T-34s burning in an open area and behind at the edge of the ravine, which ran north-south, the flashes of gunfire from the dug-in T-34s, which were answered by the assault guns of the 3rd Platoon.

The approaching assault gun was met by machine-gun fire. The squat armored vehicle rolled forward then halted by a half-destroyed building. A Leutnant ran across the open street and took cover behind the assault gun.

"What's the situation, Leutnant?"

"They have us pinned down with flanking fire, Leutnant."

"Get your people behind us. We'll drive through at a walk."

"Thank you, Leutnant." The Leutnant waved. From all sides soldiers emerged from cover. They reached the assault gun, which began to move, and walked behind it.

"Schranz! Three-hundred, one o'clock! Machine-gun nest. High-explosive shell!"

The second shell sent everything up in a cascade of rising tracer. The men behind the assault gun cheered wildly. With a leap the vehicle took a gully and climbed up the far side. Brandner involuntarily closed his eyes when a streak of flame shot over the assault gun. He saw the turret of a T-34 as it lowered its gun.

"Armor-piercing shell! Turn left!"

T-34 and assault gun fired simultaneously. While the tank's shot passed to the left of the assault gun, the latter's armor-piercing round struck the tank between the turret ring and hull and silenced it.

"Faster Rako!"

The assault gun picked up speed. The infantry behind it began to shout, then they reached the enemy position. Russians jumped up in front of the vehicle. Then the infantry reached the Russian main line of resistance. All ten vehicles of the combat echelon had set off together and they reached the enemy main line of resistance almost simultaneously. They rolled from the flanks toward the center and eliminated Soviet nests of resistance one after another. Brandner issued curt instructions to his vehicle commanders.

"They're running, sir!"

From the Soviet positions farther back everything that could move began to withdraw. The main line of resistance began to move. Brandner didn't waste much time in thinking. He had reached his assigned objective and there was no requirement for him to go any further, but this was his chance.

"Combat echelon, listen to me! We are going to follow up behind the enemy in a narrow wedge and not give him a chance to settle down. Destroy any enemy guns and equipment found. When the order 'retreat' is given pull back to the main line of resistance here."

"Damn, damn! This better work, sir. The Hauptmann ordered that we should . . ."

"Shut up, Schranz! We have been given a chance here."

They drove forward. After 300 meters Brandner left two platoons behind to secure the flanks. He himself continued after the retreating enemy with the two vehicles of his 3rd Platoon (the third had been disabled with track damage). The assault guns shot up fleeing Russian trucks, blowing them up with high-explosive shells.

"How much farther, sir?"

"The Ivans have their supply dump in the next village. That's where we're going, Marischka."

The assault guns pressed ahead to the west end of the next village. There they halted and began firing into the village with high-explosive shells. Flames rose from a fuel dump. Brandner saw burning oil drums hurled into the air. Then the first enemy artillery shells came howling in.

"The artillery spotter has seen us, sir."

"Phoenix to Marischka. Back to the main line of resistance."

The two assault guns turned. All around heavy shells rained down. Steel, stones and earth were thrown against Phoenix. It was noisy inside. The two assault guns zigzagged to the rear, firing as they went. When they had returned to their own main line of resistance Leutnant Brandner determined that they had driven more than three kilometers into enemy territory.

"Brandner to General Schaal at once!"

The Leutnant received this news when he arrived at the battery command post. Brandner set out in his Kübelwagen to the command post of the 10th Panzer Division, which had been in command of the attack.

"Leutnant Brandner of the 202nd Assault Gun Battalion reporting as ordered."

"Thank you, Brandner. Stand at ease. I wish to express my appreciation to you and your combat echelon. You made it possible for us to move back into our former main line of resistance. I have three Iron Crosses, First Class, and ten Iron Crosses, Second Class, for your brave men."

"Thank you, sir! The men have earned it."

"Listen Brandner, do you have enough fuel and ammunition to carry out another advance?"

"The combat echelon is rearming now, sir. It will be ready for action again in half an hour."

"Good. Look here: there is still a nest of resistance here in the northwest of the division's sector. We have to smoke it out immediately in order to prevent the enemy from infiltrating there during the night and strengthening his position. An assault battalion will be going with you."

Leutnant Brandner handed out the Iron Crosses in the assembly area. Then he instructed the platoon leaders. Thirty minutes later, when the rearming and refueling was completed, the combat echelon set off again in the direction of the enemy.

"How do you foresee the attack taking place, sir?"

The infantry battalion commander had come over to Brandner's assault gun; his men waited behind the slope for the order to attack. The Hauptmann pointed to the front.

"I'm going to follow you across the plain Brandner, behind your assault guns."

"Out of the question, sir! Please excuse me, but I think you should attack though the gully here while I roll across the plain and draw the enemy's fire."

"Of course that is better for my men, Leutnant. But if enemy infantry let you drive past and then attack the assault guns with explosive charges, you will be in big trouble."

"We can advance very quickly, sir."

"Very well. I will come with you now until we are in visual range."

The rules of the trade for assault artillery: Aim, fire, and hit from a concealed position!

At Brandner's order the assault guns started their engines. They began to move and rolled out of the gully. The battery commander's vehicle stopped above on the open plain.

"Your direction of attack is along there, sir."

Standing in the commander's hatch, Brandner showed the Hauptmann the direction that he intended to take. Scattered rifle shots came from the village. The bullets whizzed close past the battery commander's vehicle.

"Look out, Brandner! Snipers!" yelled the infantry officer.

At that instant Sepp Brandner felt a hard blow and blood suddenly spurted from the right side of his neck. Brandner tried to cry out, but he could not. Before he collapsed into the assault gun he felt another stabbing pain that he could not localize.

He heard the dismayed voice of Unteroffizier Schranzl: "The artery's been cut!"

In his semiconscious state Brandner heard the other assault guns move off. He heard the thunder of cannon and the sound of machine-gun fire. The strangling feeling that almost cut off his breath disappeared. Suddenly he could breathe again. He heard agitated voices. Brandner struggled to open his eyes and saw a Feldwebel of the medical platoon bending over him.

In a detached way Brandner listened to the men speaking. He heard that two more medics were coming with a panye sled. They lifted him carefully from the assault gun. Then he felt the panye sled begin to move. An icy wind blew over him. The cold cut like a knife through the blanket the medics had placed over him. The last thing he heard was the assault guns firing their cannon. Then he lost consciousness.

Brandner came to when the sled reached the village where the repair group had its quarters. The men gathered round him. Worried shouts rang out. But he was unable to speak. At the makeshift aid station the doctor decided that Brandner had to go to the main aid station in Bolkhov. Fortunately for him the road had been shoveled clear the day before. But the ambulance refused to start. At almost 50 degrees below zero the engine had become little more than a block of ice.

"Don't worry, Brandner, it will be all right. What's that on your right hand?"

The medic, who had stepped up to the litter, saw several spurts of blood. He applied a sticking plaster to the hand. "A couple of splinters, Brandner, not so bad. Now if we can just get you to the main dressing station."

As if on cue, just then the commander's car drove into the village from Bolkhov. Leutnant Brandner was put in the car immediately and the driver headed back from where he had just come. Brandner's condition was more than serious. A chaplain gave him the Last Rites. When he arrived in the operating theater it was found that a bullet had also pierced his right forearm. The entire arm was covered in blood. The first bullet had pierced his neck between the larynx and esophagus. This life-threatening wound made it necessary for Brandner to be flown back to Germany in an ambulance aircraft. But no aircraft were able to take off.

Sepp Brandner was taken to Orel by ambulance. There he waited for a hospital train for Germany. Suspended between life and death, days later he rode the train through the partisan zone near Briansk. Once the wagon in front of the locomotive struck a mine. Then partisans attacked the train. Nevertheless Sepp Brandner reached Bautzen, where he was unloaded and taken to hospital.

Brandner's recovery from this serious wound, his third, was surprisingly rapid. Several weeks later he was sent to his home town of Vienna to recuperate. He now wore the Wound Badge in Silver and the Assault Badge, which he had received in hospital on 4 April 1942. At the end of April Brandner traveled back to the replacement unit, passing on convalescent leave, and a short time later rejoined his unit, which was in Bolkhov.

✠

During the summer of 1942 Brandner's unit, the 202nd Assault Gun Battalion took part in the fighting in the central sector near Fatezh, where it was employed as a mobile fire-brigade. Then in autumn 1942 the batalion assembled in the Vyazma area. There Hauptmann Buhr, commander of the 2nd Battery, took over the battalion. As a junior Oberleutnant, Sepp Brandner assumed command of the 2nd Battery. The battalion subsequently moved into the Rzhev area, where the Soviets were preparing to launch a major offensive.

"Watch out Waldner that you don't drive the car into a tree. The night is as dark as a bear's arse!"

"Don't worry, sir. You can sleep calmly."

Sepp Brandner lay back. He closed his eyes and was soon asleep. Moments later a hard jolt woke him up.

"What's going on, Waldner?"

"We drove into a telephone pole, sir."

"How could that happen? Did you fall asleep or something?"

"No, sir! But I think I am night blind."

Oberleutnant Brandner looked aghast at his replacement driver. Then he groaned resignedly:

"And you took a chance and drove kilometers through the night without saying anything, depending solely on luck?"

The Obergefreiter, who was driving in place of Rakowitz, who was on leave, just grinned. Before he could apologize the Oberleutnant silenced him with a wave of his hand. He had heard something.

"That is a prime mover, sir," said the driver.

"Hopefully you can at least hear better than you see."

"For sure, sir. An 18-tonner. I'm certain that's what it is."

"Let's hope so for God's sake!"

They jumped from the car and Oberleutnant Brandner hurried to meet the prime mover. When he recognized the tactical symbol of the 102nd Artillery Regiment he couldn't help but grin. That was his old regiment before he moved over to assault guns.

"Hey, do you have a winch with you?" he asked the driver of the prime mover.

"No we don't" he replied at once. Sepp Brandner recognized Obergefreiter Siegl, who had given him his basic training. Siegl could not see him because Brandner was standing in the dark.

"Listen!" said Brandner, play acting, "Who's there with you now?"

"The senior NCO."

"That's Hauptwachtmeister Streit?"

"Yes, sir . . ." The driver's eyes almost fell out of head from surprise. He raised a flashlight and illuminated Sepp Brandner. But before the beam of light reached his face it illuminated the man's shoulder straps with the star.

"Forgive me, sir!"

"Yes, damn it, don't you remember me. Hey, Streit, I was your recruit, the one you worked on especially hard."

Now the senior NCO caught on as well.

"Well I'll be damned, Sepp Brandner!"

Streit leapt down from the prime mover. He hugged his former recruit who now outranked him. Two minutes later the car was back on the road. And so Sepp Brandner reacquainted himself with the 102nd Artillery Regiment in Blagusha, where he was supposed to move into his assembly area.

Oberleutnant Brandner and his battery achieved one success after another in the Rzhev area. The assault guns were often called upon to go to the aid of the infantry and eliminate enemy incursions. Small missions, large breakthroughs, whatever had to be dealt with Sepp Brandner and his assault gun Phoenix were a symbol of victory. During that fall and winter Brandner and his crew destroyed eighteen enemy tanks, from T-34s to KV-Is. The assault artillery, and in this sector the 202nd Battalion, were the mascot of the divisions they supported.

During his first major conference after assuming the post of Inspector General of Armored Forces, Generaloberst Guderian demanded that the entire assault artillery should be placed under his command. The result was a storm of protest. Apart from Speer everyone present, especially the artillery officers who were then in command of the assault artillery, were opposed. The chief adjutant at Führer Headquarters expressed the feelings of the artillerymen: "The assault artillery is the single arm in which an artillerymen can win the Knight's Cross. For this reason we wish to keep it."

Hitler, who was already half won over to Guderian's plan, thereupon turned to the panzer commander and said: "You see, Guderian, you have everyone against you. Therefore, I cannot agree." This decision was to have fateful consequences in the near future. The assault artillery remained independent and was sent wherever it was needed. Furthermore the infantry divisions, each of which was supposed to be assigned an assault gun battalion, remained without effective antitank weapons.

In December the 202nd Assault Gun Battalion was withdrawn from the combat zone and transferred to Bobichevo. There for the first time in a long time it once again had revetments for its assault guns and a bunker position for itself. From these quartering areas it conducted sorties into the surrounding area. The 202nd Battalion remained in this relatively quiet sector until spring. Then it was moved into the area south of Orel in order to take part in "Operation Citadel," the German offensive to destroy the Kursk salient. Equipped with the new long-barreled L/48 gun, it was now possible to destroy a T-34 from a distance of 1 500 meters. The assault guns had finally achieved parity in firepower.

"Sir, the village is full of T-34s!"

Hanging out of the loader's hatch, Obergefreiter Laubisch pointed forward to where the houses of the village of Oleskoye projected above the ravine. Sepp Brandner, who had been promoted to the rank of Hauptmann a few days earlier (on 1 June 1943) turned the "scissors" slightly. He saw a tank turret behind a haystack and behind a barn the nose of another.

"Battery remain in reverse slope position. Laubisch, you come with me. We'll go see where they all are."

Hauptmann Brandner left the vehicle. He turned to the dispatch rider, who was talking to the crew of Adler.

"Back to the infantry command post. Report: 'Assault guns are in the sector. Prepare to advance.'"

The motorcycle's engine roared to life and the rider headed for the rear, zigzagging around potholes. Brandner climbed down to the stream bed. He worked his way forward behind bushes and alders. Then the two men found themselves about 300 meters from the entrance to the village. Sepp Brandner marked the positions of the T-34s on his sketch map. He and Laubisch were about to head back when a Russian patrol appeared on the slope above them, not five paces away.

"Hands up!" shouted a rough voice. Brandner and Laubisch raised their submachine-guns almost simultaneously. They opened fire and the enemy above on the slope disappeared immediately.

"Go, back!" They ran on in the cover of the bushes. Bullets from a Russian submachine-gun shredded the foliage behind them and smacked into the soft ground. Then they reached a bend and were safe.

Schranzl, who had just been promoted to Wachtmeister, grinned and said to the battery commander, "Why the hurry, sir?"

"I didn't want to leave you lot alone when the shooting starts," replied Sepp Brandner without hesitation. "Platoon and gun commanders to me!"

The men formed a circle around their commanding officer, who outlined the positions of the enemy tanks and issued battle orders. The ten assault guns and three assault howitzers moved off slowly. They deployed as Brandner had ordered, the three platoons fanning out. They left the ravine and appeared on the open plain.

"1,500 meters ahead, next to the haystack, Schranzl."

"Target in sight."

"The Wachtmeister adjusted his aim and fired. The T-34 moved forward several meters. It turned and the Soviet tank's gun swung around. Obergefreiter Laubisch, who could see none of this, rammed the next shell home. The second shot thundered. A metallic bang signaled a direct hit.

"Full throttle. Continue straight ahead."

The assault guns now rolled toward the village from three directions. Flames shot from the long-barreled cannon. The first T-34s began to smoke.

"Eagle to commander: two T-34s knocked out," reported Leutnant Kirchner.

"Buzzard must soon call in too," declared driver Rakowitz. No sooner were the words out of his mouth when a voice was heard:

"Buzzard to commander. One T-34 destroyed."

"Carry on. Into the village."

"Falcon to commander. Eight enemy tanks sighted. Driving out of the village."

"Frontal attack!"

Phoenix raced straight toward the T-34s rolling out of the village. The first shot struck one of the Russian tanks, which blew apart.

"Poorly welded," commented driver Rakowitz.

A mighty blow shook the assault gun. One of the recently installed side skirts fell to the ground. Then there was another bang.

"Antitank guns, sir!"

Without waiting for orders, driver Rakowitz turned the assault gun in the direction of the shots. He saw a muzzle flash between two houses and headed straight towards it. Moving fast, the assault gun avoided the shot. Then it jerked to a stop.

"Fire!"

The shell flitted towards the enemy. A circular rosette of flames lit the morning. Farther right the howitzer fired and sent a 105-mm shell into one of the squat houses, from which an enemy machine-gun was firing.

"There they are!"

Red Army troops streamed out of the house into the open. Brandner sent the First Platoon after the fleeing enemy. The Second was sent after another antitank gun. Meanwhile Brandner and the Third Platoon advanced slowly. Shell after shell smashed into the houses. The nose of a T-34 emerged from a pile of rubble not 80 meters in front of Brandner's assault gun. Before the enemy gunner could rotate his turret the first shell from Phoenix slammed into the Russian tank. However, the shell failed to penetrate and howled away towards the sky.

"Turn left, Rako!" screamed Brandner.

A knocked out KV-II.

The assault gun turned. Rattling and roaring, the two steel giants closed on one another. But then Phoenix drove over a fence and disappeared into a side street. Then it turned again. It rumbled toward the left behind a half-destroyed farmhouse. Brandner tried to peer between the rubble and the right side. He saw rising smoke and heard the sound of his assault guns and several T-34s firing.

"Turn right, Rako. Good—stop!"

Wachtmeister Schranzl traversed the gun. Then he lowered it slightly, placing the enemy tank in his sight. Flames blasted from the barrel. The shot struck the rear of the tank just as it was about to move again. The turret hatch flipped back and flames shot out. Then the tank's ammunition went up.

"Turn, advance through the village to the east end!"

They drove on. Eagle appeared, closely followed by Buzzard. Ten meters beside it rolled Falcon.

"Drive through to the east end!" Brandner ordered by radio.

The infantry were already visible behind the assault guns. They fired at the retreating Russians. One hour later Oleskoye was cleared of the enemy. The infantry occupied the Russian positions. The Brandner battery rolled back into its assembly area. Three hours later the Russians launched a surprise attack in an attempt to retake Oleskoye. The attack force consisted of a regiment-size force of infantry supported by tanks.

✠

"Brandner, you and your battery are driving to Oleskoye in a night mission."

"Yes, sir. But that isn't simple in a surrounded village. There are still groups of German troops holding on inside. If we mistakenly fire on one by mistake . . ."

Major Buhr nodded in agreement.

"A damned difficult business, Brandner. That's why I have selected you. You know the job and you know what your assault guns can do. If there is any doubt as whether you are dealing with the enemy you will have to wait. Only fire when you are certain that the target is the enemy."

Brandner felt the weight of responsibility that had been placed upon his shoulders. Nevertheless, he was confident and believed that he and his men would do the job. He left the brigade command post and drove back to the battery in his Kübelwagen. The platoon commanders were already waiting for him.

"Comrades, we leave in an hour. Everyone top up your fuel tanks and make sure that you have a full load of ammunition. We have been ordered to attack Oleskoye and free our surrounded comrades."

Exactly one hour later the battery commander raised his right hand. The engines of the assault guns, which had been at idle, roared louder. The platoons moved off. The supply men who were staying behind saw the sharply-outlined shadow of the commander standing in the first assault gun.

Sepp Brandner tried to pierce the blackness in front of him with his eyes. The sound of exploding hand grenades could be heard from Oleskoye. Now and then a Maxim machine-gun rattled, to be answered by furious bursts of fire from the German MG 42 (rate of fire 1,500 rounds per minute).

"They're not finished yet, sir. We can get them out if we get there in time."

"We'll get there in time, Schranzl. We have no other choice but to break straight into the village and drive through as far as we can."

"To everyone: attack and drive through. Don't let yourself be stopped. Fire only on identified targets."

The drivers shifted into third gear. The assault guns rumbled up and down. The village came nearer and nearer. Fire reached out toward the commander's vehicle.

"Open fire at the enemy machine-gun!"

The second shot shattered the machine-gun and blasted it into the air. Then they reached the first houses. Groups of Russians broke in front of them and ran away. The three howitzers fired after them. Suddenly a group of German troops appeared before the assault guns. In spite of the enemy fire, Brandner emerged from his hatch.

"Right," the infantry Leutnant shouted up to him, "snipers on the water tower and in the steeple."

An order caused Phoenix to swing around.

"Follow me, men."

The Leutnant nodded. In front of him Brandner saw muzzle flashes from the water tower, which was perhaps eight meters high. The Russians had even dragged a Maxim machine-gun up there.

"There you go, Schranzl. Maximum elevation. Aim at the tower."

The cannon muzzle rose as high as it could go. Then the first shell whizzed upwards and struck the steel one meter below the top of the tower. The second and third shots landed right beside it. In the light of the fires that had broken out, Russians appeared on the tower. Dark objects flew down. Brandner immediately ducked inside the assault gun. Not a moment too soon, for at the same instant the hand grenades and several satchel charges exploded.

"Fire faster!"

Lubisch jammed his right thumb. "Damn!" he cursed. The pain shot up his arm. Nevertheless, he reached for another round and rammed it home. Schranzl backed the assault gun up a few meters. He reached a shallow depression. The vehicle's nose rose slightly. Then the gun fired, and the shell blew off the upper rim of the water tower. A loud explosion followed and bodies flew through the air. Terrible cries drowned out the noise of this pitiless night battle. Machine-guns and rifles rained down on the ground.

"Carry on! The next nest of resistance!"

"I'll lead!" the Leutnant shouted up to Hauptmann Brandner.

The Phoenix rolled onward. The remaining assault guns had also engaged the enemy. Shots rang out through the village, the signal to the surrounded German troops that salvation was at hand. The assault gun rolled past a shell crater from which was heard the relieved cry:

"It's Brandner! Our Sepp is here!"

Antitank guns opened fire, then machine-guns.

"There it is, there behind the wall!" shouted the Leutnant.

"Take cover!" Brandner shouted back. For a second he saw an assault gun appear farther south in the side street. It had to be Wachtmeister Sponsel.

"Buzzard from commander! Attack the antitank gun position in front of me, over."

Sponsel's voice came through the headset: "Target in sight, I'm attacking." Hauptmann Brandner saw the Wachtmeister's assault gun turn. Under fire from two sides, the Soviet antitank gun was soon silenced. The assault guns overran the machine-gun positions. Three men raced toward Brandner's vehicle. They were carrying explosive charges.

Hauptmann Brandner grabbed his assault rifle that hung beside him. He fired quickly, without aiming. A huge explosion blew the first enemy to pieces, but the rest kept coming. At that moment Sponsel's gun roared. The armor-piercing shell pierced the second enemy soldier. The man's charge exploded, also killing the third Russian. Five minutes later the assault guns reached the east end of the village. Some of the enemy had fled, but the rest had established themselves in the houses. The assault guns stopped for a quick conference.

"What should we do, sir?" asked Leutnant Kirchner, the commander of the 2nd Platoon.

"We have to wait until dawn. We will be able to help our comrades further when we can see more."

"Damn, the Ivans are firing into the village."

The first shells landed in Oleskoye, bringing down what was still standing. Hours passed. When the first pale light of dawn appeared in the east, Brandner turned to his platoon commanders:

"I am going back into the village to reconnoiter. If I don't return Oberleutnant Wagleitner will assume command of the battery and lead it back."

Before anyone could object, Brandner had reached Phoenix. Lubisch's head was visible in the loader's hatch.

"Let's go, sir!"

"Watch it, Lubisch! There are surely still snipers in the village."

But even though everyone else took cover Brandner could not. He had to scout the enemy positions. There was the crack of rifle shots. The bullets smacked into earth walls. Brandner was tempted to duck inside the vehicle. His fingers clutched the hatch rim. Don't weaken, he urged himself. He was responsible for the other three men in the assault gun and for all the Germans still in the hell-hole of Oleskoye. No matter how hard he looked, Brandner could not find the enemy. But he could hear them as they fired their rifles and machine-guns. Then he saw a few figures in a hastily-dug trench. Arms reached out toward him and he heard voices: "Comrades, help us."

"Wounded, Lubisch. We two will get out. Schranzl, you keep firing. Aim at the huts over there where the machine-gun is firing."

Hauptmann Brandner leapt from the hatch. When he hit the ground Lubisch was beside him. A burst of fire caused them to hit the ground simultaneously. Then they heard a crash as Phoenix fired its gun, silencing the enemy machine-gun.

The pair crept toward the wounded. An Oberfeldwebel, who wore the German Cross in Gold and the Wound Badge in Gold on his tunic, crawled out to meet them.

"Sir, we have no medics. They were killed during the night. As well we can't hold any longer, ammunition gone."

"How many are you? Who of you can still walk?"

"Six men, all wounded; none can make it back on his own."

"Then we'll drive you back."

"Thank you, sir."

One of the young lads began to sob. But he immediately suppressed this outburst, as if he was ashamed to have given expression to his emotion.

"Come, Lubisch, the boy first."

They picked up the severely-wounded soldier, ran back to the Phoenix at a crouch and laid him on the rear of the assault gun. Shots rang out. Then the wounded Oberfeldwebel fired. Brandner and Lubisch came for him but he waved them away:

"My men first!" he gasped, then fired again at the muzzle flashes from the enemy machine-gun. They eventually got everyone back to the assault gun, including the Oberfeldwebel. Sepp Brandner put his headset and throat microphone back on.

"Phoenix to everyone. We're pulling back. Drive back slowly and take the wounded with you! Out."

Brandner looked into the eyes of the badly wounded soldier. The young man stared at him with glistening eyes.

"You're getting us out of here, sir?"

"Of course, son."

Hauptmann Brandner had to look away from the overwhelming joy that beamed from the young eyes. Lubisch's head appeared in the loader's hatch.

"Have you gone crazy, Lubisch?"

"But you have your head out, sir. Two men can see more than one. We don't want to overlook any of our comrades."

Hauptmann Brandner said nothing. That was Lubisch. When he thought of his unconditional commitment and that of his other men it brought tears to his eyes. They rolled through the smoldering rubble. Snipers continued to take potshots at them. The remaining assault guns reported in. All had picked up other wounded. Sepp Brandner repeatedly tried to scan the terrain ahead through the "scissors" while Lubisch kept watch to the side.

"Sir, there's some there!"

"Where, Lubisch?"

"Behind the shot-up house. Two men. They're waving for us to pick them up."

"Turn slightly, Rako!"

The assault gun swung around. Wachtmeister Schranzl continued to fire into the midst of the witch's cauldron that the village had become. Then they stopped beside the wounded. Once again Hauptmann Brandner and Obergefreiter Lubisch got out. They picked up the two wounded, who had put makeshift dressings on each other's wounds. Then the worst was over.

Phoenix rolled on again. Rakowitz carefully avoided the worst spots. By now it was daylight. The blood-red ball of the sun had climbed over the horizon. When they reached open terrain Brandner called to his loader, "Be more careful now, Lubisch!" He could watch for wounded himself now. But still Lubisch would not lower his head for fear that they might leave a helpless comrade behind. He continued to scan the terrain. Brandner was about to repeat his warning when a shot rang out from a foxhole in front of the assault gun. Lubisch turned and for an instant Brandner could see the small hole in his forehead from which blood was dripping.

"Lubisch!" he shouted, dismayed. "Lubisch!"

But the Obergefreiter, who had been with him from the beginning, could not answer. With their dead comrade inside the assault gun and the eight wounded on it, the Phoenix arrived at the clearing station for wounded. They carefully unloaded their cargo of misery. Once again they saw the liberating looks of their rescued comrades. The other assault guns also returned with their loads of wounded. The men of the battery said goodbye to their comrade Lubisch. They buried him in Russian soil.

✠

"Everyone out of the quarters! Go, quickly!"

Hauptmann Brandner rushed through the huts, waking the men. "To the guns. We've been placed on standby alert!"

All the batteries of the brigade had been placed on alert. The men climbed into their vehicles and waited for what was to come.

"Do you know anything else, sir?" asked Obergefreiter Wimmer, who had taken Lubisch's place as loader.

"Deserters have told of a Russian attack and preparatory fire."

"Yes, if they weren't boasting and . . ."

In the distance ahead there was a flash as the Russians fired Katushas (multiple rocket launchers). The rockets smashed into the houses and turned the assembly area into hell in a matter of seconds.

"That doesn't look like boasting."

"I would rather be in a tiny foxhole than in this steel box," interjected Wachtmeister Schranzl.

"Me too, Schranzl," admitted Brandner.

The brigade commander's voice came over the radio: "Tank alert! First and Second Batteries drive out to meet the enemy head-on. Third Battery and the Brigade Headquarters stand by for my orders. All others free hunting."

"Hunting is good," murmured Wimmer. "As long as we don't become the hunted."

Soon the sound of engines was heard. Soviet tanks were trying to overrun the German main line of resistance and force a breakthrough, clearing a way for the following infantry.

"Battery, move out!"

Brandner stood in the hatch and led from the front. As his assault gun moved forward he looked around and saw the nine assault guns and three assault howitzers following. The second salvo from the Stalin Organs came roaring toward them with an ear-shattering din. Only two minutes had passed since the first had landed. One of the projectiles landed not thirty meters from Phoenix. Brandner quickly dropped inside the assault gun and closed the hatch cover tight. The tremendous force of the explosion caused the assault gun to tip steeply to the side. Brandner immediately

Sepp Brandner leading from his *Sturmgeschütz.*

reappeared in the hatch. Luckily the tracks had not been damaged. The assault gun rolled on.

"Commanders, check in. Any damage?"

The assault guns reported. None had been disabled. Now enemy tanks appeared before them in the first light of dawn.

"KV-Is in front of us."

"Twelve T-34s attacking. Following infantry."

Sepp Brandner ordered a turn as soon as he heard this report from Leutnant Kirchner. The T-34s appeared out of the morning mist. The duel between assault guns and tanks began. Star shells illuminated the battlefield. Tracer from machine-guns flitted from place to place.

Phoenix rolled right and then left. Wherever a target showed itself it was engaged and destroyed by shells from the long-barreled "seventy-fives." Within a few minutes as many as twenty enemy tanks were blazing in the brigade's area. The enemy attack ground to a halt. The Soviet tanks stopped, turned around and fled. The brigade commander rushed forward with the Third Battery to where resistance had stiffened and three assault guns had been knocked out by Russian KV-I heavy tanks. But there, too, the German counterattack got going and the enemy attack was beaten back.

When in May 1943 it became apparent that the enemy was planning a major offensive against Army Group South, it was decided to launch "Operation Citadel," which had been planned for a long time. As early as 18 April 1943 Feldmarschall von Manstein had recommended that the operation be carried out as soon as possible in order to avert the threat of an enemy offensive toward the Donets region.

Hitler ordered all commanders in chief and commanding generals of units allocated to "Citadel" to meet in his headquarters in Rastenburg on 1 July 1943. There he announced his decision to launch "Citadel" on 5 July.

The attack on the two armies' fronts began on 5 July 1943. The 9th Army, attacking from Army Group Center's area, made good initial progress and drove twenty kilometers into enemy territory in the first days of the attack. But then the 9th Army under Model stalled and could go no farther. The enemy launched a counterattack against the 2nd Panzer Army's front and achieved deep penetrations in three places. The 9th Army had to divert some of its forces to deal with these. On 13 July Feldmarschall von Kluge and Feldmarschall von Manstein were called to Führer Headquarters. After listening to what Feldmarschall von Manstein had to say, Hitler decided to call off "Operation Citadel."

But this did not mean the end of fighting in this sector of the front. Quite the contrary! The Soviets made repeated attempts to break through. Every German unit was involved in fierce defensive fighting and one of these units was the 202nd Assault Gun Brigade.

"Hauptmann Brandner?"

"What is it?"

"Runner, sir," reported Schranzl, who had come running into the command post. The runner followed behind him.

"Give it to me." Hauptmann Brandner took the message from the exhausted man's hand and read:

"Posnoye occupied by Russian troops. German strongpoint surrounded. Second Battery break through. Fire at anything that shows itself. Our forces are dug in in bunkers."

"Thank you. Kammler, write that the order is being carried out."

Five minutes after the alert the battery rolled toward Posnoye. Leading the way was the battery commander's vehicle with Hauptmann Brandner standing in the hatch. This assault gun had already destroyed 38 enemy tanks. When figures appeared in front of the assault gun, Brandner ducked involuntarily.

"Give the password!" he shouted. No reply.

"Fire!"

The assault guns fired an high-explosive shell. This was the opening act of the night battle that followed.

"All guns advance and open fire!"

One after another the assault guns joined the battle.

Over the radio came the voice of Wachtmeister Sponsel on the right flank: "Soviets are running away, sir!"

"Advance slowly and hold the village!"

In vain Sepp Brandner searched for signs of the old main line of resistance. There was nothing to be seen. Then one of the assault guns ran over a mine. On hearing the explosion Brandner gave the order to halt. Hour after hour passed. Nothing could be heard but the artillery of both sides firing. Then it became light. Through the "scissors" Brandner saw a church and in the middle of the entrance—an antitank gun!

"Schranzl, 300 meters ahead, antitank gun."

The first shell whizzed on its way and Wimmer rammed home the next round.

"Hit!"

At the same instant a gun fired to their left. The shell deflected off the side skirt.

"Back up a bit, otherwise we won't be able to get the new enemy." Phoenix rolled backwards. Rakowitz, the experienced driver, had shifted gears immediately. He stopped. There was a flash of fire and a frightful crash. A tremendous blow shook Phoenix. The four men inside the assault gun yelled simultaneously. Then they scrambled outside. Everyone was sure that the vehicle would blow up at any minute and had left the assault gun, which was still rolling backwards, through the loader's hatch.

Brandner hit the ground. Russian infantry were firing wildly in all directions. The assault gun was still rolling backwards at idle and offered the men some cover.

"Damn, it's going to roll into a big crater, sir!"

Under fire from the enemy infantry, Brandner jumped up, climbed into the assault gun and pulled out the key. Phoenix stopped just short of the crater.

The remaining assault guns succeeded in forcing the enemy back. The following infantry freed the surrounded crew. When evening came prime movers came and towed away the disabled vehicles, including Phoenix. The battery commander's vehicle was repaired during the night and was ready for action when morning came.

Two days later the enemy tried once again to break through. Twenty enemy tanks were counted opposite 2nd Battery's sector. Now they advanced, followed closely by Russian infantry.

"Don't shoot until I give the order," radioed Brandner.

"Enemy has already reached the trench fighters, sir," came the voice of Oberleutnant Wegleitner, commander of the 1st Platoon.

"Let them come, Wegleitner!"

Brandner was tempted to start the counterattack, because he knew what it meant for the infantry to lie in the trenches and allow themselves to be overrun by the T-34s. But he couldn't unless he wanted to threaten the success of his surprise tactic. He peered ahead from his haystack cover. Through the "scissors" he saw a machine-gun squad desperately firing at the leading Russian tank. The bullets bounced harmlessly off the tank's steel armor. Brandner grasped the hatch ring tighter. Then he cleared his throat.

"Attack!"

The assault guns rolled simultaneously from cover. Phoenix engaged the first enemy tank, scoring a direct hit with its first hit. The second shot was also on target. The T-34 stopped, in flames. The assault gun rolled forward, with Sepp Brandner directing the driver. He saw a T-34 in the process of collapsing a trench. The T-34's flank appeared in the sight. The shot shattered one of the Soviet tank's tracks, causing it to jerk to one side. The next shot set its engine on fire.

The assault guns drove past the infantry at top speed. Jubilantly the soldiers raised their arms in the air. Phoenix destroyed three more T-34s. Then it reached the village. There the opposing infantry forces clashed. However with its tanks gone, the Soviet assault had lost much of its impetus. When Sepp Brandner arrived back in the assembly area he was greeted by Major Buhr.

"How was it, Brandner?"

"Reporting kills forty-one to forty-five, sir."

"Brandner, I am proud of you. Once again you have foiled an enemy attack."

On 16 September Hauptmann Sepp Brandner was awarded the German Cross in Gold for this exploit.

✠

"I don't know, Sepp, there's nothing more for us to gain here. The time is past."

Oberleutnant Wegleitner raised his glass and tipped back the crystal-clear vodka. He looked at his comrade questioningly. Hauptmann Brandner nodded.

"I'm afraid you are right. The offensive has failed and now its Ivan's turn to counterattack and he has plenty of tanks."

"Then why are we letting ourselves be thrashed instead of retreating in good time?"

"God, Kirchner, we can't withdraw yet, not while our infantry are still lying in the mud ahead of us. We will have to withdraw, that is certain. But we won't go while units are still pinned down."

"Yes, we know. Whenever firepower is needed they call for the assault artillery."

"And for Sepp," interjected Wachtmeister Sponsel. Sepp Brandner waved his hand.

"Don't talk rubbish! Each of you does the same as I. Every gun has a good number of kill rings."

Then Major Buhr walked in and the Leutnant sitting next to the door shouted, "Attention!"

"Gather round everyone. Ivan has broken through and is already driving down the main road west of Orel. We have orders to cover our units' withdrawal until they are through. Here are the hot spots. 1st Battery at the crossroads, 2nd in the middle and 3rd to the left of it. Brigade headquarters with me in the assembly area to intervene at the critical points."

Major Buhr briefed the individual battery commanders. Then he stood up.

"We will do our best. Departure in ten minutes. Take 120 rounds of ammunition."

✠

"Can't hear anything, sir. The division assault team, which is supposed to inform us when the withdrawal movements are over, appears to have disappeared into thin air."

"We just have to wait, Wegleitner."

"Damn, we are last. The other two batteries have already received orders to fall back. Why hasn't the old man called us yet?"

"Because we are supposed to stay here, I imagine."

Hauptmann Brandner slowly walked back to his assault gun. The men of the assault team should have been there long ago. He wondered whether he shouldn't just give the order to withdraw. But then he dismissed the idea. Anyway, there might be units behind them, which would then be encircled. The battery moved off at dawn. There was no sign of German troops anywhere. There was now no more doubt that they really were the last ones. Now they could pull back. The assault guns drove for about one kilometer and reached the railway embankment that was their boundary. Suddenly the sound of tank engines was heard from the other side of the embankment.

"Battery go into vee formation behind the embankment!" Brandner turned to his driver. "Rako, take us up the embankment."

Phoenix's engine roared louder. The assault gun rolled briskly up the embankment. Through the "scissors" Sepp Brandner saw a Russian village and in front of it tanks, many tanks.

"Commander to everyone! Eighteen T-34s in the village in front of us. We will receive no reinforcements. Open fire on my order."

Rakowitz steered the battery commander's assault gun down the embankment in the direction of the enemy. The assault gun set off down a gully. If it was quick enough it would be able to cut off the enemy tanks, which were driving single file.

"Commander to everyone: drive 100 meters to the west behind the embankment. On my order attack north across the embankment. Out."

Brandner received the confirmation signal. Phoenix drove on alone. The noise of the T-34s driving down the road grew louder. Hadn't they heard the sound of the assault gun's engine yet?

"A little more gas, Rako!" The assault gun picked up speed. Sepp Brandner called for a slight turn. The vehicle climbed the side of the gully. Through his periscope the commander saw the round turrets of the T-34s.

"We're going to roll out of the gully now. Range to the enemy tanks 800 meters, Schranzl."

The Wachtmeister released the main gun's safety catch. Loader Wimmer stood ready with the next armor-piercing round.

This T-34/76 was knocked on its side when it was hit.

"Turn—out!" Phoenix left the gully. The cannon muzzle pointed to the sky, and when the assault gun tipped forward and was horizontal again the gunner found that he only needed to make a slight correction.

"Fire!"

The force of the recoil caused the assault gun to rock backwards on its suspension. With a crash the armor-piercing shot smashed into the armored grate over the engine of the leading Soviet tank. A whirlwind of flame shot out from the interior of the T-34.

"Commander to everyone! Fire at will!"

The Phoenix moved off with a jerk and followed an arcing course to get a clear shot at the next T-34. As it did so the rest of the assault guns rumbled over the embankment. They drove into the flank of the T-34s and opened fire from 1,000 meters. The battlefield transformed itself into a hurricane of steel and fire. There was no quarter in the duel between the assault guns and the T-34s. However, the Russians had been taken completely by surprise. The very first salvo from the assault guns destroyed several T-34s. Approximately twelve T-34s lay smoking on the plain. The rest turned and fled. One disabled an assault gun by knocking off one of its tracks then was itself destroyed by shells fired from two assault guns. The tanks driving at the end of the Soviet column accelerated in an effort to escape, but the 3rd Platoon followed at a similar speed. Again the assault guns' cannon roared. Flames shot into the sky. Then the battle was over. Seventeen T-34s had been destroyed or disabled.

"Assemble and carry on! Continue to the west!"

The battery rolled toward the rear. After an hour the outline of a village appeared.

"Eagle to Phoenix! Russian KV-I in sight ahead at the entrance to the village!"

"Turn right, Rako!" Peering through his periscope, Hauptmann Brandner now also saw the huge Russian tank. The Russian crew must have spotted the assault guns at the same time, for the tank turned and rolled back.

"After it! Fire!" Hauptmann Brandner interrupted himself, for on the hill to the left of the village he saw a large force of enemy tanks in the morning sun. The vehicles quickly spread out and cut off the Germans' line of retreat.

"Prepare to be captured!" said Sepp Brandner with resignation.

"We have to break through, sir!"

"Yes, Rako, we must. But we are surrounded by the Ivans. No matter what the outcome we have to try it, general direction west!"

The assault guns moved off and several minutes later came to a defense line in an area of terrain covered by saplings. Sepp Brandner was about to give the order to open fire when the suspected enemy threw up their arms and began to cheer.

"Don't shoot, they're ours!"

The assault guns rolled nearer. A Hauptmann emerged from cover and walked over to the battery commander's vehicle.

"You've come just in time. We are cut off. I am Hauptmann Gromel."

Sepp Brandner introduced himself. There was a smile on his face when he realized the comic nature of this situation. Hauptmann Gromel also could not help but grin.

"Where are your guns, Gromel?"

"All blown up during the night. We have to get out of here."

"Are there any of our troops anywhere nearby?"

"No, Brandner, we are the last."

"Then put your men on the assault guns. Have them take their small arms and machine-guns in case we have to break through Russian infantry."

The artillerymen climbed onto the assault guns. They had to take up as little space as possible, for there were eight to ten men on each vehicle. Then the battery rolled on.

Using his compass, Hauptmann Gromel determined the heading to be followed. The assault guns rolled fast across the open steppe, heading west. Once they got too close to a main road. Russian supply units, tanks and guns could be seen moving west. The battery turned away from the road. Hauptmann Brandner observed the enemy movements, but he saw nothing to suggest that they had been spotted.

"Forest ahead. We'll head for it. If we reach it we will have it made. According to the map there are two roads leading through it to the west."

The assault guns rumbled toward the edge of the forest. Suddenly Leutnant Kirchner shouted over the radio: "Eagle to Phoenix. Russians in the wood!"

"Hey, Brandner, they're just Russian supply columns," called Hauptmann Gromel, who had observed the enemy movements through his binoculars. "We shouldn't let them hold us up!"

"Commander to everyone: drive through, fire all weapons!"

The vehicles picked up speed, rolling toward the edge of the forest at 35 kilometers per hour.

"Soviet fuel truck ahead. Open fire from 500 meters!"

They drove straight toward the fuel truck, which grew huge in the gunsight. The first shot was fired exactly 500 meters from the target. The shell flitted into the tank truck. There was a huge explosion and white flames shot into the sky. All the other assault guns opened fire almost simultaneously. The soldiers riding on the vehicles saw the terror caused by every round.

"Ready machine-guns!" called Hauptmann Gromel.

Then they were within range. It seemed as if they were driving through the leaping flames. An ammunition truck exploded with an ear-shattering roar. Fragments howled in all directions. Then the machine-guns joined in, adding to the din. Two Maxim machine-guns opened fire and two artillerymen riding on Falcon fell to the ground, mortally wounded.

"Turn, keep turning, fire!"

The shell landed between the two closely positioned machine-guns and silenced them. Falcon stopped. Several men jumped down and picked up the wounded. Then it drove on. The assault guns fired a last few rounds into the supply column and then they were past.

An hour later, with the woods behind them, Hauptmann Gromel said, "We have to regain contact with our front."

They drove along the main road. It soon became apparent how far the enemy had advanced in the last twenty-four hours. To the right of them Russian columns moved down the road. They rolled past. The assault guns had to cross the road if they were to reach safety.

There was a final conference in a thick stand of saplings. "Why don't we just open fire and force our way across, sir?" suggested Leutnant Kirchner.

"That would be madness in our situation. The enemy would shoot us up with his tanks. We have to come up with something else."

Then one of the men standing watch shouted, "Sir, sir, aircraft!"

"We're in trouble if they're Russian close-support aircraft."

"Want to bet they're Stukas?" said Hauptmann Gromel.

"I hope you're right, Gromel."

"Break out the air identification panels so they don't bomb us," ordered Hauptmann Brandner.

When the approaching aircraft were positively identified as Stukas, the air identification panels were spread out on the ground. On seeing the panels the aircraft waggled their wings and headed for the road.

"So we still do have some aircraft," declared Obergefreiter Wimmer.

The first Stukas peeled off. One after another the dive-bombers plunged earthwards. Their furious shrieking mingled with the scream of falling bombs. After completing their dives the Stukas returned and strafed the road with their fixed weapons. The men on the assault guns could see tracer and vehicles exploding in flames.

"Let's get across, the columns have stopped!"

The assault guns crossed the road without a shot being fired. The Stukas had arrived just in time. Two hours later the vehicles reached the German lines with Hauptmann Gromel's artillerymen.

The brigade adjutant greeted the battery commander with the words: "Brandner, this means the Knight's Cross for you." Sepp Brandner shrugged off the suggestion. He was glad to have brought his men back safely. The handshakes from his comrades of the artillery meant more than any other recognition.

✠

"Brandner, Sumy has been occupied by the Soviets. You have been ordered to attack with the infantry and retake the town."

Sepp Brandner, who had taken over the 202nd Assault Gun Brigade in place of its wounded commander, nodded. The Ia of the division to which they had been assigned explained the situation. Five minutes later the brigade set out for Sumy, followed by the mounted infantry.

The assault guns stormed into Sumy, blasting clear a path for the infantry. They rolled over obstacles and blasted enemy antitank guns. Wachtmeister Sponsel destroyed another four T-34s. For this feat he was awarded the German Cross in Gold. But the attack was halted in front of the railway station, where the enemy had dug in tanks and antitank guns behind stout walls. The inhabitants of Sumy had fled. Enemy artillery began to fire. The assault guns were in action day after day. The battle raged back and forth. What the Soviets gained in night attacks had to be recovered in the morning.

Several days earlier a skull and crossbones found in a medical school had been placed on the nose of Hauptmann Brandner's assault gun. Schranzl, the born mechanic, even rigged up a light behind it, and when the first night sortie was made against Sumy the death's head led the way. With eyes lit and a small siren blaring, Phoenix rolled against the enemy positions. The results were impressive. Led by Hauptmann Brandner, the 1st Battery drove deep into the Soviet positions. Firing all guns, even though no targets were visible, the assault guns pushed on. Panic broke out among the Russians, who left their dugouts and foxholes and fled to the rear, pursued by machine-gun fire from the infantry riding on the assault guns. The following infantry were able to occupy the new main line of resistance without difficulty and dig in.

The same game was repeated several nights in a row. Then the enemy became aware of the unusual mascot. From then on Phoenix was showered with machine-gun and rifle fire whenever it appeared. But wherever it burst into a village by surprise, the enemy still broke and ran. All that summer the 202nd Assault Gun Brigade fought in the Sumy area. Then the German forces withdrew in the direction of Kiev.

✠

Between 26 August and 4 September 1943 the Russians achieved a deep penetration against Army Group Center in the direction of Konotop-Nezhin. At the end of September they reached the Dniepr where it emptied into the Pripet. Then in mid-October the Soviets began crossing the Dniepr between Dnepropetrovsk and Kremenchug. When November began the Russian divisions were nearing Kiev.

"All combat batteries into readiness positions in the north part of the city. The enemy attack is expected from the north. He must be stopped there in order to safeguard the withdrawal of the divisions from Kiev and the surrounding areas."

Hauptmann Brandner was at the division briefing along with the other unit commanders. He was still leading the assault guns as acting brigade commander.

When the floor was thrown open for discussion, Sepp Brandner spoke up: "Sir, may I make a suggestion?" The general motioned with his hand for the Hauptmann to speak his mind.

A Panzer IV in the Great Bend of the Don in 1942.

"I request permission to move my batteries to the western exit from the city. Aerial reconnaissance has shown that the Russians are building an underwater bridge at the bend in the Dniepr. If they get across there, they will be able to make a surprise advance and block the western exit from the city. We will be trapped."

The general was not convinced: "But that is absurd, Brandner. It's complete madness."

But Sepp Brandner had been in Russia a long time. He knew the tactics of the Russians very well. As a result he sent his 1st Battery to the western exit from the city on his own responsibility. Even though the situation was becoming ever more critical, life in Kiev went on as usual. The movie theaters were full. No one expected the Russian attack to come so soon.

On the evening of 3 November Sepp Brandner drove to the western part of the city with his Kfz. 15 and the two assault guns under his personal command. Leutnant Mach, who was scouting ahead in his assault gun, reported to the acting brigade commander.

Brandner said, "Well, Mach, things smell a bit fishy to me. What do you think?"

"They'll definitely be coming one night soon. Perhaps even tonight. Then . . ."

The Leutnant stopped in mid sentence, for just then he saw German vehicles approaching in a wild dash from the north.

"Damn, something's wrong there! Into the crate Mach. Order your battery to battle readiness."

Then Hauptmann Brandner ran back to his Kübelwagen and jumped into the passenger seat. All of a sudden the vehicle column scattered and seconds later the sound of tank engines was heard.

"It's the Russians, sir," Leutnant Mach called over the radio.

"Get ready!"

The last vehicle to approach was a motorcycle-sidecar. Hauptmann Brandner waved wildly in attempt to stop it, but the driver simply roared past into Kiev. The sound of tank tracks became louder. Then the shape of a tank appeared before them.

"T-34, men. We'll drive back to the security position. Mach, you take the first one, Sponsel the second in case there's another one behind it."

Wachtmeister Sponsel, who was fifty meters further back in the ditch beside the road, acknowledged immediately. The Kübelwagen drove into cover behind an overturned rail car so as not to alert the enemy prematurely. The two brigade assault guns drove back to the main body of the battery.

"Damn, why isn't Leutnant Mach shooting, sir?"

"He probably lost the T-34 in the smoke. No, there he comes."

Then suddenly Wachtmeister Sponsel's voice rang out above the rattle of tracks: "More to the right, sir, or you'll ram me!"

With a curse Hauptmann Brandner jumped out of the Kübelwagen. His driver followed as he ran over to Sponsel. "Damn it, Sponsel that was Ivan!"

Now Sponsel realized his mistake, but the Soviet tank had already rolled past.

"Go after him, Sponsel, and knock him out!"

The assault gun moved off and chased the T-34. The remaining assault guns drove into the blocking positions, barring the access road.

"Let's go, Härich, I want to go back into the city to find out what's actually happening."

The Kfz. 15 headed back into Kiev. Hauptmann Brandner called a halt after a kilometer. He had a strange feeling that danger was approaching. With a bundle of hand grenades bound with wire and his pistol in his right hand, Sepp Brandner left the vehicle. The driver also got out and covered Brandner with his pistol. Step by step the pair worked their way through the darkness. After 200 meters they suddenly heard the sound of tank tracks in front of them. Both men stood still as if rooted to the spot. Then they heard hushed voices giving orders in Russian.

"That's the T-34, sir."

Brandner nodded and dropped silently to the ground. Just as he was about to leap up and attack the enemy tank with his cluster of grenades, he heard Sponsel's voice: "Damn . . . he got away from us!"

Brandner had come within a hair's breadth of destroying one of his own assault guns. He identified himself before leaving cover. The Russian voices must have been a product of his feverish imagination.

"Let's go Härich. Sponsel, you stay here. As soon as the T-34 shows itself, knock it out. It must be in the city."

The brigade commander raced into the city. The movie theaters were just emptying. Military police stopped the car. Brandner informed the surprised men that there was a T-34 loose in the city. Then he drove back to his 1st Battery. One hour before dawn the Russian tank cannon began to roar in the western approaches to Kiev.

"Combat battery drive at once to 1st Battery in the western part of the city," ordered Brandner by radio. While the assault guns moved out to engage the enemy Brandner drove back to the division command post.

The general's first words were: "Brandner, what is going on in the west?"

"Everything's in order, sir. My 1st Battery has already engaged the T-34s."

"Then you sent the battery there on your own, Brandner?"

"Yes, sir."

"You have prevented a disaster. Brandner, I don't know how to thank you."

Three minutes later Brandner, this time in his command vehicle, was on his way to the western sector of the city. The first reports of success came in. Eight T-34s and an armored car lay burning before the western entrance to the city, through which they had wanted to break through and cut off the retreat of the German units. Kiev was on a state of alert. Trains were assembled. Supply units were already rolling down the arterial road to the west, the only place where the city was still open. Hauptmann Brandner's assault guns had been responsible for foiling this attack on the arterial road, preventing heavy casualties and unimaginable chaos.

The general recommended Sepp Brandner for the Knight's Cross, however the paperwork was lost in the Russian artillery fire. Brandner's name did appear, however, in the German Army's honor roll and he received the army's Honor Roll Clasp. By this time Brandner had destroyed fifty enemy tanks and the 202nd Brigade had achieved great success under his command.

✠

In February–March 1944 the 1st Ukrainian Front launched an all-out offensive aimed at severing the German supply lines and encircling and destroying the German forces still on the lower Dniepr. A number of German units were moved south to meet this threat, including the 202nd Assault Gun Brigade.

Near Calarasi Tag on the Kishinev-Jassy road, the brigade met the Romanian troops it was supposed to support. There were minor battles every day, but each day might also see the start of the Soviet offensive.

On 26 April 1944 the Soviets attacked between Prut and Moldau with twenty rifle and several tank brigades. All means were to be employed to force a breakthrough of the German-Romanian defensive positions. If they succeeded in breaking through the valley of the Seret they would have opened the door to Romania and the oil fields of Ploesti would lie before them. The fighting in this area saw the first employment by the Russians of the 45-ton Josef Stalin tank.

✠

"Attention, commander to everyone. Wait until I give the order. Under no conditions leave the assembly area."

The individual platoons called in to acknowledge. Russian shells rained down all around. Suddenly there was a bang on the hatch cover. Brandner seized his submachine-gun. Then he opened the hatch cover. A dark face appeared, a brown-gray uniform.

"An Ivan!" shouted Hauptmann Brandner, raising the submachine-gun. The man raised his arms simultaneously.

"Not Russian, Romanian!" he screamed. Sepp Brandner lowered his weapon and exhaled deeply.

Seeing the soldier's rank badges, Brandner asked, "What is it, captain?"

"Please follow me to our division command post. We are supposed to coordinate our counterattack," translated the Hauptmann, acting as interpreter.

Sepp Brandner followed the officer to the Romanian command post. There he was issued his orders. At first light the next morning the brigade was supposed to break into the village of Carcula, drive out the Soviets and then take the hill beyond the village from which a Soviet observer was directing their artillery fire. Romanian infantry would advance with the assault guns, take the hill and foil any attempted counterattacks by the enemy. The attack was to begin at 4 A.M.

The entire brigade moved off. Engines thundering, the assault guns rolled toward the village in the designated formation. The first enemy antitank guns began to fire. Then the assault guns opened fire, pouring shells into the enemy antitank positions. The village approached rapidly. Sepp Brandner saw that the Romanian infantry was falling further behind all the time. A burst of fire hissed over the heads of the infantry riding on the assault gun.

All hell broke loose in the village. The assault guns blasted nests of resistance. Wherever one showed itself the brigade commander and his three assault guns immediately went into action, blasting the enemy out of his hiding places. Russian troops attempting to attack the assault guns on foot were cut down by machine-gun fire. Then the enemy began to run. The brigade followed rapidly. Those Russians who could not flee surrendered. But from the hills the enemy artillery opened fire into the lost village.

"Move on to our objective men!"

Once again Phoenix took its position at the front of the assault guns. 76-mm antitank guns fired down from the hills. The German vehicles evaded the fire by changing course and then reached a defile where the enemy guns could not reach them. It opened into a ravine which led up the hill.

"We'll go up here, Rako. To 1st Battery and escorting guns: follow me. Open fire on antitank guns as soon as we reach their flank."

Rakowitz guided Phoenix through the ravine, dodging boulders. Suddenly the ground rose steeply, but they made it. Then they reached the edge of the hill and heard the antitank guns firing to their left. They were still firing down into the village.

"Turn left. All guns open fire." The attack on the antitank position proceeded. The first gun appeared not thirty meters ahead. Startled, the gun crew turned on hearing the sound of tracks. When they realized that it was a German assault gun they fled.

"After them before they warn the others."

The Phoenix turned. The next gun appeared in seconds. Russian mortars and machine-guns began to fire. Then the first shell left the barrel of the commander's gun. An antitank gun was hit as it swung around to meet this new threat. Six more antitank guns were destroyed in rapid succession. The assault guns had taken the hill. Russians jumped up and ran down the back slope. Following them, Brandner saw a group of T-34s in an assembly area. The enemy tanks fired uphill, but their shells whizzed over the assault guns, which maneuvered themselves into firing position. Within a few minutes three T-34s were ablaze.

"Commander to everyone: up the hill!"

The two batteries left in the village drove up the hill. The radio car, which followed closely, stopped beside the commander's vehicle and Brandner sent a report to the Romanian command post that the hill was in his hands. The Romanian troops appeared a few minutes later and occupied the village and the hill. An hour later a radio message was received from the Romanian command post. The Unteroffizier radio operator brought it to the brigade commander's vehicle personally. It read: "Hauptmann Josef Brandner has been awarded the Order of Michael the Brave, highest grade, for personal bravery and the tremendous success of his attack on a vital, commanding hill and its capture."

Sepp Brandner read out the message and the men in the assault gun shook his hand enthusiastically. The brigade's assault guns launched a surprise attack into the Russian tank assembly area. Once again there was a clash of armored vehicles and sixteen more T-34s were left burning and exploding. Only then did the brigade move into a good defensive position. Not until the commanding position had been completely fortified did the brigade depart to take on new duties. Brandner received an enthusiastic reception in the Romanian command post.

✠

Once more Hauptmann Brandner was recommended for the Knight's Cross, but once again, inexplicably, he failed to receive the decoration. Brandner did not complain, however. He had done his duty and got the best out of his men. A few days later he received the assault badge with the proud figure "100." Brandner had completed 100 assault missions as leader of a platoon, battery and brigade. A hundred times he had cleared the way for the infantry and panzer-grenadiers: into a new position, the old main line of resistance or to freedom.

To his surprise Brandner was then sent to the assault artillery school at Burg near Magdeburg. He was supposed to complete a brigade commander course and subsequently assume command of the newly-formed 912th Assault Gun Brigade in spring 1944. He had become one of the aces of the assault artillery. He was being given command of such an important brigade on account of his experience, even though there were other officers available who outranked him or had served longer.

At the beginning of December, with the army assault gun brigade already in action in Courland, Sepp Brandner received his last home leave before assuming command of his unit. He joined his wife in Vienna on 3 December 1944, soon after the birth of their child. Brandner was granted only a few days of rest. Then on 10 December a telegram arrived ordering him to Courland to take command of the 912th Brigade. He surely could have extended his leave, but Brandner knew that he was needed. With a heavy heart he set off for the front.

In Königsberg Brandner and his faithful Obergefreiter Hölzer embarked on the ship that was to transport them to Libau. They arrived on 12 December, joining the cut-off Army Group Courland. After reporting his arrival to the army group Brandner immediately drove to his new brigade and surveyed the territory on which it would have to fight.

✠

Sepp Brandner was constantly on the move in the days that followed. He demanded a command vehicle and as well received three assault guns for a mobile reserve. His men lived in bunkers in order to be safe from air and artillery bombardment.

Within only a few days Brandner knew almost every man in the brigade. Day after day he went out to scout the terrain. He knew how he would have to commit his brigade if the Russians launched the third battle of Courland. That day came on 21 December. After a heavy, hours-long bombardment which struck the positions of the assault gun brigade, the Russians launched their offensive. The brigade command post was showered with artillery shells.

"Listen to that. That's Stalin Organs en masse."

"It's a good thing that I ordered the brigade into readiness positions yesterday."

"You have the nose for it, sir," said Oberleutnant Opel, the operations officer.

"What about the radio reports? Do they say anything new?"

"Nothing new, sir," reported radio Unteroffizier Kaiser. "Heavy harassing fire."

"They must be drunk! That's supposed to be harassing fire? Then I wouldn't want to be around when they start barrage fire."

One of the men in the brigade command post laughed. But he stopped at once when a salvo from a Stalin Organ landed nearby, shaking the bunker. Brandner looked through the cloud of cigarette smoke and dust. Then he got up from his cot.

Brandner's *Sturmgeschütz* fords a creek.

"Make the assault guns ready for battle."

Soon afterwards the powerful Maybach engines were warming up. The radio operators set their sets to receive. The barrage was creeping ever nearer to Frauenburg, on the outskirts of which the brigade was stationed. The situation was obvious to Sepp Brandner—this was the start of the Third Battle of Courland.

"Sir, radio report from the combat battery: extremely heavy artillery fire on our readiness positions!"

"Send this: 'One-hundred percent alertness. Report the start of the attack immediately.'"

Ten minutes later it began. The first T-34s felt their way forward. The objective of the Soviet attack was obvious enough from their previous attacks, the barrage fire and the massing of enemy tanks: the Tukum-Frauenburg road. If the enemy reached it, then he would be able to split Army Group Courland in two and destroy the German forces north and south of Frauenburg piecemeal.

At this point we will turn to Sepp Brandner himself, who provided the following description of this noteworthy attack ten years later:

> It was 7:20 A.M., the focal point of the attack was clearly obvious. I received orders to lead my brigade there. Twenty minutes later the first Soviet attack was also reported there as well as the first break-

through on a one-kilometer front. The enemy had overrun our infantry with heavy and super-heavy tanks. I took my place at the head of the brigade and rolled forward to the penetration point. I knew that the enemy would know me by the brigade standard which fluttered on the right fender. Perhaps by the more than fifty rings around the barrel as well. Let him!

We drove with large intervals in order not to offer the Soviets a compact target, for in tank warfare one never knows whether the enemy's guns are not already aimed at oneself.

There was a flash from the gun of an enemy tank. Then the shell landed in front to the right. The driver realized the situation and turned to the right, placing us in position to fire at our opponent. I passed target information to the gunner. Then he got the range and the first shell left the barrel. A jet of flame from the enemy. The T-34 exploded.

Just then, straight ahead and four-hundred meters farther, the second T-34 broke through and reached the highway.

"Damn, it's jammed!" called the gunner. The loader cursed. All of this happened in a matter of seconds, our nerves were stretched to the breaking point. The two following assault guns were already engaged in combat with other T-34s and could not move in to assist us. Why didn't our T-34 shoot? What was up with the enemy?

At that moment came the shot and almost immediately thereafter the shell struck the top of a tree just above us. As I peered through the "scissors" the enemy tank looked close enough to touch. Then my vehicle gave a jerk and I saw the rosette of flame as the shell struck the front of the T-34. The crew bailed out and disappeared into the bushes.

Now a heavy artillery barrage began landing on the stretch of road in front of us. They had spotted the brigade's approach and wanted to knock us out before we could really intervene in the battle.

I received an agitated radio report from the 2nd Combat Battery: "Our infantry is abandoning its positions to the right of us and retreating from the Soviets."

But we could not support the right flank, for now the Russian tanks came. The duel began. T-34s and Josef Stalins burned. Our comrades fired, we fired as well. The gunner and loader worked feverishly. The driver turned this way and that. Shells hissed over us. Tanks, tanks, tanks. Reports poured in. Twenty enemy tanks, twenty-six enemy tanks destroyed.

I had scouted this terrain the day before and ordered the guns to the right positions. It was now do or die. The Russian barrage fire lay on our sector.

"Gas, give it gas!"

I ducked my head as we roared through the barrage fire. Shells landed ahead of and behind us, throwing fountains of dirt into the air. The gun rumbled into a crater; it leaned perilously but, engine howling, it straightened out and came out the other side.

We were now rolling toward our retreating infantry. Our comrades stopped. They were no longer alone. Now they had protection, which they needed if they were to avoid being destroyed by the massed armored assault of the enemy.

The commander of the 2nd Battery called in: "Egghart here, on the left flank."

"What's happening there?"

"Heavy fighting with tanks. Countless enemy tanks, over."

"We're coming, Egghart!"

And we roared off. We saw the flames rising into the sky from the burning tanks. That's where we had to go. Were any of our guns there? My two assault guns positioned themselves to my left and right. I called them:

"Brandner to Opel: remain here and provide covering fire. Guard the flank, I'm going to try to reach the old main line of resistance."

My command vehicle rolled forward under artillery fire which had now intensified again to full strength. Suddenly I saw them emerge from the swirling fog of smoke and flames. T-34s. There were many of them. Probably the second wave. I called: "Halt. Tanks to the left, range three-hundred. Fire!"

The first armor-piercing shell left the barrel. It struck the enemy right in the ammunition supply. There was a brilliant flash as it exploded. This discouraged the wave somewhat, but the enemy fired back. I saw their muzzle flashes, but in the excitement I did not hear the shells striking around us. Our driver circled and turned, positioning us to fire, and each time the gunner fired.

The shells flitted across to the enemy from close range and penetrated. Some T-34s burned, others were left disabled. Smoke spiraled from their hatches. Crews bailed out. Then the infantry, which had retreated, came forward again behind the other two guns of my small force and behind the assault guns of my combat batteries. They reached their former positions and overcame the enemy in close quarters fighting. Now that they had support and were not hopeless against the steel giants of the enemy, they fought with determination.

I heard the voice of Oberleutnant Egghart: 'Russian heavy mortars!' Then mortar rounds began falling around us as well. But we could not withdraw. We had to remain in this hurricane of steel. If we pulled back the enemy would break through with his tanks again and the front here would collapse.

It was the hardest test of nerve that I ever experienced. The bursts came nearer and nearer. One of my guns was hit.

But in spite of the danger we stayed, in order to see it through to the end. The Russians were also firing at us with heavy artillery. Now there was only one choice. We had to drive forward across our own main line of resistance into the midst of the Russian attack, where the enemy mortars would not expect us. And then I had to stick my head out far enough to be able to see. Once again I heard the chirp of small arms fire, just like when I had been shot in the neck. I was afraid. But what else could I do but lead my brigade properly? And so out with my head!

Then we charged forward with all of my assault guns, blazing away as we went. When we reached the Soviet trenches, the enemy retreated in panic. The plain was covered with running brown dots. We were driving point, our other guns fired at nests of resistance. We drove into the middle of the Russians. A Russian hand grenade exploded on the rear of the vehicle. Luckily I had my head inside at that time. But then I had to stick it out again, I had to be able to survey the situation. And so I saw that our large 'lunchbox' (storage bin) that we always had with us was shot full of holes.

Behind me I saw a group of our soldiers. I waved to them. They came running and jumped onto the gun. We carried on, after the fleeing enemy. My other two guns followed, keeping our flanks free.

We stopped. The enemy's artillery fire had stopped. The artillery had got scared and was changing positions out of fear that it might also be overrun. We had done it. Twilight was falling, and as it got dark our comrades of the infantry reoccupied their old positions. Food was delivered. Supplies came forward. Our call for ammunition had not gone unheard. But it was high time, too, for we were down to our emergency reserve: five armor-piercing and three high-explosive shells.

We had accomplished our mission and now we drove past our comrades, hard at work digging in, back into our assembly areas. Our engines were throttled back and there was just the rattling of the tracks. With feverish haste we checked over our faithful assault gun. The driver adjusted the steering and support brakes while we rearmed and refueled the vehicle. All four of us hauled the shells in the sled. The loader stowed as much ammunition inside the crate as he could.

It might start up again the next morning and we wanted to be ready. I had to thank my crew. Each of them had done his best.

Then the success reports came in from the various combat batteries; I only heard the most important parts. We had casualties. A number of seriously wounded. Luckily no one killed. And so I could breathe easier. Losing a man was something terrible, even if one didn't know him all that well.

Being a commander was a hard thing. For being commander meant bearing responsibility for all the men in the brigade; to be responsible for them; to the unit command and to oneself.

The brigade set up a hedgehog position in the main battlefield. Sepp Brandner drove in a Kübelwagen to each of his combat batteries.

Unteroffizier Wögel had distinguished himself once again. He already wore the German Cross in Gold and was one of the most successful gun commanders in the brigade. Sepp Brandner called the entire crew of the assault gun to attention and promoted all four men one step in rank for bravery in the face of the enemy. Then he turned to his adjutant.

"Fleige, now we're driving back to the brigade section."

The night was pitch black when they stepped outside. They could see nothing. The Kübelwagen moved off and headed back. Sepp Brandner was thinking about what the next morning was likely to bring. But then everyone in the car was startled to hear a voice shout in Russian: "Halt!"

The driver stepped on the brakes. The car squeaked to a stop in front of the Russian outpost. Brandner snatched the assault rifle from its rack and loosed off a burst. The sentry collapsed.

"Turn around, I'll cover us!"

Before the driver could answer Brandner had jumped out of the car. When he saw the approaching Russians he fired. Then he threw himself

A *Sturmgeschütz* with the so-called "pig's head" gun mantlet (*Saukopf-Blende*).

down behind a pile of snow, rammed home a fresh clip and looking to the side saw that the driver had turned the car around. The rear window shattered as the adjutant stuck out his submachine-gun and began to fire. Brandner raced back to the car with long strides and jumped in. Even before he was in his seat the driver stepped on the gas. The Kübelwagen shot forward, leaving behind it the Russian forward outpost which it had driven into by mistake. The car and its occupants arrived safely at the brigade command post. The bunker was filled with men. Brandner had to make a report to the division commander. Only then was his day over.

On 17 January 1945 Sepp Brandner was recommended for the Knight's Cross for the third time. The recommendation read:

"On the first day of the battle the 912th Assault Gun Brigade drove into the Russian attack and destroyed the enemy's armored spearhead. This first counterattack was decisive. It struck the enemy a devastating blow and frustrated his objective of splitting Army Group Courland in two."

A few days later Sepp Brandner was promoted to Major for bravery in the face of the enemy. He was ordered to Pelci Castle near Goldingen, where Army Group Courland had set up its headquarters. Just before his departure for Army Group Center, over which he was to assume command, Generaloberst Schörner proposed to the Major that he have him flown out of the pocket to form a new assault gun brigade. Although Brandner knew that this would save him from the prospect of becoming a prisoner of war and a possible death, he declined.

"Thank you, sir, but I would like to stay with my men."

His wishes were respected. Sepp Brandner remained on the Courland front.

✠

The Fourth Battle of Courland began on 23 January 1945. The 1st, 2nd and 3rd Baltic Fronts commanded by Generals Bagramian, Yeremenko, and Maslennikov attacked with a total strength of 101 rifle divisions, two tank corps, a motorized corps and eighteen independent armored formations. Facing this onslaught were the twenty-four divisions of Army Group Courland. The Soviets were determined to win a great victory and once again the fighting was fierce.

"Damn it, sir! The combat batteries are already in action. We can't withdraw a single gun."

"That's right, Opel. We'll attack them with the brigade section. Get ready, departure in five minutes."

Five minutes later the three assault guns of the brigade section moved off. For days the enemy had been trying to break through near Preekuln in the direction of Libau to capture that very important port. The battle had reached its high point. The Soviets had achieved a breakthrough west of Lielauce Lake but this had soon been partially eliminated. Repeated efforts to break through northeast of Pampali had also been frustrated; now it was obvious that the Soviets were about to try again.

"There is the enemy, sir!"

The first T-34 grew in the sight. The shell left the barrel and smashed into the Russian tank's tracks. The T-34 fired back, until a second shot finished it off. The three assault guns drove past burning German transport. A fuel truck went up in flames. The Major barked a command and the driver swung the assault gun around into firing position. The Unteroffizier-gunner fired. The turret of the T-34, which was visible above a wagon, jerked back. The next shot set the enemy tank ablaze. All three assault guns were firing now. They drove into the shattered formation of T-34s, destroying one after another.

Seeing this gave the German train personnel courage. They now went after the enemy tanks with bundles of hand grenades and Panzerfaust antitank weapons. An half hour later an explosion of flame marked the end of the last T-34. The enemy attack had been smashed. Once again the combat batteries also reported victories. They, too, had succeeded in halting the enemy and had even forced him back out of the penetration areas. Major Brandner was about to give the order to retire when he saw several more T-34s approaching. The enemy tanks were firing into the German infantry.

"Fire at the one showing us its broadside," called the Major. The crack of the shot and the impact were almost simultaneous. The tank exploded. A second was hit in the rear. Flames shot upwards from its engine compartment. The third was attacked by a Feldwebel of the train and destroyed with a hand-grenade bundle.

Major Brandner already saw another group of T-34s rumbling toward them across the snow-covered fields. The tanks appeared as dark forms against the white background. Brandner drove through a village in order to position his three assault guns on the enemy's flank. Armor-piercing shells flitted toward the enemy from the three barrels. The T-34s went up in flames and their bailed-out crews were taken prisoner.

A short time later Soviet infantry attacked. The 1st Battery appeared deep on the flank of the attacking waves. Major Brandner issued his instructions by radio: "Shoot, shoot, shoot!"

The high-explosive shells smashed into the waves of infantry. The MG 42s mounted on the 1st Battery's assault guns began to hammer away and streams of tracer reached out toward the enemy. Russian machine-guns answered this fire. They were overrun and crushed into the snow. Then the enemy began to run. German troops got up from foxholes, shell holes and positions and ran along behind the assault guns. The Soviet main line of resistance was reached. There, too, the enemy troops abandoned their positions. The decision of the day and with it the Fourth Battle of Courland had been made at that place.

When night came reports began coming in that the Soviets were infiltrating the sparsely defended farms in no-man's-land in small groups. Major Brandner called the battery commanders to his command post.

"Comrades, at dawn we attack the farms in which the enemy is hiding."

"The division's antitank resources are at your disposal, sir," reported the liaison officer.

Major Brandner replied, "Leave the men where they are. They are surely also urgently needed there."

At approximately 3 A.M. the Egghart battery moved off, led by the three assault guns of the brigade section. The farms appeared. When the first enemy guns opened fire the assault guns had already formed a semicircle around the four buildings. Advancing slowly, the assault guns opened fire. Flames rose into the morning sky. Fifty prisoners were taken and two light artillery pieces and several machine-guns were captured.

The fighting continued on 1 and 2 February. The assault guns counterattacked under fire from a rocket brigade. The entire brigade drove into the Russian main line of resistance and once again shot up the tanks which were supposed to spearhead the attack. The fighting died down. Their forces decimated, the Soviets were forced to call off the fourth Courland offensive, which they had hoped would lead to the final destruction of Army Group Courland. An army report on the Courland front stated:

> Under the impact of the heavy losses in men and materiel suffered during the previous days, the Soviets were forced to abandon their breakthrough attempts toward Libau and Frauenburg and were obliged to carry out a major reorganization. The enemy's losses in the first twelve days of the Fourth Battle of Courland were considerable, at least 45,000 men. The number of enemy tanks destroyed in the Courland during the period from 23 January to 4 February stands at 541.
>
> In the most recent fighting south of Frauenburg a south-German assault gun brigade raised its total of enemy tanks destroyed to 500. In the process its 29-year-old commander, Major Brandner of Vienna, destroyed his 57th enemy tank.

"They're the same signs that preceded the previous Courland battles. It's going to start again tomorrow."

Sepp Brandner had moved his brigade into readiness positions. Now he discussed the coming action with his battery commanders one more time and issued them their instructions.

"Hopefully we can hold, sir."

"We must hold men. Not because I believe that we can still win, but it is vital that we stand fast here until the civilians and the wounded have been shipped out of the ports still open."

The Major's face was furrowed with worry. He spent every free minute on the move, scanned the terrain, pressed his superiors to send new defensive weapons to strengthen the front.

"What shall we actually do tomorrow?" asked one of the platoon commanders. Sepp Brandner cleared his throat.

"We have only one mission, to maintain our position in the front lines and back up our comrades in the infantry. Our area of operations is wherever the enemy comes. Where the situation warrants we intervene. That is all."

The attack began at dawn the next day. Sepp Brandner had deployed the brigade exactly at the focal point of the Soviet assault. The assault guns smashed the armored spearhead which forced its way through the German main line of resistance. The assault guns were in action all day long, engaging the enemy and destroying T-34 and Josef Stalin tanks. Two of the brigade's vehicles were hit and disabled; the repair echelon recovered them during the night. Men from the supply units volunteered to take the place of killed or wounded assault gun drivers.

"Report to the brigade, sir."

"Give it here, Bayer." Major Brandner scanned the message.

"Opel and Schubert, wake the crews of your guns. A company command post has been surrounded by T-34s. Number uncertain as the tank sounds are coming from the forest around the command post."

One minute later the three assault guns roared off. Leutnant Opel followed the commander's vehicle and behind him was Hauptmann Schubert.

They reached the front lines. "Advance slowly. Make as little noise as possible," ordered Major Brandner. The company command post appeared. The company commander, a Leutnant, was waiting for them.

"Perhaps 500 meters ahead, in the wood. Three came to within 200 meters, but when one of my sentries fired an illumination flare they beat it back into the woods," reported the Leutnant.

"I'm getting out with my crew. You stay here. If you see two white flares attack the wood." The two assault guns transmitted "understood" and Major Brandner and his three men crept toward the wood. The men were armed with hand grenades and submachine-guns.

"There they are. Directly in front of us, sir!"

In their white camouflage jackets the four men of the commander's assault gun blended in with the snow. They heard a babble of voices. Major Brandner determined that the Russians were preparing to advance. He gave his men a wave and they crawled noiselessly back to their assault gun.

"Brandner to Opel and Schubert. Move forward quietly. Position yourselves to my left and right. Prepare to fire. Tanks will be advancing out of the forest at any time. Range five-hundred."

One minute later the Russian tank engines roared. Then the dark shadows appeared on the snow-covered field.

"Fire!" Three lances of flame shot from the barrels, three shells flitted towards the surprised enemy, and three T-34s were rocked by impacting shells.

"Faster loader!" shouted the Unteroffizier-gunner. The guns barked again. Then the T-34s opened fire. But they had loaded high-explosive ammunition for the command post. These burst against the forward armor of the assault guns, which advanced into the wood firing their guns.

The Russian armored spearhead was intercepted there. The 2nd and 3rd Batteries were summoned during the night, for it turned out that the enemy had planned a new attack there.

On 11 February 1945 Major Brandner was cited by name in the Wehrmacht communiqué. On 12 February he repulsed another assault by Soviet armor.

✠

"Is today the day you get your 60th victory, sir?"

"Maybe."

"Have the assault guns already received their instructions, sir?" asked the war correspondent. "I don't see a single one."

"And you're not supposed to. For if you see one than so can the Ivans. But I can promise you that all assault guns and the antitank guns are standing ready."

"There they come!"

The muffled sound of tanks grew louder from second to second. Then the first steel giants appeared.

"Oh boy! Sir, take a Josef Stalin, that will make for some wonderful pictures."

"But my dear fellow, we're not here so that you can take a few wonderful pictures." Sepp Brandner couldn't help but grin when he saw the war correspondent's disappointed face.

"Attention, everyone. Hold your fire until every shot is a sure hit."

The tanks rolled closer and closer. The enemy artillery moved its fire even further back. Then the antitank guns began to bark. The first tanks were knocked out.

"Open fire!"

The assault guns, which were hidden behind cottages and stands of saplings, in trenches and shell craters, opened fire. Soon T-34s and Josef Stalins lay burning on the fields.

"Stalin! Twelve o'clock, four-hundred meters!"

The correspondent began filming. He recorded the firing of the Russian tank's 122-mm gun. Then he heard the first shot from Brandner's assault gun and immediately afterwards there was a bang as the shell struck the vulnerable spot between the tank's turret and hull.

Sepp Brandner as commander of the 912th Assault Gun Brigade.

"They're bailing out!" screamed the correspondent enthusiastically. Then a clenched fist knocked him backwards. It belonged to the gunner manning the vehicle's machine-gun. The burst of fire from the enemy lines passed just over the assault gun. The Josef Stalin burned. The war corespondent had his pictures and it looked as if the enemy had received a tremendous shock. The units spearheading the attack turned.

"We're heading back. I will be back in half an hour. Hauptmann Schubert will be in command until then."

Ignoring the war correspondent's protests, Major Brandner ordered his driver to head back. The assault gun rumbled over the log road to the brigade command post and dropped off the correspondent. Then Brandner instructed the driver to turn around and head back.

But before the command vehicle had reached the battlefield again there was a bang, seemingly out of a clear blue sky. Brandner felt the impact below in the vehicle.

"We can't move," shouted the driver, "a track is off!"

At that very instant the assault gun was hit a second time. The shell entered the vehicle and hit its ammunition supply. Luckily for the crew there was no high-explosive ammunition left, however the powder in the armor-piercing shells produced a jet of flame.

"Get out! Get out!"

The crew jumped from the assault gun as quickly as they could. With singed uniforms, the men threw themselves into the nearest ditch. The loader had had the presence of mind to bring along a Panzerfaust.

"Stay alert! That was a tank!"

"Ivans coming, sir!"

Crouched low, Russian soldiers advanced out of the wood from which the shots had come.

"Let's go men, to the rear. I'll delay them. When you get back tell them that I'm here with the knocked-out assault gun on the log road abeam the first infantry position.

"We're not going without you, sir," declared the gunner.

"All right, we'll leave together. Loader, fire your Panzerfaust at them. As soon as the shot is fired we go."

The loader raised the antitank weapon. Bullets whizzed over him as he adjusted his aim slightly. Then the warhead flew straight toward the dense mass of Russians and exploded there. "Up! Let's go!"

The men dashed toward the rear. When the first bullet buzzed past, they began zigzagging. Seconds later the wood swallowed them up. They had made it again. German infantry in positions deeper in the wood gave suppressing machine-gun fire. The signals battalion passed on the news that the brigade commander's vehicle had been knocked out. Exactly fifteen minutes later the sound of tracked vehicles was heard from behind. It was the three assault guns of the reserve group. Riding on the vehicles was a platoon of men from the escort battery armed with assault rifles. The radio message had wrongly reported that their commanding officer was surrounded and they had come to rescue him.

The enemy quickly moved up several antitank guns and opened fire at the stranded assault gun. Sepp Brandner expressed his concern: "Hopefully we'll get our Phoenix back." But within a matter of seconds the assault gun was a blazing torch. Nevertheless, during the night the vehicle was brought back by a recovery vehicle. That same night it was delivered to the tank repair workshop.

✠

"To the division command post!"

Sepp Brandner hopped into the back seat of the Kübelwagen that was waiting in front of the brigade command post. In his hands he held his assault rifle, ready to fire, for Russian soldiers might appear anywhere. The enemy had infiltrated the main line of resistance in many places.

"I don't hear anything, Hölzel."

"It is suspiciously quiet, sir."

"Well, we'll be there soon. Another kilometer at most."

No sooner had Brandner finished his sentence when there was a tremendous explosion from the area of the division command post. Immediately afterwards there was a flurry of submachine-gun and rifle fire.

"Faster Hölzel!"

Ready to jump, the assault rifle raised, Brandner waited for the first sighting. The first bunker of the division command post appeared. They saw the cloud of smoke hanging above it and also the Russians who were storming towards it from the bushes.

"Hölzel, stop!"

The brakes squeaked as the vehicle came to a stop. Both men jumped out simultaneously and began to fire. Their fire knocked over the storming enemy. Then an MG 42 opened up from the side. A few German soldiers, who had correctly assessed the situation, appeared in the entrance to the bunker. Caught in a crossfire, the Russian attackers were pinned down. Major Brandner and his driver reported to General Feyerabend, the division commander.

"How is it that you always turn up at the right moment, Brandner?" asked the general.

"Sir, an assault gun man must always be where he is needed."

"Listen to me. We intend to eliminate a Russian salient on the right wing in the coming night. I want you and your brigade to drive through as part of the attack. The infantry will follow up and take possession of the trenches and that will be it. If we . . ."

A noise at the entrance to the bunker caused the general to stop in mid sentence. A dark shape flew into the room.

"Take cover!" Brandner shouted, and threw himself to the floor. The table tumbled over just before a hand grenade exploded, sending fragments into the walls.

Brandner and Hölzel were on their feet before the sound of the explosion died away. Several faces appeared before them. The two assault rifles opened up from point-blank range. The second Russian assault team was cut down just short of its objective.

✠

Again and again the 912th Assault Gun Brigade was called upon to intervene in the fighting. Wherever the enemy broke through, wherever the infantry needed help, Sepp Brandner and his assault guns were there.

Attacks by the brigade gave the infantry room to breathe. Twice more his assault gun was shot out from under him. On 11 April Brandner was awarded the Close Combat Clasp, unusual for the commander of an armored vehicle. On the same day his name appeared in the Wehrmacht communiqué for the second time. On 26 April 1945 Sepp Brandner became the 847th German soldier to be awarded the Knight's Cross with Oak Leaves. It was the last officially awarded Oak Leaves.

Sepp Brandner modestly attributed his success to the men under his command. After being awarded the Oak Leaves he said: "What do you want? Without my men and without their efforts I would be nothing. A commander can only achieve as much as his men are willing to give. And it is they who have given their utmost in order to save what could be saved. They deserve this decoration, my brave lads of the assault artillery!"

In a brigade order of the day Sepp Brandner promised his men that he would remain with them no matter what. His words meant more than empty promises. For a second time Brandner was urged by his superiors—virtually an order—to fly out of Courland and once again he rejected the idea. "A commander has to stay with his men, especially in their darkest hour."

The cease-fire took effect for Army Group Courland at 2 P.M. on 8 May. The guns fell silent. The war was over. The previous day General Hilpert, the last commander of Army Group Courland, radioed the Russians an offer to surrender. He drove to the enemy in a car flying a white flag. His "Ia," General Foertsch, stayed behind and took over command of the army group.

The 1st and 2nd Batteries were lined up in front of the assault gun brigade's command post. Hauptmann Egghart and Hauptmann Schubert, commander of the 1st Battery, also wore the Knight's Cross. They, too, had repeatedly distinguished themselves. The commander of the 3rd Battery, Oberleutnant Siebenbürgen, had also performed magnificently in recent months in Courland. On 8 May 1945 Major Brandner thanked all these men once more for their bravery.

When news was received that the Russians were not abiding by the terms of the agreement and were moving forward, Hauptmann Schubert moved against them. He halted the Russians without having to fire a shot. The Russians knew the assault guns all too well. They had no desire to become their last victims on the final day of the war.

Major Brandner got in touch with General Herzog's corps command post. The general confirmed Brandner's intention to hold the present positions and deny the Russians access to the bridge. Once again Sepp Brandner drove forward in his command assault gun. The white rings on the barrel stood out clearly. There were sixty, and each stood for an enemy tank destroyed. The sirens mounted on the commander's vehicle blared as the brigade advanced. The Russian commander approached with a negotiator.

"The war is over! You are prisoners!"

The Russian commander's words rang loud through the afternoon. But Sepp Brandner was not impressed.

"No surrender yet," he replied, equally laconic. "Here the Germans. There the Russians. No one crosses the bridge. We will open fire on anyone who does."

The Russian general understood what Brandner was saying. He also understood the guns aimed at the bridge. The enemy pulled back from the bridge. When Oberleutnant Ranschopf drove to the division command post he found that it had been abandoned by the senior officers.

Sepp Brandner had only one choice left. While the Schubert battery remained at the bridge, he drove back to the brigade command post and destroyed all documents to prevent the enemy from getting his hands on them. The flames also consumed the brigade chronicle, in which the unit's accomplishments were recorded. Then he drove back to the front. Brandner drove back to the brigade commanding officer one last time early on 9 May 1945. The bitterness of the moment was palpable. He assembled his men one last time. His voice wavered as he spoke his final words to them:

"Comrades, the war is over. All command authority has ceased to exist, the most difficult times lay ahead. Each man should try to do the best for himself. I can issue you no more orders. But I will try to do the best for all those who remain with me. I will do my very best to get you back to Germany, to your loved ones. That is all I have to say to you."

Hauptmann Schubert took a few steps forward. He shook hands with his commander.

"I believe that I speak for all of the men here when I say that we will all stay with you, sir."

Sepp Brandner had tears in his eyes as he listened to the men give their enthusiastic approval. This expression of trust surpassed everything and gave him the strength to hold on through captivity and try to do the best for his men. The majority of the members of the 912th Assault Gun Brigade who were taken prisoner survived, due in no small part to the efforts of Sepp Brandner.

Interrogations began. Names were demanded from Brandner, but he remained silent. When the interrogating officer asked why he hadn't deserted when the Russians were at the gates of Berlin, Brandner answered by asking the Russian officer why he hadn't deserted when the Germans were threatening Moscow.

As part of a large labor unit, Brandner passed through Moscow, Orel and Kursk to Stalinogorsk. There he was recognized by Russian civilians. Remembering how he had once helped them, they shared their pitiful rations with the column of German prisoners: an island of reconciliation in a sea of hate. Sepp Brandner repeatedly gave hope to the despairing, giving them the will to carry on and not give up. And then one day he brought the men the news they thought would never come: "We're going home!"

No one was left behind. Even the sick were smuggled out. When the prisoner transport stopped in Vienna in early 1948, Brandner's comrades bade him farewell with the words: "Long live the comradeship that you always showed us, Sepp."

Fritz Feßmann.

Fritz Feßmann

A MEMBER OF THE RECONNAISSANCE TROOPS WINS THE SWORDS

He was Leutnant of the Reserve when the German forces crossed the River Bug and began their advance into the Soviet Union on 22 June 1941 and by October he was wearing the Knight's Cross. The unit with which he served filled the same role as mounted patrols in earlier wars but its methods were different. Instead of the horse fast armored cars carried Feßmann and his comrades into the enemy rear, and every mission was a dangerous undertaking. During an advance their missions were carried out far ahead of the attack spearheads and usually the objective was to hold a strategically important bridge or some similar object. In the process they achieved feats which often seemed impossible. One such armored reconnaissance specialist was Fritz Feßmann, who in 1944 became the 103rd German soldier to be decorated with the Swords, one of Germany's highest decorations for bravery. Sadly he did not live to receive it. His path through the vast expanses of Russia to Stalingrad and back until his death is described in this chapter.

EARLY DAYS

Born in Urbach, Württemberg, on 25 December 1913, Fritz Feßmann reported for a one-year period of military service after completing his period with the Labor Service. On 1 November 1935 he joined the 7th Armored Reconnaissance Battalion in Munich. He was trained on the armored car and on 1 October 1936 he left the service a Gefreiter and officer candidate. At the beginning of 1937 he completed his first two-month reserve exercise in Munich, finishing as an Unteroffizier.

Carl Feßmann, his father and owner of a factory, gave his son a rail and steamer ticket for a round-the-world trip on the condition that he stay away for at least two years and earn his own living. The trip began in March 1937. It took the young man via China and Japan to America and then back to Europe. Feßmann met a girl in Shanghai and they were married in Wiesbaden on 12 August 1939. The young couple were forced to separate just fourteen days later, for on 23 August Feßmann was called away to attend a weapons course at the Krampnitz Cavalry School near Potsdam. During this reserve training the Second World War broke out. The course participants were immediately assigned to combat units. Feßmann went to the 7th Armored Reconnaissance Battalion, part of the 4th Panzer Division. He spent the first winter of the war in the Rhineland and on 1 March 1940 was promoted to Leutnant.

After the defeat of France the 7th Armored Reconnaissance Battalion stayed on as part of the German occupation forces. By May 1941, however, its days there were numbered. With many other divisions the 4th Panzer Division headed to East Prussia as part of the German buildup. War with the Soviet Union was imminent.

✠

Early on 22 June 1941 the XXIV Motorized Army Corps under General Geyr von Schweppenburg went to the attack on the right wing of Panzer Group 2 near Koden on the River Bug. The corps consisted of the 3rd Panzer Division under Generalleutnant Model, the 10th Motorized Infantry Division, and the 4th Panzer Division. On the day of the attack these, three divisions had the task of forcing a crossing of the Bug between Wlodawa and Okczyn and after breaking through the Soviet frontier positions on either side of the lake district north of Miedna of advancing north. The main effort would be by the 3rd Panzer Division. The assault on the fortress of Brest-Litovsk, situated between the two panzer divisions, was left to the 45th Infantry Division.

General Baron von Langermann, commander of the 4th Panzer Division, always led from the front from his command vehicle, deploying patrols to scout ahead of the division; and almost always Leutnant Feßmann and his patrol were there. By 28 June the 4th Panzer Division had reached the Beresina and was driving toward Rogachev on the Dniepr.

The struggle against the determined and tough Soviets was a new and bitter experience for the Germans, including Fritz Feßmann. He led his patrol east, concentrating on the task at hand and ignoring everything else. On 16 July he received the Iron Cross, First Class for his outstanding efforts. He also saw to that that each of his men received the awards they had earned. He was one of nine comrades, that's all he wanted to be. True, he was the leader of the patrol, but he was first to admit that the success of an operation depended equally on each of its members. And so it was that Feßmann's patrol was given the critical missions in XXIV Army Corps's (mot.) area of operations.

From Rogachev the 4th Panzer Division stormed toward Stary Bykov. The 3rd Panzer Division crossed the Dniepr River north of Stary Bykov. The XXIV Army Corps (mot.) continued its advance on 10 July. Near Propoisk the Soviets severed the 4th Panzer Division's communications with the rear. At this time Leutnant Feßmann was already in the division's bridgehead near Krichev. This was taken over by the 3rd Panzer Division while the heavy weapons and the 35th Panzer Regiment drove back and destroyed the enemy groups.

The objective of the advance was Smolensk. Together with the 3rd Panzer Division, the 4th Panzer Division took Roslavl on 1 August. Then there was a several-day rest, which the units, including Feßmann's, used to service their vehicles.

General Geyr von Schweppenburg sent his XXIV Motorized Army Corps to the attack again on 9 August. This time its objective was to advance southwest out of the Klimovichi area and make a flanking attack against the enemy forces in front of the 4th Panzer Division. The attack by the two panzer divisions was aimed at the divisions of Soviet General Timoshenko. In a battle which lasted until 13 August the Soviet 6th, 12th, 132nd, and 137th Rifle Divisions were destroyed. 16,033 prisoners were taken and many of the enemy's heavy weapons were destroyed or captured. Generaloberst Guderian, the commander of Panzer Group 2, had breached the Timoshenko Line in front of the approaches to Moscow.

Just two days later the corps attacked south in the direction of Starodub and Novo Subhov with the 3rd and 4th Panzer Divisions in the first wave followed closely by the 10th Motorized Infantry Division. The corps' right wing (the 4th Panzer Division) was supposed to turn toward Gomel after breaking through the enemy and there encircle and destroy the enemy forces in front of the German 2nd Army. However the 4th Panzer Division became hung up on 17 August. Together with the 10th Motorized Infantry Division, the 3rd Panzer Division drove forward and reached the rail junction at Unechna, severing the Gomel-Briansk railway line.

During the night of 19 August, however, the Soviets drove through between the corps two panzer divisions from the northwest, severing the link between Unechna and Mglin, where the 4th Panzer Division was stalled. There were two days of heavy defensive fighting in which the patrols of the 7th Armored Reconnaissance Battalion repeatedly drove into the enemy and finally succeeded in restoring contact with the 3rd Panzer Division.

On 21 August the German supreme command announced that it had decided to seek a decision in the Russian campaign in the Ukraine and not at Moscow. The XXIV Motorized Army Corps regrouped for the attack south. On 25 August the 3rd and 4th Panzer Divisions and the 10th Motorized Infantry Division went to the attack again. Three days later they reached the Desna. There Generaloberst Guderian paid the 4th Panzer Division a visit. The supply units were stuck in the mud, as it was raining heavily. General von Schweppenburg halted the 3rd and 10th Divisions and moved the 4th Panzer Division via Novogorod and Seversk closer to the 3rd Panzer Division. Generaloberst Guderian again appeared before Baron von Langermann for a first-hand report. The commander in chief of Panzer Group 2 gave the order for the attack south to resume. But the attack went nowhere. The Soviet units under the command of Marshall Budyenni had received the following order:

"Not one step back! Die if necessary!"

Equally determined were the divisions of Soviet Marshall Yeremenko, which the 4th Panzer Division had to face at the Desna. Fritz Feßmann made the acquaintance of the Soviet T-34 tank, which was rolling from the factories in Kharkov. On several occasions he just avoided being knocked out by shots from the Soviet super-heavy T-28 tank, but he always managed to get back with his vital reports.

This battle lasted eight days. A Soviet courier aircraft was shot down on the afternoon of 3 September. Maps found in the aircraft revealed the Soviet strength and dispositions—and a weak point between the 13th and 21st Soviet Armies. The next day Generaloberst Guderian reappeared at the corps command post. The 3rd Panzer Division was sent into the newly discovered gap and drove toward the Sjem and Konotop. The commander in chief of Panzer Group 2 also ordered the 4th Panzer Division to attack, with the Bakhmach River as its objective.

Reconnaissance revealed that the Sjem River bridge near Baturin, over which the advance toward the Bakhmach was supposed to be made, had been blown by the Soviets early on 7 September. Baturin itself was strongly occupied by enemy forces. Generalmajor von Langermann subsequently ordered that the crossing should take place near Drobzy east of Baturin. The new site offered less favorable terrain, but it was hoped that a quick crossing could be made there.

However, since it took a long time for the attack force to regroup, the enemy—as soon as he became aware of the movements—used his intact railway lines to move fresh reserves into the intended crossing site twenty kilometers to the south. Generalmajor von Langermann summoned the commander of the 7th Armored Reconnaissance Battalion and ordered him to form two well-armed patrols. Leutnant Feßmann's great test had arrived.

"Oberfeldwebel Limmer and Leutnant Feßmann to the battalion commander immediately!"

The two patrol leaders, who were just overseeing the rearming and refueling of their vehicles, went over to the command post, which had been set up in a wood approximately 300 meters farther to the rear. Hauptmann Nierle stood up when they entered. He welcomed the two men and had them sit down.

"Gentlemen! The division commander has asked for two patrols to advance south through the enemy lines and carry out a special mission. I thought of you two. If you are interested in this mission I need your approval. You can back out at any time, it is to be a voluntary mission, and I know that you have been in the thick of things in the past few days."

"We accept, of course, sir!" said Leutnant Feßmann.

"Excellent. I thank you. I will inform the division commander immediately. Be ready to move out in an hour. I will drive with you to the planned bridge site."

The two patrol leaders walked outside and went over to their makeshift quarters, where the armored cars had driven after refueling. Feldwebel Engelhard met Leutnant Feßmann.

"What's up, sir?"

A Sd.Kfz. 231 of Feßmann's unit outside a Russian farm house.

"Some sort of patrol across the Sjem to the south, Engelhard. Have everyone get ready, we leave in one hour."

"Berke is wounded, sir, we need a replacement."

"Damn, I hadn't thought of that. Do you know someone, Engelhard?"

"Unteroffizier Schweikl of the Fourth, sir."

"Good. Ask him if he would like to come along on a suicide mission. No one will be locked up for coming back." The Feldwebel grinned and disappeared.

The patrols moved out one hour later. The cannon-armed vehicle took the lead, followed by the two machine-gun vehicles. Then came Oberfeldwebel Limmer's three armored scout cars. Led by Hauptmann Nierle, they drove straight to the bridge site. When they had formed up the division commander appeared in front of them.

"Good evening, men."

"Good evening, sir."

"Men, I have a mission for you which will take you twenty kilometers inside enemy-occupied territory."

It seemed to Feßmann that his comrades held their breath; the general continued: "Your mission is to blow up the double-track railway line in the Bakhmach area and, if possible, the road crossing immediately to the south of it. This will make it impossible for the Soviets to bring in stronger forces against our division."

The division's Ia stepped forward and spread out a map on the board he had brought with him. The general had Hauptmann Nierle and the two patrol leaders move closer.

"One patrol—that's you Feßmann—will carry out the demolition of the rail line on the western outskirts of Bakhmach. The second—you, Limmer—will carry out the demolitions on the south side of Bakhmach. How you do it is up to you. And now let me wish you all the best of luck."

The division commander shook hands with the men one after the other. Then he disappeared in the direction of the division command post. Hauptmann Nierle also said goodbye to the eighteen men and wished them luck. Then Feßmann waved the crews to him. While the combat engineers brought the explosives, the men of the armored patrols discussed what they would do.

"We are all aware," said Leutnant Feßmann in closing, "that this mission is almost impossible. But we are also firmly determined to carry it out none the less. Both lines, which aerial reconnaissance confirms are in constant use, are closely watched by Russian guards. We have to slip past them unseen and place our charges on the tracks. If we succeed we will spare the entire sector heavy casualties. Therefore we must approach without delay and keep just one thing in mind: blow up the rail line. Tscherwick, you have a wife and children; if you wish to step back you may do so and we will think none the less of you for it."

"Not on your life, sir!" replied Obergefreiter Tscherwick, an Upper Silesian and the driver of the radio car.

"We will cross first as soon as it is dark. Limmer, you follow. The sentries will wake us at 3:30. Departure at 3:45. I am going across the river now to scout as far as Mitschenki, through which we will break through to the southwest."

While the men pitched in and helped stow the explosives in the scout cars, Limmer and the Leutnant went down to the riverbank. They climbed into an inflatable boat and crossed the river. The combat engineer Leutnant who was to direct the crossing by the armored cars accompanied them. They showed him the spot in the wooded valley where the armored cars were to be brought. Then they worked their way through the terrain, which was overgrown with saplings, to the southwest until they arrived at the road leading into Mitschenki.

"So it goes through, Fritz."

"Through to the rail line, Limmer."

"If we succeed, then we'll be able to celebrate two birthdays afterwards."

"We will do it."

✠

When 3:30 came the men were already standing at the riverbank. They looked at the Leutnant.

"Morning, men. What are you waiting for? Into the steamers and across with you!"

There was an occasional rumble to the south and Russian 152-mm shells soared high above their heads before landing several hundred meters to the rear. They reached the far bank, mounted up and waited. Feßmann looked at the illuminated face of his clock. When the minute hand reached 3:45 he stood up in his cannon-armed vehicle.

"Patrols—forward!"

The idling motors revved up. The column of six armored scout cars moved off into the twilight of the new day. Placing his binoculars before his eyes, Feßmann scanned the terrain in front of them. He could only see about thirty meters. The moon was hidden by clouds. Feßmann had chosen to ride in the lead radio car because from there he could remain in contact with the other crews.

Feßmann called repeated halts in order to listen. By 4:15 the visibility was already sixty to eighty meters. The cars drove through Mitschenki. The village seemed uncomfortably long to Feßmann; it was a typical Russian village strung out along the road. With map in hand he directed his driver. Soon the major east-west thoroughfare appeared before them.

"Feßmann to everyone: change in plan. We are going to cross the east-west through road and keep going through the southwest part of Mitschenki, which is a better route to our target."

"Understood!" replied Limmer.

The first two cars had just crossed the through road when the patrol leader spotted two trucks in front of the houses on the right side of the road. Seconds later a sentry came out of the house and stood in the middle of the road. The driver, Obergefreiter Tscherwick, took his foot off the gas pedal. Feßmann aimed his machine-gun at the Russian.

"Carry on, Tscherwick."

Stepping on the gas again, the driver accelerated. The Red Army soldier mumbled something to the men and left the road to return to his vehicle.

"Didn't recognize us," said one of the men, relieved. They all passed by and soon reached the south end of the village.

To the men in the steel boxes it seemed as if they were driving toward a precipice. When would the enemy become aware of them? After two kilometers herds of cattle came into view on the left. Civilians appeared. They approached readily when Feßmann waved them over.

"Where does this road go?" he asked in his halting Russian.

"To Bakhmach."

The drive continued as it gradually became lighter. Five kilometers southwest of Mitschenki Feßmann saw panye wagons on the road ahead. He tried to make out the people in the carts, but in vain.

"Weapons at the ready! Gun car to the head of the column if we stop."

The carts grew larger rapidly. Suddenly the Leutnant saw that there were soldiers in them. It was already too late to turn around.

"Stop beside the first one, Tscherwick!"

The armored car rolled up to the last vehicle. When it was alongside the Leutnant emerged from his hatch and pointed his submachine-gun at the soldiers, who stared up at him in shock and dismay.

"Ruki werch!" (hands up) he called, holding the submachine-gun where they could see it. The gun car, which was armed with a 20-mm KwK L/55, rumbled past. Its commander, Feldwebel Engelhard, signaled that everything was all right and drove forward to the leading wagon, but not so far that the carts were outside his field of fire. The Soviets offered no resistance. Oberfeldwebel Limmer, who had caught up with his three cars, disarmed them together with several of his men.

Feßmann sent the Russians to the northeast. Suddenly there was an outburst of rifle fire. It came from the east from a row of bushes; bullets whistled over the heads of the Germans. Limmer's gun car turned. The 20-millimeter cannon emptied a magazine. The shells poured into the bushes like a smoking arrow. Then they began taking fire from in front as well. Feldwebel Engelhard did not shoot back because the situation was not dangerous. There were just a few Red Army soldiers and they ran away to the south.

"We'll drive back a way and separate there. We won't get through by heading straight south. I think they now know that we're the enemy and what we're up to."

The vehicles drove 500 meters back along the road.

"Limmer we have to split up here. That gives us a double chance that one of us might reach the rail line."

"OK, Fritz. I'll head east in an arc."

The two groups separated. After driving 500 meters down a secondary road the Leutnant looked around; the vehicles of the Limmer group were just still visible. The terrain through which Feßmann's three vehicles were driving was as flat as a board. Only ahead on the left was there a group of trees. As they came nearer the patrol leader saw a village in front of the forest. It was not on the map.

One minute later the Leutnant reported to his men: "Rider approaching! Drive on, carry on as if everything is normal."

The rider approached and galloped past without giving the small column of vehicles a second glance. It was now 5:20 A.M. and completely light. And it was only because of that that none of the patrol's vehicles became bogged down. They drove around deep ruts and holes. The tires ground through sandy and muddy depressions. The 75-horsepower engines roared, driving the armored cars through the holes, spraying mud as they went.

Feßmann called to his three drivers: "The terrain is marshy in places. Make sure that you remain on the beaten path and drive carefully."

The village slid past to the column's left. Feßmann scanned the outskirts of the village through his binoculars. At the west end he saw a suspicious shape well-camouflaged beneath some trees.

"Looks like a heavy tank at the west end of the village. A few men walking around, looks like they're making breakfast."

The tension rose to the breaking point. What would happen if this giant suddenly began to move? They couldn't engage it, for they couldn't harm the tank with their "door knocker," while just one shot from its cannon would pierce their 8-mm armor like paper. They drove past the tank at a distance of about 300 meters. Nothing happened. The five Russians continued preparing their breakfast.

The Leutnant repeatedly raised the binoculars to his eyes. Fifteen minutes passed, then he saw the broad band of the main road which led from Baturin in the north to Bakhmach in the south. A glance at his watch showed the patrol leader that it was exactly 5:40 A.M. There was heavy truck traffic on the road as well as the occasional tank and field howitzer. The traffic ran in both directions.

"Into the depression there left of the road."

The three cars disappeared. Feßmann sent a report. His car was also equipped with a standard radio. He reported to division the traffic on the road and his position. Ten minutes passed. Suddenly Unteroffizier Schweikl waved from the last vehicle and pointed to the rear. The Leutnant scanned the secondary road and saw two trucks, then a third, all driving north. At almost the same time he spotted two more trucks ahead to the right. They were moving east, behind the armored cars.

"We have to withdraw. Back as far as the village."

The flat terrain offered little concealment and so they were left with the road back to the village. On the way back Feßmann identified the vehicle at the west end of the village as a heavy tank. Apparently the crew again failed to recognize them and made no move to give chase. It was a strange, unreal drive and Feßmann thought that it was like something from a dream. Five-hundred meters from the northeast end of the village there was a tall pepper field in which the three vehicles were able to take cover. They drove down a narrow side ride and then turned off. Feßmann was still able to observe the main road to Bakhmach. From then on he sent a steady stream of reports to division on the road traffic. At 6:05 A.M. he sent:

"Enemy column, motorized and horse-drawn, on the Baturin-Bakhmach road. Beginning and end not in sight."

Twenty-one minutes later he radioed:

"Reported traffic on the Baturin-Bakhmach road has stopped. Unable to get through to the west. Diverting east."

The three vehicles now drove some distance to the east. Suddenly three armored cars appeared. Feßmann identified them as belonging to his comrade Limmer; obviously he had been unable to get through to the east either.

"6:40 A.M. Limmer heading southwest. I will try to get through to the west again."

The three armored cars approached the Baturin-Bakhmach road for the second time. This time the Leutnant observed an enemy battery. Coming from the east, it drove toward Gorodishche, which was on the other side of the road, and went into position there. A short time later four guns opened fire toward the north. The heavy flow of traffic on the north-south road continued. Heavy trucks roared past the three armored cars in both directions. Occasionally a tank passed by, while now and then there was a horse-drawn vehicle, forced off to the side by the other traffic.

"Sir, sir!" called Obergefreiter Wentzel, the radio operator. "Radio message from Oberfeldwebel Limmer to the division. Limmer has set off his charges!"

"Now we have to get across. At any cost. Otherwise we'll never get through. Everyone get ready and wait for orders."

Feßmann looked across to the road. A densely-packed column of trucks was just driving past the crossing point. He had to let it pass. Then there was a gap of approximately 300 meters.

"To the road!"

The armored cars raced toward the road. The strip of pavement grew larger and then they saw the deep ditches that ran along both sides.

"Turn south!"

The three armored cars rolled south, parallel to the road and the ditches, just fifty meters away.

"Road ahead. Careful! A bridge leads over the ditch. I'll go first."

There was another gap in the traffic as Obergefreiter Tscherwick steered the car onto the bridge. The front wheels rolled onto it. Then there was a loud crash as they broke through. Tscherwick stepped on the gas, hoping that they might make it, but the vehicle was stuck. More trucks loaded with infantry appeared to the north. They were already within 300 meters. Feßmann got out. The gun car came roaring up at high speed. Feldwebel Engelhard knew what was at stake. He tossed down the tow cable while the car was still moving. The Leutnant hooked the end of the cable to his armored car.

"On my hand signal both of you engage reverse gear simultaneously!" ordered Feßmann. The Feldwebel in the commander's hatch of the scout car nodded as a signal that he understood.

The Leutnant raised his arm. Both motors howled. The armored cars vibrated and shook. The radio car slowly came free and was pulled out of the ditch. They were mobile again.

"Helmets and caps off!"

The armored cars stopped just 150 meters to the side of the road. Feldwebel Engelhard climbed down. He, too, was bare-headed. They lit cigarettes and stood smoking, in plain view of the Russians as they passed. The leading truck, which had already stopped, moved on. There was still no movement from the heavy tank at the west end of the village, behind and to the left of the armored cars.

"Drive on. Direction south. Stay 150 meters parallel to the road."

Their nerves were stretched to the breaking point. Every meter they drove took them deeper into enemy territory. But Feßmann kept his nerve, and luck was with them. After about a kilometer they came to a road which crossed the main road. The Leutnant stood up in his vehicle and waved at the drivers of the Russian vehicles approaching from the south, signaling them to halt. The first Russian truck stopped. They would have been spotted by now if they hadn't overpainted the crosses on their cars. But instead the Russian drivers cursed the delay and let the three armored cars drive across. The three armored cars then drove several hundred meters toward the west and then turned south.

The armored cars now found themselves in marshy terrain. Several times the lead car became stuck, but each time it was pulled free. The nine men strained, sweat pouring down their faces. In each case the Leutnant helped push. Now that they had crossed the road Feßmann was confident that they would make it. He had no time to worry about what was going to happen and how they were supposed to get back.

Again Feßmann's vehicle drove into a ditch. The wheels spun in the muddy bottom and once again the armored car had to be pulled out. Suddenly there was a noise behind them. It sounded like an aircraft engine. Feßmann turned around and saw three German bombers directly behind him. They were heading towards Bakhmach at an altitude of about 3 000 meters. They flew over the three scout cars and began dropping bombs on Bakhmach. Feßmann scanned the open terrain. When he spotted a train west of his position driving east—toward Bakhmach—he excitedly grasped the rim of the turret hatch. Then the radio operator called up to him: "Sir, radio message from the battalion. Question: still enemy in your rear?"

"Send the following: enemy still in Gorodishche and truck traffic in both directions two kilometers east on the Baturin-Bakhmach road."

While the radio operator transmitted the message the three armored cars rolled in a wide arc across a harvested cornfield and potato fields toward the west end of Bakhmach. The train had stopped at Chesnokovka station. North of the patrol's position several trucks were driving west and southwest. Then, about two kilometers away, Feßmann saw the linesman's cabin and several houses. The reconnaissance group had marked this spot on their maps. They were supposed to blow the track between the linesman's cabin and Bakhmach. This was their target!

The train stopped for good approximately 700 meters from the linesman's cabin. Trucks rolled from the line of freight cars to Bakhmach and vice versa. They were driving on a road on the other side of the rail line. The Leutnant could only see their superstructures. Feßmann deliberated. In this situation he could not move his three vehicles up to the railway embankment. That would be noticed at once. He had to leave them in cover. But where was even a halfway suitable place to do so? Again he scanned his immediate surroundings. His gaze fell upon a haystack.

"All three vehicles drive to the haystack and take cover there."

Moving quickly, they reached the large pile of hay.

"Both machine-gun cars stay here. I will go ahead alone in the gun car. Schweikl, you come with me, sit outside."

Unteroffizier Schweikl, the combat engineer, climbed onto the right running board, while the Leutnant got onto the left. Feldwebel Engelhard instructed his driver to advance. Quickly the embankment drew nearer. Suddenly Feßmann spotted a machine-gun emplacement about 500 meters ahead next to the embankment.

"The Russian guard position Schweikl. Pity, but we have to carry on."

When the car was within about 300 meters the Russians jumped up and eyed the approaching vehicle. The driver turned slightly to the side and then a ditch forced the men to halt approximately 400 meters from the embankment. Beyond it began a strip of swampy meadow, which the Leutnant could identify by the vegetation.

"Schweikl, we'll carry on from here on foot. Each of us will take a three-kilo charge. The gun car will stay here to cover our backs."

Feßmann and Unteroffizier Schweikl picked up the charges. Bareheaded, armed only with pistols (the Leutnant had left his submachine-gun behind in the gun car), they walked toward the railway embankment. They literally had to force themselves not to walk too fast. The Leutnant watched the movements of the trucks out of the corner of his eye. They made good progress through a turnip field. It bordered on a potato field. There the Leutnant bent over and looked back beneath his arm.

"Damn it, Schweikl, the machine-gunners behind us are going over to our gun car."

They casually placed their explosive charges on the ground. The noise of the trucks driving along the road on the other side of the tracks was loud. They lit cigarettes and blew large clouds of smoke in an attempt to make themselves seem as harmless as possible. Then they began pulling potato stalks in order to look like they were working in the fields. Perhaps this would fool the Russians.

Suddenly a civilian appeared to the left, on the near side of the embankment, dangerously near, and came toward the two Germans. The enemy machine-gunners were now behind the Leutnant. The gun car was already about 250 meters away. Schweikl muttered a curse beneath his breath.

What will Engelhard do? wondered Feßmann. If he fired he would give them away and that would make it almost impossible for him and Schweikl to get away, for he couldn't take out all five Russians simultaneously nor could he drive into the swampy area. And if he didn't shoot—what then? At that moment six horsemen rode past. Coming from the left, they rode toward the linesman's shack, passing not 200 meters from the two Germans. What followed was described by Feßmann in a report which he wrote on 9 September 1941:

> Unteroffizier Schweikl handled himself extremely well; he was as excited as I nevertheless he remained calm and cool. We pulled potato stalks and smoked cigarettes. As we did so he said: "We must do it, sir!"
>
> The enemy soldiers were within about twenty meters of my gun car. Then the unbelievable happened. My excellent Feldwebel Engelhard did not shoot. He drove slowly away, back to the north about 200 meters. Inexplicably the Russians did not recognize the armored car. The crew, who were all bare-headed, looked out. Thank God the crosses had been painted over. The Russians turned away and walked on to Bakhmach. The greatest threat was past.
>
> Schweikl and I walked on toward the small clump of bushes that stood in front of the rail line. We reached it, while the civilian strolled by us peacefully. A large number of enemy infantry, who had meanwhile disembarked from the train, marched along the road on the other side of the rail line into Bakhmach. We could hear the honking of passing trucks from the other side of the tracks.
>
> I broke the silence by saying to Schweikl, "Troops from the train."
>
> "The train is not going into Bakhmach on account of the danger of air attack," Schweikl explained correctly.
>
> "You stay here Schweikl and keep an eye on the Russians behind us."
>
> I myself crawled ahead to the embankment, behind which lay the tracks, which there were somewhat lower than the top of the embankment. The roadbed lay ten meters in front of me. On the other side thin bushes through which I could see enemy

infantry (40 meters in front of me) heading down the road to Bakhmach. To the right the terrain was open. I saw a column of about 200 men in irregular groups coming nearer, as well troop trucks heading in all directions; all, as I said, on the other side of the roadbed.

Then Unteroffizier Schweikl arrived with the charges and informed me that the five had disappeared to the east. To the right I suddenly saw three more soldiers walking straight toward us on our side of the tracks. We had to set off the charges at once!

Then we heard a noise from the right. A motor coach was roaring toward us. We took cover and it raced past. I took a brief look around and then turned to Schweikl and took my two explosive charges.

Voices to our right. I took a quick look. The three soldiers had approached to within ten meters. They were walking straight toward us. For a second I was uncertain. The entire game was at stake.

Schweikl did the only correct thing. He crawled up the embankment, which was very flat. I followed him. We were able to crawl another meter, out of sight of the Russians. The three walked right through our former hiding place.

We heard surprised shouts. Then dull thumps, apparently blows with rifle butts. This led us to think that they had discovered the explosive charges, barely three meters away from us. One can imagine our feelings.

But they walked on! Their voices faded in the distance. From the other side of the tracks we could still hear soldiers talking loudly and now and then laughter and shouts. It was an indescribable situation.

We crawled back to our explosive charges, again took a quick glance around, and then crawled to the roadbed.

"We must pull at the same time, sir," reminded Schweikl.

We worked quickly but carefully. The charges were placed on the track fishplates; each took two tracks. Then we pulled the cords and ran back.

We had run two-hundred meters through the potato field when we heard our charges go off. Pieces of iron whistled through the air.

Then the Russians began firing mortars at us. We ran and ran, gasping for breath. We had to walk the last hundred meters in

A nice view of a radio version of the Sd.Kfz. 263.

spite of the rifle fire from two sides; we simply couldn't go any faster in the heavy growth of potato plants.

When we reached the gun car the crew hauled us up. They held on to us and off we went in the direction of the haystack.

We waved to the radio and machine-gun cars as we approached. They had also had a hairy experience when enemy horsemen approached. But thanks to the excellent cover of the haystack the Russians had ridden past. Now we sent our radio report: "10 A.M.: demolition successful!"

There was still heavy traffic on the Bakhmach-Baturin road. Heavy tanks and armored cars rolled past. We succeeded in crossing the road again at the same place.

For another five hours we observed the traffic on this road from a position off to the side and were able to report more than 300 trucks and panye wagons as well as several heavy tanks and armored cars to the battalion.

Not until we were spotted by chance by enemy infantry, which attacked with antitank gun support, did we withdraw and return to our company, where we received an enthusiastic welcome from our comrades. The commander donated a bottle of champagne and some chocolate—and in Russia!

Feßmann and Limmer had successfully carried out their mission. Soon afterwards they reported to the division commander, Generalmajor von Langermann.

"I am proud of you and your men! Submit a detailed report with a map so that I can make a report to the corps headquarters. General von Geyr has already been told of your great achievement."

Only a few days later the division had a new and more dangerous mission for the "duty patrol leader."

Following the successful mission by the two patrols, on 9 September the 4th Panzer Division crossed the Sjem. The 35th Panzer Regiment fought its way forward through the freshly arrived divisions of the Soviet 40th Army, whose movements Feßmann had observed.

It had rained again. The roads were deep in mud. Marshy areas and bottomless roads hindered Panzer Group 2's drive to the south. The vehicles had to cope with deep ruts. In addition to the threat from the enemy, the dangers lurking in the tricky, swampy landscape had to be factored into the overall calculation. Nevertheless, the advance continued. Bakhmach was taken on 10 September. To its right Konotop fell on the morning of the 10th.

Russian tactical aircraft tried to halt the German advance. The Soviets were trying to keep open the last gap in the Kiev pocket as long as possible in order to allow as many of their surrounded divisions as possible to escape. Elements of no less than five Soviet armies (the 5th, 21st, 26th, 37th, and 38th) were caught in the German ring around Kiev.

At the same time the divisions of Panzer Group 1 (Generaloberst von Kleist) were driving from south to north. As soon as the two armored groups linked up the Kiev pocket would be completely closed. To that end, on that rainy 11th of September, the 3rd and 4th Panzer Divisions had to try and advance as far south as possible. On 11 September 1941 the army group gave the order for the two armored spearheads to meet near Romny. The 3rd and 4th Panzer Divisions from the north and the 9th and 19th Panzer Divisions from the south were to link up there and close the ring around Budyenny's armies.

On the evening of 11 September the 4th Panzer Division's 33rd Rifle Regiment received orders to drive further south towards Toljeki. The Feßmann armored patrol was subordinated to the regiment as its reconnaissance spearhead. Leutnant Feßmann and his three vehicles drove to the infantrymen, who welcomed them warmly. The Leutnant and his eight men had become something of a symbol of successful operations to the men of the division.

When morning came on 12 September and Feßmann gave the order to warm up the engines it was raining heavily. The 5th Panzer Brigade under Oberst Eberbach was also trying to force its way further to the south. The Oberst, an experienced commander of armor, did not want to remain behind the tanks of the 3rd Panzer Division. Once again it was Fritz Feßmann's patrol which led the way.

"Be careful, Engelhard, swampy ground!" Feßmann called to the commander of the gun car after hearing the wheels of his radio car squelching through the muck. The driver turned slightly and the ground beneath their wheels became firmer again. The cars advanced meter by meter. The rain continued to fall without letup. Even though the sun had risen it was still semi-darkness. A row of trees appeared ahead.

"There is Tolejki. Stop and observe."

The three vehicles stopped in the cover of some bushes and their commanders scanned the terrain through their binoculars.

"Sir, Ivans in front of us! Dug in to the left and right of the road!"

On hearing Engelhard's report Feßmann turned his binoculars and immediately spotted the foxholes.

"There aren't many Engelhard. Perhaps a dozen. We can take them."

"If it isn't too muddy."

"Looks good. Higher ground. Through the field, that will hold us."

The radio car led the way. The Russians in their positions on both sides of the road did not fire when the three armored cars entered the field. For fifty or sixty meters all went well. The radio car's tires spun briefly, then caught hold, but after advancing about 100 meters it was all over. The radio car was stuck fast. Before the Leutnant could warn the following gun car it spun its wheels and dug itself deeper into the mud. The 4.8 ton vehicle was simply too heavy.

"Get out and put straw under the wheels," ordered the Leutnant.

Everyone left the vehicles except the drivers. The Russians in the blocking position on the road withdrew into Tolejki without firing a shot.

"Sir, the tanks are coming behind us!"

"Damn!" cursed Feßmann. It will look bad if the tanks drive into this field. He ran back the 100 meters. The battalion commander emerged from the lead tank.

"What's up, Feßmann?"

"Russians in Tolejki. They have pulled back. Two of my cars are stuck. Pull me out of there, sir."

"I'll give you a Panzer II. It will pull you out of the mud. Then you follow us to Tolejki and take the lead again there."

One of the Panzer II tanks veered out of the column and drove across the field after the Leutnant. Its tracks ground into the soil but the tank made it. It reached the two stuck vehicles and began towing them toward the road, while the machine-gun car drove back to the road in reverse.

"Now follow me to Tolejki."

Led by the Panzer II, they drove toward the village. They reached the advance detachment and caught up with the "big brothers" on the outskirts.

"How does it look, Feßmann?"

"No sign of the enemy, sir. I'll have someone ask the inhabitants of the village what's going on."

"All right, do it quietly. It can't hurt."

German experience in Russia had shown that the best way to find out anything about the enemy was always to ask the village inhabitants. It was Feßmann's experience that the Russians in the villages—especially the women—had most often given him accurate information. They had often even warned him of mines and saved him and his crew from certain death. And that is what he intended to do on this day.

Feßmann turned to his gunner, who was from the Sudetenland and spoke Russian well, and said, "Tscherwick, get out and call over one of the Russians."

Tscherwick waved to an old Russian who was nervously chewing on sunflower seeds.

"What about the bridge ahead?" asked the driver, pointing south in the direction of the Ssula, but the man was hesitant to answer.

"Then we'll take him with us. We're going to the bridge anyway, we can ask him again there."

They placed the old man on the radio car and drove through the village toward the river and the bridge. The village was very long, which was typical of those built along the roads. There seemed to be no end to it. Beyond a corner a small wooden bridge appeared before the radio car. It did not seem to be guarded, for there were no enemy soldiers to be seen.

"On to the big bridge. Keep all weapons ready to fire."

The gun car veered out of the column in order to have a clear field of fire for its twenty-millimeter cannon. Still nothing happened. Finally, after 500 meters, the big bridge appeared ahead to the right.

"Stop! I'll have a look."

Through the binoculars Feßmann saw Red Army troops on both sides of the bridge on the far bank. He looked for antitank guns but couldn't find any. Hopefully there were none there. That would have been a disaster for them.

Sd.Kfz. 263s lined up in an open field.

"Report to advance detachment. Bridge ahead of us. Infantry on the other side. No gun positions seen."

They rolled on. Feßmann had the gun car move up alongside his radio car. Two enemy machine-guns on either side of the bridge began to fire. Tracer flitted across to the two armored cars.

"Open fire!"

The burst of fire from the radio car's machine-gun crossed with the enemy fire. Then the gun car opened fire as well. Firing short bursts, it destroyed the first machine-gun, while the radio car and the third armored car continued to fire their machine-guns. The duel lasted exactly two minutes. The enemy fire died down and the platoon leader was about to give the order to advance to the bridge when there was a tremendous explosion. Three huge pillars of flame rose up from the bridge. Then the armored cars were struck by the blast wave. The crewmen ducked inside their steel boxes as wood, rocks and steel from the wrecked bridge rained down.

"Commander to patrol: what is happening up there?"

"The enemy has blown the bridge right under our noses, sir."

"Good thing you weren't on it, Feßmann."

"Damn, damn!" cursed Feldwebel Engelhard. "The Ivans have stuck it to us again."

But as well as fury at the destruction of the bridge, his voice contained a certain degree of relief that the Russians had opened fire first, forcing them to stay where they were.

"Back to the small bridge immediately, before the enemy blows it too!"

The armored cars turned in the deep mud and drove back. When they arrived at the small bridge they found that the tanks of the advance detachment were already there. A company of infantry which had been riding on the tanks had removed the demolition charges from in front of the bridge and had gone across to secure it.

"Glad to see that you're still alive, Feßmann," called the Major on seeing the Leutnant.

"Sir, I am requesting engineers. The bridge was probably also rigged for demolition. They should also check the road on the other side of the bridge to ensure that it is clear of mines."

"Pioneer platoon forward!" ordered the commander.

The engineers arrived and found a large explosive charge which would have been set off by the weight of the tanks rolling over it. They also inspected the road. There were no mines. Apparently the enemy had not had enough time to mine the road as well. While the pioneers were inspecting the road the infantry moved forward in the ditches on both sides of the road. Five minutes later a runner came running back.

"Sir, strong enemy forces approaching from the southwest!"

"Feßmann, take your cars across the bridge, engage the enemy at the south end of the town and hold him up. Limmer, you follow the Leutnant. Feldwebel Flascher will follow to provide covering fire."

One of the Panzer IIIs separated itself from the mass of waiting armor and joined the small battle group. The six armored cars crossed the bridge and moved over to the side. The tank rolled past them, spattering them with mud, and took up position in front. The Feldwebel emerged from the turret hatch and waved to Feßmann. At the southern outskirts of the village, Feßmann saw the Feldwebel pointing to the front. Then he saw the enemy, racing south. Groups of horsemen were riding away at full gallop. Panye wagons bounced over the two dirt roads and on the road a 76.2-mm antitank gun could be seen.

"Open fire!"

Feldwebel Engelhard's gun car opened fire immediately after the order was given. The first shell flitted across to the enemy on the road. Horses reared up, whinnied and ran from the road into the cornfields. Then there were two or three flashes from the enemy positions, followed immediately by the whistle of shells, which passed over the heads of the men and struck the ground behind them. The gun of the Panzer III returned the fire. Three shots silenced one of the Russian antitank guns. The other guns fell silent as well.

"Enemy is breaking contact and withdrawing!"

Almost an entire company of infantry was on its way, riding on tanks. The men had to hold on tight when the armored cars and the Panzer III moved on. They rumbled along the south road. Wherever the enemy offered resistance he was driven from his positions by fire from the tank and the gun car.

"Now we have it!" called the Feldwebel in the tank. "What do we do now? I don't know."

"On this road straight to Hill 88. That is our objective," replied Feßmann.

While pursuing the enemy Feßmann's small armored battle group went too far west, especially from the moment when the road made a turn to the west. The fleeing Russians stopped, because they obviously had no idea how to get through the marshy terrain that bordered the road. After several final shots the patrol leader called a halt.

"We're getting away from our mission and have to go back to the bend in the road."

For better or worse the Feldwebel also had to decide to turn around. They drove to the bend in the road and then turned due south. There a smaller road branched off from the main thoroughfare. After exactly six kilometers they came to the hill. The vehicles were greeted by enemy fire. Then shells landed nearby forcing them to hastily take cover.

Feßmann reported to the battalion: "Hill 88 is strongly occupied by the enemy!"

Two minutes later the following order was received from Hauptmann Nierle: "Stay where you are. Secure the flanks of the advancing division."

While the Feßmann patrol remained in front of Hill 88, the Limmer squad and the Panzer III left with the mounted infantry for assignment elsewhere. The armored patrol's three cars sat among a group of saplings. Every ten minutes Leutnant Feßmann reported to the battalion. At one hour before dusk enemy infantry appeared. They were coming in a wide skirmish line and would certainly discover the three armored cars.

"Everyone ready to fire?" asked the Leutnant.

Several minutes later he ordered: "Open fire!" The gun car fired the first shells in a rapid salvo. The two machine-guns fired as well. The Red Army soldiers disappeared as if the earth had swallowed them up. But Feßmann knew that they definitely would not pull back but instead would soon reappear and attack the armored cars, probably with Molotov cocktails. Therefore he would have to take precautions.

"Radio operator from each car to the command car."

Feßmann got out as well. Driver Tscherwick took his place behind the machine-gun and stayed behind alone. Radio operator Wentzel left the car right after the Leutnant. The radio operators from the other two cars arrived.

"Listen up! We are going to advance in a skirmish line to the trench up ahead and stay there until the Ivans come. Lateral spacing five meters. Open fire as soon as anyone sees a Russian."

Feßmann was first to move forward through the bushes. He heard the clink of steel against steel, perhaps twenty meters ahead. He was still six or seven meters from the trench. Several strides brought him to it and he jumped inside. Mud splashed up and a burst of machine-gun fire came from the place where he had heard the noise. The bullets passed over his head. And then the brown-clad figures burst from the bushes.

The Russians shouted as they charged the Germans. The latter opened fire with four submachine-guns and the Russians fired too. A burst struck the soft ground next to the Leutnant's head. He emptied his magazine. The onrushing Russians took cover. The firing died down. Wounded called for help, then Feßmann heard the tramp of many feet.

"Back to the cars!" ordered the Leutnant.

They could see better from there. If the Russians entered their thicket again they would be able to see them. They had to wait until they were inside the tangle of bushes before they could engage them from the ground. For Feßmann, who knew all the tricks of the armored reconnaissance trade, it was obvious what he had to do. Anyone who didn't know would have been lost on armored reconnaissance duties in Russia.

The men climbed back into their vehicles and Feßmann's radio operator transmitted the Leutnant's reports. Not three minutes had passed when a pair of guns on the hill and three heavy cannon to the side of it began firing. Shells rained down on the brush-covered wilderness, shattering trees and hurling branches into the air. The shellbursts came ever nearer. A salvo of 152-mm shells landed approximately 50 meters from the armored cars. Splinters bounced off their flanks, while dirt and severed branches fell on the hatches.

"They're trying to flush us out, sir," muttered Tscherwick through his teeth. He had already taken his place again behind the driver's wheel.

"Move forward to the edge of cover."

Tscherwick applied throttle. The radio car rumbled forward. It leaned dangerously as it drove through a depression. Some distance away Feldwebel Engelhard forced his way through the undergrowth in the gun car. The machine-gun car followed.

Before the cars had reached the new position three more heavy shells came screaming in. They passed over the vehicles and landed exactly where the patrol had been just two minutes ago. Brush flew into the air and the din almost deafened the crews.

"Lucky, sir," gasped Tschwerick, "we were damned lucky."

More shells fell behind them. The barrage lasted twenty minutes, then it was abruptly shifted on to Tolejki. The dull rumble of shells passing overhead was all they could hear now, as well as the occasional explosion in the distance. Then suddenly there was another noise. The Leutnant stood up in his hatch and listened.

"To everyone: tanks!"

"Damn it!" cursed Feldwebel Engelhard when he heard the Leutnant's message. "And all we have is our door knocker!"

Feßmann's voice rang out again: "Ready the gun car."

The radio operator had already loaded a fresh magazine. Now Feldwebel Engelhard could hear the engine noise too, and then he saw the enemy vehicles appear. It was two armored cars. He was relieved, for they were on even terms with these two small crates. The first armored car rolled straight towards them, while the second turned and drove into the bushes.

"Gun car, open fire!"

Engelhard waited. When the armored car turned slightly and showed its flank he fired immediately. The shells from the first magazine flitted across to the enemy in a slightly arcing flight path. Flashes and small flames showed the Feldwebel that he had hit the target.

The Russian armed car jerked around. It fired a burst from its cannon and the first shells landed in the bushes ten meters beside the gun car.

"Magazine!"

A fresh magazine was inserted and the Feldwebel pressed the trigger. The second cluster of tracer disappeared into the rear of the Russian armored car. It began to smoke then there was a gasoline explosion.

Suddenly the gun car came under fire from the flank. The second Russian armored car's rapid-firing cannon loosed off several bursts.

"Turn!" shouted the Feldwebel. The gun car slid around on one braked wheel. A shell passed just over the car's sloped superstructure. The three men heard the squeak of the scraping steel. Then they were around and opened fire at the second enemy vehicle. It turned and fled to the east, zigzagging wildly.

The armored patrol pulled back. After about 400 meters they arrived at the last possible cover. Darkness was falling.

Turret compartment of a Sd.Kfz. 263 with the 20mm cannon visible in front of the crewmen. The coaxial machine gun can be seen off to the left.

"Radio message to battalion: 'Advance by two enemy armored cars. One destroyed by Feldwebel Engelhard. Artillery fire on position Dora-Ypsilon 12!"

The battalion commander's reply came several minutes later: "Return to the unit!"

The men in the armored cars breathed a sigh of relief. True they had gradually become accustomed to fighting in no-man's-land, nevertheless every new mission brought the question: will it turn out all right this time? Will we be lucky again? The three cars drove back and thirty minutes later reached the forward command post of the 7th Reconnaissance Battalion.

Feßmann walked over to the command post. Hauptmann Nierle stood up and took several steps toward him. Feßmann made his report, then Nierle said: "Be careful, Feßmann! I have a feeling that you are taking too many risks. Moreover, between you and me and the lamppost the division commander has recommended you for the Knight's Cross."

Feßmann was shocked and surprised. He went back to his men. Feldwebel Engelhard reported that everything was ready for the next morning.

Tscherwick kept looking at his watch. When it was several minutes before ten he jumped to his feet. Then he went over to the radio car and tuned in Belgrade. His comrades came over and gathered round the car. At exactly 10 P.M. a deep female voice began singing the song that had become a symbol to all the German servicemen at the front: "Lilli Marleen."

"Beautiful!" said Wentzel when the song was over.

✠

The next morning Feßmann was awakened by someone shaking his shoulder.

"What is it?"

"It is 6:30, sir. We leave in half an hour." It was Kämmerle, whose turn it was to wake everyone that week.

Feßmann got up. When he walked into the main room of the cottage it smelled of coffee and fried bacon. Feldwebel Engelhard, the patrol's designated cook, had prepared breakfast. They were just finishing when Oberleutnant Holzheid appeared.

"Good morning, Feßmann. Are you all set?"

"All ready, sir."

The company commander also greeted the men. Once again Feßmann outlined his plan to the company commander. When he was finished the Oberleutnant nodded in agreement.

"Looks good, Feßmann. By the way the commander of the infantry regiment wants to brief you himself. We have been split into three patrols again. I'm on my way to see Limmer. Incidentally, did you know that we'd applied to have him made an officer?"

"I'm happy for Limmer. He is a good chap, sir."

The company commander disappeared. The men hurried outside, took their places in the vehicles, and Feßmann led his three cars into the assembly area. The commander of the regiment waved them over.

"The commander, sir!" grinned Tscherwick, who was first to see the regimental commander.

The patrol leader reported to the infantry commander, to whom two batteries of an artillery regiment and a panzer company had been subordinated for the attack on Grigorovka. When the Leutnant returned to his vehicle he had to pass by the tanks.

"Hey, Fritz! Heading out with your nutshells again? Watch out the Ivans don't blow you off the field."

"Morning, Fatso!" Feßmann greeted his friend from officer school. "You'll be transferred to the kitchen if the Russians shoot another tank out from under your rear today, understood?"

Leutnant Pollmeier, known as "Fatso" within the company, grimaced. He involuntarily reached for his backside, which had been singed a few days earlier when his tank had been hit and set on fire.

"Patrol forward!"

The three cars moved out. The panzer company with mounted infantry followed at a distance. The two motorized batteries brought up the rear. The attack on Grigorovka had begun. It began to rain again. The big wheels ground through the wet ground, tossing up clumps of mud.

"Damn this weather," murmured Tscherwick.

Slowly the attack force moved forward. The enemy had to be nearby. Somewhere he was waiting for the German attack, for he had to keep this gap between Romni and Lubni open for the armies encircled near Kiev. Shortly before eight the regimental commander radioed: "Feßmann, reconnoiter to Grigorovka. A patrol has just reached Hill 88 and reports it in enemy hands; they will brief you."

The three armored cars increased speed. The main body of the attack force remained behind. Ahead the hill came into view. They headed straight toward it. Tensely the Leutnant looked and listened. They arrived at the hill and a member of the infantry patrol appeared.

"There, over the road, sir. It is passable and there is also cover on the other side."

"Where are the Russians?"

"Weak enemy forces dug in in front of Grigorovka, sir."

"Thank you . . . Move out, follow me."

The armored cars rolled up to the crest of the hill. Feßmann scanned the facing terrain to Grigorovka. He picked out the enemy positions in front of the town and in the town itself the movements of enemy forces withdrawing from north to south.

"Patrol to regimental commander: Enemy withdrawing further to the south. Infantry, panye wagons and some horsemen."

"Thank you Feßmann. Wait there. The Elbinger company is coming."

"We mustn't let them get away again, sir!" declared Tscherwick. "The damned fellows always blow the bridges under our noses and we're left empty-handed."

"That's exactly right, sir. This time it should be us who surprises the enemy."

"Very well. Here comes the panzer company." Feßmann left his armored car and waved over Oberleutnant Elbinger.

"How's it look?"

"The Russians are on the retreat to the south. They will surely blow the next bridge before we get there."

The Oberleutnant observed the enemy retreat through his binoculars. His face was very serious as he lowered the glasses.

"They will surely blow the bridge again. Damn it all, what's to be done?"

"Surprise raid, sir. Give me two of your tanks for support and we'll put the run to them."

"Hmm, sounds good, Feßmann. On your responsibility?"

"Of course, on my responsibility."

"Very well. I'll send two Panzer IIs with you, Leutnant Pollmer and Unteroffizier Drache."

The Oberleutnant went back. Soon afterwards two tanks separated themselves from the waiting column and rumbled up the slope. Standing in the hatch of the first tank was "Fatso."

"Thanks for thinking of me, Fritz."

"It wasn't me, Fatso, it was your commander. Now listen to me: we'll work our way forward in short stages. Keep a sharp eye open. When we are close enough we'll open fire. Drache, you drive behind my gun car. Fatso, you take point."

The vehicles rolled down the hill single file. They moved rapidly. The enemy infantry could now be seen clearly with the naked eye.

"Watch it, Fatso! The Ivans will have laid mines on the road ahead. Best to go around."

"Understood, Fritz."

When they had approached to within about five-hundred meters of the entrance to the village and the Russians still showed no sign of withdrawing, the vehicles fired several bursts of machine-gun fire in the direction of the enemy. The trick worked. An entire squadron of cavalry suddenly galloped out of the village. The machine-guns fired but they were soon out of range. Leutnant Feßmann observed for a good two minutes, then he gave the order to resume the advance. Nearer and nearer they came to the entrance to the village. Suddenly the patrol leader spotted fresh tank tracks.

"Looks like there were tanks in the village, Fritz."

"We have to try it. I'll take point in the radio car."

The tanks left the road and rolled into the mud to allow the patrol leader to pass. Feßmann drove into the village.

Tscherwick said to Feßmann: "We have to get through, sir. With the mud we can't turn on the narrow roads."

Elements of a motorized reconnaissance battalion prepare to move out.

"Good, then let's get through!"

They reached the first houses. Mines might explode beneath the wheels at any moment. But nothing happened. Apparently the enemy had been taken completely by surprise there and hadn't had time for the usual mine laying. The radio car moved on at a walking pace. No enemy troops had shown themselves yet and not a shot had been fired. Leutnant Pollmeier's tank now took the lead, for the armored car could barely maneuver on the muddy subsoil. They had traveled less than 200 meters when enemy infantry and cavalry appeared from the right.

"Open fire!"

The village seemed to be swarming with Russians, all trying to get to the south and put the river between them and the 4th Panzer Division's advance detachment. The Red Army troops moved in large groups from farm to farm, from garden to garden. Their rifle fire ripped through the morning, forcing the tank and armored car commanders to repeatedly duck for cover. Machine-gun and cannon fire quickly extinguished the last resistance. The enemy ran toward the bridge, which was perhaps already being prepared for demolition.

"Faster, faster! After them!"

Suddenly the bridge appeared 300 meters in front of them. The armored cars and tanks roared toward it at full speed. But then (they were perhaps still 200 meters from the entrance) the vehicles of the reinforced patrol began taking fire from the other side of the bridge. Exploding shells from heavy infantry guns began tearing up the muddy road. The enemy was firing at the spearhead of the division with five guns. Was he trying to gain time to blow the bridge?

"Tanks and gun car attack!" ordered Feßmann.

The two tanks returned the enemy's fire. Shells soared over the bridge toward the enemy positions. Meanwhile the armored cars rolled toward the bridge, which loomed larger and larger from the haze. Suddenly a heavy shell whizzed just over the leading car. Feldwebel Engelhard, who was driving just behind the radio car in his gun car, saw a muzzle flash directly ahead, at most 120 meters away. He took aim and fired an entire magazine of 20-mm ammunition. The gun fell silent.

Soon afterwards Feßmann was able to determine that three shells from this volley had scored direct hits on the enemy cannon's armored shield, killing most of its crew. The enemy fire diminished. Only the infantry guns continued to fire. The explosions on the road came nearer to the approaching cars. Suddenly Feßmann saw several Russians running toward the bridge pilings on the far side.

"The demolition team!" shouted Tscherwick.

The machine-gun swung to bear on this new threat. Two brief bursts foiled their plans. The tanks of the advance detachment now approached from the east.

"Gun car and machine-gun car stand guard. Keep the enemy busy. I'm going forward to the bridge."

Feßmann hopped out of the armored car. He heard the chirp of small caliber bullets, reached a ditch and jumped in. Radio operator Wentzel had taken Feßmann's place behind the machine-gun and now fired at any enemy troops that showed themselves. Both Panzer IIs were still firing at the infantry guns, which now fell silent. Pistol in hand, Feßmann worked his way forward until he was abeam the bridge. Let us turn to his account for a description of these critical seconds:

> I crept forward until I was level with the bridge, then peered cautiously through hedges and tall grass into the gardens to my right. Alone and on foot, I had no way of discerning the situation. Then I came to the bridge. I discovered an explosive charge on the longitudinal girder. It had to be removed. A single shot into it and the whole bridge would go up.
>
> I entered the water. Luckily it was not very deep and I made good progress. Then I reached the spot. Rifle shots were still

whizzing over the bridge, but I was too low. They couldn't reach me.

With my pocket knife, which fortunately had a strong blade, I cut through several thick wires which held the detonating cord. If some Russian were to push the plunger now . . . !

Suddenly I heard a movement behind me in the bushes. I swung round, my finger on the trigger of my pistol. But it was just brave Schweikl, my Unteroffizier. An excellent fellow! Acting on his own without orders he had followed me, for as a pioneer he definitely wanted to be there. I am proud to be allowed to lead such men.

Together we cut the wires to a second charge. Nothing happened in the meantime. Either charge would have been enough to completely destroy the bridge. But for once we had beat the Russians to a bridge and prevented it from being blown. The division would get across the river quickly here. We crept back through the ditch to our armored car. To the right I saw Russians trying to sneak away into the terrain. We fired and even though we did not have a particularly good field of fire stopped them long enough for our own infantry to take several dozen prisoners. Now the bridge was under the protection of our troops. We could move on.

Just beyond the bridge there were twenty-one metal mines lined up in a neat row on the side of the road. They were obviously supposed to be laid there. But this time we had been too quick on our feet and prevented many casualties. It was a good, liberating feeling for me and my comrades. Now we also came upon the wrecked gun. To our joy the booty was greater than expected: two 122-mm guns, one in firing position facing us and the other with the shell casing from the last round fired still in its breech.

Generalmajor von Langermann later said:

Feßmann once again spared us major casualties and assured our rapid advance to the south. Disarming the explosive charges represented a major accomplishment by this young officer, whom I consider capable of leading a larger unit.

Hauptmann Reimann, the commander of the infantry battalion, which was still engaged in battle in the village, now asked Feßmann to help his men clear the village. With the initial objective secured, Feßmann turned and supported the infantry. But soon there was another mission for the men of the patrol. The enemy had dug in on the rail line three kilometers south of Grigorovka and was firing on the division's area of operations with antitank guns and artillery.

✠

"Men, we have orders to scout the strength of the enemy opposite us and have a look at his positions. Mount up!"

The vehicles negotiated the muddy dirt road and reached the main road leading south. The wheels turned faster. They rolled south at thirty kilometers an hour, but after only a few hundred meters there were flashes from a field emplacement in front of them. A burst of machine-gun fire flashed in the direction of the patrol and passed over the vehicles. They turned onto a secondary road, which appeared to lead straight into a wood. The car's machine-guns fired as they moved and soon the enemy guns fell silent. Shells howled over the three armored cars, heading north. Feßmann could even see the muzzle flashes from the enemy guns in the tip of the wood in front of them. He radioed back:

"In front of the railway embankment, approximately one hundred meters right of the road, antitank gun position; four guns in an area seventy meters wide. On the left three Russian field guns. Forty meters from the road, eighty meters from the railway embankment."

"We'll fire a salvo of 105 millimeters, you provide corrections," came the reply.

Soon afterwards the division artillery opened fire. The fist salvo fell about 100 meters in front of the antitank position, sending fountains of mud into the air.

"Hundred more! Direction good!"

Less than a minute later the second salvo came screaming in and sent mud flying high from the area near the gun on the right flank. Then there was a flash as the shells exploded. Then the stored ammunition went up, destroying the gun position.

Feßmann gave further corrections, but only ten minutes after the guns had opened fire the enemy realized what was up and sent two scout vehicles into the wood. When they emerged from a depression Feßmann saw that they were tracked vehicles. That was bad, for they would surely get through the mud and if they cut off their avenue of escape they would be trapped there.

"Engelhard, you have to engage them before they get too close. Place the lead vehicle under fire as soon as it has reached that low rise there. Aim at the pine, that's about where he should appear."

The prospect of mines was always a nightmare to an armored crew, as demonstrated here by this *Sturmgeschütz* III from the *Großdeutschland* Assault Gun Brigade.

The Feldwebel carefully took aim at the tree based on the information from the Leutnant. The scout vehicles disappeared into a depression. When the first appeared over the low rise its nose appeared right beside the pine tree. After making a slight correction the Feldwebel fired the entire contents of the magazine. The smoke trails went straight across to the enemy vehicle. The small flames from the hits confirmed that Engelhard's aim had been good. The Soviet light tank stopped, meanwhile radio operator Reith had already loaded a fresh magazine.

Flames shot from the muzzle of the enemy tank's 45-mm gun. A shell whistled over the armored car and struck a tree trunk further back. Before the enemy could fire again, Engelhard fired off the second magazine. He had set his sights slightly lower. The small-caliber shells hammered into the enemy tank's weakest spot, the junction between the turret and hull. There was a loud bang. The tank's turret hatch flipped back and a thin stream of black smoke came out.

Then, suddenly, the second light tank appeared about forty meters to the side of the first. When it reached the top of the rise it fired its main gun and the machine-gun mounted on its turret. Machine-gun bullets struck the sloping armor of the German armored car's turret and bounced off. Flames now shot from the first enemy tank. While the gun car swung its cannon to face the second enemy tank, the reserve ammunition of the first exploded, destroying the tank.

The second enemy tank turned and before Engelhard could fire it had disappeared behind the rise. Minutes later it reappeared 500 meters further back near the railway embankment. The enemy now turned his artillery fire on the wood. After the first shells fell at the edge of the wood, Feßmann knew that they had to get out of there. He reported to division: "Enemy is ranging in on our observation position. At least four 152-mm guns on the other side of the embankment. Request permission to retire."

"Thank you, Feßmann, request granted."

By the time this message was received the armored cars had already withdrawn about 300 meters to the north through the wood. Feßmann ran ahead to see where the forest road on which they were driving led. The Leutnant reached the north end of the wood and saw that the road led straight north through a depression. He immediately ran back to his three vehicles, which were following slowly, climbed in and led the patrol down this relatively-well concealed road away from the immediate danger.

They had just left the wood and rolled through the depression when the enemy artillery began pouring shells onto the edge of the forest. Once again Feßmann's instincts had been correct and they had withdrawn just in time. The patrol's return was uneventful. Feßmann reported to the regimental commander.

"Thank you, Feßmann! Once again, you have been a great help to us. Have the field kitchen give your men something special to eat, they've earned it."

✠

On Sunday, 14 September 1941, the Feßmann patrol set off to the south again. When the day was over it had established contact with an advance detachment of the 16th Panzer Division. At the same time the leading units of the 3rd Panzer Division also made contact with the combat engineers of the 16th Panzer Division. The last remaining gap in the Kiev pocket had now been closed. Army Group Budyenny was in the bag. Late that evening Generaloberst Guderian appeared in Lokhvitsa. "Fast Heinz" wanted to be on the scene so as to be able to coordinate all operations as quickly as possible and be able to make quick decisions.

The next day the Russians attempted to break out of the Kiev pocket; as a result the entire 7th Reconnaissance Battalion became engaged in heavy fighting. The unit's light vehicles found themselves facing enemy tanks. Even Leutnant Feßmann found himself in extremely difficult situations. He nevertheless got his three vehicles out in one piece, something the eight crewmen would always be grateful for.

The Soviet breakout attempts continued in the days that followed, but the ring was closed. The 9th Panzer Division arrived to bolster the German forces as did the 25th Motorized Infantry Division. Several Russian generals were captured on 20 September while leading breakout attempts. The Feßmann patrol also brought in many prisoners.

The divisions of the XXIX Motorized Army Corps took Kiev on 19 September and on the 26th the great battle of encirclement was over. The enemy had lost one million men killed, wounded or captured. Budyenny had flown out of the pocket. 665,000 Red Army soldiers became prisoners of war. The Soviets' inability to withdraw to the east was due to the efforts of the corps, whose lightning dash to the south had closed the Kiev pocket. Fritz Feßmann and his patrol had dashed south into the wilds of Russia at the very tip of the corps.

✠

Immediately after the end of the battle of encirclement Panzer Group 2 was turned around in order to take part in "Operation Typhoon," the assault on Moscow.

The armored group headed north again. Once again the XXIV Motorized Army Corps led the way. The 3rd and 4th Panzer Divisions attacked north from the Glukhov area in the direction of Orel. The 3rd Panzer Division screened the 4th's left flank while the latter advanced as the corps' spearhead. From Glukhov, on 2 October the division reached Sevsk. Road conditions had become abominable. Rain, now and then mixed with snow, fell steadily, turning the ground into mud. With the roads transformed into rivers, the advance continued cross-country.

Feßmann was one of the first to drive into Sevsk. Under fire from the houses, he rolled through the city and stayed on the enemy's heels. Infantry riding on the vehicles exchanged fire with the enemy troops lurking in buildings.

Kromy was reached the next day. The 7th Reconnaissance Battalion stormed forward determinedly, sometimes as part of the advance detachment under Major von Jungenfeldt. When the wheeled vehicles became stuck in the mud it was the tanks under Oberst Eberbach that kept the attack going. At noon on 3 October Oberst Eberbach and his tanks reached Orel, having covered more than 130 kilometers on that day alone. The tanks drove through the surprised forward outposts straight into the city.

One of the few wheeled units with them was the Feßmann patrol. The patrol came under fire from a field emplacement but Feßmann continued to observe. But then, suddenly, shells came howling in. One landed less than 40 meters from the radio car. Before the Leutnant could duck inside the armored car splinters were flying around his head. He felt a strange pain on the left side of his head and in a semi-conscious state heard the sound of shell fragments striking the armor plate.

"Sir, you've been wounded!" shouted Tscherwick in dismay. He saw the blood running down the Leutnant's left cheek. Feßmann raised his hand and felt warm, sticky blood on his fingers.

"Can't be too bad. Over to those houses quickly."

Tscherwick turned to the side. They rolled across a meadow. While the next salvo landed behind them, hurling stones, earth and more steel fragments into the air, they reached the cover of the houses. There the Leutnant's wound was dressed. They asked him to go to the main aid station for proper dressings and a tetanus shot, but Feßmann refused.

"I already received a tetanus shot in July. I'm not leaving now, just when we're moving forward."

Feßmann did not leave. The wound healed without complications. The advance on Moscow continued. The first snow fell on the night of 7 October and the mud became worse. The division stormed through Mtsensk toward Tula. At this time Feßmann received news that his wife had given birth to a son. The advance continued through snow flurries. The armored cars literally had to plow their way through the mud. But Moscow was still far away. They hadn't even reached Tula, where the second Moscow defense line began.

Not until 23 October did the division cross the Susha. Close on the heels of the enemy the division stormed into Chern. When Leutnant Feßmann reached the city he saw a road sign: "90 kilometers to Tula." All of the wheeled vehicles became bogged down on the worsening roads. Only Oberst Eberbach's tanks continued to advance through the mud.

On 27 October Leutnant Feßmann was summoned to the division command post. General von Langermann greeted him, while Oberstleutnant Heidkämper, the division Ia, winked at him meaningfully.

"Leutnant Feßmann," began the division commander, "the supreme commander has awarded you the Knight's Cross of the Iron Cross for your actions in the blowing of the Bakhmach railway line. I have the great honor of presenting it to you today."

For a moment Feßmann was completely speechless. But then his face brightened. His eight men were standing outside. Feßmann could find no

Provisional bridge over one of Russia's many waterways.

words when Tscherwick congratulated him on behalf of the patrol. Five days later Feßmann was promoted to Oberleutnant.

The fighting went on. Nothing had changed. Feßmann continued to carry out his sorties against enemy positions and provide the division with valuable information. In spite of the mastery now established by "General Winter," Generaloberst Guderian was still determined to succeed. He assembled all the tanks of the XXIV Army Corps (mot.), the 75th Artillery Regiment, the 3rd Rifle Regiment and the Infantry Regiment "Großdeutschland" into a mobile advance guard under the command of Oberst Eberbach. He gave Oberst Heinrich Eberbach a brief but unambiguous order:

"Forward at all costs, Eberbach. Take Tula!"

On 20 October the armored spearhead was in front of Tula. Four kilometers separated it from the great industrial city at the gates of Moscow. Tula, the old silver city on the Upa, had to be taken before Moscow could be reached. The "Großdeutschland" Regiment got as far as the outskirts of the city with their workers settlements. Then it was stopped. The next morning Oberst Eberbach scouted the terrain on foot. The attack began at 5:30 A.M. When evening came the attackers had made a gain of fifty meters. The attack by Eberhard's panzers had failed. The next day Oberleutnant Feßmann also joined the battle for Tula. The offensive was suspended temporarily. For the 7th Reconnaissance Battalion it was the start of a period of positional warfare, something it was unaccustomed to.

Not until 15 November did the divisions of Army Group Center launch their assault on the Soviet capital. By the 19th all the divisions of Army Group Center were on the attack. On 18 November an assault team of the 3rd Panzer Division took the railway bridge over the Upa in a surprise raid. The Feßmann armored patrol rolled around Tula in the bitter cold. There were battles with Russian rifle divisions, but once again Feßmann and his men were unbelievably lucky. Once the machine-gun car was shot up, but the three-man crew escaped with their lives. Only Obergefreiter Bickert had to spend a few days at the main aid station, but he soon returned to his patrol.

Tula had been bypassed. The 4th Panzer Division felt its way along the rail line which led into the heart of the enemy capital from the south. It reached Aleksin Hill on the far side of the rail line facing the positions of the 49th Soviet Army. Together with the 33rd Rifle Regiment, elements of the 7th Reconnaissance Battalion took part in the encirclement of the 239th Siberian Rifle Division. However the Siberians in their white camouflage uniforms fought their way out and escaped to the east.

Feßmann and his patrol reached the rail line on 2 December 1941 and took part in its destruction, although he did not carry out the demolition himself. The armored patrol advanced as far as Kostrova. More than once enemy fire concentrated on the three small vehicles but miraculously they always came through. Fifteen kilometers south of Tula, which was still being defended, Generaloberst Guderian made the decision to withdraw the forward elements of his panzer army. He issued this order, the most difficult of his career, from the estate of the Russian author Tolstoy during the night of 6 December 1941 and a short time later announced that:

"The attack on Moscow has failed. We have suffered a defeat."

The great retreat began. Now Feßmann and his men were fighting as rear guards. These icy days and nights saw the beginning of an odyssey that was not to end until Orel. At the beginning of October 1942 Feßmann was transferred to the 14th Panzer Division, which was at Stalingrad at the time, but which was soon supposed to be withdrawn to a rest area in the rear to reequip. There Fritz Feßmann was to assume command of a company.

✠

On 7 October 1942 Oberleutnant Fritz Feßmann arrived at the division and reported to Generalmajor Heim at his command post.

"Good to have you here, Feßmann. You will immediately take over the 1st Company of the 64th Motorcycle Battalion."

That was Generalmajor Heim's greeting to the Oberleutnant. The 64th Motorcycle Battalion was the "eyes" of the 14th Panzer Division, and now an experienced armored reconnaissance officer was to take over its 1st Company.

Under the command of Major Grams, this fastest battalion in the division, equipped with armored troop carriers (halftracks), had been its point unit since July 1942. On 30 August it was in Beketovka, the southern suburb of Stalingrad. The enemy became more determined, his antitank defenses more effective. Then on 29 September the 14th Panzer Division had been transferred as army reserve into the area north of Plodovitoye. On 4 October it went to the aid of the Romanians, helping drive out Soviet troops who had broken into the positions near Sadovoye.

Meanwhile the 6th Army had reached Stalingrad. As the army was exhausted, on 9 October the 14th Panzer Division was placed under its command and moved via Voroponovo, Pitomnik and Gumrak into the area west of the big Krasnye Barrikady armament works in the northern part of Stalingrad. Commanding there was II Corps under General Seydlitz.

Feßmann joined the division as the first signs of the coming catastrophe were becoming apparent. The armored scout cars were kept busy reconnoitering the enemy's positions and strength. Feßmann, who carried out all the most difficult missions himself, soon realized what the concentration of such strong Soviet forces behind Stalingrad had to mean. He repeatedly made pointed reference to the results of his patrols, however his warnings were disregarded.

One of the Russian pincers that completed the deadly encirclement of Stalingrad passed between his company's base and the city on the Volga. Stragglers and remnants of units were placed under his command to form Battle Group Feßmann. It was a hastily thrown together outfit with a wide variety of soldiers, but when Feßmann appeared it seemed to give the men new courage. Feßmann wanted to try and stop a second Russian pincer which was driving into his rear. He had to hold his position as a bridgehead for the relief of Stalingrad. But he and his battle group were constantly forced back until they reached the Karpovka area on 19 November.

The onslaught faced by this small battle group and indeed the entire 14th Panzer Division was described by Oberstleutnant Grams in the history of the 14th Panzer Division:

> It was an eerie and nerve-wracking struggle above and below the ground, in the rubble, cellars and canals of the great city and the factories. Man against man, hero against hero. Tanks climbed over mountains of rubble, crawled squeaking through wrecked factory halls and fired from close range into rubble-filled streets and narrow factory courtyards. Many of the armored giants shook and burst under the force of exploding enemy mines. But there were also the deep and eroded loess ravines, which fell away steeply to the Volga, where a bitter battle began. If our grenadiers were lucky enough to reach the upper rim of the bank of the Volga, then at night the enemy poured out of these fissures in the earth, like an element of nature, into the rear and flanks of the Germans, and what had been won in heavy fighting during the day was lost again in the morning.
>
> The enemy could be not be seen over there in the ancient forests on the lower east bank of the Volga, neither his batteries nor his infantry. But he was there and fired, and night after night he brought reinforcements across the mighty river into the ruins of the city in hundreds of boats.

When the Russians launched their offensive against the positions of the 1st Romanian Cavalry Division in the Kletskaya area at 4 A.M. on 19 November 1942, the 103rd Panzer Grenadier Regiment under Oberstleutnant Seydel was in the Karpovka area. Under its command were the Bremer Company of the 36th Panzer Regiment and the 64th Motorcycle Battalion.

On the same day Oberleutnant Feßmann reported to his battalion commander a combat strength of 750 men. These 750 soldiers were "Battle Group Feßmann." They were supposed to halt the Russian advance, occupy the Loshki bridgehead on the Don south of Krasnoarmejskij and hold it against a fifty-fold enemy superiority. On the evening of 19 November Feßmann received word that Battle Group Sauerbruch, commanded by Hauptmann Sauerbruch (the son of the famous surgeon), was on its way and that he was being placed under its command.

The 750 soldiers under Feßmann fought desperately. They had to yield to the pressure and withdraw in steps. But along the Tsaritsa, a small river running from north to south, Feßmann succeeded in establishing a new defense line. The men of the regiment and battalion trains dug in there as did the division supply drivers, manning the foxholes and machine-gun positions. Mines were laid in front of the positions to provide a measure of protection against tank attacks.

The battle group had just established itself when the Russians attempted to break through there too. Feßmann's battle group had to hold on until the main aid station and the hospital situated in the next village behind the battle group had been evacuated. The first probing enemy forces appeared in front of the battle group's lines late on the evening of 21 November. A few hours later (at exactly one hour after midnight) the battle group commander was awakened by a tremendous explosion. Feßmann threw on his tunic and rushed outside. A Soviet heavy tank was sitting in the middle of the bridge over the Tsaritsa. It had driven over a mine which had been placed there only hours before. Blazing fiercely, the huge vehicle lit the night like a giant torch. The battle began and with it a three-day action which would demand the utmost of every member of the battle group.

For three days the Soviets tried to cross the river, once in the north, then in the middle and finally in the south, in order to roll up the battle group from the flank. By day and night Fritz Feßmann hurried to threatened sectors held by his battle group. Each fresh defensive success by the small force outdid the one before it. Following a fierce bombardment by tanks and artillery positioned on the far bank, on the evening of the third day (24 November 1942) the enemy fought his way into the south end of Lyapichev, overran the infantry defending there and captured the suburb. Feßmann, who was nearby with ten armored troop carriers, immediately attacked with riflemen from the 64th Battalion. Feßmann entered the suburb riding in the leading armored troop carrier. When the enemy concentrated his fire on the half-track, Feßmann ordered:

"Attack! Drive up to the houses! Then disembark and take out the enemy!"

The ten armored troop carriers stormed forward. Enemy tanks fired from the far bank of the river, however the intervening houses prevented them from hitting the German half-tracks. Many of the buildings went up in flames. Finally the armored troop carriers reached the enemy-occupied quarter. Feßmann jumped out. His riflemen followed. They wiped out the enemy soldiers with submachine-guns, machine-guns and hand grenades. The fighting lasted about ten minutes.

The enemy tanks also left the battlefield. The situation was in hand for the time being. Feßmann and his infantry pulled back to Novo Petrovski, eight kilometers to the south. When he arrived there his adjutant informed him that he was to report to Hauptmann Sauerbruch at five the next morning. The next morning Feßmann presented himself to General Staff Hauptmann Peter Sauerbruch, the Ib of the 14th Panzer Division.

"Good morning, Feßmann. Listen, we're pulling back our line to the prepared Loshki bridgehead. The enemy is approaching from the south with strong forces. He has already partly outflanked our division and is also pressing us from the northeast."

"Then there is nothing more to be done, sir?"

"The army has ordered this withdrawal, Feßmann. Unfortunately, the retreat has to take place by day. I don't have to tell you what that means."

"What do you want me to do?"

"I am ordering you to take your battle group, consisting of ten armored troop carriers, half of a motorcycle platoon and four antitank guns, to Lyapichev, form the rear guard there and not begin disengaging from the enemy until 10 A.M."

Feßmann repeated the order. A final handshake. Then he hurried as quickly as possible back to his command post. He summoned his junior commanders and described to them the anticipated course of the battles to come. In conclusion he said to the men:

"Comrades, we have never fought together before. Many of us have come from the trains and are not as well trained as they ought to be. Therefore I am now sending the trains back. All other non-combat elements are also going back to the west. The ration NCO will issue special

A column of Panzer IIIs moves past a burning BT-5 during the advance on Moscow.

rations for two days. Hassenpflug, you blow up all vehicles that cannot be driven or towed so that nothing usable falls into enemy hands. The battle group will move out at 8 A.M. Good luck!"

There now began an action which was so fantastic that it is best described by Fritz Feßmann himself. He wrote this report, still under the impression of the exciting events, on 5 February 1943 in Reserve Hospital II in Bamberg:

> Everything went extremely well and at 8 A.M. I drove in my armored troop carrier at the head of my battle group to the northern exit from the village. There I was stopped by the antitank gun crews on guard, who pointed out several vehicles driving around in the open terrain to our west.
>
> "Watch out they don't shoot your asses off in your tin cans!" warned the Leutnant commanding the antitank gun.
>
> I now observed these vehicles through the binoculars and identified them as tanks. They were driving in and out of the long column of trucks and cars of the division train, which was striving toward the west, knocking out vehicle after vehicle. Flames hung over the column. Flames and spirals of black smoke, and repeated flashes from the guns of the tanks and gasoline explosions from the vehicles that were hit.
>
> "Everyone stop. I'm driving forward to reconnoiter."

In my armored troop carrier I now drove straight north down the road to Lyapichev in order to get a picture of the enemy's dispositions.

After two kilometers I stopped and determined that the enemy had broken through with tanks between Lyapichev and us. I saw several Soviet tanks in the west, but several of the huge monsters were also moving to the north and northeast. I turned my halftrack around and raced back.

"Motorcycle troops follow the division trains withdrawing to the west!" I ordered. 'Silbermann, you head west with five of these armored troop carriers and two antitank guns in the direction of the Russian tanks. I will take the other five armored troop carriers and the third antitank gun onto the road north in the direction of Lyapichev. Choose your own course, but stay out of the sights of the enemy tanks.

Oberleutnant Silbermann took over the group assigned to him and drove off, while I and my group, which now consisted of five armored troop carriers and one antitank gun, set off down the road to the north in the direction of Lyapichev.

My vehicles maintained their intervals perfectly; with the antitank gun and the large armored radio vehicle we looked like a "proper army unit." The impression that we made must have been good. First one, then two and finally three Russian tanks which were west of us drove away to the north, headed northeast in a wide arc at maximum speed and rejoined their comrades there. They had therefore mistaken us for tanks and wanted to save themselves from being cut off by us.

I later learned from Oberleutnant Silbermann that the Soviets had in fact previously been driving among our train vehicles with great relish (as they could do so with no threat to themselves) and had already set several on fire.

It was due to Silbermann's daring intervention that the enemy tanks broke away from the train, even though there was little he could have done to them. One of his two antitank guns had the great misfortune to suffer a firing pin failure just as it was about to fire at one of the passing enemy tanks from ten meters.

My group and I now had the enemy tanks in front of us to the northeast and thus guarded the trains, which were behind me and still heading west in columns. The enemy tanks stayed together for some time. My vehicles and I were outside their most favorable firing range and drove quite slowly.

The Soviets fired their tank cannon now and then. Then they slowly began to move and came toward us. It was time to act. But what should I do? My armored troop carriers had just two machine-guns each, and I couldn't hope to stop the five T-34s with one antitank gun in open terrain. It was obvious that I would just be sacrificing my antitank gun for no good purpose in such an attempt. Consequently there was only one choice left to me: a stop and go war.

I moved off in my armored troop carrier and by means of hand signals I arranged the remaining vehicles to the side and behind. Driving past the Russians, I signaled for an eventual encirclement of same. They hesitated, stopped and fired.

Unfortunately, we were now in good firing range of them and shells flitted in front of and behind us, struck the ground or whizzed just over our heads. The crash of exploding high-explosive shells mingled with the smack of armor-piercing rounds hitting the soft ground. Steel shrieked, smacked against our vehicles in splinters, howled over our heads.

But this terrain was ideally suited to "tank warfare" and I was able to drive straight ahead at twenty-five to thirty kilometers an hour until it was time to reverse course.

The entire group continued to zigzag back and forth in front of the Soviet tanks, which kept up a hectic rate of fire. Once I looked back and saw shells landing in front of and behind my five armored troop carriers! Again and again the erupting fountains of dirt, powder smoke and the stink of cordite. But no hits, thank God. We were too fast for the gunners in the T-34s, who had to both command the tank and observe. They were therefore at a serious disadvantage against our tanks, which was expressed in a much slower rate of fire.

Of course we could not fire, otherwise the Russians would have caught on that we only had machine-guns. It was very exciting and made us all hot. Our zigzagging saved us time and again. And this experience of driving without being able to return fire left me with the impression that I could act, and that is always a nice feeling.

My driver drove quickly, surely and reacted immediately. He carried out the course changes I shouted to him unbelievably quickly. The men beside him were calm and collected; the cars echeloned behind me maintained their intervals magnificently. It was proof to me that these soldiers had total faith in me. What else could I do but help them and also our train? And how could I achieve this without needlessly endangering them all? It was a situation I had never experienced before.

Never before had we been in contact with the enemy in such a strange "battle order." I felt as perhaps an admiral might feel during a fleet engagement. Only, unfortunately I lacked his artillery.

Meanwhile the Soviet tanks moved to the left, then to the right again, following our zigzagging and drawing ever nearer to us. Unfortunately my previous method of driving also brought me closer to them. The situation became increasingly uncomfortable. If even one of the enemy tank commanders had had the courage to once move forward quickly, he would have at least forced us to flee but might have caught us as easy prey. And this one attack would also have had disastrous consequences for our train.

Approaching to within 1,000 meters of the Russian tanks, I ordered my driver to turn and withdrew again to 2,000 meters in order to simulate a sort of defense position behind a gentle rise.

The Soviets followed hesitantly, halting frequently to fire. It really was a gift from heaven that none of my vehicles was hit.

By means of hand signals I ordered my antitank gun to go into position and had it open fire at maximum possible range. Of course in one respect this was completely useless, however the time it gained was decisive and determined my order. Interpreting my earlier orders literally and dealing with the situation as I found it, I had to hold up these marauding Russian tanks until 10 A.M. so that not only the train units withdrawing from Novo Petrovski, but also our comrades still in Lyapichev, could get away and not have the Russian tanks arrive in their rear and destroy them.

All of a sudden the Silbermann group appeared farther to the rear on a gentle rise and came to join us. I waved to Silbermann and the Oberleutnant, whom I had come to value during my time with the 14th Panzer Division, informed me that the train had now got through, and that the last of the division's vehicles had passed the danger point and no longer needed his protection.

"Silbermann, we have to bluff the Russians here. Therefore this time we will drive north with both groups, taking no notice of them. Perhaps we will be able to get through to Lyapichev."

"Then let's go, Feßmann," was this exemplary officer's reply.

The two groups now set off to the north together. But we were not very near to Lyapichev when I was able to realize that the Soviets had surrounded the town with a thick ring of tanks. From the center of the town explosions rose into the sky. Then waves of

The attack on Moscow ground to a halt in the snow and freezing temperatures.

infantry appeared. They came out of ravines and from behind hedges.

"We can't get into Lyapichev, Silbermann."

"It looks like our comrades are pulling out of Lyapichev. The detonations suggest that."

Yes, what Silbermann was saying sounded very likely. Our comrades were disengaging from the enemy. A look at the clock showed me that it was now 11 A.M. We had held an hour longer than planned. We had thus carried out our mission to the best of our knowledge and belief and now—after being unable to see another single German soldier—withdrew to the west, where we rejoined our comrades in the Loshki bridgehead.

It turned out that the Elbinger group had disengaged from the enemy in Lyapichev in time and arrived in the bridgehead ahead of the two groups of armored troop carriers.

With the exception of the train vehicles destroyed by the Russian tanks before we intervened, we had got out of Novo Petrovski in one piece. The entire division supply train and several rifle battalions had made it through to the west. And all this because of our cheeky, unbelievable bluff.

One might get the impression from Oberleutnant Feßmann's account that the events described by him represented nothing special, but it was a decisive act that this officer had carried out with his battle group in the days of the Russian onslaught.

But in spite of Feßmann's outstanding accomplishment and those of other battle groups the 14th Panzer Division had reached a crisis situation. The confusion was further fueled by rumors. Nevertheless, the intervention of a handful of determined officers was able to prevent an outbreak of panic. The division's radio section immediately attempted to establish contact with the surrounded elements of the 103rd Regiment and K-64 inside the pocket, which it did. Soon afterwards, however, a ban on radio communications was issued.

Russian tank formations repeatedly drove into the rear of the partially surrounded units. The encirclement ring that the Soviets had thrown around Stalingrad became thicker and thicker. In powerless desperation Feßmann had to watch as all hope of rescuing his comrades in the city faded.

A Russian attack on Loshki with strong tank support on 26 November was repulsed. Oberst Tzschöckell and Hauptmann Sauerbruch, to whose battle group the Feßmann group was now subordinate, intercepted the Soviet drive. An outbreak of panic among the soldiers of the train, who were not combat troops, was prevented. When night came Loshki was in German hands again. But as the defenders were incapable of withstanding another attack, the battle groups had no choice but to withdraw to the position in the Don Bend east of Verch-Chirskaya. Oberleutnant Feßmann scouted the new position during the night of 27 November. The battle groups moved in in good order.

In the days that followed, weaker Russian attacks were repelled by mobile forces deployed in the line Demkin-Nemovski-Logovskij in order to keep the enemy in the dark concerning the true course of the 14th Panzer Division's main line of resistance for as long as possible and deceive him as to its true strength.

Late on the evening of 30 November 1942 a surprise Soviet attack overran the division's left wing. The German units shattered by Soviet tanks lay in the forest with no equipment or defensive positions. Contact with the stationary center was lost. Hauptmann Sauerbruch launched a counterattack with his last reserves. Oberleutnant Feßmann's fast armored troop carriers formed a point group.

When Feßmann advanced out of the forest into the open he was met by withering fire from an enemy antitank gun position. The shells from heavy antitank guns shattered three armored troop carriers and before Feßmann could give the order to withdraw his own vehicle was hit. Feßmann felt stabbing pains in his sacrum, pelvis, and both legs. It became dark around him. He did not know how he got back, but he woke up in the main aid station. His first question was about his comrades. They were able to tell him that Hauptmann Sauerbruch had halted the enemy and reestablished a continuous front line. Feßmann was taken by train to Kiev. He was accompanied by his faithful batman, who selflessly cared for him during the long journey. From Kiev he was flown to Lötzen in East Prussia and from there went by train via Berlin to Bamberg and the care of his family. There he was treated by an outstanding surgeon.

A long period of suffering followed. After three serious operations, each lasting several hours, he was finally out of danger. The officer slowly recovered from his wounds. The fragment that had entered his sacrum caused the greatest pain, but finally that danger too was over. On 4 January 1943 news reached Feßmann in hospital in Bamberg that he had been awarded the Oak Leaves to the Knight's Cross for his outstanding actions near Stalingrad. A few days later he was informed that he had been promoted to Hauptmann effective 1 January 1943. Feßmann was forced to remain in hospital for more months. There was even some question as to whether he would ever be fit for front-line duty again.

In June 1943 Feßmann was still not fit for combat duty. In August he was able to secure a transfer to the armored forces school at Versailles. There he taught the tactics and technology of armored reconnaissance into the enemy rear. Then at the end of January 1944 he was summoned to the armored forces school at Krampnitz near Potsdam to serve as a tactics instructor. The better his health became, the harder it was for him to remain at home. He believed that the place of every soldier who could fight was at the front and he left no stone unturned in his efforts to get back into combat.

Finally his efforts were successful. After 18 months in Germany, on 30 June 1944 he was transferred to the Eastern Front to take over a position as battalion commander in the 5th Panzer Division. It was the start of a terribly difficult period. In a very short time Feßmann won the trust of his men as commander of the 5th Armored Reconnaissance Battalion. He assumed command of the battalion during the heavy fighting in the Gomel area. Wherever there were difficult situations to master the battalion commander's vehicle was there; Feßmann led counterattacks by the rear guard, freed surrounded elements of the division and carried out reconnaissance patrols to obtain vital information.

Generalleutnant Decker, the division commander, himself a wearer of the Oak Leaves, knew that he could rely on his 5th Armored Reconnaissance Battalion in any situation and he deployed it wherever the enemy broke through with armored forces.

When enemy mobile forces broke through again on 14 July, Feßmann drove into the middle of the enemy attack force. The Panther tanks under his command destroyed seven T-34s. Maneuvering skillfully, the 5th Armored Reconnaissance Battalion foiled the enemy's plans and halted him. Standing in the open hatch of his command vehicle, Hauptmann Feßmann personally led the individual groups to the target area and deployed them against the enemy.

A shell landed near the command vehicle, showering it with hundreds of fragments. There was a bang and the vehicle shook violently. At that instant Feßmann felt a hard blow against the right side of his chest. He collapsed. His batman immediately took care of him. Luckily the shrapnel wound was a minor one. Nevertheless Feßmann was asked to go to hospital. However, as soon as his wound had been treated he returned to his battalion.

The Soviet offensive continued. The 1st Baltic Front and the 3rd White Russian Front attacked the southern wing of Army Group North and by 21 July their spearheads had reached Ponevich, approximately 150 kilometers west of Dvinsk. When the first Soviet troops reached the Bay of Riga near Tuckum on 29 July Army Group Courland was cut off. The Soviets committed strong forces in an attempt to reach Tilsit. Kovno was lost on 31 July. The German 3rd Panzer Army, of which the 5th Panzer Division was a part, was forced back behind the Dubyssa after several days of heavy fighting. Its northern flank was constantly threatened. Not until 10 August did the Soviets abandon their efforts to take Tilsit. The front came to a standstill south of Raseinen.

On 16 August Hauptmann Feßmann was wounded again, a fragment wound in the right side of the jaw, while in this area. Once again he remained with his unit. On 1 October 1944 Generalleutnant Decker summoned the brave officer. The two officers saluted. Then the general placed his hand on the younger man's shoulder.

"Feßmann, I have followed your actions of the past weeks. More than once you have saved elements of the division from total destruction

One of the final portraits of Fritz Feßmann.

through your personal actions and initiative. I have had a detailed report written up and I have recommended you to the army for the Swords."

"Sir, I don't know how to . . ."

"Not a word against it, Feßmann, the matter is clear. You will become the first officer of the 5th Panzer Division to receive this high decoration because you have earned it."

"My battalion has earned it, sir!"

"The battalion is as good as its commander, Feßmann. I know the battalion, and it was never better than now in our darkest hour. Yes, if you want to then wear the decoration for your battalion."

A few days after this conversation Hauptmann Feßmann located a strong assembly of Russian armor opposite the division's front. On the evening of that 10 October it became a certainty that the Soviets would attack in the morning—their preferred time for an attack. General Decker organized all his defense forces. It was vital that this enemy armored drive north of Tilsit be stopped.

Early the next morning the 5th Armored Reconnaissance Battalion prepared itself to meet the enemy attack behind a small wood at the crossroads north of the Pakamonen Estate. The commander's vehicle sat at the northwestern border of the wood. From there Feßmann was able to see the first enemy tank advance out of the forest from the northeast, from the direction of Kaszemeken. The division's Panthers were positioned by the road south of the wood. The battalion commander had several Panthers under his command at the northwestern end of the wood. As soon as the enemy tanks were in range Feßmann's Panthers opened fire. The tank battle near Pakamonen had begun.

Russian high-explosive shells exploded in the woods around the command vehicle. Fragments whizzed through the air. The first enemy tanks lay burning in the open fields. But German tanks had been hit too. Then, suddenly, a high-explosive shell exploded beside the commander's vehicle.

Fritz Feßmann fell backwards as if struck by lightning. The radio operator turned to him and saw the fragment wound in his head. He realized that the commander was already dead. The tank assault that Fritz Feßmann was supposed to lead now took place without him. Once again the enemy was driven back, however not even the division commander could be happy about the outcome of this day.

Two days later Generalleutnant Decker issued an order of the day in which he said:

> On 11 October 1944, wearer of the Oak Leaves Hauptmann of the Reserve Fritz Feßmann, commander of the 5th Armored Reconnaissance Battalion, died a hero's death while leading a counterattack by his battalion.
>
> With the division as commander of the armored reconnaissance battalion since July 1944, through his outstanding personal bravery and his exemplary concern for his men Hauptmann Feßmann won the hearts of his soldiers and instilled in them the highest fighting spirit. Thanks to the great skill of its commander, during the brief period under his command the battalion rushed from success to success. His tireless readiness for action spurred his men to the highest military achievements. In Hauptmann Feßmann the division has lost one of its most proven and capable commanders. In mourning we stand beside the bier of this highly deserving officer and fighter . . .

A short time later his battalion requested permission to be designated a tradition unit under the name "Armored Reconnaissance Battalion

Major Feßmann." Before the response to this request arrived, the battalion was completely wiped out in the fighting in East Prussia.

Fritz Feßmann was promoted to Major of the Reserve with an effective date of 1 October 1944. On 23 October news reached the battalion that its fallen commander had been awarded the Swords, making him the 103rd member of the armed forces and the first of the 5th Panzer Division to receive this high award.

Feßmann's remains were cremated in Tilsit. The urn containing his ashes was sent to Germany. It arrived in Bamberg on 17 October and was placed on display in the city's large auditorium. Soldiers of the panzer regiment stationed in Bamberg provided the honor guard. The population of Bamberg lined the streets as a final honor to the fallen hero.

On 17 November 1944 the commander of Military District XIII, General der Infanterie Weisenberger, presented the Oak Leaves and Swords to Mrs. Feßmann.

Kurt Knispel: The knight without the Knight's Cross.

Kurt Knispel

THE MOST SUCCESSFUL TANK DESTROYER OF THE GERMAN ARMY

Kurt Knispel was an exception in the German armored forces. He fought in virtually every type of tank as loader, gunner, and commander. He was awarded the Iron Cross, First Class after destroying his fiftieth enemy tank and the Tank Assault Badge in Gold after far more than 100 tank battles. When Knispel had destroyed 126 enemy tanks (with another 20 unconfirmed kills) he was awarded the German Cross in Gold. He became the only non-commissioned officer of the German tank arm to be named in the Wehrmacht communique. As commander of a Tiger and then a King Tiger Knispel destroyed another 42 enemy tanks. This raised his total to 168 enemy tanks destroyed, making him by far the world's top "tank killer." Knispel fought on the eastern and western fronts and continued to serve until his death on 29 April 1945. Although it was richly deserved, he was never awarded the Knight's Cross although he was reccommended four times.

KURT KNISPEL—TANK KILLER

With 168 acknowledged kills, Kurt Knispel was by far the most successful tank soldier of the Second World War. The actual number of enemy tanks destroyed by him may be nearer to 195. Beyond that he took part in a hundred minor advances and relief attacks, supporting the infantry by taking out enemy bunkers and artillery positions and helping repel infantry assaults. When he was decorated with the Iron Cross, First Class, Knispel had fifty enemy tanks to his credit, a number which won other gunners the Knight's Cross.

Knispel was a fighting man who always remained in the background. Unlike many of his contemporaries he was not consumed by the pursuit of decorations and did not suffer from a "sore throat," German Army slang for those who lusted after the Knight's Cross. Whenever there were conflicting claims for an enemy tank destroyed, Knispel always stepped back. He was always willing to credit success to someone else, when, as commander of a Tiger, he capped an unprecedented run of success.

One of his first commanders, later Oberst in the West German Bundeswehr, Alfred Rubbel, said of this absolutely unique personality:

> As a person Kurt Knispel was willing to help and unobtrusive. He shared his food and drink with his comrades and—if necessary—his last shirt. He was sincere and cheerful and all of us who knew him had the feeling that, whether on the offensive or the defensive, if Knispel was at the front to our right or left or in front of or behind us, we were safe. He never abandoned anyone no matter what the situation.
>
> He demonstated this in countless scenes and dramatic, often life threatening missions.
>
> In our three tank companies of the 503rd Heavy Panzer Battalion there were several outstanding personalities who were particularly successful against enemy tanks.
>
> One was our Oberfeldwebel Heinrich Rondorf. Another was Feldwebel Heinz Gärtner, who had a tremendous number of kills. As well there was the commanding officer, Hauptmann Clemens Graf Kageneck, who received the Knight's Cross.
>
> Knispel surpassed them all, not only in the battalion, but in the entire tank arm! In the entire German Army—to say nothing of the Allies'—there was no other tank crewman who achieved this number of kills while sitting behind the gun of his tank. All of the kills cited were confirmed. Knispel was simply unsurpassed in his success.
>
> Knispel was the gunner who did his job best. True when he finally became a tank commander—we had all been waiting a long time for this, because he was fully qualified for the job—he became somewhat more cautious. Now he had to bear responsibility for his entire crew and he took it seriously. But we all immediately recognized after his first actions as a tank commander that he was also on top of things in this position and knew what to do and did it, even acting contrary to express orders. This did not always make him the commanding officer's best friend and may also have had a negative impact on his receipt of decorations.

In his new role of tank commander Kurt Knispel confirmed all the predictions made by his objective superiors and comrades. He was an exemplary commander and often engaged superior enemy forces alone in order to give the German infantry a chance to stand fast or withdraw in good order.

Kurt Knispel was proud after he received the German Cross in Gold. To win it required six major actions, each of which would warrant the Iron Cross, First Class. To all those who knew him it was clear that he had earned the decoration many times over. For some time Knispel remained anonymous, but that changed after Snamenka, where he became an Unteroffizier and attracted attention through his outstanding feats.

Where did this soldier come from? What made him capable of such incredible performances?

THE ROAD TO THE GUNNER'S SEAT IN A PANZER

Kurt Knispel was born in 1922 in the former Sudetenland. He had a carefree childhood and grew up to be a broad-shouldered lad of medium height, whose dark hair was always a little too long, something he would be chided for later in life. After completing his apprenticeship in an automobile factory, in 1940 Knispel applied to join the armored forces. Predestined by build and training, he was accepted immediately.

For his basic training Knispel went to the Panzer Replacement Training Battalion at Sagan in Lower Silesia. There, like all other budding soldiers, he first had to learn to march and salute, then progressed to basic weapons training. This included learning to handle the Kar 98k rifle and P 08 pistol, how to throw hand grenades and how to operated the MG 34 machine-gun. Later followed training on the Panzer I, II and IV.

Commanding the 4th Company, of which Knispel was a member, was Oblt. Eckert. Platoon commanders were Leutnants Proll, Gasparin and Pardecke. Knispel's basic training lasted from 15 May until 30 September 1940, and on 1 October he was transferred to the 3rd Company of the 29th Panzer Regiment, a unit of the 12th Panzer Division based at Sagan. From this training company was created on 1 October the "field unit" of 3rd Company, 29th Panzer Regiment led by Oblt. Eckert. Finally on 15 October 1940 the 29th Panzer Regiment was complete; the following is a list of its component units and their bases:

I Battalion at Sagan
II Battalion at Lübben/Niederlausitz
III Battalion at Sprottau in Silesia.

The regiment belonged to the 12th Panzer Division, which had been formed under the command of Generalmajor Josef Harpe as part of the doubling of the panzer arm. As an Oberst Harpe had led the 1st Panzer Brigade in the campaign in France, where he won the bars to the Iron Cross, First Class and Second Class.

While serving in 3rd Company Kurt Knispel completed his training as a loader and gunner in a Panzer IV armed with the short 75-mm gun. This training lasted from 1 October 1940 until 11 June 1941 and consisted of course in Sagan and Putlos. On 2 December at Sagan there was an inspection by the division commander. The general was visibly impressed by the ability and knowledge of his tank soldiers and Knispel observed to his commander, Unteroffizier Fendesack:

"That is a real slave-driver. Want to bet that he'll soon be up for the Knight's Cross that we will earn for him?"

"Could be," replied Fendesack.

Knispel went on Christmas leave a freshly-promoted Feldwebel and spent it with his parents on their farm. He saw the 1,490-meter Altvater, the mountain covered in a thick blanket of snow, and he undertook several ski trips with a friend who was also on leave. He went to dances in several nearby towns and visited former school chums. It was his last carefree time.

After returning to his unit, in January 1941 Knispel began gunnery training at Putlos. The men lived in barracks camps, not exactly comfortable, but no one complained. It was there that Knispel first demonstrated his special abilities as a gunner. He had the gift of total three-dimensional vision and his extraordinarily quick reflexes amazed everyone. Nevertheless, to his dismay he remained a loader at first. General service duty followed until 11 March, and then on the following day the unit departed for Camp Warthe near Posen, where activities alternated between practise drives in company and larger formations and gunnery practise. On 26 March 1941 the entire battalion moved from there to "camp earthworm" near Meseritz in Grenzmark.

Meanwhile the expansion of the panzer arm from ten to twenty divisions, begun after the French campaign, had been completed. One of the new divisions was the 12th Panzer Division under Generalmajor Harpe. As of January 1941 the 29th Panzer Regiment was ready for employment in the field. The regimental commander, Dipl.Ing. Oberst Hans Stenglein, who had led 1st Battalion, 35th Panzer Regiment, before the war, worked on his regiment tirelessly, for he too was of the opinion that "sweat spares blood." The 3rd Company, to which Knispel had been assigned, was the regiment's heavy company. The short-barreled 75-mm guns which equipped the company's vehicles was already outmoded for tank-versus-tank combat.

Combat training began in spring 1941 at the Putlos training grounds in Schleswig-Holstein. This was followed by division-level training at Neuhammer in Silesia. At Easter came the sudden move into the eastern border zone. Knispel" expectations of seeing action in the Balkans went unfulfilled. "Apart from packing and unpacking nothing happened."

Transported into the Warthe District, in May 1941, the 12th Panzer Division was transferred from there, first to Arys, then to Rastenburg and Angerburg. On 12 June the division moved into its assembly areas near Rastenburg. The secret issuing of orders on 19 June showed to Knispel and his comrades that the campaign against Russia was a decided matter. Morale was high. The Wehrmacht had overrun Poland, France, Yugoslavia and Greece in lightning campaigns and it was the unanimous opinion of the personnel of the 29th Panzer Regiment that it would make short work of "Ivan" too. The lectures to the regiment concentrated on recognition of Soviet aircraft and especially tanks.

On the evening of 20 June 1941 loader Kurt Knispel sat in his tank as it rolled toward the border. The movment of the panzers turned into a "flower march through East Prussia." On the evening of 21 June everyone knew that the assault on Russia was going to begin the next morning. Kurt Knispel made his final preparations and wrote a precautionary "last letter" home without mentioning the coming action. The next day was to see the start of an operation which everyone was confident would be over by Christmas. No one could imagine that it would last almost four years.

THE WAR IN THE EAST: FROM YARZEVO TO THE GATES OF STALINGRAD

Kurt Knispel's First Action

Like the other tank soldiers of the 29th Panzer Regiment, the crew of the Hellmann tank, in which Kurt Knispel was gunner, were wakened early on 22 June, at 2:15 A.M. The tanks were fully armed and fueled and ready to go. At 4 A.M. the commanding officer read out an order of the day; by this time the Luftwaffe was already in the air and the infantry had launched their assault on the first enemy positions. The tanks did not move off until 8 A.M. Then they rolled forward through the dense mass of an army on the move, slipping between trucks and passing horse-drawn guns and infantry columns.

"How does it look, Hellmann?" Knispel asked his commander, who from his position in the open turret hatch had a clear view of what was happening.

"Nothing happening! No artillery, only a few rifle shots," he replied.

On the afternoon of 22 June the advance suddenly halted. I Battalion was alerted by radio and summoned to the front. Enemy troops in a village were holding up the advance and would have to be dislodged. When the tank was in range Knispel rammed the first shell into the breach. The gunner called to the commander: "Weapon loaded and locked."

With one company in the point position and the other two staggered to the left and right, the tanks charged toward the village. While 1st Company fired high-explosive shells at the source of the return fire while on the move, the other two engaged enemy machine-gun nests. The Hellmann crew fired a total of nine high-explosive shells and gunner Knispel was annoyed that they hadn't been allowed to fire more often.

By evening the Soviet border positions had been breached in Army Group Center's entire sector. The next day saw the beginning of the Battle of Bialystok. Commanded by Generalfeldmarschall Fedor von Bock, Army Group Center was organized as follows:

Army Group Headquarters:	Generalfeldmarschall von Bock
Chief of Staff:	Generalmajor von Greifenberg
Panzer Group 2:	Generaloberst Guderian
Chief of Staff:	General Staff Oberstleutnant Freiherr Von Liebenstein
XXIV Mot. Army Corps:	General der Panzertruppe Freiherr Geyr von Schweppenburg
1st Cavalry Division:	Generalmajor Feldt
4th Panzer Division:	Generalmajor Freiherr Von Langermann und Erlenkamp
3rd Panzer Division:	Generalleutnant Model
10th Mot. Inf. Div.:	Generalleutnant Schaal
XXXXVII Mot. Army Corps:	General der Panzertruppe Lemelsen
18th Panzer Division:	Generalmajor Nehring
17th Panzer Division:	Generalmajor von Arnim
XXXXVI Mot. Army Corps:	General der Panzertruppe von Vietinghoff
SS Pz. Div. *Das Reich*:	SS-Gruppenführer Hausser
10th Panzer Division:	Generalleutnant Schaal
Mot. Inf. Reg. *"GD"*:	Oberst Hoernlein
4th Army:	Generalfeldmarschall von Kluge
Chief of Staff:	General Staff Oberst Blumentritt
XII Army Corps:	General der Infanterie Schroth
29th Mot. Infantry Div.	
31st Infantry Division	
34th Infantry Division	

February 1942: Knispel scored his first "kill" as a gunner in this tank.

XXXXIII Army Corps:	General der Infanterie Heinrici
131st Infantry Division	
134th Infantry Division	
152nd Infantry Division	
IX Army Corps:	General der Infanterie Geyer
17th Infantry Division	
137th Infantry Division	
263rd Infantry Division	
292nd Infantry Division	
VII Army Corps:	General der Artillerie Fahrmbacher
7th Infantry Division	
23rd Infantry Division	
268th Infantry Division	
221st Security Division	
XIII Army Corps:	General der Infanterie Felber
78th Infantry Division	
LIII Army Corps:	General der Infanterie Weisenberger
45th Infantry Division	
52nd Infantry Division	
167th Infantry Division	

9th Army:	Generaloberst Strauß
Chief of Staff:	General Staff Oberst Weckmann
XXXXII Army Corps:	General der Pioniere Kuntze
XX Army Corps:	General der Infanterie Materna
VII Army Corps:	General der Artillerie Heit
V Army Corps:	General der Infanterie Ruoff
VI Army Corps:	General der Pioniere Förster
Panzer Group 3:	Generaloberst Hoth
Chief of Staff:	Gen. Staff Oberstleutnant von Hünersdorff
LVII Motorized Army Corps:	General der Panzertruppe Kuntzen
12th Panzer Division:	Generalmajor Harpe
19th Panzer Division:	Generalleutnant Otto von Knobelsdorf
18th Motorized Infantry Div.	
XXXIX Motorized Army Corps:	General der Panzertruppe Schmidt
7th Panzer Division:	Generalmajor Freiherr von Funck
14th Panzer Division:	Generalmajor Friedrich Kühn
20th Panzer Division	

Army Group Center had in reserve: the 102nd, 255th, 267th and 293rd Divisions, the 286th and 403rd Security Divisions and the 900th Instruction Brigade (mot).

Operations by the 12th Panzer Division

Under the command of Generalmajor Harpe, the 12th Panzer Division saw action within Panzer Group 3 as part of the LVII Army Corps (later renamed LVII Panzer Corps) commanded by General der Panzertruppe Adolf Kuntzen. When war broke out Kuntzen was in command of the 3rd Light Division, which was subsequently renamed the 3rd Panzer Division, and won the Knight's Cross for his actions in France in 1940. When the war against Russia began this former Hussar officer, now 53 years old, led LVII Panzer Corps with the same dash he had shown as a division commander. The 12th Panzer Division took part in the early breakthrough battles, demonstrated its tremendous striking power in the Battle of Bialystok, and performed exceedingly well during the pursuit to the Dvina.

The order for Army Group Center was:

Army Group Center will shatter the enemy forces in White Russia—driving strong units in front of its flanks—concentrate its mobile forces south and north of Minsk and take the Smolensk area quickly, and thus establish the conditions necessary for strong elements of its mobile forces to cooperate with Army Group North."

The four armies of Army Group Center were issued the necessary orders. Their initial objectives were:

Panzer Group 3 (Hoth): In the north. Area near and north of Vitebsk.
9th Army (Strauß): In the north. Dniepr crossings in the Polotsk area.
4th Army (von Kluge): In the center. Dniepr crossings near and around Mogilev.
Panzer Group 2 (Guderian): Area near and south of Smolensk.

Facing Army Group Center (contrary to some claims that there was no Russian buildup) were three Soviet armies between the tip of Suwalki in the north and the area around Brest Litovsk in the south which were under the command of the Western Military District. They were:

3rd Soviet Army: near Grodno
10th Soviet Army: around Bialystok
4th Soviet Army: east of Brest Litovsk

These formations had at their disposal 45 rifle and 15 motorized divisions as well as tank brigades (at this stage of the war the Soviets still did not have armored divisions). Since the Western Military District was faced with collapse in the very first phase of the battle, Marshall Semyon Timoshenko, Commissar for Defense (and as of 19 July 1941 commander in chief of the western front) also sent Headquarters, 13th Army into the area with strict orders to prevent the collapse of the western front no matter what the cost.

By now the German mobile units, including the 12th Panzer Division, had driven up to 200 deep into Soviet territory. At 2 A.M. on 25 June the leading units of Panzer Group 3, which was deployed in Army Group Center's north, reached the Minsk to Moscow highway, while at the same time Panzer Group 2 had achieved freedom of movement on the Brest Litovsk to Smolensk highway, which from that point on was known simply as the "rollbahn." However, on 25 June both armore dgroups had to be halted temporarily to wait for the infantry divisions, which were lagging behind, to catch up.

On 26 June the 12th Panzer Division under Generalmajor Harpe reached Minsk from the north and early the next morning it raised the war flag of the Reich over the capital of White Russia. On 28 June German forces closed the pocket around Bialystok, marking the completion of the first major encirclement of the campaign. The German offensive continued to proceed according to plan, and on 8 July Generalfeldmarschall von Bock was able to announce:

> The double battle of Bialystok and Vyazma is over. The army group engaged three Soviet armies. From these were destroyed: 22 rifle divisions, 7 tank and 6 mechanized brigades and 3 cavalry divisions.
>
> The enemy's losses in blood were heavy. He lost: 287,704 prisoners, 2,585 tanks, 1,449 guns, 245 captured aircraft.

Panzer Group 3 immediately received the following order: "Advance from Minsk to the northeast. Establish contact with the right wing of Army Group North at the Dvina."

Smashing a wide breach in the Russian front, Panzer Group 3 drove toward the Dvina. It passed through the lake narrows near Sebesh and on 8 July reached the Dvina. The city of Vitebsk was taken by the 7th Panzer Division.

With the arrival of Panzer Groups 2 and 3 at the Dvina and the Dniepr the Red Army was now fighting for its very existence. This was the decisive phase of the first year's campaign in Russia. It was here that the soldiers of the Red Army gained the time that ultimately saved Moscow. It was Marshall Timoshenko, now commander in chief of army group "Western Front," who saw the danger in time and together with his political commissar of the central committee of the Communist Party, Bulganin, took steps to bolster the new defensive front and bar the way to the "fascists" through Smolensk to the east. Army group "Central Front" under General Kuznetsov, with the 13th and 21st Armies, was also inserted into the western front. The 16th Army under Lieutenant-General Lukin defended the Smolensk land bridge. Thus the forces defending the western front had been increased to six armies with additional forces in reserve.

On 13 July the Red Army launched a counter-offensive against the two German panzer groups. The "Battle of Smolensk" developed between Vitebsk in the north and Gomel in the south. In this battle, which at first affected the German 4th Army and Panzer Group 2, Panzer Group 3 (in the north of the front) attacked Nevel with the LVIII Motorized Army Corps, while the XXXXVII Motorized Army Corps with the 29th Motorized Infantry Division under Generalleutnant von Boltenstern drove straight toward Smolensk. By the evening of 15 July the division had reached the southwestern suburbs of the city.

German froces took possession of the city the next day. The Red Army troops had withdrawn across the Dniepr (which divided the city in half) and blew the bridges behind them.

When the commanders of Panzer Groups 2 and 3, Generaloberst Guderian and Generaloberst Hoth, arrived near Smolensk on 16 July to coordinate a further advance by their tanks, they decided to drive on directly towards Moscow without waiting for the arrival of the infantry units, which were still as much as 150 kilometers behind. This was promising, because there were no more significant enemy troops in front of them that might have been able to stop these mobile forces.

It was at this very moment that the German campaign against Russia was decided. Reports by the Soviet command later showed that Moscow could not have held out and there were only weak forces facing the German panzer divisions, while the Siberian and other Far-Eastern reserves were still too far away to halt this armored drive on Moscow.

At this decisive moment the High Command of the Army inteferred in the running of the war. It ordered categorically that Panzer Group was to turn north again to support Army Group North.

The objective which the OKH had initially given Army Group Center (the land bridge near Smolensk) had been reached. Now the opportunity was there to strike the decisive blow against Moscow and achieve final victory. But this objective was abandoned and the enemy was given a chance to regroup his forces and throw his reserves into the front.

As a result of the departure of Panzer Group 3 the pocket at Smolensk was not closed. The Russian counterattack to relieve this important city, which employed all available motorized forces, was a success. Smolensk was relieved by the Red Army. The German V Army Corps under Generalmajor Allmendinger and the 36th Infantry Division led by Generalleutnant Fischer suffered heavy casualties in the onslaught by six Soviet rifle divisions.

Panzer Group 3, which was on the defensive north of Smolensk, had to advance to the Vop and there establish an eastward-facing defensive front against the Soviets. Holding the front from Lomonosowo in the north to the mouth of the Vop into the Dniepr in the south were the following german units: the 18th (Mot.) Infantry Division the 20th Panzer Division, the 900th Panzer Instruction Brigade and the 7th and 20th

Knispel's tank has reached the front at Tossno. At the time, he was assigned to the 29th Panzer Regiment's 3rd Company.

Panzer Divisions. In the last week of July seven Soviet rifle divisions and a tank brigade stormed this front, just fifty kilometers long.

The Soviets also attacked vehemently in front of Panzer Group 2. No one on the German side any longer expected to meet such resistance and counterattacks. Determined to end the confusion in the German command, on 27 July Guderian arrived at the headquarters of Army Group Center. There he learned that Hitler and the army high command no longer considered Moscow to be a vital objective. Guderian was now to turn his panzer group and head southwest—back! The precarious German situation of the was not stabilized until the infantry units arrived at the end of July.

The STAVKA now ordered the Soviet forces holding in Smolensk to break out to the east. The Red Army launched thirteen attacks in its efforts to crack the German ring around the city. The last breakout attempt was led by the V Mechanized Corps, which was wiped out in battle with the German panzers. On 5 August Feldmarschall von Bock issued an order of the day which has become well known:

> With the destruction of the Soviet divisions cut off near Smolensk the three-week battle at the Dniepr, the Dvina and Smolensk has

> concluded in a brilliant new victory for German arms and German fulfilment of duty.
>
> Taken as booty were:
>
> 309,110 prisoners.
>
> 3,205 tanks destroyed or captured.
>
> 3,200 guns and 341 aircraft.
>
> This act of yours is now part of history. I look with gratitude and pride on troops capable of such a feat.

However, according to a report by the command of Army Group Center, this success had been achieved at a cost of 74,500 officers, NCOs and enlisted men killed or wounded. After this success the army group was reorganized in preparation for a new phase of operations in the east. The two new focal points would be Leningrad and the Ukraine. Because of the heavy losses in tanks suffered by the two panzer groups, the main weight of these subsequent operations was transferred onto the infantry.

THE 29TH PANZER REGIMENT IN THE EASTERN CAMPAIGN

Kurt Knispel and his Comrades in Action

When morning dawned on 23 June the I Battalion of the 29th Panzer Regiment resumed its advance toward Minsk. As the tanks rolled forward there were repeated skirmishes with the retreating enemy. The panzers came to a swampy area which had to be crossed single file and came under fire from several dry islands in the marshes. They returned fire, eliminating the enemy resistance, and opened the way forward for the 5th and 26th Rifle Regiments as well as their division's 26th Motorcycle Battalion. After five torturous days Minsk was reached. Kurt Knispel's tank was rolling down a tree-lined boulevard when it came under fire from a fruit orchard.

Uffz. Gärtner gave the order to fire: "High-explosive shells into the garden!" The first shells smashed into the Russian machine-gun positions. When the shell casing was ejected, Knispel rammed in another and reported clear to fire. The gunner adjusted his aim slightly and fired. Less than half a second later the shell struck home and the machine-gun firing from the window of a house fell silent.

The tanks pressed ahead, providing mutual support as they drove through the city. Finally it was in their hands. Kurt Knispel and several men carried out a scouting mission from the hedgehog at the outskirts of the city. They found a brewery, which was "conquered" by them. It turned out to be a wet and happy night with plenty of beer, and the guard in front of the Minsk theater probably wouldn't have noticed if the Red Army had launched an attack to regain the city.

The next morning the men climbed into their steel boxes with "heavy heads," groaning in the heat. The tanks had been rearmed and refueled during the night. The attack on this day was aimed toward the southwest. The next day saw the long-awaited link-up with Panzer Group 2, however they advanced no further. Instead the unit was moved into a wooded area north of Minsk for several days to rest and repair its damaged tanks. The battalion sent out requisitioning detachments. Kurt Knispel, who knew a little Russian and also spoke Czech, took part and helped ensure that the foraging teams achieved good success, returning with wine, vodka, and hens.

The rest period ended on the evening of 6 July. The battalion's fighting strength had been restored enough to allow it to take part in the effort to reduce the Minsk pocket. On 7 July Kurt Knispel went to action again, "blind" in his position as loader. The tank was hit twice, once by a shell from a Russian 76.2-mm antitank gun, however no serious damage was done. That evening Hans Urban, a crewman in the tank of Knispel's friend Heinrichs, was shot from behind by a Russian commissar. He was the first fatal casualty suffered by the company. Luckily no one yet knew how many were to follow. Hans Urban had been killed while outside his tank on a patrol operation. Karl Hoffmann, Hans Kukla's driver, who also took part in the patrol, likewise died in the hail of Russian fire. They were buried near Minsk the next morning.

"They were the first, Kurt," Thaysen observed to his friend, who was standing beside him. "Hopefully the whole thing will soon be over."

"I don't believe that we'll be home again as victors by Christmas," replied Knispel skeptically. "But we'll give it a try anyway."

The tanks saw a great deal of action in the battles in the Smolensk and Vitebsk areas, mainly duels against enemy artillery. At this time and place Russian tanks were rarely met, but when they did put in an appearance dealing with them was difficult. The short 75-mm with which the panzers were armed was not an ideal weapon for tank-versus-tank combat. It was possible to follow the flight paths of the low-velocity projectiles, whose effective range against enemy tanks was limited to about 800 meters.

On one occasion the panzers were ambushed by two Soviet antitank guns concealed in their rear. Uffz. Burmeister's tank was knocked out; Burmeister and one member of his crew suffered minor injuries.

In the following days the tanks attacked and took out Russian earth bunkers which were holding up the infantry's advance. Then Knispel's tank took a serious hit. A second damaged the transmission and the tank had to go to the workshops in Borisov. Because of heavy losses in tanks and personnel the 29th Panzer Regiment's 3rd Company had to be disbanded. What was left, including Knispel's tank, was incorporated into 9th Company, helping bring that unit up to strength. The battalion remained in rest positions until 20 August.

Into the Northern Sector

The transfer of the 12th Panzer Division into the northern sector of the Eastern Front began on 20 August 1941. One week earlier, on 13 August, Generalmajor Harpe had received the Knight's Cross for his and his division's success.

When the news was released to the battalion, Kurt Knispel observed rogueishly: "Well, what did I tell you? I would like to bet that the old man ends up with even more tinsel and medals."

"But he is an old grandpa who fought in the First World War," said the tank's gunner.

"That makes no difference where this daredevil is concerned. He comes from the old cavalry and led the 12th Cavalry Regiment in the Reichswehr. They're the old soldiers who are leading the tank arm."

"Makes sense to me. Anyway he's a damned good division commander."

The 800 kilometer overland march to Leningrad began. The supreme command had thrown General der Infanterie Erich von Manstein's LVI Panzer Corps into the northern sector in order to take the top objective of Leningrad.

The 12th Panzer Division's first battle in the new sector began on 25 August. The 3rd Company had been restored and was back with I Battalion of the 29th Panzer Regiment. After his gunner was put out of action, Kurt Knispel stepped into his place and soon demonstrated his skill in that position.

Knispel was assigned to the crew of Feldwebel Hans Fendesack and on the highway south of Leningrad he destroyed his first enemy tank as a gunner. It was there that the crews encountered the T-34 for the first time. In 1941 the T-34 was superior to every German tank in terms of armor and firepower. For a Panzer IV to knock out one of these tanks it first had to approach to within 800 meters and aim at one of its vulnerable spots.

Fendesack's vehicle was hit, causing it to shed a track, and everyone except the gunner and driver got out. During the repair a T-34 was sighted emerging slowly from some bushes. Knispel reacted immediately and put the Soviet tank out of action with a well-aimed snap shot. At first it was called a "lucky shot" for no one could shoot so quickly and accurately. This would prove to be an error.

The panzers fought their way to the outskirts of Leningrad, but there they were ordered to halt. This was followed by a withdrawal of twelve to fifteen kilometers from the city. From there the men of the 12th Panzer

Division attacked toward the east. They proceeded through narrow forest lanes, fighting off surprise enemy ambushes as they went. The attack on Schlisselburg became a bloody affair. A group of German forces, including the 12th Panzer Division, was encircled near Mga. The chroniclist of the 3rd Company, 29th Panzer Regiment, the later Hauptmann Thaysen, noted: "Other units fought their way through and got us out of there."

The advance toward Schlisselburg continued along a narrow-track railway line from the northeast. West of the city the tanks came upon Russian earth bunkers and positions. Kurt Knispel shot up three or four in the first rush. After the tanks had cleared the way the infantry advanced on the city. Early the next morning Major Heinz Hogrebe and his men of 5th Company, 422nd Infantry Regiment (of the 426th Infantry Division) entered Mga and took possession of the city.

The next day Kurt Knispel and the entire company entered the city, which was running as if in peacetime. The inhabitants had been assured that the Germans would never enter the city. All the stores were open and the chocolate factory was working at full capacity. The German soldiers were all able to supply themselves with sweets.

When, following the disbandment of III Battalion, the 29th Panzer Regiment's 9th Company was incorporated into 3rd Company, Kurt Knispel came into contact with a soldier who would do more to make him into a first-class soldier than anyone else.

Unteroffizier Rubbel became the commander of the company's second tank, while Feldwebel Fendesack and gunner Knispel crewed the third. Lt. Thiele, who has platoon commander commanded the first tank, was fortunate to have such men under his command. The company subsequently took part in the big attack across the Volkhov in the direction of Tichvin.

The German command had abandoned the direct assault on Leningrad; however, a major operation by the 16th Army was to drive further east across the Volkhov, sever Leningrad's supply lines and in this way bring about the fall of the city sooner or later. The river was supposed to be crossed on a broad front. The focal point lay with XXXXIX Panzer Corps, which was to take possession of Tikhvin before driving north and finally linking up with Finnish troops, who at that time were at the Swir, between Lakes Onega and Ladoga.

In the same breath the I Army Corps was to drive down the Volkhov through Volkhovstroy and reach the south shore of Lake Ladoga, while the XXXVIII Army Corps had orders to cover the operation's southern flank by attacks east across the Volkhov.

If the operation succeeded, Leningrad would be largely cut off from its sources of supply and once its supplies of food and ammunition were

April 1942: The area around Duwobik. Knispel removes the muzzle cover from the main gun. Rubbel can be seen in the commander's hatch.

exhausted would be forced to surrender. However two factors prevented this from being realized. First Hitler overestimated the strength of the army in the east. He knew how many divisions were there, but he was not told that these divisions had lost one- to two-thirds of their fighting strength in the battles that lay behind them.

Second the unusually early and unbelievably harsh winter of 1941–42 turned out to be an insurmountable obstacle. The onset of severe cold brought the entire eastern army to the brink of a catastrophe which could only be mastered by Hitler's ruthless stand fast order and a supreme effort on the part of the German command and its soldiers.

The assault on Leningrad was led by General der Panzertruppe Georg-Hans Reinhardt and his XXXXI Panzer Corps. The attack began with the XXXIX Panzer Corps under General der Panzertruppe Hans-Jürgen von Arnim.

The 12th Panzer Division fought shoulder to shoulder with the 8th Panzer Division, the 61st Infantry Division and the 20th Motorized Infantry Division. The troops suffered badly in the minus fifty degree temperatures. Tank engines refused to start and automatic weapons froze up. Together with the 18th Motorized Infantry Division, the tanks and panzer-grenadiers of the 12th Panzer Division stormed into Tikhvin. At the end of November the 61st Infantry Division was moved to Tikhvin, partly by air, in order to release the 12th Panzer Division for mobile warfare. This move was greeted with enthusiasm, especially by the 29th Panzer Regiment.

At the beginning of December six enemy divisions attacked near Tikhvin. The city was virtually surrounded and other enemy units attacked the flanks of the corridor to Tikhvin in an effort to sever it. Finally, on 9 December, Tikhvin had to be abandoned. The objective of linking up with the Finns at the Swir had not been achieved. In a difficult and costly fighting withdrawal the XXXIX Panzer Corps made its way back to the Volkhov, often in danger of being encircled and destroyed. It was largely due to the efforts of the 12th Panzer Division that this did not happen.

Kurt Knispel Scores His Next Victories

"Supposedly only labor battalions have been reported," observed Rubbel to his comrades of 3rd Company, who were standing in a semicircle. Uffz. Rubbel had just come back from the battalion command post and was telling his friends what he had learned.

"Bless those who believe that," declared Knispel casually, "but we will see."

What they saw in the days that followed were the Russian earthworks and behind them, and amid them, tanks, tanks and more tanks. Sometimes there was freezing rain and sometimes it snowed so heavily that the commanders and drivers could scarcely see more than a meter. All throughout October the few muddy lanes they called roads were lost in mud. The tanks got through, but the wheeled elements with the supplies got stuck.

Every day they encountered enemy tanks and antitank guns, both well camouflaged. Lt. Arno Thiele and his 4th Company were always there. He destroyed a number of tanks in this area and on 29 November 1941 he became the first member of the division to win the German Cross in Gold.

The position where the 29th Panzer Regiment stood, the so-called "tube" which ran between a road and the Leningrad to Tikhvin rail line, was constantly threatened by the Soviets after the cold had made the entire marshy area passable to vehicles. Rubbel had been wounded at the end of October and had to enter hospital. Kurt Knispel, however, emerged from every combat situation unscathed.

A new attack was ordered for the beginning of November and once again 3rd Company was fully involved. 3rd Company's point tank was commanded by Lt. Meier. When the point group, which also included Fendesack's panzer, suddenly came under fire, the lead vehicle, which had just crossed a bridge, was knocked out. Four quick shots fired by a T-34 concealed in a wooded area stopped the German tank. The attack was halted and was not resumed until the assault on Tikhvin on 8 November.

This time the attack was preceded by a 20-minute barrage from 24 batteries, including the 2nd Panzer Artillery Regiment of the 12th Panzer Division. The hail of shells fell on an area 400-meters wide on either side of the road, striking the fiercely-defended wooded area. When the attack began, a Soviet 172-mm battery suddenly opened fire on the advancing grenadiers.

Fendesack alerted his company commander, who ordered his tanks to attack the enemy battery. Fendesack's driver applied throttle. The rattle of tracks mingled with the crash of exploding shells. The first enemy position was sighted and within seconds Knispel had selected his target. Several high-explosive shells struck the position and caused the Russians to flee. Then he spotted the first of four enemy guns, which were in staggered positions.

It took only seconds for him to aim and fire. Then the tank roared on and together with another of the company's vehicles approached to within 30 meters of the enemy position and destroyed the battery and overran the Russians crouching in their trenches.

"Continue to advance! Into the village!" ordered the battalion commander.

The tanks rumbled forward. They had gone about 300 meters when Knispel spotted a well-camouflaged antitank gun to the right. His first shot destroyed the weapon before it could fire a shot. With unerring accuracy Knispel destroyed a second antitank gun and then knocked out a T-34 with a single armor-piercing round.

They crossed two streams; the still-intact bridges bore the weight of the panzers. By evening they were within about 70 kilometers of Tikhvin. During the night they reached a large village. When noise was heard the tanks halted. Kurt Knispel, who spoke some Russian, went on a scouting foray with another man. They entered the village andfound that it was still occupied by the enemy. The Russians were all drunk. As Knispel was able to deduce from their conversations, they were celebrating "Red Army Day." Howling Russians staggered through the streets.

When he returned Knispel reported that part of the town was free of Ivans. They moved in as quietly as possible and prepared to assault the east end of the town. One hour later the tanks of the Third rolled around the town on the two roads they had scouted. A green flare was fired, the signal for the two tanks in the west end of the village to open fire. Several minutes later the Russian troops in the town attempted to flee east and ran straight into the fire of Knispel's and Lt. Thiele's tanks.

Trucks and limbered guns were destroyed one after another. A fuel truck went up in an ball of flames. Then, suddenly, all was quiet. The enemy surrendered. Prisoners and wounded were left in the town.

The tanks refueled and rearmed in the middle of the night. One small battle group, consisting of the remaining heavy vehicles (75-mm) of the 3rd Company, four Skoda tanks (37-mm), two antitank guns and an 88-mm flak, accompanied by four mounted infantry squads moved out at first light on 9 November. As it set off the battle group was joined by a squad of combat engineers. The enemy was blasted out of his bunkers with direct fire. The advance proceeded irresistably and when evening came the battle group was within 12 kilometers of Tikhvin.

For the past two hours the Germans had passed Russians tending fires by the side of the road. They had no idea that this was the first group of germans assaulting Tikhvin. But then enemy tanks appeared, followed by artillery, obviously bound for the front.

"Let them approach!" ordered the battalion commander.

From a range of 120 meters Kurt Knispel knocked out the first T-34, hitting it exactly between the turret and hull and jamming the turret. When the T-34 attempted to turn and flee it was hit in the rear and immediately began to burn. Ghostly figures left the tank and dashed for safety.

Platoon commander Lt. Lehmann assembled the tank commanders and said, "I believe we should drive through to Tikhvin before the night is over."

"If that's what you think, sir," replied Fendesack, "then we're with you."

"Very well, we'll push ahead quickly. No firing, but keep weapons loaded and locked. No stopping."

Ten minutes later the battle group drove on to Tikhvin, rolling past columns of enemy tanks, guns and infantry headed the other way toward the front. When they entered the city they found a peacetime atmosphere. There were no defensive preparations. Apparently the Russians were totally unaware of the 12th Panzer Division's armored raid. By now it was light, but that did not seem to bother the Russians. All the stores were open and Russian soldiers strolled through the streets.

As Knispel peered through his vision port the bridge over the Tikhvinka appeared before him. He called to his commander: "You know Hans, if I wasn't seeing this with my own eyes I couldn't believe it. Not a soul in sight."

"All right then, let's get across!" The tanks crossed the bridge unopposed. Not until they reached the center of the city did they meet any opposition. High-explosive shells and assault teams of infantry and engineers soon silenced the enemy troops firing from houses. The 12th Panzer Division had reached Tikhvin.

During the coming night of 10 November a Russian officer column approached Tikhvin. Apparently warned, it turned away. The tanks opened fire and knocked out several of the retiring vehicles. Statements by prisoners revealed that Marshall Kliment Voroshilov, the commander of the Leningrad front, had been among the officers.

Further battle groups from the division reached Tikhvin by the morning of 10 November. That afternoon Generalmajor Harpe ordered the attack continued to the northeast. Two more towns were taken after brief battles. The Russians attacked on 12 November but were repulsed. The next day they tried to soften up the village into which the 3rd Company had moved with artillery and mortar fire. When the Russians attacked, all four of the company's vehicles expended all their ammunition.

A short time later four T-34s were reported approaching. All the Third had left was a single 50-mm antitank gun. It was an uncomfortable situation for the now unarmed tank crews. The antitank gun took up the unequal battle and one of the T-34s was knocked out. The remaining three broke into the position and were destroyed with close-range weapons.

Kurt Knispel had armed himself with an antitank mine. "Listen, Willi, I'm going to take the one driving on the right. Keep the infantry's head down with your machine-gun."

Obergefreiter Willi Schrörs nodded. He swung his weapon around in the direction of the fourth approaching tank. Beyond it he could make out the brown-clad forms of Russian troops advancing in the cover of the tank.

The T-34 fired a shell that whizzed over their heads. In the pause that followed, Knispel dashed to his right. He took cover when a machine-gun sent a burst of fire in his direction, then crawled on to a grup of bushes. Knispel got to his feet and, dashing from cover to cover, reached a position in front of the enemy tank. When the T-34 began to move again, straight towards him, Knispel heaved the mine into its path and rolled to the side. Then he got up and dove for cover into a depression. The T-34 halted again. Its gun roared and then it moved forward and its left track drove over the mine. The mine exploded with an ear-shattering roar, blowing off not just the track, but the forward roadwheel as well. The tank turned on the spot. The Soviet infantry continued to advance and walked straight into the fire of the German machine-guns. Three or four bursts ended this threat and seconds later two more antitank mines exploded, disabling the last of the four attacking tanks. Gasping for breath, Knispel threw himself into the hole beside the machine-gunner.

Outside Kharkov in May 1942. Panzer IIIs moved with mounted infantry into an assembly area.

"My God, Kurt, that was amazing, you really took one out with your bare hands."

"Well the antitank mine had something to do with it, too," joked Knispel. Moments later he and the rest of the crews were called back to the tanks. The first deliveries of ammunition had reached the village, but the trucks could go no farther without being shot up by the enemy.

"Back to the village!" ordered Fendesack. The tanks turned and drove back into the village.

By morning the tanks had all been rearmed and refuelled. But the Russians had closed the ring around the village. The only remaining alternative was to order a breakout to the south towards Tikhvin. The breakthrough took place with breathtaking speed. Firing high-explosive shells and spraying machine-gun fire, the tanks broke through the siege ring and reached Tikhvin without loss. There they formed a hedgehog position.

For the next fifteen days the Red Army attacked the city repeatedly but without success. Once again the tanks were employed as mobile artillery, engaging charging infantry with high-explosive shells and destroying the attacking T-34s with armor-piercing rounds. After each Soviet attack was beaten off there followed an artillery bombardment. Then they attacked again.

In this situation Kurt Knispel spent endless hours in his cramped gunner's position. Through his commander's orders he heard what was going on outside; all that he could see of the outside was the tiny area visible through his vision port. Fortunately, inside the tank the cold was only felt when they were in rest positions, otherwise it was warm in the fighting compartment. On several occasions Knispel as gunner had to act more or less on instinct. Fendesack was constantly amazed at how quickly and precisely his gunner reacted to his orders. In those days and weeks Knispel was credited with four more confirmed kills.

Gunner Knispel in the Heat of Battle

It was 24 November 1941. The 3rd Company was placed on alert at three hours after midnight. A well-armed Russian assault force had seized a forward observer and a machine-gun crew. One member of the crew had escaped to tell what had happened.

"Let's go," said the company commander. "We're moving out in five minutes."

Cursing, Feldwebel Fendesack and his crew roused themselves. In the small cottage where they had taken shelter the men dressed quickly, picked up their weapons and hand grenades, and five minutes later were sitting in their tank.

"We'll drive in single file. Just before the sentry post Fendesack will veer off to the right, Brämer to the left, then after 200 meters turn back again. I will take point, followed by Scheffler. We will fire high-explosive for all we're worth in order to surprise the enemy. That will help you slip past, turn in and prevent the Russians from retreating as well as pin them down if there are in fact tanks there."

That ended the briefing. The four tanks were ready and the company commander raised his arm. The drivers engaged first gear and the tank engines roared as the vehicles moved off.

"Get ready!" Fendesack called to his crew. "Load high-explosive." Loader Dressel had already placed a round in the breech.

"Weapon loaded and locked!" reported Knispel.

The tanks rolled quickly along a side lane that led to the right wing of the sentry position. After following the lane for about 250 meters the tanks turned back onto their general course. The tanks rolled over the terrain which was dotted with saplings. The commander and Knispel peered ahead into the darkness but could see nothing. Even when the tanks drove past the forward sentry post there was no sign of the Russians who should have been there.

Kurt Knispel, whose gun was in the ten o'clock position, peered through his gunsight. Farther in the direction of the enemy front he saw a string of pearls of tracer from an automatic weapon but nothing else. But what was that? Directly ahead, not 200 meters away, a small glowing dot which looked like the lit end of a cigarette. He stared hard, trying to figure out the situation. Then the cigarette fell to the ground and Knispel thought he saw a movement. Acting purely on instinct, he released the safety, aimed a little lower and fired.

"Damn it, Kurt, what's going on?" called Fendesack, completely surprised. He immediately realized that there was no time for a report, for where Knispel had aimed there was a mighty explosion. Figures were tossed through the air, together with a machine-gun.

"Had no time, Hans," replied Knispel calmly, all the while peering through his gunsight.

Seconds later he called out: "Attention, enemy tank at eleven o'clock, range 500." The loader slid an armor-piercing shell into the breech, which snapped shut. While Fendesack was calling "Fire," Knispel was already pressing the firing button. Once again the shot was a direct hit. Knispel had become a dead shot, who called out each target to the exact meter and destroyed it with unerring accuracy. The tank made a dash forward, then turned left and cut off the fleeing Russians, who had meanwhile received reinforcements. The two flanking tanks destroyed the retreating enemy, while the company commander and the tanks following him blasted the Russians who had crawled into the trenches and dugouts.

All in all this speedily-executed counterattack had taken less than 15 minutes. And while the mopping-up operation was still in progress the Fendesack tank, which had taken up position several hundred meters forward, reported: "Enemy tanks with mounted infantry!"

The company commander issued his orders quickly: "Everyone prepare for defense! Scheffler tank move up and join Fendesack! Maintain at least 150 meters lateral spacing!"

Meanwhile Fendesack had moved into a good position in a shallow ravine. It was still pitch dark. Only the exhaust flames of the enemy tanks, which were rolling diagonally to the Fendesack tank's position, could be seen in the darkness. Behind them came Soviet infantry clad in their white camouflage outfits.

When the enemy had come within 450 meters and the second tank reported to Fendesack that it was in position, the order was given to open fire. A furious outburst of gunfire shattered the night. One of the Soviet tanks was hit and turned away, whereupon Knispel hit it in the rear. The tank burst into flames and illuminated a ghostly scene. Red Army troops dashed for cover in all directions. The German tanks opened fire with their machine-guns. All four Russian tankers threw themselves down and rolled on the ground, trying to extinguish the flames that enveloped them. Four T-34s turned and fled; all were hit but they were not stopped.

"That's the lot!" observed Fendesack after the firing had stopped. He turned to his crew. "You did well. Especially you, Kurt, you really let them have it again."

"One does what one can," said Knispel with a smile.

After reinforcements had arrived the tanks drove back to their quartering area, and when it was light two supply vehicles arrived with ammunition and fuel. The battalion had grown its fangs again. The panzers drove forward toward a frozen swamp where a Fieseler "Storch" had sighted a Russian observation post, from which the enemy artillery was receiving target information and corrections.

The surface crunched beneath the tracks of the tanks; it sagged but did not give way. Fendesack's panzer was in the point position. An antitank gun opened fire from a range of 350 meters and scored a hit. Fendesack's tank lost a track. One second later Knispel spotted the antitank gun, which had shed its camouflage. He took aim and fired. The high-explosive shell burst on target and disabled the crew of the antitank gun. One of the remaining tanks provided cover while Fendesack's crew carried out repairs. Meanwhile the rest raced toward the observation post. They rolled over a Maxim machine-gun mounted on a sled and heard it crushed beneath their tracks.

Several hand grenades lobbed into an earth bunker flushed out the enemy troops hiding inside. At the same time the tanks poured fire into a tree where the observer was still sitting, as in the crow's nest of a ship, trying to defend himself with an automatic rifle. He fell with the tree. After repairs to the track were completed, the Fendesack tank and its escort headed for the rear.

The next morning another still unseen observer called artillery fire down on the panzers. Salvoes of shells howled down on the positions and cottages that served as quarters. One landed near the hut being used by Fendesack and his crew and brought it down like a house of cards.

"Bunch of pigs," cursed Knispel. "We won't let you get away with that!"

"What do you intend to do? Are you planning to put them out of action with a curse?" teased one of the men of the reserve.

Knispel grinned. "Perhaps we should pay them a visit and give them a surprise serenade."

"Good idea, Kurt," agreed Fendesack. "We'll see what the commander has to say when he comes."

An hour later Oblt. Werner arrived and the Feldwebel outlined his proposal to him. "But that is sheer madness," the Oberleutnant declared and shook his head.

"But it can work if we carry it out at night and get out again immediately as soon as we have expended our ammunition."

"Not without a patrol first to scout the way and only with two tanks, if you can find a second madman."

There was no shortage of volunteers, for everyone wanted to take part. The patrol moved out as night fell in order to reconnoiter the direct route to the 172-mm battery position. The crews of the two tanks made ready.

At the same time the battalion commander contacted division and requested the division artillery to lay down a barrage on a neighboring sector in order to deceive the Russians as to the real point of attack. When the patrol returned its leader, a Leutnant from the 10th Panzer-Grenadier Regiment, climbed onto Fendesack's and briefed him. Five minutes after the barrage began the tanks moved off.

They rolled through their own forward positions, through a heavily overgrown ravine where the ground was still rather uncertain, and soon afterwards came upon a Russian field emplacement in the middle of the swampy area. The tanks drove through at high speed without firing a shot. They were challenged but gave no reply and soon they were through. Using the lane that the Russian patrols used to get to the German lines, which had been discovered by the Leutnant, the tanks cleared the minefield and drove straight toward the battery.

The tanks slowed and opened fire from barely 300 meters. They took turns firing so that when one tank fired the other was reloading. Knispel fired at the first thing that moved. He destroyed the machine-gun and rotated the turret to take aim at the battery itself.

A stockpile of Russian ammunition exploded with a thunderous roar not 50 meters to the side. The tanks spurted forward and cleared the area of raining metal. The command site with its radio antennas was spotted; the tanks rolled toward the hut and brought it crashing down. Fendesack popped up out of the turret hatch and lobbed two grenades then disappeared again.

The two panzers shot up the enemy guns and drove around the position in order to hit it again on the way back. The few shots that were fired at them missed, for the tanks rolled back the way they had come at top speed and disappeared into the darkness. All the while, to their right the division artillery continued to fire.

When the tanks returned the battalion commander was waiting to congratulate them. "Well done, men! They won't bother us for a while."

Three days later Fw. Fendesack's crew took part in another, company strength attack. This time the targets were Russian earth bunkers and field emplacements from which enemy patrols had sortied the night before. At first light the panzers set off toward the enemy positions. They were met by fire from machine-guns and a 76.2-mm antitank gun. Deployed in a wide line-abreast formation, the tanks charged onwards. One became bogged down in a swamp hole.

The tanks blazed away at the enemy. Knispel watched for muzzle flashes and immedately replied with a high-explosive shell. Suddenly four T-34s appeared. Knispel fired the high-explosive round that was already in the breech, aiming for the turret. It exploded against the side of the tank, knocking the infantry riding on its back to the ground. Then, in silent agreement with Knispel, the loader inserted an armor-piercing round. One shot was al that was neede to disable the T-34. It lost its front, left roadwheel and veered to one side. A second armor-piercing round struck its flank and set the tank on fire. The other tanks each accounted for a T-34. The last two enemy tanks turned away and escaped the shells that were fired after them by heading into a swamp with a heavy growth of young trees.

On 15 December the entire battalion was alerted, for the Russians had broken through the neighboring unit, an infantry division, with about 20 tanks and mounted infantry. The enemy tanks were now rolling toward the supply road in the German rear. The Fendesack crew learned of the situation over the tank radio. They were in the second wave, for on this day the 1st Company was leading. Fendesack listened to a report by a forward outpost: "Enemy has broken through from the northeast heading south and is trying to encircle us." Seconds later the battalion commander reported in. "Third veer south and try to stop the enemy tanks!"

The four tanks of the 3rd Company turned. Oblt. Werner ordered, "Battle readiness!" Initially all the tanks had loaded high-explosive shells.

Fendesack heard the voice of the battalion commander: "The company is fighting on its own."

"Understood, out."

The tanks drove through a small birch wood and crashed through the undergrowth. When they had cleared the stand of trees they saw the first enemy tanks, which turned, exposing their left flanks. Behind them were dense masses of Red Army with weapons at the ready.

"Open fire!" called the company commander.

One second later Knispel was the first to fire. His high-explosive shell fell among a group of charging Russians. The second round that the

This British "Matilda" was stopped with a broken tank.

loader loaded was a hollow-charge armor-piercing. Then Knispel aimed at a KV-I, allowing the necessary deflection, and fired. The Soviet tank was hit in front in the area of the left track, immobilizing it. The KV-I was still a threat, however, and its turret rotated to face its attacker. Before the other three German tanks could fire, Knispel landed another hit on the KV-I, causing it to burst into flames. Still not finished, the KV-I fired at the Fendesack tank. The tank's driver alertly moved the panzer forward several meters, causing the shot to miss.

The three remaining panzers had by now loaded armor-piercing ammunition. With the KV-I's gun still moving, Knispel fired again and this time hit the enemy tank in the rear. Flames spurted from the engine compartment, followed by thick diesel smoke. The crew bailed out and were cut down by machine-gun fire. In a brief battle lasting no more than five minutes, the Soviet attack force was destroyed. Knispel helped another tank destroy a second KV-I. He graciously stepped back and allowed the other gunner to claim the kill. It was classic Kurt Knispel, leaving something for his comrades. The next morning Knispel received the Iron Cross, Second Class from his battalion commander. Hauptmann Rothe said:

"This is just the beginning, Knispel. I think that more enemy tanks will soon follow and I wish you good hunting."

"Thank you, sir," replied the Obergefreiter drily. "We're having a small birthday party for Becker II tonight. The two of you are welcome to come."

"Who am I supposed to bring with me?" asked the commander.

"The bottle of cognac, of course, sir."

Everyone grinned.

Hauptmann Rothe nodded. "Can do, Knispel, after you brought it to my attention so discretely."

It turned out to be a lovely birthday party for their gunner Becker II.

The fighting went on and no one knew when it would end. There in the forgotten hole that was Tikhvin, which the Soviets obviously intended to make the turning point in the German offensive, the battle went inexorably. Even when the Germans were forced to abandon Tikhvin and take up positions farther to the west, the Red Army continued to attack, seeking to drive them back across the Volkhov for good.

The Red Army launched its offensive on 19 December. Advancing across the frozen marshes the Soviet forces tried to take Tikhvin. Attacks by Russian Il-2 close-support aircraft resulted in casualties. Fw. Will Klee was killed when enemy bombs fell on 2nd Company's quarters. The retreat across the Volkhov began and was completed without serious casualties. Winter quarters were occupied and early on 23 December, with the temperature at minus 38 degrees, the retreat continued to Estonia. A small Christmas party on the evening of 24 December passed quietly.

On the morning of 25 December a wold appeared in front of the crew's quarters. It stopped, raised its head and howled. The wolf was shot dead with a rifle. The drive to Estonia continued on 27 December. The next day the battalion moved into its Estonian quarters. What a difference between these solid houses and the run-down shacks in the workers' and farmers' paradise of the Soviet Union.

On 3 January the Red Army succeeded in barricading the road to Tikhvin, but several hours later the panzers opened it again. Knispel once again took part in the action, knocking out an antitank gun and blowing up a Russian ammunition dump. On 4 January rumors began to circulate that the battalion was going home to Germany to rest and reequip; however, the next morning the hopes of the soldiers were dashed. Instead of heading south, the panzers drove north and took up station at Narva, on the Soviet-Estonian border. The most recent segment of the fighting in Russia had cost Knispel's 3rd Company twenty-two men killed, forty-one wounded, and several lost to illness. The coldest recorded temperature had been minus forty-six degrees.

With the Rubbel Crew

When Obergefreiter Rubbel returned to the company on 11 January 1942 after recovering from his wound, he took over a Panzer IV armed with the long-barreled 75-mm gun, then new to the front. Kurt Knispel was assigned to the tank as gunner and Rubbel learned that Knispel had already knocked out seven enemy tanks and several antitank guns and had repulsed numerous infantry assaults. At this time the 29th Panzer Regiment had been split into two battle groups, one on the Volkhov and another at the Pogostye pocket.

At Narva, where the battle group commanded by Major Kaufmann was situated, the unit's tanks were loaded aboard a train and then unloaded at Kingisepp. From there Battle Group Kaufmann drove via Krasnogvardeysk to the front. The weather was still very cold, and initially the panzers carried out a series of small-scale actions against probing Russian patrols.

As a rule, the new tanks with the long 75-mm gun were assigned to three of 3rd Company's crews:

First Tank: commander Fendesack
driver Thaysen
gunner Giersdorf
loader and radio operator not known

Second Tank: commander Rubbel
driver Beloch
radio operator Brauner
gunner Knispel
loader Horstel

Third Tank: commander Herder
driver Opitz
radio operator Rausch
gunner and loader not known.

The battle group became involved in a series of turbulent engagements. On one occasion there was a fierce firefight with several antitank guns hidden in a wood. The Soviets opened fire on the tanks as they were driving down a forest lane. In spite of having the advantage of surprise, the antitank guns were eventually overcome.

Battle Group Kaufmann's area of operations was with the 121st Infantry Division, which it had been assigned to support in offensive and defensive operations. In the words of his commander, here Knispel "repeatedly distinguished himself as a tough yet sensible gunner, who often spotted the target faster than all the others in spite of restricted field of view."

"In the three tank-versus-tank fights that Knispel took part in as gunner at this time, he showed himself to be far superior to his opponents.

Even before they had spotted the German tanks, they were targeted by Knispel and knocked out with one or two shots. The next two engagements were similar. In them Kurt Knispel proved himself to be an unsurpassed and unerring gunner."

Since the Russians limited their attacks to small formations, they made as little forward progress as the Germans. The rumor spread that the Russian inactivity was due to a shortage of ammunition, however the fourth action was to disprove that theory.

The next German advance saw Battle Group Kaufmann support an attack by the infantry. The tanks plowed through the deep snow. Suddenly there was a tremendous crash. A frightful bang almost deafened the men inside the Rubbel tank. But fortunately the shell fired by a KV-I concealed behind a large, snow-covered bush, was a high-explosive round.

Knispel reacted instantly and hit the Soviet heavy tank with a shot between the turret and hull which put it out of action. A second shot dislodged the turret from the turret ring.

"That was a masterful shot, Kurt," Rubbel called to his gunner enthusiastically.

After this incident the battle group drove back to Narva, where it was reunited with the regiment. For the first time since the start of the Russian campaign Oberst Wahl had his entire regiment under his direct command. An attack by three tanks was soon carried out from the new base of operations. One of the panzers was Rubbel's. By now it was March; the streams were running high from the spring run-off and the mud became deeper day by day. During this attack Rubbel's tank encountered a KV-II. Knispel immediately took aim and fired. It was another of his patented "chest hits" which silenced the enemy tank. When the KV-II turned and showed its rear, Knispel hit it in the engine. Within seconds the KV-II was in flames. Three figures jumped clear and rolled on the ground in an effort to extinguish their burning clothing.

Two days later there was another tank-versus-tank duel during a night mission which saw the Rubbel tank accompany a German patrol. The sky in the east was beginning to brighten when Knispel once again was the first to sight the enemy. It was another KV-II. The huge Soviet tank was in an ambush position and was already swinging its gun around to bear on the Rubbel tank. Knispel fired while the enemy gunner was still seeking his target and scored a direct hit. The KV-II burned out. Alfred Rubbel wrote:

> Knispel's vigilance never relaxed. Whether by night or day, he commanded the entire battlefield within his field of vision. Even before I could give the order to fire, Knispel had already fired and

destroyed this giant with one shot using one of the new hollow-charge shells.

Kurt had once again recognized the situation immediately and reacted just as quickly. I never saw anyone else who combined this sureness of reaction with absolute accuracy. It was unique!

We reached a tributary of the Volkhov. It was the Tichoda, which at that time was also running high. As our tank had a fording capability of only about a meter, and as deeper water would have put it out of action, in spite of the cold—about minus twenty-five—Kurt Knispel simply pulled off his pants and waded into the water with a stick to guage the depth, seeking the shallowest spot for us to cross. In vain. If we had tried to ford the stream water would have entered the exhausts and put us out of sction.

When Knispel came out of the water he was frozen blue. But he had saved our tank, for I myself was on the verge of risking it on spec.

A quarter of a liter of rum in hot tea and plenty of movement revived Knispel and so this interlude ended relatively harmlessly, for Kurt's bear's consitution pulled him through. In general we were very lucky during this phase of the war.

The forest battles in April 1942 became bitter duels with the inventive Russians, who knew their way around the area. Snipers in the swamps and trees made life difficult for the tanks, for as soon as a commander showed his head he was fired on. A new round of forest battles broke out on 17 April and included a series of tank hunts. Rubbel's tank was knocked out and for the first time Knispel commanded a tank—albeit temporarily. Horstel and Brauner were wounded and only Knispel and the commander were able to leave the tank unhurt.

The fight went on. They had received a new tank and continued to battle the Soviets, who were highly motivated by the STAVKA, as the "fire-brigade of the north." There were repeated forays through the forest lanes. The tanks cleared a path through the moors and marshes for the 121st and 126th Infantry Divisions in an attempt to force the enemy, now consisting of an entire army, to give up. The following is a brief survey of the Soviet position in the north.

The Red Army in the Northern Sector

After the direct assault on and the capture of Leningrad had been abandoned, there followed the advance across the Volkhov and the Soviet counterattack. Army Group North's failure to link up with the Finns at the Swir had been a serious setback.

One thing very quickly became apparent during this severe winter, the worst the Soviet Union had experienced in more than fifty years: the Soviet troops were far superior to the German in training and equipment for a winter war in the severe cold. The German side lacked proper winter clothing for its troops. While the Red Army soldier wore heavy furlined boots, fur caps and padded winter coats, the Wehrmacht soldier had gone into this most severe winter still wearing his thin coat, with no lined boots or other cold-weather equipment. As a result of sabotage, dozens of transport trains carrying the German Army's winter equipment had been shunted onto various sidings in the Königsberg area. This had extremely serious consequences for the army, which suffered more than 200,000 casualties from frostbite.

Furthermore the Red Army possessed greater winter mobility, because it transported its weapons, equipment and supplies on sleighs, while the German tanks and motor vehicles proved very sensitive to the cold. The Red Army also enjoyed numerical superiority. The Soviets had demonstrated their winter superiority by attacking and encircling German strongpoints, forcing the German Army to fight their way through to relieve them. This extremely difficult and unusual style of fighting affected Army Group North's Tikhvin group of forces more tan any other.

✠

While the defensive battles in the Tikhvin and Volkhovstroy area were still raging, the inadequate German command organization was being reorganized. Already on 3 December 1941 the boundary between the 16th and 18th German Armies was moved from Babino (west of Chudovo) northeast to north of Tikhvin. This placed the lower Volkhov, the south shore of Lake Ladoga and the upper Neva in the 18th Army's sector.

In the 16th Army's sector the XXXVIII Army Corps under General von Chapius (250th Spanish Legion, 126th and 215th Infantry Divisions) held both sides of the upper and middle Volkhov to north of Chudovo, while the XXXIX Panzer Corps under General von Arnim held the extended salient at Tikvin with the 8th and 12th Panzer Divisions and the 61st and 20th (mot.) Infantry Divisions. The latter corps' forces were badly strung out along its extended front.

In the bottleneck itself was the XXVII Army Corps under General Loch, with the 223rd and 227th Infantry Divisions facing east and the 1st and 96th Infantry Divisions on the Neva facing west, fighting mainly in the Dubrovka bridgehead.

General von Boch's I Army Corps with the 11th, 21st and 254th Infantry Divisions was south of the Volkhovstroy-Mga rail line. The Oranienbaum bridgehead was held by the XXVI Army Corps under General Wodrig with the 93rd, 212th and 217th Infantry Divisions. In addition the SS Legion "Flandern" had arrived to join the 18th Army.

On 19th December, after Generalfeldmarschall Brauchitsch had requested and been granted permission to step down, Adolf Hitler had assumed the position of commander in chief of the army, which he was to hold until the end of the war and the defeat of the armed forces.

This change at the top of the army also resulted in a shakeup in the command of Army Group North. Generalfeldmarschall Ritter von Leeb left his post and was not given another. He was replaced as commander of Army Group North by Generaloberst von Küchler. General der Kavallerie Lindemann commanded the 18th Army while Generaloberst Busch stayed on as commander of the 16th Army.

It was clear to all the main participants in the north that the Red Army had siezed away the initiave. What was left were attempts to become active farther to the north and northeast. But Stalin and the STAVKA had thrown a barrier in front of these efforts, forming a new army group (the "Volkhov Front") in January 1942 and bolstering it with powerful, fresh forces.

Panzer IV (622) of the 13th Panzer Division's 4th Regiment.

The 2nd Shock Army under General Vlasov was inserted between the defending 52nd and 59th Soviet Armies. The new army included specially trained elite winter units. These included a total of eight rifle divisions, eight shock brigades each consisting of three battalions, an artillery battalion and a mortar battalion, and ten ski battalions.

Further units were moved in. The Soviet goal was to launch a major offensive to sever the 18th Army's lines of communication and destroy it at the gates of Leningrad. However the Soviet plan foundered on the German command in the north and on the outstanding fighting spirit of the German troops of all ranks and all branches of the service.

The battle began on 13 January 1942 and lasted until 4 June of that year. Before it was over the commander of the 2nd Shock Army had been captured and his entire army destroyed. The 12th Panzer Division and its two armored battle groups played a part in this German success, at the Volkhov, at Tikhvin and at the Pogostye pocket.

At the end of June resistance by the Soviet 2nd Shock Army came to an end and on 26 June the last elements went into captivity. The 2nd Shock Army had lost six rifle divisions and six brigades, while another nine units were essentially destroyed. Into German hands fell 649 guns, 171 tanks and 33,000 prisoners. The Soiviet attempt to break the German ring around Leningrad had failed. On the German side a solid front had been established which would remain essentially unchanged until January 1944.

Relief—Back to Germany

A new rumor had been making the rounds of the 12th Panzer Division since 3 May 1942—they were finally going to go home. But it was still 16 May before the units were relieved. Then I Battalion, 29th Panzer Regiment received instructions to hand its tanks and other weapons over to II Battalion. It was going home to reequip with new weapons and be reorganzed. From March to May Battle Group Kaufmann had destroyed 21 tanks and 24 guns in its new defensive area and took several hundred prisoners. This success came at a cost, however: 17 soldiers killed, 12 wounded and six tanks lost.

The general transfer back to Germany began on 17 May. The battalion was going home without weapons or equipment. Knispel and Rubbel and the men from their own and another tank initially drove as far as Tigoda on a self-propelled antitank gun. There they crossed the river in an assault boat belonging to the engineers, then proceeded along a corduroy road, used as a supply road by an infantry division. Afterwards some men rode horses, others on horse-drawn wagons, and Krasnogvardeysk was reached on the evening of 18 May. From there the men proceeded to Narva the following morning.

At the station in Narva there was a one-hour sendoff with music by the regimental band before the train set off for Germany. The route led through Reval and Dvinsk to Elbing. From there the battalion's journey continued via Frankfurt/Oder to the Neuhammer training grounds in Silesia, not far from the regiment's old garrison town of Sagan.

From there the men went on leave. Kurt Knispel was looking forward to spending the early summer at home and making the climb up Altvater Mountain with several friends, that is if there were any who hadn't been called up yet. It was a wonderful leave. Unfortunately it was too brief, for after only one week it was time to say farewell to family and friends. When Knispel and the others returned to Neuhammer they found that their tanks had not yet arrived and so to occupy the men outings were scheduled, on one occasion by car up the Bober to Oberschreiberhau in the Riesen Mountains. The drive through the Silesian countryside, which reminded Knispel very much of his home, was for him an outing in an area which had been part of Germany again since 1938.

"It is simply fantastic," he said, excited by the many sights. "All of this is Germany! It is worth fighting to hold onto this!"

The soldiers found entire German-speaking villages and Knispel learned that just as in the Altvater Mountains here the populations on both sides of the mountains spoke German. During several stops he learned that they were settlers from Zillertal, who had resettled there in the 16th and 17th Centuries. The locals were active in mining and also worked in forestry, farming and glassmaking. In a crystal shop Knispel purchased a lovely fruit bowl, which he packed well and sent home. In the local church he prayed for a safe return home from the war. Another time they set out for a nearby mountain to make an attempt on the snow-covered peak. The mountain was the tallest in the Riesen Mountains at 1,603 meters. However, the almost vertical sides defeated their best efforts and they failed to reach the top.

After the battalion had been reequipped, the combat echelon moved to Glienicke near Berlin. A visit to the Reich capital with its endless sights was a great experience for Kurt. For everyone it was like a second leave. The battalion then moved to Burg near Magdeburg. There the 3rd Company was supposed to become the last unit of I Battalion, 29th Panzer Regiment to receive its Panzer IVs. The battalion would then be fully equipped with the Panzer IV with the long gun and 100% ready for operations. But at Burg the men of I Battalion learned that they were being transferred to the 4th Panzer Regiment as that unit's III Battalion. They also learned that the 4th Regiment was the armored core of the 13th Panzer Division and had distinguished itself in action on numerous occasions.

The last leave-takers were recalled by telegraph. On 11 July the bulk of the battalion entrained. It was transported by express train, first to Dresden and then from there via Breslau to Kattowitz. The crews learned that they were destined for the southern sector of the Eastern Front. But the 3rd Company still had no tanks and following another short leave on 21 July 1942 it travelled to Biederitz near Magdeburg. At first the men of the unit were put to work by the army equipment depot in Königsberg. Finally, on 26 July, the new tanks arrived. They were immediately armed and gassed up. The next day the company was loaded aboard a train and the trip to the front began in the afternoon. Several times the train was held up by the passive resistance of Polish railway workers and the train was shunted onto a siding somewhere.

The long 75-mm tank cannon were a sight for sore eyes for the tankers. For protection against mines, the locomotive was positioned directly behind an open flatcar, which was supposed to absorb the explosion of any mines. Behind the locomotive were several sealed cars, whose contents were a mystery to the tankers. Behind them were the open flatcars for the tanks and then the passenger cars for the crews. As the weather was pleasant, the men all sat on their tanks and let the countryside slide by. There were conversations, some serious although most were light-hearted. The men played cards to pass the time.

The Incident in Cracow

When the transport train reached Cracow it was again initially shunted onto a siding. Everyone waited hours for the trip to resume. While there something happened that showed Knispel in his entire spectrum. Kurt Knispel and his friend Alfred Rubbel were sitting on one of the tanks. They were chatting when Knispel, thanks to his keen eyesight, suddenly spotted two men out of the corner of his eye. They were about 100 meters away. The one in front was wearing striped prisoner's clothes. The man behind him wore an army field uniform. The convict kept stopping, and the soldier hit him with the rifle butt and then kicked him as a signal to move on. At first it was impossible to say whether the man in uniform was a concentration camp guard or a member of the regional defense forces.

Alfred Rubbel heard his friend curse softly. "Damn it, I'm going to straighten that fellow out."

"Be careful, Kurt! He can get you in all sorts of trouble," said Rubbel, the more reasonable of the two.

"I don't care. I can't just watch and keep my mouth shut." Knispel jumped down from the tank and walked toward the two figures.

As he walked he pulled his pistol from his breast pocket, the place where tank soldiers always kept it to avoid becoming entangled while climbing in or bailing out, and pointed it at the soldier, who had just given the exhausted prisoner another kick.

"Stop, you dog!" cried Knispel furiously.

The regional defense soldier, for that is what Knispel assumed he was on account of his age, turned angrily. "What do you want, you stubble-jumper?"

"I'll soon show you!" shouted Knispel, full of rage, seeing the emaciated form of the prisoner and his furrowed face. Knispel struck the soldier with his open hand.

The regional defense soldier pointed his rifle at Knispel, who wrenched it from his hand. He swung the rifle and struck the rail, breaking off the stock. Then he administered several swift kicks to the soldier's

September 1943: The tank commanders of the 503rd Heavy Panzer Battalion's 1st Company. Of the twelve commanders, only two survived the war. Knispel is third from the left in the back.

rear. While Knispel, still burning with rage, went back to his tank, the soldier picked up what was left of his weapon and departed with his prisoner making no further use of force. Knispel would never forget the sight of that prisoner. There was such deep gratitude in his face that he could have screamed; for who would be there to protect the prisoner later?

Word of the incident soon got around. Even the battalion commander learned of it and approved. Alfred Rubbel wrote:

> Our respect for Kurt Knispel grew even higher after that, even more than for his military achievements, which were considerable. There were enough wearers of the Knight's Cross and other decorations, all soldiers of the highest standard. But in this situation Knispel had shown almost suicidal civilian courage and taught some morals to a prisoner's guard. Moreover he shamed us, for although we were upset by the scene we remained silent.

By the time Knispel climbed onto the tank he was smiling again. "If only I knew that I hadn't caused the poor devil to come to any harm," he said. "But I just saw red."

"We can only imagine what will happen to this prisoner," said Rubbel closing the incident. This was not the end of the affair, however. After the train had resumed its journey it was visited by a squad of military police at the next station. They demanded a soldier "with dark hair and about one and three-quarter meters tall."

"If you mean to take one of us with you, then one of you will have to stay here and sit in the tank," joked the company commander. And when the "highway crows" (army slang for the military police squads) made as if to carry out their threat, the commander drew his pistol.

"On this train I am in command! Anyone who sets foot on it without my permission will be shot!"

The military police withdrew. Nothing more was ever heard of the matter. Apparently the police were smart enough to report that the man they were looking for could not have been on that transport. The soldiers were all happy to leave that twilight zone between home and front. Every turn of the train's wheels was welcomed, even though an uncertain fate awaited them in the southern sector. On the way there was increased speculation as to what was in the sealed cars. They belonged to a unit of the Waffen-SS Panzer-Grenadier Division *Wiking*, which was also on the train with its tanks and like them was headed for the southern sector. One night the men got together to discuss how to unravel the mystery of the sealed cars.

"I think that Kurt can open the locks without being noticed," suggested a member of the Rubbel crew.

"Well, Kurt, would it be possible?"

"Yes, it's possible. I did learn the locksmith's trade. If you like, I can try it."

Armed with a bunch of keys from which several bits had been filed off, Knispel went to work at an hour past midnight when the SS men were dozing. His comrades carefully screened him. After several tries he opened the heavy lock. Carefully the door was opened centimeter by centimeter. When two of the men entered the first car they found themselves staring at undreamed of treasures. There were tinned goods of every kind. Alcohol, from cognac to liquor, coffee, chocolate, tobacco and cigarettes, fortified chocolate and other sweets.

Two sacks were filled to the brim with these precious commodities and hidden just in case. Then two more sacks were filled with coffee; these disappeared into the tanks' air filters, while bottles of schnaps, well-wrapped in shirts and other cloth, disappeared into the slightly elevated gun barrels. The muzzles of the guns were then capped.

Nothing was noticed and when cars carrying the Waffen-SS unit were dropped off so that it could join its unit the two units bade each other farewell with mutual respect. Everyone breathed a deep sigh of relief when the column disappeared. The company was assured morning and evening coffee for months to come.

With III Panzer Corps in the Caucasus

The 3rd Company's journey came to an end at Stalino on 4 August. From there it drove to join the 4th Panzer Regiment, which was already engaged in the advance past Rostov to the southeast. The 1st Panzer Army, commanded by Generaloberst Ewald von Kleist, had launched the drive into the Caucasus with the III Panzer Corps under General der Kavallerie von Mackensen. The battle-tested 13th Panzer Division had been placed under General von Mackensen's command once again, having been separated from the corps for seven months. Setting out from Rostov, it had joined the corps at Salsk. With the 13th Panzer Division now was the 4th Panzer Regiment, whose III Battalion was the former I Battalion, 29th Panzer Regiment, commanded by Hauptmann Schröck. Alfred Rubbel remembered:

> We were faced with a completely different picture in this sector of the Eastern Front. We saw almost tropical vegetation and encountered our first dromedaries.

When we reached the Stalin Canal near Elisat we suddenly saw villages with wonderfully cared for low stone houses. The equally well tended gardens in front of them were filled with flowers.

When we approached the first village with guns at the ready, we were greeted in pure Swabian. We had found german people, descendants of those who had been brought here by Empress Catherine of Russia to settle this almost uninhabitated land. We had stumbled across one of these Swabian settlements and received a warm welcome.

Our division was advancing on Maykop. It advanced with the 66th Rifle Regiment. This charge toward Maykop saw the 66th Regiment's I (Armored Troop Carrier) Battalion lead the way. It was led by Major Albert Brux. The battalion simply drove past Russian units at high speed and not until just outside of Maykop was it recognized as a German unit.

Firing to both sides from its armored troop carriers, the battalion raced across the bridge over the Belaya and established a strong bridgehead. General von Mackensen told the author: "An especially daring operation saved the iron road bridge from being blown by the Russians."

The next day Brux drove into the town. There was heavy fighting. Not until the next day did the panzers of the 9th Company of III Battalion, 4th Panzer Regiment, under Hauptmann Schröck roll through to the east end of the town to close the ring around the still-defending Russians. Strong enemy elements had moved into the town to bar the 13th Panzer Division's and thus the corps' way to the oil pipelines running from the Black Sea to the Caspian sea. III Battalion, 4th Panzer Regiment, was deployed at the Belaya bridge in order to prevent the Russians from escaping and prevent a counterattack toward Maykop. There were several skirmishes there provoked by the high-spirited panzer crews. Alfred Rubbel:

In Maykop we found tomatoes, grapes and melons; as well, in the cellars we found several casks of mirabelle brandy and now and then we had a few drinks. When the waves of cockiness then ran high, we challenged the Russians by riding a motorcycle we had found straight across the road and down the other side.

This goaded the Russians into a wild outburst of shooting, which usually began too late as the motorcycle driver had already reached safety. But two grazing wounds showed that it might have a different result and Hptm. Schröck soon put an end to this nonsense.

Schröck's company completed its defensive assignment without seeing any action against enemy tanks. A few days later, on 13 August, III Panzer Corps was withdrawn from the front and moved to the Terek River sector.

Leading the corps, the 13th Panzer Division arrived in the positions of the German troops stationed near Sablinskaya. The division under Generalleutnant Traugott Herr was supposed to make a quick advance and capture the entrances to the two army roads and also sieze the capital of Orzhonikidze, this while securing the flank of the 1st Panzer Army advancing along the Caucasus. Not until the start of the battles in the Mosdok bridgehead did the real purgatory begin. 9th Company, 4th Panzer Regiment was involved in day and night attacks. In these battles Lt. Heinz, who was commanding Fendesack's tank, and Uffz. Lindner were knocked out. Gerhard Opitz, Walter Blei and Walter Schulz were killed, while Vollmer, Brauner and Peucker were seriously injured.

Uffz. Rubbel repreatedly drove forward to engage the attacking Red Army forces. Gunner Knispel raised his victory total to 12 enemy tanks. Losses were heavy during the battle for Gisel airfield and the subsequent encirclement of part of the division; III Battalion, 4th Panzer Regiment suffered especially heavy losses and 9th Company under Hptm. Schröck was decimated. Finally a crisis developed when the Romanian troops abandoned their positions during a heavy Soviet attack and fled.

Kurt Knispel responded to this situation with great bravery. Not only did he repeatedly intervene at the last second in his role as gunner, but he also rescued several panzer crews after their tanks had been knocked out. It seemed as if he were invulnerable. He never suffered so much as a scratch, even though he took part in many risky undertakings such as his rescues stranded comrades.

Not until the night of 12 November did the surrounded elements of the 13th Panzer Division reestablish contact with the corps. Shoulder to shoulder with the *Wiking* Division it repulsed determined Soviet attacks. Once again Knispel's tank was employed in the role of assault gun, helping fight off repeated Russian attacks.

In mid-November a sudden change in the weather caused the mercury to plunge to minus 20 degrees and lower. All efforts to bring the operation to a successful conclusion came to an end. Until the middle of December there were only local advances, for from then on deep snow made any more ambitious attack impossible. But everyone sensed that the fortunes of war had taken a turn. It was Kurt Knispel who said to his friend Alfred Rubbel: "We individuals can still prevail, we can still do it. But the whole has gone to pot and it is doubtful whther it will ever recover."

Now and then the men heard something about Stalingrad in the Wehrmacht communiques. They had no detailed information, but the tone of the reports caused them to suspect what was happening. Everyone still hoped that the 6th Army would get out of the pocket. In any case it was still strong enough to break through any siege ring if its forces were committed in concentration. This did not happen, however. Hitler ordered the 6th Army to remain in Stalingrad and promised that it would be supplied from the air. The result is well known: the 6th Army went down in Stalingrad.

Quite suddenly the news arrived that the 9th Company, 4th Panzer Regiment, was to hand in its tanks. The unit's personnel were to go to Germany to take on a new mission and receive new tanks. The first reports of this "wonder tank" had already filtered through. Meanwhile the situation in the east had become critical. There were serious doubts whether the German forces in the Caucasus would be able to slip through the eye of the needle before the Soviets recaptured Rostov and sealed off their avenue of escape.

The Red Army was preparing not only to bring a bloody end to the 6th Army, but also to retake Rostov and trap and destroy all of the German units still to the southeast. However the men of 9th Company, 4th Panzer Regiment got out. They passed through the Fastov area, an active partisan zone, without trouble. The company was rushed home. On arriving in Cracow, from where the men were to be sent on leave, they were deloused. The familiar Führer packets were handed out. One group received marching orders while the other was issued leave passes.

Kurt Knispel, now a newly-promoted Unteroffizier, returned to his home town. His highest-ranking decoration was still the the Iron Cross, Second Class, but it had been joined by the Panzer Assault badge for 25 tank attacks and the silver braid made his uniform rather more eye-catching. His parents were happy to have their son back for a few weeks. He remained over Christmas and he was able to celebrate the new year of 1943 with two friends, who were also on leave, before travelling to the panzer gunnery school at Putlos on 10 January. When he arrived there he was surprised to learn that he was being assigned to the Tiger tank. However, since the tanks were not yet ready for the new 503rd Heavy Panzer Battalion, he and all the others were given an additional 14 days leave. And so Kurt Knispel was able to surprise his parents with his unexpected return to the Altvater Mountains.

NEW WEAPONS AND THE NEW UNIT

The New Tiger—Training—The New "Association"—New Tactics

When Kurt Knispel returned to Putlos at the end of January 1943, to his surprise he found the new champion of tank warfare, the Tiger, waiting for him there. During training and range practise with the new tank he found that it exceeded all the rumors he had heard about it. The penetrative power of the new gun and its fantastic aiming system combined with the high-speed turret rotation mechanism caused the crews to have high expectations. The results of live firing trials convinced them that they had in their hands a weapon which was superior to any tank they knew of.

The crews had to learn and practice new tactics. The first was engaging enemy tanks from long range. Then there was the fast dash from behind the front and the subsequent attack. The crews practiced attacks over and over again. It was the role of the Tigers driving on both flanks of an armored wedge formation to make quick firing halts and engage the enemy from distances of 2 000 meters and more, inflicting the initial losses on him, thus diverting his attention from the center of the attack and giving the main attacking wedge the opportunity to halt and fire en masse. The crews also had to practice driving through the enemy, double-sided envelopments, engaging antitank fronts and quick flanking attacks.

It was vital in long-range engagements to measure the range as accurately as possible. An error in range estimation meant a miss, even with the almost flat trajectory of the 88-mm tank cannon. It was here that Kurt Knispel was in his element. Once again Alfred Rubbel:

> Here my fiend Kurt Knispel proved that he not only had a good eye but also, and in particular, possessed oustanding three-dimensional vision. All of this enabled him to later emerge victorious from hundreds of engagements.

In the Caucasus, where the main role of the panzers had been high-speed raids, there had been few tank-versus-tank engagements. Not until the Red Army went on the offensive and committed more and more tank units were the panzers called upon to halt massed armored assaults by the enemy. Not until 1943 and 1944 did tank-versus-tank combat become the primary role of the German tanks. The raids were over. There followed a months-long retreat, with the German forces pursued by strong enemy tank formations. Knispel had destroyed twelve enemy tanks by this time and wore the Panzer Assault Badge.

The personnel group, which 9th Company, 4th Panzer Regiment, had accompanied back to Germany was commanded by Hptm. Schobert. The men of 9th Company went home from the Ordzhonikidze area at Christmas 1942. The group's personnel came from the 4th and 29th Panzer Regiments. The 4th's were southern Germans, Austrians and men from the Sudetenland, while those of the 29th came from the north of Germany. All of them had 18 months of combat in Russia behind them. The commander of the newly-formed 3rd Company, 503rd Heavy Panzer Battalion was Oblt. Oehmler.

One group of men was sent to the 500th Panzer Battalion at Paderborn. This group was led by Obfw. Fendesack and included Kurt Knispel. It was to become the 1st Company of the 503rd Heavy Panzer Battalion. The

May 1944: Tank commander Fendesack and gunner Knispel. Both have reason to be happy: After the bitter fighting of June 1943 in Operation Citadel, they were sent to Thuringia for rest and refitting.

commanders of the company's five Tigers were Oberfeldwebel Fendesack, Fw. Petzka, Fw. Rippl, Uffz. Rubbel and Uffz. Hermann Seidel. These experienced commanders were assigned to the three platoons of the 1st Company. Rubbel went to 1st Platoon. Lt. Jammerat was commander of Tiger 114. His gunner was Walter Junge, driver Walter Eschrich, radio operator Alfred Peuker and loader Johann Stromer.

The Tiger I and II

The Tiger was a heavily armored combat vehicle armed with a powerful, accurate gun; at the time of its service introduction it was superior to all known enemy tanks. When the Tiger was able to engage the enemy from long range it was unbeatable. With an ammunition capacity of 90 rounds it was capable of fighting for three or for days without having to rearm.

The tank's mobility was lacking, however. The components that made up the drive train had been developed in haste after a late start, and the early deployment of the vehicle meant that problems were unavoidable. This fact was known and was accepted in order to get the vehicle into service in the east, where the situation was critical, as quickly as possible. The design concept of the Tiger II, also called the King Tiger, was not surpassed until years after the Second World War. The postwar Leopard I and II tanks owed much to the Tiger II.

The inadequate mobility of the underpowered Tiger was not as serious a shortcoming as it might have been because of the tank's long-range firepower. Both versions of the 88-mm gun used in the two versions of the Tiger, the KwK 36/L 56 and the KwK 43/L 71, were the best there were. The Tiger's ability to take punishment was demonstrated by a vehicle deployed in the southeast of the Eastern Front, which in a space of six hours took 227 hits from antitank rifles, 14 from 42-mm antitank guns and 11 from the usually lethal 76.2-mm antitank gun. Not one of these hits penetrated the tank's armor.

With road wheels and connecting arms shot up, two swing arms not functioning and several direct hits on its tracks, as well as damage from three mines, this Tiger still drove 60 kilometers over difficult terrain to its own unit's workshop. The vehicle in question belonged to 1st Company, 503rd Heavy Panzer Battalion and the incident in question occurred near Proletarskaya. None of the crew sustained any kind of injury.

The example of the great tank battles during "Operation Citadel" showed how much the enemy feared the Tigers. Antitank ditches, mine fields and antitank gun positions were set up in order to stop them. Artillery of every caliber tried to halt the German panzers. The Soviets also added tank blocking units. Within a year of the Tiger's appearance the

Soviets had developed new weapons to deal with it. These included the T-34/85, KV 85, the Josef Stalin I and II tanks, the SU-85 and SU-100 assault guns, and a new 100-mm antitank gun.

For the Russians the cry "tigri" had become something to fear. Even during the basic training of Soviet tank crews, combatting the Tiger took first place. Every one of the Tiger's weak spots (of which there were few) was identified and committed to memory. In the Leningrad artillery museum there hangs a table with the title: "The weak and vulnerable points of the German 'T' tank."

The 503rd Heavy Panzer Battalion

It seems quite likely that the 503rd Heavy Panzer Battalion was the oldest Tiger battalion, as its official formation date is 4 May 1942. It is equally certain that it was not the first to take the Tiger into action.

Formation began in the 5th Panzer Regiment's peacetime garrison of Neuruppin west of Berlin. Part of the unit's personnel and the command officers came from the 5th and 6th Panzer Regiments. Initially the headquarters company, workshop company and 1st and 2nd Panzer Companies were formed. However it was not until the beginning of December 1942 that the first Hentschel Tigers reached the battalion. During this time the first Tigers were seeing action with 502nd Heavy Panzer Battalion in Army Group North's area of operations.

The Tigers were sent into action prematurely as the situation on the Eastern Front had become critical. The first three battalions were only partially equipped with the Tiger; each received twenty of the heavy tanks while the rest of the battalion was equipped with the Panzer III armed with the 75-mm gun. On 21 December 1942 the operational elements of 503rd Heavy Panzer Battalion departed for the southern sector of the Eastern Front, to Army Group South. Express trains transported the tanks into the Proletarskaya area, where they detrained. 503rd Heavy Panzer Battalion took part in the fighting at the Manich in early January 1943.

In January 1943 the 2nd Company of the 502nd Heavy Panzer Battalion, which had entrained in December, was also transported to Army Group Don and was initially attached to the 17th Panzer Division. It saw its first action in the Kalmyk Steppe under the command of Hptm. Lange. For reasons of expediency this company was incorporated into 503rd Heavy Panzer Battalion as its 3rd Company. Thus the 503rd Heavy Panzer Battalion became the first Tiger battalion to reach its authorized strength of three tank companies. In April 1943, in the Bogodukhov area, the battalion was a potent tank unit, fully equipped with a total of 45 Tiger tanks as well as other vehicles and equipment.

TIGERS IN ACTION

Knispel's Shining Hour

On 14 April 1943 the company entrained, led by company commander Oblt. Oemer. The first stop was Bogodukhov, approximately 60 kilometers south of Kharkov. Knispel had been assigned as Uffz. Rippl's gunner. Unfortunately the first calamities occurred during the trip to the front, for the composition of 1st Company was anything but ideal. The company included no less than five Stabsfeldwebel with no combat experience as well as a large number of inexperienced crewmen of other ranks. This situation should have been avoided at all costs in such an important unit, especially since more than enough experienced tank soldiers had volunteered to serve in it.

Nevertheless the three experienced crews in the company refused to put up with the nonsense of the Stabsfeldwebel in positions for which they were not qualified. They got their way and from then on the shop ran smoothly. Things settled down for good following the replacement of the company's senior NCO, Stabsfunkmeister Nega. The latter was anything but the "mother of the company," which was the role the senior non-commissioned officer was supposed to fill.

The company consisted of three platoons each with four Tigers. There was also the company commander's tank and his spare, which meant that the loss of the command tank did not necessarily mean that the company commander was put out of action too. The company commander's tank had the turret number 100, the spare 101. Hptm. Burmester led the company as Oblt. Oemler had been assigned to train additional Tiger crews.

This period in the Kharkov area was described by Franz-Wilhelm Lochmann, a member of the company commander's crew:

> From now on we lived together only as crews. This strengthened the feeling of being a team tremendously. Everyone knew the others' personalities down to the last detail.
>
> Our first order of business was looking after our own well being. We had the best of food and there was always something to drink. There were parties and anyone who wanted to could go to the opera in Kharkov. Of course, during this time we also had a wild company party.
>
> Our good life was only interrupted by drives to Chuguyev Donets, which was in the front line. There we carried out adjustment fire with the new tanks. The company was provided with aerial photos of the Russian bunkers, which made it possible to designate targets with great accuracy.

> Each tank was assigned its targets, including between the assigned sectors of the infantry positions.
>
> Feldwebel Rippl's tank achieved the best results. No wonder, for behind the aiming mechanism of this Tiger sat Kurt Knispel and he played a solo of which the other gunners, all experienced men, could only dream.
>
> No one could come close to Kurt. We acknowledged that without envy. It was a special gift which made him capable of these feats.

This statement was generally acknowledged by the other crews. With Knispel as gunner, Rippl's Tiger was unbeatable. Rippl and Knispel had known each other for along time and with their abilities the two men complemented one another. Both came from the panzer replacement training battalion at Sagan.

Before it went into action the battalion had to carry out a so-called "Turkish exercise." A simulated large-scale attack was conducted during a visit by Japanese generals following the plan for "Operation Citadel." The exercise was carried out with a high level of realism. It demonstrated close coordination between various army units and the air force. The 503rd Heavy Panzer Battalion, which was one of the forward units, came so close to the Stukas' target area that any inaccuracy in bombing could have resulted in disaster. Nevertheless, everything went well.

Several days before the start of "Citadel," the last German ofensive in the east, the battalion received a new commanding officer. He was Hauptmann Clemens-Heinrich Graf von Kageneck, who was to lead the 503rd Battalion through its most successful period. Like his successors Romme and von Diest-Koerber, he was the typical combat formation commander.

"Operation Citadel"—Knispel's Finest Hour

What Hptm. Graf Kageneck had done his best to prevent happened just before "Citadel." The three companies of his battalion were allocated to different divisions. The anticipated concentrated force of an entire Tiger battalion was frittered away.

Assigned to the 7th Panzer Division, the 1st Company rolled forward early on the morning of 5 July. The bridge over the Donets that had been erected by the engineers had been hit earlier by Russian artillery fire and it was not until the afternoon that the company was able to cross. Once they had crossed the river the tanks advanced, and after clearing the Russian antitank ditches they drove into the enemy's open flank.

The Tigers were supposed to carry the attack to the enemy in order to cover the flank of the 7th Panzer Division. The 7th Panzer Division was deployed as part of Armeeabteilung Kempf on the southern flank of the operation, the objective of which was to pinch off the Russian salient near Kursk, destroy the enemy forces inside and shorten the front by approximately 200 kilometers. The battle became a bitter struggle in which the Red Army finally won the upper hand when Hitler called off the offensive (because of the Allied landings in Sicily).

On the third day of the attack only four of the 1st Company's twelve vehicles were still serviceable. Even the company commander's tank had been hit by a Soviet artillery shell during a rest break. The crew, who were standing behind the tank, were all wounded. "Pan" Vogel and Uffz. Lochmann were both wounded in the buttocks and were sent straight from the aid station ot a hospital train. But the pair had no intention of leaving the front. Instead they grabbed their things and headed back to Belgorod, and after several days rest they rejoined the company.

The first enemy tank that Knispel got in his sights was a T-34. One shot was sufficient to knock out the enemy vehicle; the 88-mm round easily penetrated the Russian tank's frontal armor. The advance continued, passing through a total of seven villages. Thanks to General Breith the battalion had been reunited and it formed part of a wedge of German armor 40 kilometers wide which drove into the enemy's flank.

The tanks commanded by Rippl and Rubbel, called simply Max and Moritz, drove side by side. On the fourth day of the offensive Kurt Knispel destroyed seven enemy tanks. He fired from on the move as well as from great distances, but the result was the same each time: another enemy tank destroyed. On one occasion they passed a group of 14 Russian tanks heading in the opposite direction. Knispel's tank immediately gave chase. The others were witnesses as Knispel knocked out one tank after another from behind. When three T-34s turned around, they were knocked out by Rubbel's panzer, which was covering Rippl's Tiger.

Each day brought new surprises and successes for Rippl and his crew, whether attacking or simply advancing. In fast drives through enemy-held villages where enemy tanks and antitank guns lurked behind walls and hedges, Knispel was the undisputed king of gunners. It was a unique experience, not just for the Rippl crew, but for Knispel himself: with this gun he was simply unbeatable. They, too, were hit on occasion and more than once the crew had to climb out and take cover from Russian infantry. But each time they got back into their tank and drove on.

The last day of the attack saw more vicious fighting. The panzers moved out at first light. After advancing several kilometers they came upon

After 102 "kills" between spring 1942 and May 1944, Knispel (left) received the German Cross in Gold. Haase is on the right.

an antitank gun position, which was taken out quickly. As they moved on Knispel suddenly spotted a gathering of tanks to the right behind bushes and trees.

"Three o'clock, 800 meters—enemy tanks!"

"How many, Kurt?" called Rippl.

"About ten," replied Knispel.

"Max to Moritz: we have a few tanks for you. Move towards us."

"Motitz to Max," replied Rubbel, "we're coming."

Rippl's driver had already turned the Tiger; the loader held the next armor-piercing round ready and had another in the rack. The first enemy tank drove out of cover, showing its flank. Knispel looked at it for a second to confirm its identity and then called "halt!" The driver stopped, Knispel adjusted his aim then the cannon roared. The T-34's turret was blown off.

"Direct hit!" Rippl shouted to his men. But Knispel and his loader were already set to fire again. Two more shots and two more Russian tanks, which had dared try to sneak past the Tigers, sat knocked out behind the saplings.

"Max to Moritz, we have three."

"Moritz to Max, leave some for us!"

Knispel knocked out two more T-34s and Rubbel's Tiger added two more. The last T-34 turned on its heels and roared towards the rear. As it fled Knispel fired a shot from more than 2,000 meters; the shell found the mark and the Russian tank burst into flames. Rippl and Knispel, a heart and a soul in a tank, fired from every position on this day. They rescued comrades' tanks from desperate situations, brought back stranded crews under fire, and proved equal to any situation.

After eight days as attack spearhead and battering ram, the 503rd Heavy Panzer Battalion was now employed as a mobile fire-brigade. It happened when the neighboring division withdrew and an avalanche of Russian tanks poured into the resulting gap. When Graf Kageneck received the call to once again close a hole, he had just eight Tigers altogether. Among them were the tanks Max and Moritz.

The Tigers at first advanced rapidly through a swampy area. Beyond it lay a gentle, alder-covered slope. The tanks rolled to the top and then they all saw the infantry falling back. Driving through their midst were Russian tanks, firing wildly to all sides and simply running down entire squads of infantry.

"Form up, positions from right to left: First, Second and Third!" ordered the battalion commander.

The 1st Platoon's two tanks opened fire first. As the T-34s reached firing position they were knocked out by the long-ranging guns of the Tigers. Knispel destroyed three of the T-34s. The eight German tanks knocked out a total of twenty T-34s, virtually destroying the Soviet tank unit. The infantry had time to regroup and were reintegrated into the main line of resistance.

On 14 July the battalion reached the Belgorod-Kursk main road with its last ten serviceable Tigers. It was there that the main assault had begun ten days earlier. Now they were back at the same place. Without orders, the Tigers repeatedly drove back into the steppe to free other German units still lagging behind.

Kurt Knispel was always there. Rippl's tank was the only one to get through to a signals unit trapped in a burning village. The Tiger shepherded the unit back while holding the T-34s at bay. Several of the more aggressive Soviet tanks were knocked out.

The last German offensive had failed. It had turned out that the Red Army had also been preparing an offensive and that the many delays and postponements by the German side had given the Soviets the opportunity to shore up their defenses and move in large reserves, which ultimately turned the tide.

The Tiger had proved itself in every role assigned to it. But there were too few of them. The number of Tigers claimed destroyed by the Soviets far exceeded the total number produced to that point. The only Tigers to see action at Kursk were the 503rd Heavy Panzer Battalion in the southern pincer and the 505th Heavy Panzer Battalion in the north. In twelve days of action during the Kursk offensive Rippl and his crew had destroyed twenty-seven enemy tanks. Obergefreiter Knispel had been his gunner for all of these kills. He was awarded the Iron Cross, First Class and soon afterwards was promoted to Unteroffizier.

"Operation Citadel" had also cost the 503rd Heavy Panzer Battalion heavy casualties. Oblt. Scherf, commander of 3rd Company, was wounded and put out of action. Lt. Weinert was killed, and a few days later Lt. Baron von Rosen was wounded. Eleven members of 1st Company died in battle; a number were wounded but stayed with the company. For his successful command of the attack, on 4 August 1943 Hptm. Clemens Graf Kageneck was awarded the Knight's Cross.

Kursk had made Kurt Knispel's name a byword for the battalion and for all of the III Panzer Corps.

Retreat—On the Defensive

The German fighting withdrawal began on 16 July. The Soviets had launched a counteroffensive. From then on the battalion's efforts were primarily aimed at preventing the infantry from being outflanked by enemy tanks. The battalion did not see action as a unit again, instead the indidual companies and platoons were parcelled out to various units.

Once the Fegelein SS-Brigade was overrun by a mass of enemy armor. Uffz. Rubbel led the relief effort, followed closely by Rippl's Tiger with Knispel as gunner. The other tanks were still far behind, beyond radio range. Now and then a shot from a Tiger's "eighty-eight" could be heard in the distance. The two Tigers fought off pursuing enemy tanks.

Then they headed back. The next morning they came to a wooden bridge over a small stream. It looked like it could bear the Tiger's weight. Rubbel drove across, but when the Rippl tank drove onto the bridge it broke through. With the help of the tank that had made it across, the Tiger was pulled free. They drove for days, engaging the enemy frequently. The last two Tigers held off the enemy with their long-ranging "eighty-eight" cannon. There were no more massive enemy attacks; the Red Army was exhausted too. The battalion's actions became more dispersed, but wherever the Tigers appeared in twos and threes the T-34s stayed back. The Russian command had issued orders for its tanks not to engage in duels with the german Tigers.

When Rubbel and Rippl were forced to withdraw to avoid being outflanked, the commander of a regiment accused them of having failed to recover a third tank, which was sitting damaged and stranded in no-man's-land.

"We can't let them say that about us," shouted Knispel furiously. "Even though we didn't leave our tanks in the lurch, we have to recover this one if at all possible."

"You're right, Kurt," agreed Rippl and Rubbel.

The matter was closed. Under heavy fire from enemy antitank guns the two Tigers drove forward 200 meters apart. They fired high-explosive shells while on the move and knocked out several antitank guns, but they could not get to the tank. Shells ricocheted off their turrets. From a range of 1 500 meters Knispel did what he had to do. He destroyed the stranded German tank, which had been abandoned by its crew, to prevent it from falling into enemy hands. When they returned and made their report they were severely criticised by the regiment's commander for the loss of this tank. Rippl and his crew were reprimanded. Once again it was Unteroffizier Knispel, a man who had already destroyed far more than 50 enemy tanks and wore the Panzer Assault Badge in Silver, who spoke up in their defense: "I wish to inform the Oberst that this tank was abandoned by its own crew and not by us. We tried everything to get it back. This proved impossible and could only have ended with the loss of our two Tigers. We therefore had to destroy it to prevent the Russians from using it."

Somewhat placated, the Oberst said, "Very well, you are dismissed."

When the two crews had left, the regiment commander turned to his adjutant and asked, "Who was the dark-haired Unteroffizier with the Iron Cross, First Class?"

"That was Knispel of the 503rd Heavy Panzer Battalion, sir," replied the Oberleutnant.

"Damned fellow, he embarassed the hell out of me. With a mouth like that, he must be a Berliner."

"No, sir, Knispel comes from East Sudetenland."

"Forget it, it doesn't matter. But that fellow impressed the hell out of me!"

There were no more accusations and the two tanks finally succeeded in getting the infantry out of their miserable situation.

As there was no range-measuring device in the Tiger (nor in any German tanks) the distance to the target always had to be estimated. A shot could only be on target if the range was estimated precisely. At this Knispel was a master. Once he and his tank were sitting at an antitank ditch when someone called out: "Tanks from the left!"

About 3,000 meters away two tanks had rolled out of a wood. They were Churchill Iis. The armor on the front of these tanks was 100 mm thick. Before anyone else could react, Knispel opened fire and after the second shot the first Churchill went up in flames. During this engagement, which lasted only a few seconds, the second enemy tank was able to drive back into the forest.

During the fierce fighting withdrawal from July to September 1943 there was another situation which was typical Knispel. Two of the First's tanks had been assigned to infantry units withdrawing on foot. Both tanks took up position in the rear to prevent the infantry units from being overtaken by forces.

It was a hot day. In addition to the infantry, all civilians were supposed to be transported out of the evacuated area with their cattle. It became a huge column, and the two Tigers were obliged to slow their pace to match its. The troops had been instructed to march to the village of Osswetz and secure it. During the evening the sound of tracks was heard. The infantry went into position and the two Tigers drove into the ditches on either side of the very broad road. An hour earlier the two Tigers of the First had been joined by a third Tiger. When the sound of Russian deisel engines was finally heard it was already dark. The third commander was certain that the noise was coming from a German prime mover.

"We should fire signal flares so they don't miss us," he declared.

"Keep your finger off the trigger, they're Russians," warned Feldwebel Rubbel.

"Nonsense, it's one of our prime movers," the commander declared forcefully and he bagen waving a lit flashlight to identify the tanks' position.

"He's out of his mind. Get into the tank!" said Rippl. They climbed in. "Prepare to fire!" The two Tigers were ready for combat in seconds. The third Tiger continued to flash signals in the direction of the enemy.

"Stop, you idiot!" the other two commanders shouted from their open turret hatches. The sound of deisel engines moved straight towards them. The rattle of tracks became very clear and they obviously belonged to T-34s.

Rubbel's tank was right of the road, while Rippl had taken up position in the ditch to the left. The two commanders were still standing in their turret hatches, trying to see through the rising fog. The third commander

The loader in a Tiger gets ready to ram home an 88mm round.

continued to flash his signals. The crews of the Tigers had developed a special tactic for night fighting. Since vision through binoculars was limited at night and was even worse through through the gunner's sight, all observations were made with the naked eye, as this gave the best results.

Flare pistols with illumination rounds were carried in each tank to ensure a safe and illuminated field of fire. While the gunner took rough aim at the enemy based on the sounds, the two commanders each fired a green flare, as a white would have been too blinding. The two flares climbed into the night sky at 45 degrees, the best way of illuminating the terrain at night. In their light Knispel immediately spotted a T-34. He aimed and fired. Rubbel's Tiger fired fractions of a second later. Two T-34s went up in flames.

"Our Russian guide, the commander of the third vehicle Uffz. Tesmer, did not fire. Instead, in return for his unwitting aid to the Russians he was hit by a third T-34.

"Fortunately for him the 76.2-mm round did not penetrate but instead bounced off—even at that close range."

The third T-34 had moved off to the side. Seconds later a group of about twelve Russian tanks opened fire. As they moved forward they became silhouetted in the light of the blazing tanks. The Tigers opened fire again. Knispel destroyed another T-34 and when it was over eight Russian tanks had been knocked out and were on fire. Even though he had been late, but fortunately not too late, Uffz. Tesmer recognized the enemy and destroyed one of the T-34s.

The enemy tanks withdrew and finally the engine sounds from the "prime movers" died away. The infantry unit, which had gone into position, was able to go back to sleep apart from sentries. During the subsequent withdrawal Knispel's tank suffered a breakdown. Three or four of the twelve cylinders in the Tiger's engine overheated and had to be replaced. The spark plugs were removed. The cylinder pressure had forced out the cooling water and this had to be replaced. One hour later the tank continued on its way.

The conclusion of the retreat consisted of crossing the Dniepr River over the assigned bridges. 1st Company's last two tanks, Max and Moritz, drove north and reached Kremenchug. The bridgehead on the east side of the river was still held by German troops. There was no way for the two Tigers to cross the sixty-ton bridge (a railway bridge) because there was no raodway beside the tracks. Several rail cars were brought in, the tanks rolled up a hastily-fabricated ramp and were secured on the cars. The rail car bearing Rippl's Tiger was pushed across the bridge first. Knispel watched skeptically, but he assured himself that if the bridge could bear a 100-ton locomotive it would not collapse under a sixty-ton tank.

By this time Knispel had destroyed more than sixty enemy tanks during "Citadel" and another twelve in the period before it (as well as a number that were not confirmed). Consequently he easily met the requirements for the third (Gold) level of the Tank Battle Badge, which was now awarded to him. During this six-week period, however, the participating Tigers of 1st Company, 503rd Heavy Panzer Battalion were only credited with 12 days of tank combat. This shortcoming was the result of the award conditions. For a day of combat to be recognized as a tank combat day by the battalion command, at least one of the battalion's companies had to be involved. What counted was not contact with the enemy but combat with the enemy. If only a few of the battalion's tanks were committed with another unit, as was the case here with the 1st Company, it was not counted as a tank combat day even if enemy tanks had been destroyed. While this was certainly unfair, it was in keeping with the regulations. Looking back, Oberst Alfred Rubbel was convinced that Knispel must have taken part in at least 300 tank battles.

Snamenka was reached at the end of September 1943. The battalion was reunited. New Tigers arrived at the front along with replacement personnel who were integrated into the battalion. From there the unit moved into the Kiev area. The Red Army had launched a major offensive their in an attempt to retake this important city, which in 1941 had been the scene of a major battle of encirclement in which the Soviets suffered huge losses.

The defensive battle lasted until the end of 1943. It was a hard-fought small war in mud and filth and finally in ice and snow, often in completely uncertain situations. The battalion had still not been brought completely back up to its former strength. It was short on personnel and, more importantly, Tiger tanks.

The battle in Army Group South's area that broke out at the beginning of 1944 saw a confrontation with the Red Army in the southern Ukraine west of Kiev. It was a fierce struggle in which the Tigers of 503rd Heavy Panzer Battalion were in action repeatedly. The battle lasted from the start of the new year until 18 January 1944.

Kurt Knispel continued his success in this new sector. Large numbers of enemy tanks fell prey to his well-aimed shots. Thanks to his commander Rippl, Knispel was able to take the initiative, for he had been given permission to fire at his discretion without first receiving confirmation from the tank commander. That is what distinguished this tank crew; they reacted as the situation warranted without insisting on conventions of rank or the chain of command.

Following the start of a short breathing space after reaching Snamenka, the battered 1st Company, like the battalion's other companies, hoped that it would be sent on leave. Those hopes were unfounded and it would be April 1944 before the company went home. In between lay months of fierce fighting in snow and mud against an enemy growing stronger almost daily.

During January 1944 the tanks of the 503rd Heavy Panzer Battalion were placed under the command of the heavy panzer regiment formed by Oberstleutnant Dr. Franz Bäke, the commander of the Westphalian 11th Panzer Regiment. Bäke had first become noticed during "Citadel" when he was commander of the regiment's II Battalion. After he was made commander of the 11th Panzer Regiment in mid-January 1944, his first order was to form "Panzer Group Bäke" and stop the enemy forces that had advanced east of Vinnitsa, encircle and destroy them. Ther 503rd Heavy Panzer Battalion was sent to join the new battle group with its 34 Tiger tanks. In the battle against a Russian tank corps Bäke's force would destroy 267 enemy tanks in five days.

Bäke's unit was subsequently redirected to open the recently formed pocket at Cherkassy. In a few days of fighting the battle group's panzers destroyed 80, then 30, then 20 enemy tanks. As the spearhead of Battle Group Bäke the 503rd Heavy Panzer Battalion got to within eight kilometers of the encircled German forces and helped make it possible for them to break out. For this action Bäke was awarded the Swords and received a commendation from General der Panzertruppe Hube, commander in chief of the 1st Panzer Army.

Kurt Knispel performed tremendous feats in these bitter battles. He and his comrades fought without pause against the numerically superior armored forces of the enemy. What was at stake was nothing less than the survival of Army Group South.

In the months that followed his receipt of the Iron Cross, First Class Kurt Knispel destroyed no less eighty enemy tanks. His name became well known to the infantry, for whom the panzers were often the last hope of survival. Knispel surpassed every other panzer soldier on the Eastern Front in the way he destroyed enemy tanks.

On 10 February 1944 the battalion's remaining eighteen Tigers reached Schubennyj. Hptm. Scherf, who had taken over the battalion after its previous commander was wounded, reported to Oberstleutnant Bäke. The heavy battalion had been divided into four groups, which were commanded by:

1st Group:	Lt. Rondorf
2nd Group:	Obfw. And der Heiden
3rd Group:	Obfw. Fendesack
4th Group:	Obfw. Sachs

The battalion's supply base was taken over by Lt. J.J. Haß. Battalion medical officers were Oberarzt Dr. Karl Schramm and Assistenzarzt Dr. Bürg.

The order issued by Dr. Bäke on 10 February read:

> Together with the 16th Panzer Division, the regiment will attack the village of Frankovka on the Gniloy River across Hill 239 southeast of Bosovka. It is to take the village and the bridge there as well as the fording site across the Gniloy Tikich and capture the

higher ground northeast of Frankovka and establish a line of security there.

The direction of attack was changed by III Panzer Corps, to which the battle group was subordinated. At the same time the corps' panzer divisions under General Breith attacked in the same direction and covered the flank.

The corps order stated: "The next objective is the Medwin-Lysyanka-Chesnovka-Chizhintsy crossroad. Start of attack: 11 February 1944, 6:30 A.M."

Oberstleutnant Bäke showed the commanders of the Tiger and Panther battalions and the commander of the infantry battalion an aerial photo of the area. The bridges and the fording site were clearly visible. Then he said: "We have to make sure that we cross the Gniloy-Tikich on the first day and while it is still light. It will be much more difficult if we become bogged down at night before reaching it. If that happens we may lose valuable days."

RELIEF ATTACK ON THE CHERKASSY POCKET

The Battle from the 503rd Heavy Panzer Battalion's Perspective

"Ready for battle, move out!"

This radio message from Oberstleutnant Bäke set the relief force, including the 18 Tigers of the 503rd Heavy Panzer Battalion, in motion. At first they made rapid progress. On the Bosovka-Frankovka-Bushanka road, just short of Hill 239, they encountered twelve T-34s and three antitank guns.

The panzers closed in. Knispel's first two shots, high-explosive rounds, were aimed at the antitank guns, which were knocked out within thirty seconds. Then the loader switched to armor-piercing ammunition. Knispel knocked out the first T-34 from a distance of approximately 1,800 meters, even before the Tiger was within range of the Soviet tank's gun. All of the German tanks opened fire and soon seven of the enemy tanks had been destroyed, including a second by Knispel. The survivors turned and fled in the direction of Frankovka.

"Man, Kurt, that went like lightning," declared the commander of the third group, Oberfeldwebel Fendesack.

"One does what one can," replied Knispel. The Tigers loaded high-explosive rounds again and drove on, expecting a wave of enemy tanks to break from cover or for a concealed antitank gun to open fire at any second. But the Tigers advanced another two kilometers without contacting the enemy.

When the Bushanka road came into sight, Knispel instinctively knew where the enemy would be: "Ahead to the right, moving to the left, about ten enemy tanks, range 1,500!"

The Tigers, which had just taken up position there in preparation for a move on more distant Frankovka, opened fire. It was just like target practice, for the T-34s were driving down the road in single file instead of using the cover of the treed, snow-covered terrain. All four Tigers fired almost simultaneously. Once agin Knispel's aim was good. The T-34 he had selected literally blew apart when its ammunition exploded. The enemy had no opportunity to return fire; every one of the T-34s was destroyed.

While the battle was raging Knispel saw the next tank being fired on by two T-34s, which hit the Tiger in the tracks. He rotated the turret and opened fire. The first shot grazed the enemy tank, the second was a direct hit. The other T-34 turned and tried to escape, but it, too, was hit and knocked out.

Eleven T-34s were destroyed in this engagement. A brief rest stop followed, during which Dr. Bäke consulted with the 16th Panzer Division. He then instructed the Tigers to take up a covering position just beyond Hill 243 and from there place targets in and around Frankovka under fire and as well keep an eye on the slope beyond the village. Hauptmann Scherf despatched the Tigers to the specified position.

In the meantime the Panther battalions of the Bäke Regiment and of the 16th Panzer Division had advanced rapidly toward Frankovka with the infantry riding on the tanks. They siezed the village and the bridge then

A King Tiger during field gunnery exercises.

secured the area. Moments later the order "Ready for battle, move out!" was issued for the second time.

Following Hptm. Scherf's instructions, the tanks of the Tiger had laid out four to six armor-piercing and high-explosive shells. When the order to open fire came, all of the Tigers, which were in a widely spaced formation, fired at the outskirts of the village and the houses beyond with high-explosive shells. When tanks from the village appeared on the slope beyond, they were fired on with armor-piercing shells. Each tank had allocated fifteen armor-piercing rounds for this purpose. This supporting fire from the Tigers eased the task of the assault group. By noon Frankovka and its bridge were in German hands.

From Hill 243 Hptm. Scherf sent a radio message to Lt. Haß, who immediately lead the four recovery vehicles of Battle Train I and the motorcycle reconnaissance platoon to Frankovka, which they occupied as their new base of operations. When Lt. Haß arrived with the train the tanks were immediately refueled and rearmed. Afterwards the Tigers crossed the Gniloy-Tikich one after the other. The four vehicles stationed behind the hill were the last to arrive and as darkness was falling they, together with the regiment's Panther battalion, took up covering positions on the hill north of Frankovka. The corps immediately requested aerial reconnaissance, which revealed that there was a strong Russian blocking force in a shallow ravine about 3 kilometers northeast of Frankovka. A quick count revealed 80 tanks and 50 antitank guns.

The attack was resumed at 8 A.M. the next morning. The tanks of the 16th and 17th Panzer Divisions very soon became involved in the first battle with T-34s, which sortied from Dashulkovka. The panzers moved into a wedge formation and waited for a promised bombing attack by Stukas. The Tigers of the 503rd Heavy Panzer Battalion were approximately 600 meters in front of a shallow rise when Oberstleutnant Bäke gave them the following order: "503: attack frontally, the Panther battalion simultaneous flanking attack from the right. Wait for the Stuka attack. Just one squadron coming!"

The four Tigers were assigned their attack lanes and recived the order to remove armor-piercing and high-explosive shells from the storage racks in preparation for firing. They would attack as soon as the Stukas had dropped their bombs in order to exploit the resulting condusion among the enemy. When the Stukas arrived and dropped their bombs, the Soviet tank commander, contrary to his plan to let the Germans approach, immediately ordered his tanks to move forward and attack. The first wave of T-34s appeared over the crest of the hill, followed closely by a second. Both headed straight toward where the Tigers were waiting to attack.

The Bäke Regiment was immediately able to open fire along its entire width. The approaching force of thirty T-34s was almost completely wiped out. Kurt Knispel knocked out two of the attackers. Once again he had been one of the first to sight the enemy and open fire. The few survivors drove back up the hill and disappeared into the valley beyond. When the last Stukas had flown away Hptm. Scherf gave the order to attack. Firing their cannon and machine-guns, the tanks of the 503rd Heavy Panzer Battalion rolled up the hill and from there opened fire on the valley, which was jammed with enemy forces.

Antitank guns and T-34s opened fire on the Tigers from the Soviet positions on the left flank. As well, T-34s fired at the Tigers from the opposite slope, approximately 900 meters distant, and put several out of action. Four Tigers were written off as total losses during this attack, while a fifth was put out of action when it took a hit in the driver's visor. The tank was able to leave the battle zone under its own power, however two members of the crew eere dead and the rest wounded.

In following up behind the retreating T-34s, Kurt Knispel spotted one enemy tank which was in a previously invisible hiding place. The muzzle of the tank's gun was just visible. Knispel aimed about one meter higher and fired. There was a loud explosion and the gun barrel jerked upwards; he had obviously found the mark.

The Russian tank corps deployed there lost almost its entire complement of vehicles. A total of seventy Soviet tanks were destroyed as well as all fifty antitank guns, most of which fell victim to the Stuka raid. What the German tanks were lacking now was fuel and ammunition. A radio message to III Panzer Corps requesting an air drop of supplies met with the response: "Reply to follow." The Bäke regiment formed a hedgehog position 1.5 kilometers south of Chesnovka.

The battle continued in the days that followed. Bäke's armored force was unable to force a breakthrough to the trapped German divisions at Cherkassy matter how hard it tried. On 13 February a force of fifteen T-34s attacked the village of Chishinzy. Stationed there were the Tigers commanded by Lt. Rondorf and Uffz. Gärtner. They reported: "Enemy tanks with mounted infantry!"

The two Tigers opened fire from a range of 1 500 meters and knocked out four T-34s with their first volley. Seven more were fired on from 1 000 meters and were destroyed one after another. On 20 May 1944 Rondorf received the German Cross in Gold while Heinz Gärtner was awarded the decoration one month later.

On the afternoon of 13 February Ju 52 transports swooped low over German-held territory behind the security front and dropped canisters of fuel, ammunition and gasoline hand pumps. Everything was recovered, nothing was lost. Especially valuable to the tanks were the canisters of fuel and ammunition for their cannon, but the drop also included motor oil, machine-gun ammunition, hand grenades and flare pistols.

On 14 February the 503rd Heavy Panzer Battalion advanced in two columns toward Dzhurzhentsy. An antitank gun position was taken out by four Tigers. During the night the Tigers' position was attacked by T-34s, which were not spotted until their glowing red exhausts were spotted. Eight Tigers were ready to fire, among them Fendesack's tank with Knispel as gunner. Five enemy tanks were destroyed, one of which was credited to Knispel.

The next morning, the 15th of February, Oberstleutnant Bäke's command post called Hptm. Scherf recommending "maximum caution and readiness." At 8:15 A.M. instead of the expected Russians, General Breith, commanding general of III Panzer Corps, and Generalmajor Back, commander of the 16th Panzer Division, arrived at the regiment's command post. They had flown in in two Fieseler "Storks." A short time later the 503rd Heavy Panzer Battalion took up position in the direction of a reported enemy tank formation. One Tiger was knocked out in the ensuing engagement with T-34s. Four T-34s were destroyed in return.

Heavy Panzer Regiment Bäke subsequently launched the decisive attack in the attempt to break through to the units surrounded at Cherkassy. When fendesack turned toward Dzhurzhentsy at high speed his Tiger was hit in the rear. The engine caught fire and Fendesack gave the order to abandon the tank. After everyone had got out, heat from the fire detonated the Tiger's ammunition. The attempted breakthrough failed, just eight kilometers from its goal.

The attack was supposed to be repeated at 4 A.M. on 17 February. But then the forward Tiger, commanded by Fw. Sachs, fired two white flares. Then the infantry next to Sachs fired white flares. Several more were fired by the forward outposts. It was men from the pocket who had risked a final breakout from the pocket. Many were wounded, exhausted. The sight brought tears to the eyes of the tank crews.

The men who had escaped the pocket surrounded the Tigers and shook hands with the crews. They were given cigarettes and chocolate. Approximately 600 men, who made up the first group, passed by the Tigers. They were followed at approximately 5:30 A.M. by a second group of about 500 men. Further small groups continued to straggle in until evening came.

The Tigers lashed out at the purusing enemy. More groups of german soldiers continued to arrive and it was not until midnight on 18 February that the Bäke regiment withdrew to the west. The operation to relieve the men trapped in the Cherkassy pocket was over.

The German Cross in Gold for Kurt Knispel

After the conclusion of these operations the 503rd Heavy Panzer Battalion was pulled back in a fighting withdrawal from Cherkassy via Vinnitsa to Jampol and from there to Kamenets-Podolsk. During these battles Fendesack's crew, especially his gunner Kurt Knispel, distinguished themselves in defeating Russian attacks and outflanking attempts. On 23 February 1944 Oblt. Walter Scherf, who led the 503rd, was awarded the Knight's Cross for these actions.

Scherf had himself recommended Kurt Knispel for the Knight's Cross, for the latter had roughly twice as many kills as required for a tank gunner to receive the decoration. However, the recommendation did not win approval. Such was not the case with the German Cross in Gold, for which Knispel was recommended together with Lt. Rondorf. The decoration was in fact long overdue, as Knispel's actions could have won him the German Cross in Gold three times over. He had far surpassed the successes of all the tank gunners who had already received the Knight's Cross and there was no way of knowing how far he would go.

Knispel received the German Cross in Gold on 20 May 1944. Soon afterward he was promoted to Feldwebel for demonstrated bravery in the face of the enemy. As the third member of the 503rd Heavy Panzer Battalion to win the German Cross in Gold he was one of the outstanding soldiers not just of the battalion but of the entire panzer arm. Knispel had been recommended several times for the Knight's Cross, but certain imponderables always stood in the way. Its is known that Oberstleutnant Dr. Franz Bäke also submitted a proposal for the awarding of the Knight's Cross to Knispel; as he put it: "If anyone in my unit deserves the Knight's Cross one hundred percent, then it is Knispel."

Based on a report by Dr. Bäke, on 25 April 1944 the Wehrmacht communique declared: "Unteroffizier Knispel, a member of a heavy panzer battalion in the east, destroyed 101 enemy tanks during the period July 1942 to March 1943." This figure did not include the twelve tanks in whose destruction he had previously played a part as loader and gunner.

On 4 May 1944 the last member of the 503rd Heavy Panzer Battalion left the Eastern Front to return to Germany. The unit arrived in Paderborn early on 9 May. From there it was transferred to the Ohrdruf training ground, where the battalion was to rest and refit.

There was great joy when the first Tiger II, the *Königstiger* (King Tiger), arrived there on 14 May. Knispel immediately took his place as gunner. By now Oblt. Oehmer had assumed command again. The next evening there was big dinner in the mess. Among those who came to honour the 503rd Heavy Panzer Battalion were Generaloberst Heinz Guderian, Generalmajor Thomale, his chief-of-staff, two officers with the rank of Oberst and four Majore from the OKH formation staff. It was a fantastic party. The next day saw the beginning of adjustment fire with the 88-mm L/71 tank cannon. This weapon and its heavy armor made the Tiger II a mobile fortress. The 503rd Heavy Panzer Battalion was the first army battalion to equip with the new Tiger.

During his stay in germany Knispel paid several visits to his friend Alfred Rubbel in hospital. On each occasion they drank a bottle of red wine which Knispel always managed to procure somehow.

THE ALLIED INVASION OF FRANCE

The battalion completed reequipping with its new tanks several days after the start of the invasion, and it was transferred to western France, which had become a combat zone on 6 June 1944. The tanks had to detrain in Dreux, approximately eighty kilometers west of Paris. The King Tigers required four nights to cover the last 200 kilometers. Travel by day was out of the question on account of the enemy's total command of the air. A series of engine fires caused a number of the battalion's tanks to be lost. On 8 July it departed the Dreux forest for the Caen area.

Early on 11 July the battalion was placed on alert. British tanks had broken through. Knispel went into action as gunner in platoon commander Fendesack's Tiger. The 3rd Company destroyed a total of eleven enemy tanks. Knispel's share of the success that day was two tanks knocked out. The battle went on. On 30 July the battalion was forced to fall back toward St. Lô.

The battalion halted in the St. Pierre area, where it remained until the position was outflanked by british units. On 14 August the unit suffered casualties in a series of attacks by rocket-firing fighter-bombers. Obfw. Fendesack's tank was hit in the third attack. Kurt Knispel pulled his badly wounded friend and comrade in arms for four years. However, his injuries were such that Hans Fendesack died on 15 August 1944.

The next night in Ticheville French partisans surrounded the cellar in which the men had taken shelter. Knispel was among those who picked up his weapon and helped shoot the way clear. The same day tank 124 broke down and on 18 August tanks 113, 111, 100, and 122 had to be blown up inside the pocket. On 20 August two of the last King Tigers had to be blown up and the crews began the retreat on foot. Kurt Knispel climbed into the last King Tiger, this time as commander, More than once he saved the vehicle and crew from destruction. He often knocked out the enemy's point tanks from long range, from which his King Tiger was not even visible.

"Knispel's name was on everyone's lips. He was the wonder of the panzer arm."

At the end of August the battalion had to return to Germany. The many bombardments and the enemy's tremendous superiority in tank and infantry divisions had won the day. The loss of St. Lô and of many soldiers in the pocket there meant that the battle in Normandy had been lost. Following the conclusion of these battles Lt. Lochmann and Feldwebel Knispel were the only members of the who had never been wounded.

The battalion was assembled in the Paderborn area at the beginning of September. The 1st Company moved into Bentfeld, the 2nd Company into Eilsen and the 3rd Company into Hövelhof. From there Kurt Knispel, now highly decorated, went home on leave one last time.

The companies were brought up to strength. Replacements came from the 500th Panzer Replacement Training Battalion based at Paderborn. From 19 to 22 September the battalion received a complete complement of 45 new Tiger IIs. Familiariation of the newcomers, breaking-in of the new tanks and other necessary preparations lasted until 8 October. On that day the battalion entrained in pouring rain. The trains headed east to Hungary and Budapest was reached on 14 October. 1st Company moved into the Sconemedi area. Energetic German intervention temporarily prevented Hungary from leaving the alliance.

Knispel carried out the next missions with his comrade and friend Lt. Rubbel. They achieved a series of successes, but then Rubbel's tank was knocked out by an enemy tank and he was wounded for the fourth time. Rubbel remained with the unit and was named operations officer. Rubbel remembered:

> It was there that I saw Hptm. von Dienst-Körber hug our Knispel, who had just destroyed his 126th enemy tank and who had come to report, and say with emotion in his voice: "Knispel, if I had the Knight's Cross I would give it to you here and now on the spot!"
>
> "Thank you, sir," answered Knispel and one could sense the joy in this recognition from a respected commander. "But it is not the Knight's Cross that makes a soldier but his actions."
>
> "That is true, Knispel, but nevertheless: honors to those who deserve them! You have earned the Knight's Cross three times over and I will see to it that you receive it!"
>
> The application was filled out immediately and sent to the *Feldherrnhalle* Panzer Corps, to which the 503rd Heavy Panzer Battal-

ion had been subordinated and disappeared somewhere in the maze of paperwork. However several days after this request was submitted the corps' Second General Staff Officer came to the battalion. Feldwebel Kurt Knispel was brought to him and gave his smartest salute.

"Feldwebel Knispel, I congratulate you on this success, which is unique in the panzer arm, and wish you continued luck. You can be assured that I will do everything to see to it that you receive the decoration you so richly deserve."

"Thank you, sir, I will take your statement for the deed."

At first the Oberstleutnant was taken aback. When he looked questioningly at the battalion commander the latter explained: "Knispel has already been promised the Knight's Cross several times, however he has never received it."

And he was never to receive it, even though his actions as a tank commander alone were worthy of the decoration; while commanding a King Tiger he destroyed forty-two enemy tanks and a large number of antitank guns and artillery pieces. Kurt Knispel was the prototype of the tough, successful soldier. He was less concerned with general discipline and that "thwarted many of his plans." It must be said, however, that personal resentments toward this soldier should never have prevented him from being decorated with the Knight's Cross.

If this soldier is given a special place in this book, it is because there never was a German soldier like Knispel, the man from the Altvater Mountains. Any other nation on earth would have counted itself lucky to have such an uncompromising fighter in its armed forces. But back to the events in Hungary.

Knispel's good luck, which had never failed him, held true in the fighting between the Theiß and Danube Rivers. Always in the thick of things, it seemed a miracle to everyone in the battalion that he had never been wounded. Under the command of Hptm. Fromme, on 21 October the 503rd Heavy Panzer Battalion's 1st Company rolled through Mezötur in heavy street fighting. Knispel knocked out three antitank guns and a T-34. Then the attack was broken off. On 22 October the battalion attacked near Törökszentmiklos. The 3rd Company led the way with five tanks. Behind it came the 1st. During this action Lt. Fürbringer ended up behind a Russian antitank front and was fired on from all sides, but he nevertheless brought his battered Tiger back with twenty-four serious hits.

At the end of October the battalion assembled in Cegled. Beginning on 1 November it saw action between Cegled and Kekskemet. The fighting on this day saw the first appearance of the new Josef Stalin tank armed with a 122-mm gun; these, too, were destroyed by the King Tigers. During the days and weeks that followed Fw. Knispel scored further successes against Russian tanks. In some cases his kills were made from maximum range, up to 3,000 meters. His kill list grew longer and longer and everyone agreed that Knispel would soon reach the offically-recognized figure of 200 enemy tanks destroyed.

Hptm. Fromme had to leave the battalion in mid-December. Hptm. von Dienst-Körber assumed command of the battalion, which at that time was in the Lake Balaton area. The battalion was in the forefront of the effort to eliminate the dangerous Russian bridgehead across the Gran River. On one occasion Knispel charged into the bridgehead and destroyed several antitank guns, an infantry position and three tanks before moving aside and making room for the following panzer-grenadiers.

Initially subordinated to the *Feldherrnhalle* Panzer Corps, on orders of the OKH, on 19 December 1944 the 503rd Heavy Panzer Battalion was incorporated into that corps. Officially it became the "Heavy Panzer Battalion *Feldherrnhalle*," but no one called it that. It continued to be the 503rd Heavy Panzer Battalion as before. Here the battalion was reunited with Dr. Bäke, who had been appointed commander of the *Feldherrnhalle 2* Panzer Division.

On 9 January 1945 the battalion carried out an attack as part of the 23rd Panzer Division. Lt. Piepgras led the four tanks of the 1st Company. Seven enemy tanks were destroyed in combat, two of which were credited to Knispel. At the end of January in the middle of a heavy snowstorm, the Tigers were sent against enemy tanks which had broken through. Fifty enemy tanks were reported south of Gyula on 1 February. The three available Tigers under Lt. Piepgras stopped the enemy. After knocking out an enemy tank, the battalion commander's Tiger became the target of about 20 more T-34s. Hit several times in the running gear, the Tiger was disabled. Under fire Hptm. von Diest-Körber left the tank and removed a shot-up roadwheel which was jammed in the track, after which the tank was able to drive on. Lt. Otto Beyer of 2nd Company, Heavy Panzer Battalion "Feldherrnhalle" won the German Cross in Gold here. A total of 17 enemy tanks and assault guns were knocked out on this day. Three were credited to Knispel.

On 13 February 1945 the battalion moved to Csuz, where it rested for several days. Knispel procured some wine and there was a party. Not until 17 February did the battalion move into the area north of Kürt. Several tanks had returned after being repaired, raising the battalion's strength to 22 Tigers. Enemy antitank guns and mines caused the first casualties.

Hptm. von Diest-Körber was wounded while crossing enemy antitank ditches. Lt. Heerlein took over command of the battalion temporarily. The commander of the supply company, Hptm. Wiegand, immediately drove forward and assumed command of the battalion. The night attack that had been started was brought to a successful conclusion; the entire Gran bridgehead was evacuated by the Russians.

At the end of March 1945 von Diest-Körber returned from hospital, contrary to doctor's orders. It was the sart of a terrible muddy period. The battalion moved into quarters in Csuz. On 7 March the battalion had moved to Verebely, 15 kilometers behind the main line of resistance. Several limited attacks were carried out from there. On the evening of 22 March the 1st Company threw a wild party. Kurt Knispel was one of the happiest. His optimism was infectious. It was like the old days, and no one who didn't know him would have guessed that the young man in their midst was the most successful tank killer in the German Army.

Three days later began the Russian offensive all along the Gran front. The Russians succeeded in crossing the Gran at several places and establishing bridgeheads. During the night of 27 March Lt. Führlinger was killed by fragments from an exploding artillery shell in Verebely. The Tigers, which had been very successful, especially on 29 March, were the last to be withdrawn from their positions near Neutra. The last eight to ten Tigers established a blocking position near Bab Castle. The fighting continued as the German forces withdrew in steps, lasting until 13 April.

On 15 April the battalion was sent into the 357th Infantry Division's area in order to help the division establish a new defense front. On 19 April there were several sharp engagements with waves of Soviet tanks attempting to outflank the German positions. It was there that Kurt Knispel experienced something like his swansong, for he accounted for four of the thirteen enemy tanks destroyed. The fighting intensified on 21 April and Knispel knocked out four tanks and tree antitank guns. His was one of the five Tigers that the battalion was able to field. Then the small battle group was joined by three Tigers from the workshops. An entire Russian armored group with mounted infantry broke through the front, resulting in one of the last big armored engagements of the war. Ten enemy tanks were knocked out in front of a dairy farm. Then the panzers counterattacked, led by Knispel in his Tiger II. He approached a small group of enemy tanks and destroyed three. Following this smashing success the panzers assembled in Laa. Lt. Linkenbach had been seriously wounded and was put up for the Knight's Cross.

From Zingendorf, site of the battalion command post, the unit moved to Wostitz on 26 April. The next day saw a resumption of heavy fighting, which lasted until 30 April. Six enemy tanks were destroyed. According to a member of Knispel's crew, on 29 April 1945 he destroyed his 168th and last enemy tank. He was then attacked by several enemy tanks and was killed. Fw. Skoda, who had rushed to Knispel's aid, was also killed. The invulnerable Feldwebel Knispel was no more. An unsurpassed fighter had paid for his final action with his life.

"Our lives were made empty by this loss. We often thought we heard his voice on the radio, summoning the tanks of his platoon and leading his daring missions as he did in the past."

One of the best soldiers in the German Army and at the same time one of the least known had met his end after an unparalleled run of success. There was no one who even came close to him. The fact that he never received the highest German decoration proves that bravery was not the most important factor in winning the Knight's Cross, but that having the right superior who was prepared to push for the awarding of the decoration counted for more.

Nevertheless, all those who knew Kurt Knispel knew that he was a born fighter and that he had the necessary personal tools to convert these into success. In addition to his natural skills he was blessed with never failing courage, he was oblivious to danger and was always ready to help. If this work succeeds in bringing some degree of recognition to Kurt Knispel the man, the soldier and the fighter, then it will have achieved its purpose.

Johannes Kümmel, the "Lion of Cupuzzo."

Johannes Kümmel

FORCED MARCH THROUGH THE DESERT

The door to the quarters was thrown open. The regimental adjutant came rushing in. The man who was stretched out on the field cot sat up. He yawned and then rose from the cot.

"What is it?" he asked. "Has peace broken out?"

"Afraid not, Hans, but the commander wants to see all officers in exactly five minutes. In the big lecture room."

"What is it? New mission? The Balkans?" asked the officer, who was already washing the sleep from his eyes while the adjutant still stood in the door.

"Close. We're going to Africa. The commander will tell you all the rest."

Hauptmann Hans Kümmel, commander of the 8th Panzer Regiment's 1st Company, pulled on his tunic. The Iron Cross, First Class hung on the left breast. In the buttonhole was the ribbon of the Iron Cross, Second Class and beneath it the Panzer Assault Badge. The officer took a quick look in the mirror. Everything OK? One didn't want to stand out in front of the new regiment commander. He left the quarters and walked over to the lecture room. When he opened the door he could tell by the buzz of voices that many of his comrades were already there.

Kümmel walked over to the men of his battalion. "Hello, Hans, have you heard? Our days in Heidelberg are numbered."

The thirty-one-year-old officer with the two stars on his shoulderboards shrugged his shoulders. A change of quartering areas was common in war. From the luxurious surroundings of Paris, where the headquarters of the 8th Panzer Regiment had settled after the French campaign, the battalions of the regiment had gradually moved into the Dijon area. It was there that Oberstleutnant Cramer had joined them to familiarize himself with the regiment he was to command.

Then the voice of the adjutant rang out above the babble of voices: "The regimental commanding officer!"

It became still. The commander stepped inside. He was of medium height, with a wiry build and piercing eyes. Even in the black uniform of the panzer troops he could not conceal his cavalry origins. Cramer spoke:

> Gentlemen, the 15th Panzer Division has been chosen to go to Africa. It will form the second leg of the German Africa Corps. The first leg is already there. It is the 5th Light Division under Generalmajor Streich. We are forming a blocking unit to support the Italians.
>
> Preparations are under way. The division headquarters is leaving tonight. Tomorrow our regiment will be issued equipment for the tropics and the following morning wil travel by rail via Munich and the Brenner to Naples. There it will embark for the crossing.

Kümmel went back to his company. He allowed the men to go out on one last night pass. He knew how long the mission in Africa was going to last, even though initial reports from that theater were good. The next days were filled with the usual preparations: innoculations, lectures. For Kümmel this meant much hard work. Finally the train carrying the regiment's I Battalion set off in the direction of Munich. After several delays the train crossed the Brenner Pass and drove through Italy. There was a stop in Rome, during which the men made a brief visit to the Colosseum. And then Naples and the long wait for the next transport.

In Naples Kümmel learned that the ship carrying the bulk of the division headquarters had been sunk by the Royal Navy. One more piece of bad news was received: Generalmajor von Prittwitz, the division commander, had been killed during a reconnaissance sortie near Tobruk. As Oberstleutnant Cramer informed the assembled officers, von Prittwitz, a wearer of the *Pour le mérite* (Blue Max) had been ordered to scout a favorable artillery position from which to soften up Tobruk. He was told that there was still an Italian outpost on the Via Balbia. Believing this, he roared off and drove straight into the sights of a British antitank gun positioned on the road. A shell struck Generalmajor von Prittwitz in the chest and he was killed instantly. His driver was also killed.

That had been on 10 April. And on the same day, in the White House in Acroma, eighteen kilometers from Tobruk, Generalmajor Streich had assumed command of the attack on the city, port and fortress of Tobruk. As yet, however, the men of the 8th Panzer Regiment knew nothing of this. They also did not know that the 33rd Panzer Artillery Regiment under Oberstleutnant Eduard Crasemann had gone down when submarines of the 10th Malta Submarine Flotilla destroyed an Italian convoy.

✠

Finally it was time to embark. The tanks drove slowly across the pier to the ships. Cranes howled and lifted the heavy loads over the loading hatches. The tanks were loaded in such a way that they could drive straight from the pier into battle when they arrived in Tripoli. Together with the regimental commander Kümmel went aboard the Kypfel. He listened to the captain's instructions, saw the escorting Italian torpedo boats, and then they were at sea.

Once during the voyage there was a submarine alert. The two escorts dropped depth charges and raced about like two shepherd dogs. They succeeded in forcing the submarine away from the convoy. Many of the men, including Kümmel, suffered from seasickness during the crossing of the Mediterranean, but the convoy reached Tripoli safely.

The 160 vehicles of the 8th Panzer Regiment moved off. Hauptmann Kümmel drove in the command tank at the head of his company. Standing in the open turret hatch, he saw the white stone of Tripoli. The long column of brand-new tanks, all painted desert yellow, rolled out of the port toward the Via Balbia, passing wells and palm trees as they went.

"Like a fairy tale, isn't it, Toni?" said Kümmel to his driver Feldwebel Kruschinski, who had been with him since the campaign in Poland.

"Too beautiful to be true. I suspect that we're heading into a real mess, sir."

When others were listening the driver said, "Sir." The rest of the time it was Hannes and Toni.

A ghibli headed toward them. For the first time the panzer crews experienced the fury of this sandstorm. They closed the hatches, but the sand got in everywhere. And it was everywhere: in the ears, on the lips, in the nose and in the throat.

"Keep going!" odered Oberstleutnant Cramer. "Anyone left behind catch up as soon as you can and assemble in Sidi Azeiz."

The regiment passed through Tripolitania and headed into the Syrte. The tanks drove through Cyrenaica and arrived at the Africa Corps's positions near Tobruk. There the elements of the proud panzer battalions were welcomed by the new division commander, Generalmajor Hans-Karl Baron von Esebeck.

Kümmel observed the short, thin man with his glasses and the Knight's Cross at his throat. He had no way of knowing that the new division commander would only lead the division for a few days.

"We are driving past Tobruk to the south, on to Bardia. The stragglers will assemble here and follow as quickly as possible."

The general placed himself at the head of his force, which had been reduced to three panzers, and they drove through to Bardia. There Oberstleutnant Cramer received orders to attack Fort Capuzzo, which had been occupied by British forces. The three Panzer IIIs advanced in a widely-spaced vee formation. On 10 May the British 22nd Guards Brigade had thrown the German 15th Motorcycle Battalion under Oberstleutnant Knabe out of the Halfaya Pass. The three panzer crews learned this during their first stop, when they encountered the motorcycle troops, who were a part of their division and who had already been in the desert for four weeks.

"Then we'll have a go!" said Oberstleutnant Cramer. "Don't shoot until I give the order to do so."

The crews climbed back in. Still standing in the open turret hatch, Kümmel looked out at the desert, which in the area of the fort was as flat as a board. Seconds later he saw some stones fly up and suddenly muzzle flashes. Shells howled toward the tanks and landed in the sand far ahead of them.

"Battle readiness!" ordered Cramer. The hatches snapped shut.

"Weapon loaded and locked!" reported loader Behrensmann.

"Watch it Lenz!" roared Unteroffizier Hoffer, who was commanding one of the tanks. They rumbled through a hole. The limestone cracked beneath the tracks.

"Commander to everyone: full speed ahead!"

"To everyone!" repeated Hoffer, grunting lustily, for "everyone" was his tank and that of his company commander. Ahead the regimental commander's tank dashed to the side, stopped and fired the first shot. As if this had been some sort of sign, three or four more antitank guns now opened fire.

"The middle one!" Hauptmann Kümmel ordered his driver.

Feldwebel Kruschinski raced through a camelthorn bush at top speed, grinding the plant beneath the tank's tracks. Then he halted abruptly.

"Fire!" roared the Hauptmann.

There was a crack as the 50-mm gun fired. The Panzer III roacked back on its tracks.

Kümmel saw a fireball in the center of the gun position. "A hit!"

"Onward! Onward!"

The tank moved off with a jerk. It picked up speed, moving faster and faster. Then British troops appeared before them. They looked quite strange with their flat helmets. Radio operator Egon Milde fired a burst from the machine-gun. The enemy troops disappeared as they took cover. Then the tank was past them.

Three, four, then five tanks emerged from behind the white stone fort. The first shot left one in flames. Through his periscope Hauptmann Kümmel saw the crew bail out. All three of the regiment's tanks now fired simultaneously. They scored five hits on another enemy tank. The tank's hatch flipped back and a mushroom cloud of smoke rose above the doomed vehicle.

"Everyone follow me!" came the regimental commander's order. The tanks advanced and reached the smoldering British tanks. They had done it! Weaponless and arms raised, British soldiers emerged from their positions. The guns fell silent. The first action in Africa was over and they had retaken Capuzzo.

The men climbed from the tanks, limbs shaking and faces contorted. The motorcycle troops moved in to clear the fort of any remaining enemy. Kümmel breathed a sigh of relief. They had seized Fort Capuzzo. Several days of rest followed. General Rommel visited the regiment, which was back up to strength. He greeted the unit's commanding officer and said:

"Cramer, from the day you took Capuzzo with your three crates you have been in my good books!"

"Thank you, sir. One does what one can," replied the "stalwart" officer, who had fought in the First World War and who had been left badly wounded on the battlefield at Amiens on 8 August 1918.

"Yes, tomorrow you can prove that it wasn't a lucky shot. Tomorrow we are going to attack the Halfaya Pass and take it back. From Sollum you will drive south through the desert, turn north behind the pass and enter by the back door."

"And who will be coming through the front door, sir?" asked Cramer.

"Knabe and his motorcycle troops, a company of the 33rd Reconnaissance Battalion and I Battalion of the 21st Panzer Division's 104th Rifle Regiment."

"Then we will do it, sir!" replied Cramer.

THE BATTLE OF THE HALFAYA PASS

"Get ready!" said Kümmel. His tank crew crawled out from under the Panzer III and stretched their stiff limbs. The other tanks sat in a circle. Sentries had been posted some distance away in order to avoid any unpleasant surprises. Suddenly it became noisy. On the entire plateau in the Sollum-Capuzzo area, where the desert changes into a high, rocky plain, the attack forces made ready.

At the same time the men of Battle Group Herff were preparing for battle on the road leading up to the pass, two-hundred meters above, and in the wadis just in front of the western exit from the pass. They would rather be engaging the enemy. It was probably going to be difficult for them to take the British positions in a frontal attack. In front of the pass lay rising terrain littered with boulders and crisscrossed by wadis. The order was simple enough: "Battle Group Herff take the Halfaya Pass!" But carrying out this order was something else.

Also making preparations in the area southwest of Capuzzo were the elements of the 21st Panzer Division's 5th Panzer Regiment assigned to conduct a feint attack to the southeast. With them was a battery of artillery and five of the feared "eighty-eights."

✠

Oberstleutnant Hans Cramer stood in his open turret hatch and pumped his arm three times. The panzer armada moved off. Leading the way was the Panzer III of Hauptmann Kümmel. Kümmel looked around. Behind him were the tanks of 1st Company. They were crewed by experienced men, all veterans of Poland and France. They had launched the second phase of the Battle of France from the Aisne just as they were doing now.

The panzers rolled into the desert. Camelthorn bushes cracked beneath the tank tracks. Engines roared, tracks rattled. They drove at twenty kilometers per hour. The tanks rocked like huge cradles when they drove through holes. Inside everyone held on tight. Far in the east the sun was just coming up. Blood red, it emerged from the night sky on the horizon, filling the desert with fluttering red rays of light. Then it was daylight, clean and clear and glowingly beautiful, almost without a pause.

"How's it look, Kruschinski?" Kümmel asked his driver. The Feldwebel grunted something unintelligible.

"Good road, eh?" Kümmel asked again, trying to get a conversation going.

"As good as anywhere when the ground is fissured and full of holes," Kruschinski replied laconically. "If you hold on tight I won't break your ribs."

"Just don't get stuck," implored the Hauptmann.

And as if this were a signal, Oberstleutnant Cramer transmitted from the command vehicle: "I Battalion close up tighter. II Battalion move off more to the right and also stay close!"

The light wind blowing in from the sea carried with it the dull rumble of gunfire. The tanks rolled on, and half an hour later they turned north. Now they were heading uphill again. When they stopped for a brief rest the sun was already high in the sky. It shone with elementary force on the tanks and caused the steel to become hotter and hotter.

"All company commanders to me!" ordered Oberstleutnant Cramer.

Hauptmann Kümmel walked with the others over to the regiment commander, who had spread out a map on the front of his tank. "In half an hour we will be here, at the back door of the pass. There are antitank guns positioned in the old Italian positions in the rocks there. I Battalion will attack and destroy the bunkers on the right flank. II Battalion will roll past I Battalion into the pass and take out the gun positions. Destroy all enemy positions."

The men climbed back into their tanks. The next half hour would decide their fate. Antitank guns always had the advantage, because they sat in concealed positions. Their crews could let them come and then suddenly open fire. It could be too late before the tanks even had a chance to fire the first shot. Fifteen minutes later they were halfway to the pass and had not been fired on. Feldwebel Kruschinski said, "Our comrades are attacking now."

The others were probably thinking the same thing: what was happening on the other side of the pass? They heard the intensifying fire. The fire from the antitank guns and British heavy machine-guns was becoming increasingly heavy. Suddenly the artillery and anti-aircraft guns of the secondary battle group also opened fire. From the steep slopes they poured indirect fire onto the pass road. What were they doing on the other side, thought Kümmel, for he knew that his friend Oberleutnant Tocki was leading the 33rd Armored Reconnaissance Battalion's 1st Company into the teeth of the antitank guns.

The men advanced in two attack groups. I Battalion of the 104th Rifle Regiment had been ordered to make a frontal attack on the pass. They got as far as Wadi Qualala before the British guns opened fire. Field guns cracked, antitank guns barked, and as soon as a German helmet appeared above the rim of the wadi it was greeted by a burst of machine-gun fire.

Hauptmann Wilhelm Bach, who had led the battalion since Tobruk, ordered the 37-mm antitank gun forward. The sun was high in the sky. The thermometer registered 56 degrees Celsius in the shade as the soldiers manhandled the antitank gun gun to the front. But the weapon achieved nothing. During a pause in the firing Hauptmann Bach leapt onto the rim of the wadi, scanned the enemy positions, saw flashes of gunfire and quickly ducked back down again. The shots aimed at him whizzed over the rocks. He had seen the position of the the flanking gun and ordered the "thirty-seven" turned toward them. Following a brief exchange of fire that

A gun crew moves its field gun by hand through the sands of the desert.

gun and the two machine-guns were put out of action. Then Hauptmann Bach gave the order to fix bayonets, and ten seconds later he roared:

"Battalion—get ready—forward!"

Bach stood up and shouted "Hurrah!" and the others took up his battle cry. They ran on, into the enemy fire. Suddenly from the other side of the pass they heard the crack of tank cannon as well as machine-gun fire from the armored troop carriers of the 15th Motorcycle Battalion, which had moved up with the 8th Panzer Regiment.

"Keep going men!" shouted the Hauptmann. "Keep going!"

"Open fire!" Oberstleutnant Cramer gave the order as soon as he saw the first muzzle flash from the British antitank guns. Kümmel and his eight panzers led the way. Leutnant Peters and Oberfeldwebel Kruck made the first firing halt. Both shots were direct hits and the antitank guns fell silent. The tanks pressed on rapidly. The motorcycle unit roared past them on the right but was forced to take cover by enemy machine-gun fire.

Oberleutnant Stiefelmeyer called a warning to his comrade: "Kümmel, watch out, to your right!"

"Turn right!" ordered the Hauptmann. "Five-hundred—antitank gun!"

Obergefreiter Kleff had the target in his sight. But before he could fire there was a flash from the enemy position. Glowing red, the armor-piercing shot raced toward them. It struck the turret at an angle and glanced off; the noise was terrible and it left Kümmel's ears ringing. He heard his tank's 50-mm gun fire and saw a bright red fireball appear in the enemy position.

"Hit! Fire again!"

Loader Albers had loaded the next round. The breech clicked shut, the gun fired again, the tank rocked backwards and the shell exploded on target. They saw flat helmets, faces beneath them. Then the deafening clatter of the machine-guns, the rattle of tracks, all of which echoed off the steep rock walls of the pass. The advance continued. The first position was destroyed with direct fire. An ammunition supply exploded with a loud boom. Flames, smoke, sand and cordite smoke which burned the lungs.

"Kümmel company follow!"

There was the company commander's tank. Two British twin machine-guns were trying to blind it by taking out its vision ports.

"Follow! Everyone after me!"

Kruschinski turned the tank and the machine picked up speed. He spotted a 20-mm Oerlikon cannon and headed straight towards it.

"Hang on!" the commander warned the others. Then they were over, crushing everything beneath them. A few men jumped to the side, threw away their weapons and raised their arms. They were rounded up by the following motorcycle troops.

Oberstleutnant Cramer's voice rang out through the din: "Carry on, through the pass!"

Several Tommies came running, carrying mines. One of the First's tanks drove over one of the charges. It was disabled with one track blown off. Kümmel heard the voice of Feldwebel Unbescheidt order his crew to bail out. The tanks rattled on and fired at muzzle flashes. Bullets sprayed their steel armor. Inside the tank there was a cacophany of sound. The gunner saw a British truck moving a "seventy-five" into position on the right.

"Firing halt!" ordered Kümmel.

The tank halted in the middle of the paved road. Kümmel saw that the gun had been unlimbered and that it was being brought to bear on them. Kleff fired just as the first round was being loaded into the breech of the British weapon. From that close range it was a direct hit. Driver Kruschinsi saw pieces of steel thrown into the air by the force of the exploding shell, as well as shattered bodies. He bit his lip, tasted blood on his tongue and drove on into the chaos of battle.

The men of the British 3rd Guards Battalion, the famous Coldstream Guards, were now under attack from two sides. They were in a trap. It was unlikely that they would be able to hold the Halfaya Pass, considered impregnable, much longer. But they did not give up. They had orders to defend the pass no matter what, and by doing so preserve communications with Tobruk. And so they fought on two fronts, with determination and bravery.

Kümmel radioed a warning to the tank of Leutnant Peters: "Look out, to your right!"

Peters immediately instructed his driver to dodge right. The shell fired by one of the last surviving guns passed behind the tank and bounced off the rocks. Gunner Kleff fired. The first shot was high. The British gun fired again. Hit in the engine compartment, Peters' tank sat immoilized, pouring black smoke. Then Kleff fired a second time. The last enemy gun went down in a rising cascade of smoke and flame. Five of the 1st Company's tanks rolled on until sweat-streamed faces beneath German helmets appeared before them. They halted. A man in the uniform of an Hauptmann, dirty, with a bandage on one arm, came toward Kümmel's tank. It was Hauptmann Bach.

"We thank you, comrades!" said the Hauptmann and saluted.

"Nothing to thank us for," replied Kümmel. "Hopefully, we didn't arrive too late?"

"You came at just the right moment to give us the courage to attack across the open ground."

The Halfaya Pass was in German hands. The German infantry installed itself where the soldiers of Italian General Bergonzolli and then of the British had defended the pass. The tanks assembled at the west end of the pass. Far below him Hans Kümmel saw the sea. It looked blue and calm from 200 meters up.

The company had lost three tanks, one in combat and two with track damage. Two men had been killed. Kümmel helped dig the graves. He dragged stones with which to cover the graves in order to prevent jackals from getting at the bodies of their dead comrades. Then he removed his cap. He had lost two of his men. That was difficult and bitter at the same time. Kümmel feared that they would not be the last and that worse was yet to come.

✠

While the men of the 104th Rifle Regiment remained above in the pass and set up their positions, the tanks and the motorcycle battalion rolled down the steep road to the northwest and assembled south of Bardia. The next days passed quietly. Everyone suspected that this was the calm before the storm. In his tent Hans Kümmel wrote letters to the parents of the two fallen comrades. He wrote what he felt, plain and simple words. More he could not do.

When he had finished the letters he left his tent and walked to the beach. He heard Kruschinski playing his harmonica. His tank crew were sitting there. He also saw Leutnant Peters and Oberfeldwebel Kruck. It was ten minutes to ten. A figure approached from the darkness. It was Oberleutnant Stiefelmeyer.

"Want to hear 'Lili Marlene,' Hans?"

"What's that?" answered Kümmel.

"You mean to say that you've never heard it?"

"I can't remember. What is it, anyway?"

"Wait a minute, and you'll hear it. It's something, I can tell you."

One of the men turned on the backpack receiver and adjusted the fine-tuner. The set began to whistle and then came the voice of the announcer: "This is the Belgrade soldiers' station. It is now 21:57 hours." For a few seconds it was still. Then a husky female voice began to sing the words to the song "Lili Marlene." Kümmel enjoyed the song. It was seductive and he thought of home. It was quiet on the beach for quite a long time. The waves washed against the shore. Kümmel's thoughts drifted back to his earlier days as a soldier, to Böblingen and the other posts, but also to his youth. It had not been easy. He had been just nine years old when the First World War ended.

"It's time now, men," he said.

They stood up one after another, crawled into their tents and talked long into the night. Oberleutnant Stiefelmeyer and Kümmel walked up and down the beach together.

"Do you really think they have new tanks with a long 75-mm gun?" he wondered.

"I hope that they don't have anything of the sort, for if they do our crates will be hopelessly outgunned."

"By all means!" agreed Kümmel. "Only our Panzer IV with the long-barreled gun would be equal to them."

They walked on for several hundred meters, then turned toward the regiment command post. When they reached it they heard a loud jumble of voices and the clinking of glasses.

"It sounds like they're celebrating something there, Hans," observed Stiefelmeyer.

"Let's have a look," was Kümmel's reply. They walked up to the big radio truck and knocked.

"Come in!" called Oberstleutnant Cramer.

They stepped inside and Kümmel shielded his eyes from the light.

"Has peace broken out?" asked Stiefelmeyer.

"Not quite, but we have good news from Crete."

They took a drink from a spare bottle which had survived the trip from Dijon. Several minutes later Oberstleutnant Cramer brought the discussion to an end: "Time that we were getting to be. We'll find out more tomorrow."

THE BRITISH OFFENSIVE

The next day passed in the uncertainty of waiting. More and more tanks were made serviceable. Kümmel tried repeatedly to free up a few hours for the individual platoons to go swimming. On one occasion they had just entered the water when General Rommel came driving up in his "Mammoth." Kümmel was about to report, but Rommel gestured for him to stand easy.

"Are your men well on their way, Kümmel?" he asked.

"They are in top form, sir," answered the Hauptmann.

"That's good. Very well, carry on lads!"

The general drove away and his vehicle disappeared beyond the dunes in the direction of the regiment command post. In the next days Kümmel saw Rommel, or the "Desert Fox" as they called him, repeatedly. He was with the divisions south of Tobruk and he came to them in the area south of Bardia. He drove up to the Halfaya Pass and also inspected the positions between Sidi Azeiz and Capuzzo.

Erwin Rommel at the front and among his soldiers.

Once Hauptmann Kümmel drove reconnaissance and reached Hill 208, approximately eight kilometers west-southwest of Capuzzo. He saw Italian combat engineers fortifying the positions there. Then he came to the heavy flak battery which was set up in a reverse-slope position. An Oberleutnant came over to him.

"Ziemer!" he said.

"Kümmel," replied the Hauptmann. They shook hands.

"Good field of fire for the battery if the Tommies come up from the southeast." He pointed from the top of the barely 600-meter-long and roughly 400-meter-wide hilltop to the southeast, where the coast stretched into the distance. Hans Kümmel looked at the position. The four "eighty-eights" were so well camouflaged that they had virtually disapeared into the sand. Only their barrels projected beyond the sandbagged emplacements.

"It's just that I don't believe the enemy will attack right here," declared Ziemer. "They will either attack along the road through the Halfaya Pass, or they will make a wide sweep through the desert around Sidi Omar. Anything else would be rubbish."

"Yes, well one never knows that beforehand. Anyway, as a tank man this piece of desert would tempt me. For if you got pass Hafid Ridge here, you would be in Capuzzo and Sidi Azeiz in no time at all."

The two officers were joined by Oberleutnant Paulewicz, commander of the 1st Oasis Company, which was in command on this small hilltop.

"If Tommy is stopped here," he said, "then his entire offensive is down the drain."

"Well, then, Paulewicz, just make sure that they don't get through."

"If the panzers help us, we will do it," declared the Oberleutnant confidently.

Through his binoculars Kümmel observed the dust clouds in the desert.

"Something going on there, Bock," he said to his adjutant, who had accompanied Kümmel and meanwhile had driven the car forward to the southeast face of Hafid Ridge.

"Yes, it looks like a whole mahalla!" nodded the Oberleutnant.

"What are they doing? Have they received replacements for the tanks they lost?"

"We haven't heard anything about a convoy. But it is hard to say. Perhaps they have received a lot of new tanks without our knowledge."

✠

What Hauptmann Kümmel and his superiors did not know yet was that a British convoy had got through to Africa. Following the defeat of General Wavell in Cyrenaica, British prime minister Winston Churchill had done everything he could to restore the fighting power of the 8th Army. He knew that the 15th Panzer Division's 8th Panzer Regiment had been transported to Africa, raising the Africa Corps's strength in the theater to two complete panzer divisions. In the famous conference of 21 April 1941 Churchill forced the Admiralty to send the next convoy through the Strait of Gibraltar instead of around the Cape of Good Hope. This would provide a faster resupply than the Germans would be able to achieve. The convoy was dubbed "Tiger."

"Operation Tiger" was supposed to deliver 295 tanks and 50 fighter aircraft to Africa. The Admiralty required five large cargo vessels to transport these quantities of equipment. The naval forces under Admiral Somerville were to guard the vital convoy. If it got through, the British 8th Army would have enough tanks to carry out its summer campaign, codenamed "Battleaxe."

The "Battleaxe" plan called for the armored forces of the 8th Army to attack in three groups. The following units were available for the operation: the 4th Indian Division with one brigade of its own and the 22nd Guards Brigade, as well as the 7th Armoured Division with a brigade of Matilda tanks and one of Cruiser tanks. Attacking on the right flank would be a brigade of the 4th Indian Division with its own Matilda infantry tanks. It was to capture Halfaya Pass and clear the entire strip of coastline. In the central sector was the 22nd Guards Brigade with the rest of the Matildas, the 4th Armoured Brigade. Its mission was to take Capuzzo and Sollum. The 7th Armoured Brigade was ordered to advance on the left flank straight towards Hill 208 (Hafid Ridge) to take possession of this commanding high ground, and then advance toward Sidi Azeiz, linking up with the fortress garrison and closing the ring around the trapped German units.

According to General Wavell, who had assumed command in Egypt:

> In the second phase of the battle we will move up the freed-up Matilda tanks of the 4th Armoured Brigade as support for the 7th Armoured Brigade, for it is to be expected that the Germans will give battle with their two panzer divisions. If we succeed in relieving Tobruk and breaking the German siege, then we will be able to advance in the direction of Derna and Mechili in the third phase of the battle, unhinge the German positions and achieve ultimate victory in North Africa.

Such were the British hopes for "Operation Battleaxe." Air Vicemarshal Tedder had amassed 105 bombers and 98 fighters to support the ground offensive, but the decisive factor was the almost 300 tanks that had arrived on the "Tiger" convoy. The importance of this convoy is reflected in a telegram from Winston Churchill to General Wavell, in which he said:

> Should "Tiger" reach you, the moment has come to dare and to act. I have ordered the Hurricanes on Malta placed under your command as soon as "Tiger" successfully reaches its berths. These Huns are far less dangerous when they have lost the initiative. All of our best wishes go with you.

"Operation Tiger" succeeded, even though one of the ships (the *Empire Song*) hit a mine and went down with its cargo of 57 tanks and 10 aircraft. Approximately 240 tanks reached the front. This number included 135 Matilda IIs and 82 new Mark II tanks. Already on 28 May General Wavell wired London that the tanks had been assembled and their guns aligned and that with them he would be in a position to drive back the Africa Korps, relieve Tobruk and achieve total victory.

In the first days of June Radio Monitoring Section Southeast, whose leading elements were in North Africa, but whose main body was still in southern Greece and Sicily, intercepted a series of radio messages which were successfully decoded. Each of these messages indicated that the British were planning a major offensive. On 10 June 1941 there was a chart hanging in the main decoding center of the Radio Monitoring Section Southeast, which for security reasons was called "Weather Reception Station Southeast." On it could be read the following:

BATTLEAXE
Commander in Chief: General Beresford-Peirse
7th Armoured Division: General Creagh
4th Indian Division: General Messervy.

"Get ready men, we're moving into the readiness position!" Hans Kümmel woke his crew with these words. There was movement in the tents and in the holes in the sand beneath the tanks. 12 June 1941 was just three hours old. It was still dark.

"Shit!" said Feldwebel Kruschinski, digging a few sand fleas out of his skin. "Here we are out in the middle of the desert and can't even go swimming any more."

"This is no holiday at the beach, Toni," interjected Unteroffizier Milde. He took a drink from a canteen and passed it on to Theo Kleff.

The tanks were ready for action. A few days of rest had been enough for the 8th Panzer Regiment to restore full battle readiness. The routine daily flights by the British had not bothered them. The sporadic night raids were worse. The Tommies always appeared just after they had gone to sleep and dropped their bombs. The latter were a type filled with steel hooks. The hooks stuck in the sand, posing a threat to the tires of any vehicle that drove over them.

Half an hour later the two battalions of the 8th Panzer Regiment were ready to march. The two groups moved off. They drove north a ways, down the coast road toward Bardia. Halfway there the commander's vehicle stopped and allowed his force to pass by him.

"A tough character, our old man!" Theo Kleff observed to his loader.

"That's for sure," replied Albers.

Beyond the regimental commander the tanks veered west into the desert. They drove through the hilly landscape that fell away toward Fort Capuzzo and Sidi Azeiz. They rolled some distance farther down into the desert and then a halt was called and the tanks spread out.

Kümmel's crew climbed out and crawled under the rear of the tank. "In the middle of the desert, at the end of the world," declared Kruschinski.

"And not a bastard in front of us. If the Tommies come we'll be the first ones they tackle."

"Wrong men. Definitely wrong!"

Hauptmann Kümmel, who had briefed the company, returned. He brought with him news from the contact sentries.

"Who is in front of us then, apart from the flak?" asked Leutnant Peters.

"Our old friend Gustav-Georg!"

"The unholy Saint Georg!" declared Kruschinski. "Well, then we can sleep soundly. Watch out wherever he and his motorcycle troops are!"

Hauptmann Kümmel joined the group and added: "And the pastor is in the Halfaya Pass! Have you heard what the Tommies call him? 'Pastor of the sweeping fire!' "

"Tocki is there as well. Our regulation antitank officer!"

Two hours later the tank crews had dug their foxholes and pitched their tents over them. The heat drained the men. They lay in their holes wearing just their underwear. Hans Kümmel wrote a few letters, then he inspected his company. Toward evening the readiness position became a scene of hectic activity. The men crawled dazed from their holes. There was food and tea. Then they sat down together. Kruschinski played his harmonica. The drone of the familiar British night bombers caused them to fall silent. The lights went out. The noise grew louder, but the machines flew past and headed towards Gambut airfield.

"It'll be starting again there again anytime," observed Egon Milde. "Perhaps they'll be hitting Gazala-North, too."

Albers ended the conversation: "It doesn't matter to me, as long as they don't come here."

The 13th of June was another tension-filled day. Everyone waited for the order placing them on alert. But when the sun went down they came out of their holes again. Somehow they had procured some Bols liquer as well as several bottles of red wine from the Italians.

Kümmel went over to his friend Stiefelmeyer. "Well, what do you think Otto, when is it going to start?"

"Tomorrow or the day after," answered the Oberleutnant.

"I'm scared stiff, Otto," admitted Kümmel. "But damn it, one simply can't let it show."

"Who here isn't afraid? I saw the regimental commander yesterday. The old man also said that he was nervous. But when it comes down to it Hannes, when things get hot, we'll all have our feet on the ground."

"Yes, you're right. We're always afraid beforehand. And our knees don't start shaking again until it's over."

"It's a good thing that none of the lads know that, Hannes," laughed Stiefelmeyer. "They think that you are Siegfried himself."

Kümmel shrugged his shoulders but said nothing. They went on talking for a little while, their jokes expressing gallows humor. That was the only way they could bear it all: the sun, the sand, the sand fleas and the damned sandstorms.

Some time later Stiefelmeyer said, "Well, I'm going to go and get some sleep."

They said goodbye and Kümmel walked over to his tent, which was half underground behind his tank. His batman stood at the entrance.

"Do you want anything else, sir?"

"Thank you Fritz, you can lie down. Good night."

Johannes Kümmel in conversation with a Luftwaffe soldier.

"I still have one question, sir. I don't know if I should . . ."

"Out with it Fritz!" Kümmel said to his batman. "Maybe I can help you."

"Gerda has written, sir."

"Ah, your young lady, I see. Is she well?"

"Yes, sir. But she has written that something is on the way and we aren't even married."

"Well, that's not all that tragic Fritz!" said Kümmel. "That will take care of itself. As soon as you have leave . . ."

"Her parents want to kick her out, sir."

"Damn, that's a stupid way to act. Wait a minute!" Kümmel thought it over. Then he had it.

"You will be the courier, Fritz! You will travel to Wunsdorf and deliver the requisition list personally and wait until all the replacement parts are loaded and nothing is missing. That means fourteen days at home. Tomorrow morning you can set off for Gazala-North."

"Sir, I don't know how to thank you!" stammered the Obergefreiter.

"No need to, Fritz. Someone has to fly to Germany. It might as well be you."

The Obergefreiter saluted smartly and then strode off in the direction of his tent. Kümmel smiled as he watched him go. How easy it was to make a man happy. He disappeared into his tent, pulled off his boots and tunic and lay down on the field cot. Minutes later he was asleep.

✠

"Alert readiness, gentlemen!"

With these words Oberstleutnant Cramer began his briefing on the evening of 14 June 1941.

"Then it's finally starting!" called one of the company commanders, relieved.

"Gentlemen, the English have left their readiness positions. According to reports by reconnaissance machines more than 200 tanks are advancing as well as approximately twenty-five-thousand men."

✠

At the same time as Hauptmann Kümmel was alerting his company, the positions in the Halfaya Pass and on Hill 208 were scenes of hectic activity. The enemy was going to attack these critical points and everything had to be ready to meet and repulse him. The night passed. Enemy bombers flew over the assembly areas. Their targets lay in the German rear, where they bombed supply roads and troop concentrations. The panzers were ready. They had been rearmed and refuelled on the morning of the 14th. Toward four in the morning the sky began to brighten quickly. A few minutes later it was daylight. And then the men around Hauptmann Kümmel saw the huge dust clouds rising into the sky to the southeast—and they were growing larger.

Oberleutnant Mayer, the signals officer, came over to them. "Enemy tanks approaching Hill 208, presumed direction of advance: Capuzzo-Sidi Azeiz."

"Dress warmly," observed Kruschinski. "They'll be coming this way if . . . if the flak doesn't stop them."

"God alive!" said the signals officer, "you've certainly got two pieces of heavy artillery with you!" He pointed to the two Panzer IVs armed with the short 75-mm gun, the so-called "stump."

"We got them two weeks ago," replied Kümmel. "If we get close enough to the enemy we'll have a good chance with these guns."

The tension became almost unbearable during the next hours. Fresh reports continued to filter through.

"Tommy is attacking Halfaya Pass with new tanks!"

"Flak Battery Ziemer has engaged fifty Matildas."

"And we sit here and wait!" mumbled Kruschinski.

Despatch riders drove past heading to the front. Then the first ones came back. Their faces were gray.

Hauptmann Kümmel stopped one of the men: "Enemy is attacking Capuzzo with fifty tanks!" he said.

"Fifty?" asked Kümmel dismayed. And he thought of the motorcycle troops sitting in their foxholes in Capuzzo, with almost no heavy weapons.

"Sir, we have to advance, otherwise those damned fellows will grind everything into the sand," declared Leutnant Peters, who commanded the second Panzer IV.

"I would certainly like to too, Peters. But we have no order to attack, and . . ."

Kümmel fell silent, for two motorcycle-sidecars appeared ahead. Both were carrying eight soldiers and were wobbling badly as if the drivers were drunk.

Kümmel ran toward them and waved. They turned toward him and stopped. He saw that almost all the men were wounded.

"What's going on up front?" he asked.

"Tommy tanks everywhere! They are shooting up everything and chasing every single man. Oberstleutnant Knabe had to order a retreat. He's up there somewhere in the thick of it. All wounded . . . !" The man fell silent.

"Everyone in turn." Kümmel turned to the Feldwebel on the second motorcycle. "What happened?"

✠

The motorcycle troops lay waiting for the enemy in the holes and trenches on the southern half of Fort Capuzzo. Already the rattle of tracks and the howl of engines could be heard clearly. Gefreiter Kohlmann made an adjustment to his machine-gun, which was installed in a low part of the trench in such a way that it could sweep the ground in front of it.

"There they are!" shouted Unteroffizier Stein and lowered his binoculars.

They could already see them with the naked eye, and when they emerged from the dust they counted them. They stopped at thirty for there were more and more.

The leading enemy tank halted and seconds later flames shot from its main gun. "Open fire!" ordered Oberstleutnant Gustav-Georg Knabe.

Oberleutnant Tocki of the 33rd Antitank Battalion, which had moved a single "eighty-eight" forward from Bardia the evening before, was just approaching Fort Capuzzo when he heard the sharp crack of tank guns up ahead.

"Position!" he ordered, and pointed to a small gully in which they would have a measure of cover.

Farther forward, in the fort's trenches and positions, Oberstleutnant Gustav-Georg Knabe, whose motorcycle battalion was responsible for defending the fort, watched as the tanks moved toward the fort.

"Good God, Kuhnow," said the Oberstleutnant, who had worn the Knight's Cross since 1 June 1941, "as soon as they get here they'll wipe out our entire battalion. We have to withdraw!"

"Mankiewicz, Kuhnow, take the word to the left and right: prepare to retreat!"

The two Feldwebel, who led the groups of runners and radio operators, hurried, for by now the tanks were only about 600 meters away.

"Prepare to withdraw!"

The Oberstleutnant's combat vehicle rolled forward. The machine-gunners fired another belt and then loaded a fresh one; then they heard the order. At the same time the motorcycle troops in more distant positions saw the two white flares fired by the operations officer. They jumped up, ran to their motorcycles, climbed on and raced away.

When the positions had been evacuated, Oberstleutnant Knabe ordered the personnel around him to mount up and withdraw. They ran to the vehicle, whose engine was already running. They jumped in and the vehicle moved off and began to pick up speed. Just then a shell struck the rear of the command vehicle. It skidded and then came to a stop.

"Get out!"

The men jumped out and, crouched low, ran to the side. They came to a set of sewer pipes that passed under a road.

"Get in!" ordered the Oberstleutnant.

At that moment a second shell smashed into the command vehicle fifty meters behind them. They crawled into the two pipes, which fortunately were long enough. Feldwebel Mankiewicz saw comrades approach on their motorcycles. He heard the fire from the enemy tanks intensifying. A fully-manned motorcycle-sidecar was shattered by a direct hit.

The tanks rattled through the desert, still in inverted wedge formation, stopping occasionally to fire. It was like a rabbit hunt. One of the enemy tanks headed straight for the command vehicle and stopped. The British crew jumped out, pulled boxes and luggage out of the smoldering vehicle and pulled out the Oberstleutnant's clothes, which they took turns trying on. The other tanks rolled on, stopping only to fire their guns.

To the right and left and on the road itself lay shattered vehicles and dead and wounded soldiers. The others ran for their lives. Among those running for their lives was a group led by Unteroffizier Stein. They had lost their vehicle and were now running on foot. The tank nearest to them stopped. As he ran, Gefreiter Kohlmann, a machinist from Dortmund, looked around. He saw a flash from the tank's gun and instinctively jumped out of the way. He hit the ground and the shell landed to his right, knocking Hüsler and Jettkowski off their feet. Kohlmann crawled over to them. Hüsler was dead. A huge fragment had torn his throat open. But Jettkowski was alive. He had taken two fragments in the leg and one in the thigh.

"Get out of here, Bodo," he said.

"You're crazy!" replied Kohlmann. He picked up his comrade and ran on.

The tank that had fired at them began to move again. It overtook them on the right, passing 100 meters away, and headed north at high speed. After a few hundred meters Bodo Kohlmann felt as if his arms were going to drop off. Then Stein appeared out of the veil of sand. From then on they carried their wounded comrade together. They were ready to give up but then they heard a loud crack as a gun was fired, followed almost immediately by a mighty explosion. Through the sand they saw a mushroom cloud of fire.

"That was an eighty-eight! They've come. They're going to get us out of here!" roared Stein.

The two men staggered on toward where the "eighty-eight" was.

It was the "eighty-eight" under Oberleutnant Tocki, which had gone into position in the shallow gully. Paul Kühne, the gunner, saw the approaching tanks. His heart was in his throat when he saw the steel giants emerge from the veil of dust and powder smoke.

"At least a dozen, sir!"

"Range six-hundred. Twelve o'clock—fire!"

The first shell left the long barrel. It whistled toward the tank that had been selected as its target, pierced the forward armor and sent it up in flames.

"Direct hit, Kühne, now the one to its right, the one that has just halted."

Unteroffizier Kühne already had the tank in his sights. He pressed the firing button just as the enemy gunner fired his weapon. The armor-piercing shell kicked up sand ten meters to the right of the anti-aircraft gun; however, the shell from the "eighty-eight" scored a direct hit on the tank, which was destroyed when its ammunition exploded. The gun crew now turned to the third tank of the leading group. One shot, direct hit, an explosion, crew members bailing out. The entire line of tanks stopped. The British crews activated their smoke generators, and the tanks disappeared behind blue-gray swaths.

On seeing the enemy tanks making smoke, Unteroffizier Stein shouted, "We did it! We did it!" They stumbled on and reached the flak position, where Jettkowski's wounds were looked after.

A single "eighty-eight" had halted the advance of 47 enemy tanks, while at the same time preventing the total destruction of the 15th Motorcycle Battalion. Several groups reached the tank assembly areas of the 15th Panzer Division and the Kümmel company. One of the men described to Kümmel what had happened.

✠

"We have to act at once. Waiting for orders would mean a loss of time we could never recover," said Kümmel. He thought for a moment then made his decision.

"Peters, you take over the company. Oberfeldwebel Kruck to me!"

The Oberfeldwebel, who commanded the third Panzer IV, came running over to his company commander.

"Kruck, we're going to drive forward, attack the enemy tanks and stop them from destroying the rest of the motorcycle troops. If the enemy tanks break through they will destroy all our rear-echelon units and then we'll be in big trouble."

"Yes, sir, I'll follow in your wake!" called Kruck. He appeared to be enthusiastic.

They climbed into their tanks. The heat inside the vehicles was stifling when the engines were running.

"All set?" Kümmel asked the Oberfeldwebel.

"Ready to go!"

"Then move out!"

They drove quickly through the sand and reached the lone anti-aircraft gun. Oberleutnant Tocki came running.

"Hans, they're behind that wall of smoke. Forty at least! He warned.

"Thanks, Tocki, make sure that none of them moves off and gets behind me!"

The anti-aircraft gun fired at the muzzle flashes that occasionally pierced the gray cloud of smoke. Kümmel, however, ordered his Panzer IVs to turn to the left.

"Head for the end of the soup, Toni!" he instructed his driver. Feldwebel Kruschinski grunted.

"Attention, Kruck, one hundred meters lateral spacing and turn with me. Fire when you see fit."

"Understood!" replied the platoon leader.

They rolled into the smoke. The tank cannon were loaded and ready to fire. Suddenly the form of an enemy tank appeared not 150 meters in front of them. It was a Mark II! The German tank stopped. Obergefreiter Kleff already had his sight on the enemy. He adjusted his aim slightly and fired. Hubert Albers was loading the next armor-piercing round even before the first shot struck the enemy tank. Then there was an explosion and the Mark II's turret was blown off. Kümmel's tank moved on. Peering through his vision port, he saw the British crew bail out. Then the next enemy tank appeared before him.

"Fire!" ordered Kümmel.

The sound of the shot and the shell striking home came almost as one. It was a shattering double blow and another enemy tank had been destroyed. The tank turned. To Kümmel's right Kruck also opened fire. The Oberfeldwebel reported:

"Got one, sir!"

"Carry on! Roll them all up!"

They drove into the waiting mass of tanks and rolled toward the enemy, who now knew that there was a wolf loose among their herd. Shells whizzed out of the smoke, and one struck the ground beside Kümmel's tank. The stink of cordite was cold and biting in their lungs. Another flash in front of them. Kruschinski steered the tank to the side. The shell intended for them struck the upper lip of the turret and knocked the commander hard against the side. Kümmel felt a heavy blow on his shoulder. For a few seconds his arm felt paralyzed, but it was just a bruise.

"Two o'clock, the two tanks!"

They saw two Mark IIs rolling through the smoke. Flames shot from their exhausts; they were obviously after Kruck.

Kümmel called a warning to his platoon commander: "Watch out Kruck! Behind and to your left!"

Kruck radioed back, cool and collected as ever: "I also have enemy in front of me, sir!"

"Turn right. That's it. Take him Kleff!"

The gunner saw the broad rear of the enemy tank moving towards the other Panzer IV from behind. He took aim and fired. The shell struck the engine and fuel tank. A bright white gasoline flame shot up. Within a few seconds the tank was in flames. They turned slightly to the left. As they did so they were hit again. Luckily the shell struck at an oblique angle and bounced off. One shot from the Panzer IV was sufficient to disable the enemy tank. Turning on one track, it fired again. This time the shell passed just past the left flank of the command panzer. Kleff also destroyed this tank with his second shot.

Jinking constantly, they moved through the main body of tanks. The tank cannon barked repeatedly. Kruck reported destroying his second and third enemy tanks. By this time Kümmel's crew had knocked out five. The British side was a scene of confusion. Raging fires and exhaust flames shot from the mist of the artificial smoke. The gunners fired at these and scored several hits. One of the British tanks was immobilized. However its turret mechanism was still functioning and it swing its gun around and fired. The German tanks moved in quickly. Theo Kleff fired the decisive shot from 600 meters, disabling the enemy tank. Together with Oberleutnant Trocki's "eighty-eight," the two tanks rolled back to their departure point. Hauptmann Kümmel reported to the regimental commander, who had arrived in the meantime.

Oberstleutnant Cramer offered Kümmel his hand. "Well done, Kümmel! I am damn proud of you!"

The survivors of the motorcycle battalion arrived at the readiness position. They had crawled into foxholes and some had witnessed Kümmel beating back the enemy. In the middle of the night, after the two tanks had been completely rearmed and refueled, Oberstleutnant Knabe and his operations officer arrived at the 8th Panzer Regiment's outer security points, which were on the road to Capuzzo. The first phase of the British offensive had failed. Kümmel and his two panzers had dealt with a serious crisis situation. Major Günther Fenski, the battalion commander, came over to his comrades.

"Hans, I am happy that you acted as you did," he said.

"Even without your order?" Kümmel asked back with a smile.

"As if you gave yourself an order because you knew that the lives of your comrades were at stake."

They took another drink from the special bottle. Feldwebel Kruschinski took the rest of the bottle to the other crewmen.

"Here, one last drink before they kick our asses in."

"You mean that you expect they will come again after this disaster?"

"What do you think, Albers? They're coming! The Tommies are much too determined to give up yet. Do you know what it looks like in the Halfaya Pass and on Hill 208? I fear that the British have finished this hill, because while driving forward I saw that they had placed heavy artillery fire there."

"The hill will hold," said one of the others. "Oberleutnant Zimmer has reported that he stopped the group that headed for Hill 208. He reported eleven tanks destroyed."

"Yes, the eighty-eight," said Kümmel, who had joined the men. "If Tocki hadn't stopped the armada we wouldn't be sitting here now, instead we would have gone swimming somewhere on the coast."

✠

On that morning everyone was also at battle readiness in the positions of the Bach battalion. The alarm was sounded when the roar of tank engines was heard. Hauptmann Bach ran forward to where the anti-aircraft guns were sited. Through his binoculars he saw the approaching tanks of the 4th Armoured Brigade. Behind them came the transports carrying the men of the Indian Division.

"Let them come closer," said the pastor, leaning on his familiar walking stick.

The tanks rolled up the pass with the sun at their backs.

"Damn, that's a lot of crates!" called one of the runners with dismay in his voice.

"If you say damn again, I'm going to let you have it," declared the pastor.

"They're passing Halfaya, sir!"

"Look what's behind them! Infantry tanks!"

"Much too slow," declared Hauptmann Bach, unimpressed. He puffed on his cigar and then looked through his binoculars again. At that moment they heard the sound of approaching shells. There were mighty explosions, followed immediately by the whistle of more incoming rounds. The enemy had opened up with his artillery in an attempt to soften up the pass. The men took cover, while shells fell all around them. Splinters of rock whizzed through the air.

"Most of it's falling in the empty wadi between the Third and the flak, sir."

"Then it's in a good place," was his reply.

The Third, which was at the front, saw the Mark II tanks approaching. Behind them came the trucks carrying the soldiers of the 11th Indian Brigade. The infantrymen jumped down, formed up and advanced behind the tanks. As yet not a shot had been fired by the German side.

"The flak has to open fire now," said one of the soldiers.

As if on cue, the 88-mm guns now opened fire. Shell after shell left the barrels and smashed into the phalanx of armored giants. The direct hits blew off turrets, pierced the thick frontal armor. More and more British tanks were knocked out. In spite of these losses the British did not quit. They had to take the pass, that was their order. The Italian battery under Major Pardi now added its weight to the defensive barrage. The 20-mm light flak also joined in.

"Ten kills, sir," reported the adjutant. Then another enemy tank stopped, shrouded in flames, and he corrected himself: "No, eleven!"

The Pardi battery lost its gun commander. Major Pardi himself ran to the gun. He fired and scored a hit. This phase of the British assault had also been a failure. On the afternoon of this first day of the battle the British tanks attacked the Hafid Ridge for the third time. Hill 208 simply had to fall, if it was not to remain a thorn in the side of the British.

"Let them come to within 800 meters!" ordered Oberleutnant Ziemer.

Gefreiter Huebner, gunner in the crew of gun "Anton" of 3rd Battery, I Battalion, 33rd Flak Regiment, aimed at the first tank to appear from out of the dust. He made a slight correction. It was almost a repeat of the situation they had encountered twice that morning when the mass of British tanks had headed for Hill 208. Then he pressed the firing button. With a sharp crack the shell left the long barrel and scarcely a second later the 88-mm round smashed through the armor of a Mark II. Flames, smoke, fleeing figures, all jumbled together in a haze of smoke.

The sun's heat caused the sand dust to glimmer. An armor-piercing shell struck the wall of sandbags around "Anton." The men were showered with dirt. The ammunition carriers gasped for breath. All four guns were firing now. A Mark II approached at high speed. It dodged to the side. Gun commander Unteroffizier Heintze had just ordered Huebner to target this tank. The British tank halted in preparation for firing. But the Gefreiter already had it in his sights.

The enemy tank was hit square in the front and was left immobile and smoking. From that point on other Mark II tanks concentrated their fire on the German gun positions. The defenders had counted 85 tanks. But then German tanks arrived and joined the battle. They were tanks of the 5th Panzer Regiment under the command of Oberst Olbricht. The enemy tanks turned and fled. Hill 208 was saved. Gefreiter Arnold Huebner had destroyed five enemy tanks on this day.

✠

The first day of "Operation Battleaxe" was over. The enemy had achieved a success, as the British 7th Armoured Division had advanced past Capuzzo and Musaid and had almost reached the assembly areas of the 15th Panzer Division. The British were thus just short of Bardia. Advancing past the southwest decline of the Halfaya Plateau, the enemy tanks reached Upper Sollum and overran the light German forces stationed there. But the big objective, a breakthrough with all forces, had not been achieved.

At least twenty-eight of the new British tanks brought in by the "Tiger" convoy, lay shattered in front of Hill 208. The burnt-out hulks of another eleven lay in front of the Halfaya Pass and on the pass road, while ten British tanks had met their end north of Capuzzo. In spite of these losses, however, the first part of the British plan had succeeded. The 7th Armoured Division was now in the rear of the defenders of the Halfaya Pass. A major victory could still be achieved if the British succeeded in encircling the 15th Panzer Division and the 5th Light Division the next morning.

✠

"Get ready!" ordered Oberstleutnant Cramer.

The tanks of the 15th Panzer Regiment had formed up to counterattack and retake Fort Capuzzo. The advance began. The sun had already risen. The 16th of June promised to be another hot day, in more ways than one. Hauptmann Kümmel stood in the open turret hatch and observed. The dense clouds of sand were being produced by the tanks of the British 7th Armoured Division. All of the 8th Panzer Regiment's tanks were attacking today. The counterattack had to succeed. The steel giants rolled across the desert. They drove over narrow trenches then came to a wadi lying across their path and roared in.

"Hang on!" Feldwebel Kruschinski shouted to the crew. The Panzer IV leaned dangerously far to the side. The engine roared. The tank steered to the other side and rumbled out of the wadi.

Suddenly enemy tanks appeared in front of them.

Oberstleutnant Cramer's voice sounded in the headsets of the company commanders: "First Battalion, frontal attack!"

"First, Second and Third inverted wedge!" called battalion commander Major Fenski. "First drive through, Second and Third open fire! Understood? Follow me!"

Hauptmann Kümmel observed the enemy. He saw their guns fire, heard the whistle of shells. The turret hatch was still open, for it was at least sixty degrees inside the fighting compartment. The panzers drove forward at full throttle, drove under the enemy fire, reached the most favorable firing range for the "stump" (the short-barreled 75-mm tank cannon), and halted to fire. All three tank cannon fired. One of the Mark IIs exploded in a display of fireworks.

The company's Panzer IIIs reached the commander and opened fire. All around them all hell was loose. Shells smashed into the ground, sending up fountains of dirt and sand. One of the tanks behind the command vehicle was hit and immediately afterwards Kümmel heard the voice of Leutnant Peters:

"Am hit, have to bail out. Give covering fire."

"Turn, Toni!"

The tank's suspension creaked as Kruschinski hauled the vehicle around. Two Mark II tanks were firing at their comrades. Relieved, they saw the Leutnant and his radio operator pull the wounded driver to safety.

"Fire!"

The gun barked. The second Mark II was hit while in the process of turning. It was immobilized, yet it fired and hit the tank of Unteroffizier Olsberg. Flames spurted from the opened hatches. None of the crew escaped this steel coffin.

"Drive on!"

They drove forward and rattled into the midst of an antitank battery which the British had moved forward. It banged and rattled. Hauptmann Kümmel, Oberleutnant Stiefmeyer and the others heard the calls for help from comrades who had been hit.

"We can't get through, relief advance!" called Major Fenski.

"Second Battalion coming from the left flank!"

Oberstleutnant Cramer took part in the relief attack, driving at the head of II Battalion. Farther ahead to the right he saw the tanks of I Battalion being knocked out."

"Faster!" he urged the companies.

The tanks advanced in inverted wedge formation. More and more German tanks were hit. Some had one track shot up but nevertheless kept firing. Oberstleutnant Cramer suddenly found himself facing a group of at least twenty Mark IIs, which were advancing at high speed toward the left wing of the 8th Panzer Regiment. These tanks with their long-barreled 40-mm guns were obviously supposed to decide the issue in the enemy's favor. Cramer acted immediately.

"Kümmel, turn and take the twenty Mark IIs in the flank," he ordered.

Hauptmann Kümmel followed the order. He saw that half of his tanks, including the second Panzer IV, were behind him. Shots whistled from the short 75-mm gun. The first tanks from the newly-arrived group of British armor stopped. Oberstleutnant Cramer gained some breathing space. He wanted to decide the issue, as he had done in Poland with the Reconnaissance Instruction Battalion.

An armor-piercing shell struck the ground to the right of the command tank. The flash of the explosion lit the interior of the vehicle. But before this tank, which had come from the flank, could fire a second shot it was hit by Oberfeldwebel Kruck and set on fire. The crew bailed out and disappeared into the dense smoke.

Seeing that some of the enemy tanks were attempting to approach from the right, Oberstleutnant Cramer ordered: "Turn to the east!" But just as his tank was swing around to the right a heavy blow shook the vehicle. Cramer felt a jolt and then a sharp pain in his head and arm. He had been wounded by shell fragments. Seconds later Kümmel received the news that the regimental commander had been put out of action. Then he heard a call for help from Oberfeldwebel Kruck. The tank turned and headed toward the Oberfeldwebel. His tank was burning.

After Kümmel's tank had knocked out the enemy, Kruck and three of his men rose up. Kruck bent down again and came up with his wounded driver leaning on his arm. Then they climbed aboard Kümmel's panzer. Shortly thereafter they disengaged from the enemy, for orders had been received to break off the engagement. They drove back to the assembly area. Exactly half of the 1st Company's tanks were missing. The other units had suffered similar losses.

"We're not going to do it like this. If Rommel doesn't come up with something else the Tommies will pound us into the ground here," said one of the men.

Oberfeldwebel Kruck bandaged the leg of his unconscious driver. Then he carried him to a waiting ambulance.

"Good luck comrade," he said softly as the ambulance pulled away.

The panzer regiment's wounded, including Oberstleutnant Cramer, were taken by the first-aid company to the main dressing station. One of the ambulances lost its way in the dark and had to wait in the desert until daylight came on the 17th of June.

✠

The attempt to retake Capuzzo had failed with heavy losses. Realizing that this old tactic was no longer of any use, Rommel sought another solution.

"One can often decide a battle by changing the point of main effort," he said to his staff officers. "Therefore, tomorrow morning at 4:30 we will attack via Sidi Omar toward Sidi Suleiman with the 5th Light and 15th Panzer Division."

"Then we will have them in a pincers," said Generalmajor Neumann-Silkow, commander of the 15th Panzer Division.

Generalmajor von Ravenstein, who commanded the 5th Light after the relief of Generalmajor Streich, cleared his throat audibly.

"Yes?" Rommel asked the general.

"The 5th Light is ready to carry out the outflanking advance. It can turn east toward Sidi Suleiman from the Sidi Omar area tomorrow morning," declared von Ravenstein.

"Excellent! Then we will force our plan on the enemy and the battle is already half won."

During the next half hour Rommel explained his plan. Then the division commanders returned to their units to make preparations for this new surprise blow.

✠

At the same hour the British brigade and division commanders had gathered in the headquarters of the commander in chief of desert forces. General Beresford-Peirse walked over to the map and began the decisive conference: "Gentlemen, the 5th Light Division has reached Sidi Omar. Even if tomorrow's attack succeeds, we can no longer take it in a pincer movement. Swinging wide around Fort Capuzzo and Hill 208, the 15th Panzer Division has also moved south toward Sidi Omar. As a result we must immediately join the Matildas with Creagh's 7th Armoured Division in order to undertake a concentric attack against the enemy tanks. Creagh will now explain his operations to us."

The British side was also certain that it could yet achieve victory, especially since it had been learned that the 15th Panzer Division was equipped mainly with Panzer III tanks, which were clearly inferior to the new British types.

✠

"Get ready!"

This was a familiar order to the tank crews, the signal that a new mission was in the offing.

"What is it, sir?" asked Oberfeldwebel Kruck. He had assumed command of a Panzer III whose commander had been wounded.

"We are moving out to link up with the 5th Light in Sidi Omar and then take the Tommies from behind near Capuzzo and at the Halfaya Pass."

Fifteen minutes later it was time. The panzers rolled through the dark night. From the forward lines and the artillery positions came the sound of heavy harrassing fire.

"Don't we want to retake Capuzzo?" asked Leutnant Peters.

"There will be time for that after we have encircled the Tommies."

They drove visually. The panzers were packed close together. Nothing bothered them. Even if the British heard the sound of tanks, it would be some time before they realized that Rommel had pulled another rabbit from his hat. When dawn came the German front north of Capuzzo was stripped of all but a few weak forces. These elements had orders to withdraw toward Bardia at once if the British attacked.

At 4:30 A.M. Generalmajor Neumann-Silkow gave the signal to attack. The 5th Light Division, which was on the right flank, now sent its tanks in motion as well. The offensive into the enemy's rear began. It was 17 June 1941. The 1st Company followed its commander at high speed. Leading the battalion was Major Fenski. Contact was made with the first enemy tanks. The British tank commanders were shocked to find the panzers here in the British rear.

The panzers broke into the British flank and reached Sidi Suleimann. From there they rolled on to their next objective. The sun was already high in the sky. The heat dried the men's throats and Hauptmann Kümmel took a swallow from the canteen which Feldwebel Kruschinski passed up to him. It was the bitter, salty water from the desert wells, with a shot of anise added to it.

Kümmel heard Major Fenski's call for the battalion to keep moving and relayed the order to his company. The tanks raced across the undulating terrain, leaving long clouds of dust behind them. They came across British supply columns, which they shot to pieces. British tanks appeared and were met by withering fire.

The confusion grew on the enemy side. Apparently none of the British tank commanders knew anymore where the enemy was. At 9:25 A.M. General Creagh signalled the commander of desert forces that he no longer knew any way out. General Beresford-Peirse might yet come to his (Creagh's) battle headquarters. When this message was intercepted by the radio monitoring service and brought to Rommel, he observed:

"They no longer know where they stand. They won't attack again now."

A short time later tanks of the 5th Light Division reached Brigadier-General Messervey's command post and overran it. The British 4th Armoured Brigade had been deprived of its commander and had been rendered ineffective. While Kümmel and his company will still striving toward the rocky slopes of Halfaya Pass, the survivors of the 4th Armoured Brigade began a hasty retreat. A short time later (General Wavell and General Beresford-Peirse had just arrived at the command post of the British 7th Armoured Division), General Peirse had to issue the order for the other units to retreat as well.

It was General Wavell, the commander in chief in Egypt, who forced this retreat in order to save what he could. Wavell subsequently flew back to Cairo and signaled London: "I regret to have to report that 'Battleaxe' has failed."

The last British troops fought their way east and reached Sidi Barrani, battered and demoralized. The German armored forces halted wherever they were. They were exhausted. They had been in action for almost seventy-two hours without a break. In those hours the 15th Panzer Division had fought and survived its first battle as a division sized unit.

Generalmajor Neumann-Silkow, who was informed of Hauptmann Kümmel's independent and decisive action, recommended Kümmel for the Knight's Cross. The following is from his supporting letter:

> Hauptmann Kümmel's attack on the superior armored enemy west and northwest of Capuzzo on 15 June 1941 was the result of his own decision.
>
> Through the daring of this decision and its uncompromising implementation he prevented the enemy from advancing farther north, where he would have caught and destroyed the combat

trains which were in the process of moving out. Without these trains, which continually supplied the 8th Panzer Regiment with urgently needed ammunition and fuel during the three-day battle, it would not have been possible to drive back the enemy and destroy considerable numbers of his tanks.

The toughness and determination of his independent decision was responsible for preventing a potentially fatal breakthrough at that place.

Oberstleutnant Cramer, who had led the regiment until he was wounded, was also recommended for the Knight's Cross. And a third officer of the Africa Corps was found worthy of this coveted decoration: Hauptmann Wilhelm Bach, the "fighting pastor."

✠

When Kümmel woke on the morning of the 18th his replacement batman had a strange grin on his face.

"Is something going on, Zimmer?" he asked.

"Not that I know of, sir," replied the Gefreiter, continuing to grin.

Some time later Kümmel walked over to his tank and immediately made a curious discovery. A roaring lion had been painted on one side of the vehicle. There was something written beneath it. Stepping closer, he read: "The Lion of Capuzzo."

"Kruschinski!" he shouted.

The Feldwebel crawled out from under the tank and stood before his company commander.

"You called, sir?" he asked casually.

"What is that supposed to be?" asked Kümmel, pointing to the image of the lion.

"That is our emblem from now on, sir. The Hauptmann is now called the 'Lion of Capuzzo.'"

"If this puss in boots is not gone within two minutes, I will boot you in the rear end, understood?"

The Hauptmann turned around so that the stunned soldier, a veteran of many battles, could not see the smile which he could no longer suppress. While Hauptmann Hans Kümmel was able to have the painting washed off, he would never lose the nickname "Lion of Capuzzo."

All day long the men worked on the tanks, making them fully battle ready. Sweat flowed in streams down the sun-browned bodies of the work-

A Panzer III E of the 15th Panzer Division.

shop personnel. A few hours later Kümmel had an opportunity to speak to the division commander again. Then he and his crew drove to the seaside for a dip. They cavorted in the water like carefree boys, and tried to forget the horrors that lay behind them.

On 18 June Rommel wrote to his wife in Germany that the three-day battle had ended in a complete victory for Germany. He added that in the coming days he was going to visit all of the units that had taken part in order to thank them in person. He, too, had been on the battlefield for three days and nights without a rest. The next day Hauptmann Kümmel received advance warning from Major Fenski that Rommel was coming. They greeted the commander in chief with the usual ceremony. After Kümmel had reported, Rommel said: "You have a good company, Kümmel. Perhaps soon an equally good battalion."

Major Fenski winked at his comrade secretly. Feldwebel Kruschinski was called upon to give his version of the events of 15th June. The Feldwebel did this in his own way: "The commander gave the order. Full throttle and after them! Eight tanks knocked out. Tore up the Tommies and came home, sir."

Rommel laughed. He nodded to the Feldwebel, and had cigarettes and a sack of oranges passed out before leaving for Hill 208.

British prime minister Winston Churchill received news of the defeat at his estate in Chartwell. He had gone there to be alone for a few hours. Several days later he wrote in his personal diary:

> The success in the desert would have meant the destruction of Rommel's daring troops. . . . I had not yet heard anything about the events of the 17th of June, and as I knew that the outcome of the battle would be reported very soon I went to Chartwell. . . . There I learned what had happened in the Capuzzo-Sidi Suleiman-Halfaya Pass area on 17th June. Disconsolate, I wandered around in the valley for hours.

On 17 June 1941 all British hopes in the desert were dashed. Four days later Churchill telegraphed General A.P. Wavell: "I have decided that the public interest will best be served if General Auchinleck is named commander of the army in the Near East in your place."

Thus one of the most capable desert commanders was sent into the wilderness. Rommel had taken Wavell's newly-won "laurels from his head and cast them in the sand." Rommel deserved much of the credit for the German success, but so did Oberstleutnant Cramer and Gefreiter Huebner, Hauptmann Bach and Obergefreiter Ilgenroth, Oberstleutnant Knabe and Gefreiter Schulz, Hauptmann Kümmel, and Gefreiter Albers.

On 9 June 1941 Hauptmann Johannes Kümmel received the Knight's Cross of the Iron Cross. Kümmel's Knight's Cross was of course cause for a fitting celebration. Rommel appeared and congratulated the man who had risen from a common soldier to an officer and had now received this high decoration. But Kümmel remained what he was: a unit leader who did whatever he could to shield his men, who took on the most difficult tasks himself and a man who saw his subordinates as comrades in a difficult time. He was called "Lion of Capuzzo." In view of his military accomplishments it was a richly deserved nickname. Several days after receiving the Knight's Cross, Kümmel went home on leave to Coswig in Saxony.

THE BATTLE AT SIDI REZEGH

The summer of 1941 was an extremely hot one in Africa. August brought temperatures of 50 to 60 degrees Celsius in the shade. During the day the men of Panzer Group Africa remained in their foxholes to escape the heat. At night the temperature fell to ten degrees above zero. Everything they touched was hot. Everything they ate was infested with swarms of flies. Dysentery spread, as did a fever caused by the tiny pappadach fly.

The 8th Panzer Regiment had dug in in the Tobruk area. Rommel was everywhere. He gradually became a bogeyman, for he appeared from nowhere and bawled out the men if something wasn't right. He gave hell to anyone who stepped out of line and violated his directives, which had in part been issued for the protection of the men. Only in this way was it possible to assure the health of the men and also maintain discipline.

Tobruk was the objective that Rommel now had his eye on. Tobruk was the magic word, for as long as Tobruk held out Panzer Group Africa was subject to attack from two sides: from the fortress and from the east, from the area of Sidi Barrani-Marsa Matruh. Rommel's demands for supplies were largely not met. This was mainly because the war in Russia had begun and almost everything available was being sent to this new theater.

Winston Churchill wrote to general Auchinleck, the new commander in chief in the Near East, that he could now attack as soon as he was ready. But Auchinleck hesitated. He did this for four and a half months, delaying the decision in North Africa by a full year and a half.

In July 1941 Erwin Rommel was promoted to General der Panzertruppe without him knowing about it. On 3 July he wrote to his wife that he had heard about it on the radio but as yet had not received any official notification.

That was the situation when Hauptmann Kümmel returned from leave in August.

✠

The sun had already wandered far to the west. A Kübelwagen approached the 1st Company's positions.

"Visit, sir," said Unteroffizier Milde to the acting company commander.

Oberleutnant Peters nodded. He wiped the sweat from his brow and put on his pith helmet. Before he could do up the buckle the car stopped right in front of the tent and out jumped Hans Kümmel.

"The old man is back," shouted Milde. The men emerged from their holes and from beneath the tanks. They ran toward their company commander and encircled him.

"Not all at once!" cried Kümmel. "You'll pull my arm off! How are things Bock?" he asked the operations officer, who had just emerged from the tent housing the radio station.

"Good, Hannes!" replied Oberleutnant Bock. "And now they're even better. You look great!"

"It was lovely at home," replied the Hauptmann.

The crew of the company commander's tank came running. They had been farthest away to the northeast. Feldwebel Kruschinski led the way. Again there were howls of greeting, handshakes, questions and answers. Before leaving his men Kümmel said, "If the reports are correct there will be a welcome home drink behind the company command post tonight at 10:10." Kümmel unpacked his things and took out the gifts he had brought. After an hour he felt at home again in the hot desert when he ate his first meal and had to chase away the flies.

After he had eaten, Kümmel said, "Then I have come back in time for the next offensive."

"Doesn't look like it, sir," interjected Feldwebel Schnier, the orderly office chief. "Nothing is getting through. The Tommies are sinking every second ship."

"Rommel must be furious," replied Kümmel.

Kümmel and his comrades gathered late in the evening. Oberleutnant Bock appeared with Oberleutnant Thurow and Stiefelmeyer and battalion commander Major Fenski showed up. It was a pleasant gathering and Kümmel was kept busy talking about home. The next morning he held the first muster for the company. He saw that everything was in tiptop shape.

✠

"What day is it today, Becker?" Kümmel asked his adjutant. The short Leutnant looked at the calendar.

"The 21st of August 1941, sir. You are scheduled to drive to the forward outposts."

"Thank you, Becker. Afterward we're going swimming, so bring the bathing trunks."

They climbed into the fast car and drove away. Obergefreiter Albers was also along for the ride. They hadn't gone far when they sighted the first enemy aircraft.

"Bombers, sir!" declared Becker.

"With an escort of Hurricanes!" added Albers.

"They're flying too far north to be able to see us and . . ." Kümmel stopped, for several silver dots had appeared from the north.

"German fighters!" shouted Albers.

The fighters, which were flying at least 500 meters higher than the British formation, quickly grew in size. Then they dove, and the men on the ground saw flashes as they fired their cannon and watched the first Hurricane go down in a steep dive and explode on impact.

"There, the parachute!"

The parachute was clearly visible as it drifted toward the desert. A northeast wind was blowing it toward the Germans. Soon they could see the figure of the pilot swinging beneath it.

"Approach slowly," ordered Kümmel.

The car moved off and turned toward the spot where the British pilot was sure to land. A Hurricane appeared, turned and headed straight toward them.

"Get out!" roared Kümmel.

They leapt from the still moving car. The driver had pulled the hand brake and the car came to an abrupt stop. Albers was the last one out. He ran after the Hauptmann, who leapt into a cleft in the ground just as the Hurricane opened fire. Albers realized that he wasn't going to make it in time. He therefore dodged to the side and threw himself down. He heard the sound of bullets striking the ground and then felt a sharp pain in his rear.

The Hurricane roared over Albers. He felt the turbulence from the propeller. Then everything began to swim before his eyes. He heard the sound of footsteps but it was if he was hearing it through cotton. Then he felt a warm breath on his face. He heard the Hauptmann's voice telling him to hang on. He clasped his hands behind the company commander's neck and felt himself being lifted. Then he heard the drone of the returning fighter and the sound of bullets striking the ground.

Kümmel did not see the aircraft but he heard it. He ran several steps to one side and threw himself down. The bullets missed. He immediately got up again and carried the now unconscious loader to the cleft. Together with the driver he laid the wounded man on his belly. Kümmel gasped, "Have a look at him, bandage him up." Meanwhile Albers had awakened from his brief period of unconsciousness.

"Sir," he stammered, dismayed, "they've shot me in the rear end!" He gasped in pain and anger. "There of all places!"

His words produced grins all round.

"Not so bad, Albers!" said Becker. "Only a flesh wound. It will be healed in four weeks."

"Drive Becker and me to the forward outpost and then take Albers to the main dressing station," decided the Hauptmann.

"Can't I stay here, sir?" asked the loader.

"No way," replied Kümmel categorically. "There might be complications, and . . ."

"Sir, there!" shouted the driver.

Kümmel turned around again. He saw a Messerschmitt 109 turn behind a Hurricane and fire. Seconds later one of the enemy aircraft's wing broke off. It nosed down, went into a spin and blew apart in a mighty explosion. The duel between the British and German fighters continued low over the horizon.

"They're probably Redlich's boys (1/JG 27)," Leutnant Becker declared to Kümmel.

"Brave lads, Becker—on both sides. We can always climb out of our tanks and . . ."

Kümmel stopped in mid sentence, for his thoughts returned to the downed Hurricane pilot.

"Let's go, Zunkley!" he said to his driver. They drove to where the British pilot must have come down. The car stopped and Kümmel got out. He looked all around and several times called out to the British airman.

"Hello, comrade! Hello, comrade!"

Suddenly he heard a rustling sound from some camelthorn bushes about ten meters ahead. When he reached them he saw a pale face and a fist holding a pistol. It was pointed right at his belly.

"Don't shoot!" he said in broken English. "We will help you!"

Kümmel moved closer. Then there was a crack. The German heard the bullet whiz just past his head and threw himself down to the ground. As he dropped he drew his pistol and aimed at the shadow visible between the two bushes. He could have shot, too, but he didn't. Kümmel crawled on until he could see the Englishman clearly. The airman was lying on the ground, his right foot bent outwards in a strange way. The pistol was still in his hand, but he was no longer able to hold it level. The pain-contorted face turned to Kümmel.

"Help," stammered the man.

A few steps brought Kümmel to the Englishman, who was now no longer an enemy but a wounded soldier who needed help. Kümmel took his canteen and unscrewed the cap. Then he held the opening to the lips of the British airman, who drank deeply.

"Come here!" Kümmel shouted to the others.

The Kübelwagen came roaring over. Leutnant Becker got out and walked over to the Hauptmann who was inspecting the airman's leg.

"Give me a hand, Becker," he said. Together they lifted the injured man into the car and sat him beside Albers. Albers, who was smoking a cigarette, saw the longing look in the man's eyes.

"You can still have a smoke, even if you were the one who shot me in the britches," he murmured, and pulled out another cigarette. He lit it and stuck it between the Englishman's lips.

They drove straight to the forward outpost where they were greeted by Oberfeldwebel Kruck.

"Take off, Zünkley!" Kümmel ordered the driver. "And as soon as you have dropped off the two wounded come back here."

The car drove off and Kümmel inspected the position, which extended farther southeast into the desert than any other. The tanks were sitting in a depression, well camouflaged with camelthorn and other bushes. Ferdinand Kruck led the Hauptmann to the observation post, which was situated just behind the crest of a hill. A binocular periscope was mounted there.

Hauptmann Kümmel took a look. The desert spread out as far as he could see. But then, suddenly, he spotted four British armored cars. They were driving fast from southeast of the observation post toward the northwest and would surely end up behind the company command post if they continued on their present course. Kümmel reached for the crank on the field telephone. The senior NCO answered.

"Alert the heavy platoon immediately. English patrol heading northwest through grid square 2315-3510. Distance from the command post three kilometers. Heavy platoon to attack the patrol and destroy it."

Kümmel continued to observe the four intruders and saw them alter their heading slightly toward the north. They were now heading straight toward the command post.

Several minutes passed. Then the first Panzer IV appeared and rolled toward the British armored cars. The second appeared farther to the west and then the third drove into the Hauptmann's field of view.

The leading tank was already within 1,000 meters of the armored car which was leading the British patrol. By the time the enemy commander spotted the panzer it was already too late. There was a flash as the Panzer IV opened fire. The very first shell settled the fate of the British vehicle. The three following vehicles now opened fire. The shells bounced off the tank's armored sides.

Kümmel kept up a running commentary for the benefit of the others. The other two German tanks joined the battle. The British vehicles turned to flee, and as they did so one was hit and burst into flames. The other two escaped into the desert, zigzagging wildly. Kümmel saw one of his tanks drive forward and pick up the survivors from the two British vehicles.

"Looks like we were in just the right place," declared Leutnant Becker.

"Hmm," said Kümmel reflectively, "by the way where is your second tank Kruck?"

Oberfeldwebel Kruck looked at his watch.

"Should have been here some time ago, sir. It is on a routine drive through the Wadi Qualinta. That always takes an hour."

"When did it depart?"

"Nearly two hours ago, sir."

"Come on Kruck, let's go and find it."

They climbed into a tank. The camouflage was removed and then they drove off. Kümmel breathed a sigh of relief when they reached the wadi. Now they were shielded from the enemy's view. They drove another kilometer and suddenly heard the sound of gunfire.

"It's coming from the southeast end of the wadi!" called Kruck. "Full gas, Hümmelchen!"

The driver stepped on the gas pedal and the Panzer III rumbled over the rocky ground. Then they came to a spot where the wadi turned to the southeast. From there they saw Unteroffizier Kohlmann's tank. It was sitting in the open in the middle of the wadi. Flashes of gunfire were coming from the high ground on both sides. Shells hammered into the sand. Another struck the tank's turret but was deflected and smashed into the wall of the wadi.

"We're going to drive through at full speed. All set?"

Kümmel lowered the hatch cover but did not lock it.

"Weapon loaded and locked!" called the loader. Meanwhile Oberfeldwebel Kruck had already taken aim at a muzzle flash. The tank picked up speed. The enemy gunners spotted this new threat and turned their attention to it, but within seconds the panzer had already driven under their angle of fire. Kümmel ordered:

"Turn left! Up the hill and then halt!"

Kruck nodded. It was exactly what he would have done. He rotated the turret so that only a minor correction would be needed before opening fire. Driver Hümmelchen headed the tank up the slope. The engine howled as they took the hill. Once the tank slid sideways and threatened to tip over, but the driver reacted quickly and averted disaster. Then they were on top. Kruck peered through the sight and saw a British Matilda tank. He made a slight correction then pressed the firing button. The 50-mm gun barked and the armor-piercing shell struck the unprotected rear of the enemy tank. A bright flame shot out as it's gasoline tank exploded. The stricken tank turned and was hit again.

The second enemy tank, positioned fifty meters farther away, turned on the spot. Shrouded in a cloud of dust, it disappeared down the hill at high speed and left the panzer's field of fire. Without waiting to be told to do so, Hümmelchen turned the tank to the right and drove to the steep slope. Suddenly Kümmel saw eight or nine British tanks; still a good 1,000 meters away, they were rolling straight towards him.

"Turn. Back to the other tank!" ordered Kümmel. They rolled back down the hill and drove up to the Panzer III, which was sitting there like a lame duck.

"What's your situation, Kohlmann?" Kruck shouted to make himself heard above the noise from the engine.

"Can't get away, Oberfeld, the clutch has had it!"

"The Tommies are coming," Kruck shouted back. Then turning to Kümmel, he asked, "Should we take them on board and abandon the tank?"

"Out of the question. You wait here and I'll go have a look."

Hauptmann Kümmel knew about tanks and was also an expert in technical matters. Clutches had been his specialty. He jumped down and ran over to the tank, which was sitting in the middle of the gully.

"Locking ring wrench," he said, and the driver passed him the tool he wanted. Kümmel tried to make an adjustment, but the clutch had already been moved as far as it would go.

He now tried to move the tank, as the clutch had cooled of somewhat. His effort paid off. The huge vehicle turned. Applying the throttle cautiously, he succeeded in backing the tank up about 400 meters. Just then the first enemy tank appeared above on the sandy crest. It was fired on by the second panzer, which was covering Kümmel's withdrawal. The British tank backed out of sight.

"They're up above, sir," radioed Kruck.

"Hold them off Kruck, hold them off!" Then he heard the driver of the damaged tank say, "It won't work, sir, the plates slip as soon as they get hot."

"Give me a cap full of sand," ordered Kümmel.

For a second the driver stared at him as if he had lost his mind. But then he jumped out and got the sand. Kümmel stepped on the gas pedal. Then he formed a funnel from his identity disc and poured the fine sand into the clutch. Meanwhile the sound of tanks was growing louder. Instead of climbing the hill, the enemy was now trying to slip past the Germans on the other side and get behind them. It sounded as though the British were already abeam them. Hauptmann Kümmel tried it once again. The tank moved! The clutch plates had become so rough that they held even when the Hauptmann shifted into second gear. The panzers drove at a good pace to the end of the wadi and then turned toward the company command post. Ten minutes later they reached safety. The enemy tanks, whose commander had surely been hoping for easy prey, had meanwhile disappeared.

"Remove the clutch, install new clutch plates, and report to me in an hour that the tank is serviceable again!"

Kümmel disappeared into his tent and removed his sweat-soaked tunic. Leutnant Becker came in.

"Terrific, sir, just terrific!" he said enthusiastically. "Why didn't someone else come up with that idea?"

"They'd better not risk throwing sand into a clutch!" warned Kümmel.

Some time later Unteroffizier Kuhlmann came to report. He admitted knowing that the clutch was badly worn. He subsequently received a dressing-down that shook the tent but there was no formal punishment. After Kuhlmann had slinked away like a wet poodle, Kümmel turned to Leutnant Becker.

"You see, Becker," he said, "these are first-class men. But we simply can't allow such sloppiness. We could easily have lost a tank because of it."

"I will drum it into them that we have to think of our equipment, sir," replied the Leutnant.

August passed in searing heat. Twenty men of the company were stricken with diahorrea. More and more men reported sick. Only Kümmel seemed indestructible. He did not get sick. "I don't have time for it," he said.

Three weeks after he was wounded Albers returned from Benghazi. The wound in his rear end had healed, but he brought with him a ring-shaped rubber cushion to sit on whenever he was in the tank. His comrades found this most amusing and teased him mercilessly.

In September flies, ticks, sand fleas and scorpions became the 8th Panzer Regiment's chief opponents. Rommel still hoped that the supplies might yet start flowing, but he was disappointed. British submarines and aircraft were decimating the supply convoys. Between July and November of 1941 alone they sank 48 German and Italian cargo vessels carrying 200,000 tons of supplies.

On 15 September Hans Cramer returned to the regiment. Travelling by way of Crete and Derna, he rejoined the unit which was still in its old positions south and southeast of Tobruk. Everything was just as it had been four months earlier in May 1941.

✠

The 5th Light Division had been renamed the 21st Panzer Division. The 90th Light Division had been formed from the 361st Africa Regiment. In order to effectively bombard the fortress of Tobruk, General Rommel formed the 104th Artillery Detachment, which was increased in size constantly. At the beginning of November the artillery detachment had nine 210-mm howitzers, thirty-eight 150-mm howitzers and twelve 105-mm cannon-a considerable amount of firepower by African standards.

Rommel was everywhere in those weeks. He also visited the 8th Panzer Regiment several times. Once he found Feldwebel Kruschinski asleep in a foxhole, a fez perched on his head. He woke him rather harshly and ordered him to pay more attention to his appearance. Completely flabbergasted, Kruschinski stood in his foxhole with the fez on his head and tried to reply as militarily as possible. Behind Rommel everyone was grinning, but that did not make the situation any easier for Kruschinski.

Rommel turned to the commander of the First. "Kümmel, knock this fellow into shape . . ." Rommel had turned all the way round and was now looking into the sun-browned face of the tank officer which was split from ear to ear by a wide grin. He fell silent. Then he waved his hand through the air contemptuously. "What an outfit!" he said. Then he turned and walked quickly back to his command vehicle so that the men could not see that he was smiling too.

An hour later Kümmel was back with Kruschinski and took the young man to task for his earlier behavior. "Listen, Toni," he said, "that just won't do. Rommel couldn't have been too impressed to see you in that getup."

"It won't happen again, Hannes," replied Kruschinski.

"You will straighten up then?" asked a surprised Kümmel.

"Not exactly, sir, but I have promised Feldwebel Hinrichs from Rommel's staff two Tommy cap badges if he warns me by telephone in time when Rommel is coming here again."

"That is another way of not attracting attention to yourself," sighed Kümmel. "But I would rather you didn't walk around like such a good-for-nothing."

✠

Two days later Generalmajor Neumann-Silkow visited the First. It was obvious that Kruschinski's web also extended to the division headquarters, for everything was in tiptop shape. Neumann-Silkow, with the unavoidable peaked cap on his lean face, was very satisfied with the First.

As he was leaving the general observed casually to Feldwebel Kruschinski: "You are paying too much, Kruschinski! If you will get me a good 'desert rat' cap badge I will call you in advance to allow you to prepare for my arrival." Once again Kruschinski was left standing like a wet poodle and had to endure the ribbing of his comrades.

By the beginning of November Rommel, together with Oberstleutnant Siegfried Westphal, Panzer Group Africa's new First General Staff Officer had worked out the plans for attacking Tobruk. These plans were now talked through in Rommel's command vehicle, a converted bus. During the day Rommel drove to the front in a Kübelwagen. Everything was readied for the big blow against the fortress.

"It's about to start, sir!" Obergefreiter Albers said to Hans Kümmel when the latter inspected the individual groups. Kümmel said the same thing to Major Fenski when he arrived that evening. Fenski in turn said the same to the regiment's commander. Oberst Cramer already knew, for he had been ordered to attend the briefing.

Two days later all the members of the 15th Panzer Division were told. Generalmajor Neumann-Silkow set up a special formation which was supposed to function as a sort of "traffic controller." Each unit of the division was led into the attack lanes by a group from the formation and was guided to the crossings which led over the deep antitank ditches. As a result of direct action in all parts of the division's attack lane, the special unit soon knew every bunker and machine-gun position in the fortress. Route markers (canisters containing fuel to serve as light beacons) stood ready. After several postponements, 23 November 1941 was chosen as X-Day.

South of Gambut, due north of the Trigh Capuzzo, the desert road which led from Capuzzo via Sidi Azeiz and Sidi Rezegh to Tobruk, the men of the 115th Panzer-Grenadier Regiment stood ready. Hauptmann Kümmel had the entire company on line. Major Fenski came frequently to assure himself that everything was ready. But the enemy was ready too. A photocopy of Rommel's handwritten plan of attack had fallen into British hands. General Auchinleck acted immediately. He knew that he would have to strike first if he was to avoid a disaster, striking the Germans while they were in the midst of their own preparations. The British forces at

Johannes Kümmel celebrates the awarding of the Knight's Cross with his comrades.

once went into readiness positions. Clever camouflage concealed their movements. Finally, on 14 November 1941, Auchinleck was ready.

The evening of 17 November settled over the desert near Gambut. The men of the 1st Company of the 8th Panzer Regiment lay in their tents and foxholes. Hauptmann Kümmel was with his crew when it began to rain.

"Rain, sir!" Unteroffizier Milde called enthusiastically.

"It's just falling mosquitoes," replied Kruschinski.

Ten seconds later there could be no more doubt that it was in fact rain. Soon rain was pouring down from the African sky. The men poured out of their holes and ran about in the rain, bare naked. They had no idea why this was happening, for it had not rained in this area for years. After they had had enough, the soldiers returned to their tents and towelled themselves dry. All of a sudden the water came down from the Halfaya

Plateau and rushed south and west through the dry wadis. Carrying rocks and masses of sand with it, the torrent raced downwards. The first tents were swept away and a truck which was parked at the bottom of the wadi was overturned.

"Into the tanks!" ordered Kümmel. They ran to the parked armored vehicles, climbed in and shut the hatches. They were safe there. Suddenly there were explosions from the minefield in front of them.

Kümmel reassured his men: "It's just mines exploding!"

The radio operator relayed a message he had just received: "High water, high water!"

But high water was also the code word for a British attack. There was a great deal of confusion until it was confirmed that it really was high water. When day finally broke after the night of the floods, the soldiers worked like mad to free their vehicles from the mud and sand. With their vehicles bogged down and all personnel engaged in getting them out, any German attack was out of the question. At that very hour, however, the British were launching their own offensive, "Operation Crusader."

It was still raining when the British XXX Corps (the 1st South-African Division, the 7th Armoured Division and the 22nd Armoured Brigade) moved off from the Maddalena area, headed northwest and advanced past Bir Sheferzen towards Sidi Rezegh. The XXX Army Corps included 94 older versions of the Crusader tank, 210 new Crusaders and 173 Stuart tanks. Altogether the corps had 477 tanks at its disposal.

At the same time the British XIII Army Corps attacked east of Sollum. In its ranks were the 1st and 2nd Armoured Brigades with 135 and 126 Matilda and Valentine tanks respectively. General Cunningham, who had been placed in command of this attack, had another 250 tanks in reserve. At the same time a convoy was en route to Africa with another 60 Stuart tanks and 25 infantry tanks. When the British attack began, Panzer Group Africa had a total of 260 German and 154 Italian tanks at its disposal.

We've been placed on alert men! The Tommies are attacking. An armoured brigade has attacked the Ariete (Italian armored division) at Bir el Gobi. It is the 22nd Armoured Brigade. The 7th Armoured Brigade is advancing via Gabr Saleh toward Sidi Rezegh and it has just been reported that the 4th Armoured Brigade is advancing on Gambut. Our 21st Panzer Division has

> already launched a counterattack. The 5th Panzer Regiment under Oberst Stephan will halt the 4th Armoured Brigade.

With these words Oberst Cramer filled his company commanders in on the situation.

It was exactly 2:30 P.M. when Hans Kümmel returned to his company. He brought his men the news that they had been tensely awaiting: General Crüwell, the commanding general of the Africa Corps, had committed Battle Group Stephan south towards Gabr el Saleh. At that hour Rommel himself had driven to the battle group in order to personally lead its attack. The loss of the German plan of attack was made good when Auchinleck's plan was discovered in a staff vehicle of the 4th Indian Division.

"When will our turn come, sir?" asked Oberleutnant Peters, who had been promoted just fourteen weeks earlier.

"Tomorrow morning, I should imagine."

II Battalion was placed on alert and that evening engaged British tanks which had driven into the panzer regiment's picket line.

The night passed in gnawing uncertainty. Rumors made the rounds. At dawn on 19 November the enemy also appeared before I Battalion, 8th Panzer Regiment, however it proved to be nothing more than elements separated from the main force.

"The First will attack enemy armor abeam the Trigh Capuzzo!" ordered Major Fenski.

The eight panzers moved off. Kümmel deployed his vehicles. Suddenly they came under fire. The hatches clanged shut. The guns lined up on targets and the first shots rang out. One tank was disabled with a shot-up track. Then Kümmel's panzers closed with the enemy. They fired from a range of 1,400 meters.

Kümmel congratulated his gunner after the enemy tank he was firing at burst into flames following the third shot. The tank moved to the side to avoid a crossfire and then took out an enemy tank firing from the flank. Kümmel then directed his tank into the enemy's flank.

"They're retreating!" Kümmel informed the battalion commander. "Am initiating pursuit."

"Only as far as Point 106.7, Kümmel!" ordered Fenski.

The panzers raced after the fleeing enemy tanks, caught up with two of them and knocked them out. Then they turned and drove back to their assembly area. There an order had been received from the German Africa Korps. It read: "Tomorrow we will link up with the 21st Panzer Division and launch a decisive attack against the main body of the enemy armored forces."

Rumors filtered through: the 361st Africa Regiment had overrun a British tank company and had taken over its vehicles. It was now carrying out its own attack against the enemy.

✠

The next morning the 15th Panzer Regiment turned west onto the Trigh Capuzzo.

"Enemy's 7th Armoured Division has reached Sidi Rezegh!"

This news alarmed the men. The tanks rolled down the Trigh Capuzzo at top speed. Lone enemy tanks, separated from the main body, were chased off the road and destroyed. Hauptmann Kümmel's heavy tanks were once again driving point. He was one of the first to see the fires blazing on Sidi Rezegh airfield. Dust clouds revealed the presence of enemy vehicles.

"There they are, Fenski!" he reported.

Suddenly the sonorous voice of Oberst Cramer sounded in the commanders' headsets:

"Attack the enemy tanks at the southeastern and eastern outskirts of Sidi Rezegh!"

The panzer companies spread out. While the Second Battalion swung out to the southwest into the desert, the First Battalion drove straight toward the enemy. Soon the enemy antitank guns opened fire. To Kümmel's right a tank exploded. The crew were able to scramble to safety.

"Ahead, eleven o'clock, one thousand, two-hundred!"

"Target in sight!" called Theo Kleff. The gunner took aim, but before he could fire a heavy blow shook the tank. Kümmel smelled gasoline fumes. Then there was a crackling sound. The driver groaned.

Kümmel gave the order to get out and himself jumped out through the hatch. He forgot the wires of his headset; they were both torn out, but he was left with welts on both cheeks. Together with the radio operator he pulled Toni Kruschinski from the tank. The Feldwebel had a hole in his forehead but was fully conscious. They dragged their comrade to the side and saw the fire crossing. Smoke trails from tracing ammunition were visible in the daylight. Guns flashes, shells exploded, gasoline tanks blazed. Gradually the din of battle receded into the distance.

"How is it, Toni?" Kümmel asked his comrade in arms of many years.

"Don't feel anything. Apparently the splinter isn't in too deep."

They placed a temporary dressing on the wound. When they were done a lone tank came back along the track. It was Hellmigk.

"Sir, the major said I am to hand over my tank to you."

Hellmigk's face was covered in blood. It also soaked his head bandage. They climbed into the Unteroffizier's tank. Kümmel joined the regiment an hour late. By that time the battle had been decided. In spite of this setback, the next morning the British reached the Italian positions south of Sidi Rezegh and broke through. The tanks of the 8th Panzer Regiment attacked again, resulting in a short, sharp engagement. Kümmel destroyed three enemy tanks, as did Oberfeldwebel Kruck.

On the evening of 20 November the panzers stopped for a brief rest. Günther Fenski said to Hans Kümmel: "Now we have a good starting position. From here we can tear up the rearward communications of the advancing Tommies,"

"Have you heard, Günther? The 21st Panzer Division is stranded near Sidi Omar out of fuel."

"Who said that?" asked Fenski astonished.

"I heard it several times over the radio. They are in urgent need of fuel and have asked for an air drop."

"If Tommy finds out, he will step up his efforts even more and . . ."

Leutnant Becker came rushing into the tent. He waved a note pad excitedly in the air.

"What is it Becker?

"Cunningham has ordered the garrison of Tobruk to break out. It begins tomorrow morning!"

"Alarm, alarm!"

They ran into the open and jumped into their panzers, where they waited for news. It wasn't long coming.

"Reconnaissance tanks have run into the 4th Armoured Brigade!"

The tanks drove off immediately. Half an hour later they reached the battlefield, where several tanks, including two Panzer IIIs, were burning. Oberst Cramer gave the order to attack. The battle began and soon afterwards the enemy withdrew. Night settled over the battlefield.

"Everyone remain where they are!"

The crews settled in for the night of 21 November. Several platoons took up security positions and observed the desert toward the west.

"We are in the Englishmen's rear. If we strike quickly now we will have them between two fires," said Major Fenski during a conference.

"Yes, if we succeed in stopping the Tobruk garrison's attempts to break out," said Oberleutnant Stiefelmeyer. Oberleutnant Heinrich cleared his throat.

Congratulatory meeting for General Crüwell on 20 March 1942 at Umm Er Rzem. From the left: Oberst Menny; Oberst Bruer; unidentified signals officer; Generalmajor von Bismarck; Kümmel; Oberst Gerhard Müller; Oberstleutnant Pfeiffer; and Oberst Herbert Ewert.

"Yes?" said Kümmel. The commander of the 2nd Company, who had just arrived, had the latest news.

"According to English radio traffic the 22nd Armoured Brigade, which in the afternoon was fighting the Italian Ariete Division, has been turned around to reinforce the 4th Armoured Brigade."

"Then they must be here by morning," observed Fenski.

"What's the Bologna Division's situation?" asked Stiefelmeyer.

"According to the latest reports, the British 70th Infantry Division, supported by 50 tanks, has sortied from Tobruk, broken through and captured all the Italians' artillery. However the 3rd Reconnaissance Battalion under Oberstleutnant von Wechmar was able to seal off the penetration at the last second."

"Then the decision will come tomorrow comrades!" declared Major Fenski. "And I am certain that we will play a major part in the concert."

"We hope so, sir!" quipped Leutnant Becker.

✠

During the night the 15th Panzer Division regrouped again. Oberst Cramer deployed his units to the east and drove into the enemy's deep flank. The sound of tank engines and the rattle of tracks carried a considerable distance in the night. Kümmel also heard a considerable amount of noise from the direction of the enemy.

At this time General Ludwig Crüwell was at Rommel's command post. Rommel said to him:

> At first light tomorrow morning you are to attack the enemy forces driving toward Tobruk with the entire Africa Korps and destroy them! You are to retake Sidi Rezegh airfield, which was captured by Brigadier Davy's 7th Armoured Brigade yesterday morning. Sümmermann and the 90th Light Division have failed to retake the high ground near Bel Hamed. Therefore I fear that the six-kilometer-wide gap in our siege ring around Tobruk may be widened further.

According to the "official history," the combat situation on the evening of 21 November was as follows:

> The troops of both sides were scattered about in the roughly thirty-kilometer-wide strip of terrain from the front lines of the breakout gap near Tobruk to the open desert southeast of Sidi Rezegh airfield like the various layers of a Neapolitan Cassata.

✠

"We are to encircle the British 4th Armoured Brigade!" That was the order issued by Oberst Cramer on the morning of 22 November 1941. Soon afterwards the tanks moved off. Kümmel stood in the turret hatch of his tank. Off to his right in the battalion wedge formation was Oberleutnant Heinrich, commander of the Second, and to his left Oberleutnant Prion. Stiefelmeyer and his 4th Company brought up the rear.

The sun was high in the sky. It grew warmer. The sand settled in their ears, mouths, noses and eyes. The men cursed. The sound of fighting could be heard from the direction of Tobruk. Toward midday they had an opportunity to observe an air battle. British Blenheim bombers attacked the elements of the Africa Corps driving on the Acroma-El Adem road. They were escorted by Curtiss Tomahawk fighters. German fighters attacked. Two

Bf-109s each shot down a Tomahawk. Then one of the bombers exploded in flames.

In the early afternoon the panzers encountered the first enemy forces. Oberst Cramer gave the order to attack. The tank battle began. Kümmel led his tanks to the right in a flanking maneuver. They drove through a wadi and then turned west. A group of tanks appeared to the left. They were facing southeast and returning fire from the 4th Company. The attack came from the flank. One platoon halted to fire while the other advanced. The heavy platoon drove through, halted and fired. After the first salvo from the short-barreled "seventy-fives" three enemy tanks were in flames.

Suddenly Kümmel's tank was hit in the turret. The noise was terrifying. The battle came to an end. Hubert Albers rubbed his bruised thumb. The catch bag was full of casings. They had thirty armor-piercing shells left. The 15th Panzer Division's opponent had been the British 7th Armoured Division. The heavy artillery under Oberst Böttcher pounded the recognized British positions.

Oberst Cramer received orders to encircle and destroy the British 4th Armoured Brigade. His panzers moved off. Twilight set in and it soon became dark. Ten minutes later the four leading tanks reported that they had lost contact. Oberleutnant Jahns, the regimental adjutant, brought the bad news to the commanding officer. The latter summoned his battalion commanders.

"What now, sir?" asked Jahns.

"We will continue the pursuit!" decided Cramer. "Fenski and his battalion will drive point. As soon as he finds the enemy tanks he will report and try to engage the enemy. We will then follow with the II Battalion. Bolbrinker, you and your II Battalion stand ready, understood?"

Major Bolbrinker, a wearer of the Knight's Cross since 15 May 1941, nodded.

"Departure in ten minutes!"

Fenski returned to his battalion and called his company commanders.

"The pursuit of the enemy will be continued tonight. Everyone close up tight!" Then he turned to the battalion adjutant. "Bock, you are to see to it that the lateral interval between the companies doesn't become too great."

"What is it, sir?" asked Oberleutnant Peters when Kümmel walked past him toward the company commander's tank.

"Night drive, Peters. Stay alert and make sure that you and your platoon don't lag too far behind."

Kümmel climbed into his tank.

"Prepare for night drive, stay close together."

Major Fenski raised his arm and pumped it three times.

"Panzers—forward!"

The tanks rattled away and headed into the darkness. Leading the way was the battalion commander, then the 1st Company with Hauptmann Kümmel. The tanks drove in second gear. Kümmel could barely see his hand in front of his face.

"Do you have the man in front, Toni?" he asked Kruschinski. The latter had returned from the dressing station the day after he was wounded with the splinter still in his forehead.

"Have him!" called the driver.

Suddenly Kümmel saw a flash in front to the right. It looked as if someone had lit a match.

"Attention, something ahead! Damn, it's a tank!"

At that same moment the commanding officer's tank halted. Fenski saw the outline of many tanks before him.

"Attention, commander to everyone: enemy tanks in front of us. At least fifty. 1st Company turn to the left and stop exactly opposite. 2nd Company around to the right and stop within sight of the First's leading tank. 4th Company form the forward third of the circle and the Third at my disposal."

Kümmel ordered his tanks to turn to the left. He drove in a wide semicircle, remaining in sight of the enemy tanks which still made no move.

"Man," murmurred Egon Milde, "are they all sleeping on their ears?"

"They apparently can't see either," added gunner Kleff. He had rotated the turret to place the gun in the four o'clock position, always keeping one of the enemy in his sights.

After some time Kümmel's company had reached the point where the circle was half completed.

"Halt! Everyone ready to fire," ordered Kümmel.

They waited. In the east the first tanks of the 2nd Company moved into position. Kümmel radioed Oberleutnant Heinrich. The latter answered and called a halt. The tension had risen to the breaking point. It might start at any moment. All hell would break loose when the first shot was fired.

The battalion commander's voice came over the radio: "I'm going to drive through the middle of the English position. Attention, we're firing white flares." Then he said to the adjutant, "Go ahead, Bock!"

Oberleutnant Hans Bock straightened up slightly. He raised his fist holding the flare pistol. There was a bang and the flare rose into the night sky. A flash of white and then darkness again.

"They're already through, sir!" declared Kruschinski. Kümmel nodded. He was still standing in his open turret hatch staring in fascination at the flares rising at brief intervals, illuminating the entire assembly of armor.

"Commander to everyone: all headlights on!"

The tank drivers, who had by now closed the circle around the enemy, switched on their headlights. Beams of lights came from all directions, illuminating the British hedgehog position.

"Sauter, you and your people move up!" ordered Fenski.

The battalion's dispatch riders jumped from their motorcycles and advanced on the British position with submachine-guns raised.

Cries of "hands up!" rang out through the night.

Completely flabbergasted, the Tommies raised their arms.

"One of them is trying to get away!" shouted a Gefreiter. Unteroffizier Sauter leapt onto the tank, whose engine had roared to life. He opened the hatch and loosed off a short burst. The order was given to open fire on enemy tanks attempting to break out.

"There, to the right!" shouted Kümmel. But Kleff had already taken aim. The crack of the gun firing opened a brief, dramatic firefight. The chosen enemy tank was hit in the tracks. Two others that tried to run were also stopped. Then quiet returned.

"Don't shoot unless they try to get away!" Fenski ordered his company commander commanders. "Commanders and radio operators get out. Take submachine-guns with you. Loaders and gunners remain in the tanks."

Kümmel and his radio operator climbed out of the tank. The pair took several prisoners. Several crews resisted, having overcome their initial shock. Three enemy tanks went up in flames, one after the other.

"There he is!" shouted Kümmel and ran to where a British Captain was about to set a fourth tank on fire. The officer surrendered.

A report was sent to the regiment. II Battalion followed at high speed. Oberst Cramer drove up close to the ring of tanks and then stopped.

Major Fenski reported: "One brigadier-general, seventeen officers and 150 men taken prisoner. 35 tanks and 15 armored vehicles captured."

"Thank you, Fenski," said Cramer, beaming. "This is the Knight's Cross for you!

The British 4th Armoured Brigade and the command post and staff officers of the 8th Hussars Regiment were in German hands. Brigade commander Gatehouse barely avoided being captured as well, for only an hour earlier he had gone off to report to General Gott. The men were exhilarated. There were excellent cigarettes, canned pineapple and other delicacies. Kümmel had to step in several times to reign in his men, for their mood was becoming too exuberant

When the sun came up on 23 November (it was Totensonntag, the German day of remembrance) Cramer led his regiment out of the Bir Sciaf Sciuf area to the southwest. All the companies received the following radio message sent by Generalmajor Neumann-Silkow:

"The enemy must be defeated decisively today!"

Early that morning Mussolini had given Rommel command over the Italian forces of the XX Army Corps (General Gambara). The panzers set out on a wide-ranging encircling movement. Dense fog still lay over the desert, but the sun was already visible. It would soon burn through and then the heat would return. The tanks came upon supply vehicles of the British 7th Armoured Division and the 5th South-African Division. Generalmajor Neumann-Silkow wanted to pursue and destroy them. But General Crüwell ordered them to wait for the Italian Ariete Division, which was supposed to join the 15th Panzer Division.

"Attack and destroy the enemy!" ordered General Crüwell.

Oberst Cramer accompanied his regiment, driving in the center of the wedge formation. On his right was the 5th Panzer Regiment and on his left the Ariete. Once again the tank crews gave a maximum effort. They forced their way through only to run up against a barrier of antitank guns manned by the South-Africans.

Kümmel radioed his company: "Turn! Follow me to the right!" He veered off to the right, avoiding the hurricane of fire from the enemy guns. They were concentrating their fire on the 2nd and 3rd Companies and the 8th Company of II Battalion. Major Günther Fenski was killed in this attack. The battalion was left leaderless until Kümmel stepped in to take over.

Five of I Battalion's tanks already lay disabled on the battlefield. One after another the tanks were blown apart by the enemy fire. Hardest hit was the Italian Ariete Division, which lost half of its 120 tanks within half an hour. II Battalion lost Oberleutnant Wuth, commander of 8th Company, killed along with Oberleutnants Koser and Franke and Leutnants Pisat and Adam. By rapid zigzagging Kümmel managed to work his way forward. The individual companies were widely dispersed. Cramer tried to get through at one place in this wall of death. He repeatedly ordered his commanders to spread out and not offer a compact target.

The 1st Company fought in a sea of dust, flames and cordite smoke. Kümmel tried to break through. His tank was hit, but luckily none of the crew were injured. In the midst of the battle, when Kümmel's tank was

A late model, long-barreled Panzer IV of the 26th Panzer Regiment in Italy.

sitting behind a knocked-out Matilda, Kruschinski suddenly raised his hand.

"I have it, Hans!" he shouted, and showed Kümmel the shell splinter that he had dug out of his wound.

Oberst Cramer appeared. "Follow me! We're going to outflank the antitank line and attack it from the rear."

Kümmel acknowledged and called his heavy tanks. They turned, followed Cramer and drove around the line of antitank guns before which there were at least a dozen blazing tanks. Before long they were in the enemy's rear. They drove so fast and fired from such close range that the enemy had no chance. The last resistance was broken. The rest of the battalion's tanks subsequently poured through the breach and reached the South Africans' defense line.

The panzers drove through, firing at everything that moved. The sun went down on 23 November 1941. All around burning trucks and tanks lit up the darkness. Self-propelled guns sat crushed where tanks had driven over them. Some groups of British soldiers managed to escape the encirclement and fled south into the desert. When night came, the South

Africans surrendered. With losses of 3,394 men their brigade had ceased to exist. The Afrika Corps lost more than sixty tanks on this bloody Sunday. The panzer-grenadier regiments had suffered equally heavy casualties. But from a strategic point of view victory appeared to be within sight. Oberst Cramer named Hauptmann Kümmel battalion commander.

✠

The threat facing the Axis forces had been averted. The Afrika Corps had won a victory and the 8th Panzer Regiment had played a major role in it. The regiment continued its advance in the direction of Sidi Omar.

"Exploit!" Rommel had ordered. But exploitation meant staying on the enemy's heels, giving him no chance to rest but, instead, pursuing, encircling and destroying him. The days that followed were very strenuous ones for the 8th Panzer Regiment.

Leutnant Arnold had taken over Kümmel's old company. In the following days of advancing and fighting the Hauptmann proved a brilliant tank leader and commander.

The British offensive had failed. Tobruk had not been relieved. Cunningham wanted to quit, even though he still enjoyed a 2:1 superiority in tanks and artillery and a 7:1 advantage in armored cars. A few hours after Cunningham expressed his feelings in a radio message General Auchinleck appeared in his headquarters. There he declared:

"This battle must not end with a defeat! It would be the end in North Africa, it would mean the British defeat at the Nile." He concluded his speech with the words: "At this hour I am determined to sacrifice the last man and the last gun to stave off defeat. The Eighth Army will come through or it will not return."

General Cunningham was relieved. In his place General Ritchie assumed command of the Eighth Army.

✠

Following the report by General Crüwell, on the morning of 24 November Erwin Rommel drove to Sidi Omar and personally led the attack on the Halfaya Pass. He was accompanied by Generalmajor Gause, his chief of staff. However, in spite of the heroic efforts of its men the 5th Panzer Regiment could not take Sidi Omar. Oberst Stephan was killed.

Leutnant Arnold was wounded on 1 December. Kümmel subsequently placed Leutnant Thurow in command of 1st Company.

The days that followed were tense ones for the 8th Panzer Regiment. On the Trigh el Abt it ran into a far superior force of enemy armor. On 5 December the Afrika Corps attacked British forces assembled near Bir el Gobi. Once again Kümmel and his battalion led the assault. On 6 December the British 7th Armoured Division withdrew towards Bir el Gobi. General Crüwell needed the Italian XX Corps to guard the flanks so that he could launch a final decisive attack with the German Africa Corps. "Where is Gambara?" he signaled repeatedly. But the divisions of the Italian XX Corps did not come. The battle went on on 7 December. Generalmajor Neumann-Silkow drove to the front to see Cramer.

"Cramer," he said laconically, "we are going to attack and destroy the enemy."

"I believe that we can do it, sir!"

The attack began. Kümmel saw tanks hit and knocked out to his left and right and behind him. It was an almost unbearable scene.

"Tanks from the right!" reported Stiefelmeyer, who was leading his 4th Company on the near flank. Seconds later Kümmel heard that the enemy had arrived on the right. He immediately ordered I Battalion to turn towards the right flank.

Kümmel's crew knocked out the leading enemy tank, and the rest pulled back into the desert. Suddenly there was gunfire on the right flank. The division commander's tank appeared.

"Kümmel, follow me with four vehicles."

They drove toward the enemy tanks, which kept up a steady fire. Oberfeldwebel Kruck's panzer was hit in the tracks.

"We're fighting on!" reported the Oberfeldwebel. Then he heard a warning call from Oberleutnant Prion:

"Watch out Kruck! Tanks from behind!"

There were several shattering blows, then a call from Kruck:

"Sir, I . . ."

The transmission ended abruptly. Kümmel had heard the voice of his old comrade in arms Kruck for the last time. He drove on, halting and firing. All of the tanks of the 1st and 2nd Companies pressed toward the enemy. Suddenly enemy tanks appeared from clouds of dust and smoke. There were shots, shattering impacts. Through his vision port Kümmel saw Generalmajor Neumann-Silkow. He was standing in the open turret hatch, apparently in order to be in better command of the attack. Suddenly Kümmel saw him jerk backwards then collapse into the hatch. Anxious seconds passed. Then suddenly an anguished call: "The division commander has been killed!" An armor-piercing shell had struck the commanding officer in the chest, killing him instantly.

Though almost exhausted, the tank crews fought on. Near Sidi Azeiz and on the Trigh Enver Bey, near the mosque of Sidi Rezegh, and in the foothills near Tobruk and El Duda Cramer and his tanks engaged the pursuing enemy in order to buy time for the equally hard-pressed infantry to withdraw. Near victory had turned into defeat. The German Afrika Corps had to retreat if it was to avoid destruction.

Generalmajor Gustav von Vaerst was summoned to Africa to take over the 15th Panzer Division. He came from the armored forces school at Krampnitz near Potsdam. The new commanding officer arrived in the African theater on 17 December 1941. Major Kriebel, the Ia of the division, reported the unit strengths.

The 8th Panzer Regiment reached the area of Agedabia near Christmas 1941.

THE GREAT OFFENSIVE TO THE EAST

When Panzer Army Africa launched its new surprise offensive on the early morning of 21 January 1942, the 15th Panzer Division once again led the way. The enemy was taken by surprise. The divisions of the Africa Corps drove quickly in the direction of Antelat. Wherever the enemy offered resistance, it was crushed by the panzers. Oberst Cramer received orders to employ his panzer regiment to pursue and encircle the British 1st Armoured Division.

Kümmel's 4th Company under Oberleutnant Stiefelmeyer drove on the left flank, while 2nd Company formed the point and 3rd Company was staggered to the right rear. When Cramer saw that the British were retreating east into the open spaces, he ordered the panzers to advance at maximum speed. While south of Antelat elements of the Africa Corps veered east, the 8th Panzer Regiment drove toward Saunnu in a wide arc.

Black forms appeared far ahead. Kümmel looked through his binoculars. Those weren't boulders or bushes, they were British tanks! The enemy vehicles were still at least four kilometers away.

"Enemy tanks in front of us!" reported the battalion commander.

"4th Company attack frontally. All others turn toward Giof el Mater!"

"Commander to 4th Company: attack and tie down the enemy."

Kümmel saw Stiefelmeyer's company press ahead while he rolled toward Giof el Mater with the main body and the regimental commander. The vehicles raised towering dust clouds as they raced across the desert.

The 4th Company was able to carry out its assigned task. The main body of the 8th Panzer Regiment was now behind the British 1st Armoured Division. The panzer companies attacked. Kümmel led the battalion in the direction of the airfield. They came upon two British antitank guns and knocked them out. One of the panzers was hit and disabled by a third gun firing from the airfield boundary. Now it became a target.

"Range six-hundred! Twelve o'clock! Armor-piercing shell!"

The routine work of destruction began to function again. The shots came in rapid succession, followed by flashes as the shells struck home. One fundamental rule of armored warfare states: shoot first! The crews of the 8th Panzer Regiment knew this all too well. Kümmel directed the companies as the situation required. Surrounded, under fire from three sides, elements of the 1st Armoured Division surrendered.

They had done it again. Msus had fallen, the British 1st Armoured Division was destroyed. Left on the battlefield were 96 tanks and armored cars as well as 38 guns. Twelve aircraft were captured. The German attack had come so quickly that they had been unable to take off in time to escape.

While Kümmel's I Battalion had conducted the flanking attack, Cramer and his II Battalion had launched a frontal attack. Kümmel was also able to hear the regiment commander's orders by radio. The huge supply dump at Msus fell into the hands of the Africa Corps. As a result British preparations for an offensive in the Saunnu-Msus area were frustrated. This time Rommel had been the quicker. However, the "Desert Fox" was not satisfied with this success. He decided to advance from Msus in the direction of Benghazi. That city was of great importance as a supply port for the Afrika Corps and all of Panzer Army Afrika.

Kümmel's battalion stormed along the Wadi Faregh in pursuit of the fleeing enemy. Whenever the enemy stood and fought there were short, sharp engagements. The panzers remained successful. Hauptmann Kümmel destroyed more British tanks. The panzer-grenadiers of the 15th Panzer Division drove to Maraua led by Oberst Geißler and took the town. Battle Group Marcks advanced east.

Seventeen days after launching its attack, Panzer Army Africa had won back all of Cyrenaica, the same area that the then Panzer Group Africa had been force to give up in a five-week struggle. Only Tobruk could not be taken, as the available forces were insufficient. The German and Italian divisions stopped before the Gazala Line. The 8th Panzer Regiment had played a critical role in the pursuit of the enemy, mastering crisis situations through quick intervention and sparking further advances. Generalmajor von Vaerst, who had taken over the division in those difficult days of December 1941, now led it toward the Egyptian frontier.

Oberst Cramer became one of the first soldiers in the African theater to receive the German Cross in Gold, a new decoration created in autumn 1941. Soon afterwards, however, he was forced to give up his regiment. Before he left he told Hauptmann Kümmel: "I know that it was you and the other comrades who led our regiment to victory. And I ask that you maintain your attitude and aggressiveness, which I have always admired, even under a new commanding officer."

The two men said goodbye. Oberstleutnant Theege became the new regimental commander. Meanwhile Erwin Rommel, who had been promoted to Generaloberst on 20 January 1942 and the same day became the sixth recipient of the Knight's Cross with Oak Leaves and Swords, had flown to Führer Headquarters in Rastenburg with his First General Staff Officer, Oberstleutnant Westphal.

On 26 May the waiting ended for Hauptmann Kümmel and his tank crews. Rommel's plan was simple and brilliant. The two Italian infantry corps were to attack the Gazala position frontally, reinforced by the 361st Africa Regiment of the 90th Light Division led by General Crüwell. While these units were keeping the British busy, Rommel intended to carry out a great swing through the desert with the Africa Corps and the Italian XX Motorized Army Corps, go around the southern bastion of the line and then drive north into the rear of the position. This southernmost bastion was Bir Hacheim, which was defended by the French.

Punctually at 2 P.M., the Brescia, Pavia and Trento Divisions launched a frontal assault together with the German 361st Regiment.

"Make dust! Make a lot of dust!" Rommel had ordered. The siege artillery opened fire.

At approximately 8:30 in the evening the tank crews of the 15th and 21st Panzer Divisions, as well as the Ariete Armored Division and the motorized elements of the 90th Light Division, received the code word "Venezia."

The tank commanders raised their arms, the attack began. Also part of the attack force was the 8th Panzer Regiment under Oberstleutnant Theege. Ten thousand vehicles headed south into the desert, following a compass heading. The moon provided sufficient light and the drivers could tell from their odometers how much farther they had to go.

Johannes Kümmel.

By the time the sun came up on the morning of 27 May 1942, the bulk of this huge armada had completed the turn around Bir Hacheim and was already driving north, into the enemy's rear. The Afrika Corps's two panzer divisions were in the middle of the attack force, with the 15th on the right side and the 21st on the left. If he looked back, Kümmel could see the 180 tanks of the armored battle group. The regiment was at full strength in tanks for the first time ever.

"Attention, don't spread out too far!" instructed Kümmel, for he could not exceed the specified frontal width for his battalion. This was already three kilometers and he was just able to visually survey the entire area. The depth of the battalion wedge was approximately one and a half kilometers. Dense clouds of dust were visible behind to the right, indicating that II Battalion was in position.

"The Tommies are really in for something if they come now," said Kruschinski.

Kümmel nodded, switched to "Transmit" and called the regiment. "What does air reconnaissance have to say?"

"Nothing sighted yet!" Theege replied laconically.

"Pity that we don't have the 33rd Reconnaissance Battalion here, then we'd know what's in front of us," observed Oberleutnant Thurow, the new battalion adjutant.

"It's near Tobruk," said Kümmel, although everyone knew it.

"But Tommy is somewhere in front of us. Shall I drive ahead?"

"Go Siefers. But just drive ahead and if you sight the enemy report immediately and come back."

"So now at least we won't drive into an ambush," declared Kruschinski with satisfaction.

Hauptmann Kümmel raised his binoculars to his eyes. Somewhere in the vastness of the desert was the enemy. But where? There was nothing to be seen. Then, suddenly, a voice in his headset: "Enemy tanks, sir. Twelve o'clock, range three-thousand!"

"Battle readiness!"

The necessary preparations were made. Several rises appeared ahead.

"They're hiding in there, sir!" reported Siefers. And at that moment Kümmel recognized the dark shapes behind the camelthorn bushes and the huge turrets of Grant tanks.

The tanks waiting there for the Afrika Corps belonged to units of the famous 4th Armoured Brigade. They had 65 Grants and had also set up a line of antitank guns.

"Attack!" ordered Kümmel.

He led the attack, with his tanks following at high speed. Orders crackled in headsets.

"Firing halt—by platoons!"

The first shots were exchanged.

"Drive onto the rise, Toni!" Kümmel called to his driver. They raced forward at full throttle and saw the first of their own tanks catch fire.

"Was that tank or antitank gun fire?" Kümmel asked Oberleutnant Stiefelmeyer, to whose company the tank belonged.

"Tank fire!" reported the Oberleutnant.

Dark shapes emerged from the dust, half visible above the rise. Then a dozen bright flashes. A shell howled over the turret and Kümmel ducked involuntarily. Kruschinski stopped the tank. Kleff took aim at the muzzle flash and fired. On the flanks the other tanks were also halting to fire. Out of the corners of his eyes Kümmel saw flashes to his left and right: hits. A shell struck the ground just in front of his tank, then another. A third landed right beside the right track shield. Fire, smoke and dust! Kümmel coughed. Through the drifting dust clouds he saw that the enemy were now discarding their camouflage. They were tanks he had never seen before.

"Damn!" called one of the company commanders. "Those are brand new types. Long gun, at least 75 millimeters!"

"Move in closer. Real close or else we won't stand a chance."

Theo Kleff cursed. He had already hit one of the enemy tanks three times, but the steel giant was still shooting back.

"We have to have artillery fire!" called Kümmel. Radio messages were sent.

Oberstleutnant Theege called the artillery which was supposed to support the panzer regiment's attack.n On the left flank the 5th Panzer Regiment now joined the battle led by Oberst Gerhard Müller. He also ordered his tanks to attack at maximum speed in order to close the distance as rapidly as possible. Major Martin, one of his battalion commanders, was killed in the attack.

"Hang on, Kümmel. I'm coming with II Battalion!"

Oberstleutnant Theege led II Battalion in an arc around the center. Kümmel drew the enemy's concentrated fire, dodging constantly to avoid being hit; nevertheless, his losses mounted. Taking advantage of this situation, II Battalion reached a position on the enemy's flank. Its attack came as a complete surprise. Shells struck the thinly-armored sides of the Grant tanks. A number of the heavy British tanks caught fire and exploded.

A excited voice rang out in the tank commanders' headsets: "Keep going boys, keep going! We've got them on the run now!"

Kümmel led his heavy Panzer IV tanks into the enemy formation. They fired from close range. German and British tanks maneuvered, seeking favorable positions from which to fire. The dust and smoke filled battlefield was lit by flashes of gunfire, raging fires and explosions. Suddenly the British withdrew. The 8th Hussars, the core of the 4th Armoured Brigade, threw in the towel. The skilled German attack with the constant shuttling of panzers had unnerved the British. In this phase of the German attack the 3rd Company of the Royal Tank Regiment alone lost sixteen Grant tanks.

"We did it, sir, we did it!" shouted Siefers enthusiastically.

Before he could answer, Kümmel, just then emerging from the turret hatch, saw the division commander's battlefield command vehicle drive up. Generalmajor von Vaerst had come forward.

"In which direction shall we advance, sir?" asked Leutnant Max Keil, temporarily in command of 1st Company.

Before von Vaerst could reply his adjutant called out: "There, men! There goes Rommel!"

And so it was. soon afterwards Kümmel heard the voice of the Generaloberst, ordering him to close up and follow. Led by General Nehring, the advance continued toward the north. The 90th Light under Generalmajor Kleemann swung toward El Adem with the Africa Corps's three reconnaissance battalions and the Italian XX Motorized Army Corps. The 21st Panzer Division advanced to just outside Acroma. The 15th Panzer Division continued to drive north toward the sea.

It was exactly 4 P.M. when Kümmel saw the enemy attacking from the right flank: sixty-five Grant tanks were driving into the 15th Panzer Division's march columns. The German tanks which tried to stop the Grants had no chance. In this critical phase of the battle it was Generalleutnant Nehring who saved the 15th Panzer Division. I Battalion, which was at the front, could not turn and come to the aid of the elements at the rear, for Kümmel and his men were under attack from the northeast. They defended themselves grimly. Casualties were heavy.

But General Nehring, who was just then on a scouting drive with Oberst Wolz, the commander of the 135th Flak Regiment, brought a retreating flak battery into position. Soon three more guns from the Africa Korps's combat echelon also arrived. These six "eighty-eights" formed the initial barrier and soon there was a three-kilometer-wide antitank front. Every shot from the 88-mm guns was a hit, and every hit was devastating, even against the heavy enemy tanks. The flak saved the Afrika Corps, especially the 15th Panzer Division.

✠

The days that followed saw heavy fighting. Generalmajor von Vaerst was wounded near the desert fort of Got el Ualeb. Oberst Crasemann, former commander of the 33rd Panzer Artillery Regiment, assumed command of the division.

The battle went on. The Afrika Corps was surrounded and the 5th Panzer Regiment was decimated near Got el Ualeb. Generalmajor Gause was wounded as was Oberstleutnant Westphal. In the Bir el Tamar area Kümmel drove through a minefield that had not yet been fenced in with barbed wire. The 15th Panzer Division subsequently ran into the 5th Indian Division. It became a battle of bend and break. Kümmel once again displayed his tactical brilliance and skill as a commander of armor. Though badly outnumbered, he attacked and won the day.

The 10th Brigade of the 5th Indian Division was completely destroyed. The battle in the desert reached its climax in the first days of June 1942. It was then that Gefreiter Baier captured Brigadier-General Desmond Young, the commander of the shattered 10th Indian Brigade. He was the same man who would write an excellent book about Erwin Rommel after the war.

In these days the British 2nd, 4th and 22nd Armoured Brigades lost 170 tanks. The British 8th Army was practically smashed to pieces. Only Bir Hacheim held on. The Free French and the Jewish Battalion fought heroically. When this bastion finally fell too, Rommel ordered his forces to attack north again. Oberstleutnant Ernst-Günther Baade gave the signal to do so when his 115th Panzer-Grenadier Regiment took Bir Hacheim.

The 15th Panzer Division drove toward the Mediterranean coast. Once again Kümmel drove point. On the morning of 15 June 1942 he sent a radio message that would soon become famous: "First Battalion has reached the sea with six tanks."

The units drove on, feigning an attack to the east, then turned and attacked Tobruk. Through the morning fog of that Saturday, which none of the men would ever forget, on 20 June 1942 they set out to storm the fortress on the Mediterranean. With them was the 21st Panzer Division under Generalmajor von Bismarck and the 15th Rifle Brigade under Oberst Menny.

At 8:30 A.M. the first tanks, with Kümmel in the lead, rolled through the antitank ditches which the engineers had made passable. The tank destroyers of the 33rd Battalion followed. Above them flew Stukas, which were supposed to soften up Tobruk. The tanks advanced. British antitank guns fired from the flanks. Artillery pounded the attack lanes. Kümmel sent his tanks through the fire zone one company at a time. Finally they were stopped before Gabr Gasem. The afternoon sun shone down on the tanks in which the men had been fighting and slaving for almost twelve hours.

"Attack! Wedge formation and fire at the embrasures!"

Kruschinski gave it the gas. They drove toward Gabr Gasem. One of the tanks near Kümmel exploded with a thunderous roar. He now ordered his gunner to engage the enemy antitank gun. Kleff's third shot silenced it. The enemy began to run. Gabr Gasem had fallen. Kümmel urged his tank commanders onwards. They rolled toward Fort Pilastrio, which had put up such fierce resistance the previous April. At 7 P.M. its commander raised the white flag.

Two thirds of the fortress of Tobruk was in German hands. Rommel was in the front lines with the Kiehl combat echelon. He ordered the remaining bunkers taken out with pinpoint fire and helped his engineers dig out the notorious "crossroads mines." The last resistance was extinguished on the morning of 21 June. Tobruk had surrendered. Many of the men collapsed when they climbed out of the tanks. Kümmel went from company to company, making sure that they were all well cared for. His iron will allowed him to stay standing. Erwin Rommel was promoted to Generalfeldmarschall.

But the Africa Corps drove farther east. Its objective was the Nile. The tanks of the 8th Panzer Regiment advanced on the extreme southern wing, passing the Mersa Matruh telegraph road to the Siwa oasis. They encountered enemy armored forces and the 21st Panzer Division veered south. The enemy tanks belonged to the 4th and 22nd Armoured Brigades against which Kümmel had fought so often in the past. Mersa Matruh was surrounded.

Hauptmann Kümmel and his battalion had played a prominent role in difficult and decisive battles and his name had become a symbol. On 29 June, while standing in the turret hatch, Kümmel was wounded in the right arm in a surprise artillery barrage. He was supposed to be taken to the rear but he refused. After his wound was dressed in a nearby aid station he returned to his unit. His arm in a black sling, he climbed into his tank and went on leading his battalion.

Mersa Matruh had fallen the same day. The last bulwark before the El Alamein position had ceased to exist. General von Vaerst led the division to the Ruweisat Ridge, where New Zealand and Indian troops had broken in on 15 July. A counterattack drove them out again but there was a shortage of troops.

"Just one more panzer division, Kümmel," said Oberstleutnant Theege, "then we would do it."

This missing division never came, however. The German forces were just able to fight off counterattacks by British assault brigades. This time one grenadier saved the Africa Korps: Günther Halm, machine fitter and gunner on a Russian-built 76.2-mm antitank gun. He destroyed nine tanks and disabled six more. When the 21st Panzer Division arrived the attack by a hundred enemy tanks had already been stopped. The 5th Panzer Regiment was able to destroy 80 more tanks.

On 30 August 1942 the 8th Panzer Regiment rolled into the southern sector of the Alamein front with seventy tanks for the final big attack. Rommel had revealed his intentions in an order of the day: "Soldiers! Today the army, bolstered by new divisions, will set out to destroy the enemy once and for all!"

At midnight Kümmel gave the order to open fire. British antitank guns opened fire from a minefield through which the panzers had to pass.

I Battalion, 115th Panzer-Grenadier Regiment drove into the minefield. Losses were heavy. The battle had begun. Generalmajor Georg von

Bismarck was killed while leading his division. Generalmajor Kleemann was wounded, then General Nehring.

General von Vaerst took over the Africa Corps and Oberst Crasemann once again led the 15th Panzer Division. The 15th Panzer Division was stopped near Alam Halfa. The enemy had erected a miniature Tobruk there.

Oberst Crasemann attacked again on 1 September. After bitter fighting Kümmel broke through at Hill 132 and in the afternoon was eighteen kilometers from the sea behind the El Alamein front. Was this the victory? But the 5th Panzer Regiment had not got through, for the defensive positions were even stronger where it attacked. Furthermore fuel was running low and no supplies were getting through. The German forces were too weak to take this last bulwark.

Kümmel was recommended for the Knight's Cross with Oak Leaves for his decisive actions in the attack on Tobruk on 27 May and the destruction of enemy tanks south of Mersa Matruh. He had fallen ill. His arm wound refused to heal, nevertheless he remained with his men. On 11 October 1942 Hauptmann Kümmel became the 133rd recipient of the Knight's Cross with Oak Leaves. The time had come for him to leave Africa. Kümmel was sent to Germany and on 1 November 1942 was transferred to the 7th Panzer Replacement Training Battalion. There he was supposed to pass on his experiences and tactical knowledge to new tank officers. Kümmel was named in the Wehrmacht communique on 11 October 1942. While on a brief home leave he learned by telegram on 1 December that he had been promoted to Major for bravery in the face of the enemy.

BACK TO THE FRONT

On 10 June 1943 (the day of the Allied invasion of Sicily) Kümmel, now an Oberstleutnant, was transferred to Headquarters, XIV Panzer Corps in southern Italy. Two days later he and a small staff under General der Infanterie Hube went to Sicily, where the situation was already critical. There he was able to observe Hube at work. Because of him the German divisions were able to escape the inferno on Sicily after a thirty-eight-day battle.

Hube assumed command two days after the landing on Sicily. Headquarters, Italian Sixth Army, which had previously been in overall command, had not proved equal to the task. The Italian divisions no longer obeyed orders. Standing in the corps command post, Kümmel witnessed battles as a spectator for the first time in his life. The experience was not to his liking. He wanted to be back at the front. General Hube commanded on the north slope of Mount Etna, between Randazzo and Lingualossa. Feldmarschall Kesselring arrived there on 5 July to outline Hube's duties, the essence of which was:

"You are to establish a continuous front at the cost of giving ground."

Feldmarschall Kesselring greeted Kümmel, whom he knew from Africa. "Do you have any special requests?" he asked the Oberstleutnant, who only four and a half years earlier had been a non-commissioned officer.

"I would like a front-line command, sir!" answered Kümmel.

"Watch out, that won't take very long," observed "smiling Albert," as Kesselring was called by the enemy.

In the days that followed, the corps headquarters established a defense line which was to hold for some time. There Kümmel met the chief of staff of XIV Army Corps, Oberst von Bonin. He saw in this intelligent and lively spirit the moving force behind events in Sicily. Kümmel's comrade in arms from Africa, former commander of the 115th Panzer Grenadier Regiment, Oberst Ernst-Günther Baade, had been named "Commander, Straits of Messina."

One day Kümmel drove up to the fighting divisions. But then he was sent to the mainland where a new assignment was waiting. After familiarization by the current regimental commander, Oberst Otto Büsing, he was to take over the 26th Panzer Regiment of the 26th Panzer Division. This regiment, or more accurately those elements that were available, were stationed in the Rome area when Kümmel arrived at the end of July. "Battle Group Büsing" had orders to counter an enemy invasion of Italy. The 26th Panzer Division had been formed from the 23rd Infantry Division in France in summer 1942. Oberst Smilo von Lüttwitz became its first commanding officer. He was to lead the division until summer 1944.

Kümmel soon discovered that his new unit was no panzer division at all. I Battalion, which was equipped with the Panther, had been seconded to the "Großdeutschland" Division in May 1943 and it would not return until January 1945. Its departure left the division with just one battalion equipped with Panzer IV tanks. In spite of this Kümmel approached his new duties with great enthusiasm.

The division went into action for the first time following the Allied invasion of the Italian mainland. On 3 September the British 8th Army (Kümmel's opponent in North Africa) crossed the Straits of Messina and landed at Catona and Reggio Calabria. Three days later the 26th Panzer Division assumed command there. Two days after that the British 231st Infantry Brigade landed near Pizzo and on 9 September the US 5th Army came ashore near Salerno. Two days prior to this the Italians surrendered unconditionally. Kümmel was shocked. He had met some brave and exemplary Italian soldiers in Africa. And now this!

After taking part in the occupation of Rome with the Büsing group, the division was rushed to the Salerno front. However the 26th Panzer Regiment remained in its previous area of operations to guard the area and take on additional men and equipment. After the march through Rome it was situated in the Doganella-Ninfa-Sermoneta area. There it remained until the end of September. The panzers subsequently drove via Frosinone, Arce, Cassino and Venafro to Vinciaturo-Isernia.

There Oberst Büsing handed the 26th Panzer Regiment over to Kümmel: "I am going to Russia, Kümmel, and I don't know what awaits me there. But I know for certain what will happen here: you will lead this regiment, which is only a remnant, as I would have liked to have led it."

Oberst Büsing was killed in action in Russia on 8 March 1944.

On 4 November 1943 the division was assigned to the XIV Panzer Corps. The tanks had to drive more than 180 kilometers through the mountains. Kümmel got them all through. He himself climbed into a bogged down tank and got it moving again. But instead of being committed with his division, they were named corps reserve and sent to Aprilia. When he complained about this he received the following explanation: "Kümmel, we need a potent unit that is quickly, well and surely led so that we can commit it where the situation is hot. And that is your unit."

Not until the end of November did the panzer regiment, less 5th Company, return to the division formation. It was a command of make do and improvisation. Kümmel, who had wanted a regiment, led companies, at most a battalion.

In the battle of Orsogna on 8 December 1943 he succeeded in repulsing a heavy enemy attack, destroying three enemy tanks. The next day the Wehrmacht communique reported:

"In the heavy fighting of recent days, the 26th Panzer Division under Generalleutnant Baron von Lüttwitz has repulsed all attempts by the enemy to break through in the eastern sector of the Italian front, exhibiting exemplary morale and steadfastness."

On 14 December Kümmel led one of his classic attacks. At 2 P.M. he set out with three of his four companies to eliminate an enemy incursion against the 90th Panzer Grenadier Division. Panzer-grenadiers and panzer-engineers were placed under his command for the attack. It was pitch black when they moved off. The attack failed. The 6th Panzer Company did not get out of the heaps of rubble that was Orsogna. The others drove into an antitank front and lost their orientation. The engineers who were supposed to clear away the mines ran into an ambush.

Furthermore, at the time of the attack Kümmel learned that the enemy had also achieved a penetration between the 9th and 67th Panzer-Grenadier Regiments. With the 6th Company, which he had held back, he succeeded in foiling another breakthrough attempt.

On 16 December, after the 6th Parachute Regiment had arrived as reinforcements, Generalleutnant von Lüttwitz ordered Kümmel to launch a counterattack from Arielli. Generalleutnant von Lüttwitz left his regimental commander with the following words: "You must attack with your sixteen tanks and try to get through, otherwise the situation will be bad."

When morning came, Kümmel saw the attacking New Zealanders through his binoculars. "Fire! High-explosive shells!"

The remaining tanks fired into the broad waves of attackers and finally brought them to a halt. But the attack's objective, the reestablishment of the former main line of resistance, was not reached. Kümmel lost six tanks in the fearful artillery fire. He later told his adjutant, "If I had had the entire regiment we would have carried through the attack. We have even less here than in Africa."

Oberstleutnant Kümmel would always remember that they lived from hand to mouth, so to speak. They withdrew into the "Emil Line," which ran along the Foro River. On 21 December the division was ordered into a prepared intermediate position. The attack of 24 December was repulsed. Once again Kümmel's handful of tanks played a decisive role, intervening at the critical points.

Kümmel took advantage of the quiet of 25 December to visit the companies and spend some time with his men. He took small Christmas trees to the units. Perhaps he thought of the words which the chronicler of the 26th Panzer Division, Georg Staiger, wrote in the diary that day: "God, let the war end mercifully for us."

The day after Christmas brought a surprise, for it snowed unusually hard for the south of Italy. Movement came to a halt, as did the fighting. As a result the division enjoyed a two-week break. On 13 January 1944 it received advance orders for a new deployment to Pescara.

On 22 January the division was sent to the I Parachute Corps, which was in command in the new Allied landing zone at Anzio-Nettuno. The staff vehicles and the panzer regiment's heavy company were first into the new combat zone. It was the most difficult march Kümmel had ever experienced. The pass road near Popoli and Avezzano claimed victims. Vehicles overturned between Monte della Selva and Monte Veltrino; others slid off the road and, to make matters worse, Allied fighter-bombers also attacked. Thanks to the 304th Army Flak Battalion and the panzer regiment's light flak companies the air attacks did not cause much damage.

The division went to the attack on 31 January. Kümmel again had sixteen tanks at his disposal. They drove through wispy fog—in fact smoke laid by the enemy to cover his movements. When the tanks crossed the railway embankment south of Cisterna the crews saw the sea in the distance. But now they were discovered. Artillery opened fire. Fighter-bombers attacked. And then on the right flank a blocking position of tanks and antitank guns opened fire. Five of the tanks that Kümmel had deployed on the right were knocked out. Contact was lost between the tanks and the panzer-grenadiers, who had been forced to take cover.

Kümmel decided to press on. They reached Fosse Femina Morta, where they were attacked in error by their own infantry. The attack was halted. The Germans had driven into enemy preparations for an attack of their own. At 6 P.M. General von Lüttwitz called off the attack. The units had been committed with no possibility of preliminary reconnaissance. As a result the entire division came within a hair of being destroyed.

The battle for Cisterna and Iso la Bella (whose objective was the reduction of the enemy bridgehead) resulted in heavy losses. The men of the 4th Parachute Division under Oberst Trettner fought with grim determination. The men of the "Hermann Göring" Parachute-Panzer Division, the 3rd Panzer-Grenadier Division and the 114th Light Infantry Division all gave their utmost, for here there was a chance of throwing the enemy back into the sea.

On 16 February the 26th Panzer Regiment attacked once again. I Battalion, 4th Panzer Regiment (Panthers), a battalion of panzer-grenadiers, a battalion of panzer artillery and two companies of combat engineers had been placed under Oberstleutnant Kümmel's command. Everyone was confident. When General von Lüttwitz asked Kümmel if he was strong enough to break through, he replied:

"Come what may, we will get through to the sea with this bunch."

The attack began. Three infantry divisions attacked and reached the "dead road." That was as far as they got, however. Enemy artillery fire raked their ranks. Then 600 Allied bombers attacked, shattering the German command apparatus. General von Lüttwitz was wounded by bomb splinters.

Turning to the general, Leutnant Küsters, who commanded his tank, said: "It's as if we are cursed! We cannot get through! The enemy is too strong!"

Kümmel's Panthers got as far as the east-west road on 17 February. The divisions' infantry forces had not gone into action yet, therefore General von Lüttwitz ordered an attack south from the Cisterna area for the evening of 20 February. However that evening the OKH ordered the attack called off.

General von Lüttwitz was forced to leave the division on 23 February as his wound was getting worse. Oberst Hecker, a comrade of Kümmel's from Africa, took over the division. Oberstleutnant Kümmel had not even spoken with Hecker when disaster struck.

On 26 February Kümmel wanted to drive to his two full-strength companies left from I Battalion, 4th Panzer Regiment, and his own regiment. He planned to scout a new assembly area from the Cisterna area in preparation for a new attack.

Approaching a sharp curve, Kümmel warned his driver, "Watch out Würzer." The Feldwebel at the wheel of the fast command car nodded. Suddenly he saw a large hole not thirty meters ahead and hauled the wheel around. The car went into a skid, went off the curve—still at top speed—and smashed into a boulder. Kümmel was thrown clear. His adjutant, who was himself injured, crawled over to him and saw that his commander was already dead. A severe skull injury had ended the life of this successful tank commander.

Together with his driver, Kümmel was buried the next day. His tank crews carried him to his final resting place. Many of these hardened combat veterans had tears in their eyes. Recalling a poem, one of the men, a Stabsgefreiter from Saxony, spoke the following words: "Yes, we have buried a good man. And he was more to us!"

Oberstleutnant Hans Kümmel never got to lead a proper regiment. On 20 May 1944 he was promoted to Oberst posthumously. Beginning as a simple grenadier and rising to the rank of Oberst, he followed millions of other German soldiers who were claimed by this frightful war.

Karl Nicolussi-Leck in front of his Panther. In addition to the Knight's Cross, he is wearing an array of combat awards, including the Hitler Youth Proficiency Badge.

Karl Nicolussi-Leck

HIS EARLY DAYS

Karl Nicolussi-Leck was born in Pfatten near Bozen on 14 March 1917. Beginning in the autumn of 1923 he attended elementary and middle schools in Kaltern and Bozen, and on 28 July 1936 he graduated from secondary school in Bozen. From 10 October 1936 until December 1939 he studied law and science at the University of Padua in northern Italy.

The Nicolussi clan, whose members distinguished themselves through the use of a surname, consisted of 160 families in the town of Lusern alone. The name Nicolussi is derived from Niklus-Nikolaus. Variations include Nicolussi-Baiz, Nicolussi-Castellan, Nicolussi-Zom and Nicolussi-Leck. The latter family name can be traced back as far as the 15th Century. The family was one of three who were granted the entire mountainside of Lusern by the Count von Trap in 1610. In the history of the church Lusern is part of the parish of Brancafora in Val d'Astico. The people of this area spoke Old German in an Italian area. German scholars visited this linguistic island, after which the German presence in Lusern was officially recognized. As a result, in 1866 the Italian school in Lusern became a German one. The name of the first German teacher: Simon Nicolussi. "In the subsequent course of the history of this old German district, in 1899 a child of the town was ordained a priest. His name was Christian Nicolussi-Leck."

The town of Lusern, which numbered 900 inhabitants, was completely destroyed by fire on 9 August 1911. Karl Nicolussi-Leck's older sister Judith, who was already approaching nine years of age, survived that unfortunate day. During the First World War the town, which lay between old Austria and Italy, became a war zone. On 25 May 1915, two days after a secret treaty was concluded in London promising the Italians the Brenner as a boundary, resulting in an immediate Italian declaration of war against Austria, the town of Lusern was shelled from nearby Italian forts. While the Austrian fortress near the town was not hit, the town went up in flames under a hail of shells.

Many people were killed or wounded. The inhabitants of Lusern fled through the mountains to Caldonazzo. There they were packed into cattle cars and in a three-day journey were transported via Innsbruck and Salzburg to Bohemia. One of those who made the trek was Karl Nicolussi-Leck's grandmother. The Lusern families remained in a potato cellar in the village of Nestomic until 1919, when they were finally permitted to go home.

However, the entire Nicolussi-Leck family did not make this odyssey, for in 1903 shoemaker and small farmer Jakob Nicolussi-Leck had bought a small farm near Kreitern, halfway between Kalter Lake and the Leuchtenburg ruins. Ecclesiastically it was part of Kaltern and politically it belonged to Pfatten.

By 1920 the entire Nicolussi-Leck family had returned to live there, for as "Pangermanici" they were no longer welcome in Lusern after 1919. Eleven children, parents and aunts lived at Kreitern. That was also where Karl, who had been born on the farm in 1917, grew up. Much later he was to build a similar life in Hochfrangart, where he now resides.

The world in which Karl lived as a young boy and student, in kindergarten and youth and artist gatherings, shaped him as a person and implanted in him the desire for a natural way of life. From his sister Judith we know that Karl was called "the nice one," that he visited his aunt up on the Altan whenever time and his holidays permitted, loved flowers and in his sister's words "was no child." He always had something else on his mind instead of wasting time in youthful pursuits.

One person who left her mark on the young student young Nicolussi-Leck was Professor of Philosophy Rigatti. By the age of 17 he had read all the works of Plato. Even his later studies in philosophy, law and political science could not change his conviction that in terms of basic understanding the dissection and analysis of matter which was mandatory in biology did not exceed Plato. At the time he illustrated his point of view as follows: "True, the cell which was killed by the labor situation can be dissected under the microscope, but it can no longer be admired."

He continued: "Of course analytical thought imparts power in the partial sphere, but not for appreciation of the whole. Indeed in its later consequences it leads to disruption and destruction of the whole."

Karl Nicolussi-Leck accepted the limitations of our system and took it as the basis for his actions. He later said: "I am basically a conservative man. The wonder of it all for me is the law of conservation, which has kept the movements of atoms constant for billions of years in spite of their explosive power. To be conservative means to expose what exists to only minor changes and interventions in order to avoid encrustments, and in thinking and research to not always strive for increased power, in short: to fundamentally alter the nature of research and technology."

NICOLUSSI-LECK BECOMES A SOLDIER

When the then South Tyrol became a matter of prestige between Berlin and Rome and Hitler showed signs of being ready to cede the area to the Duce, the Nicolussi-Leck family opted for German and for Germany. A member of the family once said: "Even if the devil rules in Germany we must cling to her, because we are Germans."

Karl Nicolussi-Leck played a leading role in the VKS—the German People's Group for South Tyrol. In this way he saw an opportunity to "find a answer to the (Italian) fascist system of oppression; and when we all saw that Austria was returned to the German Reich we were convinced that South Tyrol would come to the Reich too. Scarcely any of us had ever been beyond South Tyrol, but every success by Germany also seemed beneficial for us."

The VKS organization was built by the political spokesmen, of whom Karl Nicolussi-Leck was one. In the plebiscite which followed many (too many for Mussolini) South Tyroleans voted for Germany and, if need be, resettlement. But even though they had opted for Germany, the people of South Tyrol wanted to stay in the area that had been their home for more than 500 years. However in spite of this Hitler signed a resettlement pact with Mussolini.

Karl Nicolussi-Leck had become something of a "red flag" to the Italian authorities. When the war broke out he abandoned his studies and went to Germany after his application to join the Waffen-SS had been accepted. And so on 10 April 1940 he joined the SS-Standarte "Deutschland," and following his basic training he was promoted to the rank of Rottenführer. Nicolussi-Leck took part in the Balkans campaign as an SS-Scharführer in the *Deutschland* Regiment and was wounded (not seriously) for the first time.

By the time the invasion of the Soviet Union began on 22 June 1941, Nicolussi-Leck was a member of the *Der Führer* SS Regiment (the former SS-Standarte *Der Führer*) of the 2nd Waffen-SS Division *Das Reich*. His regiment was deployed in the central sector and Karl Nicolussi-Leck proved himself as a soldier and comrade in the dramatic struggle up to the gates of Moscow. There he was seriously wounded. This wounded counted as the first of five which would earn him the Wound Badge in Silver.

With a high recommendation from his superiors, on 1 November 1941 the Scharführer was sent to the SS-Junkerschule at Bad Tölz to attend an officer candidate course. Nicolussi-Leck achieved outstanding results and completed the course on 30 January 1942. On 20 April he was promoted to the rank of SS-Untersturmführer. Nicolussi-Leck very quickly learned the truth of the maxim that Walter Flex, poet and front-line soldier in the First World War, had once formulated:

"Service as a lieutenant means being an example to your men.

Showing them how to die is only a part of it."

This maxim governed routine service and combat duty in the Waffen-SS Panzer-Grenadier Division *Wiking*, but with one restriction. For Felix Steiner, the division's first commander, the cardinal rule was: "to wage every battle only with the necessary, rational employment of forces and not allow oneself to be enticed into falsely understood brashness or even to disregard for life."

Of course in this division of the Waffen-SS, too, the rule of a superior leading by example was binding. Naturally this meant demanding and giving a higher degree of eagerness and willingness to see action and awareness of duty from every officer than from the men in the ranks. But there was no place in this unit for self-destructive fanaticism or a willingness to die without regard for losses. This did not alter the fact, however, that every division of the Waffen-SS maintained its fighting integrity and never gave up no matter how hopeless the situation. These characteristics are evident in the following chapter, which describes the actions of the young Untersturmführer Nicolussi-Leck while serving with the *Wiking* SS Motorized Division.

IN COMBAT WITH THE *WIKING* DIVISION

The Division: Its Formation and a Summary of Its Operations

In September 1940 Adolf Hitler,the supreme commander of the German Armed Forces, ordered the formation of a motorized SS division from the personnel flowing to the Waffen-SS from the countries of Norway, Denmark, Finland and Holland. The core of the new division was the 3rd Motorized Infantry Regiment *Germania*, which had become available following the cancellation of "Operation Sea Lion," the planned invasion of Great Britain. It was joined by the new *Westland* Regiment in Munich and the *Nordland* Regiment in Vienna and Klagenfurt.

On 9 November 1940 SS-Brigadeführer Felix Steiner was assigned the task of forming the new division, which had been designated 5th SS Division (Motorized) *Germania*. Steiner selected as his first general staff officer

SS-Sturmbannführer Ecke, who was currently serving as Waffen-SS liaison officer in Führer Headquarters. The three named regiments were soon joined by the 5th SS Artillery Regiment, which was followed by the division pioneer battalion being formed in Munich. Other elements were the 5th Reconnaissance Battalion from Munich-Freimann and the supply troops from Berlin-Lichterfelde. The choice of the title *Germania* for the division conflicted with the existing regiment of the same name, and so on 21 December 1940 a Führer order was issued changing the division's designation to 5th SS Division (Motorized) *Wiking*. The division had received its ultimate name, although it would undergo two future changes to reflect its changing role and equipment.

Beginning on 2 June 1941 the division was transported to Silesia, where it came under the command of the 1st Panzer Army commanded by Generaloberst von Kleist. In turn it was subordinate to Headquarters, XIV Army (mot.) Corps, commanded by General von Wietersheim. The campaign in the east began on the morning of 22 June 1941. The *Wiking* Division advanced behind the two panzer corps. The initial objective was Ternopol.

The following table lists the division's senior officers and regiments:

Division Commander:	Brigadeführer Steiner
Germania Regiment:	Standartenführer von Oberkamp
Westland Regiment:	Standartenführer Wäckerle (KIA 2/7/41)
	Standartenführer Phleps
Nordland Regiment:	Standartenführer von Scholz
5th Armored Artillery Rgt.:	Standartenführer Gille
5th Armored Pioneer Btn.:	Sturmbannführer Mühlenkamp
5th Armored Recon. Btn.:	Sturmbannführer von Reitzenstein
5th Antitank Battalion:	Sturmbannführer Maak
5th Flak Battalion:	Sturmbannführer Stoffers
5th Armored Signals Btn.:	Sturmbannführer Kemper
5th Medical Battalion:	Sturmbannführer Dr. Unbehaun
5th Repair Battalion:	Hauptsturmführer Sporn

By 4 July the division headquarters was already in Ternopol, as was Headquarters, XIV Army (mot.) Corps. It was there that General von Wietersheim informed SS-Brigadeführer Steiner of an order which had been issued at the corps level. For commanders' eyes only, it restricted "the authority of courts martial in the Barbarossa area" (meaning all of Russia). Punishable offenses by members of the German Armed Forces against the Russian civilian population would no longer be automatically pursued.

Brigadeführer Steiner gave General von Wietersheim the only possible answer as an officer who had served in the First and now the Second World War:

> No unit leader who respects his honor and that of his troops can give such an order. Given such methods even the best unit must run wild and collapse morally. Discipline will suffer as a result and the moral worth, as well as the fighting strength of the unit, will diminish. For these reasons I feel justified in pursing any punishable act against the population through the court-martial process in accordance with the military penal code. [This is the verbal statement which Steiner gave before the international military tribunal at Nuremberg in June 1946.]

When the Commissar Order was then received, the generals of the XIV Panzer Corps agreed to ignore it as well. Brigadeführer Steiner: "We will wage this war decently, as has always been the custom in our army."

But back to the military campaign:

From Ternopol the *Wiking* Division stormed through Saranow and Husyatin to Proskurov. Each of the division's regiments achieved great success offensively and in repulsing Soviet counterattacks. During the Battle of Uman the division repulsed the efforts of five Red Army divisions to break out, while at the same time guarding the northern flank of Panzer Group 1, which had launched an attack aimed at encircling the enemy.

Wiking advanced by way of Smelta and Korsun to Kamenka on the Dniepr River. There, on 17 August 1941, the division was relieved by the *Passubio* Division, part of the Italian expeditionary corps to Russia, after which it stormed on toward Dneproderzhinsk. Dnepropetrovsk was the next objective. Kamenka was taken and a bridgehead was established there and expanded. Three times during this phase of the fighting the enemy claimed to have destroyed the *Wiking* Division. The fighting continued and Pavlograd was taken by *Wiking*. Once again the division closed a pocket, this time by blocking the heights on both sides of the Melitopol-Stalino railway line. When it was over 65,000 Red Army soldiers were taken prisoner and 125 tanks and 500 guns were captured.

The Russian winter arrived, first with knee-deep mud which made movement almost impossible, followed by deep snow and cold which paralyzed the German armies. The advance came to an end near Astakhovo and then the first fighting withdrawal began; it ended with the division occupying winter positions along the Mius River. On 30 November 1941 the Commander-in-Chief of the 1st Panzer Army wrote the following in an order of the day addressed to the units under his command:

> You performed magnificently in the winter battle of Rostov. In icy cold, fighting day and night, you beat off the fiercest enemy attacks and carried out the withdrawals ordered by me.
>
> Now we are going over to the defensive in a new position and we will hold it.
>
> (signed)
>
> VON KLEIST.

The division received a new face. The entire headquarters staff was changed, or replaced, as First General Staff Officer Ecke had been killed. His position was filled by the Second General Staff Officer, Hauptsturmführer Reichel. Hauptsturmführer Killed became the new Second General Staff Officer. The commander of the *Germania* Regiment, Standartenführer Reichsritter von Oberkamp, went to the SS Command Office as Inspector of Infantry. Sturmbannführer von Reitzenstein took over the tank battalion and had to be replaced in his former position. The same thing happened to nearly every position. At the beginning of January 1942 an assault gun battalion under Obersturmführer Lange joined the division.

The Mius position was held against heavy enemy attacks and finally on 21 March 1942 the *Wiking* Division was relieved and was sent to Germany to rest and reequip. During this period of reorganization the division was joined by the long anticipated 5th SS Panzer Battalion under Sturmbannführer Johannes Rudolf Mühlenkamp. It possessed a complement of 40 medium and heavy tanks. One of the platoon commanders in the panzer battalion's 2nd Company was SS-Untersturmführer Nicolussi-Leck, who in the intervening period had taken two training course to acquire the knowledge required to command a small armored unit.

THE CAMPAIGN IN RUSSIA IN 1942

An Untersturmführer on the Road to Victory

Formation of the 5th SS Panzer Battalion began at the Wildflecken troop training grounds in mid-February 1942. When Untersturmführer Nicolussi-Leck arrived there the battalion commander made him a platoon commander in the 2nd Company and he proceeded with his training like everyone else. Nicolussi-Leck also accompanied the battalion when it moved to the Staumühle troop training grounds at Senne. Even there he attracted attention because of the cleverly-engineered attacks by his platoon and in the officers' lectures he was one of those who spoke about his ideas on company-level armored warfare. The agile and approachable officer from South Tyrol was liked by all the men. Though of a serious nature, he also knew how to have a good time and he was willing to take part in or at least tolerate any kind of fun.

At noon on 9 June 1942 the battalion began entraining at the Sennelager railway station. The task was completed within three and a quarter hours and the next day the trains rolled through Paderborn, Halle, Leipzig, Ratibor and Oderburg into the Debica area. In the days that followed, the transport continued through Lvov and Ternopol, Vinnitsa and Alexandria to Dnepropetrovsk. On 17 June the battalion disembarked at Amrossiyevka station. There the unit resumed a normal service routine, however after several test alerts this was ended by the first real alert at 1:00 A.M. on 20 July. At 6:00 A.M. the battalion set off for Federovka, 65 kilometers away, and from there it rolled on to Taganrog and Beiwodjem on the following day. The battalion arrived too late to take part in a counterattack against enemy forces which had broken into the old winter position, for German forces had already driven the "Ivans" back.

In the afternoon the battalion's tanks, led by 1st Company, followed up and first contact was made with the enemy at dusk. Several vehicles were knocked out and 70 prisoners taken. The next day the battalion commander ordered 1st Company to conduct an armed reconnaissance; the 1st Platoon moved off at 7:00 A.M.. The entire battalion followed soon afterward; it veered toward the northeast and in the afternoon went to the attack on the right of the 13th Panzer Division.

As soon as the attack began tank 101 was hit in the engine compartment and went up in flames. Tank 125 drove over a mine and was likewise a total write-off. The third casualty was tank 114, which was hit by a Russian 76.2-mm antitank gun, the notorious "crash-boom." Russian antitank guns were knocked out and then the men of the battalion watched as Stukas and heavy fighters took out Russian positions facing the German infantry. One of the Stukas was hit by Russian anti-aircraft fire and came down in flames behind the battalion.

Then the battalion's 2nd Company, which was in a semi-concealed position together with other tanks that had moved up, opened fire. The assault groups stormed across the first antitank ditches; these were intended to guard the position near Leniawan, which was situated between the rail line to Tschaltyr and the main road to Sultan Saly in the approaches to Rostov.

Sturmbannführer Mühlenkamp gave the order to attack the antitank ditches. The companies rolled forward cautiously, deployed into a broad firing front about 300 meters from the ditches and opened fire on enemy forces in a raised position beyond the trench, aiming at muzzle flashes.

"Nico"—as Untersturmführer Nicolussi-Leck was known to his comrades—barked out a command to his gunner: "Eleven o'clock, enemy antitank gun!"

Two seconds later the gunner replied, "Target recognized!" and two seconds after that there was a crash as the cannon of the Panzer IV fired. The shell landed just short of the antitank gun. A second shot followed just seconds later; this time it was on target and the exploding HE round put the position out of action.

Machine-gun fire from the tanks raked the enemy positions, and when these fell silent the pioneers advancing close behind the tanks rushed forward to the antitank ditch. They placed explosive charges in the walls of the ditch in order to level them for the vehicles to cross. Several explosions rang out through the morning. Then a company of grenadiers riding in armored troop carriers rolled past, through the leveled section of the ditch and secured the other side. The first tank that drove through the flattened area became hung up on the floor of the ditch. A Luftwaffe unit brought up logs, boards and beams and these were shored up with earth. The next tank crossed safely and then the entire battalion followed.

Shrouded in dense clouds of dust, the battalion rolled onward through the lanes marked in the minefield. It was about 1:00 P.M. when Sturmbannführer Mühlenkamp ordered the tanks to advance on the second Russian position. After Stukas pounded the position the tanks rolled forward. Artillery fired over the tanks, moving forward to keep pace with the advance.

The 2nd Company was on the right flank and it was first to engage the enemy. Nicolussi-Leck ordered his platoon, which was driving point, to drive through the position quickly. At 400 meters they came under fire from enemy antitank guns, whereupon the battalion commander called: "Press on, Nico, we'll cover you!"

The platoon's four tanks roared on at full speed. The tracks rattled, the engines roared, and the four tanks fired their machine-guns at the ghostly shapes of Soviet antitank and machine-gun nests as they appeared, keeping the enemy's head down. The tanks reached an area of cover and took up hull down positions. Nicolussi-Leck ordered a firing halt. All four tanks were ready and they opened fire simultaneously, pouring HE rounds into recognized positions and silencing the enemy.

A concealed Soviet antitank gun opened fire at the tanks of the Nicolussi-Leck platoon from the seven o'clock position. The tanks had already passed and were swerving around the enemy foxholes, constantly moving so as not to present a stationary target. Not until they reached a shallow ravine did the panzers stop and from there fired at groups of fleeing Russians as they streamed past.

The rest of the battalion's tanks arrived. "Well done, Nico!" radioed the battalion commander, "they've turned tail."

For this action Untersturmführer Nicolussi-Leck received the Iron Cross, Second Class, which was officially awarded on 25 July.

In the late afternoon Sturmbannführer Mühlenkamp and Sturmbannführer Dieckmann, commander of I Battalion, *Germania* and also leader of a spearhead battle group, met to discuss the next day and their joint advance. Dieckmann, a wearer of the Knight's Cross since 23 April 1942, would secure the western flank of the advance with one company, while at first light two of his assault companies would advance across the next antitank ditch riding on the tanks of the Mühlenkamp battalion, which would provide supporting fire for the infantry assault and roll up the positions of Rostov's third defensive position from west to east. A second armored battle group would drive through the cleared section of the antitank ditch and storm toward the western part of Rostov.

The tanks moved off at six o'clock the next morning and on reaching the Russian antitank ditch they swept the troops holding the position with fire and drove them out. At the third antitank ditch, the last before Rostov, the tanks once again had to stand fast in the limited cover until part of it was leveled and they were able to drive through. But when they did, they set out at maximum speed directly toward the northwest end of Rostov.

Untersturmführer Nicolussi-Leck took out an enemy antitank gun which had fired at his company's 1st Platoon, silencing it with his second shot. The advance continued. A low wall was knocked down and the tanks reached the outskirts of the city. Fire came at them from many concealed positions. The battalion called his tank commanders and urged them not to stop. The panzers rolled forward, taking fire from the first side-streets; it soon became apparent that the entire western part of the city had been turned into a fortress and that there would be no getting through here. Four of the battalion's tanks had already been knocked out and if they pressed ahead there would be many more.

The company commander asked Nico what they should do: "We have to get out of here!" he replied.

Ten seconds later the voice of the battalion commander rang out in the tank commanders' headsets: "The battalion is to pull out of Rostov. Assemble in the ravine on this side of the antitank ditch."

The tanks withdrew from the city by platoons. Nicolussi-Leck was first to reach the antitank ditch, and when he arrived he found himself facing a collection of trucks which had apparently moved in from the right. The trucks were bringing fresh troops to the third defensive position. Nico gave the order to open fire. When Russian tank-killing squads attacked he stood up in the turret hatch and lobbed a hand grenade at the leading squad. He ducked down, took a second grenade from the loader and lobbed it at a second group of Russians.

The tank's machine-guns mowed down the attacking Russians. Then his other two tanks attacked. The fourth had driven over a mine outside the city and was now stranded in no-man's-land. The crew, two of whom had been wounded, had been recovered. The attacking Russians were blown away like chaff in the wind. Several trucks blazed and ammunition exploded, making the enemy's situation even more chaotic.

Sturmbannführer Mühlenkamp received a report that the Russians, after being repulsed near Tschaltyr, were preparing to ford the Don and its tributary fourteen to fifteen kilometers west of Rostov. Without waiting for further orders, Mühlenkamp radioed the following to division: "No movement by tanks possible in the western part of Rostov. The battalion is going to fight its way along the Don with the intention of reaching the ford where, according to pilot reports, the enemy intends to cross the river."

The city of Rostov was still the scene of heavy fighting and was burning in many places. Meanwhile the tank battalion launched a direct attack. With the 2nd Company leading the way flanked on the left by the 3rd Company, the panzers overran the remaining Russians in the Tschaltyr position and engaged with machine-guns and high-explosive shells those groups that had already forded the Don. A group of Russian infantry which approached Nicolussi-Leck's vehicle was taken out by two hand grenades thrown by the commander.

On 24 July the Wehrmacht communiqué declared:

> As announced by special bulletin, troops of the army, the Waffen-SS and Slovakian units have broken through the heavily fortified, in-depth defense positions of Rostov along their entire front and after fierce fighting have taken the city, an important transportation and port facility.

It remains to be said that it was the 13th Panzer Division under General Herr which finally took possession of Rostov. The keystone of the Soviet retreat south across the Don had been removed. The goal now was to pursue the Red Army as fast as possible, in order to prevent it from retreating beyond the Kuban.

The *Wiking* Division's tank battalion spent 24 July servicing its vehicles, especially their weapons. Meanwhile the 13th Panzer Division was still engaged in street fighting in Rostov. The 5th Panzer Battalion took up position in a large park at the western outskirts of the city, where it had 48 hours in which to repair its damaged vehicles. The men gorged on the plentiful apricots which were just ripening at that time, but they soon suffered the consequences of eating too much half-ripe fruit.

The battalion moved out on 27 July. By evening the Russian blocking position near Kamyschewacha had been taken and the enemy driven off. At 6:45 the next morning Untersturmführer Nicolussi-Leck raised his right arm. The engines of his four tanks (the fourth had since rejoined the platoon) accelerated from idle to full throttle and the panzers set off at the head of 2nd Company—and the entire battalion. The tanks came upon a Russian field position. The two antitank gun positioned there were knocked out by the first salvo of HE rounds.

Then a white flag appeared from one of the field positions, a sign that the Russians there wished to surrender. Unterscharführer Scharnowski opened his turret hatch to order the Russians to throw down their weapons and advance with hands high. But before he had spoken half of the sentence a single shot was fired from the enemy position. The bullet struck Scharnowski in the temple, killing him instantly. Russian antitank guns then opened fire from several concealed positions and were joined by 80-mm mortars from a trench situated farther back. Nicolussi-Leck ordered his tanks to advance. All guns blazing, they rolled over the trenches and headed for the mortar position.

The field position was taken by storm and sentries were posted in the village of Metschedinskaja which lay just beyond. At precisely five o'clock the next morning, one hour before the tanks resumed their advance, Unterscharführer Scharnowski was buried in the village. All of 2nd Company and many members of the battalion paid their last respects to this popular tank commander. When the service was over the tanks moved on. The day's objective was Sredne Jegorlik. It was reached at 11:30 A.M., making 30 July a "fast day." The 13th Panzer Division, which had set off at the same time as *Wiking*, was still lagging 25 kilometers behind.

Nicolussi-Leck's crew and his platoon continued to make a name for themselves. Their new Panzer IVs, which were armed with the long-barreled 75-mm gun, gave them a better chance of defeating the dangerous T-34, which was appearing in larger numbers. The principal objective of the division, which several days earlier (on 21 July) had been subordinated to the LVII Panzer Corps, was the Kuban River. The division attacked at 5 A.M. on 4 August and by evening it was at the rail junction of Krapotkin, which lay north of the Kuban. Along the way there were a number of fierce clashes, in which 1st Company lost tank 111 to antitank rifle fire. The advance continued through the town in the direction of the river. Antitank guns suddenly opened fire from the raised roadway leading to the bridge and tank 115 was badly hit. The 2nd Company outflanked the enemy position and knocked out six 76.2-mm antitank guns one after the other, two of which were credited to Nicolussi-Leck. The attack was halted, however, when further concealed antitank guns intervened and disabled seven of the battalion's tanks. There was no way to bypass the position and so Sturmbannführer Mühlenkamp ordered his tanks to pull back out of range. The withdrawal from the raised roadway was a success and from then on the tanks were concealed by groups of tree and saplings. After about 10 kilometers of driving in reverse they reached cover.

The men of the *Nordland* Regiment fought in Krapotkin itself and took possession of this important town. The Luftwaffe supported the attack and when the fighting was over a number of Russian freight trains lay burnt-out on and beside the tracks. The Wehrmacht communiqué of 5 August declared: "At the Kuban the railway junction of Krapotkin was taken by storm by a unit of the Waffen-SS after heavy fighting."

At the decisive point in the attack on the town Standartenführer von Scholz had placed a company of *Nordland*'s II Battalion on the tanks of the supporting panzer company. He then led the ad hoc battle group through Krapotkin, which was swarming with Russian troops, and seized the road and rail bridge. When the leading tank reached the approach to the bridge the structure exploded with a thunderous roar. Soon afterward two freight trains loaded with gasoline and oil went up in flames. Nevertheless, by 10 A.M. on 5 August Krapotkin was firmly in the hands of von Scholz's battle group. One of the tanks that had made the advance possible was Nicolussi-Leck's. On 9 August Untersturmführer Nicolussi-Leck received the Iron Cross, First Class for his actions.

The fighting continued with undiminished ferocity. The division returned to the attack at 5 A.M. on 10 August. Grigoripolitskaya was reached and in a firefight with enemy antitank guns and several T-34s the 2nd Company, which led the attack under Obersturmführer Flügel, knocked out four antitank guns and three of the tanks. Untersturmführer Nicolussi-Leck accounted for one tank and two antitank guns.

Two of the company's tanks were knocked out. The Nicolussi-Leck platoon made a direct advance through a Russian blocking position to rescue the crews. The other two platoons engaged T-34s that appeared and covered the flanks of Nicolussi-Leck's platoon, firing HE rounds to keep the Russian tank-killing squads at bay. Nicolussi-Leck's four tanks roared

Contact ahead! A 50mm Pak is rolled forward by its crew while wheeled vehicles keep their distance. A machine gun team to the right provides security.

through the Russian troops, their machine-guns blazing. Several Russian soldiers who attempted to approach the tanks were taken out with hand grenades lobbed by Nicolussi-Leck. Finally the tanks reached their objective. The injured crewmen from the knocked-out tanks were taken inside, while the others crouched down behind the turret and fired at the onrushing Red Army troops.

The tanks roared back toward their own lines and delivered the rescued men to safety. Once again the Waffen-SS had upheld its tradition of not leaving behind any of its men—whether dead, wounded or unwounded. After the tanks had made it back Sturmbannführer Mühlenkamp wordlessly shook the hand of the young Untersturmführer who had carried out this daring rescue.

Two days later 2nd Company led another assault. The tanks moved off at 4 A.M. and the fighting began ten minutes later. Obersturmführer Flügel's tanks attacked, alternately racing ahead and halting to fire. When the company neared the Russian lines the decision was made to dash through and leave the field to the other two companies. The panzers crossed the intervening ground and cleared the second line. Then 400 meters to the right a battery of rocket launchers, the so-called "Stalin Organs," fired off a salvo.

Nicolussi-Leck asked for permission to engage and after this was received he veered to the right. The 1st and 3rd Platoons took up covering positions to the left and right and engaged the Russian antitank guns guarding the rocket battery, knocking them out one after the other. Nicolussi-Leck's tanks approached to within 200 meters then halted behind the cover of a dense stand of saplings.

"Open fire on my command, firing sequence from left to right. Load high-explosive. Fire!"

Four crashes rang out as the tanks fired their main guns; four Stalin Organs mounted on trucks took direct hits. Pieces of steel and bodies whirled through the air. A second salvo was also on target. The battery was destroyed. Nicolussi-Leck led his tanks past the shattered Soviet vehicles then swung through 180 degrees in a wide arc, bringing the four panzers into position behind the second Russian line. They rolled over communications trenches and blew up an ammunition depot. Then the fight was over and the Nicolussi-Leck platoon rejoined the rest of its company. When evening came the panzer battalion which had carried out the attack on Karabolinskaya had to halt and wait for fuel. A large hedgehog position was established around the village. Both charging assault groups and probing patrols had to be beaten off, especially from the direction of Muk.

The first order of business the next day was to rearm and refuel. All of the damaged tanks were reported serviceable and the advance resumed in the early morning. This time it was decided that 1st Company would lead. The objective was the Russian oil refinery at Muk, which the Soviets defended with particular determination. The leading tank, number 114 commanded by Untersturmführer Kollotzschy, was hit hard by a Russian light artillery piece; two rounds from tank 111 silenced the enemy weapon. Once again lack of fuel forced the panzers to halt, but during the night fuel arrived and Chatischenskaya was reached at dawn on 15 August. Once again the first order of business was to take out a battery of "Stalin Organs."

Throughout 15 August the tank units which had halted in the area of this village were showered with rocket fire. While on 16 August the 1st Company pulled back approximately ten kilometers, Flügel's 2nd Company spearheaded an attack against heavily-defended Leninaya. The village was taken, even though the Russian anti-aircraft guns positioned there had to be taken out first. Meanwhile Muk had been taken by the 13th Panzer Division. Hauptsturmführer Darjes, commander of the 1st Company, was ordered to the battalion commander to report on the situation.

On 1 September Untersturmführer Nicolussi-Leck was awarded the Panzer Assault Badge in Silver and the following day the Wound Badge in

Black for his first wound, which by then he could barely remember. On 3 September Sturmbannführer Mühlenkamp was awarded the Knight's Cross for the capture of Rostov and his battalion's daring attacks before and after. There was a fitting celebration, especially since the division had been given a rest in order to refit and reequip its units. The time off was used to further train commanders, gunners and loaders.

Untersturmführer Nicolussi-Leck had long since worked out the combat tactics of a panzer company as well as the best method of attack for any situation, and he frequently discussed these with the battalion commander. Sturmbannführer Mühlenkamp considered these ideas so important that he ordered them incorporated into the unit's manual of tactics for future use.

A new phase of the struggle began on 26 September, one which was dominated by the actions at Sagopschin and Malgobek. It would be a severe test for all the men of the *Wiking* Division and a chance for Untersturmführer Nicolussi-Leck to prove himself both as a platoon and company commander. The new area of operations was the eastern Caucasus and once again the *Wiking* Division would spearhead the German assault.

The Battles of Sagopschin and Malgobek I

The SS Panzer-Grenadier Division *Wiking* was pulled out of the line in the western Caucasus and received orders to march to the Terek. There it was placed under the LII Army Corps. In an overland march lasting from 17 to 25 September, the *Nordland* Regiment, II and III Battalions of the 5th SS Artillery Regiment and the 5th Panzer Battalion *Wiking* drove via Maykop, Labinskaya, Armavir and Mineralny Wody into the area of Pavlodolski on the north bank of the Terek. The *Westland* Regiment followed 48 hours later.

On the afternoon of 24 September division commander SS-Gruppenführer Felix Steiner, accompanied by his Ia, Obersturmbannführer Reichel, and the commander of the division's panzer battalion, Sturmbannführer Mühlenkamp, drove into the area where the attack was to be made in order to assess the terrain for himself.

The assault on Sagopschin was to begin with a diversionary attack by the *Nordland* Regiment, with two battalions on the left and one on the right on the hills which lined both sides of the long, approximately two-kilometer-wide valley. Its purpose was to tie down the enemy forces and enable the *Westland* Panzer Grenadier Regiment and the 5th Panzer Battalion to drive through the valley toward the town. Before the attack through the valley could proceed, the *Nordland* Regiment would have to eliminate enemy fire from the flanking hills. To support this important attack, II and III Battalions of the 5th SS Artillery Regiment went into position due east of Nishne Kurp while the panzer battalion assembled in the large ravine, from where it would attack directly toward the city.

At twelve noon on 25 September Gruppenführer Steiner assembled his officers for one last briefing. They were also joined at the command post of III Battalion, 5th SS Artillery Regiment by the corps artillery commander, Oberst Lukasch. The German artillery bombardment began at 5 A.M. on 26 September. Shells whistled over the heads of the waiting men toward the enemy positions. Flashes from exploding shells dotted the hills on both sides of the valley. Heavy smoke rose into the air. But as it later turned out, the Soviet troops there were in well-fortified, in-depth positions. The positions were linked by very narrow trenches and they, too, offered good protection.

The companies of the *Nordland* Regiment attacked as soon as the guns fell silent. I Battalion soon came under effective fire from the higher ground and began taking heavy casualties. Not until III Battalion succeeded in taking the higher ground was this fire eliminated. Each of the Russian positions had to be taken out individually. The regiment's commander, Oberführer von Scholz, who had worn the Knight's Cross since 18 January 1942, ran from one battalion to the other, personally encouraging his men. But then III Battalion was also pinned down and was forced to dig in. Only II Battalion *Nordland* which was advancing along the north slopes of the Musakaj, continued to gain ground. The division ordered the attack to continue in spite of the fierce resistance. Only this could enable the main thrust through the valley by the *Westland* Regiment and the panzers to succeed.

Sturmbannführer Polewacz tried again to get his battalion moving. Taking command of 1st Company, which had lost its commander, he somehow began to advance. At that very moment the infantry guns of the *Nordland* Regiment's 13th Company found the range of the Russian troops opposing the battalion and their supporting fire helped the attack begin moving again. The Russian positions were stormed and the companies of III Battalion also began advancing again.

The attack by II Battalion, *Westland* and the panzer battalion through the valley began at 7 A.M.. Sturmbannführer Mühlenkamp reached the antitank ditch near Nishne Kurp at 9:30. Under his command for the attack were the 3rd Company of the division's antitank battalion and the 3rd Company of the 5th SS Pioneer Battalion.

The tanks were halted at the antitank ditch, but the pioneers immediately went to work leveling the trench. Explosive charges brought down the walls. As the first tanks rolled through the gap the enemy opened fire with heavy 152-mm guns. The tanks of the 1st and 2nd Companies rolled forward in the previously arranged sequence. On this day the 2nd Company under Obersturmführer Flügel was supposed to lead the way, and as always the Panzer IVs of 3rd Company would reinforce the spearhead company. But this time it was different.

Since it was the birthday of Hauptsturmführer Schnabel, commander of 1st Company, he wanted his company to lead the way. Flügel had to hand over the necessary documents, aerial photos and maps to Schnabel. Then he began searching for another position from which to attack in the event that Schnabel's company became bogged down. It was 10:00 A.M. when the first tank of 1st Company rolled down into the flattened antitank ditch and crawled up the far side. The leading tank of 2nd Company under Untersturmführer Kollotzschy took a direct hit as it drove through the gap. Disabled, it lay blocking the passage. Soldiers reached the tank in seconds, but its entire crew had been killed. The passage had to be changed again. The pioneers went back to work and created another crossing point under heavy fire. 1st Company moved up once again; by the time it had cleared the antitank ditch two of its vehicles had been disabled by mines.

All the while the tanks of 2nd Company under Obersturmführer Flügel sat in their assembly area, with only limited cover, and waited for the advance to begin. Soviet Il-2 close-support aircraft flew low overhead, shooting at anything that moved. One was hit by fire from a 20-mm antiaircraft gun and turned away trailing smoke. Seconds later it exploded in a harsh red ball of fire.

Obersturmführer Flügel discussed the situation with his three platoon commanders: "What do you think, Nico?" he asked the leader of 2nd Platoon, "should we look for another way?"

"I fear that Mühlenkamp won't give us the chance. The situation is too confused. As hard as it seems we have to wait here."

"The devil knows I don't like to do it, but you are right."

Not until the last five tanks of 1st Company had rolled east at approximately 2:45 P.M. did 2nd Company received the order to move out. As soon as the tanks cleared the antitank ditch they found themselves facing an in-depth system of infantry positions.

"Open fire at your discretion! Forward as fast as possible!" ordered Flügel.

While he veered right toward a cross-trench, Nicolussi-Leck had the remaining tanks of his platoon swing left. They raced toward the trench, reached and turned right and left respectively.

"High-explosive shells into the trench!" ordered the platoon commander.

While the gunner had already loaded the round and closed the breech, the gunner used the handwheel to depress the barrel of the cannon. Then he saw the trench in his sight and fired. The shell exploded sixty meters in front of them. The casing was ejected, clanged against the guard and fell into the casings bag. The next round was loaded immediately. The second shot came less than 15 seconds later and it hammered into the trench approximately 100 meters to the side. Russian infantry poured back. The tank's machine-guns began to rattle and the brown-clad figures went to ground.

Flügel radioed Nicolussi-Leck and ordered him to advance further. The tanks raced toward a Russian heavy machine-gun. The commanders saw the shocked faces of the Red Army soldiers and then the tanks rolled over the position, grinding it into the dirt. One of the tank commanders called: "One of our sprockets has been hit." Nicolussi-Leck ordered one of his tanks to stay behind to provide cover for the disabled vehicle and he and his other two tanks set off to find the company commander.

Once the tanks halted and Nicolussi-Leck opened the hatch. Looking back, he saw that II Battalion, *Westland* had already moved up close behind them and were now trying to take cover behind the tanks. To the infantry this was something akin to a magical goal, but the young officer knew all too well that directly behind a tank was the most dangerous place, for tanks tended to draw artillery and machine-gun fire.

The tanks rolled on and came to a camouflaged dugout, from which four machine-guns were firing. They fired three or four rounds at the embrasures and when they were finished the infantry had nothing more to fear from this position. By noon the 1st Company under Hauptsturmführer Schnabel had covered half the distance to Sagopschin. When darkness fell Russian flanking forces cut off the German armored spearhead. Contact with the following units of the 5th SS Panzer Battalion was severed. The 1st Company's five tanks formed a tight hedgehog position. Russian infantry attacked and succeeded in setting one of the five tanks on fire with a Molotov cocktail. In the end, however, the Russian attack was beaten back. A Russian field kitchen, which was preparing food for the forward infantry positions, was intercepted. As a result the tank crewmen's hunger was eased for a while.

On the morning of that day the commander in chief of the 1st Panzer Army, Generaloberst von Kleist, had sent a telegram of encouragement to the *Wiking* Division. It read:

To the commander *Wiking.*

The entire army looks to your division.

Your job is to spearhead the attack on Grozny.

I expect your leading elements to reach Sagopschin by 1800 hours this evening.

(signed)

VON KLEIST.

That had not happened yet. The 2nd Company under Obersturmführer Flügel moved up behind 1st Company, followed closely by the tank destroyers of 3rd Company, 5th SS Antitank Battalion under Hauptsturmführer Oeck. The individual platoons rolled through the main valley, firing left and right into enemy-occupied ravines. The Russian heavy artillery opened up again and Sturmbannführer Mühlenkamp, who had driven to the front to assume the lead, ordered the attack force to veer south to where the artillery could not reach it.

The following account is by Obersturmführer Flügel:

My company rolled over the crest of a hill into the valley in wide formation and was about to veer toward Sagopschin. This proved impossible, however, for the steppe grass was on fire in places. Then we came under artillery fire from the south slope and from Malgobek, as well as from Sagopschin. We therefore veered into the terrain near Sagopschin and drove into the midst of a Russian defense position.

Serious dramas were played out there. I was able to follow it all over my company radio, even though I, too, was in a serious predicament.

Mines were thrown in front of our tanks. Russians climbed onto our tanks in order to drop hand grenades through the hatches. We had to keep each other clean and so I asked Nico to sweep my tank with his machine-gun. Nicolussi-Leck did this with great success, then fired several high-explosive rounds into the dense mass of Russians attacking from the right flank hoping to take us out with their gasoline bombs. Then I saw Nico swing his tank around and a long jet of fire shot from his main gun. Looking in the direction of the shot I saw a Russian 76.2-mm antitank gun, the notorious "crash-boom." Nicolussi-Leck's high-explosive round killed or wounded the entire gun crew and put it out of action.

Obersturmführer Wörmer, commander of the 1st Platoon, was wounded in the head when he tried to look out of his tank. Untersturmführer Perthes was killed.

When darkness fell we rolled behind a shallow rise and formed a large hedgehog in a cornfield. We were alone, for *Westland* was still pinned down in heavy fighting in the deep Russian defense lines, which we had simply driven through, and could not move up.

This ends the report from 2nd Company. Now an account from 1st Company which shows just how hard the fighting was. It was written by Richard Putensen, whose account from 20 February (the day the *Wiking* Division's 5th Panzer Battalion was formed) to 19 October 1942 provides a clear picture of the situation in which 1st Company found itself.

The 26th of September 1942 was a difficult, yes even a black day for our company. Our vehicle broke down with cooling system damage at the very outset of the attack. Once again it was a failure of the universal joint in the driveshaft to the radiator fan. We were disabled and had to wait for First Squad.

Of course our commander, Untersturmführer Kollotzschy, had to go on leading his platoon and so he climbed into tank 112. It would have been unthinkable for him to stay behind with the damaged tank. Such an act would have offended the honor of the platoon commander and the officers above him. The CO held another briefing, then Hauptsturmführer Schnabel came back to our company and it moved off. Behind us was the 2nd Company and we followed the progress of the battle over our radio as best we could.

The commander of the 3rd Platoon, which was now the point platoon, reported that he had driven over a mine at the antitank ditch. Thus tank 134 was also out of action. Then we heard something about tank 112, into which our commander had climbed. We could not understand all that was said. It sounded as if only two men had got out after an artillery hit. We already feared the worst and while we repaired our tank behind a low rise which blocked our view we could hear the crack of our tank cannon and the crash of Russian antitank guns and artillery, which had obviously opened fire at our tanks.

A short time later we received a report from the battalion command post. It said: "Commander, gunner and loader of tank 112 killed."

The exploding artillery round had blown away the commander's cupola and torn a great hole in the turret. The driver and radio operator suffered severe burns and received several fragment wounds. The news of the death of our comrades, and especially of our platoon commander, hit us very hard.

Russian aircraft attacked while we were getting water for our radiator. Cannon shells exploded all around but no damage was done. The few bombs that were dropped were well off target.

Now our tank was serviceable again and we set off to join the company. We arrived just as the tanks were about to move off again after having been pinned down by artillery fire and the wait for the antitank ditch to be leveled.

We first came to tank 114, which also had mechanical trouble. All around the ground had been scorched by the heavy artillery fire. We joined the company formation and a short time later crossed a hill on the right from which we were taking heavy antitank fire.

A new antitank ditch appeared before us. We continued to advance, following a line of hills. Our lead tank knocked out a concealed Russian antitank gun and immediately afterwards knocked out a speeding truck packed with Russian troops.

Our company took bitter losses and the hours seemed like an eternity.

Our artillery had been given orders to place the commanding hills and the town limits under fire. When our forward observer was put out of action the artillery fire was supposed to be directed from our company tank. This was something we rarely practiced, however, and delays in engaging the enemy were inevitable.

Then we heard a pleading call: "Hurry! Artillery fire on Sagopschin!"

Before the guns could open fire several more T-34s appeared before us. An order was passed to us from 2nd Company: "If the tank destroyers do not intervene we will have to fight to the last tank and the last round!"

The Russian batteries on the hills were silenced. Now there were only mortars and antitank guns still firing and we breathed easier.

We wanted to fight our way through to 2nd Company, which had already advanced past the village and was now standing in front of another antitank ditch, with what was left of our 1st Company. But as soon as the first of our tanks left the cover of the rise behind which we were hiding it was met by heavy antitank fire.

That meant that we had to stay in this relatively safe position for the time being. To make matters worse, the enemy guns on the hill began shelling us once again.

With the arrival of darkness our commander assembled the tanks into a hedgehog. We were ordered to take two tanks and under the cover of darkness recover the command tank and several crews who had been forced to abandon their vehicles. Just as we were about to depart our battalion commander approached and declared that the battalion was already taking care of this.

A few minutes later a voice rang out through the darkness: "Where is the 1st Company. This is the commander!"

It was our company commander, who had made it through to us together with several bailed-out crews.

Only now, after it had become somewhat quieter, could we leave our tanks; we waited for the moon to rise and then drove back to our departure positions.

There was still one more bitter event to come before this day was over. Tank 135 drove back in the darkness, taking several wounded to the rear. One of our antitank guns mistook it for a Russian tank, fired and scored a direct hit. The commander, gunner and loader were killed instantly. The driver and radio operator suffered serious and minor wounds, respectively.

On the 27th we set to work preparing the graves for our fallen comrades. We had lost three more killed in a surprise mortar barrage. They were a tank commander and two members of the headquarters section, including the driver of the CO's vehicle.

A careful inspection of our tank revealed a total of five hits, all of which had struck the right running gear and failed to penetrate the hull. Once again we had been very lucky.

On 29 September we withdrew further into a ravine which protected us from enemy fire. According to a report from battalion, a further advance could only take place when the hill positions had been taken. All around the terrain was very difficult for tanks, which was further complicated by the skillful positioning of several antitank ditches.

We were still in the same place on 30 September and we worked to restore our tank to the best possible working order. The more seriously damaged vehicles were towed away by the workshop platoon for repairs.

We looked like vagabonds. There was no water for washing, not even brackish water. The heat and the dust were something else.

With a touch of gallows humor one of the lads said that our hands were rubbing clean again in several places.

There was an alert at 4 A.M. on 1 October, but we did not withdraw again. The camp was packed up, however, so that we could leave immediately if orders were received from division or battalion. In the evening we learned that an Untersturmführer of the company had been killed by artillery fire.

Mail arrived today. It was handed out and we received the long-awaited letters from our loved ones at home.

Tanks versus Tank Combat—Twice Knocked Out

After the entire battalion had linked up with the 1st Company, Untersturmführer Nicolussi-Leck was ordered to report to his battalion commander.

"Nico," began Sturmbannführer Mühlenkamp, "a Russian antitank front has been set up in our open southern flank. This has to be eliminated during the night, for it poses a growing threat to our flank. Your platoon is at full strength, therefore I have chosen you."

Nicolussi-Leck snapped his heels together and said, "Thank you, Sturmbannführer." Mühlenkamp gestured for him to stand easy and then pointed to a map pinned to the wall of the cottage.

"These are the possibilities: either a direct frontal attack, rushing this gap, or across the right flank. I'll leave it up to you, Nico."

"Then I would propose breaking through here on the left, where the enemy has left a gap of approximately 100 meters to the rock wall, driving behind the antitank front and picking off the antitank guns one by one."

"And the guards that will surely be there?" asked Mühlenkamp.

"An assault team will have to see to them. They will have to be taken out."

"Yes, that could guarantee the element of surprise. Very well, that's how it will be done. The assault team will move out at 2245 hours. You and your platoon will have to have reached your staring position by then. The assault team will advise completion of its mission by radio and then you will move out."

"Thank you, Sturmbannführer, we will do the job."

The wiry, self-confident South Tyrolean, with the impeccable manner of a real officer, saluted and walked out. Before he reached the door Mühlenkamp raised his hand. Nicolussi-Leck stopped. "Sturmbannführer?"

The battalion commander said "Watch out for yourself and your men, Nico."

"Yes, Sturmbannführer," replied Nicolussi-Leck and walked out. He hurried back to his platoon and assembled the commanders of his four tanks. He looked into their expectant faces and knew: I can't deceive these lads. It was they, young volunteers of eighteen and nineteen years, who formed the backbone of his platoon and of 2nd Company.

The company commander joined them, summoned by a runner. "How does it look, Nico? Are you going to do it?"

"Of course, Hans," replied Nico. "This is a great chance to strike a blow at the enemy that he won't soon forget. Anyway it's necessary, because if we don't do it they'll finish us off from there one day."

"I understand. And now explain to me how you plan to do it. Like the drive through Mechetinskaya on 29 July when we drove around that awful hole, and then let the Ivans have it, driving fast and blazing away with everything we had, without losing a single tank?"

"Something like that." Then the Untersturmführer outlined his plan and the four crews listened tensely. One or two questions were posed and answered. Then came the order from Obersturmführer Flügel: "Get some sleep! I'll take care of the guard. You will be wakened at 2200 hours. First check to make sure that you have enough ammunition and fuel."

The crews were already standing by their tanks some time before they were due to be wakened. Untersturmführer Nicolussi-Leck walked over to them. He looked at his watch. The mess orderly brought them a pot of hot coffee; they recognized the aroma of real coffee.

"Drink up boys, it's going to be a cold night," declared one of the tank commanders. They held out their cups, took one of the meat-paste sandwiches and tucked in.

Then it was time. They overheard a runner telling the Obersturmführer that the assault team had moved out. The crews climbed into their tanks, started the engines and rolled single file into attack position, making as little noise as possible.

The platoon commander's voice sounded in their earphones: "To everyone: first vehicle, turret to 3 o'clock, second vehicle 11 o'clock, third and fourth vehicles 12 o'clock. Load high-explosive and lock!"

Each tank commander in turn reported: "Weapon loaded and locked."

They had been in position for several minutes, when Nicolussi-Leck heard the voice of the assault team leader in his headset: "Mission accomplished, give us another five minutes."

When the time was up Nicolussi-Leck gave the order for the tanks to advance. The motors roared as the tanks moved off in first gear, increasing their speed with each gear change. Then the panzers rolled through the gap. Not a shot had been fired and it looked as if they might get through when a Maxim machine-gun positioned on a low ridge in front of them began to rattle.

"Second gun: range 200, eleven o'clock, machine-gun nest—fire!"

The gunner saw the flash of tracer from the machine-gun. He made a slight adjustment and pressed the firing button. The high-explosive shell struck the rocks about half a meter below the machine-gun and blasted the rock and the weapon into the air.

The tanks came under fire from the right flank. "Keep going, keep going, full throttle!"

They roared past the surprised Russians, who had been rudely awakened, and reached the turning point, which was marked by a small clump of bushes.

"Turn and attack as ordered!"

Following the platoon commander's order, the tanks formed up into a line abreast formation with about thirty meters between vehicles and approached the gun positions from behind. Half-dressed Russians tumbled out of their dugouts and fled in all directions.

"There is the gun!"

"Target in sight," reported the gunner. Two seconds later the gun barked and almost simultaneously there was a crash as the high-explosive

Soldiers of the 5th SS-Panzer Division *Wiking* man a tripod-mounted MG42 at Dnepropetrowsk.

shell detonated. They rolled on, the next round already loaded. The second shot was aimed at a group of Russians storming toward the tank. The first shot by the platoon commander had been the signal for the other three tanks to open fire as well. They had already selected their targets. Piles of ammunition exploded, spraying fragments of steel through the air. Peering through his armor-glass view port, Nicolussi-Leck spotted a sentry post on the right.

"Turn right, enemy sentry post!" The tank wheeled around on one track, the gunner took aim and the gun barked again. A second round was fired into the position from 80 meters, causing it to burst into flames.

Turning again, the platoon commander set off after the other three tanks and reached the stop position at just about the same time. They rolled back to the company position, where Obersturmführer Flügel and Sturmbannführer Mühlenkamp were waiting for them.

"Well done, Nico, that was great work," said an exultant Flügel, shaking his hand vigorously.

Sturmbannführer Mühlenkamp also stepped up. "Congratulations, Nico, you did a good job."

"Exactly according to plan, Sturmbannführer," replied the platoon commander.

The men were jubilant. They had survived the attack in one piece and eliminated a serious threat to the entire battalion, indeed to the division. A few hours later the Russians moved an entire battalion into this sector, fearing another attack. The big question facing the division command was what was the enemy planning.

On 27 September the *Nordland* Regiment had advanced another few hundred meters across the plateau and the two ridges. The 5th SS Panzer Battalion remained under cover, its tanks widely-separated, while II Battalion, *Westland* fought off sporadic Russian assaults. The panzer-grenadiers moved closer to the division's antitank battalion for better protection against enemy tank attack. The new main assault was once again supposed to be carried out in the valley. At 3 P.M. Steiner asked von Scholz for his plan of attack. This time he assigned his personal adjutant, Sturmbannführer Engelhardt, to outline the plan.

Engelhardt, a former Danish general staff officer, presented the division commander with two plans, both of which he had worked out with von Scholz. While one plan proposed an attack against Malgobek, with the emphasis on III Battalion, *Nordland*, the second called for an advance across the south hills toward Kessam. Under no circumstances should they attack in the valley, as the enemy had erected a complex defensive system there.

The plans were put before the LII Army Corps. The latter liked neither, instead it favored an attack through the valley, claiming that a breakthrough could most easily be achieved there. The army command agreed with this view, because it also hoped to coordinate the attack with a simultaneous assault by III Panzer Corps. And so the already battered *Nordland* Regiment was ordered to attack through the valley.

Fritz von Scholz, who had received the Knight's Cross on 18 January 1942 as an SS-Oberführer and commander of the SS-Regiment *Nordland,* was convinced that such an attack must lead to disaster. He therefore decided that if the attack was made he would lead the assault and be killed, for—as he stressed to his friend Sturmbannführer Engelhardt—"This attack will be the end of my regiment. The only chance for a victory is to first eliminate the enemy's flanking fire. Only then can we reach Sagopschin."

Fritz von Scholz, the son of a major-general, had received the highest Austrian decoration for bravery, the Golden Medal of Bravery, while serving as an Oberleutnant in the artillery during the First World War. As a commander in the Freikorps Oberland he had helped free Upper Silesia in 1921 and in 1935 became a member of the Verfügungstruppe, the first SS combat unit. In the western campaign he won the bar to the two Iron Crosses he had won in the First World War. On 1 December 1940 von Scholz had assumed command of the *Nordland* Regiment of the *Wiking* Division at a time when both units were being formed. He subsequently led *Nordland* into the campaign against Russia. North of Rostov he won fresh laurels for the regiment. On 29 November he won the German Cross in Gold and on 18 January 1942 he was decorated with the Knight's Cross. At the very least the corps should have listened to the opinion of this soldier, who was acknowledged to be an exemplary officer, tactician and strategic thinker. But instead of consulting with him it simply ordered the attack to go ahead.

The attack on 27 September resulted in no gain. The attacking forces were showered with artillery fire from Sagopschin and Malgobek.

On the late afternoon of that day the *Westland* Regiment's I Battalion finally returned to the division from the western Caucasus. It had had to be left behind in order not to endanger the German position there. The battalion was moved up close behind the 5th SS Panzer Battalion. The *Nordland* Regiment was left in its former positions on the hills on both sides of the valley, while I Battalion, *Westland* was assigned to carry out the attack on Malgobek together with the 70th Grenadier Regiment.

After being pinned down in the valley by heavy enemy fire throughout the 27th of September, Sturmbannführer Mühlenkamp received orders from the division commander to eliminate the enemy guns which were still laying down the flanking fire from the two lines of hills before the new attack began. Oberführer Gille, commander of the 5th SS Artillery Regiment, was certain that they could do it; he assumed command of the attack. In addition to his artillery Gille also moved up anti-aircraft guns, for the Soviet air force was becoming increasingly active, striking German quartering and assembly areas. Russian fighters and close-support aircraft also intervened in the ground battle. For the first time Soviet airmen dropped phosphorus bombs, burning down the cornfields and steppe grass in the valley.

To counter this aerial onslaught the Luftwaffe had just four Bf-109 fighters of Fighter Squadron 52. Day after day they rose to intercept the incoming raids and though they took a considerable toll of the enemy they were unable to significantly affect the attacks.

During the night of 28 September the *Wiking* armored battle group, which included the self-propelled guns, had formed a large hedgehog in a huge cornfield. The *Westland* Regiment moved up close to this hedgehog and suffered further casualties from artillery fire. The company and platoon commanders went to Sturmbannführer Mühlenkamp's quarters to receive their orders. Mühlenkamp explained the plan of attack:

> First Company, 5th Panzer Battalion will make a frontal attack against Sagopschin with the bulk of the *Westland* Regiment. 2nd Company, 5th Panzer Battalion will carry out an enveloping movement to the north and reach the Sagopschin-Nizhne Atschaluki road behind Sagopschin, block the road and depending on the situation attack Sagopschin from the rear.

At the suggestion of Sturmbannführer Mühlenkamp the time of the attack was moved forward in order to take advantage of the morning fog. This had to be done in order to get close enough to the enemy tanks, as the cannon of opposing T-34s were clearly superior to those of the German tanks. The Panzer IIIs and IVs lacked the long-ranging guns of the later Tigers and Panthers.

The attack began at the prescribed time. The panzer battalion rolled forward briskly. First Company had been assigned the point position. Behind it came the point company of the *Westland* Regiment in armored troop carriers, led by Hauptsturmführer Harry Willer. Stationed behind it were I and II Battalions *Westland*, on the right and left respectively.

It was still dawn when the first positions in front of Sagopschin were reached; fortunately the first antitank ditch was not very deep and the tanks drove through. High-explosive shells and machine-gun fire drove the Red Army troops from their trenches and positions. Surprise had been achieved. Mühlenkamp's panzers rolled east past Sagopschin. Abeam the town Untersturmführer Nicolussi-Leck's platoon began taking fire from the right. Four enemy tanks were spotted. Nicolussi-Leck gave the order for his crews to open fire. In seconds the gunner of the platoon commander's tank had his sights on the first T-34. The cannon barked and the enemy tank, which was positioned in the middle of a group of four, took a direct hit and went up in flames. Then its ammunition exploded. The two tanks on either side of this first victim were also hit, while the fourth—the farthest distant—was damaged by a member of the platoon and then finished off by a well-aimed shot from the platoon commander's tank. Nicolussi-Leck ordered his tanks to press ahead at maximum speed. A fifth enemy tank was positioned several hundred meters farther east, concealed behind some bushes on the far side of a road. The Russian tank gave away its position by opening fire and the armor-piercing round passed less than half a meter over the turret of Nicolussi-Leck's tank. His gunner returned fire. The shell struck the sloping frontal armor, knocking the T-34 back, and ricocheted upwards. The T-34's second shot went wide to the left, thanks to a skillful evasive maneuver by the driver. Then Nicolussi-Leck's gunner fired a second time; the shot hit the T-34's turret ring, dislodging the turret. The enemy tank was now disabled, its gun pointing down at the ground. The crew bailed out but there were only three men. The fourth, the commander, had obviously been killed. Then a burst of machine-gun fire meted out the same fate to the others.

Following the destruction of this fifth tank the tanks proceeded quickly. Meanwhile 1st Company was bogged down in the Russian defensive system between Sagopschin and Malgobek I and was forced to defend itself against attacks from all sides. The panzer-grenadiers kept the enemy at bay with their MG 42s, but they also suffered heavy casualties. Hauptsturmführer Willer, who was leading the point company, was killed. Sturmbannführer Mühlenkamp's only hope now was that 2nd Company would succeed and that its attack would relieve some of the pressure in the valley, which as predicted had turned out to be a great trap. Soviet tanks were committed to a frontal attack against the German attack force. A total of 25 were counted. They drove out of Sagopschin toward the west with a small group to the south; further enemy tanks waited in reserve.

Obersturmführer Flügel had linked up with the Nicolussi-Leck Platoon. The entire battalion fought its way more to the north, fending off repeated assaults by enemy tanks, in an attempt to reach the dead space behind the line of hills.

Waves of Soviet tanks attacked repeatedly against the southern flank and it appeared that they would force the 5th SS Panzer Battalion to go over to the defensive. But Sturmbannführer Mühlenkamp knew that being forced onto the defensive would mean the end against the more potent guns of the T-34s. He therefore ordered his panzers to head straight for the Russian tanks and hold their fire until they were within 800 meters of the target.

The battalion's tanks rolled forward at high speed, selecting their targets as they went. True to panzer arm tradition, Sturmbannführer Mühlenkamp led the way, for only by being on the spot could a commander quickly issue appropriate orders to deal with a rapidly changing situation. The resulting action, which consisted largely of one-on-one duels between the opposing tanks, was described by Sturmbannführer Mühlenkamp:

> The sun finally broke through at 7 A.M., earlier than expected. The fog was suddenly absorbed by the warmth of the sun. We were in the midst of the outer Russian positions near Sagopschin. And what a sight we saw: everywhere the thin lines of the trenches and the higher mounds that marked machine-gun positions, all well manned. We were kept under constant machine-gun fire from the embrasures of the dugouts, with the enemy firing at hatches and vision ports. Now and then our vehicles were struck by a projectile from an antitank rifle. We could see the outlines of Red Army soldiers, stalking us with hand grenades and gasoline bombs.
>
> We drove over the trenches and ground the Russians into the mud. Enemy troops leapt at us and the only way we could help each other was for one tank to spray the other with machine-gun ammunition to keep the attacking Russians at bay. Occasionally our machine-guns succeeded in forcing a mass of attackers to go to ground.
>
> One of the tank commanders driving on the left flank reported: "Tank, on the right, three o'clock, range 800!"
>
> The battle began, occasionally interrupted by the onset of heavy enemy artillery fire.
>
> The first hit we took struck just behind my turret. The engine began to smoke, the thirteen-ton turret had been lifted from its ring, and my seat's back support had been shot off.
>
> I had been thrown forward and was lying across the cannon. "Get out!" There were sixty shells in our tank, as well as about 6,000 rounds of machine-gun ammunition, and I had placed thirty hand grenades beneath my seat for self-defense, just in case

we were attacked at close range. In the turret ring were thirty rounds of ammunition for the flare gun and as well both gasoline tanks were still almost full. It was a highly explosive, deadly cargo which could go up at any second.

Before my order to get out could be carried out we were hit a second time, on the front hatch. My driver, Fritz Kröbsch, collapsed and in seconds his head was covered in blood.

Then another shattering blow, this time a hit on the turret. The hatch, which weighed about two-hundred kilos, fell into the interior and severed the right arm of Heinze, my radio operator, who was also operating the bow machine-gun.

All of this took place in a matter of seconds, faster than I can repeat it here. I pulled the driver and radio operator out through the emergency escape hatch and dragged them several meters away from the tank.

At that moment Untersturmführer Köntrop, my regular gunner, rolled out of the command tank. He had returned with our regular tank, which had been put out of action the day before and since repaired. I gave instructions for it to destroy the enemy. Shortly before I was hit, I had spotted a Russian position nearby. You must get in there and wait until the replacement tank arrives, I thought to myself.

With my pistol in my hand I jumped into the Russian trench, ready for anything. After my regular command tank arrived we moved the wounded into the trench and tended to their wounds. All of this took one minute at most.

I also now realized how it could happen that we were struck by such a devastating barrage. While we were still advancing, two Russian T-34s had slipped past us and had positioned themselves between my panzer battalion and the following *Westland* panzergrenadiers. It was something special to meet such a well-led enemy tank force. This tank commander was a professional. He had executed a perfect ambush.

Now another T-34 appeared from the cover of some bushes behind us and opened fire at us with its machine-gun. Bullets streaked toward us. Köntrop suddenly cried out. A burst of fire had literally sheared off his right leg. I picked Köntrop up and dragged him into the Russian trench in front of us. The trench, which a short time ago had been full of Russians, was now empty. The Ivans had pulled back.

Afterwards I brought our badly wounded driver Kröbsch and radio operator Heinze into the trench.

On my instructions the so far uninjured loader had already removed the machine-gun and together with a member of *Westland* who had got through, he guarded our wounded comrades.

I was about to run back the several dozen meters to my command tank, which was engaged in a duel with a T-34, in order to take command once again, when Köntrop seized me with the last of his strength.

"I'm dying Sturmbannführer," he whispered softly. I stayed with him, holding his hand. A minute later Köntrop was dead.

Köntrop, an excellent, always cheerful young fellow and a fearless young officer, was no more. We would miss this dyed-in-the-wool Berliner with his admittedly often fresh mouth.

A short time later I reached my replacement tank. The dead and wounded members of my crew were recovered.

In the meantime Obersturmführer Flügel had advanced beyond Sagopschin and, as I could tell by the sound of tank cannon firing, was engaging further T-34s.

To my right the 1st Company had come to a halt. Several of the company's tanks had been hit in such a way that the shear pins on the sliding couplings had broken, as a result of which the cannon, with a very few exceptions, could not be moved. Hauptsturmführer Schnabel of 1st Company and Darges, commander of 3rd Company, had also been knocked out.

This ends Sturmbannführer Mühlenkamp's account. The following description of 2nd Company's role in the battle was provided by Obersturmführer Flügel:

I carried out this enveloping attack on Sagopschin with my reinforced company, which was equipped with the recently introduced Panzer IV mounting the long-barreled 75-mm gun. Compared to previous tanks this vehicle represented a decisive improvement. Now we could engage the T-34 at greater ranges and were equal to it as far as the armament was concerned. But our crews were definitely better, especially since the Russian tanks had only a four-man crew, a serious shortcoming.

Untersturmführer Schicker, Bürscher and Schuhmacher also came to the party, The self-propelled 76.2-mm guns of the

'Wespen' Battalion under Sturmbannführer Köller, but especially its 3rd Company led by Hauptsturmführer Oeck, were to support the left flank of the attack on Malgobek.

The floor of the valley had been mined across our direction of attack, which could have deadly for us had I not discovered the tall poles marked with bundles of straw just prior to the attack. Investigation of these revealed that they had been placed by the Russians to mark clear lanes that had been left through the mines. We drove through these at top speed.

I staggered our forces, with Untersturmführer Nicolussi-Leck's platoon in front, covering against any threat from the hills. I attacked sharply with the other two platoons.

When the pale light of day came up and the first ghostly outlines took on visible form, we were already exchanging fire with attacking enemy tanks. We were so interlocked during the close combat that we almost took each other's fenders off.

Driving beside me was Obersturmführer Nicolussi-Leck. He knocked out three enemy tanks before his own tank was hit in the engine from close range and began to burn. In the heat of the battle he failed to notice what had happened until he was advised by radio. Only then did the crew bail out. They headed for a hole several dozen meters behind the tank. The loader had brought along the machine-gun, and it was immediately put to use, for a group of Red Army soldiers had seen them abandon their tank and wanted to nail the crew. But they hadn't counted on Nicolussi-Leck, who was one of the best and most intelligent tank officers we had and who showed himself to be equal to any situation.

In the midst of the confusion we realized that no one was following us any more. The *Wespen* were bogged down somewhere farther back and the men of *Westland*, some of whom had been riding on the self-propelled guns, had since dismounted and were guarding the valuable vehicles.

Our attack almost became a crisis. We were exposed to the enemy's artillery salvoes like food on a serving tray and still had to fight the T-34s. Those that were still able to withdrew toward Sagopschin.

The following is a contemporary account of the Nicolussi-Leck platoon's part in the attack:

We drove through a broad minefield. Riding on our tanks was a company of *Westland* troops, who were to protect us from enemy infantry and clean out the enemy trenches when we overran them. The gunsights and sight glasses soon misted over. The fog caused large drops of water to form, which further reduced visibility, causing much cursing.

Drivers, commanders and gunners, too, strained their eyes in an effort to penetrate the pea-soup fog, but in vain.

The mounted infantry had to be doubly alert in order to deal with any unpleasant surprises. Our panzers rolled through the gray-white wall like ghostly monsters. But then the fog abruptly began to thin out. Now and then we could see approximately 100 meters ahead into the battlefield. And then the fog was gone. Everything appeared clear and bright in the brilliant sunshine. We gained ground quickly.

Then suddenly a call: "Attention! 3 o'clock, 1,500 meters, enemy tanks in the depression!"

Even though I was not wearing a headset I also heard these words clearly inside the tank. Our first encounter with enemy tanks. Everyone was tense, alert. Then our commander's instructions came down into the fighting compartment:

"Load armor-piercing, stand by to fire!"

I loaded the first armor-piercing shell and reported: "Weapon loaded and locked!"

While all this was happening I found time for a quick look out the side vision slit. A row of enemy tanks was visible in the hollow ahead and to our right at the reported distance. We counted about twenty-five. They were moving at high speed toward our lines.

Suddenly something whistled over us. Tank or antitank gun, it was impossible to say. We advanced at high speed.

"Attention! One o'clock, 400 meters, enemy tank!"

I had already placed the first armor-piercing shell in the breech. Several tanks in front of us had already initiated combat. "Open fire!" called the commander. I had already taken aim at the target; a press on the firing button and the shell shot out of the barrel, its recoil raising the front end of the tank slightly.

Seconds of tension. Next to us another of our tanks fired its gun. Then I saw a flash from the enemy tank. "Hit," shouted the commander. "He's burning!"

We drove on. Casting a quick glance through the vision slit, I saw two stationary T-34s two-hundred meters away at 2 o'clock at the edge of a field of sunflowers. Smoke was pouring from them. But we were still being fired at.

Then suddenly our commander called: "Tank 231 is on fire!"

We saw Untersturmführer Nicolussi-Leck's crew abandon their vehicle. The platoon commander climbed into one of his prime movers while his crew was left to look after the tank.

A pillar of smoke farther right showed that another T-34 had been hit. Over the radio I heard that a fourth enemy tank had been knocked out. We were happy, but the day was not over yet and this was not the last kill of the day.

The subsequent course of the battle was described graphically by gunner Neumann:

Our company commander exploited the confusion among the Russians. We drove deeper into the valley, which was opening up before us. Behind us our infantry, which had been forced to dismount at the beginning of the battle, was engaging the Russians who were emerging from their holes intent on falling upon our tanks. They were cut down by machine-gun fire and hand grenades.

We gained ground rapidly and got through the antitank gun and antitank rifle fire to the antitank ditch. It turned out to be a dried-up river bed which the Russians had turned into a dangerous tank trap by making a few additions.

Crossing it under fire was difficult and dangerous. Oberscharführer Bachschuster was killed by artillery shrapnel while standing in his tank's turret hatch. We others got through in one piece.

Meanwhile we had advanced far beyond Sagopschin. We now veered right toward our objective, the Sagopschin-Nizhne Atschaluki road. The point platoon, led by Untersturmführer Scheel, immediately engaged several more enemy tanks which were standing guard there. Within minutes four were ablaze. We drove through to the road and barricaded it. Our appearance there took the Russians completely by surprise. They imagined we were still in the valley in front of Sagopschin. There we learned the kill totals from Untersturmführer Flügel. Our company had destroyed six T-34s and five British Mark IIIs. Two other T-34s had been damaged and immobilized.

As we learned later, when we advanced past Sagopschin we had run into a second Russian tank unit which was being held in reserve. However our advance had split these two tank units apart.

Obersturmführer Flügel sent one platoon forward on the left of the road to give sufficient warning of approaching vehicles or tanks. It encountered two "crash-booms" (76-2-mm antitank guns). Then it was fired upon by two enemy tanks. The platoon was unable to return fire, however, because the enemy were out of range of the 50-mm guns with which the platoon's tanks were still equipped.

The 2nd and 3rd Companies together formed a large semicircle and secured the road.

Nothing happened for a long time. The sound of heavy fighting could be heard from Sagopschin. Orders were received by radio that the air identification panels were to be removed from the tanks and that they were to be well camouflaged, as the staff of JG52 had reported Russian aircraft in the area.

An half hour later 18 Russian aircraft appeared. However they did not attack us, but instead dropped their bombs on Sagopschin. Had the *Westland* Regiment taken the town?

Now Russian heavy artillery positioned in Malgobek also opened fire on Sagopschin. What was happening there? The Russians must have lost the picture. We attributed that to their poor communications. Based on what we knew for certain and from where the shells from our division's artillery were falling, we still had to be west of Sagopschin and the Russians in the town.

We very much hoped that our tank destroyers and self-propelled guns would soon arrive with the mounted infantry to secure the area that had been won. But instead armor-piercing shells suddenly began whizzing over us. The enemy antitank guns could still not be made out and therefore we could not engage and silence them.

All of a sudden we heard the whistle of incoming shells. Heavy artillery shells began falling among us. We were forced to withdraw and abandon our obviously recognized positions, but the Russian shells followed us. It was obvious that a well-hidden forward observer was directing the fire of the Russian 152-mm batteries. But we sat passively inside our cramped steel boxes. We heard the guns fire and waited for the shells to land. Up until this time the Russians had assumed that we were their own tanks, but the enemy antitank guns must have reported us as hostile.

It was noon when our commander decided to drive into the antitank ditch in order to get away from the heavy Russian artillery fire.

There were difficulties associated with the execution of this order, because our first tank was placed under direct fire when it drove into the dry riverbed. Nevertheless all of our tanks reached the antitank ditch, where they sat under cover up to their turrets. For the first time since we had set off early that morning we were able to leave the tank and enjoy a few deep breaths of fresh air. We camouflaged all our tanks and repaired any damage, while the gunners removed the bow machine-guns and provided close cover.

Obersturmführer Flügel went from vehicle to vehicle, checking on the condition of the wounded.

—

By now it was 4 P.M. The company commander's tank was in constant contact with the battalion and the division. The tank crews learned that the infantry had moved out but was making slow progress because of strong enemy resistance. Everyone waited for nightfall. When night fell the Russians began making feverish attempts to restore contact between their units. In some cases German forces intervened, and a number of prisoners were taken. As there was no water, ten Russian prisoners were sent to fetch some.

SS tankers share cigarettes with army and police soldiers.

"They'll never come back, Untersturmführer," declared Rottenführer Schlingmann to Nicolussi-Leck. But the latter just shook his head skeptically.

"I think that they'll feel safer here than with the others in Sagopschin," he replied. As was so often the case Nicolussi-Leck was to be proved right, for the ten Russians came back with full water canisters—and another twenty of their comrades, who also surrendered to the Germans.

During the night Obersturmführer Flügel sent the damaged tanks and the wounded back to the pole markers. He had instructions to report to the battalion. One thing was certain. If the enemy attacked before fuel and ammunition arrived, the situation would be hopeless. Obersturmführer Flügel assembled his platoon commanders and asked them what he should do.

"You have sent your report to the battalion Hans, all that is left is to bypass the chain of command and try to get in touch with General Steiner at division."

"Isn't that a very unusual method?" asked Flügel doubtfully.

"Yes, but this is a very unusual situation and as such it demands an unconventional solution."

"Nico is right," interjected another of the platoon commanders.

"Very well, but if I end up in the stockade then come visit me and bring something to smoke," replied Flügel sarcastically, before he used the last of the "juice" (the energy in the radio transmitter) to get through to the division command post. The Ia, who took the call, sent for General Steiner.

"What's going on Flügel? Are you in a jam? It had better be a very big jam if you intend to get out of this unscathed."

"Gruppenführer, we have no fuel and our ammunition is just about gone. The enemy has forced us into the antitank ditch. We need fuel and ammunition immediately as well as infantry support."

"But otherwise you are well?" inquired Steiner with a chuckle.

"Very well, sir. We can knock Ivan's block off if we get what we need."

"All right, Flügel. You will get everything. Everything you have asked for, including infantry, will come through the gap in the minefield to you tonight."

Order was restored in the battalion. After the first tank-versus-tank duel it withdrew approximately one kilometer. This was necessary in order to refuel and rearm the tanks. Sturmbannführer Mühlenkamp had entered the battle with forty tanks. One third had been put out of action by mechanical breakdowns or enemy action. Hauptsturmführer Oeck, the commander of 3rd Company, 5th SS Antitank Battalion (self-propelled), had had his vehicle shot out from under him. He hobbled off the battlefield with 14 fragment wounds in both shoulders. The *Westland* Regiment lost many men on this day. It had been showered with murderous enemy fire from the hills on both sides of the valley. Russian aircraft bombed them and close-support aircraft came down to fifty meters to strafe them with machine-guns and cannon.

The attack by I Battalion, *Westland* succeeded in clearing the first enemy trench. Then the Russians fired like mad with artillery, rocket-launchers and machine-guns and forced the attackers to go to ground. The battalion's attack between Sagopschin and Kesskem, or into the town' defenses from the right, had failed with heavy casualties. Once again the decisive blow had been struck by the enemy batteries on the hills, which fired on anything that moved in the valley.

At this point we return to Sturmbannführer Mühlenkamp's account of the battle. After his command tank was knocked out, Mühlenkamp moved over to his former command tank, which had been hit and then repaired, allowing him to return to the front. This excellent account was provided to the author by Johannes-Rudolf Mühlenkamp many years ago:

> I had just restored order to my tank unit—the Russian T-34s were no longer attacking—when I took another hit on the right side. The shell whizzed through the fighting compartment and through the buttocks of the gunner sitting to my left.
>
> At about three in the afternoon my third tank was knocked out. Soon afterwards, when I arrived at the command post of I Battalion, *Westland,* I found the battalion commander, Sturmbannführer Hadeln, completely dazed, arranging his battalion's dead and checking their names. There were several heaps of arms and legs, all from men who had been blown apart by the heavy Russian artillery shells.
>
> I will never be able to forget that horrible scene.
>
> At first I had the impression that Hadelm might have gone mad, for he was very attached to his men and had always been a caring superior and fatherly friend to them.

The *Westland* Regiment had meanwhile pulled back approximately two kilometers to the west and had found what cover it could in shallow depressions. It established a defensive position in the valley in front of Sagopschin until nightfall. The *Wiking* panzer battalion had to carry out several relief attacks to the east to free the pinned-down panzer-grenadiers.

That 28th of September was one of the bloodiest days ever for the men of the *Westland* Regiment. The attack, which had begun so well, was completely shot to pieces by the Russian artillery. All of the well-planned offensive moves had been smashed by the enemy, validating the prediction made by Oberführer von Scholz: "Without the two chains of hills we can never capture Sagopschin!"

Another important factor in this depressing defeat—for in spite of the large number of enemy tanks destroyed it was nothing less than that—was the two Russian tank attacks. Carried out in a westerly direction along the Musakaj hills south of the *Wiking* Division in the valley, their objective was to barricade the antitank ditch near Nizhne Kurp—deep in the rear of the division—and then destroy the division from two sides. That the Soviets failed to do so was attributable to the efforts of the 5th SS Panzer Battalion under Sturmbannführer Mühlenkamp.

This was Johannes-Rudolf Mühlenkamp's second great defensive success, equal in significance to the one which had won him the Knight's Cross on 3 September 1942. Years ago he told the author: "What would I have been without my men, fighters like Flügel, Schnabel and especially Nicolussi-Leck. They entered this battle and won it against an at least twofold superiority in enemy tanks." The battle had pitted forty vehicles of the 5th SS Panzer Battalion and six tank destroyers of the 5th SS Antitank Battalion's 3rd Company against at least 100 enemy tanks.

On the evening of that 28 September Oberführer von Scholz was named sector commander in the Sagopschin Valley, placing Obersturmbannführer Geißler, commander of the *Westland* Regiment, under his command. Oberführer Scholz was to remain sector commander in this hotly contested valley until 15 October and until 3 October Headquarters, LII Army Corps continued to insist that the attack had to be made in the valley. On the early morning of 29 September the corps pressed for another quick attack. General Steiner moved up I Battalion, *Nordland*, which was to carry out the attack together with II Battalion, *Westland*. II Battalion, *Nordland* was to simultaneously advance on the hills on the right toward Kesskem, while a single company of III Battalion, *Nordland*, would follow the attack on the Malgobek hills.

The attack began at 2 P.M. A preceding artillery bombardment was supposed to soften up the area, but the attack soon bogged down. The German artillery soon outpaced the attack force and at 3:30 it had to be shifted back 400 meters. Nevertheless, under the inspiring leadership of Oberführer von Scholz, at 5 P.M. the combined attack group stormed and took the Russian positions 800 meters west of Sagopschin. There the advance was halted again, but at least the troops were relatively safe from the enemy's artillery fire in the former Russian trenches.

The battle continued on 30 September and General Steiner again complained to LII Army Corps, asking for a regrouping, which in his view was the only possible way to achieve victory. This reorganized attack began on 1 October under the cover of morning fog. A small assault team lead the way for each company. At first the attack proceeded smoothly, but when the leading troops were only fifty to seventy meters from Sagopschin the fog lifted abruptly and the attackers were met by a storm of defensive fire. The leading squads were literally cut to pieces. Oberführer von Scholz, who was at the front, was forced to order a retreat. His battle group withdrew approximately 1,000 meters and the assault teams dug in.

On the morning of 2 October Oberführer von Scholz reported to General Steiner at the latter's command post; he concluded by saying:

> I reject further attacks on Sagopschin if we do not receive adequate air and artillery support. I demand as preconditions: the elimination of the flanking positions, and I propose that I attack with my regiment's II Battalion on the line of hills south of the valley near Mussakaj, if this absolutely has to be.

General Steiner endorsed the plan and suggested that they wait until 4 October to attack, because by then the batteries of I Battalion, 5th SS Artillery Regiment, which was still occupied in the western Caucasus, would have arrived. LII Army Corps pressed for the attack to be made as soon as possible and at 7:30 P.M. on 2 October the division issued orders for II Battalion, *Nordland*, to attack in the Mussakaj sector on the following day. Sturmbannführer Mühlenkamp assigned four of his tanks to support the battalion.

Under the command of Sturmbannführer Arnold Stoffers the attack made rapid progress. The Soviet 57th Brigade, which was in positions on a hill 800 meters north of Kesskem, was driven back. The Russian guns which had placed flanking fire on the German attack against Sagopschin would fire no more. But Sagopschin itself was still in Russian hands and General der Infanterie Eugen Ott, the commanding general of LII Army Corps, demanded from Steiner a new plan for continuing the attack. This time Grozny was to be taken. General Steiner pointed out that Malgobek was the key to Grozny and would have to be taken before an attack could be mounted against the main objective. The commanding heights of Malgobek also made it difficult to go on holding the projecting main line of resistance in the valley before Sagopschin.

General Ott said to the commander of the *Wiking* Division: "Your *Germania* Regiment is arriving from the west Caucasus tomorrow. With it you will take Malgobek."

The corps was dispersing its forces. The *Wiking* Division fought the ensuing battle with barely half of its forces and as a result failed to reach its objective, suffering heavy casualties which seriously weakened it. Meanwhile most of the damaged tanks of the Mühlenkamp battalion had been repaired. The panzer battalion was called upon to take part in this attack, but the terrain forced the tanks to operate single-file on narrow mountain roads. This went against all the principles of armored warfare. 1st Company, 5th SS Panzer Regiment was assigned to support the attack.

The attack began on 5 October 1942. The plan called for the *Germania* Regiment to assault Malgobek. Under the command of Hauptsturmführer Schnabel, the panzer battalion's 1st Company helped the grenadiers advance. Leading the assault force was I Battalion, *Germania*, under Sturmbannführer Dieckmann. To its left was II Battalion, *Germania*, under Sturmbannführer Jörchels, while on the right II Battalion, *Nordland*, screened the attack in the direction of Sagopschin. Bringing up the rear was the 70th Grenadier Regiment under Oberst Tronnier.

On this day 2nd Company under Obersturmführer Flügel also took part in the attack. The 1st Company was to follow. During the course of the attack Untersturmführer Nicolussi-Leck destroyed three enemy tanks which approached the advancing grenadiers from the open flank. Three more were knocked out by Obersturmführer Flügel and tank commanders Steinhaus and Weber. It was later discovered that they were all British-built Mark IIIs and Valentines.

This time six Stuka dive-bombers supported the attack, bombing nests of resistance ahead of the advance. By 11 A.M. the *Germania* Regiment was just 500 meters from Malgobek. In preparation for the final assault, one more large-scale Stuka attack was laid on against the town. It was precisely 11:20 A.M. when about twenty Stukas appeared. Over Malgobek they peeled off into vertical dives, sirens screaming, their targets the enemy batteries. One machine was hit by ground fire and veered off, trailing smoke. The exploding bombs shook the earth and were the signal for the grenadiers to attack. A huge oil tank blazed in Malgobek. The Russian infantry fought with fierce determination, but gradually their resistance weakened. By 2 P.M. Malgobek, the key to an assault on Grozny, was in German hands. Hauptsturmführer Dorr, recently decorated with the Knight's Cross for his actions in the west Caucasus, noted in his personal diary: "Our regiment paid a high price in blood. 33 killed and 200 wounded, some seriously, spilled their blood for Malgobek."

Malgobek-East fell on 6 October and by three in the afternoon the big oil tank was in the hands of the grenadiers. The tank contained a large quantity of high-quality aviation gasoline, ending the Luftwaffe's fuel worries in this area for some time. The Soviets fought desperately to halt the German advance. In the days that followed the panzers were committed several times and Nicolussi-Leck played a leading role by clearing the way for the infantry or halting Russian attacks with tank support.

11 to 14 October was a period of bitter fighting. The initiative passed over to the Red Army, which committed everything it had available. 1st Company relieved 2nd Company and supported the grenadiers in their defensive struggle. After the last unit, III Battalion, *Germania*, arrived from the western Caucasus on 14 October, a new attack was scheduled for the following day. Two points of main effort were formed. It was the beginning of a battle that would ultimately see the Untersturmführer from Tyrol at the head of his own company.

1st Company Engages the Enemy

At 9 A.M. on 15 October ten enemy tanks were reported by Battle Group Stoffers. These were met by 1st Company, as 2nd Company was supporting the attacking infantry. Hauptsturmführer Schnabel succeeded in knocking out one T-34 and one Mark III. The rest of the company accounted for three more. The Soviet armored assault was beaten back.

Sturmbannführer Mühlenkamp, who had sortied with 1st Company, summoned all of his commanders for a battlefield conference. The purpose of the meeting was to discuss a fresh assault. Less than ten minutes later the tank commanders met in the midst of the assembled panzers. 1st Company provided cover for the meeting. Just as Sturmbannführer Mühlenkamp began assigning attack lanes, the Soviets opened fire on the concentration of tanks. Their feared 172-mm guns began saturating the area with shells, and before any orders could be given one of the large-caliber shells fell in the midst of the group of panzer battalion officers.

Screams rang out through the morning and men fell to the ground, killed or wounded. Two soldiers nearest the point of impact were literally blown to bits. Sturmbannführer Mühlenkamp was thrown to the side and suffered only minor injuries. But Hauptsturmführer Schnabel, the commander of 1st Company, was dead. Untersturmführer Pinnow, who had been standing next to him, was also killed, as were Hauptsturmführer Barthold, Oberscharführer Bossel and an antitank officer. The wounded were tended to immediately. There was great confusion, for a considerable portion of the panzer battalion's officers had been put out of action with a single stroke. Tank 111, 1st Company's command vehicle, was hit twice by an enemy tank which had crept up to the edge of this gruesome scene and made the most of its opportunity. Tank 123 was seriously damaged by artillery fire. Its commander Löbelin was killed instantly as was Rottenführer Martin, while gunner Bahlinger was seriously wounded.

A total of seven of the battalion's officers were killed or wounded. The 1st Panzer Company was hardest hit; it was left without a single officer and was placed under the temporary command of the leader of the headquarters squad Großrock until a new commanding officer arrived. That evening the battalion commander's runner ran to 2nd Company. He asked Untersturmführer Nicolussi-Leck to come to the battalion.

"We won't be seeing you here any more," observed Flügel. "The old man has picked you. You're becoming a company commander."

"You're crazy, that would be much too soon."

"You should remember one thing, Nico, it's never too soon for us Vikings. It can't be soon enough. In any case I wish you the best of luck."

"But we won't be so far apart, Hans," said Nicolussi-Leck, "we'll see each other almost every day."

"All right then, but you'd better get going, for the old man doesn't like waiting for young Untersturmführer."

When Karl Nicolussi-Leck walked into the battalion command post Mühlenkamp took several steps toward him and extended his hand to the young officer.

"Well, Nico, to make this short you're moving. You're to take over 1st Company effective immediately and lead it into action tomorrow."

All that Nicolussi-Leck said in reply was, "Thank you, Sturmbannführer."

"You can stay here now, for in a half hour there is a battalion briefing on the attack." The Sturmbannführer reached for a bottle of cognac, which was always on hand, and poured a drink for himself and the Untersturmführer.

"Much success Nico. And may God watch over you."

"Thank you, Sturmbannführer!" was his simple reply. The personnel question had been settled.

Before the day was over Untersturmführer Nicolussi-Leck had to introduce himself to his new crew. He climbed into tank 111, which had been repaired. The men of his crew already knew him and were happy to be able to serve under a new commander who, though young, was rich in experience and knowledge.

Standing in the open turret hatch of his command tank, at several minutes before four in the morning on 16 October Karl Nicolussi-Leck gave the signal for his company to move out. The engines sprang from idle to full throttle. The company drove out of its assembly area and headed for the Dieckmann battalion's attack lane. First Platoon was to provide direct support to the grenadiers when they broke into the enemy positions and occupy any enemy tanks which attempted to intervene. The rest of the company was to provide supporting fire and then when the moment was right swing around to the right and join the battle, as suggested by Nicolussi-Leck. The objective was the heavily defended Hill 701.

The four tanks reached Battle Group Dieckmann and the break-in began; immediately the Soviet artillery opened fire. Hauptsturmführer Hirchenhain's tank 135 took a direct hit which knocked it out of action. Hirchenhain was killed instantly and two members of his crew were wounded. Nevertheless, thanks to direct fire from the remaining three tanks, which poured high-explosive shells and machine-gun fire into the enemy trenches, the break-in succeeded.

The other platoons rolled forward to attack. At some point Quax, the dog which always drove with Untersturmführer Max Kolodschi, had to go out, but this time he did not return. The following is from the notes of Richard Putensen, who was in the company commander's tank:

> We were stunned. Our faithful companion, who was just one of us, suddenly gone? But all of our calls did no good and we were unable to leave the tank on account of the murderous artillery fire.
>
> Then came the order to drive on. Our new company commander—we also called him "Nico"—knew nothing about the animal, and in spite of his reserve and tolerance we could see that he was slightly annoyed over our efforts to find the dog.
>
> We were about to drive away when our loader heard a howl. Nico ordered the tank to halt. The loader's hatch was opened and our Quax jumped into the crate. We closed the hatch and proceeded on our way.

At 2 P.M. the company commander received orders to carry out the attack on the hill. Nicolussi-Leck had seven tanks at his disposal when the action began. On the left flank the 1st Platoon had already turned toward Malgobek. The tanks raced forward. The commander of 2nd Platoon spotted two antitank guns just in time and knocked them out before they could fire. Then the tank which was driving on the right flank approximately 100 meters ahead of the others reported:

"Ten to twelve tanks, range 800, half-right behind the hill."

"Battle readiness! Load armor-piercing. Fire at will!"

This order from Nicolussi-Leck literally electrified the seven tank commanders. They now had to prove to their new commander that they could engage the enemy with success. The company commander had his driver continue forward at high speed for another 200 meters; meanwhile his gunner had taken aim at the second enemy tank from the left and made continuous corrections to keep it in his sight. Nicolussi-Leck ordered a firing halt and the tank came to an abrupt stop. Exactly three seconds later the round left the barrel and the recoil raised the tank slightly. The armor-piercing shell struck the enemy tank between its turret and hull and dislodged the turret from the turret ring.

"Direct hit," the company commander reported laconically. "Continue firing." The gunner had placed his sights on the tank on the left and one second after he fired the gun the second shell struck home. This time it blew off the second T-34's right track. The enemy tank turned on the spot and loosed off a shot in the general direction of its foe, but the round missed the company commander's tank by at least four meters. A second hit set the Soviet tank alight.

The crews of Schönlechner and Kürten had meanwhile knocked out two more of the tanks which the enemy had placed in the very front lines. At this point approximately ten to twelve Soviet tanks withdrew from this dangerous position and Nicolussi-Leck realized that they had been facing at least sixteen enemy tanks.

"Turn right, maximum speed," ordered the company commander. The tanks made a slight turn and drove into the second Russian line from the right flank. Enemy gun crews swung four guns around to face the approaching panzers, but two were destroyed by Nicolussi-Leck and his men before they could open fire. The tanks fired high-explosive shells into the Russian positions farther back. The enemy fled and the grenadiers, who had already reached the hill in a frontal attack, pushed through to the panzers.

The battalion commander personally thanked Nicolussi-Leck. "No need, just doing my job," joked the company commander.

The tanks rolled forward another approximately 200 meters until they found a good position in which to shelter from the enemy artillery fire. The Untersturmführer repulsed the enemy tanks still in the approaches by knocking out three. The accompanying Russian infantry jumped down from the tanks and took cover. The panzers rushed ahead and wiped them out with machine-gun fire and hand grenades.

Meanwhile the grenadiers had broken through the second trench line. They pressed forward into the system of positions beyond and cleared them. Isolated groups of enemy soldiers fought to the death, but there could be no doubt that the commanding Hill 701 had fallen.

Russian patrols probing the approaches were met by Finnish volunteers, who knew their away around the terrain extremely well. No wonder, for in his Finnish homeland Untersturmführer Pojanletho had been a senior forester. When he returned he reported that barely 2,000 meters to the rear enemy forces were preparing for a fresh counterattack.

The Russian attempt to regain Hill 701 began at five the next morning. Dense fog enabled the Russians to close within thirty meters before they were spotted. There followed a wild close-quarters battle in which the commanders of the 9th and 11th Companies of the *Nordland* Regiment, Obersturmführer Pallesche and Obersturmführer Mühlinghaus, were severely wounded. They died soon afterwards at the main dressing station. Unterscharführer Sahlmann was also killed and there were further casualties in a hand grenade duel against wildly attacking Russians.

By 7 A.M. the Russians were within twenty meters of the German positions. Nicolussi-Leck immediately dispatched two panzers to the scene. Oberscharführer Selters and Unterscharführer Willms headed for the embattled hill. They poured high-explosive shells into the waves of Russian infantry and within minutes had halted the attack. Those Russians who had almost made it to the German trenches were cut down by machine-gun fire and hand grenades lobbed by the two tank commanders.

The first attack had been beaten off. The commander of the 1st Platoon, Untersturmführer Hübner, was seriously wounded. Tank 114 commanded by an Oberscharführer was hit in the turret. Gunner Manzenrieder was killed instantly. The remaining four crewmen, all of whom were wounded, were rescued.

At 2:30 P.M. the Russians attacked again. 300 infantry assaulted the German positions supported by several antitank guns and heavy machine-guns. At 2:02 the German barrage fire was shifted forward onto the approaches, through which the Russians had to pass in order to assault the hill. Four panzers, including that of the company commander, supported the defenders. They knocked out the antitank guns one after another and then took out the mortar positions and machine-gun nests, which had been moved forward to support the attack. Untersturmführer Nicolussi-Leck ordered five tanks to counterattack. Two panzers remained in the forward positions to guard against surprises by enemy tanks. Nicolussi-Leck was the first to sight a group of Russian tanks working its way through dense brush, trailing a long column of infantry behind it.

"Open fire on the tanks!"

The panzers opened up a withering fire. The enemy tank selected as the company commander's target caught fire after the second shot. The command panzer was itself hit, but luckily the armor-piercing shell round fired by the T-34 struck at an angle and ricocheted into the sky. Another enemy tank was knocked out. The rest turned tail and at least two more were hit as they retreated, one of which disappeared trailing smoke. Fifteen minutes later the enemy artillery opened up again. Soviet antitank guns also began firing blind, hoping to force the panzers from their hiding places.

Then the Russian attack began; the attackers got so close that during pauses in the artillery fire the defenders could hear the voices of the commissars as they urged on the Red Army troops. By 4:35 P.M. the last attackers had thrown in the towel. The majority of the prisoners taken were members of the 1127th and 1129th Rifle Regiments of the 337th Soviet Rifle Division.

When the enemy attacked again on 19 October the German positions were assaulted by Soviet infantry and tank forces. Once again the 5th SS Panzer Battalion's 1st Company rolled out to meet the enemy. Untersturmführer Nicolussi-Leck destroyed two more enemy tanks and the rest of his company accounted for four more. Nicolussi-Leck's tank was hit and the engine burst into flames. "Nico" gave the order for his crew to bail out. Hectic machine-gun fire greeted the men as they exited the tank. A bullet pierced Nicolussi-Leck's upper arm. While his crew worked to ready the tank for recovery, the Untersturmführer was taken to the rear by several grenadiers.

This brought to an end the young officer's combat activities in the area of Hill 701. He was transferred via the main dressing station to the nearest field hospital and from there to Germany. For his actions during this period Nicolussi-Leck had been awarded the Iron Cross, First Class and had been recommended for the German Cross in Gold. It would be some time later before he received the "fried egg," as the latter decoration was referred to by the soldiers. To be eligible one had to have participated in at least six actions which warranted the Iron Cross, First Class.

The Russians finally gave up their effort to retake the hill after a fierce, two-day struggle. The *Wiking* Division established its winter quarters in Malgobek. The repair echelon worked tirelessly to repair the damaged equipment, while the division itself worked to improve the positions it had won. On 20 October General Steiner was summoned to panzer army headquarters in Pyatigorsk to report to the commander in chief, Generaloberst von Kleist, and the army chief of staff, General Zeitzler. General Steiner emphasized that every single member of his division had given his best and that no advance out of the Malgobek area was possible with the forces available. He made it clear that the gains that had been made had come at too high a price in blood and rejected any further attack of this type without sufficient artillery and air support.

However, regrouping in preparation for a new operation began on 21 October 1942. III Panzer Corps received instructions to make another attempt to crack the Russian front in the Baksan-Terek triangle and drive through towards Ordzhonikidze. But the *Wiking* Division's offensive battles in the Malgobek area were over and before the year was over the division would undergo some important changes.

The *Westland* Regiment received a new commanding officer in the form of Sturmbannführer Polewacz. His place as commander of I Battalion, *Nordland* was taken by Sturmbannführer Lohmann. Oberführer Fritz von Scholz went to the northern sector of the Eastern Front where he took over the newly formed Latvian Brigade. The new commander of the *Nordland* Regiment was Obersturmbannführer Joerchel. II Battalion, *Germania,* was placed under the command of Hauptsturmführer May.

KARL NICOLUSSI-LECK: IDEAS AND SUGGESTIONS FOR THE TRAINING OF OUR NEW PANZER COMPANY

A thorough review of my experiences, as well as the comparative observation of other tank units from various theaters with different levels of success, has convinced me that it is thoroughly possible to be successful on a regular basis against even a technical superior armored foe while minimizing losses in men and tanks. In order to achieve this, it is necessary that a number of simple but decisive rules of engagement, which were developed in the field, be systematically drilled into the personnel. From all areas of training the following of these rules of combat must be emphasized:

1. The thorough tactical training of commanders and drivers based on operational experience.
2. Combat training based on experience will always endow the crews with superiority in combat.
3. Technical training, which by awakening interest in technology and technical understanding, and by providing a thorough technical knowledge of the tank and its operation, makes it possible for the crew to always keep the vehicle serviceable or restore it to serviceability in the event of mechanical breakdown.

It is important to eliminate from the standard training material all that is trivial or irrelevant. These lessons of experience must be passed on to

SS panzer grenadiers are prepared to defend.

the crews of all new units in the form of clearly formulated combat rules and easily understood tactical principles. These basic rules are most effectively engrained when they are repeated before and especially during firing, weapons, radio and crew training, thus allowing them to assume tangible form.

In this context it must be stressed that the instillment of the martial spirit must take first place especially in the armored forces. Often a certain portion of courage and aggressiveness is decisive in achieving success (especially in enveloping attacks). And enveloping attacks, and this cannot be stressed often enough, are the cardinal basic principle of armored warfare. This armored spirit must be possessed by all the soldiers of the armored forces, as well as by the officers, especially tank commanders and gunners. All means are to be employed to awaken this aggressive armored spirit.

The main themes of a training program for the armored forces are: (a) Acknowledgement of the tank as the principle factor in modern land warfare. They alone make it possible to wage battles of envelopment and thus destroy the enemy and achieve victory. As well there is (b) Foundation and development of armored forces in friendly and hostile nations. (c) Armored spirit and the history of our panzer arm are key elements of the training plan. Reference should be made to soldiers like Guderian, Rommel, Hoth, von Manteuffel and Henring, who have helped the panzer arm achieve some of its most decisive successes.

Secondary lectures serve to examine and analyze typical armored battles, their development, progress and outcome. Reference is to be made to the role of the old cavalry, tank battles of the First and Second World Wars are to be examined and analyzed and the keys to their success stressed.

Tactical Rules for Platoon and Tank Commanders

The diversity and extent of the armaments potential possessed by our enemies has forced us to seek to achieve superiority on the battlefield exclusively through the leadership skills of our commanders and the willingness of our soldiers. More than anywhere else this finds expression and is valid in the panzer arm. Therefore the tactical training, not just of the platoon and company commanders, but of all commanders, is of decisive importance. The standardized, flexible command of a panzer company guarantees victory against a much stronger but inflexible opponent.

The following basic concepts are valid for a company and a platoon and they are absolutely vital in successfully carrying out those missions which are assigned to the unit. These basic concepts are not meant to be taught just as theory, rather they have to implemented during company and platoon training, both on the sand table and the training field. Use of a sketch map is always advantageous.

The Point Platoon: Its Battle Configurations:

1. Standard point platoon configuration when only roads are passable.
2. Advance in double columns when the terrain beside the road (field) is passable.
3. "W" configuration when advancing cross-country over the steppe.

Method of Advance:

In organizing the point platoon, the point tank exceeds the point speed slightly in order to reduce its time between waypoints to allow for observation stops.

The platoon commander, driving with the second tank constantly adjusts the prescribed point speed in order to ensure that the maximum interval of 150 meters is not exceeded.

In the double column and "W" configurations the company keeps pace with the point platoon, with the same maximum interval.

Conduct on Contacting the Enemy

Open fire with machine-guns immediately, even though this is inaccurate at first, in order to keep the enemy's head down. Then the platoon commander orders: "Destroy weak enemy with aimed, concentrated fire or by envelopment." If strong enemy forces are encountered request employment of the entire company.

Conduct on Encountering Fixed Obstacles (boundaries of forests and towns, hills, turns)

Observation stop, if possible in cover, spray area with machine-gun fire to draw out possible enemy.

Non-observance of this cardinal rule of the point tank makes an encounter with a frontal antitank gun from short range or with concealed antitank guns from the side or rear unavoidable (these account for 80% of all point platoon losses).

All remaining training principles retain their validity (intervals, observation sectors, methods of orientation, etc, etc).

Engaging Antitank Guns and Artillery

In general, the existing principles are valid and recommended for tactical basic training. These are:

1. Antitank gun from in front, range 1 000 m: Position - concentrated machine-gun and high-explosive shell fire.
2. Antitank gun from in front, range 400 m: Non-threatened tank opens concentrated fire. Threatened tank attacks from on the move while outflanking (if possible presenting enemy gunners with maximum deflection target).
3. Antitank gun from in front, range 60 m: Threatened tank drives straight toward the antitank gun, all guns firing, and drives over it. Non-threatened tanks place the enemy position under concentrated fire.
4. Antitank gun from the side, range 200 m: The threatened tank drives on at full speed, opens fire. Non-threatened tanks take position and open concentrated fire.
5. Antitank gun from behind, range 200m: The threatened tank drives on and away from the firing enemy at full speed, firing smoke candles and engaging the enemy with the turret at 6 o'clock. Non-threatened tanks immediately take position and open fire.

While these principles are valid, alone they are not enough to prevent the loss of the threatened tank and must be used in combination with two of the most important basic rules in engaging antitank guns:

1. As soon as the antitank gun opens fire, all tanks which can fire in the direction of the antitank gun while on the move immediately

open fire with machine-guns. This serves to distract the gun crew, which can then be destroyed by high-explosive shell fire or by envelopment.

2. Immediate concentration of all tanks, especially those not threatened, against the antitank gun. The non-threatened tanks are in the position and obligated to destroy the antitank gun, because a tank threatened from behind is most usually incapable of doing so because it must zigzag in order to evade the shells fired at it by the enemy antitank gun.

The same measures apply to combat against enemy artillery, however direct engagements must be avoided at all costs. The flanking attack must be very wide in order to always remain outside the guns' area of traverse.

This surprising and seemingly unusual proposal of first answering a firing antitank gun with immediate machine-gun fire, has been proved in practice and is based on the following facts:

1. When the antitank gun fires the tank keeps moving for at least 20 seconds. Machine-gun fire can be employed during this time.
2. At first the antitank gun's position has not been determined, only its general direction is known. An high-explosive round makes no sense in this situation; instead I use a tracing round with which I fix the target, suppress the target, and find the range. If this happens and the tank has come to a halt, then it is time to deliver a well-aimed high-explosive shell.

Breaching Enemy Infantry Positions Without Infantry Support

In spite of the best efforts of the tank commanders to avoid this type of combat, it is often unavoidable during breakthrough operations and while engaging rear guards. Units that are not specially prepared and trained for it encounter major difficulties and usually suffer casualties at the hands of enemy tank-killing squads. One tactic has proved especially effective:

Battle configuration: exclusively "W" configuration.

Procedure: First eliminate all antitank gun weapons in the area of the intended breakthrough point. Then:

1. Assault tanks drive firing to within ten to fifteen meters (hand grenade range from the turret) of the most forward trench.
2. Gunners and radio operators sweep the enemy position with machine-gun fire and high-explosive shells so that no enemy soldiers venture out of the position.

3. Tracked armored vehicles scout the flanks and deep zones for snipers which might threaten the commanders as they throw their hand grenades. Close-combat teams take out the snipers.
4. Commanders of the assault tanks lob egg-type hand grenades, well aimed, into the enemy positions and trenches until no more resistance is detectable. Then the wave of tanks drives ahead to the second enemy trench and repeats the procedure.

This procedure is quick and effective and if executed precisely costs no casualties. Precise cooperation between all crew members and all tanks is necessary, however, for in such situations there is no time for further orders.

Everyone does what he is required to do—as he has been taught. The driver drives to within ten to fifteen meters, gunner and radio operator depress the weapons toward the most forward enemy position and keep the trench under constant fire. The loader keeps the commander supplied with egg-type hand grenades, the commander pops up out of the turret, aims, throws, and ducks back into the turret. The part of the company not assigned to the breakthrough is employed by the company commander to guard the flanks.

Driving through Towns

The main rule is: if possible, every village should be bypassed and taken from behind. If this is not possible because of terrain or obstacles, the tanks must pass through the town as quickly as possible. The following is recommended:

Battle Configuration: Column or double column, with small, approximately 10-meter intervals between vehicles and columns.

Procedure: The point platoon drives through the town at maximum speed, firing all weapons to both sides. The company follows in the same manner. The town is then taken from the rear in the normal way in cooperation with the infantry and artillery, provided this has not been made unnecessary by the passage of the tanks.

This armored thrust through a town whose temporary occupation by the enemy is intended to hold up our advance is not identical to the house-to-house fighting in a conventionally defended city, where progress is slow and the tanks have to advance with the grenadiers in the fashion of the assault guns.

Supporting Our Infantry in the Attack

This mission must always be preceded by a conference with the infantry commanders and officers in which precise coordination is laid down:

Battle Configuration: "W" configuration.

Procedure:

1. From a hull-down position the entire panzer company observes as the grenadiers move out and advance.
2. When the grenadiers have reached a point 60 to 100 meters from an enemy position, one tank platoon drives forward at maximum speed and breaks into the enemy position with the grenadiers.
3. While this is taking place the company provides supporting fire from its hull-down position and engages all antitank guns which appear or have been identified.
4. If a hot spot has shown itself in the battle, or if the enemy counterattacks with tanks, the point platoon occupies the enemy while the company commander intervenes with the remaining platoons, if possible in an enveloping attack.

Supporting Infantry in the Defense

Tanks support and reinforce the defense most effectively when they are positioned one to three kilometers behind the main line of resistance as a mobile reserve. However if the infantry's limited fighting strength in the main line of resistance makes the use of tanks in front lines necessary, the following is recommended:

Battle Configuration: Firing line or "W" configuration, hull-down, 50 to 100 meters behind the main line of resistance at the most threatened spot.

Procedures:

1. When the threat of enemy tank attack exists position all panzers behind the probable break-in point, which is identified by a timely report from the infantry. Wait for the enemy tank attack in a good reverse slope (hull-down) position and then when they appear put them out of action with concentrated fire.
2. When the threat of a penetration by enemy infantry exists, carry out a local, limited counterattack with several tanks, if possible without crossing the front slope (behind which the tanks are in their hull-down position), because there they face the danger of being knocked out by antitank or anti-aircraft guns. The main purpose of this minor counterattack is to affect the enemy's morale by spreading confusion.

Only rarely and then under the most favorable conditions should the panzers leave the reverse slope to engage enemy tanks on the forward slope.

Note: These principles for the support of the infantry in the attack and the defense may also be used by a panzer platoon. In any case the company is committed as a whole for this mission.

Tank Versus Tank Combat

As long as we have tanks which are equal or superior to those of the enemy, the principles contained in the manuals retain their validity and their former significance.

Nevertheless it is advisable to retain the battle tactics which resulted from the former inferiority of our tanks. When employed with equal tanks they will make success easier to achieve than would otherwise be the case. Beyond that there is no guarantee that the enemy will not introduce new tanks which will once again be superior to ours, as in the case of the Dreadnought. The following are the most important principles of tank-versus-tank combat:

Battle Configuration: "W" configuration whenever possible.

Battle Tactics:

Under whatever conditions—favorable or unfavorable—the encounter with enemy tanks takes place, one must act immediately and either occupy the better position or carry out a lightning-quick outflanking movement. The best solution is to do both simultaneously. That means: one part of our tanks occupies the enemy from good positions, another part carries out a flanking attack.

A stationary, head-to-head confrontation in open, level terrain is usually costly and fails to produce success. It must be avoided at all costs.

Our great tactical flexibility as well as the various advantages of the commander's cupola strongly favor shortening the engagement or reducing the firing range. This is achieved by having one platoon blind the enemy with smoke shells—from long range—while a second platoon advances slightly off to the side and takes out the enemy tanks from close range. Another tactic is to lure the enemy tanks into a town or tree-covered area and then destroy them there from close range.

It is obvious that in tank-versus-tank combat the dispersal of one's own forces must lead to losses and failure, more so than in any other type of combat. On the other hand, however, a compact attack and the concentration of fire from all participating tanks leads to success, with maximum losses to the enemy and minimum casualties for us.

Important Aspects of Combat Training

There can be no doubt that the execution of these simple tactical measures is very difficult in practice. The necessary tactical flexibility and cohesion of the panzer company can only result from intensive combat training which engrains into the crew the behavior of the individual tank in combat down to the last detail. In order to make the following rules self-evident to every tank crewman during combat training, experience suggests:

1. The commander must maintain visual contact with his superior and neighbor at all times with as little radio contact as possible.
2. The commander must observe the terrain intensively in order to prevent his tank from driving into swamps, traps and communications trenches.
3. Support of assault tanks by responding immediately to flanking antitank guns and infantry tank-killing squads.
4. In combat the tank fulfills only two functions: either driving at maximum speed or stopping and firing. During observation halts or general halts it remains under cover and well camouflaged.
5. Every recognized antitank gun is immediately responded to with machine-gun fire. Not until the tank has halted or the target has been identified or registered (which means that the gunner has acquired the target and ranged in on it) is the main gun used.
6. Even in combat the gunner must leave the main gun locked for as long as possible and always re-lock in order to keep it ready for use.

The precise and immediate implementation of these simple rules of engagement has the following result: the tanks do not become separated and isolated in the field. They work together. There are no losses to enemy tank-killing squads. Only rarely is a concealed antitank gun successful. All tanks participate in the combat rather than half of them becoming bogged down.

The tank-versus-tank battle is thus already half won.

It is necessary to learn these rules of tank-versus-tank combat and armored tactics by heart and constantly repeat them. Violations are to be punished, for they could make the difference between success or failure, between victory or defeat.

Suggestions for Technical Training

The success of a panzer units depends first of all on the number of tanks taking part in the battle. However this number is reduced by mechanical breakdowns both during approach and withdrawal, more than by losses due to enemy action.

This means that a higher level of technical training for the drivers and crews is a decisive factor in the operation of a panzer company. This level of training must enable drivers and crews to prevent as many breakdowns as possible in the field and repair those that do occur. Everything possible must be done to complete the technical training. Crews must be shown training films and even taken to tank factories and repair facilities in order to instruct them in what do to deal with various defects.

It is recommended that:

The last ten days of general driving school consist of driver combat training. In this way the driver instructor familiarizes the trainee with the movements and maneuvers of the tank by issuing combat orders as they might be given by the commander in action. No measure must be left out through which every member of a tank crew is alerted to any possible breakdown, failure or malfunction and its repair is examined.

Every crew must become its own repair team and be capable of carrying out the following jobs:

Cleaning, lubrication, oil change, filter cleaning, oil and water level checks, shock absorber checks, removal and replacement of shear pins, road wheels, torsion bars and track links, adjustment of track tension and proper maintenance of the battery.

To achieve this it is necessary to allocate one day per week, or at least an half day, to maintenance. Training films and lectures should also be used to increase understanding and foster interest in technical matters, for one thing is certain: someday every tank crew will make a decision on its own in combat and based on this decision will have to work to save the tank or blow it up to prevent it falling into enemy hands. These technical requirements must become common knowledge if the crew is to cope with this serious threat to the tank and to itself.

THE BATTLE OF KOVEL

Background to the Battle

At the time of the *Wiking* Division's action, in the Kovel pocket there were a regiment of regional defense troops, a regiment of the 8th SS Cavalry Division, a battalion of the 17th SS Police Regiment, one battalion each of pioneers, flak and artillery, and approximately 300 railroad workers. The 5th Artillery Regiment under Standartenführer Richter and the 5th Panzer Regiment under Mühlenkamp made ready.

It was 9:30 A.M. on 28 March when Karl Nicolussi-Leck faced his regimental commander. "Hannes" Mühlenkamp, as he was known to his regiment, began to speak:

"Nico, you will move off at 3 P.M. and advance with your entire company to Tupaly. There you will be subordinated to the 131st Infantry Division. How many battleworthy tanks do you have?"

"Exactly seventeen Panthers, Obersturmbannführer. As well there are the recovery tanks and ten Mulis (armored tracked vehicles)."

"Outstanding," replied Mühlenkamp sarcastically. "The 434th Grenadier Regiment will provide volunteer assault teams who will ride with you on the tanks. I myself will drive ahead to Tupaly with Standartenführer Richter at 1 P.M. and scout the terrain."

The two comrades in arms said goodbye and when the tanks arrived at Tupaly only one had dropped out with damage to its main coupling. After nothing further happened on this day the tank crews began to think that perhaps things weren't so serious at Kovel after all. What they did not know, however, was that on the evening of that 28 March 1944 Gruppenführer Gille had in a radio message from Kovel described the situation inside the city as very serious and requested that the relief force "move at once."

The previous day's attack from west to east by the 131st Infantry Division and the attached III Battalion under Sturmbannführer Franz Hack together with the 190th Assault Gun Battalion had only got as far as Nowe Koszary and Stare Koszary. Therefore, on 29 March the 8th Company was placed on alert. At 8:30 A.M. Obersturmführer Nicolussi-Leck reported to Oberst Nabert.

"You will set out from near Stare Koszary at 11 A.M. You will drive by way of Czerkassy and Moszczona toward Kovel with mounted infantry—I have in mind three assault teams each of ten men. The forward units will make a frontal attack at the same time as your advance. As well you will receive artillery support from a battalion of our division artillery, which will place fire on the woods northeast and southeast of Koszary as well as on Czerkasy and Koszczone."

"Who will brief me on the attack terrain?" asked Nicolussi-Leck.

"Germania's III Battalion is forward in your assigned sector. Sturmbannführer Hack will brief you."

Having received his orders, Nicolussi-Leck left and drove to the command post of his friend Franz Hack. Sturmbannführer Hack briefed him on the terrain over which the attack would take place, making specific reference to the raised railway embankment on which the tanks would be driving: "The terrain on both sides of the embankment is damned swampy. If I may advise you, I think you should first attack the high ground and the forest edge one kilometer east of Stare Koszary. As soon as you have taken out the Russian antitank guns posted there, we will advance through the forest together along the road and try to reach Kovel."

Then Sturmbannführer Dorr, commander of the 9th SS Panzer-Grenadier Regiment Germania, declared himself satisfied with the plan. Everything seemed ready. But Obersturmbannführer Mühlenkamp, who arrived at Hack's command post a short time afterwards, decided differently, for overrunning the Russian antitank guns might result in serious, even fatal losses. He ordered:

"Nicolussi-Leck, you will first drive along the rail line to Czerkasy; reaching the town is your first objective. After scouting the terrain you will then drive through Moszczona to Kovel."

The company commander drove back to the starting position one more time before he made his mind up to set out from the crossroads at the southeast end of Stare Koszary, initially attack east and break through the forward enemy positions. Then he planned to turn north, reach the sole rail line in this swampy area, and then attack the enemy blocking positions situated right of the rail line west of Czerkasy as well as Czerkasy itself.

"Tanks advance!"

The order was received by the sixteen Panther tanks of the 8th Company, which immediately began moving. Up front in the leading tank of the 1st Platoon was Hauptscharführer Eugen Faas. He acknowledged the reports from his loader and listened as the company commander issued orders to the other platoons by VHF radio. Tracks rattling and motors roaring, the steel phalanx rumbled out of its assembly area into open ground. The light snow flurries were no hindrance to visibilty.

"Attention: enemy artillery opening fire!" transmitted Faas.

The first shells burst left and right of the advancing company, spraying the skirts of the fast Panzer V's with mud and steel splinters. Like the attack armored spearhead, the two flanking groups had also moved out. To the right of the tanks the Hack battalion and ten supporting assault guns attacked the forest, in which Soviet infantry had been spotted. On the left advanced the Bolm battalion of the 434th Grenadier Regiment. It, too, was supported by seven assault guns.

Within minutes the Soviet fire had grown in intensity to a heavy barrage. Artillery, antitank guns and mortars rained shells on the advancing soldiers. Nevertheless the 1st Platoon reached a favorable position from which to fire at the enemy trenches. Hauptscharführer Faas saw a flash as an antitank gun fired from a position ahead and to the right. An order rang out and all the tanks that had made it this far opened fire. The Panthers' 75-mm guns barked. Faas informed his crew that the antitank gun had been hit and destroyed.

The tanks joined the battle as they cleared the swamp. The company commander committed the Jauss and Scheel platoons. In a hail of shells from the fast, maneuverable Panthers the attack made rapid progress. Soviet troops began fleeing from their trenches. They disappeared into the forest, pursued by machine-gun fire and exploding high-explosive shells.

Seeing that the enemy was giving ground, Nicolussi-Leck ordered all his tanks to follow him. They rolled over the trenches, ground the machine-gun positions into the dirt, and reached the rail line. The company commander issued his next order: "That was our first objective. Now along the rail line to the enemy's blocking position west of Czerkasy."

The tanks rumbled forward to the right of the rail line. The snow flurries were becoming heavier. Large white flakes shrouded the lead tank, making it invisible to the crews of the trailing vehicles. They drove around large shell holes and soon the first Panther became stuck in the mud.

"Stuck fast. Cannot get out under own power," reported Untersturmführer Immelmann.

"Right flank cover in the direction of the wood with your cannon, for our own infantry hasn't shown up there yet."

Four more Panthers suffered the same fate. But Nicolussi-Leck made a virtue out of a bad situation, using them to screen his entire right flank. Soon afterwards the lead tank reached the enemy position about 600 meters west of Czerkasy. Twelve antitank guns were positioned there and these opened up a withering fire.

"Attack, attack the antitank guns. Knock them out as quickly as possible!"

The Panthers drove toward the antitank position in open wedge formation. A tank was hit and immobilized; nevertheless, it continued firing until a direct hit set it on fire. The crew bailed out. Then a second Panther was hit and finally a third, but the rest kept firing.

The gunner in the platoon commander's tank, Rottenführer Jürgens, saw a flash as an antitank gun fired. The shell hissed past the turret, missing by just a few centimeters. He adjusted his aim slightly and fired. The shell struck the enemy gun position and detonated the reserve ammunition stacked there.

"Do you hear, Jürgens? Two o'clock, range 800!"

"Target in sight," replied the gunner. He swung the turret around and took aim at the new target. Three times the cannon barked, three times empty shell casings clanged against the shell-catcher and fell into the casings bag. Then there was another explosion in the Russian antitank position.

The company commander had sent the 3rd Platoon to the right to outflank the enemy position, and now these Panthers opened fire, knocking out one antitank gun after another. It was over in minutes; all twelve antitank guns had been put out of action. Karl Nicolussi-Leck reached the high ground in his command tank at precisely 2:30 P.M..

"Damn, I can't see a thing Obersturmführer," called the driver. The snow was now so heavy that it was restricting visibility.

"We'll stay up here and form up. No further advance until I give the order," decided the company commander.

They waited forty-five minutes on the hill. During this time Nicolussi-Leck contacted the regiment by radio: "Company is on the hill 600 meters west of Czerkasy. Enemy position breached. Infantry still engaged. Heavy blowing snow reducing visibility. Will resume the advance as soon as the snow showers have passed. Six vehicles stuck in the mud. Recovery vehicles needed. Request doctor for the wounded."

During these forty-five minutes patrols determined that Czerkasy was surrounded by swamps on three sides and consequently was ideal terrain for any defender. They also determined that the terrain made a further attack to the northeast impossible. It was 3:30 P.M. when Obersturmführer Nicolussi-Leck resumed his attack toward Czerkasy. This time his intention was to take the town by enveloping it from the right. But after only a few dozen meters three more tanks were stuck in the marshy ground and it became obvious that this attack would never get through.

The Obersturmführer immediately swung the company around and sent his remaining tanks across the embankment to outflank the town to the left. Enemy guns opened fire when the tanks appeared in front of the town. The battle between the tanks and the artillery and antitank guns was short and sharp. Eight German tanks were hit, but most were able to continue fighting and provide the others with needed supporting fire.

The firefight lasted fifteen minutes. The gunners and loaders in the Panthers worked hard, firing and loading again and again. One after another the enemy guns were put out of action. By this time the entire west end of the town was in flames, and dense groups of Soviet infantry streamed out to the north and northeast, seeking to escape into the forest.

"In we go, everyone! Watch out for concealed artillery and antitank guns. Forward, follow me."

Eight tanks were left. They set off behind Hauptscharführer Faas, who had assumed the lead after the company commander's tank had become stuck in the soft ground. But the "old man" soon got free and dispatched four Panthers to scout in the direction of Moszczona. Before long they came to the first barrier of antitank guns. They knocked out two of the enemy weapons but two more tanks became stuck in the mud. Not long afterwards the infantry of the Bolm battalion succeeded in catching up with the Nicolussi-Leck panzer company. Under covering fire from the tanks they cleared the remaining Red Army troops from the town.

At about 6 P.M. the commander of the Eighth received a radio message: "Company remain in Czerkasy and secure to the north, east and southeast."

Karl Nicolussi-Leck now ordered those tanks which were still serviceable to form a protective front to the north and east. The tanks stuck in the swamp to the right of the rail line were ordered to screen to the south. When darkness fell the recovery vehicles went to work and during the night freed several tanks from the mud. In the village itself Nicolussi-Leck's men

MG34 machine-gun team in action.

were able to take possession of two abandoned anti-aircraft guns, four light artillery pieces, a number of mortars and antitank rifles, numerous small arms and a number of horse-drawn panye wagons. Based on the signal flares they had fired, the infantry units which were supposed to have advanced south of the rail line were still pinned down far to the west.

At about 7 P.M., by which time things had quieted down, the commander of the Eighth transmitted the following situation report:

> The objective of Czerkasy assigned to me by the last radioed order from the regimental commander has been reached. At the moment I have six fully battle ready tanks. I will be able to recover four more from the swamps in the next four hours. I cannot count on deliveries of fuel and ammunition on account of the swamp, as the tracked trucks cannot get through. Our infantry has caught up to me on the left and is occupying Szerkasy. On the right they are far behind based on their signal flares.
>
> My reconnaissance advance in the direction of Moszczona has shown that a further advance toward Kovel in that direction is almost impossible, first because of the swamp, second because of lack of fuel, and third because of the strong antitank defense which is present there, suggesting that the enemy is expecting us in that direction.

> The terrain is equally impassible to the east; likewise south of the railway embankment to the forest edge. On the other hand, after the destruction of the antitank position west of Czerkasy, which consisted of 16 guns in three lines, the enemy does not appear to have established further antitank positions farther south or east, as my bogged-down tanks have not been fired upon in spite of favorable firing range.
>
> It is unlikely that antitank guns will be moved up during the night to block the raised rail embankment because of the difficult terrain. As well, based on my reconnaissance probe the enemy is expecting me in the direction of Moszczona, which is where the enemy troops fleeing Czerkassy moved to.
>
> The railway embankment is therefore the sole passable and least defended route to Kovel, provided it is used by night. The situation of the garrison of Kovel, of which I was informed by radio, is so serious that the sending of heavy weapons seems imperative. Therefore I am going to set out at 10 P.M. and drive along the embankment to Kovel. True this means that I am abandoning my last-received assignment, to defend Czerkasy, however I am acting in the spirit of the original plan of attack, to reach Kovel.

This daring plan was almost frustrated by a message from the regiment, for an hour and a half after midnight on 30 March orders were sent by radio for the 8th Company not to take any action on that day. It was division reserve and was to move to Stare Koszary at dawn. The grenadiers of the 434th Grenadier Regiment who were to have ridden on the tanks were to be sent back to their regiment. However the message did not get through, and it was not until 5:10 P.M. that Unterscharführer Heins reported in. He had been ordered into the Tupaly-Stare Koszary area with a one-ton prime mover equipped with a radio set, in order to pass the regimental commander's order to the Nicolussi-Leck company. When he checked in the regiment learned that the 8th Company was on the railway embankment just two kilometers west of Kovel.

The early morning of 30 March found nine serviceable tanks lined up in a row along the railway embankment. Obersturmführer Nicolussi-Leck gave the order to move out. As he had done on the previous day, Hauptscharführer Eugen Faas led the way as the nine tanks set off down the railway embankment. The grenadiers of Hauptmann Bolm followed to the left of the embankment; they deployed in the direction of the forest and tried to keep pace on foot. It was still dark. The roar of engines shattered the morning stillness. Standing in the turrets of their tanks, the commanders strained their eyes in an effort to penetrate the darkness. Standing in the lead vehicle was Eugen Faas. Suddenly the medium-sized, stalky Hauptscharführer saw muzzle flashes from tanks and antitank guns about 400 meters west of Czerkasy station.

"Battle readiness!" he shouted, closing the turret hatch above him. "Turret three o'clock!"

Gunner Jürgens rotated the turret in the specified direction. Through the optical sight he recognized the outline of a tank. He made a slight correction and fired. The force of the recoil raised the Panther's nose slightly.

"A hit!" reported the Hauptscharführer. From a range of just 400 meters the enemy tank had been an easy target. The second enemy tank, a T-34, fired its gun and almost simultaneously took a direct hit from the "seventy-five" of Unterscharführer Herbert's Panther. The Soviet tank immediately caught fre and seconds later its ammunition exploded.

"Tanks destroyed," Faas reported back to his company commander. "We are pressing on."

The tanks began to move again, but after only 100 meters the point tank ran over a mine. With an ear-shattering roar it detonated beneath the Panther's left track, blowing it into pieces.

"Have track damage, have to remain here," reported Faas.

The Eighth's remaining eight tanks swung out to the right to bypass the disabled point vehicle. In doing so a second tank drove over a mine and was also disabled. Its commander reported that he, too, was unable to continue.

Nicolussi-Leck, who had left his own tank and come forward on foot, said to the Hauptscharführer, "Faas, form a strongpoint with the two disabled vehicles and keep this rail line open no matter what. I will leave you sixteen grenadiers to guard your right flank and to handle any Ivans who might want to take a crack at you."

The company commander had already sent the pioneer squad ahead to look for additional mines. Those that they found were soon cleared. The infantry, which had also arrived by this time, formed a security screen in front of the tanks incorporating the railway station grounds and the wooded area to the east including the ammunition dump to the right of the rail line. When the mines had all been cleared at 6 A.M. Hauptmann Bolm advised the commander of the panzer company that he had received orders not to advance any farther with the tanks.

"I cannot stay here, Bolm," replied the panzer officer. "I will continue on immediately with the mounted assault teams which have been placed under my command."

Nicolussi-Leck resumed his drive toward Kovel with seven tanks. The Panthers pushed forward, every minute bringing them nearer to their objective. But just one hour after their departure all hell broke loose at the strongpoint. The two immobilized Panthers came under fire from antitank guns, artillery, mortars and finally even from "Stalin Organs."

"Take cover!" shouted Scharführer Herberts as the first salvo from the Katyushas came in. Four salvoes, each of sixteen rocket projectiles, struck the ground in a rectangular pattern, shrouding the area in smoke and flame. Countless fragments struck the tanks and they were shaken by the force of the explosions.

The five men in each Panther felt the tension mounting. They sat in their steel boxes, unable to do defend themselves. They had to endure it all, unable to do anything to hit back. That was the worst.

Suddenly the enemy fire abated and then stopped. "They'll be attacking soon," observed Rottenführer Rohlfs, the driver of Herberts' tank.

Hauptscharführer Faas' voice came over the radio: "Stay alert, stay very alert. The Ivans will be coming now. Load high-explosive. Herberts, you take the left side, I'll take the right."

And they did come. Soviet troops emerged from the forest in a skirmishing line and ran toward the two immobile panzers.

"Open fire!" called Faas and almost immediately the first shots were fired. The gunners saw the high-explosive shells explode in the midst of the masses of charging Red Army soldiers. But fresh groups appeared from behind to fill the gaps; they were running for their lives, for to survive they had to run beneath the fire from the two German tanks.

Thirty seconds later, with the charging Russians approximately 300 meters away, Faas' voice rang out again: "Machine-guns—open fire!" The two radio operators opened fire. Their bursts raked the broad lines of infantry.

The shouts of the attacking Russians could already be heard above the sound of the gunfire, and through their vision ports the commander could see the contorted faces of the enemy.

"Hand grenades and submachine-guns ready, Herberts?" Faas asked his comrade in the second Panther.

"Already in action!" reported Herberts, for he had flipped back the hatch cover and fired several quick bursts at a squad of Russians nearing the tank with Molotov cocktails. One of the Russians was hit, and the gasoline-filled bottle he was carrying exploded, enveloping him in flames. His screams were drowned out by the shouts of the next wave of attackers.

When the attackers were near enough, hand grenades were lobbed from both tanks. Three Rusians reached Faas' tank and clambered up onto the track fenders, only to be cut down by a burst of submachine-gun fire.

"Turn on the spot!" Faas shouted to his driver. The latter succeeded in turning the vehicle. For several seconds the enemy were once again in radio operator Rynzec's sights and he was able to send a burst their way. Hand grenades exploded against the armor of the two Panthers, but these were no more than pinpricks. Soon afterwards the enemy retreated into the nearby forest, pursued by machine-gun fire from the two radio operators.

While the two tanks had been employing all the means at their disposal to defend themselves, the sixteen grenadiers assigned to support the Panthers had succeeded in keeping three or four tank-killing squads at bay. Had it not been for them the two tanks of the 1st Platoon would probably have succumbed to close-range attack. When the enemy withdrew the support troops had lost one man killed. All the others had withstood the assault in their foxholes. Several minutes later Herberts heard the sound of antitank rifles firing from the woods, dangerously near. He radioed to his platoon commander, 'It's not over yet Faas." Armor-piercing projectiles struck the side skirts and bounced off.

Small arms fire sprang up between shots from the antitank rifles. Three slow-firing Maxim machine-guns opened up; however they posed no serious threat to the Germans, who were in good cover. Then the enemy artillery opened fire. The Russians had also moved forward two antitank guns and these also began firing at the small German force. But the antitank guns were at too great a range to be of any serious threat to the two Panthers.

One hour after the first attack Herberts called: "They're coming again!"

A dense wave of brown-clad Russian soldiers broke out of the forest, disappeared into a stand of saplings and then reemerged. The two bow machine-guns opened up again. The two main guns also opened fire and the Red Army troops went to ground. The second attack was halted barely thirty meters from the first tank. The wounded Russian soldiers crawled away and disappeared into the swamp. Suddenly Eugen Faas established radio contact with Unterscharführer Kasper, who was southwest of Czerkasy with the four tanks that had bogged down earlier.

"Kasper, can you tell our Ari (artillery) to lay down fire on the forest here? I am under continuous attack from there and am stuck here with two tanks."

"Consider it done, Faas! Transmit your position and that of the forest. You can make corrections through me."

Three minutes later the first shells from division artillery howled over the tanks and struck the ground just in front of the forest.

"Two-hundred more!" transmitted Faas. "Direction is good."

The next salvo fell in the woods, severing the tops of trees.

Moments later Kasper called again. "I have the artillery's forward observer here with me. If you can locate specific targets he can put a fill salvo onto them."

As soon as an enemy strongpoint revealed itself it was placed under artillery fire. The Russian force, whose numbers had been increasing steadily, was increasingly diverted from the two tanks, which now once again came under fire from "Stalin Organs." Whole squadrons of these fiery-tailed rocket projectiles streaked through the air and exploded all around the two German tanks, which though literally showered with fire received no direct hits. The ear-shattering noise drew nearer and nearer to the tanks. And then suddenly a salvo of sixteen rockets struck the ground right beside the platoon commander's vehicle. The tank was rocked so severely that Faas and the four men inside the steel giant felt as if they were in a nutshell on a heavy sea. The stink of burnt powder entered the fighting compartment and the crew could see the glow of fire from the explosions.

"Faas to Ari: 'Stalin Organ' position 300 meters half-right from your last salvo. We are under heavy fire, in danger if you can not eliminate it."

The artillery observer replied: "We'll open fire on it. You transmit corrections."

They saw that the first shells must have fallen close to the enemy position, for the explosions were very near the flashes from the next salvo of rockets. Once again the tanks were shaken.

"Fifty more and exactly fifty right," Faas called above the roar of exploding rockets.

Kasper acknowledged and then a fresh salvo slammed into the middle of the "Stalin Organ" position. Pillars of fire rose into the air, indicating that the rocket launchers' ammunition store had gone up.

"Direct hit!" roared Faas. ""Stalin Organs" silenced. Large munitions explosions."

The battle for the two tanks raged on into the evening hours, then Faas had to report that his two tanks were running low on ammunition.

"We're coming to relieve you Faas. When it gets dark we'll come to you and bring ammunition and infantry with us."

"Be careful, the ring around us is strong. You will run into the Ivans as soon as you near the railway embankment," replied the Hauptsturmführer.

"Understood, Faas, we'll get through. Until then!"

"What is the Eighth doing? Have you heard anything?" asked Faas, who was rather concerned about the uncertainty as to the fate of his comrades.

"Nothing heard yet. But if I know Nicolussi-Leck, he will soon be in Kovel."

"Hopefully," observed Faas before he signed off.

✠

The 8th Company panzers were still advancing in the direction of Kovel. Obersturmführer Nicolussi-Leck had assumed the point position. Meeting no opposition, they rolled on at a steady pace. It looked as if they had overcome the enemy at that spot and could now drive into the city unopposed. When the seven tanks were within about two kilometers of Kovel a dispatch rider came roaring up to the last tank from behind. The tank's commander, Scharführer Hugo Möller, had to listen three times before he grasped the seemingly impossible order and was able to transmit it ahead by radio:

"End vehicle to commander: order from battalion commander Bolm: The tanks are to halt. Over."

The company commander could not believe his ears when he was ordered to stop so near to his objective. For at precisely that moment the enemy had opened fire at the point vehicle with small arms and antitank rifles.

"Those are the enemy troops blocking the northwest exit from Kovel Obersturmführer," radioed Oberscharführer Jauss.

"Attention: engage the antitank rifle teams."

The Panthers's cannon opened fire at the antitank rifle crews that were visible and took them out one after another. Nicolussi-Leck glanced at his watch and saw that it was not yet 7:30 A.M.

"Commander to end vehicle: message to Hauptmann Bolm: panzer company carrying on, cannot disengage. Furthermore have not been subordinated to you."

The company commander had made an independent decision to press ahead without infantry. At the same moment that Nicolussi-Leck transmitted his decision, ten to twelve anti-aircraft guns opened up from the general line Kovel-Moszczona. Shells struck the Panther's frontal armor and ricocheted into the sky or whizzed close past the tanks and struck the ground far behind them.

"Open fire!"

The tank gunners selected their targets. Fire flashed from the muzzles of the tank cannon and shells whistled toward the enemy positions, which had almost disappeared in a sudden snow shower. But the snow also concealed the tanks from the threat on their left flank.

"Everyone advance together, into them!"

The tank engines roared at full power and the vehicles leapt forward. Soon afterwards they reached the Soviet blocking position in front of the German strongpoint Strecker. They rolled over the Russian trenches, crushing gun positions and machine-gun nests, and then German steel helmets appeared before them. One man shouted something to them. Others cheered for joy and waved their arms. They had done it and had breached the enemy's ring around the city. They were inside the pocket. The infantry squads that had accompanied the tanks had never left them and had played a major role in the success of this quick and courageous breakthrough attempt. It was exactly 7:30 A.M. when the tanks under Nicolussi-Leck reached the Kovel railway loop and established contact with Hauptmann Strecker.

"You've come just in time Nicolussi-Leck. You must take out two antitank guns which are dug in behind the ruins. They are constantly taking out our corner positions."

"Of course, we'd be pleased to take care of it."

Nicolussi-Leck barked a command and two Panthers turned toward the position described by the Hauptmann. They were briefed on the target and after four shots each the two antitank guns had been silenced. After granting Hauptmann Strecker's request the tanks formed up and drove straight to the center of Kovel. At 8:10 A.M. they stopped in front of Gruppenführer Gille's command post.

"Gruppenführer, I wish to report the arrival of the Eighth Company with seven panzers."

Gille shook hands with the Tirolean. "Thank you, Nicolussi-Leck! You have helped us a great deal. Now I am certain that we will make it."

✠

During its assault, which has gone down in history as the "panther leap to Kovel," the *Wiking* Division's 8th Panzer Company put out of action sixteen antitank guns, two anti-aircraft guns, two American-built Sherman tanks (the first to be seen on that front) and forty antitank rifles, as well as a large number of mortars and light infantry weapons. It also captured numerous panye wagons as well as transport carrying food and supplies. Not a single one of the company's tanks was a total loss. All of its Panthers were repaired and returned to action a few days later. Gruppenführer Herbert Gille submitted the paperwork for the Knight's Cross, which Obersturmführer Karl Nicolussi-Leck received on 25 April 1944. He was the first participant in the Battle of Kovel to receive the Knight's Cross.

With the breakthrough and the establishment of a pipeline into the city, the threat to the pocket was eliminated for the time being. But the permament threatening position remained in place, and there was a pressing need to expand this first breakthrough, as well as open the pocket and send in the entire *Wiking* Division battle group. At this time the Fourth Army also dispatched the 4th and 5th Panzer Divisions to Kovel.

But what had happened to Faas in the meantime?

✠

Darkness had fallen over the hedgehog held by the sixteen grenadiers and two Panthers. Hauptscharführer Faas had left his tank to reconnoiter on foot. With him were Scharführer Kuntze and Rottenführer Petersmann, They reached the forward position of the grenadiers, warned the Obergefreiter standing guard that they were not Russians, and then set out through the saplings until they reached the most forward Russian positions in front of the forest's edge. Shells from the enemy's harrassing fire howled over the men's heads, but they were in no danger.

"All quiet, Hauptscharführer," whispered Kuntze.

"But they have moved strong forces into the forest," replied the platoon commander, "listen to that."

From the forest they heard the sound of Russian tanks moving their way. Orders rang out. It was obvious that the Russians were massing, probably in preparation for an attack on their position at first light. Several minutes later they crept back to their position. Eugen Faas contacted Kasper.

"Listen, pal," he began, "the Russians are obviously trying to seal off the area to the west of me and cut me off. They will attack in the morning. You have to break through with the infantry before then, is that clear?"

"Understood, Eugen. We will be moving out at 2 A.M. The infantry company is ready to go."

"Good luck!" said Faas before signing off.

Several minutes later Faas held a short conference with the Feldwebel of the infantry and Scharführer Herberts. "Now we have to wait until Kasper arrives. As soon as they attack it will be up to us to take the enemy in the flank from here and let them have our last few high-explosive rounds."

Several minutes after two the wide-awake tank crews and the remaining fifteen infantrymen heard their four tanks approaching and then the sound of battle flaring up.

"Russians! They're trying to stop Kasper!" called one of the lookouts. But Faas had already spotted the enemy and and he quickly assigned his gunner the target. The big guns of the two Panthers fired their last rounds of high-explosive ammunition.

The crash of tank cannon from the four approaching Panthers mingled with the sound of antitank guns and antitank rifles firing. The noise grew steadily louder and the men in the small pocket knew that relief was at hand. The battle lasted four and a half hours, but then the four panzers and the infantry following in their wake appeared before the two stranded Panthers.

As soon as the relief force arrived Faas ordered: "Kasper, secure the rail line to all sides immediately, and have your remaining infantry dig in around the tanks!"

This order came not a minute too soon, for scarcely had the panzers taken up their positions, scarcely had the crew of the ammunition vehicle that had accompanied the relief force heaved the first shells through the turret hatch of the platoon commander's tank, than enemy infantry stormed out of the woods due south of the rail line against their tiny defensive position. The defensive battle broke out and only then was it discovered that the ammunition vehicle had only a few rounds of ammunition left. The rest had been consumed by the four Panthers in their battle to break through the Russian ring.

"Radio message to Standartenführer Richter," Faas called to his radio operator. "Ammunition situation serious. Urgently require resupply, otherwise strongpoint can no longer be held."

Meanwhile Kaspers' tank was also almost out of ammunition and the onrushing waves of Russian infantry were becoming ever denser.

"Break through the enemy ring with two tanks and establish a supply line to the strongpoint" was the answer received from Joachim Richter, commanding officer of the 5th SS Artillery Regiment *Wiking* and now commander of a battle group.

One minute after receiving the order, Faas declared, "I will carry out the breakthrough myself. Becker will follow me in his tank."

Meanwhile he had transferred to another of the tanks and gave the commanders of the remaining vehicles one last order: "You cover us while Becker and I head out, concentrating on the woods south of the rail line. All right then, see you later!"

The two Panthers moved out. "Cannon at nine o'clock," Faas instructed Rottenführer Becker. The tanks rumbled west, scanning the edge of the forest for enemy machine-gun or antitank rifle positions. Faas was approximately 1,200 meters from the breakout point when several heavy antitank guns opened fire simultaneously from the left flank. The first hit hammered into the side skirts, the second set the Panther on fire. The tank ground to a halt.

"Becker, take out the position and the antitank guns, we have to bail out."

The five men in the platoon commander's vehicle got out of the burning Panther; three suffered burns but they were rescued. While they took cover they heard the gun of the second Panther firing. But then it, too, was hit and began to burn.

"Hopefully Becker and his men will get out," called Scharführer Kuntze.

Small arms fire began coming in. While running across a small clearing radio operator Rynzec was hit in the head and killed instantly. The crew of Becker's tank got out safely. The men were in the middle of the enemy-held area, heading for the German lines, when the first He 111 bombers appeared in the early light and attacked the enemy with bombs and machine-guns. But they also opened fire on the bailed-out tank crews, and the gunner from Becker's tank was wounded.

"Back to our strongpoint," ordered Faas, for it was obvious that they were not going to get through the enemy lines. Not until they were back in their strongpoint was it noticed that the wounded gunner was absent.

"Assault team to get him out. I need two men."

The missing gunner's two friends volunteered at once. Together with Faas they worked their way through a ravine overgrown with saplings, ran into a Russian patrol, shot their way out and reached the wounded man. They then laid him in a tent square and carried him back. Safe and sound they arrived back at the strongpoint for the second time.

It was evening now at the critical point in the corridor to Kovel, which had to be kept open. The enemy fire, which had previously almost died down, now intensified until it became a heavy artillery, antitank gun and mortar barrage against the German position held by just a few tanks and the company of infantry.

"I believe that the heavy antitank gun—they are least 91-mm guns—will be moved during the night in order to bring them closer to our position and put us in their sights," said Faas. "Therefore we have to move about 200 meters to the west and take up positions in the station buildings, where there is perfect cover and camouflage for the tanks. Furthermore we will be better able to defend the rail line and the corridor from there."

Meanwhile a recovery party had repaired one of the two Panthers disabled with track damage, and Faas was able to return to his command tank. However, because of transmission damage it could not cover any more distance than the 200 meters to the railway station buildings. Faas now had three tanks with which to defend the new strngpoint at the station. The fourth Panther, whose tracks and running gear had been shot up, had to be left behind on the rail line. The radio and all important components were removed. Then Scharführer Herberts blew up his vehicle before falling back to the station.

While the strongpoint consolidated itself, Faas continued his efforts to obtain ammunition. But there was still no way to send the urgently needed supplies. The enemy was pressing nearer from all sides. From the south he had reached the defensive position itself and during the night a ring was closed around the small battle group. It was guarded only by the infantry company's machine-gun squads, which kept the enemy at bay with rapid fire.

The railway station lay under heavy artillery fire all through the night. When dawn came the next morning—it was now 31 March—strong enemy troop movements could be seen in the woods south and southwest of the strongpoint.

"If we don't get ammunition soon, we've had it," observed Scharführer Herberts, who together with his crew was manning a machine-gun.

"What did Faas say? He's going to try it alone?" asked Rottenführer Rohlfs with a grin.

"Rubbish! Faas sent a situation report to the regiment and a radio message to Sturmbannführer Hack. They know what's happening and will surely help us."

"Hopefully, Scharführer," said Rohlfs skeptically.

Fifteen minutes later the Red Army forces attacked with several battalions from a position 800 meters west of Czerkasy.

"All machine-guns ready to fire!! Hold your fire until every shot is on target. Tanks—open fire!"

Under this concentrated defensive fire the assault collapsed approximately 100 meters from the strongpoint. The Soviet troops withdrew into the woods due south and 300 meters to the west of the strongpoint. A short time later the enemy launched a second attack along the rail line. The Soviets got to within 300 meters of the strongpoint and then dug in where they were.

By now it was noon and the situation of the defenders was almost hopeless. The enemy had moved up another battalion of rocket launchers, further strengthening their barrage. Mortars pounded the strongpoint, whose dimensions had now shrunk to about 40 by 80 meters, while bursts of machine-gun fire struck the remains of the station's walls and ricocheted in all directions.

Suddenly, from the edge of the forest, barely 150 meters south of the strongpoint, several Soviet 76.2-mm antitank guns opened fire.

"To Panthers one and four: the antitank guns have to be put out of action!"

The two designated Panther crews returned fire. They succeeded in knocking out the antitank guns with several quick and well-aimed shots before they could pose a serious threat to the position. By now the ammunition was almost all gone. Eugen Faas, who had orders to hold the strongpoint at all costs, sent alarm calls and requests for help to everyone he could think of. No one answered. Finally, at 4:30 P.M., he got through to the regiment. Obersturmbannführer Mühlenkamp ordered him to break through to Kovel with all his serviceable tanks and blow up the rest.

Since the enemy had intensified his fire to a barrage at 2 P.M., there were numerous casualties. Faas set aside a well-protected air raid shelter in the station building for the wounded. But in the meantime Obersturmbannführer Mühlenkamp had pulled every possible string and had arranged for a supply drop to the embattled force. The supply aircraft arrived at approximately 4:15 P.M. but, instead of circling in order to fix the position's location by locating its ground markers, they simply dropped the supply canisters on their first pass. The vitally-needed supplies fell into Russian hands.

Fifteen minutes later Faas ordered the breakout. He ordered the few remaining armor-piercing shells brought to the last driveable Panther. Then he ordered the remaining vehicles blown up. Since the Hauptscharführer had no idea of the way to Kovel, following a brief conference with Hauptsturmführer Treucker, the commander of the panzer-grenadier company (who had been sent by Sturmbannführer Hack), he decided to break out to the west again.

"All wounded onto the tank," he ordered. "We are going to break out as soon as it's dark."

At approximately 5 P.M. the enemy fire intensified again. Faas ordered several rounds fired in order to deceive the enemy. They were about to move out when word was received that Hauptsturmführer Treucker had been wounded. He, too, was hoisted onto the Panther. An Obersturmführer assumed command of the decimated company and they moved out.

As commander of the sole remaining tank, Faas stood in the open turret hatch. When he saw that the only tracks were blocked by a barricade, he knew that the Russians were waiting for them.

"Drive over and through it!" he ordered, then raised his submachine-gun to firing position. The machine-gun began to rattle and the Panther rumbled over the barricade. It tilted dangerously but the tank crushed the barricade. Eugen Faas fired at red Army troops as they appeared. He heard shots and bullets whizzed past his head. The following infantry fired their MG 42s from the hip. They had passed the barricade but they were not yet through the entire encircling ring.

Antitank guns opened fire. Several hits from light and medium antitank guns struck the Panther's side armor. It was a miracle that all the wounded were not knocked off the tank. The Panther kept moving until it struck a mine. Now a stationary target, it took several direct hits from the antitank guns and caught fire.

"Bail out!" shouted Faas. Four men got out, but the driver had sustained a fatal head wound and the wounded were cut down by an attacking Russian tank-killing squad. One seriously wounded man was burned to death in the tank.

The survivors continued on foot. As the enemy was himself carrying out an attack toward the west, the infantry company and the surviving tank

Soldiers of the 5th SS-Panzer Regiment *Wiking* during the attack over the Armawir-Maikop rail line in August 1942. Nicolussi-Leck's tanks supported this attack.

crewmen were able to infiltrate the assault groups and advance with them until they reached their own lines. During the last phase of the breakthrough through the swamp they were recognized and came under heavy small arms fire. Enemy mortars and artillery took aim at the individual groups and as a result the Faas group suffered casualties of five dead and six wounded from the tank crews. The fact that they got through alive at all was due to the daring raid carried out by Unterscharführer Kasper. The Faas platoon's part in the breakthrough to Kovel was now over.

While the battle for the hedgehog at Czerkasy was raging on 31 March 1944, at 11 A.M. the tanks of the 7th Company, 5th SS Panzer Regiment *Wiking* were detraining at Maciejow station. An hour later one platoon was ordered to defend against an enemy attack near Berewisy. The rest drove to an assembly area in a wooded area two kilometers east of Tupaly.

"Hannes" Mühlenkamp, who had been ordered to Cholm for a briefing on 30 March, arrived at the regimental command post at 1:10 P.M. on this day. Fifteen minutes later he and the commander of the 131st Infantry Division set off to drive to Tupaly and at the same time scout the terrain to the southeast of that town. Meanwhile 7th Company under the command of Obersturmführer Otto Schneider had driven into the assigned areas, and the 1st Platoon, led by the company commander, had gone out to face the enemy attack. The Panthers shot up the advancing enemy vehicles and within an hour had halted the attack. At 5:10 P.M. Obersturmführer Schneider reported that the enemy forces attacking at Berewisy had been repulsed, whereupon he was ordered back and instructed to attack and take the village of Kalinovka on 1 April. The tanks would be supported by the 431st Grenadier Regiment. At approximately 10 P.M. on this day an army ski battalion, which was directly subordinated to Headquarters, Fourth Army, set out in the direction of Kovel. Obersturmbannführer Mühlenkamp succeeded in having two panye wagons loaded with ammunition for the hedgehog position near Czerkasy accompany the battalion. The 7th Company was subordinated to Battle Group Hack for the attack on the following day.

Early on the morning of 1 April, at precisely thirty minutes past midnight, Otto Schneider arrived at the command post of Sturmbannführer Hack. His company arrived seventy-five minutes later. At 3:15 A.M., while orders were still being issued, the sound of heavy fighting was suddenly heard from the area of Czerkasy, and a half hour later the 434th Infantry

Regiment reported that the enemy had broken through near Czerkasy and had taken possession of this stopping point on the rail line. Sturmbannführer Hack ordered: "Schneider, you will send your company to counterattack toward Czerkasy. The Eppighaus battalion will provide infantry support. First, however, there will be a Stuka attack at 5 A.M."

As the tanks drove forward into their readiness positions their crews saw the Stukas approaching. They heard the low drone of aircraft engines and saw the Ju-87s peel off one after the other and plunge toward the earth, sirens wailing. The dive-bombers released their bombs, pulled out low over the forest and climbed away.

"Attack, attack," ordered Otto Schneider,

The Seventh's panzers rolled forward. After only a few hundred meters they began taking heavy antitank fire from the south. They returned fire. The Panthers began moving again, to resume their attack and evade the enemy fire, and it was at this point that the first tanks became bogged down in the marshy ground. Within half an hour six tanks had been temporarily put out of action in this way. Two more Panthers drove over mines and were disabled with track and running gear damage, while another two were knocked out by enemy fire. Two Panthers managed to fight their way through and link up with I Battalion of the 434th Grenadier Regiment. Three other tanks had moved into good cover and were still available to the company commander.

When Obersturmführer Schneider passed on this news at approximately 7:10 A.M., there followed a telephone conference between the Ia of the 131st Infantry Division and Oberst Naber (commander of the 434th Gren.Rgt.), Obersturmbannführer Mühlenkamp and Sturmbannführer Hack. Meanwhile they had learned that the ski battalion had been pinned down south of Czerkasy during the night. Obersturmbannführer Mühlenkamp then issued the following order to the 7th Company:

"Attack with the remaining five serviceable Panthers, direction of advance Czerkasy! All infantry units to accompany the advance and retake Czerkasy."

The attack began. The five Panthers advanced, providing mutual covering fire. They reached the pinned-down infantry.

The tank commanders stuck their heads out of the turret hatches briefly and shouted, "Join up, join up! We'll cover you!"

The combined force advanced. Enemy resistance was broken by accurate, pinpoint fire, machine-gun nests were taken out, antitank gun positions smashed. Meter by meter the tanks and infantry advanced against the heavy resistance until they reached Czerkasy and the enemy finally broke and ran.

At 12:30 P.M. Obersturmführer Schneider reported: "Czerkasy is in our hands."

✠

Early on the morning of 2 April Obersturmbannführer Mühlenkamp, whose panzer regiment was to carry out the final breakthrough to Kovel, sent the commander of the armored reconnaissance platoon, Untersturmführer Manfred Renz, to reconnoiter in preparation for the armored breakthrough to Kovel. The purpose of this sortie was to find the ultimate direction of attack for the Panthers through the marshy terrain.

Mühlenkamp had selected Manfred Renz for this mission because this young tank commander had been with him through the campaign in the Balkans and the *Das Reich* Division's battles in Russia in 1941, when he, Mühlenkamp, had commanded that unit's reconnaissance battalion. Right up to the gates of Moscow Mühlenkamp had found Renz to be a dependable assault team leader. The personal ties that developed at that time and the absolute trust between the two men led to Mühlenkamp's decision to entrust Renz with this difficult assignment—on which the success of the entire attack would ultimately depend.

At this point we turn to Manfred Renz for his description of this mission:

> Creaking and waddling like a duck, our Panther, which wore a coat of white camouflage paint, ground its way along the muddy, narrow streets of Stare Koscary, which were lined on both sides by wooden houses. The huts with their straw roofs lay under heavy artillery fire, which the Soviet 143rd Rifle Division was sending at us from its positions east of Kovel in order to disrupt the approach of the rest of the Panzer Division *Wiking*, as well as the 4th and 5th Panzer Divisions sent by the Fourth Army, and the 131st Infantry Division in the areas of Maciejow, Milanowicze, Tupaly and Koscary.
>
> A large snow-covered plain, which spread itself out like a white shroud, stretched from the villages of Nowe and Stary Koscary to the swamp city of Kovel ten kilometers farther east. Bitter cold still lay over the countryside on that 2 April 1944, turning the few huts as well as the trees and saplings into bizarre shapes.
>
> Dense swaths of smoke from the burning cottages crawled along just above the ground in the direction of the Soviet positions to the east. Light fog shrouded the landscape and we were fortunate to have these favorable conditions in which to carry out

our mission. We were to scout the terrain conditions—as well and as far as the enemy permitted—for our Panthers breakthrough to Kovel.

Four of my reconnaissance platoon's Panthers were left behind in order to avoid unnecessary noise. My fifth tank's camouflage coat was touched up and special sound insulation was installed on the engine. So prepared, my driver Hoffmann carefully guided the giant up to the first houses of Stare Koscary, in order to be able to make our initial inspection of the terrain from the best possible cover.

Before us the tracks left by the 8th Company were visible, stretching along the Koscary-Kovel railway embankment until they disappeared in the fog and snow. I decided to first take the Panther into the wood which lay at the railway embankment north of Stare Koscary in order to assess the possibilities for a passage by tanks. There was sufficient cover there to prevent being seen by the enemy.

Following a hard dirt road at the east end of the wood, which linked Stare and Nowe Koscary, we succeeded in crossing the embankment and immediately ducked back into the woods.

So far the Soviets had not stirred. It was vital that we find a relatively solid subsurface for the crossing of the swamp in the direction of Moszczona. From the wood, whose last trees stood just a few hundred meters from Nowe Koscary, I risked a further advance through the village to its northeastern boundary. From there I hoped to reach the forest of Warazyk, at the same time checking the condition of the road southeast of Nowe Koscary from Warazyk to Moszczona. Four to five kilometers away, the ridge from Dubowa to Point 192.7 offered the Soviets a favorable ambush position.

Staying close to the wall of a house, we first spent a long time observing the terrain in front of us to the ridge, which extended between Moszczona and Dubowa. At the same time the ground between Moszczona and the northwest end of Kovel was appraised for a passage by tanks. I decided to advance along the Nowe Koscary-Moszczony road in a northeasterly direction and take up a final observation position at the west end south of Warazyk. I had to try and avoid flanking fire from the enemy, and therefore I swung out between the lines of houses somewhat before heading for a wood at high speed—in doing so showing the Russians only a part of the tank's right flank.

Not a shot was fired while we executed this turn. The tall tree trunks offered sufficient protection and very soon we had reached a most favorable position which allowed to virtually control the entire area near Moszczona and Czerkasy with our 75-mm gun and two machine-guns. It was clear that an attack could be made toward Kovel with two wedges of tanks. Moszczona and Dubowa with the intervening ridge offered the Soviets a favorable defensive position. The east end of Moszczona and the ridge were, as I could see through my binoculars, heavily defended by antitank guns.

This threat from the flank would absolutely have to be eliminated before any breakthrough to Kovel. Only the Nowe Koscary-Moszczona-Dubowa and Moszczona-Kovel roads marked on a 1:100,000 scale map, the ridge, and part of the terrain between Nowe Koscary, Moszczona and Czerkasy could be considered suitable for tanks.

The swampy area in front of us offered no other possibilities. Most of all, in my opinion a loose deployment of the tanks was impossible. In this case, if they wanted to avoid becoming stuck in the swamp, they would have to fight their way forward caterpillar fashion along the few poor roads.

I drove back to the battalion command post with the results of my reconnaissance and there I gave a detailed report to Obersturmbannführer Mühlenkamp with reference to the map. Obersturmbannführer Otto Paetsch, the commander of our II Battalion, was also present.

Untersturmführer Manfred Renz had brought back the information needed for the final breakthrough to Kovel, and "Hannes" Mühlenkamp did not hesitate to order it to go forward.

During 3 April Obersturmbannführer Mühlenkamp had his hands full making preparations for the attack on Kovel and the link-up with the elements of his 8th Company encircled there. He could not help thinking what it would be like if his I Battalion was available to him. But I Battalion was in Cholm waiting for new tanks. Hauptsturmführer Kümmel, who commanded the battalion, had moved into Cholm's west barracks, and on 22 March he had sent twenty-two panzer crews to the army ordnance depot at Magdeburg-Königsborn to pick up twenty-two Panzer IV tanks, enough for just one company. On 31 March two tanks were issued to the headquarters company and five each to the 1st to 4th Companies for training purposes. That was all.

I Battalion was therefore lost to Hannes Mühlenkamp and he had to carry out the attack on Kovel with just his II Battalion. However the 5th Company had arrived just in time with thirteen tanks, as had II Battalion's headquarters company with five Panthers, three armored prime movers, a four-barreled flak and three Kfz fifteen vehicles. And finally 6th Company had arrived in the concentration area with ten tanks.

The entire battalion took shelter in the forest two kilometers east of Tupaly. The battalion command post was also set up in Tupaly. At approximately 11 P.M. on 3 April Hannes Mühlenkamp summoned the commander of II Battalion, Obersturmbannführer Paetsch, and Obersturmführer Schneider, the commander of 7th Company, to the regimental command post. There he revealed his plan of attack.

> The 4th Panzer Division, which had since arrived, will attack north from Stare Koscary toward the ridge northwest of Moszczona, passing through Nowe Koscary. One company, in this case yours, Schneider, will support this attack from the position near Krasnoduby by supressing the enemy in Kruhel and eliminating the threat from the flank.
>
> One platoon from your battalion, Paetsch, will stand ready at the northeast end of Stare Koscary near the cemetery in order to deal with any opposition that might appear on the right flank of the 4th Panzer Division in the area north of Czerkasy and later near Moszczona. The purpose of all of these operations is to solidify our starting position for the big attack on Kovel the day after tomorrow.

Everything was now set for the attack to begin. But at 9:15 the next morning the following message was received by radio from the Ia of the 4th Panzer Division: "4th Panzer Division's attack postponed by 24 hours. Panther battalion will provide supporting fire for 5th Panzer Division's attack on Kruhel."

As soon as the radio message was received Obersturmbannführer Mühlenkamp informed the battalion of the changed situation, and Obersturmbannführer Paetsch ordered his 6th Company under Hauptsturmführer Alois Reicher to support the attack by the panzer-grenadiers of the 5th Panzer Division from its position on Hill 196.1. However Alois Reicher waited in vain for the German infantry. Now and then he took fire from the village and replied with high-explosive shells. Finally, at 1:45 P.M. on 3 April, he reported: "No sign of our infantry attack. Enemy infantry in Kruhel."

Hannes Mühlenkamp subsequently had 6th Company sent back to II Battalion's area. Thus everything was set for the attack on 4 April. Early on this day Obersturmbannführer Mühlenkamp and the regimental operations staff arrived in Stare Koscary and established contact with the command posts of the panzer-grenadiers. The German artillery opened fire at 3:15 A.M. and when dawn arrived at 5:13 the individual panzer companies set out toward Kovel with their respective attack groups.

The 5th Company moved off from the southeastern boundary of Stare Koscary with orders to spearhead the attack against the forest and the hills 2.5 kilometers southeast of Koscary by II Battalion, SS Panzer-Grenadier Regiment "Germania." The 6th Company began the assault on the hill 500 meters south of Krasnoduby, with orders to suppress the enemy in Kruhel and on the hill to the north of it and prevent the 4th Panzer Division from being taken in the flank as it attacked the forest and the land bridge 3 kilometers northeast of Tupaly. The 7th Company sat at readiness in the wood 2.5 kilometers southeast of Tupaly, positioned behind the 431st Grenadier Regiment. Once the reinforced 2nd Ski Infantry Regiment, II Battalion, SS Panzer-Grenadier Regiment *Westland* and III Battalion, SS Panzer-Grenadier Regiment *Germania* had reached their objectives it would attack to the southeast towards Kalinovka and the cemeteries to the south.

The attack could begin.

✠

"Panzers forward!"

The high-pitched voice of Obersturmführer Jesser rang out through the morning. Still standing in the turret hatches of their Panthers, the tank commanders saw the company commander raise his arm. The previously idling tank engines roared louder. The giants jerked and jolted into motion. Behind them the panzer-grenadiers left cover and joined the tanks. After advancing a few hundred meters they began taking fire from the Russian positions in front of the forest edge.

"Battle readiness!" The company commander's order rang out in the tank commanders' headsets. Hatches slammed shut and the loaders reported the weapons clear.

"Advance by platoons. Halt and fire one platoon at a time, all others continue to advance!"

The 1st Platoon halted. The 75-mm guns cracked. Shells howled toward the enemy positions, shattering breastworks, scattering barbed-wire and destroying machine-gun nests. Halting and firing in turn, the platoons of the 5th Company worked their way toward the enemy positions, which spewed machine-gun and mortar fire as well as small arms fire from Russian automatic rifles. The panzer-grenadiers advanced behind the tanks, taking cover whenever they stopped to fire.

"Attention, calling Battleaxe. Ahead half-right, range 600—machine-gun nests!"

Tank "Battleaxe" halted, took aim at the fire-spewing enemy position and fired three high-explosive rounds in rapid succession. The machine-gun position was destroyed. Soon afterwards the attackers reached the first forward foxholes and rolled over them. A Red Army soldier rose up behind the first tank, intending to lob a dynamite charge onto the rear decking. But the second Panther moved in quickly and ground the enemy soldier into the dirt beneath its left track. Meanwhile the tanks had reached the trenches. They drove parallel to them, collapsing them, and fired their machine-guns at the Soviet troops withdrawing toward the forest. The panzer-grenadiers took the position in close combat.

"Radio message to regiment," ordered Obersturmführer Jessen. "Have broken through the enemy positions situated in front of the forest edge. Our escorting infantry has occupied these positions. One battalion has succeeded in entering the northern tip of the forest."

While the 5th Company had reached its initial objective, it now also had to occupy the forest, in which the Russians were sitting in cleverly camouflaged positions. The 6th Company, commanded by Hauptsturmführer Reicher, advanced with the infantry toward Kruhel after it had eliminated recognized enemy positions. The individual tanks shot up Russian machine-gun positions at the outskirts of the town and then rolled into Kruhel from both flanks. The town was cleared of enemy troops by the infantry. As the attack continued III Battalion, *Germania* was halted in front of the forest edge. II Battalion, *Westland* also failed to get through, even though 7th Company provided all the assistance it could.

Dense groups of enemy infantry stormed out of the forest, counterattacking in an attempt to retake the positions that had been lost. The attack was beaten off by pinpoint fire from the panzers. But then Soviet machine-guns began to rattle. Russian snipers perched in trees began picking off the grenadiers. A frontal attack against these well-fortified positions, invisible fifty meters deep in the forest, was doomed to fail.

The 5th Company had meanwhile approached to within about 400 meters of these positions on both sides of the Stare Koscary-Kovel road when Obersturmführer Jessen saw muzzle flashes from approximately ten previously hidden guns. Shells howled toward them, knocking out one tank and forcing the others to retreat to cover. An advance through the forest would have led to the loss of all the tanks. Informed of this situation,

Obersturmbannführer Mühlenkamp requested artillery fire on the forest. He also received a promise of Stukas. Unfortunately neither the artillery nor the Stuka attack which followed thirty minutes later could dislodge the enemy.

The division's assault battalion now entered the forest from the north. It soon encountered very strong opposition. There were dramatic battles in the forest in the twilight of the dense undergrowth. Man against man, pistol against pistol, hand grenade against hand grenade, following the pitiless rule "you or me." The fighting men of both sides crept through the forest, took fire, dodged into cover, crawled on, found an exposed enemy and exploited their opportunities. This battle frayed the nerves of the soldiers and it looked as if no progress was possible.

Calling in tanks was also out of the question, for every company was reporting Soviet counterattacks aimed at recapturing the ground taken by the panzers. Soviet assault troops repeatedly tried to recapture the commanding hill position held by 5th Company. But repeatedly they were beaten back with severe losses. One of 5th Company's tanks was knocked out, while two others were damaged when hit in the turret and running gear by antitank fire.

"We need the Stuka attack now," said Obersturmbannführer Mühlenkamp to his adjutant, Hauptsturmführer Fritz Zimmermann. The latter glanced at his watch.

"Any second, Obersturmbannführer," he replied, and as if that was the key word, they heard the drone of engines. A short time later twelve Stukas appeared over the western forest, identifiable by their cranked wings and fixed undercarriages. Then they peeled off over the forest, screamed down toward the Soviet positions and dropped their bombs. The dive bombers pulled up, seemingly threatened by the explosions from their own bombs, then turned west and disappeared.

"That did the trick, Obersturmbannführer," observed Zimmermann, but Mühlenkamp shook his head skeptically.

"Yes, it looks good, but we'll find out if it had any effect when we attack again."

"Attack," said Zimmermann, and the tanks rolled forward. They reached the edge of the forest, fired at the muzzle flashes they saw and disappeared into the woods. Trees toppling before them, the panzers approached the first log bunkers. Shells blasted them apart. The infantry followed, engaged the enemy in hand-to-hand combat and occupied the enemy positions. This time they had done it.

When he received the report of this success Obersturmbannführer Mühlenkamp drove to the command post of the 4th Panzer Division. The division Ia, Oberstleutnant Peter Sauerbruch, received him. He escorted him to the command post, where Generalleutnant Dietrich von Saucken, a monocle in one eye, greeted him. Mühlenkamp saw the Knight's Cross with Oak Leaves and Swords at the general's throat; von Saucken was well known as one of Germany's most skillful commanders of armored forces.

"Well, Mühlenkamp," said the general, "if we want to get to Kovel quickly then we have to make a concentrated assault now. The panzer-grenadiers of our 12th Panzer-Grenadier Regiment's II Battalion have taken "Egg Hill," the most strongly fortified section of the enemy's defenses. I Battalion overcame the enemy in house-to-house fighting in the Warszyk colony at the southeast corner of the forest, but my I Battalion of the panzer regiment is stuck in a dense minefield. The armored pioneers are clearing the field in order to allow the tanks to pass through. Therefore we have to concentrate all our forces. Your 5th Company will turn around to the north with the 4th Panzer Division if it can disengage itself from the enemy. Otherwise your regiment will follow immediately behind the 4th Panzer Division and reach Moszczona as quickly as possible."

An inquiry by Mühlenkamp revealed that the Fifth could not be pulled back until darkness fell, because sniper and machine-gun fire were making it impossible to recover the tanks and the wounded during daylight. Therefore the 5th Company would be subordinated to the 131st Infantry Division after it had successfully carried out all recoveries during the night.

II Battalion, SS PR *Wiking*, reached Moszczona at 5:45 P.M. Mühlenkamp immediately sent it advancing south along the Moszczona road, with 6th Company screening to the southeast and east and 7th Company to the northeast and east.

The breakthrough to Kovel planned for 4 April had already failed. The attack had gained ground, but that was not enough; for all hell had broken loose in Kovel itself. The Soviets were trying to overrun the weak forces defending the city before they were relieved from outside. The handful of tanks of the 8th Company were the main reason that General Gille was repeatedly able to master crisis situations.

Obersturmführer Nicolussi-Leck struck determined blows, engaging and destroying the enemy at the decisive phase of his attacks against the German lines. In the course of this heavy fighting he lost five of his Panthers. There in Kovel, in the notorious center of the Pripet Marshes, inadequately trained soldiers stood shoulder to shoulder with railway workers and police in a desperate battle.

General Gille's willingness to fly into the city and lead the defense with his Waffen-SS men was a noteworthy factor in raising the morale of the defenders. "My division is coming and the 4th Panzer Division is also on its way. We have to hold for the next few days, then we will be freed." The men believed this promise, and Gille meant every word. For days the defenders holding out in the ruined houses could hear the waxing and waning sound of fighting to the west.

The Soviet divisions stormed onward. Their objective was the River Bug at Brest Litovsk, and there was no one but the tiny garrison of Kovel to stop them. If Kovel fell it would release the eight Soviet divisions laying siege to the city and increase the pressure to the west. Kovel was also an important railway junction for the enemy, one which he needed badly to supply his advancing divisions in their continuing offensive. As the cold eased at the beginning of April, turning the area into a muddy hell, the garrison held on to prevent a catastrophe, as well as to save the more than 1,500 wounded who lay in makeshift cellar infirmaries, awaiting evacuation.

Mud and water—plenty of water—characterized the situation in those April days, when Soviet forces of the 1st, 2nd, 3rd, and 4th Ukrainian Fronts and the 1st White Russian Front launched a general offensive in the direction of the Carpathians. In the wet triangle between the Dniepr and Pripet the Soviet 13th Army had gone to the attack against the defending German XIII Army Corps and had set its sights on Kovel.

General Arthur Hauffe was unable to halt the vastly superior enemy with his three infantry divisions and was forced to retreat. And now two panzer divisions were approaching from the west to save Kovel. They were determined to crack the ring of steel around the city and save the Waffen-SS men, police troops and railway workers, and especially the many wounded, whatever the cost.

Obersturmbannführer Mühlenkamp had planned the breakthrough to Kovel for the 5th of April. He anticipated an attack by his regiment in two wedges so as to clear the widest possible corridor into the city. Following the firm land bridge, the southern wedge was to drive past the northwestern outskirts of Kovel along the Dobowa-Kovel road to its northeastern outskirts at the Kovel-Dorotycze road, then veer south and attack the city from the northeast. One company was to screen to the north and east in the area of the brickworks and prevent additional enemy forces from being fed in from the east toward Dubowa.

The northern attack wedge was supposed to operate from Moszczona along the ridge to the east toward Dobowa and there screen to the north and east. I Battalion, SS Panzer-Grenadier Regiment *Germania* was to attack from the tanks' security position (approximately 1.5 kilometers southwest of Kovel), advance southeast against the railway loop and rail crossing at the northwestern outskirts of Kovel under cover of darkness, and go over to the defensive there when daylight came. From there it would be possible to establish contact with the defenders of Kovel, link up with them and screen to the northeast and southwest. During the night all of the tanks were refueled and rearmed.

✠

It was 3:15 A.M. when Hannes Mühlenkamp's command tank moved of with the 1st Panzer-Grenadier Battalion of the *Germania* Regiment. With him in the tank were Obersturmführer Sepp Martin, his operations officer and two combat messengers. A second Panther accompanied the command vehicle to provide cover.

"We are going to advance straight towards the northwestern outskirts of Kovel!" declared Mühlenkamp.

The vehicles began to move. One behind the other the armored troop carriers moved forward. The darkness restricted them to a walking pace, but the distance they had to cover was not so great and they would be able to make it by daybreak. Once tank noises were heard ahead and to the northeast, however they moved away again. One hour later the attack wedge reached the northwestern outskirts of Kovel unopposed; the infantry dug in.

"Dispatch patrols at once to establish contact," ordered Mühlenkamp.

The patrols set off and soon afterwards the battle group, which had escaped detection by the enemy, established contact with the defenders of Kovel.

"All right, now you climb into the second command tank, Martin! We're driving in the direction of the center of the city. Battle readiness! And if the enemy shows himself we'll blast our way through."

The two command tanks rumbled forward through the still dark suburb. Suddenly there was a powerful blast beneath the right track of the command tank—a mine. The regimental commander's tank sat disabled one kilometer southeast of the rail crossing. A platoon of infantry and the tank's crew stood guard over the vehicle until it could be towed away and repaired. Following this incident Mühlenkamp transferred to the second Panther.

When it became light the two panzer companies moved out in two armored wedges. Advancing rapidly, the Sixth crossed the Dubowa-Kovel road. Taking fire from an enemy battery, it turned and attacked. The Panthers approached from three sides, moving and firing. Their accurate fire silenced the first enemy gun. A stack of artillery shells went up with a loud roar and two more Russian guns were put out of action. The fourth scored a hit on one of the tanks, but the projectile struck the turret at a sharp angle and bounced off. Moments later this gun, too, was knocked out by a direct hit.

"Onward, everyone follow me!" called Hauptsturmführer Reicher.

The tanks rattled up to an enemy obstacle and simply drove over it. The two machine-guns that were emplaced there were crushed beneath the tracks of the tanks. Several of the Soviet troops manning the position suffered the same fate. Finally the small armada reached the cemetery at the northwestern outskirts of Kovel, and soon afterwards the first soldiers wearing German steel helmets appeared before the tanks.

"It's good that you've come. We've had to wait for you a damned long time!" said a Feldwebel with a hollow, bearded face.

The tank commanders were briefed and the tanks took up their security positions facing north. Alois Richter dispatched a radio message to his commanding officer, reporting that they had made it. Seventh Company had moved out simultaneously with the Sixth. Due west of Dubowa it ran into a formidable Soviet strongpoint of antitank guns. A determined attack by the panzers overran and destroyed the position, after which Obersturmführer Otto Schneider ordered his tanks forward toward the rail line one kilometer west of Dubowa. When they had reached the line the Panthers swung out to the south and drove toward the city from a southerly direction.

Johannes Rudolf Mühlenkamp was a bulwark in a crisis while commanding the 5th SS-Panzer Regiment *Wiking*.

Artillery and antitank guns opened fire. The tanks split up into small groups and took aim at the muzzle flashes from the Soviet guns. The duel between the tanks and the enemy artillery and antitank guns lasted ten minutes. Obersturmführer Schneider's command tank was hit three times. But "Iron Otto," as he was known, ordered his tanks to press on. They blasted the enemy positions and rolled into Dubowa. A Panther struck one of the cottages at the east end of the village and brought it crashing to the ground. Red Army troops tried to retreat, pursued by bursts of machine-gun fire. Dubowa was in the Seventh's hands. When Hannes Mühlenkamp received this news he was certain that he could now drive straight into the city, for the 6th Company's screening line at the northeastern outskirts of Kovel would prevent his attack from being flanked from the northeast and east.

Untersturmführer Manfred Renz, who participated in the events of 4 and 5 April 1944, described the breakthrough by the Panzer Regiment *Wiking* from the perspective of the commander of an armored reconnaissance platoon:

> During the afternoon hours of 4 April I was ordered to the battalion commander, Obersturmbannführer Paetsch, who informed me that my two reconnaissance Panthers (the others still had not arrived) were to accompany the attack and that I was to act as adjutant as Obersturmführer Förster was sick and out of action.
>
> We moved off at 4:35 P.M., positioned behind the 6th and 7th Companies, and advancing at high speed we soon reached Moszczona, the starting point of our main attack.
>
> At first the two companies had only light resistance to overcome and by evening they and the battalion headquarters were in the area of Moszczona. Security was posted and at the same time the starting position was identified for the breakthrough to Kovel. I myself received permission from the battalion commander to take part in 6th Company's attack, which was led by Hauptsturmführer Reicher, as part of the Grossrock platoon.
>
> Because of my precise knowledge of the terrain, if the opportunity presented itself I was to scout out the best route for the southern armored wedge at the northern outskirts of Kovel.
>
> The regimental commander had already succeeded in getting through to the northwest of Kovel with two command tanks in the early morning hours without contacting the enemy. However the commanding officer's tank struck a mine and had to be placed under guard.

We moved off at daybreak on 5 April and attempted to gain ground to the southeast and east by driving along the secondary road from Moszczona to Kovel.

"Eagle—Eagle—Falcon and Sparrow Hawk are taking the lead—over!" With this radio transmission I inserted myself into 6th Company's attack.

The contours of the low-lying city of Kovel, situated in the center of the marsh with the Turja River flowing through it from north to south, were just visible in the morning twilight. With its numerous branches and tributaries, this river cut through the wooded, marshy area that surrounded the city of Kovel. All around the city separate marshes extended between the larger wooded areas, creating an almost impossible obstacle for a large-scale armored assault.

As one of the most important rail junctions in White Russia, the city was an important strategic point for all military operations. The raised embankment of the Lublin-Kovel rail line formed a natural barrier to the north and northwest of the city, but at the same time it provided a rail connection.

The outlines of the barracks installations in the north part of the city were just visible in the morning mist. They rose artificially from that part of the city and formed a natural defensive bulwark. At the same time the hill on which the barracks stood commanded all the northern and some of the eastern approach routes to the city.

My men sat tensely in the tank and observed the road and the battlefield terrain. Radio communications between the individual units of the regiment were excellent, and the deployment of our armored wedge southeast along the Moszczona-Kovel road was completed in near textbook fashion with no serious difficulties.

In the meantime I drove up through the company in order to reach the point as quickly as possible, however the terain limited speeds to less than 30 kilometers per hour. Often it was less than 20 kilometers per hour. The main reason for this was that the tank drivers proceeded very carefully in order to take advantage of every dry piece of ground, for every wet piece could mean getting stuck and the loss of the vehicle. Fortunately, in spite of the recent warmer weather the ground was still frozen and was only slippery on the surface.

Then I heard: "Buzzard to Falcon." What was up now?

It was a call for help from Hauptsturmführer Reicher. His tank had become bogged down in the swamp to the tops of its tracks.

Luckily for the company's progress the commander and his Panther had not broken through on the firm road but rather just off to the right of it. The remaining tanks rolled past the stuck command vehicle in first gear, and the crews saw driver Bahrmann and another member of the crew walking around the tank with the tow cable.

I called a halt at a dry-looking place and cautiously backed up toward Reicher's Panther in order to pull it free. Falcon's 700-horsepower motor roared; much too loud for our ears, and the enemy immediately began shooting at us. Under enemy fire we cautiously moved forward and then the tow cable broke with a loud snap. Reicher's Panther, slipped backwards onto its old track.

But we had been lucky, for by applying full throttle my skilled driver had brought our 'Falcon' out of the danger zone. Nevertheless, the enemy was now raking us with fire from the northern outskirts of Kovel.

I summoned a second Panther by radio and then I crawled back to Bahrmann and his comrade, taking them the ends of two tow cables. In the midst of this maneuver a third cable was thrown to us from a tank of the Grossrock platoon.

The men worked quickly. They did their best at attaching the tow cable. And in spite of the heavy enemy fire we still had not taken any losses. The enemy's view was partially blocked by the rising terrain, which was lucky for us.

With three tow cables attached we succeeded: the tank came free.

The terrain became somewhat better and by driving faster I was able to catch up to Untersturmführer Grossrock, who was still advancing slowly. With a few words we laid down our subsequent tactics. Driving in an accordion formation, we advanced at high speed, always at full throttle, across the difficult terrain to Kovel. Escorted by my second reconnaissance tank, I led the way for Grossrock's five Panthers.

Meanwhile it had become fully light. The enemy, who knew our intentions, now employed all his weapons in an effort to stop us. Our guns went into action and the clusters of houses in Dobowa, which were studded with antitank guns, were placed under fire. The firing grew more intense. We soon realized that the enemy had set up several antitank barriers there one behind the other in order to prevent our breakthrough.

The fire from the enemy antitank guns was quite accurate. While making a fast dash forward we received a hit, but it merely shook our tank and failed to penetrate the armor. My gunner reacted quickly. Tapping his shoulder with my right hand, I guided him precisely to the target.

High-explosive 800—antitank guns in front of a group of houses. Open fire!

With these words the battle began. The first shot fell in the middle of the target. A large cloud of dust, mixed with pieces of trees and buildings, flew into the air.

As the lead tank I now directed all the firing by 6th Company. Grossrock and his five Panthers immediately took their cues from my first shots and within a few minutes we were able to silence the enemy antitank guns and tanks. It later turned out that we had destroyed several enemy tanks and ten antitank guns as well as numerous light and heavy machine-guns. I wasn't about to let anything stop me now.

"Sparrow," I called. "Sparrow, come in!"

"Sparrow here, we hear you, Falcon!" replied the tank commander.

"Request covering fire for dash across the Kovel-Brest Litovsk road to the northern edge of the barracks."

Grossrock and my companion vehicle Sparrow gave me covering fire. Moving fast, our tank became the first to try and cross the dangerous road as quickly as possible. I noticed that the enemy had not been completely silenced, for several impacting antitank shells whirled up dirt and mud around my tank.

The entire 6th Company, which had overheard, now opened fire with all guns and also gave me good cover by firing smoke shells. But suddenly, at the northern outskirts of Kovel, a mighty, ringing explosion right in front of us. A huge cloud of smoke, mixed with long swaths of flame, rose from the north end of the city. A fuel and ammunition dump had exploded.

"We're seizing this opportunity to break through!" I reported to Reicher. We drove faster, but just short of the embankment there was a crash. We had been hit, but our armor withstood this blow too. However, we had to immediately return fire, which my gunner did without waiting for my order, for he had spotted the antitank nest.

Within a few seconds, before it could fire again, the antitank gun was put out of action by a single shot fired point-blank from a range of 400 meters. We made smoke in an effort to avoid being hit again, and in fact we did succeed in crossing the road on the embankment and reached a hull-down position.

Now the Red Army troops withdrew. The Russian infantry attempted to retreat to the east. Under covering fire from the remaining tanks Grossrock now also ventured across the roadway and within fifteen minutes we had six panzers east of the road. After another thirty minutes the remaining enemy resistance at the north end of Kovel was broken, after which we were able to deploy north of the barracks for safety. From these positions we were able to keep the enemy fleeing into the woods north of Kovel under fire for quite some time.

The 6th Company now received orders from the regimental commander to remain where it was until the arrival of 7th Company. But suddenly an armored troop carrier with an unusual-looking superstructure appeared on the road. Our lookout tank first fired a warning shot across its bows from 500 meters. Recognition flares were promptly fired from the armored reconnaissance vehicle.

It turned out that it was Oberstleutnant Hoffmann, commander of the 12th Panzer-Grenadier Regiment of the 4th Panzer Division. He had a film correspondent with him and was on his way to Gille's command post in Kovel.

Toward evening we, too, were moved into Kovel, where we were given an enthusiastic welcome by the liberated garrison.

✠

With the 7th Company acting as a steel wedge, at 3:10 P.M. the Panzer Regiment *Wiking* moved off from Dubowa at 3:10 P.M. and after clearing a mine barrier and breaking the enemy resistance, at 5 P.M. it reached the center of Kovel.

"Expand the breakthrough to the east and west together with the garrison of Kovel."

This order from General Gille confirmed the fact that the garrison was now certain to be able to withstand the tremendous Soviet pressure with the assistance of their comrades outside the pocket. Hannes Mühlenkamp reported to Gille and soon afterwards he was able to greet the commander of his 8th Company after long, worrisome days of separation.

"Nicolussi-Leck, I am happy to see you whole and healthy again," he called, and shook the hand of his comrade in arms.

"The pleasure belongs to me and my men," replied the Tirolean and then laughed.

Kovel had been relieved, however the danger was scarcely diminished, for after a three-week defense by the garrison, at the cost of mounting casualties, the stocks of ammunition and food had dropped alarmingly.

Bit by bit, the Soviets succeeded in taking pieces of the outer defense line and the defenders were gradually forced back into the city. Then Soviet assault troops broke into the inner defense hedgehog and established themselves in several blocks of houses. From there they advanced step by step until they had taken entire rows of houses and were able to place the remaining sections of the city under fire from commanding positions.

In leaflets and radio broadcasts the Soviet high command had already announced the imminent fall of Kovel and the destruction of the garrison of the city. But now a link had been forged to the embattled defenders. In addition to the tanks and panzer-grenadiers of the *Wiking* Division it had been the soldiers of the 4th Panzer Division who had helped relieve Kovel. It was I Battalion, 35th Panzer Regiment under Stabsarzt Dr. Schulz-Merkel which attacked on the early morning of 5 April in order to take possession of the village of Dubowa. Dr. Schulz-Merkel wrote:

> The night of 5 April was spent regrouping, rearming, refueling and cooking. One by one the commanders of the participating units came to me in the potato cellar. The briefing for the coming attack took place at roughly 2 A.M.
>
> General Saucken informed us that the Führer had issued another order. We were supposed to turn south along the rail line. Our division commander knew the situation first-hand, and he also had the courage to order the attack to go ahead, not according to the wishes of the higher-ups, but where the facts indicated that casualties would be less and the chance of success were greatest.
>
> The panzer companies were in position behind the railway embankment before dawn. First objective was the village of Dubowa and the cemetery wood to the south of it. The enemy had so heavily armed the place with artillery, antitank guns and antiaircraft guns that the attack had to be well prepared if it was not to become very costly.
>
> The panzer-grenadiers moved out while it was still dark and their surprise attack enabled them to take out a field position in

front of the village. The tanks, which had supported the attack with their fire, were not to advance until ordered to do so.

A Waffen-SS Panther company with eight tanks was assigned to support us. It was assigned its target area at the east end of the village and likewise took up position behind the embankment.

There were flashes from the outskirts of the village as the enemy opened fire at us; we replied, and the lighter it became the more accurate was our fire. The panzer-grenadiers rolled up position after position, effectively supported by our panzers. Now tanks and grenadiers also approached the village from the north. The enemy had not counted on this. The fierce battle lasted almost four hours, then the cemetery wood and with it the road from Brest-Litovsk to Kovel was in our hands.

The elimination of the "armored citadel of Dubowa," as this bastion was often referred to in reports, was a decisive success in the Battle of Kovel.

Following this success the German forces regrouped for the ultimate assault on Kovel. At 11:30 A.M. on 5 April the Schulz-Merkel battalion moved off in order to take out the bunkers blocking the way into the city. The panzers subsequently reached the area of the brickworks in the northeast part of the city. The battle there lasted two hours, before the tanks of I Battalion, 35th Panzer Regiment reached the last barricade. From there Oberstleutnant Hoffmann, the commander of the 12th Panzer-Grenadier Regiment, drove into Kovel with his grenadiers riding on the tanks. He was accompanied by a cameraman from the propaganda service.

Ernst-Wilhelm Hoffmann, who had won the Knight's Cross while serving as a Major and company commander in the 12th Rifle on 4 September 1940, received a jubilant welcome from the bearded defenders of Kovel as he drove to see the commander of the forces defending the city.

In the late afternoon Gille also received a visit from Generalleutnant von Saucken. Kovel had finally been relieved and a corridor established through which the medical officer of the 4th Panzer Division, Dr. Paechner, immediately set about evacuating the 1,500 wounded in armored troop carriers. All of the transports of wounded got through, in spite of the terrible roads.

Kovel had been saved for the time being. But the enemy did not give up. We had only delayed the inevitable. And if they did succeed in closing their ring around the city once more, even more German soldiers would be caught in the trap. The Soviet high command therefore sent a stream of new units into the Kovel area to join the six rifle divisions, the assault brigade, the three tank regiments and the antitank artillery regiment already arrayed around the city.

A difficult, weeks-long battle still lay ahead.

✠

"Comrades, I have summoned you here to discuss with you the next steps in Kovel. I am happy to see you here again Nicolussi-Leck and to have your Eighth here, even if five of your tanks were knocked out during the time when you were on your own." Obersturmbannführer Mühlenkamp, freshly shaved, had assembled the commanders of the panzer companies and the regimental headquarters in the old school. The stresses of recent days, the efforts to find and exploit a gap in the enemy's ring around the city, were visible in their faces.

"Effective immediately," continued Mühlenkamp, "the Seventh is assigned to I Battalion of the *Germania* Regiment. It will support that battalion's attack west along the Kovel-Stare Koscary rail line, whose purpose is to expand and secure the corridor.

Untersturmführer Niemann, you will immediately dispatch a Panzer IV of your platoon to provide additional protection for the disabled command tank. It is sitting roughly here, at this position."

Horst Niemann stepped up beside Mühlenkamp and looked at the map of Kovel with the enemy penetrations penciled in. Then he nodded in confirmation and said, "I'll get going straight away."

Mühlenkamp nodded to him, satisfied. That's how his tank commanders had to be: always ready to take on even the most difficult assignments.

"Two Panthers from your company, Jessen, are to join the unit of Hauptmann Olbricht, which is defending the Monopol barracks in the southern part of Kovel. Look for two good positions from which you can engage the attacking enemy from the flank and destroy him. Good luck!"

Platoon by platoon the officers received their assignments. They looked at Mühlenkamp and saw how seriously he aproached the task at hand. The briefing was interrupted by a telephone call. Mühlenkamp heard the voice of Gruppenführer Gille. Then he hung up and turned to Hauptsturmführer Reicher.

"Reicher, you and your Sixth are also to support the attack by I Battalion of *Germania.* You are to drive along the railway line."

No sooner had Untersturmführer Niemann departed when a call for help came in from the southeastern part of the city. Ten minutes later the five tanks of the regimental headquarters company under Obersturmführer Lüthgarth roared off to intervene there and restore the situation.

When the briefing and the allocation of forces was over, Mühlenkamp drove out to his various units in order to see for himself that his company commanders had selected the proper positions. There were confident faces everywhere he went. The bearded railway workers, who had dug in in positions in the center of the city, waved to him as he rolled past standing in the turret of his tank. The Soviets did not launch an attack toward the center of Kovel on this day. Apparently the breakthrough by elements of two German armored divisions had given them something more to think about.

✠

Untersturmführer Niemann, the leader of the motorcycle reconnaissance platoon, had taken his Panther to stand guard over the disabled command tank. He was just speaking to the reconnaissance tank's driver when a flash of gunfire was seen approximately two-and-a-half kilometers away.

The shell fell a few meters in front of the disabled tank. "Kurt, watch out, enemy Pak!" he warned the driver. The gunner took aim at the muzzle flash from the antitank gun's second shot, but before he could fire the round from the Soviet gun pierced the hull of the command tank. The loader was hit and fell backwards, while at the same time gunner Kuddernatsch pressed the firing button. He watched as his shot fell short, kicking up dirt several dozen meters in front of the system of positions.

The next shell from the Russian antitank gun struck close beside the Panther and shook it hard. Flames shot into the fighting compartment and the choking smell of cordite almost took the men's breath away. Nevertheless, Kuddernatsch succeeded in loading another round himself and then fired a second time.

Suddenly a tremendous impact shook the tank. The commander felt a hard blow against his head. He heard the sound of an armor-piercing shell ricocheting off the armored turret and shouted for the crew to bail out. They jumped out, took cover in a ditch a few meters beside the Panther and watched as Untersturmführer Niemann engaged the enemy and soon afterwards knocked out one of the antitank guns.

"Goshawk to Commander: command tank has been knocked out by an antitank gun from 2,500 meters. Command tank has hits in the hull and turret, crew wounded but bailed out. Am currently in a firefight with enemy antitank guns."

Hannes Mühlenkamp received this report at 5:10 P.M. He immediately ordered Jessen to dispatch a platoon from his 5th Company to the command tank and support the Panther in its struggle with the enemy guns. As soon as Jessen acknowledged, Mühlenkamp alerted the recovery platoon and ordered it to begin recovery as soon as darkness fell and repair the command tank as quickly as possible. The recovery effort was a success and one hour later the men of the workshop company, which was commanded by Obersturmführer Erich Weisse, was at work. Mühlenkamp now tackled some paperwork, completing the requisitions for ammunition and fuel. He was just beginning to write a letter when the telephone in the anteroom rang. The signals NCO came in.

"Obersturmbannführer, it's the division commander."

Hannes Mühlenkamp went over to the telephone, took the receiver and identified himself. On the other end of the line was the Ia of Battle Group Gille. "Listen Mühlenkamp, Gruppenführer Gille has just been informed that the enemy is attacking Dubowa with strong infantry and armored units and at the same time is also advancing on the brickworks at the northeast end of Kovel. Your regiment is ordered to immediately dispatch a company to Dubowa. There the company is to report to Hauptmann Weide. The company's orders are: 1. To smash the enemy attack, especially the armored units, and guard Dubowa to the north and east. 2. Remain there until further orders are received. In order to secure the brickworks, you must send another company of your regiment to the northeast outskirts of Kovel and deploy it near the brickworks with its front facing north and east."

Mühlenkamp immediately put together what was still available from the elements of his regiment and dispatched the tanks to the two specified points. The two panzer companies spent the night of 7 April in these positions, but the enemy had obviously smelled a rat and did not come. Now and then there was a duel between an antitank gun and one of the tanks, until morning came and all fighting there ended.

During the next two days the commander of forces in Kovel, Gruppenführer Gille, successfully deployed his few remaining tanks at the trouble spots in his defense system. Gille himself drove to the various positions to inspect them. What he saw filled him with confidence, for in addition to his own troops the units of the 4th Panzer Division were also manning positions in the city and on the commanding hills west of Kovel, keeping the vital supply corridor open.

Mühlenkamp was now able to begin the task of bringing his companies back up to strength. Almost all of the damaged tanks were repaired. The troops were confident and for the first time after long, desperate weeks the defenders were able to sleep at night. The situation inside Kovel stabilized noticeably. The enemy seemed to have realized that he could do nothing there, at least for the next few days. Then on the early morning of 12 April Russian assault units stormed toward Hill 179 from the north. Seconds after enemy tanks were spotted the telephone rang in Obersturmbannführer Mühlenkamp's command post.

"Request tank support as soon as possible, Obersturmbannführer. Enemy attacking hill with large numbers of tanks. Without antitank weapons unable to stop them."

"We'll send you 6th Company. Make sure there is someone there to guide us in—out!"

Once again Mühlenkamp selected the 6th Company under Obersturmführer Jessen, as it had the most tanks. The company, which two days earlier had retaken Hill 179.4 northwest of Kovel and Bachow together with a battalion of panzer-grenadiers, immediately left its assembly area.

"Grossrock platoon outflank the infantry to the left, Jensen platoon drive past on the right and keep the tanks busy."

This order from Hauptsturmführer Reicher was passed on several minutes later, when the Sixth could already see the enemy.

Then another report came in: "There are at least thirty tanks. They are driving widely separated."

"Attack the last tanks in the column. We will separate the infantry from the tanks and stop them."

Untersturmführer Grossrock sent his five Panthers sweeping around in a wide arc, and when the enemy's flank was before them they opened fire. Flames shot from the muzzles of five tank cannon and shells whistled toward the enemy. The first T-34 took a direct hit and was blown apart in the explosion of its ammunition. A second T-34 was left blazing fiercely after the first shot. The crew tumbled from the hatches, their clothing on fire, and rolled on the ground.

The battle continued. The Jensen platoon went into action on the other flank. Moments later four enemy tanks which were bringing up the rear lay shot-up and burning on the gentle slope of the hill. The enemy infantry were pinned down. But their tanks, those that had survived the initial onslaught, continued to drive south toward the German positions on the hill.

"Let them go!" radioed Reicher. "We'll get them later. Take care of the infantry first."

The Panthers fired high-explosive shells, drove over machine-gun positions, and poured fire into the bushes from which Russian antitank rifles had opened fire. Finally this phase of the battle, too, was over and Reicher radioed to his company commander: "Enemy infantry separated from the tanks. Enemy tanks continuing to roll south. We are about to attack them en masse."

Now, for the first time, the sector of the front near Hill 179 witnessed a true tank-versus-tank battle. The German Panthers' superiority over the Soviet T-34s was a decisive factor in the eventual outcome of the battle.

Untersturmführer Grossrock and his crews engaged a group of ten enemy tanks. They fired a salvo into the enemy vehicles and then changed direction and roared across the steppe, their tracks throwing up clumps of sod. While turning the Panthers were fired at by three T-34s that had gone into a ravine; hull-down, all that was visible of them were their turrets and the long barrels of their cannon.

"Hollermann and Berke swing out to the right. Everyone else back!" ordered Grossrock.

The tanks turned, taking several hits in the process; Fortunately,the shells detonated against their side skirts. A mighty blow shook the platoon commander's tank. Grossrock saw a wall of flame just in front of him, and the driver cried out, but once again the crew was lucky. Seconds later the Panther disappeared into a hollow in the ground and rolled along it at full throttle. When they saw the muzzle flashes from the three T-34s to their left, they rattled out of the ravine and found themselves behind the enemy tanks.

"Fire and make it count, men," called the Untersturmführer. And that is exactly what they did. The three T-34s were hit. One began to burn, the other two drove away and were engaged by Hollermann and Berke.

Grossrock shouted a warning to his gunner: "Look out! Right at twelve o'clock, four-hundred!" The driver turned the tank slightly.

"Target in sight!" called the Rottenführer, and seconds later the Panther's 75-mm gun barked.

The Russian T-34, which had appeared from the other side, took a direct hit. It stopped, the hatch snapped back and the commander jumped on to the tank. Then he was caught by a burst of fire which toppled him to the rear. Seconds later the ammunition stored inside the tank exploded, tearing it to pieces. By 10:30 A.M. the tanks of 6th Company had destroyed nine enemy tanks and had hit several others. While the infantry on the hill fought off the attacking Red Army troops and beat them back, the Sixth continued to battle the enemy tanks, which had taken cover in the terrain.

One hour later Hans-Georg Jensen, the commander of the 2nd Platoon, destroyed two T-34s one after another. The two tanks had rolled out of the forest directly in front of him and had then tried to dash back to safety. But Scharführer Rix met his fate. His Panther was hit in the right track. Firing in all directions, and turning in circles on the one still intact track, the crew fought on. Their tank took hit after hit until finally it was in flames. No one escaped from the blazing steel coffin. Two more Panthers were hit and disabled; their crews were able to get themselves to safety. Both tanks were recovered during the night.

The battle lasted until 1 P.M., when the last enemy tanks disappeared. Fifteen smoldering wrecks littered the battlefield, shrouded in clouds of black smoke. The 6th Company had beaten off the Soviet attack and destroyed fifteen enemy tanks. Untersturmführer Grossrock had distinguished himself once again, and Mühlenkamp submitted a recommendation for the Knight's Cross for the brave panzer soldier.

The next four days went by in what passed for the "routine" of the Battle of Kovel. The Soviets fired into the city, while patrols and small assault units probed the German lines for weak spots; wherever they appeared they were met by a hail of small arms fire and sent reeling back.

The reduction in the Soviet pressure was due to the withdrawal from the encircling ring of the 143rd Rifle Division, which took up positions on both sides of the rail line to Czerkasy, its front facing west, in order to reduce the corridor. As well, the 243rd Rifle Division was sent around Kovel and drove into the area northwest of the city to threaten the corridor from there. In spite of this relaxation, the German defenders had to use extreme caution, for Kovel was still extremely important to the Soviets.

On the afternoon of 16 April all unit commanders were assembled in Gruppenführer Gille's command post to receive orders for a new attack which was to be carried out the following morning. Herbert Gille, his wire-rimmed glasses on his rather large nose, stood at the map table and nodded to the officers as they entered. The General, who had come from the cadet corps, knew that he could depend on each of his commanders one hundred percent. Those who stood before him—Richter, Hack and Dorr, Mühlenkamp, Paetsch and the others—were all veterans who had proved themselves in many battles.

"Gentlemen," began Gille, "at one hour after midnight we will set out to clear the western part of Kovel and Hills 189.5 and 188 which lie west of Kovel. We have to take these hills, which represent a permanent danger to us, from the enemy. We have to gain a firm hold on the access road and the Brest-Litovsk-Kovel rail line, and furthermore it is necessary to show the enemy who is calling the tune here."

SS-Gruppenführer Gille and SS-Obersturmbannführer Dorr.

Gille issued brief, concise instructions to each of the units. The enemy situation was clear, for the Ic of the division and his staff had been able to come up with a precise picture of the enemy from prisoners' statements and captured documents. He outlined the plan of attack as follows: "Battle Group Dorr will attack from the rail loop northwest of Kovel and will advance along the rail line under cover of darkness," continued the general. "The regimental headquarters and 5th and 6th Companies of Panzer Regiment *Wiking* will go into position directly behind the 50th Pioneer Battalion at the western boundary of Kovel. As soon as the pioneers have established a bridgehead across the Turja and have found a way from the western part of the city across the southern foothills of Hill 189.5, they will advance and take the south barracks with the hill."

At one hour after midnight the tanks of II Battalion, which was fighting for the entire regiment, together with those of the regimental headquarters, were ready. Ahead the sounds could be heard of the pioneers at work as they labored to bridge the west arm of the Turja for the tanks while it was still dark.

"Do you think it will work, Obersturmbannführer," asked Hauptsturmführer Zimmermann, the regimental adjutant.

"Why shouldn't it work, Zimmermann?" replied Mühlenkamp, then seconds later he raised his hand to signal quiet.

From ahead, where the pioneers had moved into the departure positions, a Russian Maxim machine-gun had begun to rattle. Another joined in and in a matter of seconds the night was filled with the sounds of combat.

"Damn!" cursed the adjutant softly, "the Russians have spotted our pioneers."

Instead of replying Mühlenkamp ordered: "Patrol forward!"

Three members of the headquarters climbed down and crept forward in the direction of the fighting. When they reached a position level with the pioneers they saw lances of fire from bursts of machine-gun fire and now and then tracers flitting through the darkness. They were being fired on from the enemy positions toward where the German pioneers were.

Moments later Untersturmführer Scholk came upon the pioneer Leutnant in a ditch. "How does it look?" he asked.

"Terrible. The Ivans are giving it to us. We can't go any farther. Sixty meters more and we would have done it."

"I will call for tanks," offered the Untersturmführer.

"That would be good, for we have to do a good job."

The runner headed to the rear and moments later came upon the regimental commander, who had moved his command vehicle forward to the edge of a small forest. He made his report and Mühlenkamp ordered two tanks from 6th Company to move forward over the narrow embankment in the direction of the pioneers.

"Attention, Vulture to Eagle, have reached the pioneers, move up."

With these words Oberscharführer Knut Petersen summoned forward the Panther of Unterscharführer Gustav Kern, which had been following at a distance of several hundred meters. Gustav Kern instructed his driver to move forward at full throttle. The tank reached the bend in the embankment and Kern saw Petersen talking to the commander of the pioneer company, Hauptsturmführer Schliack.

"How does it look?" he asked after the tank's engine had come back to idle.

"The road in front of us is mined and is defended by two barricades. Our pioneers have cleared a lane. An assault team will lead us through and we will get rid of the barricades. First we will silence several machine-gun positions that are making things difficult for our pioneers."

"Very well, let's get started!"

"You take the right flank, Gustel, and good luck!"

"Same to you," Gustav Kern called after the Oberscharführer, who had already moved off in his Panther guided by one of the engineers.

"Turn right, follow the engineer," Kern instructed his driver. Hubert von Alfriend turned the Panther and drove behind the man at a walking pace. After about forty meters the man took cover and pointed ahead to the right. Kern guided the tank forward a little farther, then saw the sudden flash as a machine-gun opened fire from the dense brush.

"One o'clock! Two-hundred and fifty!"

"Target in sight!" called gunner Adolf Truppner.

The first shell crashed into the bushes, followed by a second. Bursts of machine-gun fire clattered against the armor plate. Then antitank rifles opened fire and armor-piercing projectiles struck the tank and bounced off. To the five men inside the steel box it sounded as if bells were being rung very close to their ears. The Panther rattled across the open terrain for a few meters and then halted again. Two more shots were fired from its main gun. A projectile from an antitank rifle struck the bulletproof glass of a vision block and glanced off to the side.

"Forward, quickly, we're going to run over them!"

Truppner engaged first gear. He shifted gears and the tank rolling faster and faster then plunged into the bushes. Kern saw startled faces appear before the tank, ineffective bursts of machine-gun fire. The Panther rolled over a machine-gun position and then wheeled around to the right.

"Look out, Ivans!" shouted the driver.

Kern had seen them coming. He opened the hatch cover, because the enemy were already beneath the range of his guns. He stood up and fired his submachine-gun as he saw the first enemy soldier leap onto the track shield less than two meters away. The man fell backwards and dropped to the ground. At that instant something struck him in the back like a giant fist and knocked him forward over the rim of the hatch. Kern probably felt nothing more; he sagged into the tank and blood from his neck wound dripped onto the driver's shoulder. Seconds later two hand grenades exploded in the interior of the tank, killing everyone. A Russian tank-killing squad had "cracked" the Panther.

The second Panther under Oberscharführer Petersen made it to the first barricade. It opened fire but then itself became the target of four antitank guns. Petersen succeeded in knocking out two of the enemy guns but then the Panther was hit in the turret ring, jamming the turret. Petersen withdrew and sent the following radio message to the regimental commander:

"Enemy behind two thick barricades with antitank and anti-aircraft guns. Cannot get through."

On receiving this message Mühlenkamp ordered the 6th Company to prepare for action. Seconds later Hauptsturmführer Reicher radioed that the Sixth was ready to move.

"Swing north and support the attack north of the pioneers. It is important that we win a crossing over the Turja."

The company moved off, followed an arcing course and at 4:45 A.M., exactly fifteen minutes after receiving the order, it began taking fire.

"Everyone select their own targets! Attack everything that fires!"

The Panthers rolled forward in platoons. Untersturmführer Grossrock, who had swung the widest and was on the extreme right flank, saw one of the antitank guns to his left front.

"Forward quickly. Firing halt at the round bush!" he ordered.

The gunner aimed roughly as the Panther rolled over the bushes. When the tank stopped the target was already in his sight. He made a slight correction and pressed the firing button. The first shell was a direct hit. A fierce battle now developed in the western part of Kovel. The enemy defended with all the means at his disposal. Nevertheless the Soviets were forced back step by step, and wherever they held onto an island of resistance they were outflanked and flushed out by several Panthers. The battle lasted three hours. The pioneers, who had meanwhile cleared the road of mines, followed up. They assaulted the remaining nests of resistance and silenced those that refused to surrender.

At 8 A.M. the crews of the leading panzers—this time the Jensen platoon was leading the way—saw the river shimmering in the morning light before them. They halted, shot up a fleeing enemy train column, and reached a crossing site that had been used by the enemy. One after another the company's tanks drove across the log road thrown up by the engineers. They had reached the departure position. But what was happening on Hill 188, their next objective? And when would Battle Group Dorr, which was deployed on Hill 189.5, arrive?

✠

After moving out from the rail loop northwest of Kovel, the battle group commanded by Sturmbannführer Hans Dorr had crept forward along the rail line and reached the first enemy positions while it was still dark.

"In we go men, everyone follow me!"

Hans Dorr, a farmer's son from Sontheim in the Allgaü district, had forced a crossing of the Kuban, for which he received the Knight's Cross on 2 October 1942. On 15 November 1943 he had become the 327th recipient of the Knight's Cross with Oak Leaves. Now he led another assault by his panzer-grenadiers. The small force of barely two-hundred and thirty soldiers knew what was at stake and they took their lead from their commander. They stormed the enemy positions shouting battle cries, lobbed hand grenades as they ran, leapt into the trenches and overpowered the enemy in hand-to-hand combat.

"Report to Obersturmbannführer Mühlenkamp: Battle Group Dorr has reached and taken the first enemy strongpoint, is advancing on Hill 189.5."

The panzer-grenadiers resumed their advance. By now it was 6 A.M. and the first light was visible in the east. The next two hours turned into a dramatic duel with Russian units which tried to bar the battle group's way to the hill. The companies fought their way through. They were deployed skillfully by Sturmbannführer Dorr and when they reached the foot of Hill 189.5 the companies had it three-quarters surrounded.

Dorr passed the word: "Simultaneous attack up the hill. That will split the defenders' fire."

The panzer-grenadiers rose and charged up the hill. While they were halted on the southeast side, on the northeast side the men of 3rd Company reached the upper rim of the hill. They rushed over the crest, took some fire and leapt into Soviet trenches and blasted a path clear. It was exactly 7 A.M. when Sturmbannführer Dorr reported the capture of the hill. According to his radio message, his leading elements were already at the railway line 1 000 meters southwest of Hill 189.5.

The two battle groups linked up two-and-a-half hours later. Now the movements of the two formations could be coordinated. With 6th Company already across the river, 5th Company now followed. At the western outskirts of Kovel it turned south to clear the western part of the city. A company of infantry from Battle Group Dorr was assigned to it for this purpose as was a platoon of pioneers.

But the 6th Company rolled on, straight toward Hill 188, which lay south of Hill 189.5. It reached its objective and drove away the weak Russian screening force there. Hauptsturmführer Reicher immediately dispatched a patrol to reconnoiter to the southeast.

After driving through the western part of Kovel, the 5th Company had reached the line of hills to the left of the Sixth. With its left wing in the south barracks, it was able to scout toward the southwest in the direction of Horodelec.

This attack had turned into a major success. The enemy had been driven back. One by one, his last fiercely-defended strongpoints were taken out by the panzer-grenadiers. Kovel was once again totally in the possession of the defenders. For the time being II Battalion of the Panzer Regiment *Wiking* remained in Battle Group Dorr's security sector.

Nothing extraordinary happened until 20 April, except that now it was the Germans who were mining and fortifying their positions. On the afternoon of 20 April the men in Fortress Kovel learned that Gruppenführer Herbert Gille had become the twelfth member of the German Armed Forces and first soldier of the Waffen-SS to receive the Knight's Cross with Oak Leaves, Swords and Diamonds. He was awarded the decoration for the successful relief and defense of Kovel.

In the same hour Hannes Mühlenkamp received a radio message informing him that he had been promoted to the rank of Standartenführer. The fighting inside Kovel itself had swung in favor of the defenders, but this did not end the struggle. For the Soviets continued their efforts to bypass Kovel and once again encircle the embattled city.

✠

The next few days were quiet in Kovel. On 25 April the 7th Company of the SS Panzer Division *Wiking* was subordinated to the 4th Panzer Division. In return the 2nd Company of the 46th Antitank Battalion was placed under Standartenführer Mühlenkamp's command and moved into Kovel. On 26 April the unit commanders were ordered to report to the commander of forces in the city. There Mühlenkamp learned that an attack operation code-named "Ilse" had been laid on for the next day. His regiment was given the following assignment: in cooperation with an infantry group commanded by Major Quehl, it was to advance from the southern approaches to Hill 189 along the rail line to Lubliniec, then swing toward the southeast, take Hill 193.3 and barricade the crossing over the Turja River near Korodelec.

Early on the morning of the 27th the battle group moved into attack positions near the windmill at the southwestern outskirts of Kovel. Available to Standartenführer Mühlenkamp for the attack were the following units:

Regimental headquarters
Headquarters, II Battalion, SS Panzer Regiment *Wiking*
Armored pioneer company
8th Company, Panzer Regiment *Wiking*
2nd Company, 49th Antitank Battalion (tank-destroyers)
one platoon of I Battalion, 66th Flak Regiment

At 6:10 A.M., one hour after reaching the assembly area, the infantry moved out from the rail crossing (three kilometers southwest of Kovel) in order to capture the marshy area between the rail crossing and the village of Lubliniec and establish a starting point for the subsequent attack by the tanks and tank-destroyers.

Mühlenkamp had assigned a road scouting detachment from the armored pioneers to assist the infantry; its mission was to locate suitable passages and then guide the tanks through these passable routes. "Infantry Group Quehl" also moved out, and at 7:15 A.M. Major Quehl reported: "Village of Lubliniec is firmly in our hands. Stiff enemy resistance in the forest east of the rail line."

7th Company's attack began at 7 A.M.

"Attention, commander to all commanders: three enemy antitank guns in flanking positions to the west." Untersturmführer Grossrock had been first to spot the enemy. As he had done so often in the past, he had led the way toward the marshy area after the infantry reported that it was in their hands.

The flashes of gunfire from the enemy antitank guns were clearly visible. The leading tanks had already opened fire on these, when suddenly three more antitank guns opened up from the south, in the area of Lubliniec. The Panthers took evasive action and their commanders realized that they could go no farther. The swamp was very close to the land bridge there and to make matters worse one of the tanks drove over a mine. Grossrock radioed for pioneers to come forward. When the pioneer squad arrived it was discovered that the entire intervening ground was infested with enemy troops. Machine-gun fire and bursts from automatic rifles caused the pioneers to immediately take cover.

"The pioneers haven't the slightest chance," declared Grossrock an hour later after he and Untersturmführer Jensen had been ordered to the company commander.

"Maybe we can give them one by forcing the Russians to keep their noses buried in the dirt," interjected Jensen.

"But the rail crossing! If we cross it they'll get us for sure," replied Grossrock.

"We'll fire off smoke shells and drop smoke dischargers as well, then we can slip across unseen," decided Alois Reicher.

The first smoke shells were fired. One of the pioneers positioned smoke dischargers and soon a dense gray cloud of smoke hung over the railway embankment, becoming a dense curtain of smoke that obscured everything.

"1st Platoon cross one at a time and take up supporting fire positions!"

Grossrock set his panzers in motion. They rumbled up the railway embankment. Everyone was alert and tense. Would the enemy see them and open fire? The platoon commander's tank crossed the embankment and rolled another 150 meters east into the saplings, where it took up position.

"Next vehicle follow!" ordered Grossrock.

Once again there was the same tension, which eased only when the second Panther had crossed safely under cover of the wall of smoke. And so the Sixth crossed the railway embankment without being fired at directly. Several random shots were fired by the enemy, however these all fell wide of the mark and caused no damage. However, if Reicher thought that the worst difficulties had been overcome he was soon proved wrong. Progress became increasingly difficult. Enemy artillery opened fire and several Russian antitank guns began finding the range. One of the Panthers got stuck in the swamp and immediately became their target. Then mines began to go off.

"Pioneer squad up! Clear mines from the attack lanes. We'll provide covering fire."

The pioneers came and went to work in the intervening ground. They came under fire from all directions as they cleared the mines. The Panthers opened fire on any enemy movement with their turret and bow machine-guns and occasionally fired high-explosive shells as well. Slowly the attack gained ground. Wherever there was a hold-up Alfred Grossrock appeared to clear away the obstacle and get the attack moving again. The Panthers worked their way forward,exchanging fire with enemy antitank guns, mortar positions and machine-gun squads. The pioneers removed the mines, the tanks took care of enemy opposition. Lubliniec and Dolhonosy, the attack's objectives, moved nearer and nearer. Before the Sixth whole columns of enemy infantry retreated toward the southeast.

"Report from the Gille group, Hauptsturmführer" said the radio operator, handing his commander a message. It read:

"Lubliniec and Dolhonosy have been taken by elements of the 131st Infantry Division."

"This is crazy," called a furious Reicher. "Then who is still shooting the hell out of us from there?"

It later turned out that the villages in question had been taken by the 131st Infantry Division. For example Major Quehl had reached Lubliniec at 7:15 A.M. However, the Soviets later launched a strong counterattack which retook the village. They had outflanked Quehl's force on both sides at the moment that the latter was about to clear the forest east of the rail line.

The spring sun emerged from the clouds and warmed the men, who had now (it was precisely 3 P.M.) moved out of the swamp and were preparing to assault Lubliniec. However seven of 6th Company's tanks were no longer there. They were in the swamp on both sides of the rail line and could not free themselves under their own power. Not until darkness fell would it be possible to pull them out and return them to action.

New orders were received: "Attack on Lubliniec! Advance on a wide front and destroy everything that gets in your way. Break through from the limits of the village straight through the center to the opposite end and trap the enemy!"

The Jensen platoon rolled down the left lane toward the village, assuming the point position in front of the remaining tanks. They approached to within 2,000 meters, then the enemy defensive fire opened up. Muzzle flashes indicated the presence of seven antitank guns in well-camouflaged positions at the outskirts of the village. The tanks returned the fire. In minutes the duel was in full swing and the first village houses caught fire. Trees were felled and mortar rounds sprayed the tanks with steel splinters.

On the right the Grossrock platoon had also reached firing position. When their cannon joined in the enemy fire became noticeably weaker. Hard blows struck the armor of Jensen's command tank, however the driver reported that the vehicle remained driveable. They fired at the enemy, knocking out one gun after another. As the tanks moved closer the Russian troops began to run. Then the first Panther roared into the village. An antitank gun was run over before it could fire again. Then finally they were through and had reached the opposite end of the village.

Reicher dispatched the following message: "Have taken Lubliniec. Seven enemy antitank guns and a number of antitank rifles destroyed. Ready to advance on Hill 191.5 to facilitate passage of our infantry through the forest south of Hill 180.5."

"Sending you 5th Company. It will set off southeast from Lubliniec against Hill 193.3 and take possession of it. Conduct armed reconnaissance to Horodelec."

"Now things are happening Hauptsturmführer," said Untersturmführer Jensen.

"It's about damned time," called out one of the men.

"How about it, Jensen? Reconnaissance to Horodelec with your platoon?"

"I am ready, Hauptsturmführer," replied Jensen immediately.

"Then off you go. It's a long way there."

Reicher pointed to the narrow lane that ran through the forest in the direction of the village in question.

"2nd Platoon form up behind me. Turrets to eleven and one o'clock alternately!" ordered Jensen.

The turrets of the Panthers moved until their guns were pointing ahead to the left and right. Lined up in this way, Jensen's tanks were ready to engage a threat on either flank. Jensen reported that his platoon was departing and the tanks disappeared into the forest.

"We're now heading for Hill 191.5. Panzers advance!"

The tanks moved off. They followed a straight course toward the east, now and then coming under fire from Russian antitank rifle squads. The Panthers cleared the way and quickly forced the enemy back. An half-hour later they were in the assigned positions and from there fired into the flanks of the enemy who was trying to hold up the German infantry with heavy machine-gun and mortar fire. In this way they enabled the infantry to occupy Hill 188.5 and the forest to its south. Meanwhile Standartenführer Mühlenkamp had moved forward his regiment's 8th Company as well as the 2nd Company of the 49th Antitank Battalion and a flak platoon of I Battalion, 64th Flak Regiment and had sent them into positions west of Lubliniec to screen toward the west and southwest.

"All in order, Reicher," Mühlenkamp asked his company commander on reaching his assigned position.

"With us yes, Standartenführer. But I haven't heard anything from Jensen yet."

"If Jensen succeeds in taking Horodelec and barricading the Turja crossing beyond it, 'Operation Ilse' will have been a complete success."

"If only he would send a radio message," said Reicher.

"He would if he had anything to report," answered Mühlenkamp, who could understand his company commander's concern for his 2nd Platoon.

"Get everything ready to recover the stuck vehicles, Reicher."

Mühlenkamp intended the order to take his friend's mind off the whereabouts of his 2nd Platoon.

✠

"Attention, Horodelec ahead! We are going to try and seize it quickly. All tanks follow me in single file. Fire as soon as targets become visible, not before. Forward!"

The tanks advanced, moving faster and faster, and drove toward the village. Two machine-guns opened fire and then a few antitank rifles, but without effect.

"Keep going, don't stop!" called Jensen.

The tanks rumbled on, reached the outskirts of the village and found themselves facing a lone antitank gun.

"Kröte, halt and fire."

The Panther stopped and took aim at the antitank gun. The latter got off a shot which bounced off the German tank's sloping frontal armor. The Panther's long cannon belched fire and the antitank gun was destroyed.

"Onward, onward, onward!"

Driving down the broad village street, the tanks came to a square. From there the tank commanders suddenly saw a long column of trucks with twelve limbered antitank guns. The vehicles were just preparing to drive away toward the Turja crossing.

"Open fire on the first truck!"

The first shell blew off one pair of the truck's wheels and it ground to a halt. Then the tanks drew level with the Russians. Machine-guns rattled and Red Army soldiers leapt at the tanks and tried to knock them out from close range, but the crews defended themselves. Only Rottenführer Lohrer's tank was disabled.

Some time later the remaining antitank gun crews surrendered, and the crew of the disabled Panther stood guard over them while Jensen led the remaining tanks toward the Turja crossing. Before they reached it they came upon the transport column, which had fled in the direction of the river. Jensen rolled left past the column until he had reached the bridge. There he knocked out the first trucks in front of the bridge. The Turja crossing had been barricaded. The soldiers from the Russian column ran toward a wood on the bank of the Turja.

Radio message to the commander: "Jensen platoon has taken Horodelec and barricaded the Turja crossing. 12 antitank guns captured intact."

The operation had been brought to a successful conclusion. No fewer than forty-three heavy antitank guns had been destroyed or captured, as well as six light antitank guns, seven heavy mortars, four infantry guns, eighteen antitank rifles, twenty-eight trucks, three light anti-aircraft guns, twenty-five panye wagons, three tanks and countless small arms. The attack's objective—to destroy the strongpoints needed by the enemy for a further drive into the city—had been achieved.

At eleven the next morning an order was received from the Ia of Battle Group Gille for the units of the Mühlenkamp group to return to Kovel by companies. By approximately 10:30 P.M. all units were back in Kovel and were occupying their former positions. The enemy had suffered serious setbacks which made it painfully obvious that the defenders of Kovel were not a spent force yet.

✠

The 28th of April was a day of rest for all the crews of the tanks of the *Wiking* Regiment. For the first time in weeks they could write a long overdue letter or have a proper bath. But this quiet was short-lived, for the next morning 8th Company was placed on alert. A Soviet assault force had achieved a penetration at the eastern outskirts of Kovel. A strong enemy group with tank support had established itself due east of the dirt road, north of the rail siding, and had gone over to the defensive. Within a few hours the Red Army troops had turned the houses there into proper bunkers. An attempt by German infantry to lance this "festering sore" had failed. The counterattack failed to force the enemy back a single meter and the attackers suffered heavy casualties.

At a staff conference Generalmajor Weber, the commander of the 131st Infantry Division, declared. "Gille, we have to have tanks and assault guns if we're to iron out this penetration."

"You will get them tomorrow morning!" was Gille's reply. Subsequently the "Eighth" and the 1st Company of the *Wiking* Division's 5th Assault Gun Battalion were released and moved forward into an assembly area.

✠

"Your tanks, Oberscharführer Scheel, and the six assault guns will support the four attack groups. That means that each assault group will have one Panther and one assault gun. The remaining Panthers and the two extra assault guns will remain in reserve. They will be committed where massed fire is required. I wish you all good luck," said the general.

The assault group leaders returned to their formations and received the promised tanks and assault guns. It was 6:30 P.M. on 30 April, and in minutes the assault against the enemy penetration would begin.

"Tanks forward!"

Three of the five Panthers of the Scheel platoon rolled forward down the railway road followed by their respective assault groups of infantry. The fourth set off toward the enemy-held tracks and the fifth followed close behind to help engage any recognized enemy positions. Scheel saw muzzle flashes from the cellars of the houses and ordered his crew to open fire.

Panzer grenadiers prepare to mount up.

His tank selected as its target the house on the street corner to the right. It fired two high-explosive rounds into the cellar and the machine-guns fire ceased. Then it fired two armor-piercing rounds through the wall of the second story below the eaves and there, too, the return fire ceased.

The four groups moved forward in steps. Evening twilight was already falling. Two previously unseen antitank guns opened fire. The crews silenced them with machine-gun fire. Enemy tank-killing squads were intercepted by the infantry and wiped out. The battle was an extremely bitterly-fought one. The Soviet strongpoints were overcome only after the last man had been killed or badly wounded. The German assault groups came under machine-gun and automatic rifle fire and were repeatedly forced to take cover. These delays also slowed the pace of the tanks and assault guns and enemy resistance stiffened even more.

Oberscharführer Scheel cursed beneath his breath when he realized that the infantry was no longer providing close-in protection for the tanks. A few seconds later he saw a tank-killing squad approaching one of his own vehicles. Unterscharführer Billerbeck had driven across the tracks and having passed the switchbox was now in an exposed position.

"Radio operator: open fire on the attacking enemy!"

"Target in sight!" replied the radio operator. His MG42 fired short bursts at the other tank and the Russian squad that was about to blow it up.

"Do you know that you're shooting at your own tank?" called Schober furiously.

"We know it," replied Scheel. "But the Russians who want to take you out are already on it."

After a few seconds of silence Schober called back: "Thank you, Fritz!"

After reflecting for a few seconds Scheer ordered: "We're pulling back to the switchbox to rearm."

The five Panthers drove back and replenished their ammunition stocks. When this was done they headed back into the night and went into position abeam the enemy-held tracks. At one in the morning Mühlenkamp and Obersturmführer Nicolussi-Leck went forward to where the tanks were. Scheel and the commanders of the remaining four tanks gathered round to receive their orders.

"Everyone listen to me," said Mühlenkamp. "At 4:20 A.M. our tanks and assault guns will open the attack with a barrage on the bunkers and enemy positions. The tanks will then drive beside the pumphouse and try to reach the entrance to the treed street and the end of the station street in order to take the enemy bulwark from both flanks."

Everything was clear. The crews had three hours to rest before the attack began. Soon all but the men on guard duty were fast asleep.

✠

The tanks and assault guns opened fire promptly at 4:20 A.M. Shells hissed through the pale morning light and smashed into the enemy-held houses and bunkers.

"Maximum rate of fire. Neutralize the machine-gun positions with machine-gun fire so that the infantry can move up and take out the houses," ordered Scheel.

One after another shells crashed into the enemy-occupied houses. This prevented the enemy from returning fire and the German infantry were able to rush forward. They reached the first bunkers and lobbed explosives through the embrasures and back doors. Explosions shook the ground. The Russians fled their holes and came out to surrender. But farther back the next line of strongpoints opened fire and forced the German infantry back into cover.

"Three tanks advance beside the 'enemy tracks' and two beside the pumphouse and open fire."

Oberscharführer Scheel drove forward on the right towards the pumphouse. Unterscharführer Schober took the left flank and rolled across the railway embankment to within 50 meters of the entrance to the tree-lined street. At the same time Scheel reached a position about 50 meters from the end of the station street. Now it all came down to one last dash.

"Platoon commander to all tank commanders: advance and reach departure position."

Scheel had scarcely given the order when heavy artillery fire began falling on the left group of tanks.

Unable to spot any target that he might be able to shoot at, Schober called desperately: "Schober to Scheel: do you see anything? No matter how hard I look I cannot make out the enemy from here!"

"Move forward a bit, then you will see them!" advised Scheel.

"Max, forward thirty meters, until we can see the entrance to the street," Schober instructed his driver.

The 700-horsepower motor, which had been at idle, roared as Max Freinecke moved the tank ahead. After barely twenty meters there were two heavy bangs. A jolt shook the tank and the driver reported: "Have driven over mines. Both tracks gone!"

"Damn and blast!" cursed Schober, "That's all we need!"

"Gunner, stay sharp. Open fire immediately on any recognized target, otherwise they'll take us out here."

Gunner Karlheinz Pötter peered through his sight, its crosshairs pointing in the direction of the enemy. But he could see nothing but the shells which came howling over a shattered wall. They hammered into the railway embankment to the left and right, showering the tank with clumps of debris.

"Disabled with mine damage to both tracks," reported Unterscharführer Schober.

"Continue to screen there in the direction of the poplar street," ordered Oberscharführer Scheel.

Fifteen minutes passed. Twice Schober thought he saw something and ordered Potter to open fire, but each time it was a false alarm. Then, suddenly, heavy artillery fire began falling on the railway embankment.

"They've got wise to us," called radio operator Kersten furiously. Shells exploded and the bursts crept ever nearer to the Panther.

Suddenly the driver called out: "Unterscharführer, I see the observer!"

"Call out the target!"

"House with the open chimney, right beside the round tree, third floor, right window."

"Target in sight!" shouted Holm, and his machine-gun opened fire. He fired four long bursts in succession. From then on the artillery fire became sporadic and no longer reached them.

One at a time the crews picked out various targets and destroyed them. One group of Russian infantry that tried to cross in front of them to attack the tanks and assault guns on the other flank was destroyed with high-explosive shells. Ammunition began to run low, and eventually only Schober could continue to engage targets freely. Then, at exactly 3:30 P.M., a Russian heavy antitank gun which had not been heard from before suddenly opened fire.

The first shell showered the front of the tank with mud and bushes and shook the Panther. The second, fired not twenty seconds later, was a direct hit. It penetrated the armor plate, dislodged the turret and wounded Potter, Meyer and driver Freinecke. Schober and Holms escaped injury. Several of the tank's smoke candles caught fire. The dense smoke threatened to choke the men, but Holm and Schober took advantage of the cover it provided to rescue their wounded comrades from the tank, which otherwise would surely have become their coffin.

Holm climbed back into the tank and managed to get off one last message: "We have been badly hit, have to bail out!"

The reply: "We're sending infantry!"

An infantry assault team came forward and took up covering positions forty meters behind and to the left of the knocked-out Panther. The heavy enemy fire had also made things more difficult for the remaining tanks and assault guns. One tank was so badly hit by artillery fire that it was forced to withdraw. A third Panther was hit and was supposed to be towed into cover behind the pumphouse. But before the Sturmmann could attach the tow cable he was shot in the head and chest and was killed instantly. A fourth tank developed radio trouble. It picked up all the wounded infantry it could find and drove back with them. And finally Oberscharführer Scheel's tank was hit in the turret machine-gun and put out of action.

The two still-serviceable tanks moved into positions from which they could protect the disabled vehicles against infantry attack. When darkness fell German infantry moved up into a trench that had been dug fifty meters in front of the tanks. Under their protection the disabled tanks were recovered by the technical sergeant during the night. The two serviceable tanks were also withdrawn while it was dark. The attempt to eject the enemy from this heavily-defended position had failed. Instead tank 814 had been knocked out by antitank guns and mines and 834 by artillery fire. The platoon suffered casualties of one killed and five wounded.

This supporting attack had shown one thing clearly: the Panther was unsuited to such tasks. It was also apparent that the attack had been doomed to failure by the hesitant advance by the infantry assault groups. Nevertheless, as a result of this operation the enemy did not try to continue his advance, restricting himself instead to improving and fortifying his positions.

✠

It was quiet in Kovel for the next eight days. The enemy's efforts slackened noticeably and there were rumors that the Red Army was preparing a major offensive. The high commands of the armed forces (OKW) and the army (OKH) were convinced that it was going to come in the Kovel-Ternopol area and would thus be directed mainly against Army Group North Ukraine. Following the pitiless and desperate fighting southwest of Kovel during the winter and spring of 1944, intelligence confirmed the buildup of enemy forces opposite Army Group North Ukraine. No one knew that this was an elaborate ruse on the part of the Soviets. They had simulated a massive buildup by running numerous empty trains into this area. As a result, the German command decided to launch a major asault to clear the situation in the Kovel area. The attack, which was proposed by Feldmarschall Model (the commander in chief of Army Group North Ukraine), required the transfer south of significant tank forces from Army Group Center.

In Army Group North Ukraine's sector a total of eight panzer and two panzer-grenadier divisions were supposed to prevent the enemy from breaking through Lvov and Warsaw to Königsberg and cutting off both Army Group North and Army Group Center.

As part of this concentration of forces on 8 May the Panzer Regiment *Wiking* was withdrawn from Fortress Kovel and was moved to Maciejow as corps reserve. At 4:30 P.M. on that May day—exactly one year before the end of the war—Standartenführer Hannes Mühlenkamp reported to the command post of the LVI Panzer Corps. The corps, which was commanded by General Hossbach, had been reduced to the 4th Panzer Division, the 101st Mountain Division and the 26th and 131st Infantry Divisions. The corps' chief of staff, General Staff Oberst von Bonin, explained the situation to Standartenführer Mühlenkamp:

"Mühlenkamp, as your regiment is the armored reserve group I am giving it the job of conducting reconnaissance for counterattacks by the 4th Panzer Division and the 26th, 131st and 342nd Infantry Divisions. You are to scout all the roads thoroughly and establish contact with the named divisions immediately."

The Panzer Regiment *Wiking* had become the "corps fire-brigade."

✠

The Soviet offensive began early on the morning of 22 June 1944. The Germans were taken completely by surprise, for instead of Army Group North Ukraine the attack struck the entire front of Army Group Center.

Thirty-eight German divisions (not one of which was a panzer division) manning an arc-shaped sector of front 1,100 kilometers long faced an onslaught by 185 Russian divisions with approximately 2,500,000 men attacking on a 700-kilometer front. This huge army was spearheaded by 6,100 tanks and self-propelled guns. 45,000 guns began the offensive with a barrage that lasted up to 14 hours. 7,000 Soviet aircraft of all types, including the feared Il-2 "Butchers," supported the attack. Never before had the Russian theater seen such a concentration of men and arms.

Facing this tremendous military force were 500,000 German troops, of whom 400,000 were in defensive positions. At this critical hour Army Group Center lacked the armored divisions which had been transferred to the northern Ukraine. It lacked the heavy weapons which were necessary to halt the Russian steamroller.

✠

At approximately 10 P.M. on 22 June 1944 the decimated II Battalion was handed over to Hauptsturmführer Reicher. At that point in time none of the men were aware of the catastrophe that was taking place to the north of them. All remained quiet in the Kovel area. This was exactly the opposite of what the OKH had predicted. The experts had made a fundamental miscalculation. In no way was Kovel the beginning or the end point of the Soviet offensive.

Bit by bit reports of the catastrophic events of the Russian offensive trickled through to the officers of the Mühlenkamp regiment. When the regiment was then moved into a quartering area west of Kovel and was subordinated to the LVI Panzer Corps again, everyone was convinced that things were going to "get going" there too.

The units moved into their old quartering areas near Maciejow and Tupaly. There followed a time of hectic transfers and subordinations, however the tank crews were unaffected. There were several minor actions in the period until 6 July, but then all hell broke loose in the Kovel area again. The men of the Panzer Regiment *Wiking* were called upon to fight one more battle near Kovel, which would demand the utmost of all of them.

✠

"Gentlemen, the situation of Army Group Center forces us to also withdraw our lines step by step. On 6 July we fall back to the Red Line, one day later to the Green Line, and so on. 'Battle Group Mühlenkamp' will remain in the Kovel area to cover our withdrawal movements until all of the infantry units have gone. Standartenführer Mühlenkamp, your job is to hold the enemy until the infantry has reached the new line and dug itself in." Hannes Mühlenkamp now had a clear picture of the situation. Army Group Center's situation was desperate. On 5 July it had just six infantry divisions left. The huge pocket between Minsk and Baranovichi had been closed and it could be only hours before the last divisions were destroyed.

At 1:15 P.M. II Battalion reported through Obersturmführer Nicolussi-Leck that enemy infantry assembly areas had been located in the Dolhonosy area.

"Place artillery fire on those assembly areas," ordered Mühlenkamp. The few guns available now tried to destroy the enemy positions, but the blows they inflicted on the enemy were little more than fly bites.

Russian bombers flew over the positions and bombed II Battalion's assembly areas. At 2:45 P.M. it was reported to Hauptsturmführer Reicher, the new battalion commander, that the enemy was attacking from the wood northeast of Nowe Koscary with seventeen tanks and infantry.

Just as he was about to issue the order for a company to prepare to head for the threatened area, the entire "Battle Group Mühlenkamp" received the following radio message from LVI Panzer Corps: "The battle group is to transfer into the Smydin area immediately."

That was at 2:50. Ten minutes later the regiment's operations section and II Battalion, Panzer Regiment *Wiking* departed for the assigned area. Two-and-a-half hours later the battle group, which was still corps reserve, readied itself in a wood south of Smydin. The regiment's armored pioneer company received orders to immediately scout bridges and roads for the Panthers. Hauptsturmführer Schliack, the company commander, set to work at once.

While the period of Battle Group Mühlenkamp's preparations had been relatively quiet, during the night of 6 July the sporadic artillery fire intensified all along the front. The first enemy attacks followed, on the left sector of the division's front. At 4:35 A.M. the Division Ia called. He said: "The enemy attacked during the night from the wood northeast of Kruhel towards Kruhel and has broken into the main line of resistance. He is now contnuing to advance south from the eastern outskirts of Kruhel towards the wooded area west of Novy Koscary and has already destroyed two forward antitank guns. There exists the danger that the enemy will advance farther to the west towards Krasnoduby."

The first II Battalion tanks went into action, but it soon became apparent that the enemy was not going to attack on this day, for his tanks only felt their way forward, apparently seeking a weak spot. Further withdrawals followed during the night, but at 4:30 A.M. 7th Company was ordered into the Smydin bridgehead and subordinated to III Battalion, *Germania* Regiment. The rest of the operational Panther battalion took shelter in Maciejow. During this night the enemy artillery fire intensified to near barrage level. Shells howled down on the assembly areas and plowed up the ground. Miraculously only minor damage was done and there were no serious casualties.

A message arrived from the 4th Panzer Division: "Maximum readiness! The enemy will probably soon begin his breakthrough attempt at this spot."

Mühlenkamp passed the word for everyone to remain on defensive alert. Days earlier he had reported an amazing discovery to General Hossbach and his chief of staff: "The terrain facing our front, which is considered too swampy for tanks to cross, has been drying up so much that tanks can drive 100 meters farther every day. A surprise attack must be expected soon."

But Oberst von Bonin, who usually received such information by telephone or telex, obviously did not take the report seriously. On 6 July General Hossbach came and together with Mühlenkamp watched a test drive a Panther. These firsthand investigations and their results were more persuasive than the dissenting views of his chief of staff. In fact the swamps had dried up so much that a general attack by the enemy had to be expected. Furthermore, increasing tank noises had been heard from the forests southwest of Kovel in recent nights. The enemy was believed to be massing strong armored forces there.

"What do you think the enemy will try, Mühlenkamp?" the commanding general asked the battle group commander.

"I expect that the enemy will try to break through to the Bug in the direction of Cholm in one go. That would explain the strong concentration of tanks opposite our front. Afterwards the enemy will try to close the bag around our entire corps."

"Is that your whole supporting argument?"

"Reconnaissance results also clearly point toward it. I must therefore request that I be allowed to redirect my tanks, which might be simply overrun here in the forest positions, to more favorable positions."

"Well, we will see," said General Hossbach. The general drove back to his corps headquarters and only after much back and forth was the order for the requested change of positions issued by the chief of staff, Oberst von Bonin.

Mühlenkamp moved his panzers into the back slope position in the Maciejow area. This was his only chance of stopping the expected armored assault by the enemy. The move was carried out during the afternoon hours of 6 July. Prior to this, however, 8th Company determined that the enemy was massing infantry forces in front of it in the Dolhonosy area.

A heavy air raid struck the German main line of resistance at 12:15 P.M. on 7 July. Heavy bombs fell southeast of the tank assembly area. This had to be the attack!

"Attention, enemy tanks ahead!"

The commander of the Eighth had been the first to spot the 17 heavy tanks and following infantry which had set off from the wood south of Novy Koscary.

"To all tanks: fire at will!"

The first armor-piercing shells were fired at the enemy. Several Russian tanks were disabled with track and roadwheel damage, while others caught fire before they could open fire on the defenders' favorable position. The surviving Soviet tanks pulled back. Then came hundreds of bombers and close-support aircraft. They attacked the positions, but fortunately Mühlenkamp, the consummate chess player, had moved his tanks elsewhere. The attack forced the infantry to take cover. Bombs howled earthward and explosions shook the ground. The "butchers" raked the German positions with cannon and machine-gun fire. The attempt to force a breakthrough was in full swing.

Now the main force of Soviet tanks—more than 400 vehicles—attacked north of Maciejow. Their direction of advance was due west. They rolled past the Panthers of II Battalion waiting in their hull-down positions. The tank commanders and gunners could scarcely believe their eyes when they saw this seemingly endless mass of steel.

"Olin, where are you?" Have you reached your position?" Mühlenkamp called to the Finnish Obersturmführer. The latter had remained with the panzer regiment after the Finnish battalion had returned to the division.

"Olin to commander: have reached the special position, see the tanks, are in good firing range.Request permission for my five Panthers to fire."

"Let the first ten pass by. Then knock out the first and the last, the rest will be stuck."

"As you order, Standartenführer."

Seconds later Mühlenkamp heard and saw the flash of gunfire from the direction of the Finn's position and soon the first Soviet tank was in flames. Thirty seconds later the tenth was knocked out and Olin's Panthers destroyed the rest in succession. The full attention of the Soviet tank units was then directed at Olin, and it was at that moment that Mühlenkamp acted.

"All tanks open fire. Maximum rate of fire, aim carefully!"

The Panthers in the hull-down position fired their 75-mm guns almost simultaneously. After the first salvo the battlefield resembled a huge junk yard. Dozens of enemy tanks lay on the plain, shot-up, burning, ammunition exploding. Then the second salvo went out, inflicting the same devastation and soon fifty of the at least 400 enemy tanks were in flames or disabled wrecks. The Panthers fired for thirty minutes and for thirty minutes the Soviet tanks attempted to escape. They rolled into ravines but were pursued and knocked out. When the sound of battle ebbed, 103 enemy tanks, including some of the newest and heaviest types, lay destroyed on the battlefield.

Mühlenkamp's report of the destruction of 103 enemy tanks appears to have met with disbelief from General Hossbach, for he sent Oberstleutnant Peter Sauerbruch to count the knocked-out tanks on the battlefield. When the officer was finished he had counted—103 wrecks. At least 150 more enemy tanks had been damaged in this duel of armor and had sought shelter in the forests. The regimental commander of one of these units was found in his shot-up tank. Found on him was a situation map, on which was marked the main direction of the Russian tank attack: Kovel-Cholm-Bug!

The Soviet tank units had been ordered to avoid costly battles and instead drive through as quickly as possible and at all costs seize the sole still intact bridge over the Bug, and establish a bridgehead for the infantry on the far side. Had the enemy succeeded in accomplishing this, all of the Hossbach corps and possible even the entire 4th Panzer Army would have been lost. Mühlenkamp had averted this threat with his tactical chess move and had inflicted a severe blow on the enemy. For the second time he had saved Kovel and the German front there. For this feat he was recommended for the Oak Leaves and he was awarded the coveted decoration on 29 September 1944.

The second great defensive success at Kovel was announced in the Wehrmacht communique of 11 July 1944 and the battle group of the *Wiking* Division under Standartenführer Mühlenkamp was identified by name.

Several days later in an interview for German radio, Mühlenkamp revealed the secret of his success: "Standartenführer," they asked him, "your battle group was deployed to cover the withdrawal movements here in the Kovel area. This movement has since been completed with no pressure from the enemy and was also planned without pressure from the enemy. How did you manage to turn this plan into reality?"

"The Soviets appeared here with masses of tanks such as, to my knowledge, had never been seen before. They had new guns and heavier armor. But this battle of a few against many demonstrated the superiority of our new Panther tank. It is especially significant that not one of our tanks became a total loss in this tough battle.

This is due to the bravery and steadfastness of our crews as well as to the quality of our equipment. They are all men who have been with me for years and whose soldierly behaviour and accomplishments are beyond praise. My special thanks go to these brave tank soldiers, and I am glad that I can speak to you at this place once again."

The following members of the Waffen-SS were decorated with the Knight's Cross or a higher grade of this decoration for their actions in the Battle of Kovel:

Knight's Cross with Oak Leaves, Swords and Diamonds:
Herbert Gille, SS-Gruppenführer, on 20/4/1944
Knight's Cross with Swords:
Hans Dorr, SS-Sturmbannführer, on 9/7/1944
Knight's Cross with Oak Leaves:
Johann Mühlenkamp, SS-Standartenführer, on 21/9/1944
Knight's Cross:
SS-Obersturmführer Karl Nicolussi-Leck, on 9/4/1944
SS-Obersturmführer Otto Schneider, on 4/5/1944
SS-Untersturmführer Alfred Grossrock, on 12/8/1944
SS-Sturmbannführer Franz Hack, on 14/5/1944

THE KNIGHT'S CROSS FOR OBERSTURMFÜHRER NICOLUSSI-LECK

At 9:10 on the evening of 1 April 1944 the division commander sent a telex to Sturmbannführer Kment, the Waffen-SS liaison officer in the Army High Command. It was logged as message number 8980. The text of the message read:

> The Division requests the award of the Knight's Cross of the Iron Cross to

SS-Obersturmführer Karl Nicolussi-Leck,
commander of 8th Company, 5th SS Panzer Regiment.
Born on 14/3/1917 in Pfatten.
In present service position since 1/5/1943.
Occupation political officer.
Father's occupation: wine grower.
Decorations received:

25/7/1942:	Iron Cross, 2nd Class
9/8/1942:	Iron Cross, 1st Class
1/9/1942:	Wound Badge in Black
	Wound Badge in Silver
1/9/1942:	Tank Assault Badge

Justification:

Acting on his own initiative and taking advantage of favorable battle and weather conditions, on the morning of 30/3 he led the armored group and handful of infantry under his command in a breakthrough from the existing main line of resistance to the city of Kovel, eight kilometers away, which had been encircled for days. After the determined enemy resistance was broken—during which combat two of 14 attacking tanks were knocked out—and after numerous mine obstacles were cleared, the small battle group reached Kovel thanks to the outstanding bravery and skillful command of Obersturmführer Nicolussi-Leck.

This action brought noticeable relief to the surrounded battle group as it had no antitank weapons. On 31/3 N. succeeded in knocking out 16 enemy tanks in Kovel.

5th SS Panzer Division WIKING
signed REICHER
SS-Standartenführer and acting division commander.
Verified by:
SS-Sturmbannführer and Division Adjutant Schulze.

On 3 April 1944 the Wehrmacht communique declared:

Repeated attacks by the Bolsheviks against the city of Kovel were thwarted by the determined resistance of the defenders. Our troops took several important hill positions in the area north of the city. In the recent days' fighting there SS-Obersturmführer Nicolussi-Leck, company commander in a panzer regiment, and Obergefteriter Pollack of the headquarters of a grenadier regiment have especially distinguished themselves.

As usual the new hero's hometown newspaper and the other organs of the German press were issued a press release describing the capable officer's actions in detail. It was mentioned that at the age of 14 the young officer had "played an active part in the struggle for freedom by the people of the South Tirol" and that in 1934 he had been called to provide political instruction to the German people. The following is Nicolussi-Leck's own account of the decisive days that led to him receiving the coveted Knight's Cross.

How I Won the Knight's Cross

> I received the Knight's Cross at the end of March 1944 for the armored breakthrough to Kovel, a city in the middle of the Pripet Marshes. At that time Kovel was an important rail and road junction. In Kovel there were a number of supply units and more than 2,000 wounded in the hospitals.
>
> When at the end of March 1944 strong Russian armored forces advanced thirty kilometers west of Kovel, reached the city and then infiltrated into the city core, which was defended only by railway workers and other replacement units, Kovel was declared a "fortified place" by Hitler.

SS tankers share a cigarette with army infantry after an operation.

Karl Nicolussi-Leck was given the order to drive through the Russian forces into the city and hold it until the Russian siege ring could be cracked by a counterattack. The breakthrough turned out to be not only time-consuming but costly as well, on account of the strong enemy forces in the city and the treacherous, snow-covered swamps. After ten hours the battle group had only covered half the distance and about a third of the tanks committed had been lost, some stuck in the swamps, some disabled by mines.

Since in this situation the breakthrough to Kovel appeared hopeless to all of his superiors, the battle group commander received orders to withdraw and return to the starting position. Although the radio message was repeated three times, Obersturmführer Nicolussi-Leck did not let his radio operator acknowledge it, for he hoped to make it nevertheless.

> Aware of the desperate, hopeless situation of the surrounded men, with whom I was in radio contact, I continued the breakthrough into the city during the night.
>
> Thanks to heavy snow showers, which concealed us, and the fact that the bridges into the city had not been blown, finally, after an eighteen-hour battle, I was able to reach the city at dawn, although with only half my tanks. My men and I went into position and supported the defense at the most vital positions under Russian attack.
>
> For one whole week we fought under unspeakable hardships against the far superior Russian siege ring and forces which attacked without letup.

A BRIEF OVERVIEW OF NICOLUSSI-LECK'S CAREER

After being wounded and sent to hospital in Germany, Untersturmführer Karl Nicolussi-Leck remained with the division nominally until 1 December 1942, when (as was standard practise) he was transferred to the SS panzer Replacement Training Battalion, where he remained until 25 January 1943. There followed a further transfer to the SS Main Office, where he assumed command of the guard unit. This was intended to allow him to recuperate further before returning to combat duty. He served there until 10 March 1943 and came to know many of the outstanding soldiers of the Waffen-SS, with whom he later stayed in touch.

On 1 May 1943 he assumed command of the newly formed 8th Company of the *Wiking* Division's 5th Panzer Regiment. As company commander he took the unit through its training on the new Panther, forging

8th Company into a tightly-knit unit. This would later pay off in numerous critical situations. After the intensive training and the formation of the 5th SS Panzer Regiment under Johannes Rudolf Mühlenkamp, he had to complete a chemical weapons course at Celle from 8 to 12 November before he was allowed to go home on leave. His marriage took place on 25 January 1944. His daughter Reinhilde had already been born on 21 October 1943.

Since 9 November Karl Nicolussi-Leck had been an Obersturmführer and at the end of January 1944 the time came for the regiment to transfer to the front and join the rest of the division. Departure was delayed by several weeks as the company was not yet 100% equipped. It was March 1944 before the 8th Company left by fast train for the Eastern Front. The front was ablaze and the *Wiking* Division had drawn a special assignment: to strike the blow that would free the enemy-encircled city of Kovel.

The Division Commander: SS-Obergruppenführer Herbert Gille

On 12 March 1944 SS-Gruppenführer Herbert Gille received the order by telephone from Führer Headquarters to go with his division to Kovel. The city, one of the most important rail juctions in White Russia, had to be held against the Red Army. When the order reached Gille German forces in and around Kovel consisted only of the 17th SS Cavalry Regiment, a regional defense regiment, an SS police regiment, a pioneer battalion, a light artillery battalion with six guns, a delousing unit and approximately 300 older railway workers. All in all it was about 4,500 men.

In overall command of this motley force, which had no combat experience, was the leader of the German anti-partisan units, Obergruppenführer von dem Bach-Zelewski. He had to be flown out of the city on account of illness. Gruppenführer Gille was to take over in his place. He expressed serious reservations in Berlin and Führer Headquarters and to the chief of staff of the army about his battle-weary division being sent into combat again so soon. Nevertheless Gille also saw that they could not simply abandon the soldiers in Kovel to their fate.

Beginning on 16 March his division's still weak *Germania* and *Westland* Regiments departed for Kovel, however they did not get through. At his initial briefing Gille learned that four Soviet divisions had by now encircled the city. The resulting pocket, just three kilometers wide and two long, was very small. The four Soviet rifle divisions on the outside were bolstered by several tank regiments. Herbert Gille had no intention of commanding from outside the pocket, and so he and Hauptsturmführer Westphal flew into Kovel in a Fieseler Storch. It was his way of letting the surrounded troops know: "We will do it! We will all get out of here!"

As a result of a special initiative surgeons and assistants flew into the beleaguered city with medical supplies. In spite of enemy flak and fighters the Luftwaffe's KG 55 flew 270 tons of supplies into the city in 255 missions. The first unit to come from the Reich was 8th Company, 5th SS Panzer Regiment, which arrived outside Kovel with 16 Panthers. This company was supposed to drive through to Kovel, which it did.

In July 1944 Gille was named commanding general of the IV SS Panzer Corps. On 10 August, on the order of Generalfeldmarschall Model, the corps headquarters, whose formation was still incomplete, was placed in command of the 3rd SS Panzer Division "Totenkopf" and the 5th SS Panzer Division *Wiking*. Both units were engaged in fierce defensive fighting in the Siedlce and Brest-Litovsk areas.

Gille's military career began in 1911 when he joined the Bensberg Cadet Corps. Three years later he was transferred to the main cadet academy in Berlin-Lichterfelde. On 1 September 1914 Fähnrich Gille was transferred to the 2nd Baden Field Artillery Regiment 30 in Rastatt and eight weeks later he went into the field with Reserve Field Artillery Regiment 55 of the 75th Reserve Division. Gille was promoted to Leutnant on 27 January 1915. He served as a platoon and battery commander and received both Iron Crosses.

After the war Gille studied agriculture and served as an administrator and inspector on several estates. On 20 March 1934 Herbert Gille was accepted into the SS-Verfügungstruppe as an Obersturmführer and served with the 19th Machine-gun Company at Ellwangen. On 15 February 1937 he took over II Battalion of the SS-Standarte *Germania* at Arolsen. Beginning in May 1939 he was charged with the formation of the first artillery regiment of the Waffen-SS. Gille commanded a battalion of this regiment through the campaign against Poland and added the bar to both Iron Crosses.

Gille also served as a battalion commander in the SS-Verfügungstruppe during the western campaign of 1940. From this unit would soon emerge the *Das Reich* Division. With the formation of the 5th SS Divison *Wiking* by Felix Steiner, Gille was placed in charge of forming the division's 5th Artillery Regiment. In June 1941 the division, and with it the 5th SS Artillery Regiment *Wiking*, went into action in the campaign against Russia. After numerous feats of personal bravery, on 28 February 1942 Herbert Gille was awarded the German Cross in Gold.

After months of defensive fighting at the Mius River, in spring 1942 the Wehrmacht launched a new offensive to the south and east. The *Wiking* Division and the 13th Panzer Division under Generalmajor Herr advanced on Rostov. The troops crossed the Don and continued south. Several cities fell to their rapid advance, until the Kuban was reached. One of the leaders of this operation was SS-Oberführer Gille, who received the Knight's Cross for his efforts.

In May 1943 Gruppenführer Steiner had to leave his division to take over the III (Germanic) SS Panzer Corps. In his place Herbert Gille was named division commander. At that time the division was on the defensive at the Donets and near Izyum. The "Vikings" were facing a vastly superior foe and were often left on their own in small groups. They constantly formed the rear guard and when the soldiers heard "The Vikings are holding!" they knew that they would not be encircled or outflanked. This steadfast division was the last to reach the Dniepr.

On 1 November 1943 Brigadeführer Gille became the 315th German soldier to receive the Knight's Cross with Oak Leaves. When he read the telex he blurted out impulsively: "I am pleased that the feats of my Vikings have been recognized in this way!"

Gille had risen from leader of an artillery unit to commander of a division and had matured into a strategist and above all an exemplary soldier. His division once again formed the rear guard when the time came to evacuate the city of Kharkov. In the Cherkassy Pocket his division fought at the critical points of Seblov and Olshana. It fought shoulder to shoulder with the men of the Belgian volunteer brigade *Wallonien* and those of the German Army. The battle went on for two weeks before the troops inside the pocket received the order to break out toward the relief force attacking from outside. The "old man" marched along with his troops, his unmistakable walking stick pointing the way. With them he swam the ice-cold, raging Gniloi-Tikich.

Immediately after fighting his way to freedom Gruppenführer Gille was ordered to Führer Headquarters. After listening to his account Hitler spontaneously awarded him the Knight's Cross with Oak Leaves and Swords. Hauptsturmführer Leon Degrelle, who had accompanied Gille, received the Knight's Cross for his actions and that of the *Wallonien* Brigade.

The *Wiking* Division assembled behind the III Panzer Corps's front to rest and refit. The entire division had 350 infantrymen and 50 submachine-guns but no vehicles or equipment. New units, such as II Battalion, 5th Panzer Regiment, were training and equipping with new weapons in the Reich. II Battalion was issued the new Panther tank. The *Wiking* Division was reorganized following the dramatic Battle of Kovel. It reequipped and trained at the Heidelager training grounds in Poland, and on 30 June the division was once again at full strength with 17,368 men.

In July 1944 Gille was named commanding general of the IV SS Panzer Corps. During the defensive battles for Warsaw the corps held its positions stubbornly. It subsequently fought in the Modlin area. On 9 November 1944 Herbert Gille was promoted to SS-Obergruppenführer. He received instructions from the OKW to immediately take his corps to Hungary in order to relieve the besieged garrison of Budapest.

On 1 January 1945 the corps attacked through the Vertes Mountains. After initial success the attack had to be called off on 9 January. The corps was withdrawn and ordered to attack on the extreme wing through the Pilis Mountains. The attack began on the evening of 10 January. It, too, made good initial progress, however the army called it to a halt 20 kilometers short of its objective. The army group planned to start a new offensive from the area north of Lake Balaton. This attack began on 18 January 1945. Strong Soviet armored forces drove into the flank of Gille's corps and there was a major tank battle near Pettend. Two-hundred enemy tanks were destroyed and the front was preserved, although the positions won could not be held.

Budapest fell on 12 February 1945. The battle in Hungary became a retreat to avoid Soviet encirclement. The *Wiking* Division was surrounded near Stuhlweissenburg. The breakout succeeded thanks to the "Hohenstaufen" Division, which had held its position on the north side of Lake Balaton in spite of the order to retreat. The division fell back through Steinamanger into Steiermark and the last big defensive battles were fought near Graz.

Obergruppenführer Gille was captured by the Americans near Rastadt. He was taken to Salzburg prison. All of his decorations were stolen in Augsburg. Because of his membership in the Waffen-SS, Gille was sentenced to eighteen months in prison. Finally, on 21 May 1948, he was released to his family. Herbert Gille died of heart failure on 26 December 1966 in Stemmen near Hanover. More than 800 former comrades from all European nations accompanied the general to his final resting place. Former Oberführer Karl Ullrich, the last commander of the *Wiking* Division, spoke the eulogy at the graveside of this unforgettable soldier.

The Commander of the 5th SS Panzer Regiment: Standartenführer Johannes Rudolf Mühlenkamp

Johannes Rudolf Mühlenkamp, the commander of the *Wiking* Division's Panzer Regiment, which had carried out the breakthrough to Kovel, had been born in Metz-Moligny on 9 October 1910. He entered the Wehrmacht after completing his schooling and even as a young officer he proved to be an outstanding trainer of his men.

Mühlenkamp saw action in Poland, first as a platoon commander and later as commander of the 15th Motorcycle Company of the *Germania* Standarte. He was one of the first members of the Waffen-SS to win both Iron Crosses. In the western campaign he continued to lead his 15th Company, which often formed the advance guard. For several weeks he served as adjutant under "Papa" Hausser before he took command of the reconnaissance battalion of the *Das Reich* Division.

In the Balkans campaign Mühlenkamp led his battalion in several daring exploits. It was there that he first demonstrated his affinity for mobile, armored warfare, and it was a sure bet that when the Waffen-SS acquired armored units he would be one of the leaders.

When the invasion of the Soviet Union began, Mühlenkamp held the rank of Sturmbannführer. Leading his reconnaissance battalion, he was always up front, in direct contact with the enemy. Mühlenkamp often drove deep into hostile territory to scout the terrain, and on one such occasion he was seriously wounded in a Soviet mortar barrage.

Mühlenkamp was back within a few months. While still in hospital he became one of the first recipients of the German Cross in Gold. While there he was also informed that when he was released he was to form the first panzer battalion of the Waffen-SS. The battalion, originally slated for the *Das Reich* Division, was assigned instead to the *Wiking* Division.

In summer of 1942 the battalion stormed southeast through Rostov into the Caucasus. Rostov was a high point for Mühlenkamp and his men, who tipped the balance in Germany's favor. In recognition of this, on 3 September 1942 he was awarded the Knight's Cross. Mühlenkamp led his battalion until March 1943, when it was expanded into a regiment.

Mühlenkamp assumed command of the *Wiking* Division in July 1944. When on 8 July 1944 the enemy attacked with ten rifle divisions, which were soon joined by a tank corps with three tank brigades, Mühlenkamp succeeded in holding the front together with the 26th and 342nd Infantry Divisions. His flexible method of command, always at the front so as to be able to react to changing situations, enabled the 5th Panzer Regiment to score a major victory over the enemy, destroying more than 100 enemy tanks. Johannes Rudolf Mühlenkamp personally took part in this action from a command tank. Thanks to his determined efforts the main line of resistance was held. On 11 July the SS Panzer Division *Wiking* was named in the Wehrmacht communique "because of its exceptional steadfastness under the command of Obersturmbannführer Mühlenkamp."

During the battles between the rivers Vistula and Bug, attacking enemy forces were once again savaged by the 5th SS Panzer Division. The Red

Army's surprise drive on Warsaw was beaten back. During the fighting, which lasted from 4 August until 3 September 1944, the "Vikings" destroyed or captured 151 enemy tanks, 19 assault guns, 13 self-propelled guns and armored cars, 176 artillery pieces, 94 machine-guns and antitank rifles and five aircraft. Standartenführer Mühlenkamp's forces fought successfully against overwhelming odds, and while serving as acting commander of the *Wiking* Division, on 21 September 1944 he was awarded the Knight's Cross with Oak Leaves. Mühlenkamp remained as leader of the *Wiking* Division until 9 October.

From January until 5 February 1945 he led the 32nd SS Panzer-Grenadier Division "30th January," which was still in the process of being formed. As well he was named Waffen-SS Inspector of Armored Troops in the SS Operational Headquarters. Until the end of the war Mühlenkamp worked tirelessly to provide the hard-pressed divisions of the Waffen SS with the panzers they needed. In Berlin he achieved some success in representing the interests of the Waffen-SS and thus helped his comrades at the front.

Johannes-Rudolf Mühlenkamp died at Goslar on 23 September 1986.

Sturmbannführer Franz Hack: With the 3rd Battalion *Germania* at Kovel

When the Soviets acquired a hill position from which they could threaten the supply road to Kovel, Sturmbannführer Franz Hack carried out a night attack. His two assault teams, consisting of volunteers from his battalion, worked their way close to the first strongpoint then attacked simultaneously and overwhelmed the enemy. A second strongpoint was taken from the Russians in hand-to-hand fighting, after which his battalion, which was waiting nearby, moved forward and captured the entire hill. For this daring action Franz Hack was awarded the Knight's Cross on 14 May 1944.

Born the son of an innkeeper in Mannheim on 3 February 1915, after completing his schooling Hack joined the SS-Verfügungstruppe on 1 October 1934. After completing the second course at the SS-Junkerschule at Bad Tölz, on 20 May 1936 he was promoted to Untersturmführer.

Hack took part in the western campaign as a member of the *Germania* Regiment, winning both Iron Crosses. He took part in all the *Wiking* Division's operations in the east, where he was wounded no less than ten times! On 18 April 1945, now an SS-Obersturmbannführer and commander of his division's 10th SS Panzer-Grenadier Regiment *Westland*, he was awarded the Knight's Cross with Oak Leaves. On 8 May 1945 he was taken prisoner by the Americans near Mauterndorf in Austria.

SUPPORTING ATTACK BY THE SCHNEIDER COMPANY

After the 5th SS Panzer Regiment's 8th Company had broken through to Kovel and joined the city's defenses, the newly-formed 7th Company under the command of Obersturmführer Otto Schneider also arrived in the Kovel battle zone. With its potent new Panther tanks, the company represented a welcome addition to the *Wiking* battle group, which together with the 131st Infantry Division and the 4th and 5th Panzer Divisions ultimately attacked and liberated the city of Kovel. Consequently Obersturmführer Schneider was worthy to join the ranks of the fighting men who had distinguished themselves at Kovel.

On 4 May Schneider received the Knight's Cross for his efforts. The most sincere congratulations came from his comrade Nicolussi-Leck, who knew very well the difficulties of going into battle with brand-new tanks.

With the war over, in May 1945 Schneider and a group of his men tried to slip through the American lines. There was an exchange of fire in a forest and Schneider and the others took cover. He must have been fatally wounded, for he was not seen again. It seems certain that Schneider was killed there.

Between Kovel and the Home Front

The reorganization of *Wiking* from an SS panzer grenadier division into an SS panzer division began in November 1943. This resulted in the expansion of the former 5th Panzer Battalion into the 5th Panzer Regiment, still under the command of Sturmbannführer Mühlenkamp.

The conclusion of the fighting at Kovel and the awarding of the Diamonds to the division commander did not result in the "Vikings" being withdrawn from combat. On 24 April Amored Battle Group Mühlenkamp, which consisted of Headquarters, 5th Panzer Regiment, the regiment's II Battalion with the 5th, 6th and 8th Companies, a pioneer company, an army antitank company and II Battalion of the 434th Infantry Regiment, attacked the Lubliniec hills. In this action Nicolussi-Leck's company, which had been brought partially back up to strength, succeeded in destroying a number of artillery pieces and antitank guns as well as one enemy tank. The battle group's total at the end of the day was 51 antitank guns, eight artillery pieces and three tanks. The Turja was reached 10 kilometers south of Kovel and was barricaded near Korodelec. This success enabled the defensive positions around Kovel to be pushed approximately 10 kilometers beyond the city to the southeast and northwest, relieving it from its close encirclement.

Although its I Battalion was absent, the panzer regiment, bolstered by III (Armored) Battalion, *Germania* and subordinated to the LVI Panzer

Corps, participated in the fierce fighting during the tank battle near Maciejow. Standartenführer Mühlenkamp suggested to the corps' commanding officer, Generalleutnant Hossbach, that he position his tanks in cover in the Maciejow area in such a way that he could intercept an enemy tank attack from the area north of the Kovel-Lublin rail line and smash it. Hossbach agreed.

But first, however, at about noon on 6 July 1944 the Soviets attacked near Novy Koscary with seventeen T-34s and mounted infantry. Out of a bright, clear sky enemy artillery suddenly fell and soon afterwards swarms of Soviet aircraft began strafing ground targets. Several minutes later the sound of tanks was heard and three T-34s suddenly appeared. They were knocked out, one by Mühlenkamp's command tank.

II Battalion was placed on alert one minute later and was soon ready and waiting in good cover. Obersturmführer Olin of the Nicolussi-Leck company had led several Panthers to a good position. He allowed ten enemy tanks to pass, knocked out the first and the last, and then destroyed the rest.

The following Russian tanks oriented themselves on the wrong side and Obersturmführer Nicolussi-Leck brought his battalion into a favorable position. The first two salvoes from the guns of the Panthers accounted for fifty enemy tanks. When the one-sided battle was over the plain was littered with the blazing, smoking hulks of T-34s. 103 knocked-out enemy tanks were counted on the battlefield. The Wehrmacht communique of 11 July 1944 has this to say about the tank battle: "The 342nd Infantry Division from the Rhine-Moselle area under the command of Generalmajor Nickel, the 26th Infantry Division from Rhineland-Westphalia under the command of Oberst Frommberger and a battle group of the 5th SS Panzer Division *Wiking* under the command of SS-Standartenführer Mühlenkamp have distinguished themselves through their exemplary steadfastness."

Johannes-Rudolf Mühlenkamp was awarded the Knight's Cross with Oak Leaves for this outstanding feat of arms.

One of the superbly-trained men under Nicolussi-Leck was Oberscharführer Alfred Grossrock, platoon commander in II Battalion's 6th Company. He and his platoon alone destroyed 26 enemy tanks. This, together with his previous successes, resulted in Grossrock being recommended for the Knight's Cross, which he received on 12 August 1944.

The battalion did suffer some painful losses, however. II Battalion, 5th Panzer Regiment was withdrawn from the 4th Panzer Army's front and Standartenführer Mühlenkamp moved the core of his regiment and the entire *Wiking* Division into the Bialystok area in order to halt enemy forces that had broken out of the Polish lowlands to the west and northwest.

It was there that I Battalion rejoined the regiment. Under Hauptsturmführer Säumenicht this fresh battalion engaged the enemy south of the Lesna and in a short, sharp tank-versus-tank duels halted him until II Battalion also arrived with its Panthers and destroyed the enemy.

Bitter fighting took place in the Warsaw area in July and August 1944 and Obersturmführer Nicolussi-Leck was wounded again. On 25 August his old 8th Company had to fight another difficult battle. Following the defeat of 20 August, the Red Army attacked in the Bug bridgehead near Laskow and Kochovo, once again following a heavy artillery barrage. II Battalion, 5th Panzer Regiment destroyed another 15 Soviet tanks in this action. On the 25th a shell fired by a Russian tank scored a direct hit on a demolition charge on the Bug bridge, setting it off and bringing down the structure. As there was no ford, the panzer regiment's I Battalion had to attack west of Cernow in order to establish a bridgehead. In the fighting that ensued there the commander of I Battalion, Hauptsturmführer Säumenicht, was killed. The bridgehead was lost. The crews of I Battalion had to blow up their 12 still serviceable tanks and then cross the river over the remains of the blown bridge.

On this day 8th Company succeeded in destroying five Sherman tanks and several T-34s. Tank commander Unterscharführer Tausend of the Eighth alone accounted for eight enemy tanks.

Obersturmführer Olin also went into action again, destroying eleven enemy tanks near Male on 6 September. Nicolussi-Leck later said: "My good friend and comrade Olin had deserved the Knight's Cross for a long time. But finally there was no question that he should have received it. Why he did not is simply incomprehensible, for in addition to a number of antitank guns, he had already destroyed 25 to 30 enemy tanks. A soldier like him was deserving of these victor's laurels." On 7 September 1944 Standartenführer Mühlenkamp issued an order of the day in which he announced the 500th tank "kill" by his regiment. On 9 October 1944 Standartenführer Karl Ullrich took over command of the *Wiking* Division. He came from the "Totenkopf" Division, where he had served as pioneer commander and regimental commander for a long time. Ullrich already wore the Oak Leaves and was to lead the division until the bitter end.

Christmas 1944 found the *Wiking* Division northeast of Warsaw after hard and costly fighting. The division had been given several days of rest. Obersturmführer Nicolussi-Leck had returned; he had been placed in command of II Battalion and had the unit firmly in hand. At approximately 9 P.M. the telephone rang in the division command post. The O1, Obersturmführer Schönfelder, picked up the receiver. The call was from "above" and said that the IV SS Panzer Corps and its cadre divisions, *Totenkopf* and

Wiking, had to transfer into the Komarom-Raab area of Hungary immediately. Its mission was to relieve the soldiers of the IX SS Corps under Obergruppenführer von Pfeffer-Wildenbruch surrounded in Budapest. Instructions to move the two Waffen-SS divisions had been issued by Hitler personally. The Führer was determined to free Budapest at all costs.

The headquarters of the *Wiking* Division reached Raab on 1 January 1945 and by 6 P.M. the entire division had arrived in Hungary. The next morning the 5th Panzer Regiment, commanded by Obersturmbannführer Darges, attacked along the Tata-Felsögalla road, while II Battalion. *Germania* assaulted the village of Agostian. By 5 January the division reached Bicske, west of Budapest. But Bicske held. A tank battle developed near the Hegyks estate. Twenty enemy tanks came upon Obersturmführer Nicolussi-Leck's Panthers, resulting in a short, sharp engagement. The leading Soviet tank took a direct hit and lost its turret. Two more followed and the surviving enemy tanks turned tail and fled, some of them hit and smoking.

The first direct Soviet assault on the castle began shortly before midnight. All tanks maintained their maximum rate of fire. The attack was beaten off at the castle walls by hand grenades and bursts of submachinegun fire. The tanks of II Battalion attacked repeatedly, until they were each down to their last three high-explosive shells. In front of the walls approximately 20 enemy tanks tried to force a breach in the defense lines. An

Nicolussi-Leck (center) poses in front of his Panther with two of his crew. Note the three different uniforms worn within a single crew.

armored convoy arrived at one hour after midnight. It brought ammunition, fuel and food. The troops defending the castle held out for days in spite of being outnumbered ten or twenty to one. Nevertheless it was apparent that the first relief attempt had failed. Within five days the IV SS Panzer Corps had destroyed 79 enemy tanks, 160 artillery pieces and 107 antitank guns, but the Red Army seemed to have inexhaustible reserves.

On 9 January the "Vikings" were relieved and moved into the Estergom area in preparation for a second relief attempt which began at 1 A.M. on 10 January. By the 12th the leading elements of the *Wiking* Division were within twenty-one kilometers of Budapest. Everyone, including Nicolussi-Leck, was confident that they would be in Budapest in another day. They could already see the tall church spires of the city. Enemy resistance was decreasing but then something inexplicable happened. It was precisely 8 P.M. on 12 January 1945 when General Gille received the order to halt the attack and pull back his panzer corps. The general argued that they could still do it, but in vain; the army group insisted that the order be carried out. The division fell back, and on 12 January it drove to Veszprem. A third relief attempt was now to begin from the Stuhlweissenburg area, for which the 3rd Panzer Division under Generalmajor Söth was placed under the IV SS Panzer Corps's command.

The attack began on 18 January. The next day the spearhead of the *Wiking* Division was cut off in the Sarosd area. The enemy occupied the town temporarily but was thrown out again. Nevertheless that Sunday, 21 January 1945, became a day of disaster, the climax of which was the death of several officers of the *Wiking* Division as a result of a direct hit from an enemy antitank gun. The commander of the *Germania* Regiment, Obersturmbannführer Hans Dorr was wounded in his command post, where a division briefing was being held. He died of his wounds in April 1945.

Stuhlweisenburg was captured and the watchword now was: "On to Budapest!"

On 23 January the "Vikings" reached the Danube near Adony, but by the 29th the situation of the German troops had become critical and the end in Budapest was near. On the morning of 29 January, just as the *Wiking* Division was about to attack, the Red Army launched its own attack spearheaded by a tank corps with about 180 vehicles. The drive on Budapest had to be abandoned in order to preserve the cohesion of the German units. On 30 January the *Wiking* Division had just 14 tanks. On 1 February it had to leave its positions on the Danube and withdraw to the west. The division conducted a fighting withdrawal under heavy pressure from the enemy and by 15 February reached Falubattian.

The surviving garrison of Budapest broke out on 12 February 1945. Only 785 men escaped and made it to the German lines on 13 February. In this situation Obersturmführer Nicolussi-Leck was given a new mission. It took him to Germany, which meant that he experienced the final phase of the struggle in battle against the British and Americans in northern Germany.

BATTLE GROUP NICOLUSSI-LECK IN ACTION IN GERMANY

The *Wiking* Division's operations in Hungary had been extremely costly in terms of personnel, especially in armored vehicles, and the unit urgently required replacements. Standartenführer Ullrich, who led the division with great courage and inspiration, ordered a collection detachment to Germany, for that was the only way to speed up the delivery of the new tanks to the front. The detachment, consisting of 150 selected tank soldiers under the command of Obersturmführer Nicolussi-Leck, set off from Györ in Hungary. Nicolussi-Leck, who had been wounded a fifth time in Hungary, knew what was at stake.

The detachment disembarked at Hesselteich near Gütersloh. From there it was supposed to go to Paderborn to collect the tanks. As there was no way of getting from Hesselteich to Paderborn with 150 troops, "Nico" ordered the Finnish Obersturmführer Ola Olin to take 30 men to Harsewinkel in order to investigate the possibility of transport from there to Paderborn.

Obersturmführer Olin reached Harsewinkel at the same time as the first tank units of the US 5th Armored Division. The enemy opened fire on the small group, resulting in casualties. Olin withdrew with his remaining men via Versmold and Melle to Lübbecke.

The group from the Nicolussi-Leck battalion, with no tanks or heavy weapons and armed only with pistols, departed. In Lübbecke the Olin group requisitioned several wood-gas powered trucks and drove back to the main group. The armored battle group without tanks then drove in these and other vehicles to Minden, arriving there on 4 April. Part of Minden was already occupied by the enemy, in this case British units. One of the bridges over the Weser-Ems Canal had not been blown yet. Oberst Wiese, the commander of the Weser crossings, had pushed for the crossings to be destroyed in good time, but the mayor of Minden, Dr. Holle, was against it.

When the soldiers of the British 6th Airborne Division appeared before the bridge, Obersturmführer Olin was in the loft of a house with a rifle equipped with a telescopic sight. He hoped to be able to spot the explosive charges and set them off with several shots from the rifle. Through his telescopic sight Olin saw the British (whose red berets identified them as paratroopers) proceeding toward a house only a few dozen meters from the other end of the bridge. He took aim at the officer in charge of the group. The latter walked up to an old woman who was standing in front of the house at the bridge, weeping bitterly. Olin had the British officer's head in his crosshairs, the range was only 100 to 120 meters. But then he carefully stroked both of her cheeks and Olin lowered the weapon. In his words: "Who could have shot after seeing that?"

A little later a Wehrmacht truck appeared followed closely by a Panzer IV. The tank had been taken over by British soldiers, who shot up the truck with high-explosive shells. Now the truck's driver and co-driver lay dying on the street. Olin's men, who had rounded up some panzerfausts, knocked the tank out with one shot. The Panzer IV went up in flames, taking the five British soldiers with it.

The next day the collection detachment, still without tanks, drove through Bückeburg. When the local population told them there was a vehicle depot nearby, Nicolussi-Leck called a halt. There they found thirteen serviceable armored troop carriers, two of which were armed with 20-mm cannon. This was the first assistance they had been able to secure. On 6 April Nicolussi-Leck's group drove through Hanover in the vehicles. Orders were received by radio for the group to go into action, along with assessments of the situation and information on the position of the enemy. The battle group's orders read:

"Strike hard and fast, disengage quickly from the enemy who has at least a tenfold superiority in numbers and arms. Mobility is the watchword of action and survival.

Attempt to establish and maintain constant contact with neighboring battle groups."

But these were just empty slogans, for this tiny battle group's flanks were completely open to the north and south. The drive through Hanover was one great triumphal march. A member of the Nicolussi-Leck group remembered:

"The queues of people standing in front of the few still-intact stores waved to us and cheered. We almost believed that we had won the war."

The men of the Waffen-SS found Hanover a great desert of rubble. Approximately 80% of all the houses had been destroyed and approximately 5,000 dead lay buried under the rubble. At least 250,000 people had been rendered homeless and most had to be fed from makeshift kitchens. Some of the homeless lived in the city's fifty large air raid shelters. Since the first major air raid on Hanover on 26 July 1943 the city had been attacked thirteen times, the last taking place on 28 March 1945. A total of 30,000 tons of bombs had fallen on Hanover. Nevertheless the armaments factories there had continued to operate at full capacity. Not until 28 March did the Allied air forces succeed in hitting the Conti rubber company and the Misburg oil refinery.

In command of the city and armed forces of Hanover was Generalmajor Paul Loehning. He had earlier served as military commandant of Stalingrad, Kharkov, Poltava and other towns and since the summer of 1943 he had resided in the Frederick Castle on Waterloo Square. A battalion of 700 convalescents and 400 firemen had been placed under his command for the defense of the city. On paper there were 25 Volkssturm battalions, however none existed in fact. The 25th Flak Regiment commanded by Oberstleutnant Wilhelm-Gerhard Röttger was the only unit with any significant firepower, with more than 258 guns in the Hanover area. With these he had succeeded in shooting down every tenth aircraft that attacked Hanover. Now his 88-mm and 105-mm guns were to be used in a ground role. However the crews of the various flak batteries were not made up of trained flak soldiers; instead they consisted mainly of students from the city's high schools, Soviet auxiliaries and a core of experienced flak personnel. The telephone exchanges, range-finders and searchlights were for the most part manned by women and girls from Hanover serving as flak and signals auxiliaries.

When Hauptsturmführer Nicolussi-Leck rolled through the city with his 13 armored troop carriers, the city commandant left the Frederick Castle and set up his command post in the bunker of the Gau command post. Nicolussi-Leck reported to him and received orders to go into position along Reichstrasse 6 northwest of Stöcken at 6 A.M. the next morning and from there watch over the Reichsautobahn and the bridge over the Weser-Elbe canal.

After spending the night in the Prince Albert barracks, the next morning the "Vikings" drove into the Berenbostel area, where they took up position between the local brickworks and the former Marieenwerder national forest. The US 84th Infantry Division was expected to attack from the west.

Two attacks by American troops were beaten off on this day. The defenders knocked out a number of enemy tanks with panzerfaust antitank weapons, including one by the Hauptsturmführer. Once again the men around Nicolussi-Leck demonstrated their iron nerve, allowing the enemy tanks to approach to forty to fifty meters before firing a lethal shot.

On the morning of 8 April Nicolussi-Leck learned from an employee of the Hanomag firm that there were several serviceable tanks on the factory grounds. Hauptsturmführer Nicolussi-Leck immediately put together several tank crews and sent them there. When they arrived at the factory the men could scarcely believe their eyes, for sitting there were seven brand-new Jagdpanther tank-destroyers, a pre-production batch with an 88-mm gun in a fixed superstructure on a Panther chassis. There was also a recovery tank.

One of the men remembered: "We took charge of the vehicles, fueled them and made them ready to go, signed the acceptance slips and immediately drove away in these potent tank destroyers."

Before the tanks could be used in combat, the crews had to collect ammunition and gunsights from Scheue near Celle. This was done one hour later, and large quantities of fuel were also found there. The battle group had transformed itself into a beast of prey, ready to strike. The guns were test fired in the afternoon and proved to be deadly accurate. After the sights had been adjusted, the test shots fired from 1500 meters were dead on target. Nicolussi-Leck's battle group was the only mobile panzer unit in the Hanover area.

Nicolussi-Leck said, "We occupied carefully chosen positions in the south, as a massed enemy attack with tanks was expected from the Hildesheim area."

The attack against Hanover began a short time later from Bad Nenndorf, headquarters of the US 84th Infantry Division under Major-General Alexander R. Bolling. In addition to the 15,300 men of his division, Bolling could call upon the 771st Armored Battalion, which had 53 tanks. On the morning of 8 April the point units of the 84th Division were near Weetzen. According to his diary entries, Major-General Bolling intended to advance along the Reichstrassen (present-day Bundesstrassen 65, 217 and 3).

The attack planned for the early morning of 9 April did not take place, because a prisoner had stated that there were German antitank guns near Hemmingen, which was in the planned attack zone. That seemed too great a threat. The attack force was reorganized and the next morning, bolstered by the addition of M-10 tank destroyers and tanks, the 334th Regiment attacked from Engelbostel. The 335th Regiment attacked simultaneously from Kirchwehren. The two flak batteries stationed near Dedensen and Lathwehren fought until their ammunition was gone, then they wrecked their guns. The anti-aircraft guns under Oberstleutnant Röttger, which fought from Heisterberg and later Langenhagen, achieved good success but were eventually wiped out.

The *Wiking* battle group was absent as that morning it had been moved forward with its thirteen armored troop carriers and seven Jagdpanthers to Frielingen and Recklungen in order to tie up the American attacks across the Leine bridges near Bordenau and Ricklingen. This proved to be a clever tactical move on the part of the experienced Hauptsturmführer. As soon as it was regrouped, Bolling's main force ran straight into this strong bulwark. Men of the 11th Armored Reconnaissance Regiment of the US 13th Corps, which had been subordinated to Bolling, suddenly came under fire from three Jagdpanthers in camouflaged positions at the entrance to Ricklingen. The leading enemy tanks were knocked out, but then the US troops called down heavy artillery fire on Ricklingen.

The Jagdpanthers were successful from ranges of 2,000 meters and more but the artillery fire forced them to withdraw into the village of Horst. The American armored reconnaissance force tried approaching from three sides, but wherever they attacked they were met by devastating fire from Nicolussi-Leck's well-sited tank-destroyers.

The combat experience and iron nerves of the Vikings did not abandon them, even in this unequal contest, and they celebrated a great victory. In this tank battle, their first in a long time, the enemy lost approximately sixty tanks and armored vehicles. While a prisoner of war Nicolussi-Leck was told by the interrogation officer: "You and your boys destroyed one of our best regiments."

The surviving companies were sent by Colonel Fierson to Bordenau to drive across the Leine bridge there. They got as far as Bordenau without meeting resistance, but then on the way to Frielingen they again came under fire from the Jagdpanthers, which opened fire from maximum range. It was four of these giants which ultimately brought the American advance there to a halt. One of the most forward sited Jagdpanthers destroyed six enemy tanks singlehanded, before it was itself hit and burned out. Nicolussi-Leck also lost one of his armored troop carriers. The *Wiking* battle group had destroyed another 30 enemy tanks. From the burning villages of Frielingen and Horst it withdrew east toward Vinnhorst and Nordhafen.

The next morning, still before dawn, American troops entered Hanover. There was no resistance. Pleas from Mayor Börner, District President Binding and Police Chief Deutschbein had led Generalmajor Loehning to order his troops to lay down their arms. As a result of this the *Wiking* battle group's positions were outflanked to the west. Nicolussi-Leck ordered his force to pull back toward the city center. The battle group would have to pass through the center of the city if it wished to avoid capture. Therefore the Hauptsturmführer ordered his vehicles to drive through Hanover as quickly as possible. The chief of the Hanover fire department, Richard Bange, offered to lead the battle group safely out of the city. He led the way in an open vehicle with Nicolussi-Leck. They drove to the Stein gate. There civilians shouted to them that the Americans were already at the main train station. This caused some detouring. Then several Americans stopped the car; Bange and Hauptsturmführer Nicolussi-Leck had to get out.

In this critical situation the nearest tank destroyer, which was commanded by Obersturmführer Olin, opened fire with its machine-gun. Nicolussi-Leck leapt onto Olin's vehicle. Bange tried to reach safety in a doorway; he was badly wounded in the chest but made it.

The *Wiking* battle group now roared down the Georgstrasse to the Aegi. When they turned on to the Marienstrasse American Sherman tanks came into view. The crews were standing beside their vehicles and were scattered to the four winds by machine-gun fire. The battle group was through.

Then in the village of Bissendorf Americans of the 11th Cavalry Group committed an atrocity. They arrested the mayor, Otto Knibbe, and master ironworker Hans Riecke after they were denounced as "Nazis." Otto Knibbe was shot dead near the Grossburgwedel Mill on 10 April. Hans Riecke died the same way on the Natelheide Road. Both men had been murdered in cold blood. This incident is mentioned in order to point out the senselessness of many combat- and non-combat-related incidents during this late stage of the war.

For a description of the battle group's activities during the final days of the war let us turn to Hauptsturmführer Nicolussi-Leck:

> We arrived in the Celle area and were ordered to carry out harrassing attacks in order to slow the advance of US forces north of the autobahn. In the process it proved inevitable that we caught and captured small contingents of US troops. In each case the officers and their men were released the next night to return to their units, leaving behind their vehicles and their provisions, which we needed. We could not burden ourselves with them and we did not want to turn them over to some unauthorized person and leave them to an uncertain fate. But we could not take them along. So we decided to set them free.
>
> Details of our fighting methods are revealed in a report written by the then Lieutenant Albert A. Robbins, who was our prisoner for a day and a night. He wrote impressively of the crossing over the Aller, which was shown to us by a woman called Anna, who led us there and guided us across the Aller under heavy artillery fire.
>
> I and my adjutant, Lt. Willers of the army, were taken prisoner when I left my battle group to go to a farm from where I planned to reconnoiter the area. A Polish farm worker alerted a squad of US military police. We managed to evade them, but on our way

> back to our men we were spotted and caught after a four-hour chase.
>
> The lengthy interrogations, to which we were subjected in a "wild west" manner, were rough. I later learned that the Americans were unaware of any difference between the "black" (general) and "armed" SS. Anyway they could see from our war decorations that we were a combat unit.
>
> My impression was that the Americans hated us because of our great defensive success near Hanover and did not want to believe that we were just a small unit. They babbled on and on about a panzer division, whose whereabouts they were seeking. But we could not help them, we were the panzer division.
>
> Colonel P. Hofmann, whom we had released to return to his unit and who struck me only by the naievete of his proposal that I return his Jeep to him for his return to his unit, was the first to grasp that we were a combat unit. The colonel, who spoke quite good German, cleared up the situation and the tricks stopped.

The American assumption that they had come up against an entire panzer division is further proof of Nicolussi-Leck's excellence as a tank commander and tactical leader of armored forces. When the war was over Major Albert Robbins tracked down the German tank commander from Hanover. The two soldiers began exchanging letters and invited each other to their respective homes for a long visit.

REBUILDING AFTER THE WAR

Nicolussi-Leck's fruit and wine businesses in the Hochfrangart area were ecologically-friendly operations at a time when the word ecology was not even used in many nations. First, however, there were long years of building before he could realize a decades old dream. Hochfrangart became an operation with a view to the future and an emphasis on quality.

In his fifties and sixties Nicolussi-Leck did much to assist the Germans displaced from Tirol. In 1971 he headed up the South Tirol Building Center. In its more than twenty years of existence the center progressed from trades training to university training. The facility was attended by thousands of students and had a staff of thirty-five to fifty professors. Thanks to Nicolussi-Leck's initiative an empty hospital in Bozen was converted to accept two schools and later a museum of modern art.

Throughout his wartime service and postwar rebuilding efforts, Karl Nicolussi-Leck remained true to his motto: "There is always plenty to do, let's get at it!"

Hermann von Oppeln-Bronikowski after receiving the Oak Leaves.

Hermann von Oppeln-Bronikowski

THE FIRST WORLD WAR—THE REICHSWEHR—THE BERLIN OLYMPICS—THE CAMPAIGN IN POLAND

"Oberstleutnant von Oppeln-Bronikowski reporting to Panzer Brigade Eberbach for practical training in the command of tanks."

Oberst Heinrich Eberbach, who had just moved into his new division command post at the northeast boundary of Orel in the central sector of the Eastern Front, walked over to the slender officer with the hooked nose and the thick, bushy eyebrows. He extended his hand.

"Good to have you here, Oppeln. We can always use a man like you."

"Is something special going on, sir?"

"Expansion of our Orel bridgehead north across the Oka and preparation for the assault on Tula."

Panzer Brigade Eberbach had been in Orel for one day. In the last days of September it had advanced northeast from Sevsk and had broken through the front of General Yeremenko's 13th Army. By 3 October 1941 the brigade had covered 130 kilometers and took Orel the same day.

"So we are headed for Moscow then, sir?"

"First we have to prevent the Russians trapped near Briansk from escaping, Oppeln."

The operations officer appeared with a welcoming drink.

"Where have you come from, Oppeln," said Eberbach, continuing the conversation.

"From the OKH, where I was active as the cavalry specialist in the staff of the General of Fast Troops, sir."

"Well, that must have been a nice job for a cavalryman, von Oppeln."

"Nice but rather tiring, for there was always office work to do, sir. Especially after commanding a front-line detachment."

"The 24th Reconnaissance Battalion, if I am not mistaken?"

"You are definitely not mistaken. And if I may say so, you are very well informed about your new arrival."

Oberst Eberbach smiled and raised his glass to his young comrade. "One is always curious about whom one is dealing with, Oppeln. And what I have heard gives me confidence. I will assign you to the heavy battalion. You will receive a Panzer IV. This is somewhat different than a horse; but the days of the cavalry are numbered. It won't be long before the last cavalryman dismounts and takes off his saddle for good. The sooner you do so, the better. We need the cavalry spirit, Oppeln. You must transplant it into your tank and then things will roll."

"I have learned, at least theoretically, the latest experiences in the panzer arm first hand. Now I have to try find the synthesis between theory and practice."

✠

Oberst Eberbach had of course already informed himself about the forty-two-year-old Oberstleutnant. But then, it was not possible to learn everything about Hermann von Oppeln-Bronikowski from the official records. Oppeln-Bronikowski came from a military family. His father had been an officer. When his son Hermann was born he was a Major commanding a battalion of the 4th Foot Guards Regiment. In the First World War the senior von Oppeln-Bronikowski rose to the rank of General and commanded an infantry division.

Hermann von Oppeln-Bronikowski was also to become a soldier. On 1 April 1912 he entered the Bensberg Cadet School near Cologne. Two years later he was transferred to the main cadet institute at Groß-Lichterfelde near Berlin. On 23 March 1917 the cadet reported to Ulan Regiment No. 10 at Züllichau in East Brandenburg. A few weeks later he was transferred from the reserve troop to the active regiment, which was stationed in Poland as part of the occupying force there.

Von Oppeln-Bronikowski volunteered for front-line service in the infantry and was transferred to the Western Front. He saw continuous action in the spring of 1918 as a platoon and assault team commander in Line Infantry Regiment No. 118. In six months of action in the Champagne and in the Argonne, he demonstrated his ability. When the regiment deployed an assault team it was almost always led by Leutnant von Oppeln-Bronikowski. He received the Iron Cross, Second Class and three months later became one of the youngest Leutnants ever to receive the Iron Cross, First Class. This was followed on 14 October 1918 by the Hessian Medal of Bravery.

Immediately afterwards he returned to his old regiment, the 10th Uhlan, which was now in Estonia. As a fast, mobile unit, the regiment, together with other cavalry units, had the task of squashing resistance by Bolshevik revolutionaries in the extreme north of the Eastern Front and launching a surprise attack on Petrograd (later Leningrad). But the war ended before this audacious plan could be executed, and von Oppeln-Bronikowski's regiment was in the Estonian capital of Reval (present-day Tallin) when the cease-fire was announced.

Together with his regiment von Oppeln-Bronikowski returned to the unit's peacetime garrison in Züllichau, arriving there on 17 December 1918. When at the beginning of 1919 Polish revolutionaries seized the province of Posen, conflict flared up at the garrison's doorstep once again. A call for help reached the Hussars and the 1st Troop, which was made up of volunteers, left for the disputed area under the command of Rittmeister von Kleist. Among the volunteers was Hermann von Oppeln-Bronikowski. Unruhstadt and Bombst were retaken on 12 February 1919. As commander of the 1st Troop von Oppeln-Bronikowski was awarded the Merit Badge of the V Corps. Later he became adjutant of the southern sector. Thus this regiment, which was later disbanded, was one of the few regiments in the east that had to defend its own garrison. Beginning in autumn 1919 the Uhlan regiment was incorporated into Cavalry Regiment No. 10. Von Oppeln-Bronikowski belonged to this regiment for twenty years, interrupted only by temporary assignments elsewhere.

Because of his cavalry experience in 1923 von Oppeln-Bronikowski was sent to the Ohrdruff Infantry School in Thuringia as a riding instructor and supervisory officer. On 1 April 1925 he was promoted to Oberleutnant. He achieved his greatest riding success when he was seconded to the then world-famous Hanover Cavalry School. He initially served there as battalion adjutant, but then as a riding instructor again and finally became head of the training program. During this time he rode as a member of the German dressage team and won many proud victories.

Oppeln-Bronikowski's riding abilities were recognized when he was chosen to represent Germany in the 1936 Olympics. He became a member of the dressage team, along with Oberleutnant Pollay and Major Gerhard. The three riders demonstrated their proficiency in numerous displays and exercises. Oppeln-Bronikowski's mount was the 18-year-old "Gimpel." These three riders won the Gold Medal in dressage for Germany in the Olympic Games.

✠

Following his Olympic triumph von Oppeln-Bronikowski returned to the cavalry school in Hanover. Then on 31 September 1936 he returned to the 10th Cavalry Regiment at Torgau as a troop commander. On 1 March 1937 he was promoted to Major and took over II (Bicycle) Battalion of the 10th Cavalry Regiment. Prior to the entry into Czechoslovakia in March 1939 several reconnaissance battalions were formed from the 10th Cavalry Regiment. Major von Oppeln-Bronikowski became commander of the 24th Reconnaissance Battalion of the 24th (Polar Bear) Infantry Division.

These reconnaissance battalions consisted of a headquarters, a cavalry troop, a bicycle troop and a motorized troop (consisting of reconnaissance vehicles and antitank guns). The trains were horse drawn. Thus there were four different march speeds within the battalion, which complicated the job of the commander. In spite of this Oppeln-Bronikowski had soon turned his battalion into a capable fighting unit.

The 24th Infantry Division was transferred east in the summer of 1939. Like all the other divisions on the Polish frontier, it received the following order at 4:55 P.M. on 31 August 1939: "Case White 1 September 1939 at 4:45 P.M."

The die had been cast. The attack on Poland, and with it the Second World War, was about to begin.

✠

Commanding the 24th Infantry Division was Generalleutnant Olbricht, who was later hung for being a member of the resistance. This officer was an example to the officer corps and every soldier under his command. He became one of the first German soldiers to receive the Knight's Cross, on 27 September 1939 following the Polish campaign.

Major von Oppeln-Bronikowski and his 24th Reconnaissance Battalion were constantly at the front of the division. They carried out their reconnaissance missions with dash and daring. More than once Oppeln-Bronikowski accompanied the motorized troop far ahead of his battalion. He also led the cavalry troop on sorties deep into enemy territory. Then one day he received an order from the division commander which would demand everything of him: "Oppeln, before us lies the Wartha bridge near Warta. The Poles have occupied it. If we don't seize it it will be blown and that will mean a delay in the completion of our assignment."

Von Oppeln-Bronikowski assembled his forces. He himself drove in the lead vehicle of his battalion's fastest unit, the motorized troop. They drove past Polish resistance groups and came under fire. The vehicles turned off the road, bypassed the opposition and then came back on the road again. But then they were halted by a major obstacle.

"Antitank guns shoot up the barricade. Assault team follow! Cavalry troop is to move up to this position."

While the antitank guns (which were later sarcastically referred to as "tank door knockers") convinced the enemy that the battalion was pinned down, von Oppeln-Bronikowski went around the barricade and regained the road 800 meters beyond it.

"Full throttle!" he ordered.

The small assault group raced towards the Warthe bridge. Ahead the Polish bridge guard opened fire. The armored cars kept moving, returning the Polish fire with their machine-guns and 20-mm cannon. Then the wheels of the fast armored cars were on the bridge. Would the Poles blow it up? The far end of the bridge appeared. The Poles were still shooting. The leader of the German assault team, who was driving close behind the battalion commander, took out the bunker crews with his men. Hand grenades exploded, rifles cracked. Then the bridge was in the hands of the reconnaissance battalion and Major von Oppeln-Bronikowski was able to signal the division: "Warthe bridge near Warta in our hands undamaged."

Thanks to the 24th Reconnaissance Battalion the advance could continue. Hermann von Oppeln-Bronikowski received the bars to both Iron Crosses from the hand of his commanding officer. The commander of the motorized patrol received the Iron Cross, First Class.

✠

After the end of the campaign in Poland, Major von Oppeln-Bronikowski was transferred to the OKH to the staff of the "General of Fast Troops." His top superior there was General Ritter von Thoma, then General Breith.

These and similar staffs for other branches of the service, for instance the infantry, the artillery and the engineers, were supposed to recruit experienced front-line officers to evaluate the experiences of their units and make suggestions for the organization, armaments and equipment of new panzer or other divisions for the benefit of the OKH and the General Staff. There Major von Oppeln-Bronikowski learned all about the creation and organization of the tank arm and its optimal employment. His area of specialization was "all reconnaissance activities by the army." He was given the task of preparing the remaining cavalry divisions for conversion into Panzer divisions. He was responsible for reequipping the 24th Cavalry Division to become the 24th Panzer Division. On completion of this task, on 1 August 1941 he volunteered for the Panzer arm. Von Oppeln-Bronikowski had just been promoted to Oberstleutnant.

THE OBERSTLEUTNANT AS "STUDENT"—FROM OREL TO TULA WITH PANZER BRIGADE EBERBACH—THE WINTER BATTLE FOR MOSCOW—COMMANDER OF THE 35TH PANZER REGIMENT

Oberstleutnant von Oppeln-Bronikowski had returned to the front, for the first time as commander of a pure armored unit, in order to learn the art of "commanding armored forces." He carried out his first attack in Russia on 25 October 1941. From the Orel bridgehead the brigade was to advance to Tula. Ultimate objective: Moscow, capital of the Soviet Union. It snowed that day, although it was still not yet cold. In spite of the snow the feared "General Winter" had not yet intervened in the battle. But the snow flurries restricted visibility, and Oppeln's driver, Feldwebel Bille, had to strain his eyes so as not to miss any obstacles. Thus it was he who first spotted the enemy.

"Attention! Sir, enemy tanks in front of us!"

Oberstleutnant von Oppeln-Bronikowski peered through his periscope. But the falling snow and the vibration of the tank prevented him from seeing anything.

"Stop, Bille!" he ordered.

The tank halted, rocking on its tracks for a moment. The Oppeln was presented with an unmistakable scene through the periscope in spite of the snow.

"Go, drive on!"

The tank gave a jerk and moved off again, while the Oberstleutnant passed along his observations by radio.

"Oppeln to commander First Battalion: group of enemy tanks moving from the river toward your right flank."

"Thank you," came the reply. "We will attack at once. Swing out to the left with your group and then take the enemy in the flank."

"Oppeln group: battle readiness!"

The eight panzer commanders, who had been deployed to guard the left flank of the advancing tank column, reported ready for battle.

The Oberstleutnant heard the voice of the brigade commander: "Oppeln, outflank them from the left and attack!"

"Follow me!"

They left the snow-covered road and drove through a depression. The thin ice crunched beneath the tracks. Bushes slipped past. The tanks drove through a pool, crushing the thin covering of ice.

The 1936 Olympics in Berlin: von Oppeln-Bronikowski won the gold medal in the dressage event.

"To everyone: we will follow the depression to Point 110. Then turn east in battle formation."

A few birch trees in the path of the panzers were crushed beneath the tank tracks. Snow rained down from their branches, obscuring the commander's view for a moment.

Then the sound of cannon fire was heard.

"The First Battalion is attacking, sir!"

"We just made it! Full throttle Bille!"

Feldwebel Bille increased power. The engine roared and propelled the steel giant forwards. They were driving a Panzer IV, one of the most modern German tanks, however the bulk of the 35th Panzer Regiment was still equipped with the PzKfw. 38(t), a Czech-built vehicle. The tank roared up the slope. Behind it followed the phalanx of eight squat Panzer IVs, armed with the short-barreled 75-mm gun. Oppeln's tank reached the top and he had a clear view. A city lay before him.

"It's Chern, sir."

Flashes appeared from the edge of the town at brief intervals and then shells smashed into the leading German vehicles on the main road.

"They are giving it to the advance detachment, sir!"

But before von Oppeln could reply he heard the voice of Major von Jungenfeldt: "Advance detachment in front of a heavy Soviet tank barricade. We are turning and going around the city."

"Good, Jungenfeldt!" said the voice of Oberst Eberbach, "forwards and after them!"

"Turn right!"

The nine tanks of the Oppeln group turned. After a few meters they cleared a stand of trees which had been blocking their view to the east and saw the tanks of I Battalion. Then, suddenly, directly in their direction of travel, huge tanks emerged from the snow-covered bushes and headed towards the Germans. Most wore a coat of white winter camouflage paint, while a few still had their dark summer camouflage. The tanks had a pugnacious and powerful, yet curiously elegant appearance. Their front, rear and side armor was sloped as was that of the turret housing the long-barreled 76.2-mm cannon. Compared to them the boxy, heavy Panzer IV looked clumsy and obsolete. One of the enemy tanks raced ahead of its companions, straight toward the German tanks.

"That must be the Russian command tank, sir. We have to knock it out first."

"Turret eleven o'clock. Eight-hundred. Fire!"

For the first time von Oppeln-Bronikowski felt the recoil of a tank cannon in tank-versus-tank combat. He followed the path of the smoking shell, which struck the ground to the right of the enemy tank, which had just come to a halt. At that instant flames shot from the muzzle of the 76.2-mm gun of the Russian tank. One of 2nd Company's tanks was hit just as it began to move. The panzer immediately ground to a halt, one of its tracks shattered. Four others fired at the Soviet vehicles as they broke out of the forest. The objective of the enemy attack was to halt the advance of Panzer Group 2 and enable their own infantry to carry out an orderly retreat. There was no doubt: the Soviet tanks were examples of the new T-34, a highly modern, twenty-seven-ton combat vehicle with an aluminum diesel motor. German troops who had already encountered the T-34 spoke highly of its capabilities.

In the few seconds it took the loader to place the next shell in the breech, Hermann von Oppeln-Bronikowski was able to take in the sweeping picture of the tank-versus-tank battle. A loud bang resounded through the interior of the Panzer IV as the gunner fired the second shot. The armor-piercing shell struck the enemy tank just beneath its turret. The turret was lifted from the turret ring and was left sitting ajar. Smoke rolled out of the crevice. Then the turret hatch snapped back and a lance of flame shot up. Then there was an ear-shattering bang as a shell struck the turret of von Oppeln-Bronikowski's tank. Fortunately the shell struck at an angle and was deflected by the armor plate.

"Full throttle, after them!"

All nine tanks rolled up the hill to where Soviet and German tanks were locked in battle. Cannon roared to the left and right of and behind the command tank. They had to close the range, for in terms of firepower the German panzers were clearly inferior to the T-34. The third shot by Unteroffizier Krämer, gunner in the battalion commander's tank, was aimed at some bushes above which the turret of a T-34 was visible.

The brigade commander's voice rang out: "Oppeln, break through to the Chir!"

An order from von Oppeln-Bronikowski caused the tanks to veer to the left and they now drove straight east toward the riverbank. Oberstleutnant von Oppeln-Bronikowski was about to acknowledge the order when three tank turrets emerged from the gully surrounding a tributary of the river.

"Fire!"

Shells whizzed over the armored turrets. Shrubbery was thrown up, sailing high into the air. Smoke spiraled into the cloudy midday sky, a signal to the Oberstleutnant that the massed fire was claiming victims. Just as he was about to order the following panzer to roll to the right and take the T-34s, which had withdrawn back into the gully, in the flank, the three Soviets emerged from the gully again at full throttle, firing wildly.

There was an explosion behind Oppeln's Panzer IV. Flames shot into the sky. The second shell from the leading Russian whizzed past the command tank. Unteroffizier lowered the elevation of the tank's main gun. He saw the front of the T-34 in his sight. He made a slight adjustment and fired. The shell struck the side of the T-34's engine compartment, and following an explosion of diesel fuel the tank was left standing. The Soviet tank crew bailed out and disappeared into the bushes along the stream. Meanwhile the fire from the surviving T-34s intensified into a veritable storm, audible even through the steel walls of the panzers. Shells whizzed towards them and smashed into their frontal armor.

"Those are T-26s, they can't penetrate!" cried the driver. He then turned hard in an attempt to steer the tank around a deep, water-filled hole. The tank's right track slid downward. For a moment Oppeln thought the tank might tip over. But then it righted itself and roared out of the hole. Almost immediately the T-26s opened fire again. The noise was such that von Oppeln-Bronikowski could not hear his own voice when he ordered a turn on seeing that the last enemy tank had been destroyed by the other panzers.

"Brigade commander to Oppeln: Turn onto the road, take the point position, take out enemy antitank guns at the exit from the town and take Chir."

The tanks turned. When he received the reports from his commanders von Oppeln realized that his group had been reduced to seven tanks. Two panzers had been knocked out by enemy fire. They drove in a wide arc. Once Oppeln's tank became stuck in a marshy meadow. The engine howled wildly. Clumps of dirt were cast to the sides. The two tracks dug deeper and deeper into the soft ground.

"Reverse gear, Bille!" Oppeln ordered his driver.

The tank finally extricated itself. It rolled to the left across a ditch and reached the road. Several vehicles of the advance detachment pulled over to allow the tanks to pass.

"Attack the antitank guns. Each vehicle take one gun!"

The tanks spread out. They drove through harvested fields, across an open area, through a wood and opened fire. An antitank gun opened fire. "Faster, Bille!" ordered Oppeln. The tank rumbled forward at full throttle. Gunner Krämer was ready to fire again. He turned the fine adjustment handwheel. The antitank gun fired again just as Krämer was preparing to do the same. However, the tank gunner's shot was a direct hit. Brown-clad figures ran crouched toward the nearest houses, pursued by machine-gun fire from the motorcycle troops of the advance detachment, who were advancing behind the tanks and drawing ever nearer to the Chir.

"There, sir! The machine-gun!"

A Russian Maxim heavy MG began to rattle slowly; to the right, fountains of snow whirled up behind a snow-covered hedge where a squad of infantry had just taken cover. Men fell to the ground.

"Six-hundred. Twelve o'clock. Fire!"

The shell smashed into a cottage at the edge of the village and blew apart one wall. The machine-gun fell silent.

"Forward! Into the village!"

The seven tanks rumbled on, firing high-explosive shells into the houses as they advanced. Flames rose up as the straw-thatched roofs caught fire. Smoke rose into the sky in dense clouds. An antitank gun opened fire from a sort of marketplace in the center of the village. A shell from a panzer put it out of action. The tank was closing rapidly on the wall of a house. Driver Bille turned hard to the right. Too late! The bow of the tank crashed into the side of the house. Chunks of masonry thundered down on the turret, making it sound to those inside as if they were in an earthquake.

Russians crossed the street in front of the tank. The following advance detachment opened fire with machine-guns. The Red Army men fled into one of the houses. Several rounds from a tank sent it up in flames. German infantry surrounded the house. Hand grenades exploded. The battle for the Chir was in full swing. Suddenly there was an explosion in front of the tank, leaving a crater in the street. "Artillery!" roared Krämer. The next shell landed just a few meters in front of the tank. The front of the tank rose sharply. Hermann von Oppeln-Bronikowski felt his stomach heave. Then the panzer crashed back down onto its tracks, and the next shell fell about fifty meters behind it on the cottage they had rammed earlier. Tracer flitted through the streets. The tank crashed through a fence and sent several high-explosive shells in the direction of the fleeing enemy.

"Brigade commander, this is Oppeln: Chir is in our hands."

"Halt in a favorable position 300 meters beyond the end of the village."

They reached the exit from the village and worked their way along a hedge until they came to a birch wood, where they went into position. The nose of the command tank laboriously worked its way through the dense wall of bushes and then stopped. Far ahead on the main road von Oppeln-Bronikowski saw the retreating Soviets.

"In position 300 meters beyond the northern end of Chir," Oppeln reported to the brigade commander. "In front of us on the main road retreating Russian infantry. There are panye wagons, trucks and guns mixed in with them."

"I'm coming Oppeln," replied Oberst Eberbach. "Stay where you are until I arrive."

Oppeln acknowledged and then issued the following order to his tanks: "Everyone open fire on the road. High-explosive shells!"

The guns of the panzers barked. Shells smashed into the vehicles moving along the road and set them ablaze. The crews abandoned their vehicles and sought cover in the woods along the river. The tank's fighting compartment was cramped. Powder smoke entered the Oberstleutnant's lungs, making him cough. Empty shell casings clanged against the shell catcher and tumbled onto the others in the bag.

"Plug your ears!" ordered the Oberstleutnant.

All that could be heard now was the whine of Soviet artillery shells passing overhead. They smashed into the village, setting more houses on fire. The tanks of the First Battalion that had previously been firing fell silent. They had probably already silenced the enemy. A command car drove out of the village at high speed. Once it looked as if it had been caught by an exploding shell, but when the smoke and dust cleared it was still moving. One of the infantrymen who had taken cover in the wood pointed the way for the brigade commander. The car stopped behind the command tank. Oberstleutnant von Oppeln-Bronikowski opened the hatch and gave his report.

"Well done, Oppeln. We're to keep moving forward."

"Then why are we waiting here, sir?"

"The Generaloberst is coming to see us, Oppeln."

"I am anxious to see what orders he gives us."

"Not me. I know him. He will say exactly the same thing that he said to me at the windmill hill near Sevsk: 'Onward, onward!'"

The advance detachment, which had been held up and battered by the enemy, now reformed. Russian prisoners were brought back. Then a dispatch rider arrived, completely covered in mud.

"Sir, the general will be arriving in five minutes."

It was exactly four and a half minutes before Generaloberst Guderian arrived.

"Congratulations, Eberbach! And now onwards, even if the weather warms up again. I hereby create the 'fast advance detachment Eberbach.' You will have at your disposal all the tanks of the XXIV Army Corps, elements of the 75th Artillery Regiment, the 3rd Rifle Regiment and the Infantry Regiment *Großdeutschland*. You are to advance ruthlessly with these troops and take Tula. It is exactly eighty-nine kilometers away."

Oberstleutnant von Oppeln-Bronikowski saluted the Generaloberst. He read concern in the furrowed face of the panzer general. Then Guderian drove on to the 3rd Panzer Division.

"So we carry on, Oppeln. Now you get a foretaste of what tank soldiers can do. Wait until you see how it is tomorrow."

"Yes, sir!"

The next morning, the 26th of October, the "Fast Advance Detachment Eberbach" resumed the advance. After only a few kilometers the leading elements, men of the Infantry Regiment *Großdeutschland,* came upon a strong Soviet field emplacement. Positioned there were several batteries of 76.2-mm dual-purpose guns, weapons which were much feared for their effectiveness.

Given the potency of the Soviet guns, it seemed foolhardy to launch a tank assault against the well-fortified and concealed Soviet position. But the Germans had an ace up their sleeve in the form of their air force, which then enjoyed air superiority. A request was made to the air fleet command for dive-bombers to attack the field positions. The Stukas soon appeared and dove like ravens on the Soviet gun batteries. Their bombs knocked out one battery after another.

The victorious 1936 dressage team: Oberleutnant Pollay, Hauptmann Gerhard, and Rittmeister von Oppeln-Bronikowski.

When the Soviet guns ceased firing von Oppeln-Bronikowski gave the order for the panzers to advance. Warmer weather had set in and the passage of the tanks turned the roads into muddy morasses. Deep holes had to be skirted and repeatedly stuck vehicles had to be pulled free. Oberst Eberbach drove along the edge of the road in his all-terrain command car. Several times he got out to help free a stuck vehicle. The battle group finally reached Tula and seized the town; the next objective was Moscow. In the leading panzer von Oppeln-Bronikowski experienced the helplessness of tanks in mud such as this. General Mud had marshaled his regiments and it looked as if he intended to contest a quick German victory.

"St. Gorbachevo ahead of us, sir."

"Oppeln to everyone: through to Gorbachevo. Don't let anything stop you!"

The tanks were still more than 500 meters from the village when enemy antitank guns began to fire. One of the first shots was a hit. The command tank was immobilized with a shot-up track. There was another loud bang as a shell struck the side of the tank.

"Get out!" ordered Oberstleutnant von Oppeln-Bronikowski.

Under Russian machine-gun fire the crew forced themselves through the narrow hatches and ran to a dense row of willows. A burst of fire shot from right to left. Seeing that the fire was meant for them, the Oberstleutnant threw himself down in a ditch beside the trees. Behind him a tank fired its gun. The sound virtually deafened him for a moment. A thousand bells rang in his ears. Feldwebel Bille landed in the ditch beside him. Then Obergefreiter Scholtz, the loader, appeared, and a moment later Krämer and radio operator Herbertz.

The other panzers moved in from three sides and poured shells into the village. Flames shot high into the air. One after another the enemy guns fell silent. Then the enemy tanks also ceased firing; they had apparently been in a readiness position on the other side of the village but had not attacked. They had probably now withdrawn. Oberst Eberbach's command car appeared on the road, followed closely by a radio car. Oberstleutnant von Oppeln was just walking over to his commanding officer's vehicle when a machine-gun began firing from one of the last houses. The first burst passed over Oppeln's head. The machine-gun in the sidecars of the two escorting motorcycles returned fire. Oppeln leapt back into the ditch. Then the enemy fire stopped and he reemerged to report to his commanding officer.

"Having your first tank shot out from under you is half a birthday, Oppeln. See what your crew can do. If nothing can be done I will call for a replacement vehicle."

"I can't wait that long, sir."

"Very well! As you wish, Oppeln."

Oberst Eberbach gave his radio operator an order. He called the First Battalion and a short time later a new tank arrived and Oberstleutnant von Oppeln-Bronikowski and his crew climbed aboard. The tank's previous crew got out and grudgingly set to work repairing the shot-up track of Oppeln's panzer.

"Will you give them a few cigarettes?"

The Oberstleutnant had his driver steer the tank toward his disabled vehicle, where he handed out packs of cigarettes to the tank men. Then he joined the rest of the tanks, which were driving down the main road. The tanks drove through St. Gorbachevo. Far ahead could be seen the muzzle flashes from the Soviet tanks, which were now defending themselves. Armor-piercing shells began falling among the leading group of tanks.

"Go! After them!" the Oberstleutnant ordered his driver. Then: "Oppeln to everyone, I'm coming up and taking over command again."

It took an hour to reach the front of the column. Panye wagons drove off the road before them. They were shot up as the tanks passed. Then they came to a stuck truck. The nose of the tank struck the vehicle and knocked it aside. Suddenly a Soviet gun opened fire from some dense bushes 200 meters ahead to the right. The shell struck a motorcycle, which was destroyed in a ball of fire. Unteroffizier Krämer rotated the turret while simultaneously lowering the main gun. The boom of the gun firing mixed with the crack of the enemy high-velocity gun. The shell struck the enemy gun's ammunition supply, which went up, taking the gun with it.

Behind the leading group of the "Fast Forward Detachment" the road was reduced to a muddy track. The potholes grew deeper and deeper. Trucks became stuck and the tanks had difficulty pulling them out. Everything was sprayed all over with mud. Dispatch riders struggled past, covered in mud, became stuck and went down. And all the while the Soviets fired at the point group from their flanking positions. Casualties mounted among the infantry of the Infantry Regiment *Großdeutschland.*

✠

Oppeln had found his place in the tank arm. It was just like in the cavalry: be mobile, recognize and exploit every opportunity and attack, attack! Quick decisions were required, for instance in the decisive moment when the leading group of the *Großdeutschland* threw itself against a Russian tank battalion. That was at Plavskoye, one day later on 27 October 1941.

Acting on his own initiative, as soon as the radio report came in from the infantry von Oppeln immediately turned around on the road. His tanks smashed the enemy and caused him to withdraw. The tanks drove through another Russian village. Just beyond the village fleeing Russian columns had once again turned the road into a knee-deep morass. The advance detachment with its wheeled vehicles became bogged down. Only tracked and half-tracked vehicles could extricate themselves from the clinging mud.

There was a lengthy halt near Chukina. There the Soviets had set up a wide blocking position. Antitank guns and field artillery, bunker positions and deep minefields halted the advance detachment. Oppeln received orders to outflank the position to the west with the tanks of I Battalion and overrun it from behind. The Oberstleutnant assembled the tanks, which were strung out along a fifteen-kilometer stretch pulling stuck vehicles from the mud. A platoon of motorcycle troops on Kettenkräder followed the tanks.

Swinging far out to the right, Oberstleutnant von Oppeln had the tanks drive along a secondary road; after the steel giants had passed the road looked like it had been trampled by a herd of elephants. After about 2,000 meters a rise appeared before the tanks and on it a large, permanent structure. Using his periscope Oppeln scanned the rise, which was covered with a dense growth of bushes. Once he saw something flash. He immediately concentrated on that area. Then he recognized a gun shield, part of which was just visible above its otherwise effective camouflage, and then the barrel of a Russian field gun.

"Attention, Oppeln to everyone: hill is manned by the enemy. Observe and report!"

"202 to commander. Thumb jump to the left, left corner of the house, bunkers fifty meters below it."

The Oberstleutnant whistled shrilly through his teeth. He turned his periscope and saw the embrasures.

"Spread out. In exactly ten minutes make a frontal attack against the hill. Open fire at your discretion."

Hidden from view by a small wood, the tanks spread out to the left and right. The ten minutes passed in oppressive silence. Now and then there was a clang as the loader removed armor-piercing rounds from the ammunition rack.

"Ten minutes are up. Up the hill at full throttle, go!"

Engines roaring, the tanks leapt forward. They left cover and rolled up the hill, followed by the motorcycle troops. But at that moment fire spat from many concealed positions on the hill. The Russian field guns fired shrapnel, which made a rattling sound as its sprayed the sides of the tank. Seeking cover, the motorcycle troops drove up close to the tanks. Exactly 100 meters in front of the command tank there was a flash as a Russian 76.2-mm gun fired. The shell whizzed past the turret. Unteroffizier Krämer aimed and fired. From that range the shot was a direct hit, blowing away the gun's camouflage and silencing it.

Bursts of machine-gun fire whistled down from the hill. Russians positioned in the house fired without pause. Suddenly a group of Russians fled a bunker approximately 30 meters in front of the command tank. A burst of fire from the motorcycle troops behind the tank caused them to go to ground. Then Oppeln's tank reached the top of the hill and stopped. At that moment the Oberstleutnant saw the enemy tanks waiting in the large garden behind the building. Again they were T-34s, with their squat, angular turrets.

"Attention, enemy tanks!" called the driver.

"Turn left, Bille! Go, go!"

The Feldwebel turned the tank on its left track. They drove along in the shadow of the building, which was much larger than it had looked from a distance at the bottom of the hill. Then antitank rifles opened fire from an out-building to their right. The rounds from the dangerous infantry weapons struck the steel of the German tank but failed to penetrate. Now Oppeln's Panzer IV was behind the building and turned back to the right toward the enemy tanks.

"The closest one Krämer!" the Oberstleutnant ordered his gunner.

Unteroffizier Krämer knew as well as the Oberstleutnant that only the Russian command tank had a transmitter, while the rest could only receive. If they knocked out the Russian commander, the other tanks would be leaderless, with no one to coordinate their actions. The shot rang out and dislodged the turret of the enemy tank. Nevertheless, it continued to close with undiminished speed, followed by six or seven other T-34s.

"First Company turn left around the building. Enemy tanks attacking!"

Now it was all or nothing. Whoever shot faster would survive. Hesitation was suicide. This was shown by the example of the tank which had just rounded the building and now rolled toward the Russian tanks from the right flank. Before it could fire, the long guns of several T-34s turned toward it. There were three shots and three shells struck the German tank almost simultaneously. Under cover of the smoke and flames the German tank crew tried to escape. A burst of machine-gun fire from the building knocked them to the ground.

Shells hissed past the German command tank. One struck the front of the tank, bounced off and howled over the turret into the air. Then the tanks of 1st Company arrived. Several seconds after they arrived the brigade commander, acting on his own, led the rest of his tanks into the enemy's flank from the southwest. Ten minutes later the tank battle was over. The large building turned out to be the barracks of a Russian tank unit, whose T-34s had gone into position there to guard the outer fortifications of Tula. A call from the brigade commander summoned the tanks of the advance detachment back to the road before they had completed outflanking the enemy. The Russians had abandoned their positions and fled along the northeast road.

Near Kolpna, Oberstleutnant von Oppeln's tank drove over a mine. Oppeln transferred to an armored troop carrier and continued to lead. The vehicles drove through the village. Beyond the village Russian tanks attacked again. They appeared suddenly over a hill. Fifteen tanks were counted. They were obviously attempting to break into the flank of the "Fast Advance detachment." The Germans accepted battle. The duel lasted half an hour. Then the Soviets withdrew their surviving tanks. Burning T-34s littered the landscape; but there were destroyed German tanks as well. Nevertheless, the advance continued.

The shattering impacts of the armor-piercing shells, which howled through the air at terrific speed, sounded twice as loud to von Oppeln's ears in the open armored troop carrier. But if he wanted to be successful, a tank commander had to be at the front with his men, for the changeable nature of a tank battle called for quick decisions to exploit a gap in the enemy position or a favorable situation. Tanks could only be led from the front.

On the evening of 28 October Kosayagora also fell into the hands of the "Fast Advance Detachment Eberbach." Generaloberst Guderian ordered the advance on Tula to begin the next day. The armored force set off on the last leg in the early morning hours. Once again the tanks rolled close behind the motorized infantry of the *Großdeutschland* Regiment. By noon they had reached a point ten kilometers south of Tula.

"We will be there by evening, Oppeln."

"The enemy is retreating rather too quickly for my liking, sir. I fear that we will meet stiffer resistance in Tula."

"If the infantry divisions follow up quickly enough it won't matter. Then we'll take Tula for sure. But first we will try to take it by surprise."

Oberst Eberbach's confidence infected every member of the armored attack force, which was already operating 200 kilometers ahead of the rest of the army. Once again the object was to breach an enemy blocking line, and when evening came on 29 October and mist began to form, the squat buildings of a workers settlement appeared before the leading tanks. Beyond it lay the vast complex of an industrial city—Tula—the reason they had been struggling through the mud for days. Tula was the weapons forge of the Czarist empire. And Tula, as everyone knew, was the last major Soviet position southwest of Moscow. The Soviet capital lay just 160 kilometers to the north. If Moscow was reached the war should be over. The soldiers thought of nothing else, for then they would go home again. And they would rather have been with their families than facing the cold, rain and mud—to say nothing of the Russian rounds and machine-gun fire.

"There is our target, Oppeln."

"And we have only sixteen tanks left, sir."

In the shimmering evening light they could see the Kremlin of Tula. The sound of fighting was coming from the workers settlement in front of the city. There infantry of the *Großdeutschland* Regiment was engaged in hand grenade and pistol duels with the stubborn defenders. Then a howling sound came from the city, swelling and filling the air. Rocket launchers of all calibers had opened fire on the attackers. Projectiles smashed into the following columns.

Horst Niemack (center) as commander of the Panzer Fusilier Regiment *Großdeutschland*.

"Tomorrow is another day Oppeln. First we will assemble and then attack with concentrated force." Then Eberbach radioed an order to his men: "Commander to everyone: stop, halt the attack!"

The company leading the assault grumbled about its fate.

"Come on Oppeln, we'll drive over there."

The two officers set off in the commander's car and reached the sixty men, all that was left of the *Großdeutschland* Infantry Regiment's 2nd Company.

"We'll do it tomorrow Oppeln. We attack tomorrow morning at 5:30."

"Perhaps we've already done it, sir."

Oberst Eberbach shook his head. He knew that none of the men had survived the assault on the fortress.

"Try to reconnoiter all enemy positions. Report to me tomorrow morning."

The next morning Oberst Eberbach and Oberstleutnant von Oppeln returned to the point group.

"There, behind that pile of wood, are the Russian forward outposts, sir. That red brick building is probably a barracks. It is like a small fortress, with antitank guns, mortars and snipers."

Oberst Hoernlein, who had only recently assumed command of the *Großdeutschland* Infantry Regiment, walked up and saluted the panzer commander. Then Hoernlein looked at his watch.

"Just 5:30!" he said curtly. "Attack! MG company position yourself on the Second's right. Go!"

The tanks could not attack, because antitank barricades had been erected on the outskirts of the town. The road there led through open terrain. The massed antitank fire would decimate them before they reached the town limits. Oberstleutnant von Oppeln followed the two Obersten as they ran along a hedge crouched low. The infantry worked their way toward the woodpile. A Maxim machine-gun opened fire, forcing the men of 2nd Company to take cover. The burst seemed to be a signal, for now the enemy opened up with everything he had. The officers ran with the men in the cover of the houses of the workers settlement. They worked their way forward in stages. Then Oberst Eberbach and Oberstleutnant von Oppeln (Hoernlein had left them by this time) reached the north end of the settlement. Now there were just 500 meters of open ground in front of them. But 200 meters away there was a deep and wide antitank ditch, which the commanders of the armored cars had described as impassible by tanks during the night advance. Another 300 meters beyond that stood the large building made of bright red brick.

The men of the 2nd Company were pinned down in the antitank ditch. Soviet snipers fired at any sign of movement. The 3rd Company was likewise pinned down before the red brick building. A request was made for supporting fire from tanks and artillery. The officers crawled and ran back to their tanks. The commanders could only fire sporadically as ammunition was running low. Because of the deep mud only a few supply trucks had gotten through.

Led by Oberstleutnant von Oppeln, the remaining sixteen tanks tried in vain to breach the Soviet defense line to the side of the antitank ditch. One after another they were knocked out. They did succeed in destroying several antitank guns, but the tank officers were finally forced to realize that the Soviets were defending Tula with everything at their disposal. The city was something of a symbol to the Russians. If Tula fell then the panzer divisions could advance farther to the east, turn north, and then Moscow would be encircled.

Antitank and antiaircraft guns fired at every German tank that showed itself. There was no getting through; the German advance forces were too weak. The previous defense by the enemy was not the cause of this weakness, instead it was the deep, clinging mud that was the decisive factor. It had brought all movement to a halt. There was no more ammunition. Knocked-out tanks could not be repaired because the mobile workshops could not get to the front. Only large tracked vehicles and horse-drawn panye wagons could get through this wasteland of mud. Everything else became stuck fast.

Even after the 3rd Panzer Division under Generalmajor Breith arrived to support the attack there was no progress. The enemy was so well entrenched with numerous antitank and antiaircraft guns in the city that the joint attack in the next days also failed. The 3rd Panzer Division lost some of its tanks in the battle. By the evening of 31 October it had just forty left. One hundred and ten had been lost during the advance on Tula and the battle in the city itself.

The Soviets deployed every unit to Tula that they could muster. It was there that Oberstleutnant von Oppeln-Bronikowski first experienced a barrage from a battalion of multiple rocket launchers, called "Katyusha" (the diminutive form of Kathryn—"little Katy") by the Soviets and "Stalin Organs" by the Germans. While the Soviet expenditure of artillery ammunition was profligate, the artillery of the two German divisions had to count every shell. There were no deliveries of food either. Finally the few remaining tanks were immobilized for lack of fuel.

✠

None of the German troops bogged down in front of Tula could know that it would be 19 November before a new attack was made. After this began, by 24 November the 4th Panzer Division, with the Eberbach brigade leading the way, went around Tula and advanced as far as the Aleksin Heights, east of the rail line to Moscow. When the Soviet 49th Army, which had halted the main assault with its Siberian divisions, began to falter, the 50th Army came out of the Moscow defense ring to support it. Lieutenant-General Boldin, the army's commander in chief, had received orders to halt, encircle and destroy the German 2nd Panzer Army. Here Oberstleutnant von Oppeln-Bronikowski learned what it meant to take part in a deep raid by tanks and finally to stand up to an enemy counterattack with wide-open flanks. The situation of the German forces was made even worse by the onset of unusually cold weather, for they were still without winter equipment.

On 27 November the 131st Infantry Division took Aleksin. Leading the last panzers, Oberstleutnant von Oppeln stormed ahead to the Tula-Moscow rail line. Demolition teams blew up the tracks. Kostrova was taken the next day, blocking the Tula-Serpukhov-Moscow road to the enemy. On 3 December the members of the 31st Infantry Division, advancing from west to east and trying to link up with the 4th Panzer Division, got to within 15 kilometers of the road before they were forced to halt their attack. The arctic cold reached temperatures of minus forty-five degrees. The tanks simply refused to move. Gunsights iced up, the engines refused to start, vacuum tubes in the radios burst.

Early on the morning of 6 December 1941, fifteen kilometers south of Tula at Yasnaya Polyana, the estate of the Russian poet Tolstoy, Generaloberst Guderian made the decision to call off the attack. He was forced to withdraw the forward elements of the 2nd Panzer Army and go over to the defensive in order to prevent the destruction of the entire army. Guderian sent the following signal to the OKH: "The attack on Moscow has failed."

At the beginning of December the attacking German armies held a 300-kilometer front in front of Moscow. A few days later the Soviets launched their great counteroffensive, a pincer movement by the Northern and Southwestern Fronts. Colonel-General Konev led the northern group of forces, while the Southwestern Front was commanded by Marshal Zhukov.

When the order finally came for the 4th Panzer Division to withdraw, virtually the entire 2nd Panzer Army had already been cut off. Fresh Soviet divisions, well-armed and wearing warm winter clothing, struck the overextended and exhausted troops of the 2nd Panzer Army. Casualties from frostbite reached unheard of levels. There was fierce fighting all along the army group's front.

Later General von Oppeln-Bronikowski said of those December days: "We often saw the ghost of Napoleon's defeat of 1812 walking about."

While the order to fall back reached the division, the engines of most of its vehicles were already hopelessly frozen. Entire tank columns were rendered immobile and had to be blown up. The division command ordered the Eberbach panzer brigade to form the 2nd Panzer Army's rear guard and cover its withdrawal. Generalmajor Baron von Langermann und Erlenkamp knew exactly what he was demanding of the brigade. But he also knew that Oberst Eberbach would complete this task. The 2nd Panzer Army retreated southwest over what had earlier been its advance road. Leading the 35th Panzer Regiment, Oberst Eberbach held off the pursuing Russians.

As a result of the southwestward retreat contact was lost with the 4th Army in the north. This resulted in a gap through which Marshal Zhukov sent his forces in a drive toward Vyazma. On 26 December 1941 Generaloberst Guderian was relieved of his command by Hitler as a result of a complaint by Feldmarschall Kluge. In his last order of the day to the troops the Generaloberst wrote: "My thoughts go with you on your difficult journey."

On 13 January 1942 Oberst Eberbach took over the 4th Panzer Division from General von Langermann und Erlenkamp, who had been selected to command a panzer corps. Eberbach was promoted to Generalmajor on 1 March 1942. Before he left, Eberback recommended Oppeln-Bronikowski to succeed him. On 1 February 1942 Hermann von Oppeln-Bronikowski was promoted to the rank of Oberst. He and his regiment were engaged in heavy defensive fighting against the hard-charging Soviets east of Bryansk. He later said of this phase of the battle, which was characterized by small unit actions and steady casualties:

> Now the German Army had to pay for continuing to attack into the winter instead of going over to the defensive at the proper time in a suitable front, pulling out reserves and securing the areas behind the front.
>
> Partisan groups, which had laid low behind he advancing German troops and bolstered their ranks, now began an intensified campaign of sabotage. They ambushed runners, sentries, quarters and transports. They laid mines on the roads, destroyed railway lines, cisterns, and bridges. This battle against the partisans was extraordinarily vicious and cruel. They were disguised as harmless

civilians and could not be identified as combatants. No prisoners were taken.

To deal with this serious threat to our rear communications we set up special roads. These were strongly defended supply roads. They led through the partisan zone and could only be traveled in convoy.

Of his "learning stage" General von Oppeln said:

General Eberbach (later commander of an army) was an especially capable, extraordinarily brave and proven commander of armored forces, from whom I learned absolutely everything that a tank commander could learn. In particular he taught me how to conduct night tank attacks.

The precondition for this most difficult style of battle is a reliable, disciplined group of men who work well together. The enemy and the terrain also play important roles.

In the defensive fighting east of Briansk Oberst von Oppeln-Bronikowski earned the reputation of being a cautious but at the same time fearless commander. He and his experienced tank commanders received the Panzer Close Combat Badges in Bronze and Silver. At the end of September, on completion of home leave, he received orders to join the 22nd Panzer Division and take over the 204th Panzer Regiment.

Russian Lend-Lease Shermans knocked out or disabled by the tanks of von Oppeln-Bronikowski.

COMMANDER OF THE 204TH PANZER REGIMENT—THE KNIGHT'S CROSS—WOUNDED IN ACTION

When Oberst von Oppeln-Bronikowski reached the 22nd Panzer Division, which was stationed between the Don and Donets Rivers, he learned at the division command post that the present regimental commander was still unaware that he was to be relieved. Almost all regimental commanders had already been relieved. Only Oberst Eberhard Rodt, commander of the division's 22nd Rifle Brigade, was left, but he had been named division commander.

When the Oberst reported to his division commander, the latter said to him: "Oppeln, we are going to be in a difficult position. The OKW believes that our division let the side down in the Crimea. It is up to us to win back the reputation of the division and its soldiers, who fought just as bravely as the soldiers of the other divisions."

"When did all this happen, Rodt?"

"I came to the division in February 1942 to take over the 22nd Rifle Brigade, which at the time was still in the formation and training stage in France. The already combat-ready elements of the division were transported into the Odessa area at the end of February, first of March. On 20 March they were committed to an attack in the Crimea even though the division and brigade commanders objected strongly on the grounds that the enemy would be able to see them from far away on the flat terrain chosen for the attack. After one and a half kilometers of open terrain there was a wide ravine with a deep antitank ditch. Beyond it lay Russian field emplacements. Our artillery had not yet arrived. The artillery assigned to us had insufficient stocks of ammunition. The army nevertheless ordered the attack to go ahead because it did not believe that the antitank ditch was there as the Soviets had only recently seized the area from the Romanians. There was dense fog when the attack began. The few tanks got lost and when it cleared up they came under heavy fire from antitank and field guns. The tanks were forced to turn back, the grenadiers followed; the result was a difficult situation which threatened to turn into panic."

"And what happened then?" asked von Oppeln, fascinated by his commanding officer's account.

"Because I was not involved in the attack, my staff and I set up an observation post on the hill behind which the attack force was marshaled. My men and I succeeded in stopping the division's flight-like retreat. That was all."

"Well, it surely wasn't easy."

"It was done. The division was pulled out of the combat zone and carried out battle exercises in the rear area. Things improved after that. The conquest of the Crimea and the capture of Bulganak, Kerch and the entire east coast of the Crimea was its work."

Oberst Rodt's report was over.

"And my panzer regiment?"

"Sixty percent of your tanks are Czech Skoda 38s, which though maneuverable are old and poorly armored. Only forty percent are German Panzer IVs. Drive to your regiment tomorrow morning and take command."

"Thank you for your frank account, Rodt."

"Nothing to thank me for Oppeln. Here's hoping we work well together in the future."

The two colonels said goodbye and Oppeln drove to his new regiment. He found the regiment spread out in a village which was divided into two parts by an overgrown ravine.

The Oberst called a regiment parade on 6 October. He introduced himself and concluded his brief address with the words:

"Don't think that we are in quiet winter quarters here. One day the Soviets will attack here and then we will all have to do our best, officers and men."

What Oberst von Oppeln experienced there in those October days would have been material for a gothic novel. He found that the important tank workshop was still in front of the division behind the front held by their Italian allies. When he tried to withdraw it he learned that it did not have a drop of fuel. He asked for fuel but received just fifty liters—and this after urgent requests—with which he was supposed to find and greet the units of his regiment. The entire regiment had no fuel. The tanks could not be moved nor could they be repaired or checked. The firewood needed by the field kitchens had to be brought in daily by sleighs drawn by cows.

On top of this there was the uncertainty of the situation, for there, above the deep northern flank of the 6th Army fighting in Stalingrad, the line was being held by the forces of Germany's allies: the 2nd Hungarian Army, the Romanian 3rd Army and the Italian 8th Army. Oberst von Oppeln was terrified when he thought of the consequences for the 6th Army of a Soviet assault on this unstable sector of the front. Generalmajor von Oppeln said of that front: "Hitler committed a serious mistake when he gave into the demands of the allied governments to commit their divisions in complete armies instead of deploying them by divisions in quiet sectors of the front. And this mistake was further aggravated by placing the armies of all three allies side by side and in a place where the Soviets were likely to launch an offensive."

In an effort to provide "corset stays" to hold these three armies together, the XXXXVIII Panzer Corps under Generalleutnant Heim, with the weak 22nd Panzer Division, the Romanian 1st Armored Division and elements of the 14th Panzer Division, was deployed close behind them. The corps headquarters was located in Serafimovichi.

Oberst von Oppeln now tried to acquire the fuel that he needed so badly. The tanks had to be moved to avoid damage. But initially Oppeln's most dangerous foe turned out to be mice. The men of 1st Company, 204th Panzer Regiment, became mouse catchers. They became so proficient that in one night they caught over 600 mice using traps consisting of trap doors with water-filled gas canisters beneath them. Oberst von Oppeln received his mission orders on 10 November 1942. His regiment was to lead the division into the area of the Romanian army, more than 250 kilometers away, reach the Kalachev area and report to Headquarters, Romanian 3rd Army. He alerted his units. Oppeln himself drove to 1st Company. He watched as the tanks were towed out of their makeshift shelters, however their engines refused to start. It was late in the evening. Temperatures fell to minus twenty degrees.

Oppeln turned to his operations officer: "What's going on, Becker? Go and find out and then report back to me at once."

Oberleutnant Becker returned several minutes later.

"Only 39 of the regiment's 104 tanks have started, sir."

Oppeln cursed under his breath. He set off in his command car to drive to the individual companies. The situation was the same everywhere he went: several tanks warming up their engines, the rest sitting immobile in their shelters.

"All company commanders report to me in ten minutes. I want to know what the problem is."

"This is the result of conservation measures, Becker," Oppeln said to his operations officer bitterly. "Now we sit here. Imagine such a situation should the Russians break through on this front."

A muffled explosion caused the windows of the regiment command post to rattle. At the same time men jumped up and ran for cover. One of 2nd Company's tanks was ablaze. The driver rolled in the snow in order to extinguish his burning clothes. Another threw a coat over him and extinguished the flames.

"What was that?"

"Tank exploded while they were trying to start it, sir. It is inexplicable, and . . ."

Then there was a second explosion.

"Damned mess! Get over there Becker!"

But the Oberleutnant did not have to go and see what was happening, for just then a runner arrived from 3rd Company.

"Sir, sir!" he gasped. "Two panzers out of action. One is on fire, the other exploded."

"Thank you," said Oppeln. He fought back his rage. He had to maintain his composure in front of his men if he was to prevent this confusion from turning into chaos.

"Inspect all tanks before trying to start them!" he ordered.

Von Oppeln walked back into his command post with long strides.

"The division commander, hurry Heintze!"

Unteroffizier Heintze, leader of the radio team, made the connection. Oberst Rodt came on the line and he passed the receiver to his commanding officer.

"What's going on, Oppeln? What's the cause for all the noise?"

"Four of my tanks have exploded, sir. Only thirty-nine have started and are warming their engines. We have to determine the cause for this disastrous fiasco. Request permission to delay departure until tomorrow morning."

"I have already asked corps to delay the departure time until tomorrow morning, in vain. But I will try again, Oppeln, and call you back. In any case look into the matter as quickly as possible, so that we can put everything possible into the report. You know of course that they are looking down their noses at us."

"I will do everything in my power, sir."

Five minutes later the senior technical sergeant from the repair company came rushing into the command post. He had a few cables and wires in his hand.

"Here, sir! Mice! The mice have chewed through the cables!"

Lost in thought, Oberst von Oppeln picked up his eraser from the desk in front of him. Mice had been gnawing on it, too.

"I understand. The beasts have gnawed away the insulation, causing short-circuits. Sparks fly and then there's an explosion."

"That's it, sir."

"Inspect that all the tanks that did not start immediately. Remove all electrical cables and replace them."

The technical sergeant left. There was no need for Oberst von Oppeln to remind him how important it was to repair the tanks quickly.

"Report to division. Take this down Mündelein!"

In brief sentences Oberst von Oppeln described the severe consequences that had resulted from the withholding of fuel and the weeks-long languishing of the tanks in their straw-filled pens. Periodic test drives would have scared the mice away or at least revealed the defects in time. The telephone rang. Unteroffizier Heintze answered.

"Sir, it's the division commander."

Oppeln took the receiver.

"Listen Oppeln. You are to depart at 21:30 hours with all your serviceable tanks. All the others must be repaired as quickly as possible and try to catch up during the night or tomorrow morning. No delay is possible. The Romanians are in trouble. We have to get there as quickly as possible to put out the fire. Have you found the cause for the tank problem, Oppeln?"

"Mice, sir. They have gnawed through the rubber cables, causing short-circuits."

"Send me a report at once. Out!"

Precisely at 9:30 P.M., Oberst von Oppeln, standing in the open turret hatch of his PzKfw. 38(t) tank, raised his arm and pumped it up and down three times.

"Panzers, move out!"

The serviceable tanks moved off. It was the beginning of a night drive that would seem like a nightmare to all the men. Without snow cleats the tanks slid like crazy on the icy road. Now and then one became stuck and was pulled free again. Then one tank exploded. It, too, had become a victim of the mice. But it was not just tanks that broke down along the way. The other vehicles suffered even more badly from the cold and the icy roads. The division commander came forward in his fast armored troop carrier; von Oppeln described the misery of this drive.

"I have lost three more, sir, and the worst thing about it is that my tank workshop has to be stranded because of lack of fuel. All manner of improvisation has to be used to get the unserviceable tanks moving again. In any case Oberleutnant Blöcker has reported that eleven tanks are already on their way to join us."

"One bit of good news at least. We have to keep a stiff upper lip, Oppeln."

The area of operations was reached on 11 November 1942 following a drive of 250 kilometers. But the division, which was already weakened, had lost many more vehicles along the way. Once again it became apparent that the chain of command was too long. The winter equipment for vehicles and tanks, ordered weeks earlier, was still on a train somewhere between Germany and the front. Instead of 104 tanks, on the evening of 11 November Oberst von Oppeln had just 31 at his disposal. They took up quarters in the specified assembly area behind the Romanians, in the

A column of T-34/85s at Heiligenbeil, Germany.

XXXXVIII Panzer Corps' area of operations. Oberst von Oppeln worked hard to get further tanks operational. One day later he was about to leave his command post for the front lines when he received a visit from a Major and an Hauptmann from corps.

"Show the officers in, Becker."

The two officers entered the command post. They identified themselves and asked the Oberst for a conversation involving just the three of them. The regiment commander gave a wave and his staff disappeared into an adjoining room.

"Now, gentlemen, what do you have to say to me?"

"The commanding general is dismayed by your report. He thinks that you are ill. The OKH has already initiated court martial proceedings. No one believes this mouse story, and after all the division is known as . . ."

With a decisive movement of his hand, Oberst von Oppeln halted the Major in mid-sentence.

"Not one word of reproach against the men of this division, gentlemen. I am standing by my report one hundred percent. What do you know of the front? What do you know of the terrible mouse plague? Here are the chewed-up cables, take them with you and place them on the table at home. And don't forget to add that the division commander and I have been requesting fuel for weeks and haven't received a drop. But now I have to go to the front. You can come along if you want to and examine the situation on the spot."

The Oberst stood up brusquely and walked out of the command post, where his command tank was waiting.

"Well, what will it be?"

"Regretfully, sir, we must return to the corps and make our report. I cannot hide my concern from you."

The two officers saluted and disappeared into their half-tracked vehicle.

"We've shaken them off, Becker."

"But not for long, sir."

Oberleutnant Becker was soon proved right. The next officer arrived two days later. This time he came direct from the OKH. When Oberst von Oppeln recognized the Major in his command post a smile came over his now haggard features.

"For God's sake, Burr, you're here? But not because of the damned mice again?"

"That's exactly why, sir. At the OKH they're saying that to make such a report you must be seeing white mice."

"Very well, then see the situation for yourself, Burr!"

"That's no longer necessary. I flew in from Berlin. At the Smolensk airfield I saw a large number of unserviceable machines. I will give you three guesses as to what they told me the cause was, sir."

"If you ask such suggestive questions, Burr, I would guess it was the work of mice."

"And you would be right. They also told me there that the mice had chewed through the rubber insulation on the wires."

"Very well then, let's have a drink."

Following a visit to the front Major Burr considered his mission completed and the next day he flew back to the OKH. The story had a happy ending and even the OKH was forced to realize that in addition to Generals "Mud" and "Winter," the Soviets now also had General "Mouse" working for them. The whole affair resulted in Oppeln acquiring a new nickname to go along with his others, one that would stay with him until the end of the war. From then on he was known as the "Mouse Commander."

✠

"Alert, sir. Several Soviet armies have broken through between Kletskaya and Blinov. Waves of tanks have already reached Blinov and are driving towards Petschany!"

"Becker, alert the regiment. Departure in thirty minutes. Have the command tank in front of the command post fueled and armed."

The alert roused the men from their rest. It was exactly 0905 hours when the alert came. Thirty minutes later when Oberst von Oppeln left his command post, he already knew more. The army group had committed the XXXXVIII Panzer Corps to counterattack toward the north. But contact with the Romanian 1st Armored Division, which was also subordinate to the corps, had been lost immediately after the announcement of the breakthrough. The tanks moved off. Soon they met Romanian units streaming towards the rear. In vain Oppeln tried to stop them. There was panic in the eyes of these men, who had faced the first great assault by the Soviets.

Seeing the chaos, Oppeln said, "I have never seen such a catastrophe, neither in the First World War nor in this one."

"Now we will have to restore the situation alone, sir."

"First we'll drive a bit farther, Becker, then we'll see."

A radioed order was received from Oberst Rodt: "Division commander to panzer regiment: veer northwest. Order from corps: advance towards

Peschany. Units of the Soviet 5th Shock Army are already advancing from there through Blinov. The danger exists that they may drive through as far as Kalach and link up there with the Russian forces coming from the east."

Oppeln turned to his adjutant.

"That means a 180-degree turn, Becker!"

"But that's impossible! It's crazy, sir, we can't . . ."

They did it nevertheless. One hour later the bulk of the regiment had turned towards its new objective. There now began a drive which was to put even the march of 10 November in the shade. The fast reconnaissance tanks in front, the regiment rolled towards Peschany. Once again the roads were icy tracks, and still there were no snow cleats for the tanks. The heavy guns and the flak were even worse off. Then, suddenly, a gaping, ice-covered ravine appeared before the panzers.

"Through, Spangenberg!"

The Oberfeldwebel at the controls of the Skoda tank was an outstanding driver; but when he saw the steep slope and the glistening surface he shook his head doubtfully.

Then he said, "in the name of God!" and felt sweat running down his back. He shifted back into first gear and drove over the last meters of level ground. Then the nose of the tank tipped forward and it went down as if on skis. A tree raced toward it.

"Slowly left, Spangenberg!"

The driver cautiously braked the left track. The tree moved out of their path centimeter by centimeter. Then the right side glanced against the tree and the tank began to turn. In seconds it was heading down the slope tail first. The tank continued to spin slowly and soon it was sliding sideways. But finally it straightened out and reached the bottom of the ravine.

"Up, get up!"

The tank's engine roared as it headed up the opposite slope. It climbed several meters before sliding back down again.

"Damn it to hell!" the Oberfeldwebel cursed beneath his breath. "Turn right and drive along the floor of the ravine!"

The heavy tank turned. Up above the next tank headed down into the ravine. The command tank drove a few hundred meters, came to a side-gully and drove out there. The tanks forced their way through the ravine, laboriously, one after the other. The division headquarters, which was following close behind, also made it through. Then came the antitank battalion and the panzer-grenadier battalion. A light battery also made it through the icy obstacle, solely because of the efforts of one man.

Late in the afternoon a village appeared before the tanks.

"That is Peschany, sir, and . . ."

The Oberleutnant fell silent, for just then something resembling a great chase broke out of the village toward the south.

"They're Romanians! Well, that tears it!"

Yes, it was the division headquarters and elements of the Romanian 14th Infantry Division which were leaving Peschany in such a hurry. Why they were in such a hurry soon became apparent to the tank commanders standing in their turrets. Tanks emerged from the towering shadows of the town. Within minutes they could see as many as thirty, widely spaced. Flames shot from their long guns, shells howled toward the fleeing Romanians. The blazing hulks of trucks were left sitting by the roadside.

"Report to division commander: Russian armored spearhead in Peschany!"

Thirty seconds after the message was sent, Oberst von Oppeln gave the order to counterattack. He could wait no longer.

"Spread out! Engage the enemy tanks and stop them!"

"Tank destroyers move left past the panzer regiment and bring the enemy tank spearhead to a halt!" Seconds later orders arrived from the division commander.

The first T-34 was only 600 meters from the leading German tank, which was almost invisible behind several groups of bushes.

"Open fire!"

Gunner Unteroffizier Kernlein depressed the gun slightly. The dark shadow of the enemy tank loomed huge in his sight. The T-34 halted. It fired at a fleeing truck, which was hit and blown to pieces. Now Kernlein fired. The shot struck the front of the Soviet tank, precisely between the turret and hull. The turret was lifted slightly. Then for a few seconds nothing happened, until the turret hatch suddenly snapped back and a jet of flame shot out.

The Russian tankers tried to get out. They were met by fire from the advancing grenadiers, who now took cover to the right and left of the panzers and dug into the snowdrifts. Some of the Soviet infantry ran behind their tanks. Others pulled Maxim machine-guns on squat sleighs, while others continued to fire wildly at the Romanians, who were still emerging from side roads and behind haystacks, running for their lives. The sky gradually grew darker. Tracer crisscrossed the plain in front of the town, weaving itself into a fiery carpet. All of the tanks were now engaged, but the Skodas were inferior to the robust T-34s. They had to close to within 600 meters for their 37-mm guns to be effective.

"Change position Spangenberg! To the right, over to that hay rick!"

The Oberfeldwebel steered the tank in the assigned direction. He suddenly shifted up, because five or six T-34s were concentrating their fire on the German tank which had just broken cover. This move by Oppeln took the pressure off the hard-pressed 1st Company, but it exposed him to a storm of enemy fire. They reached the hay rick but they were only safe for a few seconds. Three or four shells raced in and the rick was soon in flames.

"Get out of here and move over to the first houses!"

Once again the command tank leapt forward. It raced toward a fence and crushed it into the snow.

"First Company follow!"

The tanks of the 1st Company followed. On a front of 200 meters they drove toward the command panzer, which was far ahead and firing at other Soviet tanks. Three Soviets tanks which were preparing to open fire at the approaching company were forced away by the command tank's rapid fire. Then there were six or seven shots from the left in rapid succession.

"The tank destroyers, sir!"

"Great! Now forward, we're taking the village!"

The tanks rolled forward in a semicircle. The Soviet tanks halted. Caught in a crossfire from the panzers and tank destroyers, they were knocked out one after another. The command tank encountered a T-34 in the middle of Peschany. The Soviet crew were still firing into the Romanian headquarters. The enemy tank was only 150 meters away when Kernlein took aim at it. The first round sent flames spurting from its engine compartment. The second killed the crew.

"Everyone move up! Assemble into battle formation at the north end of the village!"

The tanks reached the north end of the village. Their shells hissed through the darkness after the fleeing Soviet tanks, recognizable by their glowing exhausts.

"Panzer regiment to division commander. Village is cleared of the enemy!"

"Stay there Oppeln. I'm sending the 24th Motorcycle Battalion to provide infantry support and I'm coming with it."

Oberst von Oppeln inspected the entire defense front. He directed the tanks into the most favorable positions and had recognized enemy machine-gun positions placed under fire followed by an immediate change of position. In this way the tanks escaped the retaliatory artillery fire by the Russians. Soon afterwards Oberst Rodt arrived up front. He had brought the motorcycle troops with him. They took up positions all around the village, from the northwest through north to the northeast, and set up flanking machine-gun positions.

"One more panzer division, Oppeln, and we would be able to stop the enemy here. But we are too weak as we are. The Soviets will bypass us on the left and right."

"They will attack us at dawn, sir."

"I think so. We have to commit everything to meet this Russian attack."

"How many tanks do you have left, Oppeln?"

"Exactly twenty, sir."

"Twenty of 104. If we had the entire regiment here . . ."

"Our eastern neighbor is the Romanian 1st Armored Division. General Radu is a good man, one we can depend on. He won't abandon his positions. So, Oppeln, report to me as soon as you see anything. I have to go and see how the motorcycle troops are settling in."

While Oberst Rodt went over to the motorcycle troops, Oberst von Oppeln visited his tank crews. The last of the cigarettes were passed out. Then the Oberst went over to his makeshift command post, where the signals men had already established contact with the division.

✠

At dawn on 20 November Oberst von Oppeln was roused from his sleep roughly. With a mighty roar the Soviet artillery opened fire on the village. One minute after the start of the barrage a salvo from a "Katyusha" battalion howled toward the German positions. The rocket projectiles landed just behind the tanks, falling within a several-hundred-meter circle. Flames rose from the houses of Peschany.

"We're driving to the First!" Oppeln shouted to his driver.

The command tank rolled into the combat position, followed by the operations officer and battlefield messengers in an armored troop carrier. The commander of 1st Company reported. Everyone stared tensely into the gray darkness of the early morning. They could see nothing, apart from the occasional rocket salvoes passing overhead and the tracer.

"Tanks open fire on attacking enemy tanks!" ordered Oppeln.

As if on cue, huge shadows emerged from the mist and began to close on the German positions, engines roaring. A wave of fast T-26 tanks approached on the far left flank. When they came within range the tank destroyers opened fire. The shells smashed into the lightly armored vehicles and sent them up in flames. A mass of T-34s immediately veered towards the tank destroyers and opened fire. Then with a loud crack the German command tank also opened fire. At once flames also shot from the muzzles of the other German tanks. Twenty shells raced toward the approaching enemy. A number of tanks were knocked out, but the rest continued to come nearer and nearer. As soon as they were within range of the German tanks they began dodging to the left and right. Soviet assault troops followed in dense waves, shouting their battle cry. Wearing white snow smocks, in the semi-darkness they were almost invisible against the background.

"Ten o'clock. Eight-hundred. Two tanks."

The turret rotated in the direction given by the commander. Two enemy tanks and a whole company of following infantry were trying to break into Peschany from the northwest. Unteroffizier Kernlein fired. The shell passed over the rear of the Soviet tank and disappeared. He immediately adjusted his aim, leading the enemy tank, and fired when the forward third of the vehicle appeared in his sight. The shell shattered one of the T-34's tracks. Nevertheless, the squat turret housing the long tank cannon swung toward the German command tank. The next shot jammed the turret of the Russian tank just in time. Then the crew heard the sound of an explosion. A jet of red flame shot up from the crippled T-34.

"That was the antitank guns!"

The Soviets reached the northwest end of the village and through the rumble of the heavy guns, the howling of the rockets and the bark of tank

Tanks on the move on the steppes of Russia.

cannon the crews could hear the sound of small arms fire and exploding hand grenades.

"They're trapped now, sir!" gasped the driver.

"First Company counterattack the northwest end with me and drive the Soviets out!" ordered Oppeln.

The tank engines roared louder. They moved off, picked up speed, and headed to where the infantry battle was raging. A group of Russians jumped behind a wall.

"Load high-explosive!"

The first shot smashed into the side of a house. The second passed through a door hanging off its hinges. The German motorcycle troops saw their tanks, followed and wiped out the Soviet troops who had occupied the first houses.

"The Russians have broken through to the center of town, sir!"

"Turn! Back into the center of town."

They drove back the T-34s, losing three tanks in the process. Fortunately two had only track damage, which could be repaired in a few hours. The Soviets repeated their attack. Once again thirty or more tanks approached in a broad semicircle. The German tanks and antitank guns fired as fast as they could. Once again a number of enemy tanks were destroyed before the northern exit from the village. In the first light of day Oberst von Oppeln counted more than twenty Russian tanks burning, smoking and immobilized outside the village.

"Fourth to commander. Only six rounds of armor-piercing left for each tank!"

The third wave of the Soviet attack, at least a division strong, fought its way into the first houses along the entire width of the village. The German tanks had to fight their way back step by step to avoid being encircled and destroyed. Gradually the Soviets gained control of the village. The German tanks and antitank guns had already withdrawn to the south end of the village when the division commander came roaring up from the southwest in his armored troop carrier.

"Oppeln, to the west our motorcycle troops are pinned down in the houses behind the brickworks."

"We'll get them out and cover the withdrawal."

With his last sixteen tanks Oberst von Oppeln drove into the Russian armored wedge again and then veered off to the west. They reached the spot where the men of the 24th Motorcycle Battalion had been cut off. Placing itself between the motorcycle troops and the pressing Soviets like an iron shield, von Oppeln's regiment covered their withdrawal. Facing the massed Soviet assault, the infantry had been decimated and, discouraged, were almost at the end of their strength.

"Everyone assemble on the two hills south of the village!" Oberst von Oppeln called to the men as they passed by his tank.

They picked up the 1st Battalion of the 129th Panzer-Grenadier Regiment. The artillery, which had finally arrived on the scene, was deployed to cover the flanks by Oberst Rodt. When the enemy attempted to advance south from Peschany the division was able to prevent another breakthrough. Once again the tank destroyers and tanks played equal roles in deflecting the Soviet tank attack. Together they destroyed a total of twenty-six enemy tanks on 20 November 1942. Reconnaissance revealed that the enemy had already bypassed the division to the east and west. All that was left of the Romanian 14th Infantry Division was a few stragglers. To the west the Romanian 7th Cavalry Division was also retreating rapidly south.

"If we stay here any longer," Oberst von Oppeln-Bronikowski said to the division commander, his voice filled with concern, "we will soon be trapped and will be of no further use to the 6th Army."

"I am expecting orders from corps at any minute, Oppeln. I was told to expect new orders an hour ago."

Oberst von Oppeln had arrived at the division command post to confer with the division commander and the commander of the artillery regiment. Luckily, several minutes after their arrival a radio message arrived from corps headquarters. It said:

"Twenty-second Panzer Division is to disengage from the enemy and withdraw. Occupy new positions between Donshchina and Hill 191.2. These are to be held!"

When darkness came Oberst Rodt ordered elements of the division to pull back to the specified line and reconnoiter and occupy the new positions. Only then did the main body of the division disengage and pull back. The enemy discovered the withdrawal on the right wing. He immediately attacked with tanks and infantry and tried to take Donshchina. Once again von Oppeln and his tanks intervened. The enemy was halted and thrown back.

All day long the Soviets kept trying to break through. Once they came with infantry, then with tanks, and finally a cavalry regiment approached. It looked as if the horsemen intended to charge the division's tanks and antitank guns. Shells ripped gaping holes in the ranks of the approaching riders. Horses fell tossing their Cossack riders forward over their heads. It was a grim scene of destruction. Finally the remnants of the decimated regiment fled to the north.

Luckily Oberst von Oppeln began receiving supplies again. He urged his tank crews to stay alert, for a decisive Russian tank attack had to follow soon. The armored reconnaissance vehicles, which had driven out through the enemy fire, returned. They reported strong enemy movements from Pschany to the southwest. At approximately 2:30 P.M. the Soviets attacked with another large formation of cavalry. This time the attack was spotted earlier than on the previous occasion and the artillery scattered the horsemen.

"They've gone crazy!" said Oberst von Oppeln, dismayed at such profligacy in human life. "All those brave riders and their horses!"

When the enemy cavalry withdrew Oberst von Oppeln had four panzers make preparations to sortie. They drove north at high speed, reached the southeast and southwest roads from Peschany and saw that there was heavy truck and horse-drawn traffic on both.

"To division commander. Heavy enemy traffic on both roads out of Peschany. Request artillery and air support."

The four tanks fired into the columns until a hail of rocket projectiles landed on the spot where they had just turned. They subsequently headed back at high speed, zigzagging as they went. A heavy blow against the rear of the command tank knocked it off course, Oppeln smelled gasoline fumes.

"Get out!" he ordered.

The men jumped out through the commander's and driver's hatches. Shells fell nearby. One came howling straight toward the commander. He leapt into a shallow shell crater and felt the blast wave. The sound of the exploding shell deafened him for a few seconds. A tank rolled up. Its commander must have seen that the crew of Oppeln's tank had abandoned their vehicle. Von Oppeln and his men climbed onto the rear of the tank. Turning around, he saw smoke and flames belching from his own vehicle. They finally reached the German positions. Above them shells from the division artillery and flak flew toward the enemy. Both Russian columns were halted by the barrage. The enemy advance ground to a halt. One hour later dense waves of enemy infantry broke into the lines of the 129 Grenadier Regiment's I Battalion.

Oppeln led all of his remaining tanks out of the assembly area. They came upon the Soviets, who had occupied the first line of German trenches, and drove them back. The trenches were collapsed and filled in by the tank tracks. Behind the tanks the counterattack reserve moved up and drove back the last Russians who had allowed the tanks to overrun them. Then the former main line of resistance was firmly in German hands again. Soviet tanks attacked again and nine were destroyed by the

German tanks and the flak, which was still with the antitank guns. In the late afternoon Oberst Rodt described the situation in this position to the corps headquarters with the following words:

"As a result of heavy casualties and because of the need to extend the wings, especially the west wing, the position is very weakly manned by the infantry. One really cannot speak of a position any more. In reality it is a thin screen of infantry bolstered by heavy weapons."

A short time later corps headquarters ordered a withdrawal to a position south of Kurtlak. As the division was already aware from intercepted radio messages that enemy tanks were advancing on Kalachev from the east, Oberst Rodt had the motorcycle troops and flak leave the position first and sent them to secure the crossings over the Kurtlak. When this was done another order was received from corps headquarters. It read:

"The division is to hold in its present position. If the Kurtlak river line has already been reached, the division is to attack again to the north the next morning."

After the war Generalmajor von Oppeln-Bronikowski said: "The 22nd Panzer Division was given tasks which were in no way in keeping with its fighting strength. Not only was it inadequately equipped, but it had the strength of only half a division and the fighting of the previous two days had taken a heavy toll on these few soldiers."

The bulk of the division was already pulling back when this order arrived. Only weak rear guards were still in contact with the enemy. Nevertheless, the division command succeeded in stopping them in the Medweshij area and during the night deploying them on the hills on either side of the town.

✠

For the battered division 22 November 1942 became an inferno the like of which it had not experienced before. It had orders to advance north and make contact with the Romanian 1st Armored Division, which was (or more accurately was thought to be) in the Donshchinski area. Early morning reconnaissance revealed that the Soviets were already deep in the western flank and rear of the division. Daumov was already occupied. Petrovka was under attack. On the Kurtlak as well, the enemy was advancing west and had already reached Golbinski. The Soviets had also occupied the heights north and northeast of Medweshij. And still an unending torrent of motorized columns, tanks and cavalry continued to pour south.

All the incoming reports eventually revealed a shocking picture of the situation. The enemy ring had closed around all the units in the area of

Donshchinka-Medweshij-Malaya-Donshchinski. Division ordered all secret papers destroyed. Among the articles that went into the fire was the division war diary.

✠

Precisely at 11 A.M. Oberst von Oppeln, who was leading the forward armored group, gave the order to move out. A few minutes later Soviet cavalry units attacked again from the north and west. They galloped toward the armored spearhead over the frozen ground. Before Oppeln could give the order to fire, the artillery, which was still with the rear guard, opened up. Once again men and horses fell to the ground. Anything left to face the tanks was blasted with high-explosive shells. Then it was over.

"Reconnaissance platoon up! Becker, reconnoiter in the direction of Perelasovski!"

The armored scout cars, escorted by two gun cars, rolled forward. The crews soon returned and reported Perelasovski occupied by the enemy. The division reached the high ground east of Donshchinski without meeting the enemy. There a report was received which confirmed that the Soviets had advanced via Petrovka into the Chernyshevskaya area behind them.

"That means that the division's supply road has been cut, Becker. The ring around us has been closed to the south."

"We will fight our way through somehow, sir."

"Now we have to seek out a position where we can set up an all-round defense. The Soviets will attack."

Oppeln drove to the division commander. Oberst Rodt had reached the same conclusions. He pointed to the map which one of his battlefield messengers was holding on his back while the operations officer steadied it.

"Here, on Hill 168.9 west of Perelasovski, is the best possibility for us."

"Then let's go there, sir!"

They reached the target area by nightfall. The entire division occupied a large circular position. The units were positioned for all-round defense. Security screens were thrown up all around with orders to open fire as soon as the enemy was sighted and thus alert the division. Two-thirds of the division was on duty at any one time, allowing the other third to rest.

The infantry had a hard job digging foxholes. The ground was frozen hard. As there was no water atop the hill, melted snow had to be used to fill the canteens. Tent squares and blankets were used to shield the field kitchen fires. The men of the panzer regiment spent their rest period inside the tanks. At first the tanks were still warm from the drive, but they soon cooled off.

Another opponent of the tank forces von Oppeln-Bronikowski commanded: the T-34/76.

When morning came everyone breathed a sigh of relief. The expected enemy attack had not come. The planned "Armored Group von Oppeln" was now formed. It was to consist of off-road-capable vehicles only: tanks, armored troop carriers with mounted infantry, combat engineers, also in armored troop carriers, self-propelled artillery and several assault guns. From this day until well into spring 1943 "Armored Group von Oppeln" would be the main striking force of the entire XXXXVIII Panzer Corps.

In addition to his tanks von Oppeln received twenty-five armored troop carriers with grenadiers and ten with combat engineers. As there was no self-propelled artillery to begin with, Oppeln dispensed with allocating a towed battery as it would reduce his group's speed and especially its mobility, and mobility was an armored group's biggest plus. Wheeled vehicles would have made it dependent on roads, a deadly risk here where the Soviets might appear from any direction.

Oberst Rodt gave the commander of the armored group the following order: "Oppeln, in one hour you will attack in the direction of Donshchinka. Support the Romanians. They are supposed to be establishing a local defense."

The group moved out. Led by the tanks, it rolled straight toward the nearest Soviet positions. Antitank rifle opened fire. Some of the armored troop carriers were hit and disabled. Russian machine-guns fired at the armored troop carriers, which answered with cannon and machine-gun fire. Advancing northwest, the armored group quickly forced the enemy back. The village was reached. The grenadiers were ordered to dismount and clear the houses. Some Soviets resisted and were flushed out. Soon the village was in German hands. Then the Romanians appeared.

"Do you intend to defend the village, sir?" Oppeln asked the Romanian commander.

"The Soviets will soon throw us out again," declared the latter, resignation in his voice.

"We're going to chase them down off the commanding hills west of the village too. Send infantry after us to occupy them. Then you will be completely safe here."

The general promised to do so and the tanks and armored troop carriers rolled on. Soon they came within range of the antitank guns on the hill.

"Direct assault on the hill. They won't be able to do anything to us once we've driven under their fire," ordered Oppeln.

The command tank drove toward the hill at full throttle. Antitank and field guns fired so quickly that the noise sounded like a heavy thunderstorm. One tank was hit and ground to a halt. Two armored troop carriers also stopped. One was completely destroyed when its fuel tank exploded. None of the occupants escaped alive. Then they reached the guns' blind spot. The enemy could not depress his guns enough to reach them. But he had placed mines. A tank drove over one and had one of its tracks shattered by the explosion. The rest reached the hill, drove around there and forced the Soviets out of their earth bunkers. The hill was in German hands. Romanian infantry arrived and occupied the Soviet positions. Everything appeared to be normal.

Small reconnaissance headed north and northeast, from where the enemy was expected to attack. One sighted columns of tanks and trucks moving west from Perelasowski. German artillery opened fire immediately and scattered the enemy. In the afternoon the armored group engaged enemy tanks northeast of Donshchinka and north of Perelasovski. Once again several T-34s were destroyed.

In the evening von Oppeln received orders to withdraw to the bank of the Donshchinka for the night. The Romanians misunderstood this move. To them it appeared to be the final withdrawal and so they left their positions without orders and fled south past the 22nd Panzer Division. To make matters worse, they made so much noise as they retreated that they alerted the enemy. The Soviets exploited the situation at once. They immediately gave chase with tanks and antitank guns and assault groups quickly occupied the western and northern exits from the village.

Oberst Rodt committed the free elements of the 129th Grenadier Regiment. Together with a courageous Romanian light infantry battalion they held out for a long time against the Soviets, were surrounded and finally fought their way through the Soviet ring on the hills east of Donshchinka. As only the baggage train and other second-line elements of the Romanian 1st Armored Division had been met so far, it was assumed that the bulk of the division was still to the north. "Armored Group von Oppeln" was ordered to carry out an advance to the north on 24 November in order to make contact with Romanian combat units.

During the night the Soviets attacked the division again. They were beaten back. Residents of Medweshij stated that approximately thirty Romanian tanks had passed through the village on the night of 23 November heading south. Accordingly these tanks must have broken through the Soviet ring. There was also not much point in looking for them in the north.

The corps headquarters subsequently ordered the 22nd Panzer Division to disengage from the enemy during the night of 25 November, to break through the enemy encirclement near Chernyshevskaya and join the defense on the Chir. The armored elements of the division were placed under the direct command of the corps. They were ordered to force the breakthrough near Chernyshevskaya by launching a surprise attack. All of the remaining elements, including the Romanians under the division's command, were to follow in the second march group under the division commander.

By the time darkness came the Soviets had succeeded in closing to assault range in the east, north and west. The enemy artillery began a barrage. A concentric attack was expected no later than dawn.

On receiving the latest reconnaissance results Oberst Rodt ordered the commander of the armored group to report to him. Oberst von Oppeln appeared at the command post five minutes later. He already suspected what was coming, therefore he was not surprised when Oberst von Rodt gave him a new assignment.

"You know, Oppeln, that there is only one possible way of enabling the entire division to get through the Soviet ring."

"Counterattack, sir. Drive the enemy back so that he can't pursue as soon as we depart, separate units and destroy them."

"Correct! All armored units must be committed. We have to attack from three directions simultaneously and disrupt the enemy assault."

Once again "Armored Group von Oppeln" intervened decisively in events. The enemy was thrown back with heavy losses. The tanks and armored troop carriers advanced so quickly that the enemy was taken completely by surprise. The division was subsequently able to disengage without fighting and depart. Not even the rear guards were attacked by the shattered enemy. Hours later they quietly abandoned their positions and followed the division.

Not until morning did the last German forces hear the sound of fighting from their old positions. The Soviet combat groups fought each other in the darkness before they realized their mistake. The vehicles drove over icy tracks. Steeps sections had to be negotiated with care. But when dawn came on 25 November the leading tanks were at the north bank of the Chir, north of Chernyshevskaya. The corps commander assembled his formation commanders there.

"Gentlemen, as initially planned we are going to first drive through the village with 'Armored Group von Oppeln.' While it is doing so, Rodt you will wait with the rest of the division north of the village and only follow when they are through."

The command tank moved off at 5 A.M. Oberst von Oppeln led the attack force. At first it rolled unopposed through the village. Then at the south end the enemy opened fire. Fire came down at the tanks from the surrounding hills, especially from the western flank. Soviet artillery, tanks and antiaircraft guns fired at the armored group as it drove along the valley floor. Armored troop carriers were hit and burst into flames. Tanks were knocked out. Oberst von Oppeln had to lead the group back as quickly as possible if it was to avoid total destruction. He therefore ordered a retreat to the starting position. The entire division was preparing to attack when motorized forces were reported nearing the rear of the division.

"We must not jump the gun. Attack on the suburb of Russakov with tanks and armored troop carriers at 11 A.M. I will lead the attack," ordered Oppeln.

Oberst Rodt placed himself at the head of the division. This officer was one commander who always led from the front. When the tanks rolled forward to attack all of the division's heavy weapons opened fire. Two batteries of "eighty-eights" engaged enemy tanks on the western hills. Oberst von Oppeln and his tanks drove straight through Russakov. The bridge over the Chir appeared before them.

Orders were received: "Drive across and into Chernyshevskaya!"

A Russian demolition squad ran onto the bridge at the last minute in an attempt to destroy it. The tank's machine-gun mowed the Russians down. Then the tanks drove onto the bridge. Would it blow up under them? But they crossed safely and rolled toward the town. Antitank guns fired from streets and hiding places. The tanks silenced them. More armored troop carriers were lost, knocked out by fire from Soviet antitank rifles. Once, when the advance faltered, Oberst Rodt ordered, "Drive through to the south end!"

The tanks pressed ahead. Sitting behind the controls of the tank, driver Spangenberg saw flashes as several antitank guns fired. He realized that they must be hit if they continued to drive straight ahead. He turned into a side street, drove approximately 300 meters and then turned right. The two antitank guns appeared directly ahead.

"Now Kernlein!"

The Unteroffizier fired. He saw a burst of flame as the shell struck the target. The second shot caused a series of explosions in the antitank position.

"Now through!"

The tanks rolled on, firing as they went. The enemy ceased firing. Had they already breached the antitank barricades or were the enemy guns merely waiting for them to get closer? Oberst von Oppeln tried to see something through his periscope. In spite of the cold he was suddenly hot inside his camouflage suit.

"There, sir!" screamed Oberfeldwebel Spangenberg. At that instant a cleverly-concealed antitank gun opened fire 300 meters away, betraying its position.

A mighty crash shook the tank. Oberst von Oppeln felt a heavy blow against his foot. Below him loader Dümmer screamed in pain. The tank abruptly came to a stop.

"We've been hit, Oberst. We're losing fuel. We have to get out."

Before he bailed out the commander radioed: "Have been hit. Battalion commander assume command of the battle group."

The wounded driver was being lifted out through the driver's hatch. Hermann von Oppeln stood up to leave the tank through the turret hatch. Just then there was an explosion in the antitank gun position. The following tank had silenced the enemy weapon with a single shot. The Oberst could not get out. His thick camouflage suit became caught on the turret hatch. Meanwhile, further to the rear four more antitank guns had opened fire on the tank.

"Sir, get out! Get out!"

"I'm trying," thought Oppeln. "I wish I could get out."

"The Oberst is caught!" The shouts by Oberfeldwebel Spangenberg brought two of the following tanks to the scene. They placed themselves in front of the command tank and fired at the antitank guns. The shots rang loud in Oppeln's ears. He pulled and pulled. His foot felt as if it were made of lead. But the harder he pulled the harder his camouflage suit became stuck.

Spangenberg and Kernlein came running. They clambered onto the tank. Machine-gun fire flitted toward them from a nearby house. One burst just missed the head of the commander, who tried to make himself as small as possible. The gun of the tank on the left turned toward the enemy machine-gun. The crack of the shot and the impact were almost simultaneous. The machine-gun was silenced. Together the two men pulled the Oberst out of the tank. When he was free Oppeln jumped down onto the ground. Pain shot through one leg.

"Sir, you're wounded!"

"Quick, put a dressing on it, Kernlein."

When his wound was dressed the men walked over to Dümmer, who was lying on a blanket in the cover of a shattered house. Nollmann was with him.

"How goes it, Dümmer?"

"Lousy, sir!"

"Here, have a cigarette, it will do you good and help you pass the time until the medics arrive. Nollmann, you stay here. Kernlein, go fetch an ambulance. Spangenberg come with me."

They left the house. One of the two tanks had moved on. Oberst von Oppeln and Spangenberg clambered onto the remaining tank. Without a word the tank commander gave his place to his commanding officer.

"Move on, driver. After the rest with full throttle!"

They headed toward the sound of fighting. Once they had to intervene when the armored troop carriers, which had arrived in the meantime, were held up by Russian machine-guns. They shot up the Soviet positions. The Red Army men came out with arms raised and were taken prisoner by the grenadiers. Then they reached the tanks, which had driven ahead to the south end of the village and occupied the exit road. The enemy there had already been eliminated.

Oppeln turned to the young Leutnant who had immediately given up his seat. "Thank you Richter. You and Markwarth did a good job rescuing me. If you hadn't come things might have gone badly for us."

"If it wasn't for you, sir, then the majority of the men wouldn't be here any more," replied the Leutnant. He had merely stated what most of the other commanders believed.

A short time later von Oppeln reported: "Breakthrough achieved. Armored group occupying the hills south of the town."

Hermann von Oppeln-Bronikowski with Hauptmann von Gottberg (left).

The panzer-grenadiers fought in the town until afternoon, flushing Soviet troops from their hiding places in cellars and elsewhere. The enemy soldiers defended every house as if it was a fortress. A Soviet attack from the west with tanks and infantry was repulsed. During the night the Soviets bombarded the city with rockets, artillery fire and mortars. The division command post received a direct hit. A tank patrol reported the road to Kuteinikov free of the enemy. That was important, for the supply and ammunition columns, without which a further defense was impossible, had to come from there. The supply columns arrived on 26 November.

The commanding general of the corps lauded the actions of the much-maligned division in an order of the day:

> Fate has linked me with the 22nd Panzer Division in several difficult and memorable days. I express my special appreciation and my thanks to the division for its soldierly composure, for its fighting spirit and its skillful conduct in engagements and movements.
>
> The division can be proud to be in such good shape after its extraordinary accomplishments in a situation never before experienced by German soldiers.

> Now it is vital to regain the initiative. I am convinced that in spite of all that lies behind us, the 22nd Panzer Division will pull its weight.

In the attacks of the next few days the villages of Paramonov, Leontyevski and Chistyakovka on the Chir were taken. A continuous front was established along the river. On 1 December contact was made with the 1st Romanian Armored Division on the right and the 14th Romanian Infantry Division on the left.

While in the coming days the division's infantry units expanded the main line of resistance on the Chir, "Armored Group von Oppeln" was repeatedly given "fire-brigade" missions. In the following weeks it was in action almost daily against vastly superior enemy forces. On 2 December von Oppeln advanced on Warlamov with just seven tanks. They were met by heavy fire. The first tank reported a hit. Seconds later it fell silent for ever. A second tank was hit right beside Oppeln and seconds later it was in flames. The village was taken, but when Oppeln assembled his forces he had just three tanks left.

The corps ordered: "Continue the attack on 3 December!"

The 204th Panzer Regiment had four serviceable tanks left. As the XXXXVIII Army Corps was withdraw for other employment, as of 4 December 1942 the 22nd Panzer Division was subordinate to the Romanian II Army Corps of the Hollidt Group. General der Infanterie Hollidt also made the 22nd Panzer Division responsible for the Romanian 1st Armored Division's sector. He used Oppeln's battle group as a permanent reserve attack force.

It was bolstered through the addition of the armored elements of II Battalion, 129th Regiment and elements of the 24th Motorcycle Battalion, which was assigned to von Oppeln as the "von Poschinger Group." From this point on this "armored group" was in continuous contact with the enemy for more than two months. As a rear guard it had to cover the withdrawals of the infantry divisions, often after first making them possible. Repeatedly it was the last hope of the hard-pressed infantry. While the latter withdrew during the night, the tanks had to halt the enemy and save their own hide by launching repeated night attacks. In almost every case this resulted in encirclement, so that when morning came Oppeln usually had to order a breakout.

In the battles at the Chir and Don rivers Oppeln and his unit were a tower of strength. The Oberst led the group from battle to battle in his Skoda tank. It became the "fire-brigade" on the Chir, and when German General Staff Oberst Wenck, who had joined the Romanian 3rd Army as chief of staff at the end of November, needed a potent combat unit he also turned to "Armored Group von Oppeln."

On Christmas Eve the Soviets wished the 22nd Panzer Division a "Merry Christmas" and soon afterwards announced over their broadcasting system that the 22nd Panzer Division had been destroyed. At the same time Oberst von Oppeln was handing out his meager Christmas presents to his men, five cigarettes and a candle each. In Torgau, where von Oppeln's wife happened to hear the Russian report, there was great concern. She called the OKH and asked about the status of her husband. A radio search was subsequently begun and von Oppeln was found.

✠

Oberst von Oppeln's battle group carried out many missions in December 1942, however the action described in the following account represented a high point.

"Sir, order from the Hollidt Group. Together with the von Poschinger Group we are to move to Bokovskaya today and be placed under the command of the 294th Infantry Division."

"Good, Becker. Get ready. Departure in half an hour."

Thirty-five minutes after the order was received the group set off for Bokovskaya. Before the village and the command post of General Block, the commanding officer of the 294th Infantry Division, were reached, a Soviet tank column emerged from the mist and barred its way. Oberst von Oppeln moved toward the enemy phalanx with his tanks in front, followed by the armored troop carriers. Standing in his open turret hatch the Oberst peered into the gloom. When the fog suddenly lifted slightly he saw the Russian tanks about 500 meters ahead. The majority were T-34s, but the column also included T-26s, KV-Is and KV-IIs.

"To everyone: open fire!"

The turret hatch slammed shut. Peering through his periscope, Oberst von Oppeln saw the enemy tanks turn.

"Twelve o'clock. Armor-piercing 40,500, fire!"

The first round flitted from the barrel, tore a narrow strip of glowing red brightness through the gloom and struck the side of the first T-34. All of the group's seven tanks fired simultaneously. Flames shot into the sky.

"To everyone: breakthrough to Bokovskaya!"

They charged forward on a front of two-hundred meters. A T-34 barred the command tank's way. It took two hits and was disabled with a shattered track. Another shell hit the frontal armor and was deflected. Behind Oppeln's vehicle one of his tanks blew apart.

"Full throttle Spangenberg!"

Spangenberg increased power. Suddenly a T-34 emerged from a gully. Its shell flew over von Oppeln's turret. The T-34 drove toward the Germans and cut off the small command tank, apparently with the intention of ramming it. But before the astonished Spangenberg could react, the nose of the light 9-ton tank rammed the side of the T-34, which was at least three times heavier. The shock of the impact tossed the men about inside the tank.

"Watch out, Nollmann!" called Oppeln.

The radio operator grabbed the machine-gun. Suddenly he saw both hatches on the enemy tank flip open. The Soviet tank crew emerged and opened fire with submachine-guns. A burst from Nollmann's machine-gun knocked them back inside. A squad of Russian infantry rushed toward the scene.

"Reverse gear!"

Spangenberg restarted the stalled motor. The Skoda rolled back thirty meters then the Soviets appeared in front of the tank. Spangenberg quickly shifted gears and headed straight towards them. The Russian soldiers scrambled out of the way. A T-26 came out of the gully. Before it could fire a shot it was itself hit and burst into flames.

"Did everyone make it? Report!"

Oberst von Oppeln listed as his commanders checked in. They had in fact broken through the enemy blocking position. Five minutes later Oppeln reported to the commander of the 294th Infantry Division: "Armored Group von Oppeln reporting as ordered, sir."

"Good to have you here, Oppeln. Things are hot here and we need heavy weapons more than we need bread."

The von Oppeln group repulsed every Soviet attack on Bakovskaya. When the enemy did achieve a penetration an immediate counterattack drove him out again. There followed days of tough action against a numerically superior foe. Every tank and armored troop carrier that returned from the repair shops was assigned to von Oppeln's group.

Early on 23 December General Block arrived at the command post of the 22nd Panzer Division in Paramov while his division went into position there. He presented Oberst Rodt with a report which detailed the efforts of Oberst von Oppeln and underlined his successes.

"That would be a report for the awarding of the Knight's Cross to Oppeln, sir," said Oberst Rodt. "I would most warmly recommend him."

"You are right, it is a proposal for the Knight's Cross for Oberst von Oppeln, and I will send it to the corps immediately, Rodt."

The same day Generalmajor von Choltitz appeared at the command post. He and his units had intervened in the fighting in the sector of the Romanian 14th Infantry Division and had restored order to the division. Neither he nor the 22nd Panzer Division nor the 294th Infantry Division were still in communication with the corps of Army Group Hollidt. All commanding officers were present when under the command of General von Choltitz the decision was reached to act independently and withdraw into the Yasenovski-Shirokov area during the night of 24 December.

On 1 January 1943 Hermann von Oppeln-Bronikowski received the Knight's Cross for his tireless efforts "which were decisive at this sector of the front."

Withdrawal movement "Falcon" took place during the night of 3 January. The German forces retreated farther and farther, constantly pressured by the enemy. The Don front had collapsed and in view of the threat of being outflanked from the west the Chir line was untenable. No one knew how the enemy was supposed to be halted between the Don and the Donets. Generalmajor von Oppeln later described the situation as follows:

> On the left flank there was a gap of 100 kilometers, and the right flank, too, was hanging in the air. Only with difficulty were the exhausted and weakened troops able to withstand the Soviet onslaught against the front and the flanks repeatedly able to avoid Soviet attempts to encircle and destroy them.
>
> The obvious thing to do would have been to retreat beyond the lower Don and the Donets as quickly as possible, but with the air supply of the 6th Army in Stalingrad in mind Hitler would not allow this.
>
> The 4th Army and Army Group Hollidt withdrew step by step, continuously fending off heavy enemy attacks with strength ratios of 10 to 1 and 12 to 1; always in danger of being outflanked from the south or west, or of being barred from the Don by a Soviet thrust along the river.

The fact that the retreat succeeded at all is due to the efforts of the XXXXVIII Panzer Corps, which formed the backbone of Army Group Hollidt. But the XXXXVIII Panzer Corps was the 22nd Panzer Division, in particular "Armored Group von Oppeln."

During the period from 6 December 1942 until 5 January 1943 the weak corps fought off twelve enemy rifle and five cavalry divisions as well as ten Soviet tank and sixteen mechanized brigades. A total of 451 Soviet tanks had been destroyed (the majority by "Armored Group von Oppeln") and 209 guns and 752 heavy infantry weapons were either destroyed or captured.

The 22nd Panzer Division and its 204th Panzer Regiment fought on against a twelve-fold enemy superiority until 25 February 1943. On 20 February von Oppeln repulsed the last major Soviet attack on the recently occupied Mius position. Finally, on 25 February, the Soviets, decimated and exhausted, called off the attack. On that date the 204th Panzer Regiment had one tank left. It had literally fought to the last tank.

COMMANDER OF THE 11TH PANZER REGIMENT—ARMORED GROUP VON OPPELN—COUNTERATTACK ON KHARKOV—"OPERATION CITADEL"—THE GERMAN CROSS IN GOLD

The 204th Panzer Regiment no longer existed. But for Oberst von Oppeln there was another new command waiting. Oberst von Hünersdorf, the former commander of the 11th Panzer Regiment (6th Panzer Division), a friend of Oppeln's, took over the 6th Panzer Division from General Raus on the battlefield, while General Raus took over the XI Army Corps. Von Hünersdorf suggested Oberst von Oppeln to succeed him as commander of the 11th Panzer Regiment. The cavalry officer took over the regiment and at the same time the "armored group" of the 6th Panzer Division, which was the main striking force of the division and corps. Feldmarschall Manstein ordered the corps to launch an attack against the flank of the enemy offensive.

With his new group von Oppeln stormed and took Bogdanovka and Krinitschki. The regiment soon realized that its new commander was no mere "replacement." Leading his panzers, von Oppeln forced the enemy back in the direction of Balakleia. The German offensive was already nearing the Donets on a broad front. But Soviet resistance was stiffening. The battle for Taranovka lasted three days. Not until 6 March did the city fall. There followed a bitter struggle for possession of the Msah river line.

The river was crossed on 10 March 1943. Four days later "Armored Group von Oppeln" smashed the strong enemy rear guards in the Udy sector and when the Donets was reached east and northeast of Kharkov the German offensive ran down. With the 6th Panzer Division and 106th Infantry Division attacking from the south and the SS Panzer Corps attacking from the north, major Soviet forces were encircled and destroyed southeast of Kharkov.

Three Olympic victors from 1936 meet on the Don: from the left, Walter Steffen (gymnastics), von Oppeln-Bronikowski, and Gerhard Stöck (javelin).

In a four-week battle Army Group Don under Feldmarschall von Manstein had won a classic victory. The surprise counterattack struck the enemy at the height of his success and he was severely battered. When the battle was over the German forces were back where the summer offensive of 1942 had begun. In spite of this success it was obvious to Oberst von Oppeln that the ratio of strengths was now firmly in the favor of the Soviets. He later said of this:

> The German divisions which were sucked into the maelstrom of operations on the southern front were completely burnt out. As a result scarcely anything was left of the old cadre of experienced, well-trained soldiers, especially NCOs. The feeling of absolute security was lost, because German divisions had been abandoned to be surrounded and destroyed by the Soviets. The troops were flank-sensitive and trust in the command was increasingly shaken.
>
> Instead of bringing the old divisions back up to strength, these were in some cases allowed to be destroyed and were then disbanded. A series of new formations of poorly and inadequately trained divisions followed.

> After the Luftwaffe enlisted far more men than it needed for its purposes, they came to the essentially correct decision to employ them in a ground role. But instead of transferring these good and in some cases excellent men to the army, at Göring's urging Luftwaffe field divisions were formed. But in spite of all the best intentions and the bravery of the men, these units were completely unsuited to land warfare on account of their inadequate training and experience.

✠

"We are going to take the village in front of us and establish ourselves there."

Major Bäke, one of the battalion commanders, was sending the lead group on its way when suddenly a dispatch rider roared up and stopped beside von Oppeln's tank.

"Sir, the commanding general wants to speak to you!"

"Thank you."

Oberst von Oppeln radioed Major Bäke and ordered him to halt the point until he arrived. The Austrian general greeted the Oberst when he pulled up beside him.

"Good day, sir."

General der Panzertruppe Otto Knobelsdorff, an officer who preferred rapid armored thrusts, shook the colonel's hand.

"You are to take the town and establish a position between Point 167.1 and the two points there. Patrols are to scout the approaches, Oppeln."

Oppeln spoke to the general for fifteen minutes then climbed into his tank and with a final salute said goodbye to General Knobelsdorff.

"Let's go, Spangenberg. After them like a fire-brigade. Direction Langdorff!"

Spangenberg was the only member of the 204th Panzer Regiment that Oberst von Oppeln had been able to take with him. The driver increased power. Squatting in the cramped confines of the command vehicle, Oppeln struggled to see ahead. There was no sign of the enemy. His own tanks also appeared to have driven through the village that was appearing ahead. There was no sign of them either.

"What's going on, Spangenberg? Are we heading the right way?"

"This is the road, sir."

Oppeln thought about what would happen if the Soviets found them now. His vehicle, an armored troop carrier, did not even have a cannon, just a dummy gun in the turret and a single machine-gun. Almost all of the space inside was occupied by the many radio sets.

"Bäke battalion report!"

Three times the Oberst called, but no one answered. The entrance to the village appeared ahead. Spangenberg drove on at a good clip. The road through the village was long and straight. Everything looked peaceful, until suddenly von Oppeln sighted an enemy antitank gun only meters away.

"Drive over it, Spangenberg!"

The driver advanced the throttle to full power. He turned slightly to the right and headed straight toward the antitank gun. If it fired now it would all be over. But the gun crew saw the half-track appear, lost its nerve and fled. With an ear-shattering crash the antitank gun was crushed beneath the armored troop carrier. But just as Spangenberg turned back onto the road Oppeln spotted another antitank gun two-hundred meters ahead, then another one hundred meters beyond it.

"Right, Spangenberg. Turn behind that house!"

The armored troop carrier was travelling too fast to turn in time, but Spangenberg tried it. The vehicle groaned and squeaked, but it just got past the house and reached cover behind it. The noise of the vehicle's engine sounded very loud. The antitank guns had ceased firing because they could no longer get their sights on the half-track. There was no sign of their own tanks.

"To Bäke battalion! We are trapped. Attention, Russian antitank guns on the village street!"

Several red Army soldiers appeared around the corner of the house. The radio operator, who was manning the machine-gun, fired quickly. The Soviets disappeared. Then suddenly Major Bäke reported in.

"We're coming!"

Three minutes later they heard the dull roar of tank engines. Then the panzers appeared on the right flank and turned onto the village street. Tank cannon barked. Mingled with the sound was the crack of antitank guns firing and ammunition exploding. The battle between the tank battalion and the antitank guns lasted ten minutes. When it was over all the antitank guns had been destroyed. Major Bäke reported to the commanding officer that when the lead vehicle came under fire he had veered away, intending to go around the village.

"But that was close, Bäke! We thought the street was clear and that you and your tanks had already passed through."

"One simply shouldn't drive alone, sir," said the Major smiling.

Thirty minutes later the panzer regiment reached its assigned position. Tank patrols set out to scout the enemy situation. One day later Oberst von

Oppeln arranged his tanks on the west bank of the Donets like pieces on a chessboard and had them dig in up to their turrets. The result was a strong defensive position. With their rotating turrets the tanks could provide mutual protection and also engage an opponent coming from any direction. As well, in their hull-down positions the tanks presented a small target.

✠

With the start of "Operation Citadel" on 4 and 5 July 1943, the XXXXVIII Panzer-Korps, commanded by Generalleutnant Dietrich von Choltitz, went to the attack from the Belgorod area. A makeshift bridge had been erected over the Donets there. When Hermann von Oppeln drove onto the bridge with the first of his tanks, the structure collapsed under the load. The advance was halted for the time being. "Armored Group Oppeln" was sent across the Donets farther south and was placed under the command of the 7th Panzer Division, Rommel's old "ghost division."

Together with Oberst Adalbert Schulz, later Generalmajor and wearer of the Diamonds, von Oppeln carried out a tank attack on a broad front. It was the biggest he ever experienced. 240 German tanks broke through the Soviet positions in front of the Pena river line. The cannon fire seemed like a great lightning storm. Bunkers and Soviet antitank guns were smashed by concentrated fire. German tanks drove over mines and were immobilized. Others were knocked out by antitank guns. Smoke rose from numerous wrecked tanks, symbols of destruction and death. Nevertheless, the tanks fought their way through the in-depth system of Soviet positions. But then the enemy committed his strategic reserve of tanks, the 2nd Guards Tank Corps and the 3rd Mechanized Corps.

Oppeln was ordered to outflank the Russian tank forces situated farther west and to cut off and destroy them. Then he was to establish contact with the German units attacking from the west. Oberst von Oppeln summoned his battalion commanders to his command post.

"Gentlemen, we will carry out our mission in a big night attack. The terrain suits such an attack. Our night advance road is also a Russian route of retreat. We will not attack the Russian columns at first in order to conceal our movements for as long as possible. And now everyone get ready. Departure after darkness falls. Bäke, you and your battalion will drive point, I will join you in my command vehicle."

The summer night had fallen when the tanks moved off. They reached the road and soon afterwards were driving side by side with Russian truck columns. Now and then there were only a few meters between the German tanks and the Russian trucks. Everything went smoothly. The tension became unbearable, for with every meter the tanks advance the Russian armored divisions were getting closer. They were just preparing to depart when the German tanks appeared.

"Attack!"

The night was suddenly shattered by the crash of gunfire. The roar of engines was drowned out by the inferno of shots and explosions. Major Bäke had his battalion drive around the totally surprised enemy and then open fire. Explosions rang out. Tanks sat blazing on the battlefield. Major Bäke, whose command tank also lacked a cannon, left his vehicle. Armed with a Panzerfaust antitank weapon, he attacked the enemy tanks which counterattacked his battalion. Bäke destroyed three T-34s from very close range.

Oberst von Oppeln drove into the midst of the enemy tank movements. His machine-gunner fired at Soviet infantry which attacked the tanks with Molotov Cocktails. One tank made a sharp turn and drove over a tank-killing squad as it neared the command vehicle. When morning came and von Oppeln received the reports from his battalions, he found to his immense relief that the night attack had not cost a single one of his tanks. But no fewer than 27 Soviet tanks lay destroyed on the scene of the nocturnal battle. Von Oppeln recommended Major Bäke for the Knight's Cross with Oak Leaves. On 1 August 1943 Bäke became the 262nd recipient of the award. Oberst von Oppeln was awarded the German Cross in Gold on 7 August of that year.

A short time later von Oppeln received a radio message ordering him to report to Generalmajor von Hünersdorff's command post immediately. The general had been wounded and wanted to speak with him at once.

"Turn, Spangenberg, we have to drive over that hill."

"It's occupied by the enemy, sir," warned the operations officer.

"But we'll save a great deal of time. Get going!"

Travelling at full speed, the armored troop carrier reached the hill. At that moment an antitank gun opened fire. The first shell struck just behind the half-track and threw the rear end of the command vehicle around. But the next was a direct hit. A flash of fire blinded von Oppeln. He felt a sharp blow against his foot, heard cries and smelled the odor of burnt powder. Flames licked high.

"Get out!"

Two members of the crew were wounded, but they could still walk. Oppeln was helped by his operations officer and Oberfeldwebel Spangenberg as he walked over to the road. Shells forced them to take cover. They crawled into a ravine and crept to the road. Sitting in a ditch, von Oppeln

During the invasion of France in 1944, von Oppeln-Bronikowski reported to Rommel.

had his wound dressed. Suddenly Generalmajor von Hünersdorff appeared in his staff car. Messengers had informed him of the attack on von Oppeln's command vehicle.

"That looks pretty bad, Oppeln. You should go to hospital. Luckily I have only a minor head wound and will remain with my men."

"Then I will say goodbye, sir. Here's hoping that we see each other again soon."

Oppeln was taken to Kharkov hospital and from there was sent to Germany. However, on 13 July General von Hünersdorff's command vehicle was hit again. Shrapnel pierced his steel helmet and entered his head. He died on 17 July 1943 in hospital at Kharkov. He was succeeded temporarily by Oberst Wilhelm Crisoli until 22 August, when Oberst Baron von Waldenfels took over command of the division.

After a brief period of recuperation Oberst von Oppeln was supposed to receive a new regiment. In spite of the briefness of his stay, von Oppeln had made many friends in the 11th Panzer Regiment. Oberst von Oppeln-Bronikowski had been in continuous action from October 1941 until July 1943. He was always in the front lines and had played a decisive role in the actions. As a result, when he returned from convalescent leave in September he was assigned to the officer reserve.

During his leave in the old cavalry and peacetime garrison of Torgau, after four weeks of rest in October 1943 he was named commander of the 100th Panzer Regiment, with which he transferred to France in spring 1944. In order to avoid confusion with the independent 100th Panzer Battalion, which was also in France, the panzer regiment was renumbered number 22. The regiment was assigned to the 21st Panzer Division under General Feuchtinger.

Oppeln worked tirelessly to obtain better equipment. He managed to have his entire regiment equipped with Panzer IV tanks. Panthers and Tigers were not available. When the invasion began the 22nd Panzer Regiment was strung out along the line Tours-Le Mans. The unit's command post was in Falaise.

IN THE INFERNO OF THE INVASION FRONT—THE OAK LEAVES FOR OBERST VON OPPELN

It was 2:01 in the morning when the phone rang in the regiment command post in Falaise. The man on night duty heard the voice of General Feuchtinger, who asked for Oberst von Oppeln. One minute later the Oberst picked up the receiver.

"Oppeln here!"

"Oppeln, the invasion is under way. Place everyone on alert at once. General Marcks has ordered Alert Level II."

"Thank you, General. I will issue the alert."

When the general hung up von Oppeln called the 1st Battalion. There was no need to say anything to Hauptmann von Gottberg, its commanding officer.

"I heard, sir. My battalion has just been placed on alert. It will be ready to go in fifteen minutes."

"Thank you, Gottberg. Out!"

"Second Battalion here, Major Vierzig."

"Vierzig, the 2nd Battalion must break off its night exercise and immediately take on live ammunition. Send the companies back immediately and report when ready for battle."

One hour later the entire 22nd Panzer Regiment was ready for action. Ninety-eight Panzer IVs waited with engines running for the order to counterattack to the coast. As he sat and waited, Oberst von Oppeln listened to reports that the British were taking bridge after bridge. Finally, after four hours of waiting, he received the order to attack east of the Orne.

"Gottberg, you and your battalion move out. I will follow right behind you. Maintain air attack interval. Move from cover to cover."

Oberst von Oppeln and his staff drove to the 1st Battalion. He rolled along the column, urging haste. But during the advance he received orders not to attack Allied airborne troops east of the Orne but instead to strike at the main opponent west of the Orne. This turn placed the commander of the 1st Battalion and his operations staff at the rear of the column. Oberst von Oppeln and his staff came behind the 2nd Battalion.

Nevertheless the change in direction proceeded relatively smoothly. Passing the bomb-ravaged city of Caen, the panzer regiment arrived at the Orne bridge near Le Rouville, which was still intact and not occupied by the enemy. The regiment crossed the Orne and there made preparations to attack north in the direction of Nouville-Beuville. So far the regiment had not lost a vehicle to air attack. By 2:30 P.M. the forty tanks of the 2nd Battalion were ready for action. However contact had been lost with the Gottberg battalion and since there was no contact with the enemy radio silence still had to be maintained. Oberst von Oppeln sent runners and officers to restore communications with the unit. At that moment General Feuchtinger appeared. He walked over to the regimental commander.

"Oppeln, if you don't succeed in driving the English back into the sea we have lost the war."

"I will attack!" said the Oberst, stone-faced. No one knew what he was thinking.

"Regimental commander to everyone: drive to the coast. Tanks move out!"

It was the first time the Oberst had seen his commanding officer in the front lines. It was also the last, for General Feuchtinger never showed himself at the front again. Followed by the regimental headquarters platoon, Oberst von Oppeln rolled forward. His thrust was aimed precisely at the gap between the two landing zones "Juno" and "Sword."

The tanks were forced to drive over a hill in front of Bieville and they were met there by British antitank guns. Within minutes the command tank of the regimental headquarters platoon and five other tanks had been destroyed by direct hits. The tanks had run into elements of the 3rd British and 3rd Canadian Divisions.

"We cannot get through here, sir!" reported Major Vierzig.

"Dig in, dig in. We must wait for reinforcements. Choose a defensive position there in front of the wood."

"Too narrow a field of fire, sir!"

"Yes, but there we will be so close to the enemy that we will be safe from the naval gunfire and bombers."

They drove close to the enemy-held wood. The tank crews dug in their vehicles. Oppeln's command tank was dug in just 100 meters behind the main line of resistance.

The order was given: "Stand fast, no matter what the enemy side does."

What Oberst von Oppeln did not know was that the 1st Battalion of the 192nd Panzer-Grenadier Regiment had reached the coast near Lion sur Mer and was waiting for tank support, while they sat here near Bieville and Beuville. The 2nd Battalion of the 192nd Regiment was positioned on the panzer regiments' right near Benouville. The 8th Company in particular waited for tank support. At the same time the British 27th Infantry Brigade launched a quick attack against von Oppeln's defense line. The attack was repulsed. Enemy barrage fire intensified, but the panzer regiment held its position north of Caen.

Meanwhile the 12th SS Panzer Division had also been alerted and had been deployed in the direction of Caen. An attack was ordered for twelve noon on 7 June. The 12th SS Panzer Division was supposed to attack to the left of the 21st Panzer Division and drive the enemy landing force into the sea. But the SS division was also unable to advance, and General Witt was forced to call off the attack on the evening of 7 June. All hopes now rested on the coming day. On that 8 June three panzer divisions, which had been stationed in the rear as the OKW reserve, were finally to arrive for a combined counterattack. A major attack was supposed to crush the British beachhead, now ten kilometers deep.

But there was no concentrated attack on 8 June. Instead the Allies continued to bomb and the British tried to break through the 22nd Panzer Division's front. A naval artillery barrage destroyed the regimental command post, wounding the adjutant, operations officer and signals officer. Oberst von Oppeln escaped injury. The 22nd Panzer Division held its defense position for no less than sixteen days against the growing attacks by Montgomery's divisions. Counterattacks were launched in support of the flanking panzer-grenadier battalions.

Finally, on 7 July, the remains of von Oppeln's panzer regiment was pulled out of the positions north of Caen. It was relieved by the 16th Luftwaffe Field Division. Oberst von Oppeln had held for thirty-two days without yielding a single meter of ground. On 28 July von Oppeln was awarded the Knight's Cross with Oak Leaves. As usual he attributed his success to the men under his command.

The regiment had suffered fifty percent casualties. The remaining forty-eight tanks were concentrated in I Battalion while von Oppeln led II Battalion to Chalons sur Marne to reequip. When he returned he found that I Battalion had been struck by a massed bombing raid. Working feverishly, von Oppeln succeeded in repairing twenty tanks. A major British offensive was expected at any time.

Code-named "Operation Goodwood," two army corps attacked the German divisions positioned east of the Orne, including the 21st Panzer Division. There was bitter fighting. The famous 11th Armoured Division lost 126 tanks, the Guards Armoured Brigade 60. The British offensive had to be called off. St. Lô fell on 19 July, one day before the attempt on Hitler's life. Included in the 150,000 German troops trapped in the Falaise pocket was the 22nd Panzer Regiment, now with just eight tanks.

In the fighting withdrawal from Caen via Falaise to the east bank of the Seine the panzer regiment fought British, Canadian and American troops. The panzer-grenadier regiments were down to 40 to 60 men. The 1st Panzer Battalion under Hauptmann von Gottberg had just eight Panzer IV tanks. It now proved extremely fortunate that von Oppeln had sent the 2nd Battalion to refit. He drove there to see what was going on. When he stopped in Paris on the way back he learned that the pocket had been closed for good. He was told that a return to his regiment was impossible. The Oberst made it possible. He drove through the enemy and received a warm welcome from his men.

A breakout from the pocket was ordered. After the 22nd Panzer Regiment had lost its last tank von Oppeln, together with two officers and a driver, set out for the Seine using side roads. In Vesoul von Oppeln received orders to report to Führer Headquarters to receive the Oak

Leaves. The ceremony took place in the same room in which the attempt on Hitler's life had taken place.

✠

In the headquarters Oberst von Oppeln-Bronikowski learned that he was to take command of a panzer division. He was sent on a division commander course, however this was cut short after only eight days. Oberst von Oppeln traveled to his new division's command post in Arys, East Prussia. He first assumed command of the elements of the 20th Panzer Division deployed south of Tilsit until he officially assumed command of the division. Oberst von Oppeln tackled his new command with customary vigor, spending a great deal of his time at the front. He organized his forces into an "armored group" and two less mobile battle groups. The former regimental commanders and their staffs were placed in command of the three groups. On 30 January 1945 Hermann von Oppeln-Bronikowski was promoted to the rank of Generalmajor.

Soon afterward the 20th Panzer Division was rushed to Upper Silesia, for powerful Soviet forces had reached the industrial region. The division went into action in Gleiwitz. Enemy tanks overran the reconnaissance battalion's columns. Von Oppeln requested permission to break out. However General der Infanterie Schulz could not approve the request as he had been forbidden to do so by the OKH. Not even the commander of an army had freedom of action. Precious hours were lost. Not until night came did Oppeln receive authorization for a breakout. The columns drove down the one open road under cover of darkness. Several tanks guarded the flanks.

The division commander and his small force rejoined the division in the morning. As a result of the delay in gaining approval for a breakout the division's reconnaissance battalion had lost almost all of its vehicles. Two vehicles were shot out from under von Oppeln, raising his total to ten.

The 20th Panzer Division was under the command of the XXIV Panzer Corps. General der Artillerie Hartmann had commanded the artillery forces of the 24th Infantry Division during the Polish campaign. Hartmann ordered von Oppeln to attack the Russian forces that had crossed the Oder and drive them back again. The division attacked the enemy's flanks and completed its mission.

Meanwhile the Soviets were closing in on the city of Neiße. They already controlled the commanding hills. Consequently the 20th Panzer Division's attack was halted and it was sent to Neiße. The city could not be saved but positions were held west and southwest of Neiße. The situation stabilized and Oppeln received orders to free "Fortress Breslau," which had been surrounded by the Soviets.

In a night attack von Oppeln succeeded in opening a narrow corridor to the city, however it was soon closed again. The division fought on, staging a slow withdrawal. On 18 April 1945 Generalmajor Hermann von Oppeln-Bronikowski was awarded the Swords.

The division passed through Dresden, seeing first-hand the devastating effects of the Allied terror bombing. The Soviets were storming toward Prague. The Vlasov Army rebelled and the Czech uprising began.

On 8 May Generalmajor von Oppeln was summoned to the command post of the *Hermann Göring* Parachute-Panzer Corps. There he learned that Germany was about to surrender. Von Oppeln disbanded his division and he and his men set out for home. On 18 May 1945 von Oppeln's small group was spotted and captured by the crew of an American jeep. He was taken to the POW camp at Plauen and from there to Staumühle transit camp near Paderborn. Von Oppeln finally ended up in POW Camp No. 2224 near Brugges in Belgium. The food was so "good" there that the six-foot general ultimately weighed just 110 pounds.

On 26 April 1946 he was shipped back to Staumühle in Germany. After two years as a prisoner, on 22 May 1947 General von Oppeln received his first hearing on charges of being a war criminal. He was found totally innocent and was released on 4 August 1947. He died on 18 September 1966.

Appendix

RANK COMPARISONS

ENLISTED

US Army	German Army	Waffen-SS
Private	*Schütze*	*SS-Schütze*
Private First Class	*Oberschütze*	*SS-Oberschütze*
Corporal	*Gefreiter*	*SS-Sturmmann*
(Senior Corporal)	*Obergefreiter*	*SS-Rottenführer*
(Staff Corporal)	*Stabsgefreiter*	(None)

NONCOMMISSIONED OFFICERS

US Army	German Army	Waffen-SS
Sergeant	*Unteroffizier*	*SS-Unterscharführer*
Staff Sergeant	*Feldwebel*	*SS-Oberscharführer*
Sergeant First Class	*Oberfeldwebel*	*SS-Hauptscharführer*
Master Sergeant	*Hauptfeldwebel*	*SS-Sturmscharführer*
Sergeant Major	*Stabsfeldwebel*	(None)

OFFICERS

US Army	German Army	Waffen-SS
Lieutenant	*Leutnant*	*SS-Untersturmführer*
First Lieutenant	*Oberleutnant*	*SS-Obersturmführer*
Captain	*Hauptmann*	*SS-Hauptsturmführer*
Major	*Major*	*SS-Sturmbannführer*
Lieutenant Colonel	*Oberstleutnant*	*SS-Obersturmbannführer*
Colonel	*Oberst*	*SS-Oberführer* or *SS-Standartenführer*
Brigadier General	*Generalmajor*	*SS-Brigadeführer*
Major General	*Generalleutnant*	*SS-Gruppenführer*
Lieutenant General	*General der Panzertruppen* etc.	*SS-Obergruppenführer*
General	*Generaloberst*	*SS-Oberstgruppenführer*
General of the Army	*Feldmarschall*	*Reichsführer-SS*

Index